to J. M. Buchanan

compliments of M. R. Colberg

BUSINESS ECONOMICS

PRINCIPLES AND CASES

BUSINESS ECONOMICS

PRINCIPLES AND CASES

BY MARSHALL R. COLBERG

Professor of Economics and Chairman,
Department of Economics
Florida State University

WILLIAM C. BRADFORD

Professor of Business Economics
Northwestern University

AND

RICHARD M. ALT

Director of Research
New England Mutual Life Insurance Company

REVISED EDITION

1957

RICHARD D. IRWIN, INC.

HOMEWOOD, ILLINOIS

REVISED EDITION

First Printing, June, 1957

Library of Congress Catalogue Card No. 57–10202

PRINTED IN THE UNITED STATES OF AMERICA

PREFACE

THIS book combines text and case materials for use in courses in which economic analysis is applied to the solution of business problems. These courses appear in university and college bulletins under a variety of names, such as "Business Economics," "Price Policies," "Economics of Enterprise," "Economics of the Firm," etc. They are offered both by schools of business administration and by departments of economics. Usually, they are junior, senior, or first-year graduate courses and have as a prerequisite the principles course in economics. Frequently students in these courses have had some training in accounting, finance, marketing, and statistics; however, a background of these subjects is not essential to an understanding of this volume.

The point of view taken in this book is that of the executive responsible for making decisions which guide the business enterprise. The authors' purpose is to use techniques of economic analysis to solve—or at least to throw some light upon—problems of business management. These problems are of two sorts: those that can be called *internal* because many factors in the situation are within control of the business firm; and those that are *external,* involving conditions which business management cannot control but to which it must adjust.

The organization of this book differs from the 1951 edition in several respects. The text material has been arranged in Chapters instead of Sections to permit greater flexibility of assignment. Several cases of the original edition have been retained, but new questions have been added. In some instances the original cases have been placed in a different topical arrangement with the hope that they will be more useful and pertinent. Where new cases have been added an effort was made to use experiences of business firms of various sizes. A number of topics not covered in the first edition have been included.

A casebook must necessarily be limited both as to the number of situations covered and as to the variety and technicality of the economic issues treated. This book is not intended therefore to present cases which cover all areas of economic activity. All cases are based upon actual business experiences, or government records, although, in many cases, fictitious names have been used at the request of the companies studied. We are indebted to the following companies and individuals for their generous assistance in providing source material: American

v

Airlines, Inc.; Baltimore and Ohio Railroad Company; Capital Airlines; Commonwealth Edison Company; Marshall Field & Company; Glenn L. Martin Company; Maryland State Planning Commission; Nash-Kelvinator Corporation; New York, New Haven, and Hartford Railroad; Northern Illinois Gas Company; Standard Brands; Tanis Company; United Airlines; and the Wall Street Journal. We also wish to acknowledge the provision of materials by several firms who, for their own reasons, wish to remain anonymous.

An undertaking of this sort owes much to the work of others. Eugene C. Holshouser has given us permission to use material from his statistical demand study for frozen orange concentrate. Excerpts from a statistical investigation of long-run cost of production by Joel Dean have been used in the present edition as well as in the first edition. Charles B. Franklin made valuable suggestions pertaining to the chapter on the theory of games. Professor Melvin L. Greenhut generously read the chapter on plant location and prepared a preliminary draft of the summary which appears at the end of the chapter.

We are grateful to Dean Richard Donham of Northwestern University for the privilege of testing many of the cases in the classroom. Professor Dascomb R. Forbush of Northwestern University has been most helpful with many suggestions, criticisms, and materials. Professor Clark L. Allen of North Carolina State College first suggested the present combination of authors for the revised edition. We wish also to thank our loyal assistants, Mrs. Gennelle Jordan, Miss Betty June Bishop, Mr. Warren Pillsbury, Mr. Joseph DiBerardino, Mrs. Marjorie B. McKiblin, and Mrs. Jean Joyce for their assistance in preparing the manuscript and helping to keep the work moving toward final publication.

MARSHALL R. COLBERG
May 1957   WILLIAM C. BRADFORD
RICHARD M. ALT

TABLE OF CONTENTS

Mergers. Nature of Gains to Firms. Mergers and the Public Interest. Exclusive-Dealer Contracts. Interlocking Directorates. Significance of Interlocking Directorates. The Fair-Trade Philosophy. Economic Forces Hamper-
ing Fair Trade. Manufacturers' Actions Regarding Fair Trade.

Case 14–1. *Standard Oil Company of California et al.* v. *United States,*
337 U.S. 293, 519
Case 14–2. Schwegmann Bros., Inc., 523

Chapter I

~~~~~~

UNCERTAINTY AND PROFIT

ECONOMICS is the study of the optimal use of scarce resources to satisfy human wants. It consequently deals with both the extent to which labor and capital are employed and the way in which these factors are allocated among alternative goods and services. Economics is primarily a social science rather than one which has as its purpose the analysis of efficient behavior on the part of the individual business firm. Nevertheless, social economy requires that business enterprises be alert to the demands of consumers, be of efficient size, be operated efficiently, and be compelled by competition to pass on to buyers the advantages of their efficiency. A good deal of economic analysis is concerned, consequently, with principles of efficient action applicable to the firm. This book will discuss some of these principles and will present business cases the solution of which should be facilitated by the application of the associated analysis. A good businessman need not be an economist, but a knowledge of economics is likely to sharpen his thinking about his own firm's problems and sometimes will aid him in making wise decisions which would not otherwise be obvious. Certain types of business decisions are sufficiently difficult and important to justify use not only of all relevant theoretical analysis but also of expensive empirical investigation.

Only Uncertainty Is Certain

It is often said that nothing is certain except death and taxes. In an important sense, not even these qualifications need be made. The entire institution of life insurance is based on the uncertainty of the date of death of the individual in comparison with the calculability of mortality rates for large numbers of persons within various age groups. Also, the amount and nature of the taxes which will be assessed by governmental bodies are often important uncertainties of life.

If the future could be known with certainty, correct economic decisions could be made by everyone. The worker could know precisely where and how to earn the largest income, the business executive would know in advance the outcome of alternative ventures which he

1

might undertake, and the investor would be fully cognizant of the relative desirability of the various investment opportunities open to him. Decision making would not be difficult, and professional decision makers (business executives) would not be highly paid. Investment in a newly formed uranium mining company would be as safe as investment in a well-established utility company.

In the actual world the existence of uncertainty causes future incomes to be imperfectly predictable. Often, it is possible for the individual to choose between receiving income which is definite in amount according to terms either of a contract or of an unwritten agreement, or receiving income which depends, instead, on the outcome of the economic activity in which he participates. In the first case the individual can be fairly sure as to what his income will be in the near future, while in the second case the degree of predictability is lower. A fisherman, for example, may work for a regular daily wage or, alternatively, may share in the proceeds of the sale of the catch. The latter arrangement is very common because of the unusually high degree of uncertainty regarding the production function (relation of output to input) in the fishing industry. Similarly, a manager may be employed at a specific salary rate by a chain grocery store or, alternatively, may operate his own store where the return for his labor and capital investment depend on the success of the operation. Similarly, a person wanting to invest funds in a particular corporation may become a bondholder, a preferred stockholder, or a common stockholder. In the first case, he would be a creditor of the firm, receiving interest in a fixed annual amount. His income would not depend on the success of the firm except that a sufficiently unprofitable situation might endanger both his receipt of interest and the safety of his principal. As a preferred stockholder the degree of uncertainty of his return would be somewhat lower, while as a common stockholder the investor faces the greatest degree of uncertainty, both as to return and as to safety of principal.[1]

Hired and Self-Employed Resources

Labor contracted for at a specific wage or salary rate, a rented building or machine, and funds borrowed from bondholders or banks may conveniently be considered to be examples of "hired" resources. Labor

---

[1] Over a long period of rising prices, however, common stock may offer the investor more nearly a guarantee of stability or gain in *real* income and real value of principal than either bonds or preferred stock. Many managers of pension funds, for example, are investing in common stocks for this reason.

secured on an income-sharing basis, capital contributed by stockholders, partners, or individual proprietors, and labor services furnished by owners of enterprises may be termed "unhired" or "self-employed" resources or factors of production. Persons who dislike uncertainty are likely to take steps to receive their income primarily as a contractual return, while those with less aversion to uncertainty are likely to prefer to receive a larger proportion of their income on a noncontractual basis.

In a competitive economic system the payments to hired factors of production are based on the estimated marginal revenue productivity of these resources—that is, on the additional revenue which firms expect to secure from the sale of the additional output attributable to a unit of a resource, other productive inputs remaining unchanged in amount. Since contractual payments must be arranged in advance, and since firms compete with one another in hiring factors of production, the payments to hired resources represent businessmen's anticipation as to the worth of these resources. In business, as elsewhere in life, expected and realized situations frequently differ. If a favorable turn of events—a sudden increase in people's willingness to spend their money for goods and services, for example—causes firms' incomes to exceed expectations, increased residuals are left over after all costs have been deducted from gross income. An unfavorable turn of events, or overoptimism on the part of businessmen in bidding up the prices of factors of production, will reduce the size of the residuals which remain to firms after paying for all hired inputs. The "self-employed" or "unhired" resources receive their incomes out of these amounts which remain after hired resources are paid off at contractual rates.

Accounting and Economic Profit

The accountant designates as "profit" or "net income" the amount which is left over out of gross income after all payments to hired factors.[2] The economist points out that further deductions must be made from this amount in order to get a somewhat less arbitrary picture of the success of the firm's operations in any period. The accountant's measurement, while suited to the purpose for which it is made,

---

[2] The materials used up in manufacturing and the fixed plant may be considered to be "hired" resources even if they are owned by the firm at the time of use. The productive powers of the materials and plant will have been paid for at a definite rate determined by their purchase price. The net income of the firm depends to an important degree on the actual productivity of the plant compared with the annual depreciation which must be charged on the books in order to reflect the loss of service capacity.

is greatly affected by the extent to which resources are remunerated on a contractual basis. Other things being equal, the greater the extent to which the needed resources are hired rather than self-employed, the lower will be the net income shown in the accounting records. In order to avoid this arbitrary element, the cost of self-employed resources, evaluated by determining what they could earn if employed on a contractual basis instead, must also be deducted. The alternative earnings of unhired factors are often called "implicit costs." Hence, deduction of implicit as well as explicit costs from gross income gives "economic profit." Deduction of explicit costs alone gives accounting profit.

The above distinction is of great practical importance because of the existence of a heavy federal tax on corporation "profits." Often, it is possible for a firm to raise additional capital funds by selling either bonds or common stock. If it sells bonds, the funds are "hired," and the interest is an explicit cost of doing business. If, instead, stocks are sold, the funds are owned, and there is no explicit interest cost which can be deducted in arriving at accounting profit. There is an implicit cost involved in that the funds raised by selling stock could instead have earned some contractual rate in an alternative employment. By selling stock instead of bonds, the corporation subjects itself to a larger corporate income tax. In recent years, many firms have raised additional capital funds by means of bonds rather than stock, in order to secure this tax advantage. In other cases, firms have converted preferred stock into bonds for the same reason.[3]

Accounting profits of corporations in the United States in recent years are shown graphically in Exhibit 1. Federal corporate income taxes have amounted to almost half of aggregate profits over the period covered by the chart. A little less than half of the corporate profits after taxes have been paid out to stockholders in dividends, the remainder having been "plowed back" into the companies, chiefly as a means of financing plant expansion. The same data are shown in Exhibit 2, which also includes information for selected earlier years. The dampening effect of the long and severe depression of the 1930's is reflected in the low corporate profits earned in 1939, despite the considerable recovery which had occurred since 1932.

The distinction between economic and accounting profit is also of

---

[3] It is quite apparent that a corporation income tax should tax economic profit rather than accounting profit in order not to affect the relative desirability of different types of securities from the corporation's point of view. In practice, however, a knotty problem of calculating appropriate alternative contractual rates of return on securities would exist.

Exhibit 1

CORPORATE PROFITS AND THEIR DISPOSITION

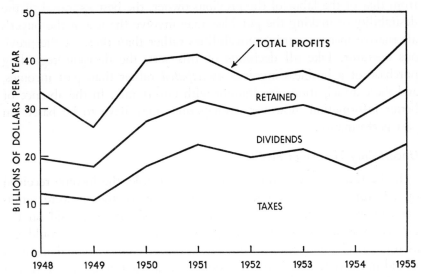

importance in evaluating the worth of a small enterprise which is for sale. Typically, the individual enterpriser contributes his own labor and some capital to the operation of his firm. This involves an implicit cost, since his labor and capital could, alternatively, earn income elsewhere on a contractual basis. Since no explicit cost is involved, the enterpriser is unlikely to show any cost on his books for the use of his own resources. If the firm is offered for sale, it becomes important

Exhibit 2

CORPORATION PROFITS, TAXES, AND DIVIDENDS
(Billions of Dollars)

Year	Corporation Profits before Taxes	Corporate Tax Liability	Dividend Payments	Undistributed Profits
1939	$ 6.4	$ 1.4	$ 3.8	$ 1.2
1944	23.3	12.9	4.7	5.7
1946	22.6	9.1	5.8	7.7
1948	32.8	12.5	7.2	13.0
1949	26.2	10.4	7.5	8.3
1950	40.0	17.8	9.2	12.9
1951	41.2	22.5	9.1	9.6
1952	35.9	19.8	9.0	7.1
1953	38.3	21.3	9.3	7.7
1954	34.0	17.1	10.0	7.0
1955	43.8	22.0	11.2	10.6

Source: *Economic Indicators*, June, 1956, Joint Council of Economic Advisers (Washington, D.C.: U.S. Government Printing Office, 1955), p. 22.

for a potential buyer to keep in mind the exclusion of these costs. Since the alternative earning power of the buyer's labor may differ from that of the labor of the previous owner, the best appraisal of the desirability of making the purchase may involve the use of the buyer's alternative income-earning possibilities rather than those of the previous operator. Like all decisions of this sort, the decision regarding purchase of a business involves *anticipated* rather than past incomes, and these anticipations are fraught with uncertainty. In the absence of better information, however, anticipations may have to be based on past performance.

Uncertainty Theory of Profit

If the future were always perfectly predictable, the income received by a factor of production would be the same whether it were remunerated on a contractual or on a residual basis. Persons paid on the former basis would not be willing to accept less than they could get as residual claimants; and, similarly, those receiving residual incomes would not accept less than they could earn at contractual rates. In the actual, uncertain world, there is usually a difference between the income which resources earn on a contractual and self-employed basis —that is, economic profits (positive or negative) usually exist. In a year of especially good business, for example, economic profits generally are likely to be positive. Most stockholders will receive better rates of return than bondholders, while persons in business for themselves may do better, on the average, than if they had worked for someone else. In a year of depressed business activity the situation is likely to be just the opposite—that is, economic profits in most lines are apt to be negative.[4]

Since there would be no economic profits in a perfectly predictable world, uncertainty is the basic reason for the existence of profits in the actual world. It is necessary, however, to distinguish between true uncertainties and those more manageable uncertainties which can be insured against. Examples of the latter are uncertainty as to the duration of life, uncertainty as to whether a particular house will burn,

---

[4] Professor Frank H. Knight of the University of Chicago, the originator of the uncertainty theory of profit, has stated that, in his opinion, "business as a whole suffers a loss." This he attributes to such factors as an irrationally high confidence which most men feel in their own abilities, the excessive stimulation received from competitors in bidding for resources, and the tenacity with which most men stick to a business even when it is doing poorly. See F. H. Knight, *Risk, Uncertainty, and Profit* (Boston and New York: Houghton Mifflin Co., 1921), p. 366. This observation seems questionable, however, if applied to the post-World War II economy.

and uncertainty as to whether a car or truck will be involved in an accident. If statistical probabilities have been worked out with sufficient accuracy to make it possible for a company to sell insurance against occurrences of a particular contingency, a definite contractual payment by the firm to the insurance company will guard against financial loss on this account. Professor Knight has termed such insurable uncertainties "risks," in order to distinguish them from the uninsurable uncertainties which must be faced by those who receive their incomes on a noncontractual basis. The two types of uncertainties can also be usefully distinguished as "transformable" and "nontransformable," the former being those which can be avoided at a definite cost by means of insurance or hedging (to be described later in this chapter), and the latter being those which cannot be sidestepped by the businessman by means of transformation into a definite cost.[5] Shifts in tastes, inventions, discoveries of new natural resources, and interruptions in the state of peace or war are changes which can neither be anticipated nor be insured against. They are examples of the true uncertainties which cause economic profits—positive and negative—to exist.

Innovation Profits

The innovation theory of profits is concerned with the impact of changes which occur with the passage of time. Perhaps the most widely known statement of the theory is that of the late Professor Schumpeter, who attributed economic profits to innovations made by businessmen.[6]

The innovation theory can be described as follows: A firm introduces a new product or a new idea, which results in yielding an existing product at a lower cost; or differentiates its product, which results in a wider acceptance by consumers; or promotes various combinations of these ideas, which gives the firm an advantage over its competitors. As a result, the firm enjoys an economic surplus from this advantage. Eventually, either new firms are attracted to the field by the profits of the successful firm, or competitors produce close substitutes and thus reduce the sales of the innovator. Or competitors may adopt the cost-reducing methods of the innovating firm, causing the latter to lose its temporary advantage. All this requires the passage of

---

[5] J. F. Weston, "A Generalized Uncertainty Theory of Profit," *American Economic Review*, March, 1950, p. 44, suggests this terminology.

[6] Joseph S. Schumpeter, *The Theory of Economic Development* (Cambridge, Mass.: Harvard University Press, 1934), chap. v.

time; but when the adjustment has worked itself out, the advantageous position of the innovating firm has been lost, and its economic surplus has disappeared. As the number of firms adopting the innovation or producing a sufficiently close substitute increases, the profits of all firms tend to decline.

Such a theory implies the freedom of new firms to enter the field without restriction other than that imposed by time—a lag during which the profits of innovation can be received. So long as such a condition exists, and all potential competitors possess complete knowledge of past events in the business world, no firm can enjoy innovation profits indefinitely.

The innovation theory is logically part of the broader uncertainty theory of profit. Innovations in methods and products are one of the great unpredictables which cause positive and negative economic profits to exist. If innovations could be fully foreseen, they would not have this effect. All firms would be ready to introduce a new production method, for example, as soon as it was available, and no special advantages would accrue from the method. Since such prediction is not possible, and since adjustments take time, innovations would occasion profits even if our economic system were highly competitive in all respects.

Profits and Liquidity

Another theory of profit has been set forth by Professor Boulding.[7] He emphasizes that the ownership of goods of any sort—factories, inventories of finished products, goods in process—involves the sacrifice of liquidity. That is, an alternative on the part of the owner would be the holding of cash instead of goods. Boulding points out that even holding cash involves risk of loss because the general price level may go up, thereby reducing the real value (purchasing power) of a stock of cash. He believes, however, that greater risk is involved in holding any particular good because the good may not only decline in value because of a fall in the general level of prices but it may also decline because of supply-demand conditions peculiar to that commodity.[8] Also, the holding of liquid purchasing power permits the snapping-up of

---

[7] K. E. Boulding, *Economic Analysis* (New York: Harper & Bros., 1948), pp. 429–31.

[8] It should be noted, however, that the modern tendency of government to follow inflationary monetary and fiscal policies reduces the riskiness of holding goods and increases the chance of loss by holding cash.

bargains which may become available, and quick entry into fields where innovations offer a favorable opportunity. Because of these advantages of liquidity, Professor Boulding has stated that profits can be considered to be the necessary reward to induce firms to hold goods, and he points out that this ownership of goods is indispensable to the existence of enterprise. It should be noted that this theory hinges on uncertainty regarding future prices; consequently, it is logically a part of the broader uncertainty theory of profit.

Monopoly Profits

Although economic profits would exist in a completely competitive economy, monopolistic advantages of various sorts are a great source of profit in the real world. Cartel agreements, whereby firms in a particular field (e.g., dry cleaning) set prices above the competitive level, are an important source of profit. Exclusive franchises are common in the utility and transportation fields; and these, of course, confer monopoly power on their owners. While public regulation of privately owned transportation and utility systems does much to prevent franchise holders from securing very large profits, such public regulation often is not sufficiently effective to prevent above-normal returns. Also, monopoly profits are frequently made by governments which sell such commodities as electric power and water in noncompetitive situations, such profits frequently being used as a partial substitute for taxes.

Patents give their holders exclusive monopoly powers for a period of time. These powers and the associated profits have been considered to be appropriate as a reward for the creative effort of their holders. It should be noted, however, that patent monopoly is not always profitable. Many patents are never exploited commercially because, while they may be technologically unique, the demand-cost situation is not sufficiently favorable.

Product differentiation by such means as trade names, distinctive packaging, and highly publicized differences (real or fictitious) from rival commodities give some degree of monopoly power to a great many firms. This source of monopoly profits is often less dependable than that of a franchise or patent, and heavy advertising may be necessary to maintain the advantage over time. However, the importance of a well-known slogan, picture, or package should not be underestimated.

A particularly advantageous location can also bring monopoly profits to a firm. This is especially likely to be true if the site is owned by the enterprise itself, since otherwise the rental charged by the owner is apt to be so large as to make the location no more favorable than some poorer site which could be rented more cheaply. However, if the enterpriser in question—say, a clothing retailer—owns the store and the land, he could, alternatively, lease this property to another firm and secure a favorable rental income. Monopoly profits due to locational advantages are, consequently, difficult to distinguish from rental income. Since economic profit is the difference between a firm's income and its explicit and implicit costs, it can be argued that locational monopoly is not really a source of profits. Many questions of this type are mainly matters of definition of terms rather than matters of real economic importance.

The Transforming of Uncertainties

As was pointed out earlier, it is useful to distinguish between "transformable" and "nontransformable" uncertainties. The latter provide the basic explanation for the existence of profits in an economy of private, competitive industry. Nevertheless, a good deal of knowledge and judgment are required by businessmen in order successfully and economically to transform the types of uncertainties which are avoidable at a certain cost. The time and effort which must be spent in this type of activity varies a great deal from business to business. The process of transforming uncertainties into definite costs can be called "hedging."

Hedging, in essence, involves the purposive holding of two opposite positions at the same time. Roughly, it can be described as betting in two opposite ways at the same time. The purchase of insurance is of this nature and hence is a variety of hedging. When a businessman buys fire insurance, he is, essentially, betting that a fire will occur on his premises; the insurance company is betting that this will not happen. Even if the fire does occur, the directors of the insurance company are unlikely to be dismayed because the company will undoubtedly win its bets with numerous other persons who bought fire insurance, and the successful wagers should at least offset the unsuccessful ones. As the owner of a building and its contents the businessman is, of course, hoping that no fire will occur, since this would bring financial loss. In order to protect himself in this position, he must take an opposite stand—that is, he must bet that a fire will occur. Whatever the actual outcome, he should not fare too badly, since he will have converted an important uncertainty into a definite cost—the cost of the insurance premiums.[9]

Hedging is often possible even when insurance cannot be purchased against occurrence of an unfavorable event. Instead of betting with an insurance company, one can often place a bet with someone else. For example, suppose a young man attends a ball game with the president of his company, who is a Dodger fan. And suppose that at the start of the game the boss places a bet of $100 on the Dodgers to beat the Giants with a wealthy individual in the next box. The young man can then improve his prospects with the company by boldly placing a similar bet with the stranger. While waiting at the refreshment stand to have the boss's order filled, however, he may bet $100 on the Giants. Assuming that the odds are even on both teams, he has avoided the risk of loss (and the possibility of gain) but has advanced a notch in the president's esteem (provided that the latter does not learn about the hedge).

Long and Short Positions

An important variety of hedging in the business world consists of taking offsetting "long" and "short" positions. Like the offsetting $100 bets on the Dodgers and Giants, this is not sensible unless the firm is forced into one position as an incident to doing business. If the position is a dangerously speculative one, it is conservative to hedge against it, thereby incurring a small, certain cost rather than risking a large, speculative loss.

An individual is in a "long" position whenever he owns any commodity, security, or other asset of value. His hope is then that the asset will increase in money value as a result of the operation of supply-demand forces.[10] His fear is that market forces will reduce the value of his asset. On the other hand, a person in a "short" position hopes that the market price will decline rather than rise, since he has made a contract to deliver a commodity, security, or other asset at a future

---

[9] Even apart from the consequences of the disruption of business, the insured person is apt not to recover his entire loss, since insurance companies normally do not sell policies to cover the whole value of inflammable property. To do so might place too much temptation in the way of some policyholders to win their bets with the company. Even beneficiaries of life insurance policies have been known to take steps to secure the proceeds prematurely.

[10] It is also possible to be long on money itself. This occurs whenever a cash balance is held. The hope of the individual is then that the purchasing power of the cash will increase—i.e., that prices will fall. Conversely, one is "short" on money when in debt, since it is necessary to make future delivery of principal and interest to a creditor.

date for a specific price. The more cheaply he can purchase the asset when the delivery date rolls around, or the more cheaply he can produce it in time to meet the delivery requirement, the larger his gain will be. A contractor, for example, who has agreed to construct a building, road, or other project for a specified sum may be considered to be in a "short" position with respect to that asset. One of his problems, once the contract has been signed, is that the cost of materials, labor, and other inputs may increase during the construction period, so as to make the job an unprofitable one. In order to hedge against this contingency, he must take a long position with respect to the needed inputs. He may, for example, sign a lease to rent the needed equipment at a specified price for the period of construction; or, alternatively, he may buy the equipment. He may attempt to secure a contract with the labor unions involved, which will make his labor costs more predictable. With respect to materials he has two alternatives: (1) He may buy all of the necessary materials ahead of time, storing them until needed; or (2) he may contract to have them delivered to him at specified prices at specified future dates. Either way, he would have a hedge against an increase in their price. Once the contractor had assumed correct "long" positions on most of the inputs required for construction of the project, he would be fairly well hedged against unfavorable price changes. He would have transformed some uncertain costs into predictable ones.

Futures Markets

Hedging operations on the part of businessmen in many lines of activity are made possible by the existence of organized markets in which commodities are traded both at "spot" or "cash" prices for immediate delivery and at "futures" prices for deferred delivery.[11] Futures contracts are regularly made for some dozens of relatively

---

[11] Holbrook Working, in an informative article entitled "Futures Trading and Hedging," *American Economic Review*, July, 1953, p. 315, points out that it is not accurate to state that a futures contract *always* involves deferred delivery because, for example, some sellers of September wheat futures in September may intend to make immediate delivery. It is safe to say, however, that most futures contracts do involve deferred rather than immediate delivery. Unfortunately, from a pedagogic point of view, much trading which is not in the futures markets also involves deferred rather than immediate delivery. International commodity trading and purchase and sale of many manufactured goods regularly involve deferred delivery. Also, commodities bought in the "cash" market are frequently sold on terms providing for 30-, 60-, and 90-day credit. Fortunately, most of the confusing terminological problems do not seriously hamper the student who wishes to acquire a general understanding of commodity markets and their importance to business. The problem of terminology can, however, be a serious obstacle to the acquiring of a detailed knowledge of the workings of any particular commodity market.

homogeneous and storable commodities such as wheat, corn, oats, lard, cottonseed oil, cotton, cocoa, coffee, refrigerated eggs, Maine potatoes, lead, zinc, and copper. In the month of April, for example, Mr. A may contract to buy, and Mr. B to sell, a specified quantity of wheat during the month of December at a specified price. The seller has the option of making delivery on any day within the month of December, delivery actually taking the form of delivery of warehouse receipts for the commodity. Mr. B also has the option of delivering any of several grades of wheat rather than just a specified grade; and a discount or premium from the agreed price then is effective, since the agreed price relates to a standard grade.

The financial pages of certain newspapers regularly carry quotations of both spot and futures prices. In April, for example, prices of spot May, July, September, and December wheat are quoted. Since quoted futures prices are based on anticipated demand-supply conditions in those future months, they may be thought of as traders' present expectations as to what spot prices will be for the same grade when those months roll around. In an uncertain world, these expectations are seldom entirely correct. The constant changes in futures prices reflect the buying and selling actions which are constantly taking place, the price movements generally being in the direction of more correctly reflecting the cash prices which will actually prevail in the future months, since later quotations are based on later information. Quoted futures prices are, therefore, likely to be a good forecast of price movements. If, for example, May coffee is selling at 55 cents, July coffee at 51 cents, September coffee at 47 cents, and December coffee at 45 cents a pound, a housewife can look forward with some confidence to a reduction in the cost of coffee in her budget.

Spot and Futures Prices

The "spot" or "cash" market for a commodity differs in important ways from the futures market. Whereas a futures contract can generally be satisfied by delivery of any of the grades of the commodity, a spot transaction pertains to the transfer of a specific lot of a specific grade, the transaction often being consummated in a face-to-face meeting of buyer and seller. When a spot transaction is made, the buyer actually wants to receive delivery of the commodity, and delivery will be made unless the contract is canceled by subsequent agreement between the two parties. On the other hand, most of the buyers of futures do not actually want to take delivery on these contracts, nor do sellers usually want to make actual delivery. Instead, the buyer of a futures contract usually "offsets" this contract by a similar futures sale prior to delivery time; if the price has gone up, he makes a gain equal to the difference in price (less commissions and taxes). Similarly, the seller of a futures contract usually offsets the contract with a purchase of futures prior to delivery time; he gains if the purchase can be made at a lower price than he has sold for, and he loses in the opposite case.

Speculation and Arbitrage

The futures market is a great convenience to both speculators and hedgers, since the actual commodity need not be handled, and since buyers and sellers normally do not have to be concerned about selection of the specific grade, place of delivery, and other details. A speculator who believes that a presently quoted futures price is too low—that is, that demand will be stronger in relation to supply than present quotations indicate—is likely to *buy* a futures contract. If his expectation is correct, he can later offset this purchase with a similar sale at a higher price. On the other hand, a speculator who believes that a presently quoted futures price is too high can *sell* futures, profiting by a later offsetting purchase if his "bearish" expectation turns out to be correct.

Instead of attempting to take advantage of a change in a single price over time, a speculator may, instead, attempt to turn to his advantage a difference between two prices when that difference appears to be out of line. Suppose that a study of market conditions suggests strongly that July oats futures are underpriced relative to September oats. This would suggest an arbitrage transaction in which July oats would be bought and September oats would be simultaneously sold. It would then not matter whether the more normal differential were established by a rise in the price of July oats, by a fall in September oats, or any other combination of change, so long as a smaller difference in price came to be established. The arbitrager would gain on either the long or short transaction and lose or break even on the other one, but his gain would exceed his loss. Similarly, an improper differential between two markets—say, between the New York and the New Orleans cotton markets—could be turned into an arbitrage profit by a simultaneous purchase in the relatively low market and a sale in the relatively high market.

The arbitrager can be considered to be "betting two ways at once." His action differs, however, from that of the hedger in that the latter is forced to assume one of his positions (make one of his bets) as an incident to carrying on his regular line of business activity. The arbitrager takes both of his positions as a speculative matter. In practice, it is often impossible to characterize an individual as purely a hedger or purely an arbitrager on a particular transaction, since a hedger is not averse, of course, to making an arbitrage profit, whenever possible, in the process of protecting himself against an adverse price change.

Hedging by Selling Futures

A wheat farmer, contemplating his growing crop in July, realizes that he is an involuntary speculator in wheat on the "long" side. He may decide to hedge by selling September wheat, perhaps in about

Exhibit 3

Date	Transaction	Farmer Receives	Farmer Pays
July 20..............	Farmer has growing wheat which will yield an estimated 10,000 bushels when harvested. Cash price of wheat is $1.80 per bushel.		
July 20..............	Farmer sells 10,000 bushels of September wheat at $1.85 per bushel.	$18,500	
September 10........	Farmer buys 10,000 bushels of September wheat at $1.70 per bushel.		$17,000
September 10........	Farmer sells his own wheat in cash market (10,000 bushels at $1.70 per bushel).	17,000	
		$35,500	$17,000

the quantity he expects to harvest in that month. By taking this action he has, roughly speaking, already sold his growing crop at a specific price for delivery at harvest time, and he is in no danger of suffering a speculative loss between July and September. Actually, he is unlikely to deliver his own wheat on the futures contract; he will probably off-set his short position in late August or September by buying September futures in the same amount he had previously sold. Then he will sell his own wheat in the cash market.

If we assume that the quantity of wheat involved was 10,000 bushels and make certain price assumptions, the transactions can be summarized as shown in Exhibit 3.

In the situation pictured, the farmer would be glad that he hedged, since he has a net gain of $18,500 (from which, however, commissions and taxes must be deducted), whereas his crop would have brought him $17,000 if he had not hedged. The cash price of wheat declined 10 cents a bushel between July 20 and September 10, but this was more than offset by the 15-cent decline in September futures over the same period. The protection received from this sort of hedging is based on the fact that cash and futures prices generally move in the same direction. These two prices may, however, not move by the same amount; consequently, the hedger is apt to make either a speculative gain or a loss of moderate proportions.[12] If the price of cash wheat had increased from, say, $1.80 per bushel on July 20 to $1.90, the farmer would have a larger net income by not hedging. The existence of government price supports at some designated percentage of "parity" may make hedging by farmers less necessary. (However, both spot and futures prices can fall below support levels.) The price-support program thus places part of the speculative risk of a price decline on the shoulders of the taxpayers.

Hedging is practiced extensively by certain types of processors. For example, the practice has expanded in recent years in the case of southern textile mills.[13] These mills buy spot cotton early in the season and sell cotton futures as a hedge. Offsetting futures purchases are made as orders are received for textiles. This gives them substantial protection against losses on their long position in cotton. If cotton has declined in price between the time it is purchased and a textile order is received, the mill may have to quote a price on textiles which reflects the lower price of cotton. In this case, however, a profit will be made on the futures transactions, and this may equal or even exceed the reduction in revenue occasioned by the need to cut the price of textiles.

Hedging by Buying Futures

Much of the hedging which occurs involves the initial purchase, instead of sale, of futures. This method is followed when the businessman has taken a short position in a raw material or finished good. Suppose a candy manufacturer receives large orders in September for

---

[12] Actually, the farmer did not engage in a pure hedging transaction, since he was short on mature wheat but long on immature wheat prior to harvest time. If he had held wheat in storage and had sold wheat futures in the same amount, the long and short positions would have been more definitely offsetting.

[13] J. B. Bear and O. G. Saxon, *Commodity Exchanges and Futures Trading* (New York: Harper & Bros., 1949), p. 242.

delivery of his product in time for the Christmas season. He is obliged to quote a definite price on the future delivery of candy and is, therefore, in a short position. He can hedge against a rise in his production costs by adopting a long position in sugar, his principal raw material. If spot and futures prices for sugar move in a parallel fashion during the next few months, as they generally do, an increase in his production costs due to a rise in the price of cash sugar should be quite closely offset by his profit on the purchase and sale of sugar futures. If, on the other hand, spot sugar declines in price, the candy manufacturer would

Exhibit 4

Date	Transaction	Manu-facturer Receives	Manu-facturer Pays
September 15........	Candy manufacturer sells candy which will require 112,000 pounds of sugar, the candy to be delivered early in December.		
September 15........	Candy manufacturer buys 112,000 pounds of November sugar at 6 cents a pound.		$ 6,720
November 15........	Candy manufacturer sells 112,000 pounds of November sugar at 7 cents a pound.	$7,840	
November 15........	Candy manufacturer buys 112,000 pounds of spot sugar at 7 cents a pound.		7,840
	.	$7,840	$14,560

have been better off had he not hedged. An added inducement to hedging, however, is that banks may be willing to make loans for working capital purposes only when the borrower has hedged appropriately against unfavorable price changes.

The candy manufacturer's transaction might be summarized as shown in Exhibit 4.

In spite of the increase in the price of sugar, the candy maker should receive an adequate net return for his product. He has secured the needed sugar for $6,720 (the difference between his payments and receipts in the sugar transactions). This is a price of 6 cents a pound (plus commissions and taxes on the sugar transactions), which is the price he was able to anticipate in September when he fixed his candy prices. If November sugar had been selling at a price which appeared to be too high, he could have hedged instead by buying spot sugar in September and storing it until he needed it. It is usually more convenient, however, to hedge by means of futures transactions.

Such businessmen as bakers, bottlers of soft drinks, coffee and cocoa importers, flour millers, cold-storers of eggs, cottonseed and soybean crushers, copper smelters, and many others make extensive use of hedging. Often, the choice of whether to hedge at all, and if so, what sort of hedge to use, hinges on the relation between spot and futures prices. If futures prices appear to be abnormally low relative to spot prices, it may not be wise to hedge by selling futures; the chance of their declining further may be too poor. In this situation, it may be best to attempt to arrange short and long positions which call instead for purchasing the underpriced futures.

Financial Hedging

Any individual or firm holding a considerable amount of assets should give thought to the problem of diversification—usually, not all of the eggs should be put in one basket. From the point of view of the consumer, the danger is that an increase in the cost of living will lower the real value of cash assets or of assets which have a specified value in dollars (such as U.S. Savings Bonds and mortgages). The manager of a financial institution such as an insurance company or building and loan association faces a different sort of uncertainty— uncertainty as to the future course of interest rates. A rise in interest rates is equivalent to a decline in bond prices. When interest rates go up, bonds with more distant maturity dates (e.g., 1980) fall more in market price than bonds which will pay off their face value in the near future. Cash, of course, does not fall in face value at all when interest rates rise. As a consequence, a proper hedging of asset holdings may call for a portfolio which includes both long- and short-term bonds or mortgages, cash, and perhaps common and preferred stocks (where the law permits the institution to invest in stocks). The low rate of interest secured on short-term bonds and the zero rate received on cash may be considered to be the cost of hedging against a rise in market interest rates. This sort of hedging has less definite guides than hedging on the commodity markets. Two individuals faced with hedging their holdings of soybeans might act in precisely the same way, whereas two managers of financial institutions faced with the same uncertainties are unlikely to reach the same compromise between income and protection.

The holding of a portion of assets in the form of common stocks is especially attractive for pension funds, which have an obligation to protect the real purchasing power of contributions made by workers. Common stock prices are likely to keep up with, or more than keep up with, increases in the cost of living. In recent decades the federal government has shown much more interest in maintaining full employment than in maintaining stable prices. In such a political climate, stock ownership has assumed great importance as protection against inflation.

Since the owner of stocks is "long" on these securities, it is possible for him to hedge by taking an offsetting short position (betting that his stocks will go down). Since there is no futures market for stocks, a short position is assumed in a somewhat different way than in the commodities markets. A short seller informs his broker of his wish to sell a certain number of shares at the current price or near the current price. The broker then arranges to borrow the shares so they can be delivered to the one who buys from the short seller. At a later date, it is necessary for the short seller to "cover," buying the stock at its market price in order to return the shares to the lender. If the stock has declined in price between the time of sale and covering, the short seller profits by the difference in price (less commissions). In the opposite case, he loses by the amount of the price increase. When this type of hedging is carried out, the short seller may choose to turn over his own stocks to repay his loan. This would be apt to happen if his outlook became more pessimistic subsequent to his short sale.

Hedging with Put and Call Options

"Put and call" options are an old financial device which has recently attained increased importance in the United States in connection with the stock market. Such options were formerly used in commodity markets in this country but are no longer so employed. Like commodity futures, put and call options on stocks can be used both for speculation and for hedging.

A "put" is a contract under the terms of which the buyer has the option of delivering to the seller a specified number of shares of a certain stock at a specified price within a certain period of time; that is, the buyer of such a contract may, if he finds it advantageous to do so, "put" the stock to the seller of the contract at a certain price. The purchase of a put is a transaction which resembles a short sale in that a speculator who buys a put is hoping that the stock to which it applies will fall in price. Suppose a put option were purchased on Chrysler common stock at $70, the put costing $325 and being good for 60 days. The market price of Chrysler at the same time would be near $70 also. Suppose that Chrysler declined to $65 per share within the option period. The buyer of the option could then legally deliver (put) 100 shares of this stock to the seller of the option, receiving $7,000 for the shares which he would buy for $6,500. His profit would be $500, less the $325 cost of the option, less the broker's commissions on the option and on the stock purchases.

The purchase of a call option is a "bullish" transaction which, if made by a speculator, means that he expects the stock concerned to go up in price. The buyer of a call is buying the right to purchase (call for) a particular stock at a specified price during the life of the contract if he finds it advantageous to do so. The seller of the option must stand ready to deliver the stock if it is called for. Suppose General Dynamics is currently selling at $65 per common share. A call option at $65 good for about three months might sell for about $600. An individual who believed that the stock was going to rise in price during the period could buy a call. If he was correct and the stock rose to $80, he would exercise his option to buy 100 shares at $65. His capital gain would then be $1,500, less $600, less commissions and taxes. If the stock did not rise in price, he would not exercise his option and would lose the $600 cost of the option, plus commissions and taxes.

A call on stocks is similar in nature to the sort of option frequently used in real estate transactions, in mining, and in other business ventures. An option to lease or buy a certain piece of property at a definite rental or price is a "call" on the property, and the seller of the option is legally obligated to carry out the transaction if called upon by the buyer to do so.

The seller of a put option must stand ready to buy the stock at the stipulated price if the buyer chooses to exercise his option. The chance he takes is that the buyer of the option will "put" stock to him which, at the time it is delivered, is worth less than the price stipulated in the contract. For taking this risk, he receives the proceeds of the option sale as compensation.

The seller of a call option takes the risk that the buyer of the option will call for delivery of securities which have a greater market value than the buyer will pay. That is, he takes the risk that he will be deprived of a capital gain which he would otherwise have enjoyed. However, the seller of the call receives the proceeds of the option sale as a compensation for facing this uncertainty.

Purchases of puts are sometimes useful as a way of hedging against a decline in the market value of stockholdings. (At the present time, this practice is not widespread, however.) Pension funds, mutual investment funds, estates, individuals, and others may have large asset holdings in the form of common stocks. Especially after substantial paper capital gains have been made, the manager of a portfolio of stocks may be tempted to buy put options which match all or some of the stocks held. This protects against a decline in market value, since the profit which could be made by delivering stock in the event of a market decline would roughly offset the loss in value of the securities held. Should the market continue to advance, however, the put contracts would not be exercised, and their cost would constitute a sort of insurance premium. The practical problem facing the manager of a pension fund, for example, is that of deciding when it is better to hedge by buying puts and when it is better to risk the possibility of a fall in the stock market. When the decision is to hedge, the purchase of puts provides a way of transforming a possible large loss into an ascertainable cost. The substantial cost of put and call options, and the lack of general knowledge as to their uses, however, tend to limit their employment in hedging operations. Actually, most buyers of put and call options have a speculative motive, while the original sellers (makers) of the options are interested in the income which can thus be earned.

CASE 1-1: THE KOWMAN CORPORATION

The Kowman Corporation, established in 1938, was a family-owned corporation engaged in the business of warehousing. At the time of incorporation the firm was authorized to issue 50,000 shares of common stock with a par value of $10 per share and 1,000 shares of preferred stock at $100 per share. The latter stock bore a dividend rate of 6 per cent on a cumulative basis. When the firm. commenced operations, Mr. Kowman was named president of the corporation and was issued 500 shares of common stock. Mr. Kowman's two sons and two daughters were issued 100 shares each. No further issues of stock had been made since.

Late in 1937, Mr. Kowman had purchased at a bankrupt sale, for $89,000, an eight-story building which had been used as a factory. It contained 320,000 square feet of floor space, and was equipped with one large freight elevator and a smaller combination freight and passenger elevator. It was remodeled at a cost of $14,250 and turned over to the Kowman Corporation in exchange for the 1,000 shares of preferred stock. With this building the corporation entered the business of warehousing both commercial and household goods.

In 1946, Mr. Kowman acquired another building at a war-surplus sale at a price of $210,000. This building had 255,000 square feet of floor space, consisting of three stories and a large loading platform at the rear. It was equipped with one large freight elevator as well as a truck ramp to the second floor. In 1950 the corporation erected a third building, two stories high, with a freight elevator, containing 183,000 square feet of floor space, at a cost of $191,000. This building was located adjacent to that purchased by Mr. Kowman at the war-surplus sale. Both of these buildings were located at the edge of the city, while the original building was approximately four blocks from the main business section of the city. The second building was leased by Mr. Kowman to the Kowman Corporation for $15,000 per year for a 20-year period, the corporation to pay all costs of remodeling, maintenance, insurance, and taxes. Remodeling costs were $23,000 and were charged off as current expenses in the 1947 fiscal year. The buildings were identified on the books of the corporation as buildings A, B, and C, in the order of their acquisition.

The business was operated by Mr. Kowman's two sons. Each had received, since 1952, a salary of $25,000 per year. One of Mr. Kowman's daughters was secretary of the corporation at a salary of $7,500 per year, while the other daughter served as treasurer at a similar salary. Neither of the two daughters performed actual service for the firm other than signing documents in their official capacities. Until 1950, Mr. Kowman himself had received no salary; but effective that fiscal year, he had since drawn an annual salary of $10,000, although his services were chiefly advisory and of a perfunctory nature.

The initial capital of the company was supplied by the amounts paid in at par value for the common stock outstanding and by loans from Mr. Kowman as the need arose. The funds for Building C were provided by Mr. Kowman without interest. These funds were being repaid out of profits. After the profit-and-loss statement was prepared each year, exclusive of dividends on the preferred stock, all profits above $1,000 were paid to Mr. Kowman on this note. At the end of 1954, $41,000 had been repaid to Mr. Kowman toward the cost of Building C.

The company had shown a small profit each year since its beginning. Dividends on the preferred stock were paid each year, and none are now in arrears. The building for which this stock was issued was recently appraised at $250,000 when the company was approached by a prospective purchaser who desired the building for business use. As the profits remaining after dividend payments on the preferred stock had increased over the years, executive salaries had been adjusted upward.

In the spring of 1955 a national warehousing and van service company approached Mr. Kowman with a proposal to purchase the

Exhibit 1

THE KOWMAN CORPORATION

Statement of Profit and Loss, January 1, 1954, to December 31, 1954

Storage receipts	$232,492.57	
Miscellaneous receipts	1,352.39	
Total Receipts		$233,844.96
Expenses:		
Executive salaries	$ 75,000.00	
Operating salaries and wages	39,423.64	
Insurance	21,535.62	
Telephone	1,686.17	
Taxes*	14,319.26	
Heat, light, and power	6,231.75	
Maintenance†	21,472.05	
Miscellaneous expense	1,124.35	
Supplies	7,461.41	
Depreciation:		
Building A	5,000.00	
Building C	9,550.00	
Trucks and vans	3,000.00	
Rental expense, Building B	15,000.00	
Total Expense		220,804.25
Total Profit		$ 13,040.71
Less: Dividend on preferred stock		6,000.00
Net Profit		$ 7,040.71

* Includes social security, real estate, and transactions taxes, but not income taxes.
† Includes $7,335.50 for a new roof on Building A.

Kowman Corporation. This national company had one warehouse in the same city as the Kowman Corporation, with approximately one third as much space as Kowman. This warehouse was supervised by a local manager at a salary of $12,000 per year. In the event the purchase was completed, the national company proposed to increase this manager's salary to $15,000 per year and to dispense with the various executives currently with the Kowman Corporation. In reply to a request from the national company for a profit-and-loss statement, together with some other nonstatistical information, the Kowman Corporation submitted its profit-and-loss statement, as shown in Exhibit 1.

After an analysis of this information the national company made an offer of $750,000. This price would include the purchase of Building B and also the surrender of all outstanding capital stock to the purchaser.

QUESTIONS

1. Is the statement of profit and loss, as shown in Exhibit 1, acceptable to you? Why? If this statement is not acceptable, prepare one which is, and explain your corrections.
2. Would you, as the chief executive officer of the national company, have made an offer of $750,000? Why? Would you offer more or less?
3. Assume that the purchase offer valued Building A at $300,000, Building B at $250,000, and Building C at $200,000. On the basis of the remaining data in Exhibit 1, prepare a profit-and-loss statement for the national company, and explain any differences in results. Compute depreciation on the three buildings on a 20-year basis, using the straight-line method.

CASE 1–2: CHARLES F. DARRELL AND SONS

For many years the firm of Charles F. Darrell and Sons had been engaged in the wholesale distribution of butter, eggs, and poultry in Chicago, Illinois. Although the firm had only a few employees and a relatively small amount of fixed capital, its total volume of business exceeded $4 million annually. The bulk of its operations was in butter and eggs; poultry constituted only a small part of the business. The firm was founded by Charles F. Darrell during the latter part of the nineteenth century and had been managed by John Darrell, a son, since 1920.

Since both butter and eggs were seasonal in production, the firm always had purchased heavily of these two items during peak production periods and placed them in cold storage, to be drawn out as needed in off-peak seasons. For this purpose the firm had for many years used the facilities of the Ace Warehouse and Cold Storage Company, a bonded warehouse. As shown in Exhibit 1, the production of butter and eggs tended to rise about the first of April, and to exceed the amount consumed throughout the spring and early summer. In August and September, production tended to level out and decline until it came into balance with current consumption. During the remainder of the year, consumption ordinarily exceeded production, and butter and eggs in cold storage were withdrawn to meet the excess of consumption over production. This practice of storage and withdrawal tended to insure a steady flow of butter and eggs to

Exhibit 1

BUTTER AND EGG COLD STORAGE MOVEMENT, CHICAGO, 1948

WEEK ENDED	BUTTER (POUNDS)			EGGS (CASES)		
	In	Out	On Hand	In	Out	On Hand
Jan. 3	104,290	855,263	2,412,780	68	3,952	60,450
10	122,319	867,276	1,667,823	1,201	6,172	55,479
17	183,022	525,574	1,325,271	3,481	6,498	52,462
24	98,328	315,905	1,107,694	6,037	2,405	56,094
31	148,956	403,256	853,394	19,437	6,538	68,993
Feb. 7	83,119	274,067	662,446	22,204	10,019	81,178
14	170,942	291,221	542,167	27,456	16,218	92,416
21	269,385	231,177	580,375	20,115	22,482	90,049
28	146,197	228,259	498,313	6,213	13,867	82,395
Mar. 6	88,012	314,839	271,486	3,045	6,400	79,040
13	75,168	194,601	152,053	11,241	2,788	87,493
20	57,290	131,818	77,525	19,307	2,125	104,675
27	51,584	42,012	87,097	47,011	675	151,011
Apr. 3	88,830	47,731	128,196	77,801	560	228,252
10	202,607	169,096	161,707	73,360	683	300,929
17	204,012	269,975	95,744	95,497	1,501	394,925
24	142,166	127,923	109,987	110,443	378	504,990
May 1	236,899	130,810	216,076	159,355	357	663,988
8	500,064	139,310	576,830	184,471	658	847,801
15	799,350	191,256	1,184,924	164,163	716	1,011,248
22	927,907	241,138	1,871,693	132,870	866	1,143,252
29	1,677,793	208,436	3,341,050	126,993	2,338	1,267,907
June 5	1,640,919	153,914	4,828,055	93,004	883	1,360,028
12	1,269,487	289,997	5,807,545	101,356	1,065	1,460,319
19	1,415,778	200,040	7,023,283	103,941	2,081	1,562,179
26	1,515,764	113,601	8,425,446	56,570	1,611	1,617,138
July 3	1,584,097	279,769	9,729,774	36,301	2,103	1,651,336
10	1,973,599	148,287	11,555,086	35,532	2,951	1,683,917
17	1,682,285	413,782	12,823,589	25,553	10,710	1,698,760
24	1,555,396	235,149	14,143,836	16,144	3,314	1,711,590
31	1,398,316	336,256	15,205,896	9,257	8,632	1,712,215
Aug. 7	1,220,225	114,051	16,312,070	10,101	13,718	1,708,598
14	843,311	92,475	17,062,906	4,476	25,471	1,687,603
21	1,236,377	174,117	18,125,166	1,693	36,722	1,652,574
28	850,316	292,949	18,682,533	5,221	44,406	1,613,389
Sept. 4	637,389	283,353	19,036,569	6,750	62,840	1,557,299
11	454,577	194,761	19,296,385	6,913	58,646	1,505,566
18	505,414	512,942	19,287,857	2,048	89,397	1,418,217
25	526,413	410,986	19,403,284	1,096	89,533	1,329,780
Oct. 2	225,898	480,597	19,148,585	30	111,148	1,218,662
9	110,316	579,511	18,679,390	121	110,140	1,108,643
16	287,345	952,740	18,013,995	216	146,823	962,036
23	409,429	775,293	17,648,131	287	146,497	815,826
30	380,421	761,473	17,267,079	960	145,106	671,680
Nov. 6	275,834	837,462	16,705,451	....	157,785	513,895
13	82,730	736,091	16,052,090	518	125,900	388,513
20	66,465	1,114,703	15,003,852	189	117,244	271,458
27	51,444	1,571,379	13,483,917	270	65,078	206,650
Dec. 4	69,958	1,686,064	11,867,451	631	59,616	147,665
11	99,620	1,480,576	10,486,495	....	25,046	122,619
18	352,576	2,114,203	8,724,868	....	24,693	97,926
25	406,598	1,487,875	7,643,591	....	8,435	89,491

Source: *Dairy and Poultry Yearbook* (Chicago, 1949).

consumers throughout the year and to some extent leveled out the fluctuation in prices which would otherwise have occurred.

Eggs were purchased by the firm from country suppliers, local egg buyers, and local co-operatives. These contacts had been built up as a result of long years of experience. Local suppliers and buyers accumulated their purchases until a freight car had been filled and then offered the entire lot for sale to a dealer such as Darrell and Sons. A carload of eggs consisted of 480 cases of 30 dozen each, a total of 14,400 dozen. The firm in a year handled approximately 300 carloads of eggs, most of which were purchased and placed in storage between April 1 and August 1. A very small amount of eggs was delivered in less-than-carload lots locally by near-by farmers. During periods of peak production, eggs were shipped in carload lots to the firm without a formal offer of sale. Such shipments were usually accepted and, if Darrell and Sons were unable to handle them, were easily disposed of to another dealer. Occasionally, it was necessary to request formal offer of sale from local buyers and co-operatives if the market showed any indication of inability to absorb an unlimited quantity. When such conditions existed, the firm tended to refuse offers from local buyers with whom they did only occasional business.

Although Darrell and Sons had been a successful and reputable firm, its working capital requirements were far in excess of its available cash. It was, therefore, necessary to finance the purchase of eggs for storage by means of loans from banks. The carrying of large storage stocks involved the risk of price changes from the time of purchase until the stocks were withdrawn and sold. There was also the risk of deterioration of the eggs as a result of the passage of time, an ordinary business hazard covered by normal markups. Banks and other lending agencies were reluctant to extend a great deal of credit unless the loans were secured by a hedge on the Chicago Mercantile Exchange. It was the policy of most of these agencies to lend up to approximately 90 per cent of the value of the purchase at the time it was placed in storage, provided that the loan was secured by a hedge and the warehouse receipt. Accordingly, the firm had made it a practice, since the egg futures market had been organized in 1918, to sell egg futures as it purchased eggs for storage in the spring and early summer, provided that the futures contract price reflected all charges and normal markup. To finance these purchases, the firm borrowed at its bank. In August of each year the firm had outstanding loans which varied from $1.5 million to $2 million, depending upon the price of eggs. As eggs were withdrawn from storage during the winter and futures contracts fulfilled, either by delivery or by repurchase, the loans were repaid, so that by February of each year the firm had no obligations at its bank.

Exhibit 2 shows the expenses which were incurred by local egg buyers and co-operatives in preparing and transporting eggs to the

Exhibit 2
COSTS TO LOCAL BUYERS OF PREPARING AND TRANSPORTING EGGS TO CHICAGO
(Per Dozen)

	Cents
Collecting costs at country points (including local transportation and containers)	2.5– 3.0
Grading	1.5– 2.0
Candling	1.0– 1.5
Country overhead	1.0– 1.5
Packing	2.0– 2.5
Freight to market	1.0– 1.5
Total	9.0–12.0

wholesaler in Chicago as current supply or for storage. These expenses were in addition to the price paid to the producer for his eggs. Thus, if the price paid to the producer was 40 cents per dozen, the cash price paid by the wholesaler in Chicago would range from 49 to 52 cents per dozen. If the eggs were placed in storage, the cost of storage, insurance, repacking, etc., would be approximately $\frac{1}{4}$ to $\frac{3}{8}$ cent per dozen per month of storage. It was a sort of tradition of the trade that the expected price of eggs at the time of withdrawal from storage—i.e., the futures contract price—must be at least 3 cents per dozen above the prevailing cash price to break even on the purchase and storage of eggs. Any smaller margin was considered unprofitable by the trade, since eggs were in storage for approximately six months. While there was still some margin between the costs of storage and insurance and the minimum 3-cent margin, the trade did not consider it worth while to risk the exploitation of such a small margin.

Early in April, 1949, the firm began to receive eggs in excess of demand and made preparation for storage. No eggs had been placed in storage by them since August, 1948, demand having been met by current receipts and withdrawals from storage stocks. All obligations had been paid at the bank when due. Several hundred cases of eggs were prepared and placed in storage, but no hedge was placed against them on the Chicago Mercantile Exchange. Mr. Darrell had been aware for some time that the price of October futures was less than

3 cents per dozen more than the current cash price. He attributed this to several causes, such as possible flush production in the fall months, general lack of confidence in current levels of commodity prices, and possible amendment of the government purchase program which could provide subsidies to producers instead of support prices, with resulting serious price declines in the market. By April 4, 1949, the firm had placed 34 carloads of eggs in storage but had not yet hedged them. This inventory required almost all the working capital of the firm. The bank advised Mr. Darrell that it would be unable to extend credit to cover purchases without a hedge.

Exhibit 3

QUOTATIONS OF OCTOBER EGG FUTURES ON CHICAGO MERCANTILE EXCHANGE AND CASH PRICES OF CURRENT RECEIPTS, MARCH, 1949
(Cents per Dozen)

Date	October Futures (Close)	Cash Price (70% Grade A and Over) Naturals*	Date	October Futures (Close)	Cash Price (70% Grade A and Over) Naturals*
Mar. 1.........	46.85	45.50	Mar. 16.........	47.00	44.50
2.........	47.00	44.50	17.........	46.95	44.50
3.........	47.05	44.75	18.........	47.00	44.50
4.........	47.10	44.75			
			21.........	47.20	44.50
7.........	47.35	44.75	22.........	47.40	44.50
8.........	47.30	45.00	23.........	47.55	45.00
9.........	47.20	45.00	24.........	47.60	45.00
10.........	47.25	45.00	25.........	47.85	45.50
11.........	47.25	45.00			
			28.........	48.15	46.00
14.........	47.20	45.00	29.........	48.00	46.00
15.........	47.15	44.50	30.........	48.20	46.50
			31.........	48.35	46.50

* Processed or treated eggs command a premium of about ½ cent per dozen. Eggs packed in wood cases command about ¼-cent premium over fiber cases.
Source: *Chicago Tribune* (daily quotations).

Exhibit 3 shows the March quotations for October egg futures on the Chicago Mercantile Exchange as well as the current cash price for eggs during the same period.

QUESTIONS

1. Would you recommend that Darrell and Sons hedge their egg purchases regardless of future prices? Why?
2. Should the firm continue to buy eggs if financing can be secured without hedging? What effect would this have upon the firm's profits? Would

you, as the officer of a bank, be willing to extend credit to this firm without a hedge? Why?

3. In view of the conditions outlined above, what action would you recommend that the firm take?

4. Are there any indications as to why the difference between the cash and futures prices for the month of March, 1949, is insufficient to cover the costs of carrying eggs in storage?

APPENDIX A TO CASE 1–2: THE EGG FUTURES MARKET

Eggs are used primarily as food or as an ingredient in the preparation of foodstuffs. Liquid, frozen, and dried eggs, which constitute about 13 per cent of production, are utilized by commercial bakers and by manufacturers of candy and confections, salad dressings, egg noodles, and similar products. A little less than 3 per cent of the total egg supply is bought by hatcheries or held by farmers to replenish stocks. Additional uses of eggs are found in the preparation of feed, pharmaceutical and photographic supplies, leather tanning, textile dyeing, bookbinding, and ink manufacturing.

As a rule, eggs are sold by farmers to a local concentration point, such as a country store, egg buyer, co-operative, creamery, or packing-plant station. These buyers usually pass their accumulations to larger concentration points, where the eggs are graded, packed, and shipped in carload lots to the large centers.

Because a handler who accumulates eggs for carload shipments usually has a substantial inventory (approximately $6,000 tied up in each carload), it is advantageous for him to sell a contract for future delivery of the eggs at the time that he stores them, thereby insuring against a decrease in price during his period of ownership. For the same reason, many users or distributors of large quantities of eggs buy futures contracts, so that they may be sure of the availability of eggs for their use or sale. Such a purchase also makes possible to them a normal manufacturing or operating profit and insures them against an increase in raw-material prices.

The market for egg futures is traditionally an active one, with fluctuations registered monthly, weekly, daily, and even hourly. There are two primary classes of traders—speculators and hedgers. The speculator finds the futures contract to be of sufficiently long term for him to make use of his knowledge and study of the egg market. Acting on this study, he assumes the market risk when the hedger sells futures contracts as a hedge against his unsold stock or when another hedger buys futures contracts to protect his supply. The presence of these speculators in the futures market in large numbers—always willing to buy and sell at a price—makes it possible for the hedger to pass on the risk of price changes.

Egg handlers, wholesalers, and processors insure their warehouse stocks against price drops over the summer period by selling futures contracts on the Chicago Mercantile Exchange. Conversely, manufacturers, distributors, and others with future sale commitments, but without stocks of eggs, insure themselves against price increases by buying futures. Each has thus executed a hedge, the object of which is to eliminate or reduce his price risk.

The *Commodity Yearbook,* published by the Commodity Research Bureau, states that "studies of the results of futures trading in eggs in the nearly thirty years since the Chicago Mercantile Exchange was founded, demonstrate conclusively that great benefits are assured for both farmers and the consuming public through the price stabilization, insurance of normal operating profits and reduced costs which result from this link in the distributing system." This statement has been subjected to some criticism from various sources. On several occasions when the price of eggs has moved toward unusually high levels, speculators in the futures market have been singled out as the cause. While speculators make possible the futures markets, it is not certain that their role has always been one of benefit to those affected by the market.

APPENDIX B TO CASE 1–2: FEDERAL PRICE-SUPPORT PROGRAM FOR EGGS

Under Section I of Title I of the Agricultural Act of 1948, eggs were supported at 90 per cent of parity until January 1, 1950. Monthly the parity price was adjusted for seasonal variations. Purchases were, therefore, made by the government at prices which were estimated to yield 90 per cent of parity. Throughout 1949 a support price of 35 cents per dozen at the farm yielded this percentage.

The general purpose of all price supports is to maintain the purchasing power of agricultural products in relation to that of industrial products. During the war emergency, supports were used to stimulate production. The program was continued to aid reconversion to a peacetime production basis and to help avoid the possibility of repeating the disastrous price declines which followed World War I.

The method used to support the egg market is at the discretion of the United States Department of Agriculture. The department's current policy is first to purchase dried eggs from driers who certify that they have paid support prices to the producers. The program is centered mostly in surplus-producing areas in the Midwest, and should be reflected throughout the country. It was felt that it would be impracticable to give individual support to the 4.5 million farms that now contribute to the bulk of production.

If support through driers does not achieve the desired result, then purchases of frozen eggs will be made from breakers who have similarly certified to prices paid to the producers. As a last resort, shell eggs may be purchased in areas not served by driers and breakers.

In 1948 the department bought the equivalent of about 2.8 million cases of shell eggs, or 1.7 per cent of the total production of that year. The program for 1949 was an extension of the 1948 program and continued on the 35-cent basis with a 2-cent premium paid to producers who delivered their own eggs to processors. The department had bought, through April 27, 1949, approximately 39 million pounds of dried eggs, equivalent to roughly 4 million cases of shell eggs.

In putting into effect the support program for eggs, the department, through the Commodity Credit Corporation, offered to buy in unlimited quantities dried eggs from driers in accordance with regulations set forth above. The department paid the dried-egg processors $1.26 per pound for powdered eggs in barrels or $1.28 per pound when packaged in 14-pound containers.

These prices are calculated to yield a price of 35 cents per dozen to producers on the assumption that one case of shell eggs will yield 10 pounds of egg powder. The actual result has been a yield of $10\frac{1}{2}$ to 11 pounds of powder per case. Consequently, the profit on dried eggs is actually greater than anticipated. In order to take advantage of this extra profit, driers have tended to offer country producers more than 35 cents per dozen, which, in turn, affects the cash price of eggs in Chicago.

CASE 1–3: CALKINS-WALKER, INC.

Calkins-Walker, Inc., was a ladies' apparel and specialty store which carried a complete line of ladies' furnishings, notions, and cosmetics of high quality only. Prices ranged from the upper-medium lines to the high-priced luxury lines. More than 60 per cent of its business was on an open-account basis, and more than 25,000 accounts were currently active. The company was located in the main downtown business and shopping district of a large metropolitan area. The population of the city proper was approximately 3 million, with another 2.5 million persons in the adjoining suburbs.

The firm had been in its present location for more than 35 years. It occupied the first four floors of a seven-story building, the remainder being used as office space from a separate entrance on the street fronting the building. The space occupied by Calkins-Walker was leased on a 30-year basis. The lease agreement provided for a basic rental of $85,000 per year when annual net sales were $750,000 or less, plus 2 per cent of net sales when net sales exceeded $750,000 but were less than $1.5 million, and plus 3 per cent of net sales in excess of $1.5 million. This lease had been renewed in 1949. The original lease contained lower rentals than the current one.

Within a five-block radius of Calkins-Walker, there were three department stores which carried similar merchandise in the same price range. These stores also carried less expensive lines. There were several smaller specialty shops in the same area which carried many of the same lines as Calkins-Walker, but none carried a complete line. There were also a few shops which carried higher-priced lines than Calkins-Walker, but they were comparatively small and catered almost exclusively to the luxury trade.

The suburban areas surrounding the city had developed to a large extent according to income level. To the north, there were several communities with the highest income level of the metropolitan area. On the western side was another group with only slightly lower incomes, and to the south was a smaller number of areas with high incomes. Within the city itself the higher-income groups lived in the north and northwest portions of the city. The southern and eastern portions of the city were inhabited primarily by an industrial population. In the higher-income suburban areas were a few old and well-established shopping centers. In two of these areas, there were branches of two of the large downtown department stores. In addition, there were several of the smaller, higher-priced ladies' specialty shops, among them several of the nationally better-known ladies' ready-to-wear firms.

From 1932 to 1935 the company suffered losses on operations and showed only a small profit in the years which followed. No dividends were declared from 1932 to 1939. Although it was difficult to obtain adequate supplies of all lines of merchandise during the period of World War II, the company earned good profits in spite of price controls. From the end of the war until 1949 the company enjoyed a substantial increase in sales each year. Sales reached a new high in 1948, at $2,421,335.27. In 1949, there was a decline to $1,947,-217.31. Recovery followed in 1950, with sales increasing to $2,003,-112.53. Beginning with 1951, sales began to decline, in spite of the fact that incomes in the area were increasing.

The decline in sales prompted Mr. Frederick, the president and general manager of Calkins-Walker, to investigate. He observed that there had been a large growth of population but learned that it was concentrated in the suburbs. By 1948, there had been some net loss of population by the city to the suburbs, especially in the middle and upper-middle income groups. To the northwest, west, and south of the city, entire communities were being erected. The established suburbs were also growing and developing much of their vacant land. Mr. Frederick believed that the growth of the suburbs had only begun and was concerned by the effect of their growth upon downtown shopping areas.

The growth of the suburbs had far exceeded the development of public transportation, so that by early 1949 the private automobile was the primary means of suburban transport. The increase in the number of motorcars resulted in overcrowded traffic and parking conditions in the downtown areas. It was feared that this situation would discourage shoppers from the suburbs, and various studies had been made or were under consideration. To date, nothing concrete had developed.

In the new communities, shopping centers were rising. In some cases, they were planned and included in the original blueprints of the community. In others, they had grown independently and unplanned. Mr. Frederick was of the opinion that the conventional, planned shopping center was not the proper location for a suburban store of Calkins-Walker. He felt that the clientele of his store was not attracted by a shopping center, but that better results could be obtained by a store separate from a center if a suburban location was decided upon. He felt that there was no place at all for a store in the newer communities, but that the greatest possibilities lay in the growing and older high-income suburbs.

In order to protect the company against possible loss of markets and declining sales and profits, Mr. Frederick proposed that the firm select now the best possible locations and secure them by option until such time as the future of the downtown shopping area became more discernible. His position was that with the options the company would be assured of three possible alternatives: (1) suburban expansion with eventual abandonment of the downtown location, (2) more intensive downtown development and abandonment of suburban expansion, and (3) an integration of both urban and suburban developments.

Three desirable parcels of land in three different suburbs were currently available by option. They could be optioned either for purchase or for long-term lease. The initial option period would run for one year at a fee of $2,000 per month, renewable in six-month periods, but with the renewal fee open at the end of each option. Mr. Frederick recommended that the company acquire these options at the stated fee. Three directors of the company objected on the grounds that it was "throwing money down the drain."

QUESTIONS

1. Would you acquire the options? Explain.
2. If the options are acquired, would you say Mr. Frederick has hedged? (Do you find him simultaneously taking long and short positions?)
3. Are the options under consideration comparable to "puts" or to "calls"? Why?
4. Would you classify the taking-up of these options as "insurance"? Explain.
5. What sort of developments within the city proper might increase the value of the downtown location, making a move to the suburbs less desirable?

Chapter 2

ECONOMIC AND BUSINESS FORECASTING

In the previous chapter, it was pointed out that many businessmen protect themselves from unfavorable price changes by means of hedging. If hedging is "pure"—that is, if it does not at the same time include an element of speculation—it does not require that a forecast be made, because the businessman is protected regardless of which way the relevant price moves. For most business decisions, however, no perfect hedge is available, and reasonably accurate forecasting is necessary for profitable operations. The typical businessman must constantly "stick out his neck," and careful forecasting may help him keep ahead.

Forecasting is not always carried out as an explicit function, but it is necessarily implicit in numerous decisions which must be made within the firm. If forecasting is not a centralized, explicit activity, there is danger that important forecasts will be made, in effect, by persons who are not in the best position to engage in this activity. For example, the sales forecast may be implicit in the decisions made by the order clerk who, upon investigation, would probably be found to be using rule-of-thumb methods rather than to be making use of all of the information which might be brought to bear on the problem.[1]

A recent *Fortune* magazine survey of 405 companies (accounting for one fourth of all United States industrial assets) revealed that 141 of these companies employ staff economists and that an additional 55 firms use outside consultants.[2] While these economists and consultants engage in many different kinds of analysis (plant location, pricing, financing, etc.), most of them are active to some degree in economic and business forecasting. The former consists of making forecasts of *general* business activity such as movements of national income, ag-

---

[1] This is suggested by Carl A. Dauten, *Business Fluctuations and Forecasting* (Cincinnati: South-Western Publishing Co., 1954), p. 6.

[2] Charles E. Silberman and Sanford S. Parker, "The Economy's Scouts," *Fortune,* December, 1955, p. 100.

gregate industrial production or employment, total exports or imports, or fluctuation in security price indexes. Business forecasting pertains more directly to the activity of the particular firm, consisting of short- and long-term forecasts of sales, price forecasts for important raw materials and equipment, availability of resources at plant sites under investigation, and a host of other matters of specific interest. The separation between economic and business forecasting is not always sharp, however. From the point of view of a firm which is one of a substantial number of companies in an industry, a forecast of sales for the entire industry lies somewhere between a forecast of general business activity and of activity specific to the firm. While the firm's sales are likely to be highly correlated with the sales of the industry of which it is a member, this relation will not necessarily hold, especially over the longer run (during which new firms may enter or leave the field). In view of this difficulty of classification, no sharp dividing line will be drawn in this chapter between economic and business forecasting. Instead, the various popular methods of forecasting will be discussed separately. Most of these are applicable both to general and to specific prediction.

Uses of Forecasting

The value of economic forecasting to the federal government is quite obvious to the extent that the prevailing policy is to use fiscal and monetary measures to prevent depressions and severe price inflation. Substantial changes in federal spending and taxing may take many months to put into effect, especially if Congress is not in session at the right time, and this means that a serious downturn in business would have to be predicted far ahead of time if fiscal measures were to prevent its actual occurrence. Monetary policy can be changed more quickly and is consequently less dependent on effective forecasting.

The deliberate use of monetary and fiscal policy to prevent undesirable fluctuations in over-all economic activity and prices suggests an interesting problem in verification of the accuracy of forecasts. A correct forecast of a coming depression might appear to have been incorrect if prompt and adequate governmental efforts actually prevented its occurrence. Yet the forecast would actually have been instrumental in preventing the decline in economic activity.

The same caution in evaluating the accuracy of a forecast must be exercised when an individual firm is large enough to affect by its own actions the event which is predicted. A forecast of an insufficient capacity to meet demand in five years might itself be sufficient to cause a firm to build enough new capacity to meet the demand. (This self-defeating effect of the forecast would be amplified if rival firms were induced by the firm's actions also to expand their plant capacity.) Usually, however, the individual firm is not sufficiently important to affect the outcome by its own reactions to a forecast. If inflationary monetary policy on the part of the federal government caused a general rise in raw-material prices, for example, the power of the individual firm to prevent such a price rise would be negligible.

The uses of forecasting to the firm are many. As has already been suggested, plant expansion (or contraction) plans should be based on a long-term forecast of demand for output.[3] In order to be fully relevant for this purpose, a forecast should cover the period during which fixed capital equipment is normally amortized. Short-term price movements are of great importance to the businessman with respect to inventory holdings. Normally, an expected increase in price will make it advantageous to build up stocks in advance of the price rise (provided carrying costs are not too great). In general, the expectation of inflation will make it desirable for a firm to place itself in more of a debtor position by means of such actions as borrowing and reducing its holdings of cash and accounts receivable. A forecast of general deflation will make it desirable for the firm to attain more of a creditor position by means of building up cash, accounts and notes receivable, and other assets whose value is fixed in dollars, and to substitute common stock for bonds in its own capital structure.[4]

Forecasting the appropriate rate of production for a number of months into the future may be extremely important as an aid to procurement of materials and components which must be ordered far in advance of their use. The same is true of workers who require a period of training before they are useful to a company. On the other hand, ordinary supplies and unskilled labor may usually be purchased as the need arises, and forecasting is of little importance in relation to their acquisition.

---

[3] The term "output" should be considered to comprehend not only the product of a manufacturing firm but also the services furnished by a retailer or wholesaler, the transportation furnished by a truck or train, the housing services provided by apartment buildings, etc.

[4] An interesting empirical study of the effect of debtor and creditor positions on the firm is described by Reuben A. Kessel, "Inflation-Caused Wealth Redistribution: A Test of a Hypothesis," *American Economic Review*, March, 1956, p. 128. He found that the debtor-creditor hypothesis has predictive usefulness. Kessel's results are in keeping with the old idea that there is more "leverage" behind a stock when the company also has bonds outstanding; his analysis is, however, more thorough and more sophisticated.

Trend Projection

Probably the most common way of forecasting the future is simply to construct a chart depicting the actual movement of a series and then to project (extrapolate) the apparent trend of the data as far into the future as is desired for the purpose at hand. The projection is usually a straight line, but it may instead be curvilinear. This is sometimes classified as a "naïve" method of forecasting, since it is based on no particular theory as to what causes the variable to change but merely assumes that whatever forces contributed to change in the recent past will continue to have the same effect. Trend projectors are often able to show a high percentage of forecasts which are correct in direction, at least; but the method has the serious defect of missing all of the sudden downturns or upturns—and these are just the changes which it is most important to predict correctly.[5]

On the other hand, trend projection may be about the only available method when the variable under consideration is affected by a large number of factors the separate influence of which cannot readily be measured because of lack of data, lack of time, or other reasons. The analyst may, for example, have a feeling that a series is affected by the general growth of the economy as population increases, capital accumulates, and technology improves; and if he has confidence in this underlying growth, he may feel, quite rationally, that the observed upward trend in the series in which he is interested will continue. His simple extrapolation is then not entirely naïve, although he might be able to do better by using more complicated methods, provided the necessary data are available—and available on time. As in using any method of forecasting, it is important that the analyst be familiar with the field with which he is working. It would, for example, be ridiculous to measure the increase in retail toy sales in December over November and to project this increase in order to predict the January sales.

A simple example of forecasting by means of trend projection is given in Exhibit 1. Actual total consumer credit outstanding, as reported by the *Federal Reserve Bulletin* (April, 1956) is plotted as of the ends of the years 1949 through 1955. Over this period, there was a rapid increase in consumer credit, with the increase in 1955 being especially rapid, the gain for this year amounting to $6.1 billion. A straight-line projection of the apparent trend is made for the years 1956 through 1958. This demonstrates the sort of problem which

---

[5] This is pointed out by Charles F. Roos in a useful article, "Survey of Economic Forecasting Techniques," *Econometrica*, October, 1955, p. 366.

confronts the trend projector. It is an arbitrary matter whether one projects the trend as computed over the entire period (as has been done) or considers that the upward trend has accelerated, as indicated by the upsurge in 1955. If one were influenced strongly by the latter, he would tilt the extrapolation more sharply upward, perhaps using a curve concave on the upside. Actually, the entire projection is unusually hazardous because of the mounting fear of many important officials that installment buying is getting out of hand and the increasing possibility that effective steps may be taken to check the rise.

Exhibit 1

TREND PROJECTION—QUICK BUT DANGEROUS

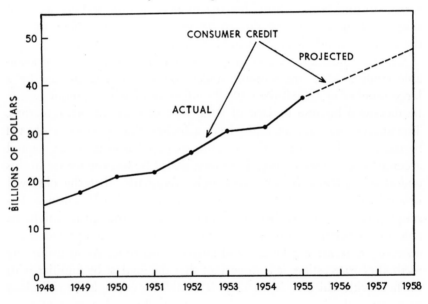

The Federal Reserve banks raised the rediscount rate five times between April 14, 1955, and April 12, 1956. This sort of monetary action, if continued, might make consumer credit sufficiently tight and sufficiently costly to reverse the trend. Such information, however, is not necessarily in the possession of the trend projector unless he has adequate time for research. It is cited to illustrate why trend projection may be extremely naïve. At the same time, if a quick estimate is needed for 1956, 1957, and 1958, projection of the trend does offer a way of getting some answers which at least reflect the current tendency of the American people to live beyond their present incomes, and the general propensity of the federal government and banking system to go along with their desires and make the desired borrowing possible. It will be noted that such monetary restriction as took place in 1955 did not stem the tide of installment credit, and it might not be incorrect to assume tacitly that further increases in interest rates would also prove ineffectual in this respect.

Leading Indexes

As has been suggested, a main shortcoming of trend projection as a forecasting technique is that it necessarily fails to foresee the vital turns, downward and upward, in the series under consideration. It is these turns which call for the most important changes in inventory policy, hiring policy, capital budgeting, debtor-creditor position adjustment, and other matters. A great deal of statistical research has been devoted to the problem of finding "leading indexes"—that is, sensitive series which tend to turn up or down in advance of other series. The value of such indicators (if reliable) is obvious. If one could discover a series which would reliably lead stock or commodity price indexes, it would not be difficult to become rich (that is, if this method of prediction did not come into general use; in that event, it would cease to lead these speculative prices). Actually, stock prices themselves have been found to be significant leading series for industrial production and for other important indicators of business health. For example, the stock market crash of 1929 preceded the calamitous depression of the 1930's. However, stock market price movements reflect the opinions and actions of speculators and investors; and the more basic question still remains as to what information affects, or should affect, the opinions of the most alert and best-informed speculators.

In 1950, Dr. Geoffrey Moore of the National Bureau of Economic Research tested the cyclical behavior of over 800 statistical series. He selected 18 monthly and three quarterly series which appeared to be outstanding business indicators. The Federal Reserve Bank of New York, in its *Monthly Review of Credit and Business Conditions,* publishes "Selected Economic Indicators" which correspond closely with Dr. Moore's indicators, except for certain omissions.[6] These are not all leading indexes, however; some are coincident with business fluctuations, and others lag behind general business activity. Earlier work along this line was done by Charles F. Roos, who in 1938 examined

---

[6] The statistical series regularly published by the Federal Reserve Bank of New York are described in a booklet entitled *Selected Economic Indicators,* published by that bank in December, 1954.

248 monthly indexes in an effort to find which ones had lead characteristics.[7]

The publicly available series found by Moore to have lead characteristics were (1) new orders for durable goods, (2) residential building contracts, (3) commercial and industrial building contracts, (4) prices of industrial common stocks, (5) wholesale prices of basic commodities, (6) average work week in manufacturing, (7) number of new incorporations, and (8) liabilities of industrial and commercial business failures. Of these, the "Selected Economic Indicators" exclude industrial common stock prices, liabilities of business failures, and new incorporations. The five leading indexes which are regularly

Exhibit 2

SELECTED LEADING INDEXES

Year 1956	Manufacturers' New Orders, Durable Goods (Billions of Dollars)	Residential Construction Contracts (1947–49 = 100)	Nonresidential Construction Contracts (1947–49 = 100)	Wholesale Prices (1947–49 = 100)	Average Hours Worked per Week, Manufacturing
January.........	$14.7	290	306	111.9	40.6
February........	14.3	318	298	112.4	40.5
March..........	13.3	317	267	112.8	40.3
April..........	14.1	315	252	113.6	40.3
May...........	14.9	286	237	114.4	40.0
June...........	14.4	280	253	114.2	40.1

published by the Federal Reserve Bank of New York are shown in Exhibit 2 for the first six months of 1956. All are adjusted for seasonal variation. One difficulty is immediately apparent: The leading indexes often point in different directions at the same time, so that until their movements become substantial in magnitude and similar in direction, it is hard to know where they are leading. Nevertheless, a downturn of some of these indicators after a consistent rise might at least warn the businessman that a general turn is more likely than before. A downturn of all five might well be a signal for action in anticipation of lower prices and reduced business activity.

---

[7] Roos, *op. cit.*, p. 369. Roos states that series which he found in 1938 to have lead characteristics still retained these characteristics in 1954.

Manufacturers' New Orders

New orders placed with manufacturers should clearly have lead characteristics.[8] Orders are an early reflection of the demand for a product; and a sizeable change in the volume of orders is very likely to be followed by changes in purchases of raw materials, in employment, in rate of production, and perhaps in the demand for loans or equity capital. New orders for *durable goods* should be especially valuable to the forecaster of general economic conditions because they reflect investment decisions, and such decisions are of great importance in generating changes in national income. Also, if the information can be secured by industry totals, such new orders may be valuable to the firm which sells materials or equipment to a durable goods manufacturer. An increase in orders for merchant ships, for example, should eventually lead to increased orders for steel, wood, turbines, radio equipment, lifeboats, etc.; and the producers of such materials and equipment may find it desirable to take steps in anticipation of their receipt of orders from the shipbuilders.

The lead characteristics of new orders which are of importance to firms selling to capital goods producers should depend not on the durability of the good once it is produced but rather on its "period of production" (in the sense of the lag between receipt of an order and completion of shipment) and on the timing of the need for materials in the production process. For example, knowledge of the volume of new orders for merchant ships might not be very important to the producers of steel for the hulls, since these steel producers would quickly receive their orders from the shipbuilders, anyway. The knowledge might be more valuable to firms which build marine radio and radar equipment, because they might not so quickly receive orders from the shipbuilders.

The Department of Commerce publishes separate series on new orders received monthly by all manufacturers and new orders received by durable goods manufacturers. These are shown in the well-known *Survey of Current Business*. The Department of Commerce computes its new orders series from reported unfilled orders and sales, using the formula: Unfilled orders at end of Month 1, plus net sales during Month 2, minus unfilled orders at end of Month 2, equal new orders during Month 2. This method is preferable to a direct reporting of the

---

[8] Roos, *op. cit.*, pp. 372–73, considers new orders to be the outstanding leading index. He points out that new orders for capital goods usually turn down before important declines occur in production and even in stock prices.

Exhibit 3

NEW ORDERS FOR, AND SALES OF, DURABLE GOODS,
1953–55

(In Billions of Dollars, Adjusted for Seasonal Variations)

Month	New Orders	Sales
1953:		
January	$12.8	$12.5
February	12.3	12.7
March	13.4	13.1
April	13.0	13.4
May	12.2	13.1
June	13.0	13.2
July	11.6	13.4
August	10.1	12.7
September	10.1	12.7
October	9.8	12.4
November	8.9	11.9
December	9.3	11.6
1954:		
January	8.7	11.6
February	9.6	11.3
March	10.2	11.4
April	10.0	11.5
May	10.0	11.3
June	9.9	11.4
July	9.7	11.3
August	10.0	11.0
September	11.7	10.9
October	11.5	10.6
November	11.5	11.6
December	12.3	12.0
1955:		
January	12.1	12.3
February	12.2	12.0
March	13.4	12.9
April	12.9	12.8
May	14.3	13.3
June	14.0	13.5
July	13.6	13.5
August	15.1	13.7
September	14.9	13.7
October	14.1	13.3
November	14.7	13.7
December	15.6	13.7

Source: *Survey of Current Business*, U.S. Department of Commerce, Office of Business Economics.

new orders as indicated each month by the sample of firms (which is "blown up" to give totals), because it eliminates cumulative errors and provides consistent series on sales, new orders, and unfilled orders.

Data for manufacturers' new orders and sales of all durable goods are given by months in Exhibit 3 for the years 1953, 1954, and 1955. These series are plotted in Exhibit 4. The data have been adjusted by

Exhibit 4

MANUFACTURERS' NEW ORDERS FOR DURABLE GOODS TEND TO LEAD DURABLE GOODS SALES

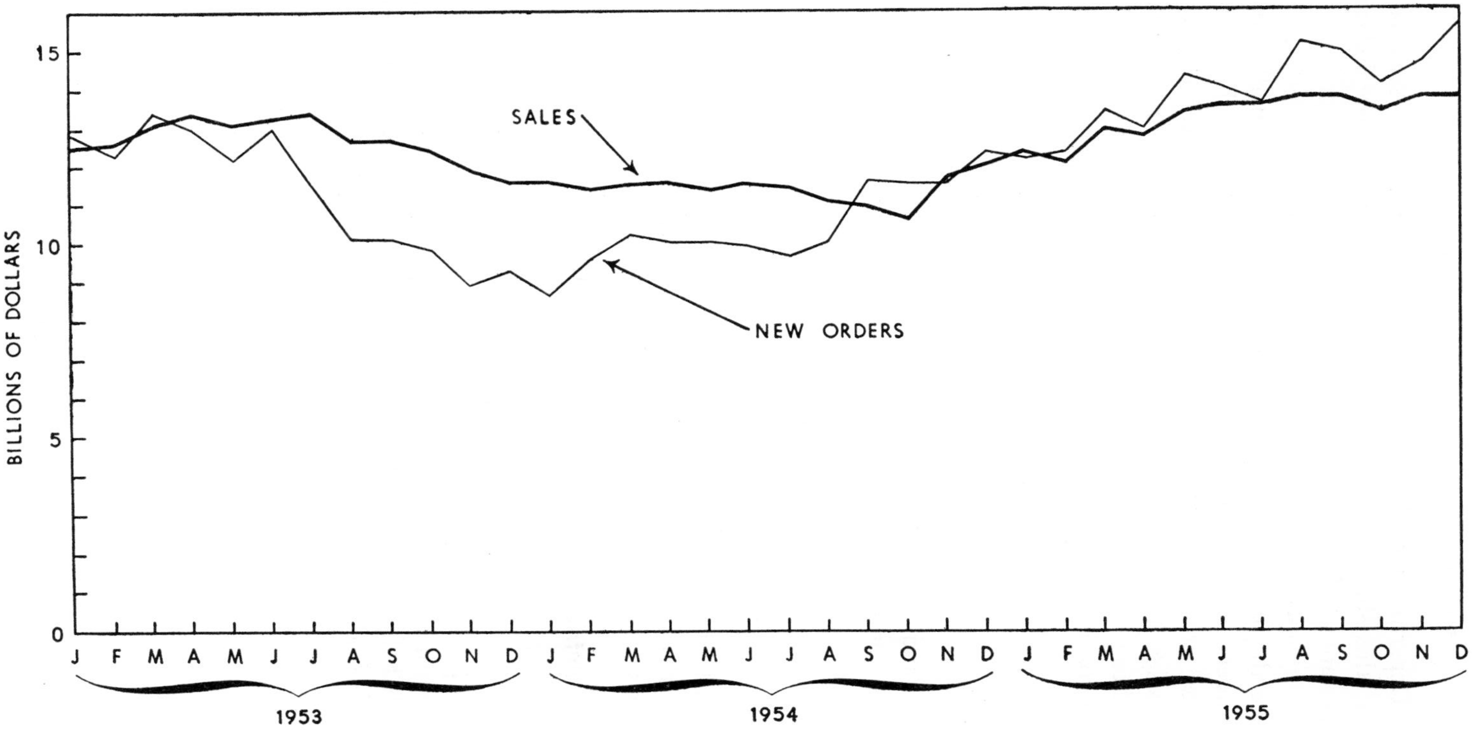

the Department of Commerce to eliminate the usual seasonal variations; this should make month-to-month changes more indicative of
important changes in the economic climate. An examination of the
data suggests that new orders are a useful leading index, but also
warns the analyst not to pay too much attention to small fluctuations
in orders; these need not affect future sales since the backlog of
unfilled orders furnishes the means for producers to keep up production
and sales in the face of falling orders. It will be noted that sales
ran ahead of new orders during most of the two-year period 1953–54.
As a consequence, unfilled orders fell from $72.9 billion at the end
of January, 1953, to $44.5 billion at the end of December, 1954.
This led some economists to expect a recession in 1955. However,
new orders and sales both increased markedly that year.

A sharp decline in new orders for durable goods began in April,
1953, and the decline continued until November, 1953, when new
orders were only $8.9 billion compared with $13.4 billion in March,
1953. Sales did not begin to decline significantly until August, 1953,
but fell quite steadily for about 14 months. By September, 1954, new
orders were clearly on the way up, but sales did not turn up until
November, 1954. The climb in new orders late in 1955 suggests an
upward turn of sales in 1956. Exhibit 4 tends to substantiate the
belief that new orders for durable goods have important lead characteristics.

Econometric Methods

The most elegant (and sometimes the best) method of forecasting is
by the use of econometrics. This term covers a variety of analytical
techniques, most of them being a blending of economics, statistics,
and mathematics. Econometric models of the entire economy are constantly being worked upon and improved. These models contain among
their variables such factors as net investment, consumption, government expenditures, taxes, and net export or import balance, since these
are key determinants of national income according to the prevailing
theory of income determination. To the extent that some of the
determining variables can be predicted, the econometric model may
be useful in forecasting such over-all measures of economic activity
as gross national product and national income. If, for example, it
could be shown by statistical study of the past that investment in
one year is largely determined by profits of the previous year and
that consumption is heavily influenced by the amount of liquid savings
accumulated before January 1 of the year in question, the econom-

etrician could use these relationships in his forecasting model. If past relationships continued to hold true (which may be a big "if"), he could make a usefully accurate prediction.

One danger in the use of econometric models of the economy is that they appear so elegant and so esoteric that they may give a false impression of infallibility. During World War II, several influential economists used econometric models to predict that there would be mass unemployment after the war. Instead, the actual problem turned out to be one of excessively full employment in the sense that total demand was so great as to bring about not only full employment but also inflation. Both consumption expenditures and private investment expenditures for the immediate postwar period were seriously under-estimated by the model builders, and this led to their erroneous forecasts.[9] Their error stemmed especially from the assumption that observed prewar relationships would persist after the war, whereas, in fact, such factors as accumulated shortages and large supplies of liquid savings brought about drastic upward shifts in consumption patterns.

Development of a relatively dependable econometric model for the United States economy is a difficult problem, and one which requires constant attention. In each period, as new observations are secured, the equations should be recomputed so that "structural change will manifest itself as it occurs."[10] At the University of Michigan's Survey Research Center, econometricians have built a 25-equation model of the United States economy.[11] They are continually revising this model as new data come in and as weaknesses appear.

Much simpler econometric techniques are frequently valuable, especially for forecasting which is of narrower scope than the Michigan economywide model. Suppose one is interested in forecasting total expenditures on tobacco products. One might theorize that of the variables which probably influence such expenditures, disposable personal income should be an outstanding candidate. From publications of the United States Department of Commerce, one could secure the data shown in Exhibit 5. These can then usefully be plotted against one another, as in Exhibit 6.

It is apparent that there has been a rather close straight-line cor-

---

[9] This situation is described in considerable detail by Frank D. Newbury, *Business Forecasting* (New York: McGraw-Hill Book Co., Inc., 1952), chap. 7.

[10] Lawrence R. Klein, *Econometrics* (Evanston, Ill.: Row, Peterson & Co., 1953), p. 264. Klein is one of the leading model builders.

[11] "Business Forecasting," *Business Week*, September 24, 1955, p. 8. This article contains a "Junior Econometrician's Work Kit" which provides an interesting exercise in prediction of gross national product and other measures for the entire economy.

Exhibit 5

TOBACCO SALES AND DISPOSABLE INCOME

(Billions of Dollars)

Year	Disposable Personal Income	Expenditures on Tobacco Products
1930	$74.4	$1.5
1935	58.3	1.4
1940	76.1	1.9
1941	93.0	2.1
1942	117.5	2.4
1943	133.5	2.7
1944	146.8	2.7
1945	150.4	3.0
1946	159.2	3.5
1947	169.0	3.9
1948	187.6	4.1
1949	188.2	4.3
1950	206.1	4.4
1951	226.1	4.7
1952	236.9	5.1
1953	250.1	5.3

Source: U.S. Department of Commerce, Office of Business Economics, *National Income, 1954* (Washington, D.C.: U.S. Government Printing Office, 1955).

relation between disposable personal income and consumer expenditures on tobacco. This sort of simple correlation analysis may help a businessman understand the forces which affect his sales and, perhaps, help him in his planning for the future. To the extent that the statisticians who compile national income statistics make forecasts of disposable personal income, these could readily be translated into forecasts of tobacco sales on an over-all basis. This would be done by locating the predicted disposable personal income on the horizontal scale and moving up to the straight line in Exhibit 6.

Other factors which might, in theory, affect expenditures on tobacco products should also be investigated. If, for example, the age distribution of the population, the number of men in the military services, and the sales of candy should also be found to be significant, the analyst might make a multiple-correlation study (using familiar statistical techniques) in order to discover their past effect on tobacco sales. If these relationships remained reasonably constant in the near future, and if some forecasts of the independent variables could be secured,[12] the correlation study would make possible a forecast of tobacco

[12] It would not be difficult, for example, to forecast the age distribution of the population which would consume tobacco products in the near future, since these people would already be living, and since death rates are quite predictable.

consumption. (This forecast might, of course, be rendered very in-accurate by either adverse or favorable medical reports on the effects of tobacco.)

Or suppose it were important to forecast the consumption of gasoline by private automobiles for one year into the future. (This forecast might be required by the United States Treasury to help that agency

Exhibit 6

EXPENDITURES ON TOBACCO PRODUCTS FOLLOW DISPOSABLE PERSONAL INCOME

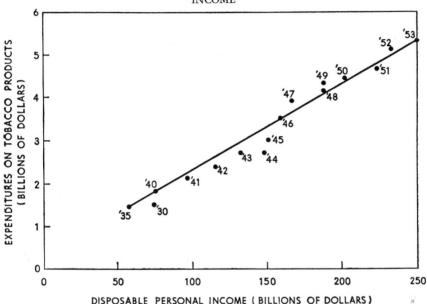

estimate receipts from an actual or proposed gasoline excise tax.) One would immediately realize that gasoline consumption can be considered to be a function of the average number of cars in the hands of users during the coming year and the average gasoline consumption per car for the year. Each of these averages could be estimated separately and then multiplied.

The average number of cars in the hands of users next year might be considered to be a function of the inventory in owners' hands at the end of the current year, plus half of the estimated sales during the following year, plus half of the estimated number of cars to be scrapped during the coming year.[13] Inventory data could be secured

---

[13] This assumes sales and scrappings to be evenly distributed between the first and second halves of the year. If this assumption did not appear to be justified from an examination of available data, it could be modified.

accurately; scrappings could probably be estimated quite closely from past records. Sales of new cars would be most subject to error; but these are much less important, anyway, than the inventory of old cars. The analyst would probably rely on automobile sales as predicted by the automobile industry itself, since in this way he would be incorporating the results of analysis which is probably superior to that which he could turn out himself (and which procedure would, in any case, be timesaving).

In order to estimate gasoline consumption per car, it would be desirable to make a correlation study for the recent past, relating this variable to such independent variables as disposable personal income, price of gasoline, and the ratio of primary road mileage to number of vehicles. (The latter might be a rough measure of congestion, which should affect gasoline consumption per car.) To the extent that the important factors were included, to the extent that past relationships continued to hold true, and to the extent that some of the independent variables were predictable, a suitable forecast of average yearly use of gasoline per car could be obtained. This prediction, plus that of the average number of cars in the hands of users, would permit a prediction of gasoline consumption and gasoline tax collections.

Survey Methods

It has been pointed out that the forecaster who wishes to make optimum use of econometric methods must constantly recompute his equations as later data become available. Also, he should often be willing to incorporate the work of others into his own system if he has reason to believe that their estimates are better than those which he could make or if this procedure will be worth while as a timesaver. Similarly, he should be willing to substitute the results of intentions surveys on such matters as planned investment and consumption if he feels that such data are more accurate than those which he can compute from past relationships. On the other hand, the analyst is free to use computed relationships if he does not have sufficient faith in the predictive value of a survey.[14]

Intentions surveys seem to have increased in popularity in recent years as a basis for forecasting important economic variables. The Department of Commerce and the Securities and Exchange Commission conduct a joint quarterly survey in order to ascertain recent and anticipated expenditures for plant and equipment. More highly publicized surveys of planned investment are made by the McGraw-Hill

---

[14] The flexibility of the econometric approach is described by Klein, *op. cit.*, p. 271.

Department of Economics. This private survey is made in October and published in November. Also, a survey is made after the year opens to cover that year and to give preliminary estimates of planned investment outlays for the next three years. The more distant plans probably have less predictive value than the near-term plans. McGraw-Hill surveys mainly the larger companies in the larger industries. These not only account for a very substantial part of total investment

Exhibit 7

ACTUAL AND PLANNED INVESTMENT SPENDING, 1954–56
(Millions of Dollars)

Industry	1954 Actual	1955 Estimated	1956 Planned
Manufacturing:			
Iron and steel	$ 676	$ 865	$ 1,488
Nonferrous metals	209	320	493
Machinery	694	788	846
Electrical machinery	439	449	507
Automobiles	1,295	1,145	1,924
Transportation equipment	191	280	319
Other metalworking	630	680	802
Chemicals	1,130	1,032	1,383
Paper	455	492	640
Rubber	131	152	188
Stone, clay, and glass	361	461	493
Petroleum refining	800	728	825
Food and beverages	765	706	743
Textiles	331	331	363
Miscellaneous manufacturing	932	870	1,076
All Manufacturing	$9,039	$9,299	$12,090
Other Industries:			
Petroleum	$4,850	$5,026	$5,320
Mining	396	358	304
Railroads	854	910	1,156
Other transportation and communication	2,954	3,143	3,647
Electric and gas utilities	4,219	4,445	4,001
Commercial	6,379	6,971	7,668

Source: "New Burst of Capital Spending," *Business Week*, November 12, 1955.

but also are likely to have more carefully formulated plans than smaller firms, plus greater ability actually to effectuate investment decisions. Separate data on actual and planned investment are published by *Business Week* magazine, showing data by industry and estimated totals for the economy as a whole.

Results of the October, 1955, McGraw-Hill survey are shown in Exhibit 7. The survey indicated that very large increases in investment spending were planned for 1956 by the iron and steel industry, the automobile industry, chemicals producers, and the petroleum industry. For manufacturing as a whole the indicated increase in investment spending in 1956 over 1955 was 23 per cent, while for all industries the planned increase was 13 per cent. These results, along with the expected increase in residential construction activity, caused some economists to predict continuation of a high level of economic activity in 1956, despite the expected slump in automobile output.[15]

A later survey of investment intentions for 1956 was released jointly by the Securities and Exchange Commission and the Department of Commerce in March, 1956. For manufacturing as a whole, this survey indicated investment of $15 billion compared with McGraw-Hill's $12.1 billion. This substantial discrepancy serves as a warning of the extent of error which may be involved in the estimates derived from such surveys.[16] Further, there is little similarity between the SEC-Commerce estimate of $1.1 billion of new investment in mining in 1956 and McGraw-Hill's figure of $304 million. It should also be kept in mind that investment plans are often quickly shelved if business activity turns down and that the necessary financing is sometimes not forthcoming. On the other side of the picture, tending to make investment surveys conservative, is the fact that some investment need not be planned very far ahead of time. For example, some commercial construction might be put in place in 1956 which was not even contemplated as early as October, 1955. Nevertheless, the survey method of forecasting investment expenditures represents a promising approach to an important problem.

A well-known survey of consumers' spending intentions is made by the Federal Reserve System in co-operation with the Survey Research Center of the University of Michigan. Findings are published in the *Federal Reserve Bulletin*. In 1955, for example, four separate issues of this publication set forth the results of the 1955 survey of consumer finances which was made in January and February of that year. The 1955 survey was based on 3,119 interviews with consumers located in the 12 largest metropolitan areas and in 54 additional sampling areas. The 1956 survey was based on 2,800 interviews. This is obviously a very small sample of the entire consuming population of the

---

[15] The decline in automobile production and sales in 1956 was due in part to expectations of unusually drastic model changes in 1957—an expectation fortified by the heavy expected investment in new machine tools and other equipment by the automobile industry.

[16] *Business Week* attributes the difference to "changes in the mood" of businessmen between the time of their reply to the McGraw-Hill survey and their reply to the SEC-Commerce survey. While this may be partially true, it probably does not account for the larger part of the discrepancy.

nation and encounters the further difficulty that consumers often do not "plan" the purchase of a new car, for example, but buy on the spur of the moment. Also, many consumers do not have financial records in good enough shape even to know what they have bought in the recent past, much less what they plan to buy. Further, some consumers are undoubtedly apprehensive of a possible connection between their answers to financial questions and their income tax liability. Nevertheless, it has been observed that the survey results have proved reliable as predictors of the direction of movement of consumers' purchases of durable goods.[17] Probably the tendency of consumers to "keep up with the Joneses" brings about sufficiently uniform behavior on the part of consumers to make a small, carefully selected sample more nearly indicative of the behavior of the entire consuming population than one would at first be inclined to believe.

Exhibit 8

INTENTIONS TO PURCHASE DURABLE GOODS
(Percentage of Spending Units)

Item	1956	1955	1954	1953	1952	1951	1950	1949
House................	9.6%	9.4%	6.6%	8.8%	6.4%	8.5%	8.4%	7.0%
New automobile......	8.2	8.2	7.9	9.0	6.8	6.6	10.6	11.8
Used automobile......	7.2	7.5	6.4	6.2	6.0	5.5	6.9	6.8
Furniture and appli- ances..........	28.0	28.5	26.9	31.9	23.2	27.4	28.4	30.9

Source: *Federal Reserve Bulletin*, March, 1956, p. 226.

One of the tables from the preliminary findings of the 1956 survey of consumer finances has been reproduced as Exhibit 8. This table shows the percentage of spending units that reported they would, probably would, or possibly would buy the indicated items in each of the years 1949 through 1956.

The percentage of consumers indicating that they might buy a house increased in 1955 and 1956, and the market for new residential construction has actually been quite active in 1956, although below 1955. It should, however, be noted that the percentage of persons indicating an intention to buy a new automobile remained the same in 1956 as in 1955. Actually, automobile sales slumped seriously in 1956, indicating either that the sample surveyed was inadequate or that consumers' statements regarding their intentions may be unde-

---

[17] James H. Lorie, "Forecasting the Demand for Consumer Durable Goods," *Journal of Business,* January, 1954, p. 66. This entire issue is devoted to forecasting in various areas of the economy.

pendable or subject to rapid amendment. In general, consumers' intention surveys are probably less dependable than firms' investment intention surveys, because the latter are more necessarily engaged in constant planning for the future. Also, firms are more likely to be compelled to take preliminary steps (such as land acquisition) well in advance of the main action which they report to the survey takers.

Requirements Forecasting

An important and very common type of sales forecasting is quite obviously open to firms selling materials or components to other firms which set up production schedules for end items. Firms which regularly supply General Motors with components can clearly gauge their future sales prospects by securing the General Motors output schedules— assuming, of course, that these schedules are sufficiently "firm," that General Motors will not decide to make its own components, and that the company in question will continue to get the General Motors business.

In recent years an allied form of forecasting has become possible to the extent that the federal government establishes production programs and schedules. During World War II, for example, President Roosevelt called for the production of 60,000 military airplanes in 1942 and 125,000 in 1943. These goals were followed by detailed production schedules which were supposed to add up to these totals. (Actually, they did not, especially for 1942.) From the detailed schedules of airplane production the federal statisticians were able to compute requirements for aluminum, engines, propellers, radio equipment, and thousands of other components. To the extent that end-product schedules were realistic for airplanes and other munitions, the detailed requirements schedules gave firms producing materials and components an excellent forecast of their own sales possibilities.

A similar situation existed just after the war, when the "Veterans Emergency Housing Program" was put into effect by Congress. Unlike the wartime munitions programs, this program did not call for government purchase of the end product. Rather, it was an attempt to use priority ratings, allocation orders, limitation orders applied to less essential construction, subsidies on building materials, and other unusual measures to secure the rapid construction of homes for purchase by veterans. To the extent that realistic housing schedules were set up by the government (and here, too, schedules tended to be over-optimistic), it was possible for industries supplying such materials as brick, tile, nails, wallboard, and clay sewer pipe to compute their probable sales to the housing industry.

Recently, the federal government has formulated a huge interstate highway program. This clearly makes it possible for the portland cement industry, asphalt industry, aggregates producers, pipe producers, steel industry, and others to make approximate calculations of their probable sales in support of this tremendous program. An advantage of this sort of program from the view of materials suppliers is its recession-proof nature. In fact, a business recession would probably increase their sales on this account, since the highway program would probably be speeded up as an emergency public work.

The firm faces a number of problems in forecasting its sales as related to a government production program:

1. The end-item schedules usually reflect a combination of political, administrative, and economic considerations. They are likely to be placed deliberately too high in order to stimulate private firms to set their sights high. Often, the end-item schedules reflect more what government officials believe is required than what can actually be produced within the specified time period.

2. The firm may not get its share of the industry sales in support of a government program. (Or it may be able to get more than its share.)

3. There are usually some opportunities for substitution of one material for another. Computation of requirements is complicated by this possibility, since there is usually no set "bill of materials" which can be depended upon. Portland cement and asphalt are examples of substitute materials.

4. "Pipe-line" requirements create difficulties. It is necessary for producers not only to turn out the materials and components needed for incorporation in end items, but also to build up inventories at various stages in the transportation-production process. In part, these inventories are needed to "fill the pipe line," so that a steady input into end items can be secured. These inventory needs are often especially difficult to predict.

In general, as government activities have come to loom larger in our economy, it has become more and more important for firms in many lines to gear their activities to government procurement programs or to government scheduling of some private activities. This requires a sort of forecasting and suggests the importance of following not only federal governmental activities, but also those of state and local governments. States usually budget on a two-year basis; New York and California, however, budget annually. Also, about 115,000 local governments have budgets.[18] An examination of available pertinent budgets may give valuable hints to the businessman as to

---

[18] George W. Mitchell, "Forecasting State and Local Expenditures," *Journal of Business,* January, 1954, p. 18.

sales possibilities. Budget proposals are usually not supported fully by legislative bodies, of course, so actual appropriations details may give more accurate (but less early) information. Also, the businessman may do well to follow the progress of bond issues of state and local governments, since these are often made for specific capital purposes and have, therefore, some predictive significance.

Political Climate

The businessman interested in predicting the future should constantly keep his finger on the political pulse. Our federal government wields important economic powers and at the same time is sensitive to the wishes of the electorate. This makes its economic actions somewhat predictable, on the assumption that there will be certain actions designed more to get votes than to regulate economic activity in a socially optimal manner. Or if vote-getting actions happen to coincide with socially desirable actions, the imminence of national elections may serve to accelerate and make more certain the appropriate governmental actions.

A case in point is related to Federal Reserve actions in the monetary sphere. Although privately owned, the Federal Reserve System is a quasigovernmental institution and is subjected to a certain amount of political pressure. At times, this has seriously hampered its power to exercise appropriate monetary policy. For example, the Federal Reserve System should, in theory, have sold government bonds on the open market during and just after the Korean War as a means of inhibiting inflation. Actually, under pressure from the United States Treasury Department, the Federal Reserve banks operated a price-support program for government bonds somewhat akin to the government's price-support programs for farm products and gold.[19] Similarly, there may be pressure on the Federal Reserve authorities to ease credit conditions prior to an important federal election. This is because those in office usually fear recession and unemployment more than inflation. Since the prospect of lower interest rates means, for example, that a firm contemplating the issuance of bonds would lower its interest costs by waiting until interest rates have actually fallen, the value of correct anticipation of Federal Reserve actions is evident. Similarly, it may be possible to anticipate congressional action on such matters as farm legislation, and such anticipation may be a useful guide to

---

[19] This is described by Clark L. Allen, James M. Buchanan, and Marshall R. Colberg, *Prices, Income, and Public Policy* (New York: McGraw-Hill Book Co., Inc., 1954), p. 234.

business policy.[20] Various private publications emanating from Washington can be useful in predicting the outcome of legislation which is in progress.

Loaded-Dice Techniques

Numerous other ways of looking into the future—some of which are more ethical than others—are based on getting information which is not generally available or on securing information sooner than other people get it. An interesting historical example of the latter occurred in 1815. By using their own carrier pigeons, the Rothschilds received advance news of the Battle of Waterloo, which gave them their chance to make a fortune on the London Stock Exchange.[21] A similar situation in which advance news has value to speculators occurs when the United States Department of Agriculture compiles its crop estimates in Washington, D.C. If the estimates are larger than has been expected, futures prices will fall, and the speculator with advance news can profit by selling grain futures before the new estimates are publicly released. The opposite is true if the estimates are lower than had been expected. This situation has led some persons to attempt to communicate with cohorts outside the building as soon as the estimates have been assembled. It is said that a man was once caught passing a signal from a washroom by means of adjusting the height of the window shade. Strict security measures are employed by the Department of Agriculture to prevent the premature exporting of crop-estimate data from the building.

"Forecasting the forecast" obviously presents another possibility along these lines. If, for example, an individual were able to come up with a close approximation of his own to the federal crop estimate and were able to make the estimate soon enough, he might be in a position to make speculative profits. (Actually, the cost of gathering and analyzing the necessary data would, in this particular case, probably bring a net loss rather than a profit.)

Methods of securing advance information vary from those which merely require alertness to those which are downright dishonest. Alertness was displayed by Andrew Carnegie, who secured advance information on industrial production by counting the number of smoking chimneys.[22] A less clearly ethical way of forecasting land values is

---

[20] A more powerful device, of course, is the employment of lobbyists to *influence* legislation.

[21] "Business Forecasting," *Business Week*, September 24, 1955, p. 4.

[22] *Ibid.*, p. 6.

employed in the oil industry, where men are regularly employed to watch the drill rigs of other companies through field glasses and to rush to the nearest phone to take up all available options on adjacent land if they see oil struck.[23]

At the bottom of the list ethically are a variety of sharp and often illegal practices which may be ways either of ascertaining what exists or of forecasting what is coming. Engineering employees of rival firms are sometimes asked in job interviews to answer questions designed to disclose products and processes rather than to ascertain the men's fitness for employment. Telephone wires may be tapped or a tiny portable transmitter planted under an executive's desk. Or industrial secrets may be stolen in outright cases of breaking into and entering premises. It is strongly recommended, however, that only the legitimate means of forecasting be studied further by the student. Otherwise, his forecasting career may be a discouragingly brief one.

CASE 2–1: A & B APPLIANCE SALES COMPANY

The A & B Appliance Sales Company was formed as a partnership by two brothers, Howard and Francis Welch, in 1937. It began operations as a radio repair shop and carried several lines of nationally advertised brands. A very small stock was carried, since distributors for most of the lines were located near by and any model not carried in stock by the company could be secured from the inventory of the distributor in a few hours. In 1938 the firm expanded into the general field of small electrical household appliances, such as toasters, coffee makers, waffle irons, hand irons, etc. The repair service was also expanded to cover these new items. Early in 1939 the firm began the installation of automobile radios for a local automobile dealer. Later in the same year, the firm acquired an exclusive contract to sell, install, and service the Motorola automobile radio. As a result, it installed automobile radios for several dealers in its locality.

Late in 1942, Howard Welch was recruited into the armed services. During his absence the firm continued to operate under the supervision of Francis, who specialized in repair work, since the manufacture of practically all electrical appliances had been discontinued for the duration of the war. During this period, Francis sought to obtain franchises to handle certain lines when such products were again available. By June, 1944, he had obtained franchises for Servel refrigerators and

---

[23] Richard Austin Smith, "Business Espionage," *Fortune*, May, 1956, p. 119.

water heaters, Westinghouse refrigerators, washing machines and dryers, electric ranges, and radio and television sets. In addition, he arranged to stock, on a nonexclusive basis, a large selection of Hotpoint products, such as dishwashers, electric ranges, and small appliances. With the return of Howard Welch from military service in October, 1944, the firm undertook, under agreement with a local plumber and electrician, the establishment of a kitchen planning and installation service. From one of the manufacturers of kitchen equipment the firm was able to obtain free counsel as to kitchen planning.

The building in which the business was housed was owned by the Welch brothers. It was located several blocks from the center of the city but on one of the main thoroughfares. In the rear of the building was the repair shop, which was large enough to accommodate six automobiles as well as the necessary benches and cabinets. Across the alley from the rear of the building was another building which had once been used as a garage by a local delivery service but was vacated when the delivery firm moved to larger quarters. This space was rented by the Welch brothers for warehouse purposes in January, 1945, in anticipation of larger operations. At this time the firm had in its employ one mechanic-electrician, a clerk who served in the store, and a part-time janitor, in addition to the services of the Welch brothers, who worked on sales and installations, together with the plumber and electrician under contract. Prior to the war, sales were made through personal contacts by the Welch brothers, and an advertisement was run continuously in the weekly paper which was published locally. The city in which the firm was located was a large suburb of a metropolitan area, but no advertisements were placed in any of the large daily papers serving the area. The brothers had grown up in the suburb and enjoyed a wide acquaintance.

In order to finance the postwar expansion, the brothers sold an apartment building in which they had an equity of $35,000. They retained three other small apartment houses which they jointly owned. For many years, they had enjoyed good banking relations with a local bank, which agreed to extend the firm a line of credit in the amount of $25,000, exclusive of contingent liability arising from indorsement of installment paper which the firm might discount at the bank. At the suggestion of the bank, the firm was incorporated in February, 1945, with each brother holding 50 per cent of the stock. The original firm name was retained. The large increase in capital was deemed desirable so that the firm could purchase several items in carload lots. This resulted in a substantial discount per item, in contrast to purchasing in small lots through a distributor or wholesaler. From his contacts made in 1943 and 1944, Francis Welch was able to obtain two carloads of refrigerators and one carload of washing machines in February, 1945.

Exhibits 1 and 2 show the condensed balance sheets and profit-and-loss statements, respectively, for 1945–48, inclusive. Exhibit 3 shows monthly sales for the same period. Early in 1949, Howard

Exhibit 1

A & B APPLIANCE SALES COMPANY, INC.

Condensed Balance Sheet as of December 31, for the Years 1945–48, Inclusive

Item	1945	1946	1947	1948
Assets:				
Cash....................	$ 4,221.91	$ 6,121.95	$ 5,382.36	$ 3,191.57
Accounts receivable........	2,927.33	3,025.71	4,271.14	5,815.78
Merchandise inventory.....	77,933.26	81,721.25	88,164.51	94,117.05
Parts inventory...........	8,525.95	8,737.61	7,929.22	8,402.61
Land and building........	15,342.95	15,342.95	15,342.95	15,342.95
Total Assets.........	$108,951.40	$114,949.47	$121,090.18	$126,869.96
Liabilities:				
Notes payable............	$ 25,000.00	$ 25,000.00	$21,250.00	$ 18,000.00
Accounts payable.........	18,750.65	15,583.55	21,934.01	17,352.21
Capital stock.............	50,000.00	50,000.00	50,000.00	50,000.00
Surplus..................	15,200.75	24,365.92	27,906.17	41,517.75
Total Liabilities.......	$108,951.40	$114,949.47	$121,090.18	$126,869.96

Welch observed that sales were showing a noticeable decline and by April, 1949, had dropped to an alarmingly low level. He drew off the balance sheet shown in Exhibit 4, as of April 1, 1949. Inquiry from the electric appliance trade association showed a similar decline in the industry. From some of his competitors, he heard the same story of decreasing sales. Of the total indebtedness shown due the bank in Exhibit 4, $8,500 was due on June 1, 1949, and $3,500 on July 1, 1949. The bank notified the firm on March 30, 1949, that it had received a sight draft with bill of lading attached in the amount of $11,000, covering two carloads of washing machines consigned to the firm, and requested advice as to its acceptance. The shipment was en route and was expected to arrive in a few days.

Because of the changed character of the firm's business in the postwar period compared to the prewar period, the Welch brothers felt they were unable to draw conclusions as to whether the decline was

Exhibit 2

A & B APPLIANCE SALES COMPANY, INC.

Condensed Profit-and-Loss Statement, 1945–48, Inclusive

Item	1945		1946	
Sales		$112,521.78		$117,595.51
Cost of goods sold		71,547.55		79,003.27
Gross Profit		$ 40,974.23		$ 38,592.24
Expenses:				
Salaries	$18,528.50		$20,024.20	
Taxes	3,687.22		4,125.89	
Miscellaneous expense	4,872.31		5,286.98	
Total Expenses		27,088.03		29,437.07
Net Profit		$ 13,886.20		$ 9,155.17

Item	1947		1948	
Sales		$124,887.33		$139,473.85
Cost of goods sold		83,072.15		89,303.91
Gross Profit		$ 41,815.18		$ 50,169.94
Expenses:				
Salaries	$21,217.30		$23,421.75	
Taxes	4,381.95		5,122.39	
Miscellaneous expense	9,924.76		4,764.22	
Total Expenses		35,524.01		33,308.36
Net Profit		$ 6,291.17		$ 16,861.58

Exhibit 3

A & B APPLIANCE SALES COMPANY, INC.

Total Sales, by Months, January, 1945, to March, 1949, Inclusive

Month	1945	1946	1947	1948	1949
January	$ 6,271.83	$ 9,155.63	$ 9,258.91	$10,002.73	$9,438.21
February	6,589.31	9,021.54	9,378.52	10,616.51	8,715.62
March	6,922.53	9,291.55	9,528.91	10,492.55	6,937.49
April	7,215.27	9,655.33	9,672.33	10,487.31	. . . . . .
May	7,583.51	9,799.21	9,895.18	10,287.27	. . . . . .
June	8,122.81	9,931.47	9,840.37	10,793.34	. . . . . .
July	8,733.46	9,806.28	9,921.32	11,173.56	. . . . . .
August	9,152.32	9,913.57	10,919.48	11,792.36	. . . . . .
September	9,935.71	9,935.61	10,845.56	12,637.28	. . . . . .
October	10,457.19	9,978.54	11,311.29	12,885.93	. . . . . .
November	10,801.32	9,981.21	11,287.63	12,921.59	. . . . . .
December	11,436.53	10,825.57	13,027.83	15,393.42	. . . . . .

of a temporary nature or something more serious. The radio business had shown some seasonality of movement prior to the war. There was a rise in the spring, followed by a summer decline, with recovery in the fall months. The present experience showed a slump coming in the spring, when the prewar experience had been in the opposite direction. From their trade association and near-by competitors, they learned that there had been some seasonal movement in washing machines and refrigerators prior to the war but that it was not always consistent. Electric ranges and refrigerators appeared to show some

Exhibit 4

A & B APPLIANCE SALES COMPANY, INC.

Condensed Balance Sheet, April 1, 1949

Assets:		Liabilities:	
Cash	$ 1,411.23	Notes payable	$ 15,000.00
Accounts receivable	4,137.29	Accounts payable	18,427.91
Merchandise inventory	95,580.62	Capital stock	50,000.00
Parts inventory	9,311.17	Surplus	42,355.35
Land and buildings	15,342.95		
Total Assets	$125,783.26	Total Liabilities	$125,783.26

correlation with new building prior to the war, but this relationship was somewhat cloudy in the postwar period, owing to the large replacement demand. It was observed that a similar decline was occurring in residential building in the spring of 1949, and this at a time when it was generally stated that there was a serious shortage of housing and a large backlog of demand for new homes.

Howard Welch felt it necessary to accept the sight draft, in order not to impair his credit standing with the bank. The original line of credit had recently been renewed by the bank. While all obligations had been met on time, he was of the opinion that the bank would be reluctant to extend additional credit on inventory at a time when sales were slow and there was some occasional price cutting in the electrical appliance field. At the same time, there was great need of obtaining sufficient cash with which to carry on operations and also to build up a balance with which to meet maturing obligations at the bank in the near future. Mr. Welch believed there were several alternative solutions to the situation confronting him. First, the decline in sales could be interpreted as temporary because of the federal restrictions on installment credit which would expire on June 30, 1949, unless renewed by Congress. He felt, as did many others in the industry, that the relatively high down payments of 20 per cent of the purchase price, together with a maximum payment period of twelve months, was one of the main reasons for the decline in sales. He might, under this assumption, seek an extension of the maturity dates of his notes at the bank. Second, the decline in sales might be in the nature of a downward trend, reflecting substantial satisfaction of the backlog of demand. This would call for a reduction in inventory within a short period of time in order to obtain sufficient cash. With declining sales, this would entail some drastic price reductions. Since about 75 per cent of the heaviest-selling items were priced by the manufacturer under resale price-maintenance acts, this would add to problems of price reductions. Third, if the decline were of a seasonal nature, a recovery would be anticipated in late summer or early fall. If this were the correct appraisal of the situation, a sharp reduction in inventory at present would forego profits which could be made during the recovery period.

QUESTIONS

1. What possible types of economic fluctuations face the A & B Appliance Sales Company? What additional information, if any, would you seek in an attempt to determine the cause of the decline in early 1949?
2. What recommendations would you make if the decline were attributed to seasonal influences? To cyclical factors?
3. If a seasonal pattern of sales were established, would you recommend that inventory policy be based on this factor alone?
4. What would you suggest as the most promising way of forecasting the demand for appliances in the near future?
5. What other forecasting techniques might be worth investigating in this case?

CASE 2–2: LARSON AND WOLF, INC.

Henry Wolf, son of the former owner of Larson and Wolf, Inc., a retail jewelry store, returned from military service in the fall of 1945. At that time, he was considering two alternative business opportunities for himself. The first was an offer from a manufacturing jeweler in an east coast city. The firm wanted Mr. Wolf to assume the duties of vice-president in charge of sales, at a starting salary of $8,500. The second alternative was entering business on his own through purchase of the Larson and Wolf jewelry store.

Larson and Wolf, Inc., was situated in a thriving midwestern industrial city of about 100,000 population. The firm had been founded in 1910 by Henry Wolf, Sr., and a partner, George Larson. By the end of World War I the store had an established clientele among the middle- and upper-income groups. The business had been energetically but conservatively managed. In 1924, Henry Wolf, Sr., acquired the interest of his partner, who thereupon retired from the jewelry business. Under Mr. Wolf's management the store continued to enjoy increasing sales volume and good profits. As the main retail shopping center migrated uptown in the late twenties, Larson and Wolf planned to follow; but in 1929 the downturn in business adversely affected retail sales of jewelry, and Mr. Wolf deferred moving to a new location.

In 1933, Henry Wolf, Jr., graduated from college, where he had made a creditable record in the study of marketing. Immediately, he went to work in the family jewelry store which, after several lean years, was beginning to feel the upturn of business activity which started in the spring of 1933. After two years of diligent effort in all phases of store work, Henry, Jr., through a business connection of his father's, went to New York, where he worked for a manufacturing jeweler in the production department and later in the sales division.

Henry Wolf, Sr., died in the spring of 1941, leaving the business jointly to his widow and to his son, Henry, Jr. It was decided that the business should be sold, since there was a purchaser who had on several previous occasions attempted to buy Larson and Wolf, Inc. The jewelry store was sold to this purchaser, a middle-aged man of considerable experience in the retail jewelry trade. The successor owner was regarded as a sound buyer and manager but was not thought to have much ability in sales promotion. He was also limited in capital resources.

When the purchaser's health failed in 1945, he communicated with Henry Wolf, Jr., who at that time was serving in the United States Army, offering to resell the business on very advantageous terms. Negotiations were still being carried on in the fall of 1945, when Wolf received an honorable discharge from the armed forces.

As he reviewed the alternative business ventures, Wolf anticipated that, should he accept the post of vice-president of the manufacturing jewelry concern, he would average $10,000 annually in salary during the first five years. It seemed unlikely that he would be taken in as a member of the firm because it was a closely held family corporation. Were he to purchase Larson and Wolf, Inc., he believed he could raise the sales volume by at least 20 per cent over the next five years. This, he thought, was a reasonable estimate, because his youth and wide personal acquaintance in his home town would place him at a great advantage over his competitors, chief of whom was a branch store of a regional chain with headquarters in Chicago. Wolf believed, also, that a shift of store location, contemplated in 1929 but never carried out, would compensate for any downtrend which might be experienced as the result of a postwar recession. If sales volume attained the level of $100,000 annually over the next five years, Wolf reasoned that he could net $15,000 as salary and profit.

In reviewing trade papers, Mr. Wolf noticed that it was freely predicted that the heavy wartime excise taxes on jewelry would be lowered or repealed. Trade sources also indicated that lower-priced merchandise would be generally available by late summer of 1946. Moreover, Wolf was aware of the tremendous backlog of savings created by the unavailability of many consumer goods during the war, and he believed that this would stimulate jewelry sales in the postwar period. At this time the article reproduced in the Appendix to Case 2–2 came to Mr. Wolf's attention.

Sales of Larson and Wolf, Inc., from 1929 to 1944 were as follows:

1929........$59,555	1937........$38,633	1941........$65,222
1933......... 19,760	1938......... 33,225	1942......... 68,617
1935......... 26,110	1939......... 30,219	1943......... 72,300
1936......... 33,102	1940......... 37,313	1944......... 76,004

QUESTIONS

1. Why were Larson and Wolf's jewelry sales stimulated by World War II, whereas sales of automobiles, appliances, and similar goods fell off?
2. Were expectations of a postwar decline in business activity justified?
3. In 1950, a postwar year, personal consumption expenditures on jewelry were $1,328 million, while disposable income was about $206 billion. Does this observation fit closely the relationship shown in Exhibit 2 of the Appendix to this case?
4. Using the National Income Edition which is published annually by the Department of Commerce as a supplement to the *Survey of Current Business,* find the latest year's disposable income and personal consumption expenditures on jewelry; and by drawing a chart, determine how closely this observation would fit the relation shown in Exhibit 2 of the Appendix. Do this also by using the equation shown in footnote 25 of the Appendix. Comment on your findings.

APPENDIX TO CASE 2–2: THE OUTLOOK FOR
POSTWAR SALES OF JEWELRY[24]

With the favorable events on the military fronts it is natural for jewelers at this time to be wondering about the sales prospects in the postwar period. In order to make an intelligent appraisal of the prospects for jewelry store sales it is necessary to determine what are the major economic factors affecting the fluctuations in sales.

---

[24] Excerpts from a report published by the U.S. Department of Commerce, *Survey of Current Business,* March, 1945.

Every jeweler knows that the most important factor affecting sales for the trade as a whole is the general condition of business. In good times sales and profits are high while in depressed periods they drop to unfavorable levels. Of course, the ability, location and capital of the individual retailer partly determine how the ups and downs of general business affect him personally. However, for the total jewelry trade sales volumes are conditioned by the general level of prosperity.

Since this is a problem concerning the demand for a consumer good the most important factor affecting the volume of dollar sales is the income of consumers which in turn is dependent on the course of general business activity.

A comparison of the data shown in Exhibit 1 on sales of jewelry stores and consumer income for the past 15-year period from 1929 to 1944, in-

Exhibit 1

SALES OF RETAIL JEWELRY STORES AND CONSUMER INCOMES

Year	Sales of Jewelry Stores (Millions of Dollars)	Disposable Income of Individuals (Billions of Dollars)*	Year	Sales of Jewelry Stores (Millions of Dollars)	Disposable Income of Individuals (Billions of Dollars)*
1929.......	$536	$79.6	1939.......	$ 362	$ 67.7
1933.......	175	44.5	1940.......	426	72.9
1935.......	235	56.3	1941.......	587	88.7
1936.......	297	65.2	1942.......	753	110.4
1937.......	347	69.2	1943.......	964	124.2
1938.......	299	62.9	1944.......	1,002	137.5

* Note: Represents income payments less tax payments.

dicates that sales went up and down as the incomes increased or decreased. This is clearly brought out in Exhibit 2 which shows the relation between sales of jewelry stores and the disposable income of individuals. The disposable income is the income left to individuals after payment of taxes.

The striking fact in this exhibit is that sales and incomes are intimately related according to a definite pattern. The points tend to fall very closely along a straight line. The line shown in the exhibit, represents the relationship and was computed by statistical methods. Essentially the same line, however, can be drawn in by inspection.[25]

The average percentage deviation or error of the actual sales from the corresponding sales as calculated from the straight line for the entire period from 1929 to 1944 is only 5 percent indicating that sales have been almost completely determined by the changes in consumer income. Furthermore, more important from the point of view of post-war considerations, sales in the war years were not out of line from the pre-war relation. In other words,

---

[25] The formula representing the line on the exhibit is given by: Sales of jewelry stores (in millions of dollars) $= -388 + 10 \times$ disposable income (in billions of dollars). This implies that whenever consumer incomes change by $10 billion, sales of jewelry stores can be expected to change by $100 million.

the tremendous wartime expansion in sales kept pace with expanding incomes in about the same way as would be expected on the basis of the pre-war experience.

Another striking point shown by the relation is that sales of jewelry stores are very sensitive to changes in consumer income. For example, from 1933

Exhibit 2

RELATION OF JEWELRY STORE SALES TO CONSUMER INCOME

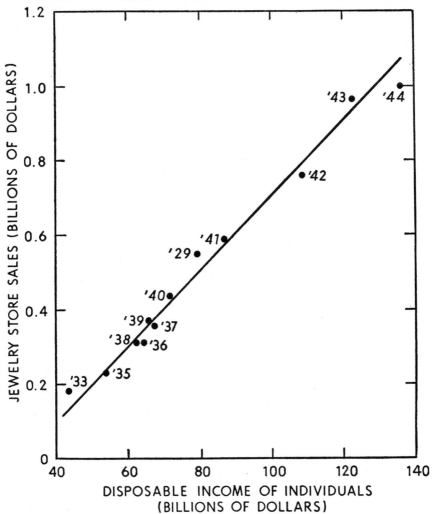

to 1937 consumer incomes increased by 55 percent, whereas jewelry store sales increased by 100 percent, or almost double the relative increase in income. In general, on the basis of this past relation it can be shown that on the average a change of 10 percent in disposable income was associated with nearly a 20 percent change in sales.

This is an important conclusion for the post-war business of jewelers. It means that when consumer income is high and increasing, jewelry stores will gain tremendously since their sales increase in greater proportion to the rise in income.

On the other hand, jewelers are at a disadvantage relative to other retailers when incomes and employment shrink since their sales drop more precipitously than the relative decline in income. Indeed, as shown in a previous study jewelry stores stand at the top of the list of major retail outlets when classified according to the response in sales to a change in consumer income.

Jewelers will find many uses for these results. A particular jeweler can compare his sales with total sales for the trade. If he finds, for example, that

Exhibit 3

POSTWAR SALES OF JEWELRY
STORES IN RELATION TO CON-
SUMER INCOME

Assumed Disposable Income (Billions of Dollars)	Estimated Sales of Jewelry Stores* (Millions of Dollars)
100	680
110	780
120	880
130	980

* Since the average percentage error of the formula was 5 percent, an allowance for a probable error of about this magnitude up or down must be made in these estimates.

his share of total national business has been in the same proportion over the years, then the conclusions stated above would apply to his case. If, on the other hand, he was doing better or worse than the trade as a whole, then he would modify the results accordingly.

For the total jewelry business, an important application is the appraisal of post-war prospects. The record of the past provides the basis for gauging the probable range of the post-war volume of jewelry store sales. Since sales have been related to income it is necessary to determine the prospects for income. This, of course, cannot be done precisely but a probable range may serve as a guide.

If there is relatively full employment after the war the disposable income of consumers is estimated at approximately 130 billion dollars at the present level of wage and tax rates. Even if this high level is not achieved there is reason to believe that the income would not fall to disastrously low levels.

Deferred demands for consumer and producer goods will be great because of wartime shortages and these will be backed up by a substantial volume of individual savings and business savings which can make them effective. Furthermore, our social insurance system, by providing unemployment insurance and old-age pensions, will act as a brake on declining incomes. Finally, business and government are laying plans for maintaining a high level of economic activity after the war. This suggests that a business firm can figure limits of, say, from 100 billion dollars to 130 billion, for purposes of calculating possibilities, and use its own forecasting to fix the probable total.

For jewelers, this range of income can be translated into the corresponding volume of sales on the basis of the relationship shown in Exhibit 3.

. . . .

The conclusion is that jewelers will have good business in the postwar years, provided income is maintained reasonably well.

CASE 2–3: NORTHSIDE INSULATION COMPANY, INC.

In November, 1942, Model Rebuilders, Inc., of Chicago, Illinois, was organized by Mr. John Wilson, Mr. Carl Svendlun, and Mr. Richard Klein. Mr. Wilson was a carpenter and mechanic by trade, Mr. Svendlun had most recently worked as a plumber and electrician but had been in business as a plumbing and heating contractor several years earlier, and Mr. Klein was employed as a salesman for a metals novelty company until that company was forced to suspend operations because of the war. Model Rebuilders, Inc., was organized primarily for the purpose of remodeling old, large homes into small apartments to meet the increased demand for housing because of wartime activity. The government had established priorities for all the necessary materials to permit such work. The three incorporators each contributed $5,000 in cash toward the capital of the firm. In addition, Mr. Svendlun contributed some material in his possession which was suitable for use by the firm, so that the total original capital was $28,500. Mr. Wilson and Mr. Svendlun made estimates and performed work on the various projects of the corporation, while Mr. Klein concentrated upon sales and the obtaining of priorities.

The company prospered under this arrangement. Each incorporator was paid a salary for his services, and profits were reinvested in the firm. By September, 1945, the company had accumulated a capital and surplus of $193,457.20 and had an average of 61 employees on its payroll. Practically all its work had been of an interior nature—that is, the removing and building of partitions, construction of new bathrooms and kitchens, resetting of windows, etc. The firm had never undertaken any new building of any kind, although it had taken several subcontracts from builders who were working on government construction projects during the war. All three of the original incorporators were now engaged in supervisory work only, and Mr. Klein had two assistants.

In October, 1945, Mr. Klein called to the attention of Mr. Svendlun and Mr. Wilson the fact that there was a decline in the amount of remodeling work available. Mr. Klein was of the opinion that, with the end of the war, people were anxious to get out of small living quarters and into larger apartments or individual homes. In addition, there seemed to be a growing shortage of certain materials, many having been freed of priorities by the government. After several conferences, it was agreed that the firm should either enter the general contracting business to build new and complete structures or seek another field of specialization where materials were more easily obtainable.

Among the materials in most plentiful supply were rock-wool insulation, roofing materials, and certain types of windows and doors, particularly those made of aluminum. After some preliminary negotiations, the firm obtained a franchise to distribute and install a combination storm and screen window made of aluminum, metal thresholds, weather stripping, insulation, and roofing, and to sell and maintain oil and gas furnaces and boilers. The combination storm windows, thresholds, weather stripping, furnaces, and boilers were produced by a manufacturer with a national reputation for quality products. The insulating and roofing material was purchased by the firm from various manufacturers according to desired specifications. On January 1, 1946, the firm was reorganized and its name changed to the Northside Insulation Company, Inc. With the exception of furnaces and boilers, all products were promptly delivered, and the company enjoyed a profitable business.

Subsequent to its reorganization in January, 1946, the company employed 10 salesmen on a salary and commission basis. An average of 75 employees was retained on its payrolls. Skilled labor was hired at straight salary on a weekly basis, while unskilled labor was hired by the hour as needed. Skilled labor consisted of carpenters, mechanics, steam fitters, drivers, and office employees. Unskilled labor was used principally in loading operations. Mr. Wilson was quite insistent upon work of only the highest quality, since that was one of the company's main selling points. Orders were sufficient to maintain a backlog of 30–90 days. This situation prevailed until the fall of 1948.

In March, 1949, Mr. Klein called a meeting of the owners of the firm to discuss what he considered to be a troublesome situation. He noted that sales had been declining for several months and that backlogs of orders had completely disappeared except on some special items which required some time for processing at the factory. This had brought about considerable idle time among the skilled labor. Mr. Klein was uncertain as to whether the situation was temporary or whether it was the beginning of a postwar depression, which for several months had been forecast. Mr. Wilson and Mr. Svendlun were of the opinion that to protect the company's interest, there should be an immediate reduction in the skilled labor, so as to reduce costs in line with the reduction in sales. Mr. Klein was somewhat hesitant about this policy, since the market for skilled labor in the building trades was rather tight; and if such labor were released now, it might be difficult to obtain satisfactory replacements if business should pick up later. Company sales, by months, are shown in Exhibit 1. The monthly

Exhibit 1

NORTHSIDE INSULATION COMPANY, INC.

Monthly Sales of Insulation and Heating Divisions, January 1, 1946, to February 28, 1949
(00's Omitted)

Month	1946		1947		1948		1949	
	Insula-tion Div.	Heating Div.	Insula-tion Div.	Heating Div.	Insula-tion Div.	Heating Div.	Insula-tion Div.	Heating Div.
January	$14,126	$ 6,354	$25,119	$ 9,211	$30,792	$12,683	$25,311	$10,051
February	15,963	6,391	24,996	9,371	30,514	13,119	23,657	8,735
March	16,004	7,119	25,314	9,514	32,718	15,212	......	......
April	18,327	7,812	26,111	9,569	33,511	16,109	......	......
May	21,571	7,903	26,413	9,741	32,573	17,911	......	......
June	21,439	7,907	27,004	9,855	32,419	18,304	......	......
July	21,783	7,962	28,119	9,867	33,479	18,115	......	......
August	21,799	7,993	29,535	10,053	32,135	17,215	......	......
September	23,801	8,573	30,007	12,519	31,419	15,219	......	......
October	26,591	10,270	30,459	12,314	30,515	13,211	......	......
November	25,935	9,971	30,231	12,692	28,433	13,733	......	......
December	26,011	9,431	31,115	12,703	27,116	11,179	......	......

volume of business transacted by the predecessor company, Model Rebuilders, Inc., is shown in Exhibit 2.

From his salesmen and company records, Mr. Klein learned that about 75 per cent of the total business in the insulation division was on homes already built. The storm sash could be custom-fitted to windows of any size or shape and was easily changed from winter to summer use merely by raising the storm window section and lowering the screen. In existing structures, insulation was blown in by means of pressure machinery which the company owned; while in new buildings, it was applied in "bats" or sheets. Both of these items were relatively expensive and were more in the nature of a capital outlay by a home owner than a current expense.

From January, 1946, to January, 1948, about 90 per cent of these sales were for cash or payment in 90 days. By December, 1948, cash sales had decreased to about 70 per cent of total sales. Credit sales were handled primarily through Section I of the Federal Housing Act, which permitted the purchaser to make installment payments over a maximum period of 36 months. Actual financing was done through the firm's bank, and such loans were guaranteed by the FHA. The remainder of the credit sales was financed by the same bank over a 12-month

Exhibit 2

MODEL REBUILDERS, INC.

Total Volume of Business, Monthly, 1942–45, Inclusive
(00's Omitted)

Month	1942	1943	1944	1945
January...........	....	$15,543	$41,782	$50,152
February..........	....	17,961	42,385	49,131
March............	....	19,547	47,981	45,119
April.............	....	23,615	49,583	45,060
May..............	....	27,435	51,572	45,111
June.............	....	31,693	53,591	45,139
July.............	....	37,591	54,352	43,176
August...........	....	39,983	55,131	42,915
September.........	....	41,573	55,431	39,325
October..........	....	41,374	55,019	37,192
November.........	....	41,561	53,215	33,251
December.........	$11,542	40,963	51,901	30,197

period. Such installment notes were indorsed, with full recourse, by the Northside Insulation Company, Inc.

Sales in the heating division were about 50 per cent replacement in existing structures and the balance in new construction. The firm usually bid for the new construction business on a subcontract basis to local general contractors. Sales for new construction were almost all cash on a 30- to 60-day basis. Payment was made by the contractor within a reasonable period after installation was completed. Sales for replacement were about half cash and half credit, the latter being financed on an installment basis similar to those in the insulation division.

From the information outlined, Mr. Klein considered the following possibilities: (1) that prospective purchasers had less cash to spend than formerly and were reluctant to go into debt (salesmen's reports did not confirm the latter), (2) that the decline might be of a seasonal character in the process of development, (3) that the replacement market was becoming saturated, or (4) that a general decline in economic activity was developing. Each of these possibilities was looked upon as an alternative and, therefore, would require different courses of action. From trade sources, Mr. Klein learned that other firms in the industry were undergoing similar experiences. Mr. Svendlun, on the basis of his previous business experience, was of the opinion that it was a seasonal factor which had not yet appeared because of the postwar backlog of demand. None of the owners of the firm gave much weight to the idea of saturation of the replacement market, while the fourth possibility was strongly discounted.

Mr. Klein believed that more liberal credit terms as to length of installment contract and size of monthly payment would alleviate the first condition, while the second would require either some effort to prevent the seasonal pattern from developing or possibly the addition, of some other line to offset the seasonal decline. Mr. Klein proposed that, as an inducement to have insulation and storm sash installed during the spring months, the firm offer to make the installations immediately, with no payment due until October 1 following. The customer would have the option of making a cash payment in full on that date or having the first payment of an installment loan fall due on the same date. The firm would provide the credit without charge until October 1. If the customer preferred an installment contract, the firm could sell the note to its bank in the ordinary manner. Mr. Klein believed that as long as the prospective purchaser would probably buy in the summer or early fall anyhow, he would be equally willing to purchase at an earlier date if no additional cost were involved. If such a plan were successful, the firm would be able to schedule its installations in such a manner as to make more efficient use of its labor force and permit the retention of its present staff of workers. In presenting the plan, it was pointed out that the gross margin of profit in the insulation division was about 50 per cent, and in the heating division about 35 per cent. The firm possessed government bonds in excess of $200,000, which bore interest at a rate of slightly more than 2 per cent.

QUESTIONS

1. What action would you propose the company undertake?
2. From the information presented, do you believe the decline in sales was a seasonal or a trend factor? How do you reach such a conclusion?
3. Would you recommend the use of the company's funds in the manner proposed? Why? Would you suggest that the firm carry its own installment paper at the going rate of $4\frac{1}{2}$ per cent rather than finance it through a bank?
4. What additional information do you feel the company should have had before reaching a decision? How would you make use of such information?

CASE 2–4: CONTINENTAL RADIO AND TELEVISION CORPORATION

In 1924 the Landle Electric Company was manufacturing a line of electric motors, condensers, switches, and transformers which it sold to other manufacturers and industrial users. In November of that year the company began to manufacture radio receiving sets and speakers. At the time, radio sets were a relatively recent invention, and it was the company's first venture into the consumer market. Distribution of these sets was made through wholesalers and jobbers.

The first models produced by Landle Electric were priced at $555, exclusive of aerial. Radio sets were well received by the public so that by 1928, there were several hundred companies producing more than 1,000 different brands. The Landle Company manufactured all the components for its sets except tubes, cabinets, and speakers. These were purchased from other manufacturers. The earliest sets were practically handmade, but by 1929 the company was using assembly-line operations. Sales in 1928 were more than 9,000 sets.

In July, 1927, largely because of its success in the consumer market with radios, the company began the manufacture and sale of electric refrigerators, another consumer item which had been introduced to the public within the preceding few years. Using its present facilities and some newly constructed ones, the company manufactured its own compressors and motors, but purchased the boxes from another manufacturer. Sales of refrigerators also expanded until the depression which began in 1929.

The Landle Company suffered sharp declines in sales and profits immediately following the economic collapse in 1929. In addition, prices of all the items it produced declined approximately 50 per cent. Price declines in radios, however, had begun in 1925; but this was due, in large measure, to technological improvements in both design and methods of production. Early in 1930 the company found itself with a large inventory on its own account as well as in the hands of its dealers. About 20 per cent of the radio inventory was eventually junked because of obsolescence.

In 1934, Landle Electric Company merged with the Nadine Corporation, a producer of commercial refrigerators and milk coolers. In 1935, another merger was completed with a producer of home laundry equipment. Thereafter, the company was known as the Continental Radio Corporation.

During World War II the company devoted almost all of its facilities to the production of military goods, manufacturing various types of electronic equipment. A limited quantity of repair parts was produced for its consumer line. In 1946, after reconversion to its line of industrial and consumer goods, the company was among the first to place television sets on the market. The name of the company was then changed to Continental Radio and Television Corporation. In 1947 the company added electric dryers, electric ranges, and home freezers to its line.

The initial stages of television production presented several problems. Whereas the company had originally made almost all of the component parts of its radio sets, it now made relatively few of them. Other than condensers, transformers, and switches, it purchased its parts from other producers and assembled the sets. Television parts were deeply involved in patent rights, so that it was decided to purchase an many as possible of the components and assemble the sets. Furthermore, recalling its early experience in the production of radios, expensive research in electronics was necessary to develop and produce many parts in television sets. It was anticipated that, like radios, television sets would undergo considerable improvement in design and performance which would result in changes in methods of production. The company's 1947 sets were priced from $395 to $795, depending upon screen size and cabinet style. By 1950 the company's prices ranged from $209.95 to $495 for sets with much larger viewing screens and more efficient performance. Prices continued their decline to mid-1954, as shown in Exhibit 1.

In March of 1956 the sales manager was requested to provide a forecast of the number of television sets to be produced for the 1957-model year, together with suggested prices. Because so many of the components of sets were purchased from other manufacturers, it was necessary to place orders for the year's requirements in April for July delivery. New-model sets were usually introduced in September of each year. About two months' production was necessary to provide dealers with sufficient inventory at the time the new line was announced.

Continental Radio and Television Corporation sold all of its products in the national market. Approximately 2 per cent of its total output was for export. In the television market the company accounted for about 5 to 8 per cent of the total market. Exhibit 2 shows shipments of television sets by the firm from 1947 through 1955. As indicated in Exhibit 3, production of television sets experienced a phenomenal growth, from 178,800 in 1947 to 7,464,000 in 1950. Because of material restrictions following the outbreak of the Korean

Exhibit 1

WHOLESALE PRICE INDEX OF TELEVISION RECEIVERS
(1947–49 = 100)

Month	1947*	1948*	1949*	1950*	1951*	1952*	1953†	1954†	1955†
January	....	.....	.....	....	....	....	74.5	73.5	69.0
February	....	.....	.....	....	....	....	75.6	73.8	68.8
March	....	.....	.....	....	....	....	74.9	73.8	68.8
April	96.3‡	100.1‡	103.6‡	96.8‡	92.8‡	92.9‡	74.9	73.8	68.8
May	....	.....	.....	....	....	....	74.9	73.8	69.0
June	....	.....	.....	....	....	....	75.0	70.6	68.8
July	....	.....	.....	....	....	....	74.3	70.3	68.9
August	....	.....	.....	....	....	....	74.0	68.5	68.9
September	....	.....	.....	....	....	....	74.2	68.7	69.3
October	....	.....	.....	....	....	....	74.2	68.7	69.5
November	....	.....	.....	....	....	....	74.2	69.2	69.5
December	....	.....	.....	....	....	....	74.0	69.2	69.7

* Not available on a monthly basis.
† Prices of television sets only.
‡ Yearly average of radio, phonograph, and television sets.

Exhibit 2

SHIPMENTS OF TELEVISION RECEIVERS, 1947-55

1947	7,152
1948	43,902
1949	135,307
1950	447,840
1951	376,999
1952	426,748
1953	577,264
1954	551,002
1955	681,745

Exhibit 3

MONTHLY PRODUCTION OF TELEVISION RECEIVERS, 1947-55

Month	1947*	1948*	1949*	1950*	1951	1952	1953	1954	1955
January	....	....	....	....	650,700	404,900	719,200	420,600	654,600
February	....	....	....	....	679,300	409,300	730,600	426,900	702,500
March	....	....	....	....	870,000	510,600	810,100	599,600	831,200
April	....	....	....	....	500,000	322,900	567,900	457,600	583,200
May	....	....	....	....	406,000	309,400	481,900	396,300	467,400
June	....	....	....	....	352,500	361,200	524,500	544,100	590,000
July	....	....	....	....	148,900	198,900	316,300	307,000	344,300
August	....	....	....	....	146,700	397,800	603,800	633,400	647,900
September	....	....	....	....	337,300	755,700	770,100	947,800	939,500
October	....	....	....	....	411,900	724,100	680,400	921,500	759,700
November	....	....	....	....	415,300	780,500	561,200	858,500	631,700
December	....	....	....	....	467,100	921,100	449,800	833,400	604,600
Total	178,800	975,600	3,000,000	7,464,000	5,385,700	6,096,400	7,215,800	7,346,700	7,756,600

* Not available on a monthly basis.
Source: U.S. Department of Commerce.

War in 1950, production declined in 1951 and did not again exceed 7 million until 1953. Production had since increased only slightly.

In preparing his forecast, the sales manager was aware of several developments in the market. The rapid growth from 1947 to 1950 was clearly the result of the introduction of a new medium of communication. The growth was not dampened by the Korean War alone but was limited by the fact that relatively few new television broadcasting stations had been approved by the Federal Communications Commission since 1948. A large number of applications was still pending, but new stations were usually approved only in areas where there was no station. Many areas had only one station, so that the choice of programs was limited. After 1948 the Federal Communications Commission had approved a number of applications for ultrahigh-frequency stations; but, in the sales manager's opinion, these had not been successful. Many of the ultrahigh-frequency stations shortly went out of business. It had been necessary to build sets which would receive high-frequency signals as well as ultrahigh-frequency signals, and also to produce adapters for sets which were manufactured prior to the establishment of ultrahigh-frequency stations. Very few of the adapters were sold.

Another factor in the market was that much of the replacement of sets sold from 1947 to 1949 had been completed. The earlier sets had small screens and required installation charges and, frequently, expensive servicing. Sets produced after 1949 had larger screens comparable in size to the 1956 sets and required little servicing. In 1954 the company, along with several of its competitors, had promoted the sale of a second television set with some results. The 1956 line of Continental carried a portable set in two screen sizes, and these models had sold more than any others in the line.

Since mid-1954, price cutting had broken out at the dealer level, and there was some pressure to push it back to the manufacturers' level. Sales had been lagging, and price concessions by dealers soon appeared. The growth of discount houses in the larger urban centers had maintained the price cutting in those areas through all of 1955. At the end of 1955 the company itself had an inventory of 2,250 of the 1955 models and 59,000 of the 1956 models. Dealers had another 71,000 sets on hand. This was far above the desired level of inventory. Sharp price reductions had failed to clear the 1955 models, most of which were the large console type and radio-phonograph-television combinations. Some of this sluggishness in sales was attributed to the uncertainty over color television. Continental had assembled 450 color television sets in 1955 under royalty arrangements with another manufacturer. Forty-two of these sets were still on hand. They were priced at $995 each. From time to time the public was confused by conflicting statements as to the time of availability of color receivers and prices. Some people predicted that color sets would be available at popular prices within the next year or two, while others publicly stated that color was at least five or six years away. Some sets were currently on the market at $595. Color sets, like the sets of 1947 to 1950, were in need of frequent and expensive service. There was also only a limited number of programs broadcast in color at that time, although the schedules of one of the major television networks included a sharp increase in the number of programs in color. Should color sets be introduced at popular prices, the entire industry agreed that black-and-white sets would almost immediately become obsolete.

Exhibit 4

DISPOSABLE INCOME, CONSUMER EXPENDITURES, CONSUMER SAVING, GROSS PRIVATE INVESTMENT ANNUALLY, 1946–55
(Millions of Dollars)

Year	Disposable Income	Consumer Expenditures	Consumer Savings	Gross Private Investment
1946	$159,182	$146,617	$12,565	$27,125
1947	169,016	164,973	4,043	29,705
1948	187,601	177,609	9,992	41,176
1949	188,157	180,598	7,559	32,549
1950	206,130	194,026	12,104	51,219
1951	226,069	208,342	17,727	56,684
1952	237,374	218,328	19,046	49,808
1953	250,235	230,542	19,693	50,325
1954	254,403	236,513	17,890	48,032
1955	270,573	253,971	16,602	60,557

Source: U.S. Department of Commerce.

As far as price considerations were concerned, the company anticipated increased costs of production. A large number of its employees were members of an electrical workers' union whose annual contract would expire on June 30, 1956. It was anticipated that a wage increase would be written into the new contract. The contract between the steel industry and the United Steel Workers of America also would expire in July, 1956. There was the possibility of a strike as well as an expected increase in steel workers' wages, both of which would be reflected in higher prices for steel, which in turn would affect the cost of materials. The sales manager suggested that the price of the company's Model A set be increased by $10. A similar increase was suggested for all other sets in the line except Model B, which he suggested be retained at its present price because of the severe competition in this model.

The general business outlook itself was somewhat mixed. There were indicators of both inflation and deflation. The consumer price index had been creeping upward, while farm prices had been declining. Housing starts were below the level of 1955, and there appeared to be a growing scarcity of mortgage funds. There were also indications

Exhibit 5

CONSUMER CREDIT OUTSTANDING, 1955

(Millions of Dollars)

Month	Total	Consumer Durables Other than Automobiles
January	$29,760	$5,609
February	29,518	5,484
March	29,948	5,479
April	30,655	5,492
May	31,568	5,555
June	32,471	5,639
July	32,896	5,676
August	33,636	5,762
September	34,293	5,848
October	34,640	5,917
November	35,059	6,057
December	36,225	6,435

Source: U.S. Department of Commerce.

Exhibit 6

ACTUAL COSTS, MODEL A AND MODEL B TELEVISION RECEIVERS, 1954 AND 1955

ITEM	1954		1955		1956*	
	Model A	Model B	Model A	Model B	Model A	Model B
Materials	$ 30.18	$ 21.46	$ 30.97	$ 21.55	$ 32.01	$ 22.19
Labor	17.22	13.51	17.09	13.71	18.46	14.06
Depreciation	1.42	1.42	1.47	1.39	1.49	1.44
Indirect labor	5.01	3.87	5.02	3.82	5.73	3.99
Factory overhead	2.74	2.01	2.77	2.07	2.89	2.09
Administrative and selling expense	2.16	2.04	2.18	2.00	2.07	2.00
Total Cost	$ 58.73	$ 44.31	$ 59.50	$ 44.54	$ 62.65	$ 45.77
Suggested retail price	$199.95	$129.95	$199.95	$129.95	$209.95	$129.95

* Estimated.

that money might become more expensive, as reflected by rising interest rates. The Federal Reserve System had recently raised the rediscount rate by one fourth of 1 per cent. On the other hand, it was predicted by several sources that investment in new plant and equipment in 1956 would exceed that of 1955 by approximately $4 to $6 billion.

Exhibit 3 shows annual and monthly production of television sets for the industry. Exhibit 4 provides data on income, consumer spending, and saving. Exhibit 5 shows the amount of consumer installment credit outstanding, as well as that pertaining to durables other than automobiles. Exhibit 6 shows the cost of production of Model A and Model B television sets by Continental. Also shown are suggested prices for these respective models.

QUESTIONS

1. How many television sets would you recommend for 1957 production? Why?
2. Do you agree with the sales manager's proposed prices? Why?
3. What relation is there between television sales and disposable national income?
4. What possible relationships exist between consumer installment credit, the money market, and television sales?
5. Of what importance is the amount of investment in making a forecast? Explain carefully.
6. Would you agree that a mere projection of past performance is an adequate forecast? Explain.

Chapter 3

THE DEMAND FOR BUSINESS OUTPUT

ONE GREAT advantage of an economic system based on private enterprise is the importance of the role which it allows consumers to play in guiding production. Businessmen can continue to produce only those items for which consumers are willing and able to pay enough at least to cover all of the necessary costs. The modern institution of advertising, however, frequently makes it unnecessary for the firm merely to accept demand as it is; rather, consumer expenditures can be influenced to a greater or lesser degree by advertising outlays and other selling efforts.

A businessman who attempts to estimate how many units of a product he can sell during a certain period of time is immediately aware that the amount will depend on the price at which he offers the good. At a high price, it is usually possible to sell fewer units than can be sold at a low price. The fact that price is so influential in determining the amount which is demanded led economists at first to concentrate attention chiefly on the price-quantity relationship. Demand came to mean a *system* of prices and quantities, more being demanded at a lower price, less at a higher one.

While market demand curves "exist" for all commodities at all times, the problem of making the necessary measurements to determine their nature is a complex one (which will be examined briefly in the Appendix to this chapter). For many analytical purposes, it is sufficient to draw purely hypothetical demand curves. In any event, it is important that the basic theory of demand be understood before any statistical measurements are made, since theory must underlie all useful empirical work.

A hypothetical demand schedule for wheat is shown in Exhibit 1. It will be noted that the quantity which buyers are willing to purchase varies inversely with the price. This is an almost universal rule with respect to market demand for any commodity, the inverse relationship being traceable to two factors: (1) As price is reduced, the commodity is substituted for others; and (2) as price is lowered, buyers can afford to buy more of the commodity. It should be noted that the demand schedule shown in Exhibit 1 is greatly simplified, showing price only at 50-cent intervals. Also, "wheat" is not a strictly homogeneous commodity (there being several grades), nor is it sold only in a single market. Further, "price" must relate to an average price per month; or, alternatively, the quantity demanded must be interpreted as the

Exhibit 1

MARKET DEMAND SCHEDULE

Row	Price of Wheat (per Bushel)	Quantity Demanded (Millions of Bushels per Month)	Value (Millions of Dollars)
A.	$4.00	50	$200
B.	3.50	60	210
C.	3.00	70	210
D.	2.50	80	200
E.	2.00	90	180
F.	1.50	100	150
G.	1.00	110	110

monthly rate of purchase which would take place at a particular price at a moment of time.

The market demand schedule of Exhibit 1 is plotted as a demand curve in Exhibit 2. For analytical purposes, this is usually a more convenient form than a demand schedule. Since the demand curve connects the various price-quantity combinations, it is drawn on the assumption that no irregularities occur in the relationship between the plotted points. The hypothetical data used in this example provide a straight-line relationship between price and quantity purchased. An actual demand curve for wheat may well exhibit some curvature; however, a straight-line relationship is more convenient to use, and most statistical demand studies for agricultural products have disclosed that a straight line fits the data about as well as more complex curves.

Slope and Elasticity

An examination of the demand schedule shows that a decrease in price of 50 cents per bushel is associated with an increase of 10 million bushels per month in quantity demanded. This relationship is unchanging throughout the demand schedule, giving the demand curve a slope of -5 ($-50 \div 10$).[1] This may be interpreted as meaning that a

---

[1] If this demand curve is considered to extend along the same straight line until it touches both axes, its equation becomes $P = 650 - 5Q$. Where P (price) is measured in cents per bushel and Q (quantity) is in millions of bushels. The slope (-5) appears as the coefficient of Q.

decrease of 5 cents a bushel will occasion an increase of 1 million bushels in the quantity purchased monthly.

Although the physical volume of sales is related linearly to price, the same is not true of the value of sales. This is evident from an inspection of the Value column of Exhibit 1 (this column being the prod-

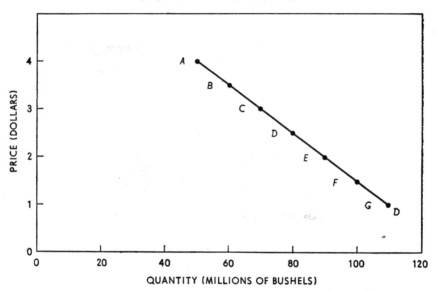

uct of price and quantity). Except at the top of the table, smaller quantities are worth more to the sellers than larger quantities. This is because the *percentage* decrease from 100 million to 90 million bushels, for example, is smaller than the *percentage* increase in price from $1.50 to $2.00 per bushel; that is, a 10 per cent decrease in quantity is associated with a $33\frac{1}{3}$ per cent increase in price, and this causes the smaller quantity to bring a higher monetary return to sellers.

The dependence of total value on the relative percentage change of quantity and price often makes the measure of "elasticity" of demand a more useful one than the measure of slope. Elasticity of demand can be defined as the ratio of the percentage change in quantity demanded to the corresponding percentage change in price. It is mathematically necessary, however, to take the ratios of very small (strictly, infinitesimally small) percentage changes in order to measure elasticity at a particular price.[2] Along a downsloping straight-line demand curve, elasticity of demand differs at every point and is negative in sign. For convenience, however, the negative sign will be disregarded in the rest of the discussion.

Elasticity and Revenue

The easiest way to compute elasticity of demand at a particular price involves use of a chart. The method can be demonstrated by reference

Exhibit 3

TOTAL REVENUE IS AT A MAXIMUM—WHERE ELASTICITY
OF DEMAND IS UNITARY

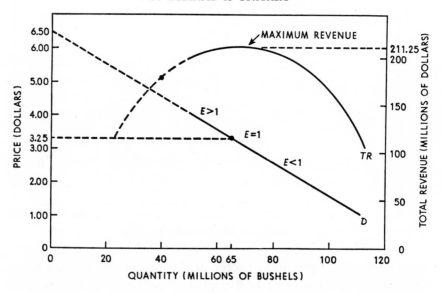

to Exhibit 3. Curve *D* is a repetition of the demand curve drawn in Exhibit 2, except that it has been extended (by a broken line) until it crosses the vertical axis (at the price of $6.50).[3] Once this intersection has been ascertained, it is easy to find the elasticity at any price along the demand curve: Simply divide the price by the difference be-

---

[2] If $\frac{dq}{q}$ denotes a very small percentage change in quantity demanded and $\frac{dp}{p}$ denotes a very small percentage change in price, elasticity of demand $(E) = \frac{dq}{q} \div \frac{dp}{p}$ This is usually written $E = \frac{dq}{dp} \cdot \frac{p}{q}$

[3] If the demand curve is not a straight line, the pertinent intersection with the vertical axis can be found by drawing a tangent to the demand curve at the price at which elasticity is to be measured and extending this tangent up to the *Y*-axis.

tween that price and the price at the intersection. At a price of $4.00, for example, the elasticity of demand is $4.00 \div 2.50 = 1.6$. Since this coefficient exceeds one, demand is said to be "elastic." At a price of $1.00 the elasticity of demand is $1.00 \div 5.50$, or a little less than 0.2. This is denoted as "inelastic" demand. "Unitary" elasticity of demand comes at a price of $3.25, since $3.25 \div 3.25 = 1$.

Sellers of wheat could maximize their income by setting a price of $3.25 per bushel, under the demand assumptions which we are using. Alternatively, it can be said that they can maximize their income by marketing 65 million bushels per month. This can easily be seen in Exhibit 3, since the total revenue curve (which is plotted against the bottom and right-hand scales) reaches a maximum at a quantity of 65 million bushels. It is also apparent from this chart that a reduction in sales from 100 million to 80 million bushels, for example, will increase the total revenue received by sellers. This is because demand is inelastic in this region. On the other hand, a reduction in sales from 60 million to 40 million bushels would reduce total revenue, because demand is elastic in this region. It should be realized that sellers who are in competition with one another cannot choose the price or quantity which will bring the greatest total revenue to the group. Competitive wheat producers normally produce and market a greater quantity than the profit-maximizing amount, and society benefits from this greater output. However, from the point of view of the producers alone, it is advantageous to restrict output to the quantity at which elasticity of demand is unitary, or to a quantity which is less than this amount.[4] Such restriction of output to maximize sellers' incomes is only possible when control is exercised by means of private or governmental action which is cartel-like in nature.

Demand Facing a Monopolist

It should be kept in mind that the demand which has been discussed so far is *market* demand rather than the demand for the product of an individual company. Where the entire output of the commodity is accounted for by a single firm, however, it is clear that demand facing such a monopolistic seller is identical with the market demand. Monopoly demand curves consequently slope downward to the right.

It is useful, in analyzing the monopolist's economic behavior, to em-

---

[4] When cost of production is a consideration, the most profitable quantity to sell is less than the quantity which brings greatest total revenue. Optimum sales volume can normally be found only by considering cost as well as revenue, as will be noted in a later chapter.

ploy the concept of "marginal revenue" as well as that of the demand schedule. Marginal revenue is simply the *additional* revenue secured by a seller from the sale of an additional unit of product. (Strictly, the unit should again be infinitesimally small.) If there were only one producer of wheat—an unrealistic assumption but one which is no longer unimportant, since farmers act somewhat in concert through the federal farm program and by means of private marketing agreements—the market demand schedule which we have been using would be the demand curve facing that firm. Marginal revenue from the sale of additional output would be found by taking the difference between successive total revenues and dividing these by the differences between successive quantities demanded. These calculations are shown in Exhibit 4.

Exhibit 4

COMPUTATION OF MARGINAL REVENUE

Row	(1) Change in Quantity (Millions of Bushels)	(2) Change in Total Revenue (Millions of Dollars)	(Col. 2 ÷ Col. 1) Marginal Revenue per Bushel
A...............	10	$20	$2
B...............	10	10	1
C...............	10	0	0
D...............	10	−10	−1
E...............	10	−20	−2
F...............	10	−30	−3
G...............	10	−40	−4

In order to get the change in quantity and in total revenue for Row A, it is necessary to assume that a quantity of 40 million bushels would have been demanded at a price of $4.50 per bushel. This would have yielded a total revenue of $180 million, and the difference between this amount and $200 million is $20 million. Division of $20 million by the quantity increase of 10 million bushels means that each additional bushel sold added an average of $2.00 to sellers' aggregate revenue. In Row D through Row G, marginal revenue is negative, showing that additional units sold actually reduce the total income of sellers (make negative additions to income).

It is clear that a monopolist seeking to maximize his profits would not sell any units which, through their depressing influence on price, would reduce his total revenue. That is, the monopolist will not operate in the region of negative marginal revenue. His price will be set at

$3.25 per bushel or higher, and his sales will be 65 million bushels per month or less. (The exact optimum cannot be defined until cost is brought into the picture.) Reference to Exhibit 3 suggests that he should operate in the region where demand is of unitary elasticity or higher, rather than where demand is inelastic. Although total revenue would be the same at quantities of 50 and 80 million bushels, for example, the cost of producing the smaller amount would obviously be less.

Demand and marginal revenue for the hypothetical wheat monopolist are shown in Exhibit 5. The dotted portions indicate the course

Exhibit 5

PRICE EXCEEDS MARGINAL REVENUE FOR MONOPOLISTIC SELLER

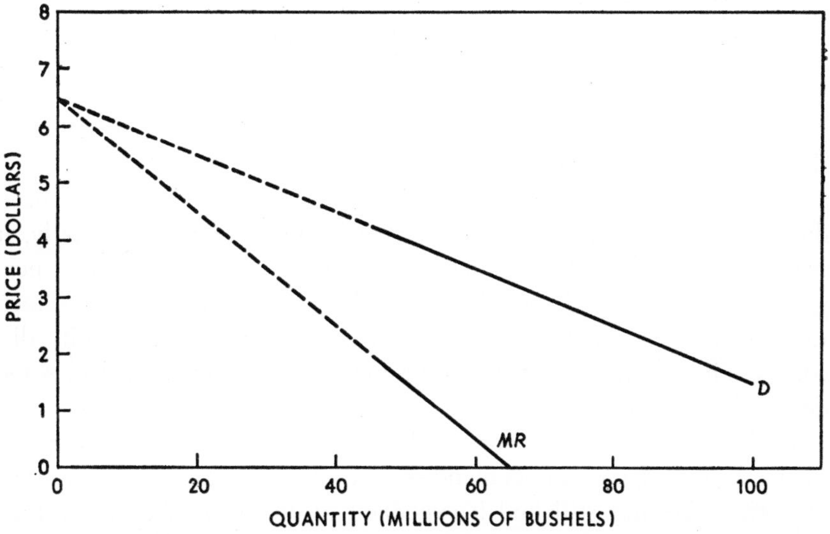

of the curves at quantities below 50 million bushels, assuming that the same linear relationship holds true. It can be seen that marginal revenue is zero at a quantity of 65 million bushels. It was noted earlier that elasticity of demand is unitary at this quantity. Consequently, it is clear that unitary elasticity and a marginal revenue of zero exist at the same output. When demand is elastic, marginal revenue is greater than one; while in the region of inelastic demand, marginal revenue is negative. The logic of this last relationship is not difficult to understand: When demand is inelastic, it is necessary to cut price sharply on all units in order to sell a little more; hence, the additional sale will decrease the total value of sales—i.e., bring in negative marginal revenue.

Some Qualifications

The demand curves which have been used so far show highly simplified "static" relationships which are especially useful in the economic theory of price determination. While they may also be useful to the businessman, it is likely to be important for him to keep in mind some complicating qualifications.

First, a reduction in price may temporarily reduce sales rather than increase them, since buyers may be led to expect further price cuts. This is a "dynamic" consideration which is neglected in the static theory of demand. Similarly, a price cut may "spoil the market," so that return to a higher price previously charged may not be feasible. Buyers are frequently more sensitive to changes in price than to the absolute level of price.

Second, even when some buyers immediately begin to buy more in response to a price cut, other buyers may be slower in changing their buying habits, so that a considerable period of time may elapse before the full effect of the price change works itself out.

Third, the demand and marginal revenue curves which have been drawn assume that all buyers are charged the same price. Actually, it may be possible to sell additional units by reducing price only to a new group of buyers, or only on additional sales to existing customers. Block rates used by public-utility firms are a good example of quantity discounts. The practice of price discrimination will be examined in some detail in a separate chapter.

Fourth, although it is theoretically irrational for a monopolist to sell in the region of inelastic demand—since he can gain revenue by raising price—he may still find it expedient to do so. By charging a less-than-optimum price, he may be able to discourage would-be competitors, build up consumer goodwill for the long run, and perhaps reduce the likelihood of prosecution under the federal antitrust laws if he is selling in interstate commerce. (There are seldom laws against intrastate monopoly.)

Demand Facing Pure Competition

Economists define "perfect" or "pure" competition as a situation in which there are so many sellers of a particular commodity that none can individually affect the price. In the absence of governmental interference, many agricultural commodities are produced under such conditions. Even today, truck-garden vegetables, poultry, eggs, and fish, for example, are often turned out by perfectly competitive firms.

Under pure competition the demand curve for the product of the individual firm is simply a horizontal line drawn at the price determined in the market. That is to say, market price is determined by over-all supply and demand, and the individual firm can sell as much as it wishes at this price. It cannot charge more than the market price without losing all of its customers (who are assumed to be both rational and mobile) and need not, of course, accept less than the prevailing price.

Exhibit 6

INFINITELY ELASTIC DEMAND FACES PERFECTLY COMPETITIVE FIRM

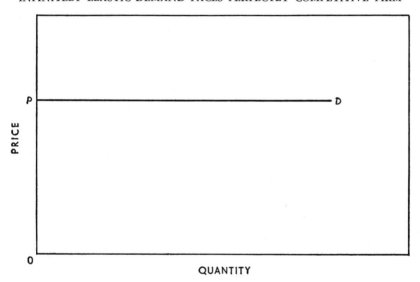

The demand for the product of a purely competitive firm is represented in Exhibit 6. Such a horizontal curve is infinitely elastic along its entire range.[5] The firm has no control over price and can be designated as a "price taker" rather than as a "price maker." (The latter term is appropriate for a monopolistic firm.)

Pure Competition Is Uncommon

The case of pure competition is, in practice, much less common than that of monopoly, when the latter term is used to cover all situations in which the demand facing the individual firm is downsloping rather than horizontal. Most firms have some power to fix price, within lim-

---

[5] This can easily be verified by reference to the geometrical test described earlier. Since the horizontal demand curve intersects the vertical axis at the market price, the divisor is zero. Consequently, OP divided by zero gives an infinite elasticity.

its, and hence are not fully competitive with others. The amount of this price-making power may be great—for example, in the case of a city-owned electric-utility system, where the rates set by the municipal authorities may be subject to no check by a regulatory commission. Or the amount of price-making power may be severely limited by the existence of close substitutes, as in the case of a seller of a particular breakfast cereal or sardines.

Some writers use the term "monopolistic competition" to denote the situation of a firm which has some monopoly power—due, perhaps, to selling under a brand name which no one else can use—but which faces the competition of more or less similar products. No clear line can be drawn between "monopoly" and "monopolistic competition," however, since every monopolist faces some competition. The prewar Aluminum Company of America had great monopoly power in the production of this metal but nevertheless encountered a measure of competition from other metals produced both domestically and abroad.

In order to operate under conditions of perfect competition, a firm must sell an unbranded commodity (such as sweet corn) and must not be significantly separated spatially from other sellers of the same good. Many firms have a degree of locational monopoly due to their greater convenience to buyers. Venders of refreshments at a football game, for example, have a separateness from other sellers which permits them to charge higher prices than those on the outside. Much advertising is designed simply to imprint brand names on the public mind, in order to lessen the severity of competition from similar or even identical goods.

Demand under Oligopoly

The demand curves which have been drawn so far were necessarily based on the assumption of *ceterus paribus*—i.e., all other factors which would affect the quantity demanded were held constant. These include prices of competing products, incomes and their distribution, and consumers' tastes. Where there are only a few sellers of a particular commodity, however, this assumption is not useful. Instead, it must be recognized that each seller will carefully watch the actions of his close competitors and frequently will react to any change which they make in price, quality, or selling effort. This is called an "oligopolistic" situation—the case of a few sellers. It is an extremely common real-world situation. Oligopolistic firms may turn out identical homogeneous products (e.g., brass tubing, aluminum sheets, or copper wire); or they may sell closely related but somewhat dissimilar goods (e.g., trucks, airplanes, typewriters, or soap powder).

A single demand curve cannot depict the price-quantity relationship for a commodity sold oligopolistically. If price is changed, the response of sales depends heavily on the actions which close rivals are induced to take. If, for example, price is lowered by one firm but rivals choose to maintain their prices and quality unchanged, the amount which buyers will purchase from the price cutter is likely to expand quite sharply. If rivals match a price cut, sales of the first

Exhibit 7

OLIGOPOLY DEMAND CURVES—SALES DEPEND ON RIVALS' REACTIONS

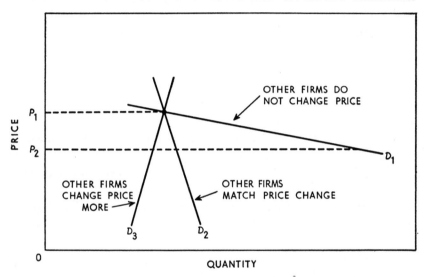

price cutter are likely to increase only moderately, since others will share in the larger total sales volume. If rivals more than meet a price cut, the physical volume sold by the first price cutter may even fall off.

A general picture of the demand situation under oligopoly can be shown graphically. Such a chart is suggestive only, since it cannot show the results of all of the possible combinations of action and reaction on the part of oligopolistic rivals. Exhibit 7 pertains to an individual firm which is assumed, first, to be charging price OP_1. If the firm then lowers its price to OP_2 and its rivals do not change their prices, the physical sales of the price cutter may expand sharply, as indicated by curve D_1. (Since this curve is elastic between prices

OP_1 and OP_2, total revenue received by the firm will rise.) If, instead, rival firms match the price cut, the volume of sales may expand only moderately, as indicated by D_2. (Since this curve, as drawn, is inelastic between prices OP_1 and OP_2, the dollar volume of sales would be down, despite the rise in physical volume.) It is even possible that the firm under consideration will encounter a positive sloping demand curve such as D_3. This is only likely if rivals more than match the first firm's price cut.

Above the original price OP the demand curves can be interpreted in a similar way. If our firm raises its price and its close rivals do not do so, sales may fall off quite sharply, as suggested by curve D_1. If the other sellers match the price increase, sales may fall off only moderately, as along D_2. If rivals should decide to raise their prices more than the first firm, that firm may enjoy higher physical and dollar sales, as indicated by D_3.

It is clear that there are so many possible combinations of oligopolistic price behavior (to say nothing of changes in such variables as quality, amount of advertising, premiums, credit terms, etc.) that demand curves for the individual firm are of limited usefulness. The same is not true of *market* demand curves for oligopolistic industries, however, and considerable effort has been expended in deriving statistical demand curves for such commodities as steel and cigarettes, where the number of producers is relatively small.

The consequences of the complex nature of demand under oligopoly will be examined in some detail in subsequent chapters. It is readily apparent, though, that a great many different results may ensue from a price change. The uncertainties inherent in the situation are conducive to the maintenance of stable prices through overt or tacit agreements between sellers. When such agreements break down, however, price wars may follow, especially when excess capacity exists.

Changes in Demand

For purposes of clear thinking, it is important to distinguish between movement along a particular demand curve and a shift in the entire curve. If, in Exhibit 8, market demand is represented by curve D_1 and price is at the level OP, an increase in price to OP' will reduce sales from OX to OX'. This can best be designated as a "decrease in amount demanded." On the other hand, a movement of the entire curve downward and to the left constitutes a "decrease in demand." This sort of change is represented by a movement of the curve from D_1 to D_2. When demand decreases, consumers are willing to buy less at *all prices* than they were previously ready to buy. An increase in demand is reflected in a shift of the entire curve upward and to the right.

A great many factors affect the demand for every commodity. Where a company carries a number of lines, as in the case of a department store, even internal competition may be important. This is sometimes a problem also between major divisions of a large manufacturing corporation, where the desire of managers of the several divisions to

Exhibit 8

CHANGE IN DEMAND MEANS SHIFT OF DEMAND CURVE

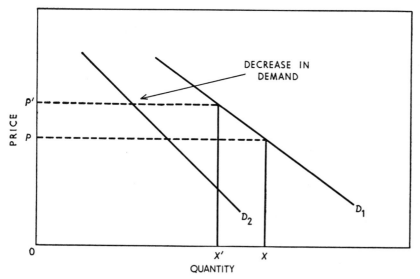

make a good showing may lead, if unchecked, to policies which are not optimal from the point of view of the firm as a whole.[6]

Most commodities are virtually independent of one another in demand except as general competitors for purchasing power. Other commodities—such as butter and oleomargarine, Fords and Chevrolets, and television and moving pictures—are close substitutes for one another. In this situation a decline in the price of one commodity tends to reduce the demand for the other. Other goods are complementary in nature, in that increased sales of one tend to increase the demand for the other. Examples are coffee and cream, tires and

---

[6] Costly competition between the various divisions of a particular government agency is also common, especially because the check of declining profits is not present. A limited amount of intra-agency competition is sometimes useful, however, since each office may provide a check on ill-considered actions of the others.

gasoline, electric power and appliances, and seed and fertilizer. In recent years, it has become apparent that television and certain types of motion pictures are complementary rather than substitutive, since the films are shown on TV. A difficult and important problem for promoters of professional sporting events is whether the televised event is a substitute for the performance itself. Careful statistical study may shed light on this sort of problem.

Many consumer and capital goods are complementary in a very important way. An increase in the demand for shoes increases the demand for shoe machinery. A change in the demand for housing affects the demand for a host of building materials and equipment, as well as construction labor. A decline in the demand for bread or cigarettes reduces the demand for wheat, tobacco, paper, etc.

Timing of Shifts

Changes in demand sometimes follow more or less regular patterns over time. Some of these patterns recur annually and are called "seasonal variations." A peak of sales just before Christmas in the department store trade represents a positive seasonal shift of demand, while a slackening of sales after the first of the year represents a negative shift of demand. Marked seasonal patterns of demand exist for such commodities as candy, portland cement, skis, automobiles, and firecrackers.

Companies engaged in the manufacture of drugs, chemicals, and nylon and other new fabrics, to name only a few, have experienced a growing demand in recent years which has persisted even in periods when sales of most other goods have marked time or fallen off. These are examples of a long-term or *secular* increase in demand. The bituminous coal and silk hosiery industries present instances of secular declines in demand.

During World War II, there was a dramatic increase in the demand for many products. Aircraft producers, mining firms, textile mills, and building contractors were among those who experienced booms which, in some cases, reversed long-run secular declines in demand. Other products experienced strong postwar demand under the stimulus of the rearmament program. Such shifts can be called "erratic movements" of demand because they follow no regular pattern of recurrence or growth.

Of particular analytical importance because it affects the demand for *all* commodities is the level of economic activity within the nation. This relation exists because production of all sorts of goods and services is the source of the income with which the goods and services may be purchased. The best measures of general economic activity are the national income estimates compiled by the Department of Commerce. These are the end product of a system of national economic accounting which has been developed only in recent decades and which is steadily being refined. National income data have two main purposes: (1) to provide a picture of what is happening, so that government can take monetary, fiscal, and other actions to counteract undesirable changes; and (2) to enable businessmen and others to adapt their actions to the economic environment in which they must operate.

The Principal National Income Measures

Gross national product (GNP) is one of the best known of the measures of economic activity. It consists of the summed values of all final goods and services produced during a given period. Only "final" products are included, in order to avoid double counting. Thus, the value of all new farm machinery, bread, and pretzels is included; but the steel, flour, and salt which enter into their manufacture must be excluded.

National income (NI) is also a well-known and somewhat more refined measure. Much of the capital equipment turned out during any year goes just to replace similar equipment worn out during the same period. This involves a sort of double counting which can be removed by deducting aggregate depreciation from gross national product. Another large adjustment must also be made in order to go from gross national product to national income. This involves subtraction of aggregate indirect business taxes (such as the cigarette and liquor excise taxes). These taxes are included in the prices at which commodities are counted in gross national product; but they should properly be excluded, since they are not part of the basic cost of producing the commodities. National income represents the net value of final goods and services produced during a year. It can also be computed as the sum of all income payments made to those who contribute to production. Regarded in this way, national income is the sum of all wages, salaries, interest, rent, and business profits earned during a period. The government statisticians obtain the same figure working from the goods side and the payments side. (When the totals are not the same, they simply put in an adjustment of $1 or $2 billion for errors and omissions which, ingeniously, brings about perfect balance.)

Personal income (PI) is a third measure of national income and one which is more closely related to the demand for consumer goods than gross national product or national income. It consists of national income less the profits which are retained or "plowed back" by business firms. These undistributed profits are available for the purchase of capital goods by firms, but not for immediate consumption. Personal income, however, includes an important category of disbursements which are not included in national income. These are "transfer

Exhibit 9

GROSS NATIONAL PRODUCT (GNP) —VALUE OF ALL FINAL PRODUCTS

NATIONAL INCOME (NI)—GNP LESS DEPRECIATION AND INDIRECT BUSINESS TAXES

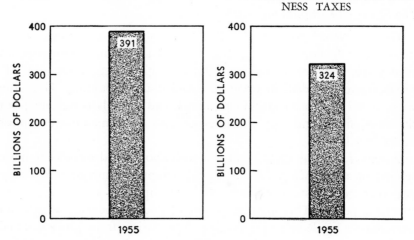

PERSONAL INCOME (PI)—NI LESS UNDISTRIBUTED PROFITS PLUS TRANSFER PAYMENTS

DISPOSABLE PERSONAL INCOME—PI LESS PERSONAL TAXES

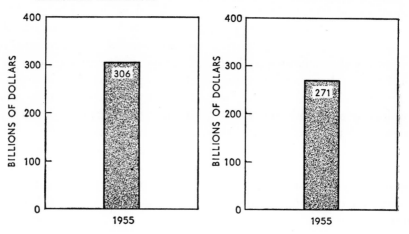

payments" of all types—payments which are in the nature of transfers between individuals for which no current productive services are rendered. These include federal old-age and survivors' social security benefits, state unemployment insurance benefits, relief payments, military pensions, and interest on the public debt. Such receipts are actually available for spending by individuals.

Since transfer payments are financed chiefly by means of taxes paid by individuals and corporations, it may be misleading to include such transfers without deducting the taxes. *Disposable personal income* (DPI) makes this final adjustment, total personal taxes being subtracted from total personal income. The resulting figure comes close to representing the dollar income actually available to individuals for the purchase of goods which are bought as a matter of private choice. (It is not a measure of national economic welfare, since many goods—such as schools, post offices, and highways—are purchased collectively rather than individually.)

The principal national income measurements can be compared graphically in Exhibit 9. Gross national product in 1955 amounted to $391 billion. Subtraction of aggregate depreciation and indirect business taxes left national income of $324 billion. Subtraction of undistributed profits and addition of transfer payments gave personal income of $306 billion, and subtraction of income taxes and other personal taxes left disposable personal income of $271 billion.

These over-all measures of economic activity have a great many uses, both descriptive and analytical. Many businessmen keep a close watch on their movements for a clue as to the macroeconomic forces which are likely to affect their own operations. Also, forecasting techniques make much use of these measures, as was indicated in Chapter 2.

CASE 3-1: NEW YORK, NEW HAVEN, AND HARTFORD
RAILROAD (1)

The management of the New Haven Railroad anticipated that, with the opening of the World's Fair in New York in April, 1939, the railroad would be unable to handle the probable volume of travel at existing rates. It was believed that the greatest pressure would arise as a result of the low Sunday excursion rates, which were calculated at about 1 cent a mile. Excursion rates usually drew peak traffic in summer time. The railroad therefore raised these rates for

Exhibit 1

EXCURSION FARES AND TRAFFIC TO NEW YORK CITY,
NEW HAVEN RAILROAD, 1939

ORIGIN	EXCURSION ROUND-TRIP FARE	SPECIAL EXCURSION FARE, APRIL 30– AUGUST 6, 1939	NUMBER OF PASSENGERS		
			Av. Sunday, Month before April 30, 1939	Av. Sunday, April 30– August 6, 1939	Av. Sunday, 3 Months after August 6, 1939
Bridgeport........	$1.25	$1.50	401	312	596
New Haven.......	1.50	1.95	560	401	915
Providence.......	3.50	4.75	75	30	150
Boston..........	3.50	5.85	502	114	891

Source: William J. Dixon, *The Elasticity of Demand for Railroad Passenger Transportation* (New Haven: Yale University Press, 1941). Mimeographed.

travel into, but not out of, New York. The higher fares went into effect on April 30 and continued to August 6, 1939 (see Exhibit 1).

QUESTIONS

1. Was the demand for excursion travel on the New Haven Railroad elastic or inelastic? On what assumptions do you base your answer?
2. Is it probable that excursion travel is more sensitive to rate changes than regular travel? Why?
3. What does the volume of travel after August 6 indicate about the nature of demand?
4. When the railroads request the Interstate Commerce Commission to grant a rate increase for passenger or freight travel, what are they assuming about the nature of demand over the relevant price range?

CASE 3–2: NEW YORK, NEW HAVEN, AND HARTFORD
RAILROAD (2)

Prior to June 1, 1936, the basic passenger fare for railroad travel in the eastern United States was 3.6 cents per mile. For Pullman travel, there was a surcharge above this basic rate. On June 1, 1936, by order of the Interstate Commerce Commission, the basic rate was lowered to 2 cents per mile for coach travel. The Pullman rate was reduced to 3 cents per mile, and the surcharge was abolished. These fares continued in effect until July 25, 1938, when the Interstate Commerce Commission authorized an increase in the coach rate to 2.5 cents per mile. The Pullman rate remained at 3 cents per mile. On March 25, 1940, the commission restored the basic rate of 2 cents for coach travel. (See Exhibits 1 and 2.)

It was generally believed by officials of the Interstate Commerce

Commission that a reduction of railroad passenger rates would, under many conditions, serve to increase total revenues. This view was not shared by officers of the New Haven Railroad.[7] A study of the demand for passenger travel on the New Haven by William J. Dixon of Yale University threw some light on this problem. The Dixon

Exhibit 1

OPERATING REVENUES OF THE NEW HAVEN RAILROAD,
1935–40

Years	Freight	Passenger	Other	Total	Net Railway Operating Income
1935........	$40,834,001	$22,108,806	$8,170,473	$71,113,280	$8,179,548
1936........	44,880,649	24,996,101	8,990,399	78,867,149	8,036,300
1937........	45,150,055	26,892,165	9,100,367	81,142,587	4,591,390
1938........	38,809,938	26,329,579	7,940,624	73,080,141	517,047
1939........	47,525,678	27,381,782	8,511,016	83,418,476	8,462,922
1940........	50,512,702	26,342,490	8,748,917	85,604,109	9,274,354

Source: *Moody's Manual of Investments: Railroad Securities.*

Exhibit 2

AVERAGE FARES AND PASSENGER TRAFFIC ON THE NEW
HAVEN RAILROAD, 1935–40

Years	Average Rate per Passenger per Mile (Cents)	Passengers Carried	Passenger-Miles	Average Miles per Passenger
1935..............	2.13	30,920,975	1,036,305,605	33.51
1936..............	1.97	34,551,901	1,268,606,403	36.72
1937..............	1.87	37,188,689	1,438,562,921	38.68
1938..............	1.92	37,705,865	1,371,825,004	36.38
1939..............	1.99	36,197,090	1,373,887,509	37.96
1940..............	1.83	36,713,912	1,437,484,656	39.15

Source: *Moody's Manual of Investments: Railroad Securities.*

study was confined to one part of the New Haven system—the heavily traveled Shore Line, running from New York to Boston through the cities of Bridgeport, New Haven, New London, and Providence.[8]

The Shore Line of the New Haven Railroad (see Exhibit 3) traversed the heavily industrialized sections of southern Connecticut

---

[7] For statements of views of the commission and of the management of the New Haven Railroad, see *Interstate Commerce Commission Reports,* Vol. CCXIV, No. 26550, "Passenger Fares and Surcharges" (February 28, 1936), pp. 174 ff. The opinion of Commissioner Meyer is reproduced in the Appendix to Case 3–2.

[8] Many of the facts contained in the present case are derived from Willian J. Dixon's essay, *The Elasticity of Demand for Railroad Passenger Transportation* (New Haven: Yale University Press, 1941). Mimeographed.

bordering Long Island Sound, and the populous manufacturing areas of Rhode Island and eastern Massachusetts. In the period 1935–40, this region experienced little change in population, the six principal cities on the route of the New Haven having the following populations in 1940:

New London	48,000	Providence	444,000
Bridgeport	170,000	Boston	1,570,000
New Haven	230,000	New York	7,455,000

Exhibit 3

MAP OF THE SHORE LINE OF THE NEW HAVEN RAILROAD*

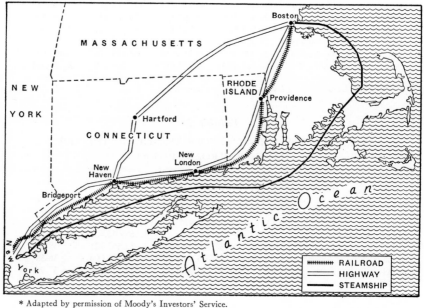

* Adapted by permission of Moody's Investors' Service.

These cities provided the New Haven Railroad with a high density of traffic, amounting to 2,742,293 local passengers, or 325,546,000 passenger-miles in 1940.

In order to determine the effect of rate changes on volume of traffic, the survey covered only local traffic—that is, the traffic which originated in the six principal cities of the Shore Line and which had as destinations some one of these cities. Interline and commuting traffic was excluded. Ticket-sales data were collected from station accounts by months for the years 1935–40, inclusive.

The New Haven offered four types of passenger service: regular coach, regular Pullman, limited Pullman, and excursion. Regular-fare traffic, both coach and Pullman, accounted for the largest part of total passenger revenue. For this reason, it was decided to study the relationship of the volume of this traffic to rate changes. For purposes of this study the weighted averages of regular coach and regular Pullman fares were determined by giving effect to the number of passenger-miles actually recorded for each type of traffic. The result was a weighted average fare actually moving traffic in each period.

As noted above, there were three primary rate changes in the period 1935–40; and from time to time, minor changes of rate were introduced by the railroad. Prior to the Interstate Commerce Commission ruling of June 1, 1936, there was a 3-cent rate for 30-day round-trip and summer travel, and a 2.5-cent rate for week-end trips, valid both in coaches and in Pullman cars. Between Providence and Boston, the 2.5-cent rate also prevailed in five-trip form; and on June 5, 1935, a one-day round-trip ticket was established between these two points, computed at approximately 2 cents a mile. When the New York World's Fair opened on April 30, 1939, the New Haven introduced 60-day round-trip coach tickets at 2.25 cents per mile. These were at first good only for trips into New York; but two months later, they were placed on a system-wide basis. During the Christmas season in both 1938 and 1939, special round-trip coach tickets with limited return were sold for 2 cents a mile. During the entire period, Sunday and holiday popular excursion tickets between certain points, priced at approximately 1 cent a mile, were on sale, as well as some special two-day excursion tickets at somewhat higher rates. Except for the excursion rates, all of these minor fare changes, as well as the three primary changes of June 1, 1936, July 25, 1938, and March 25, 1940, were included in the weighted average fares for regular traffic.

For each of the years 1935–40, weighted average fares of regular traffic were computed for the winter months (January, February, and March); for the summer months (June, July, and August); and for the entire year. These several average fares were then placed against the respective traffic volumes for each of the years under study, as shown by Exhibit 4. Graphic presentation of these data in Exhibit 5 reveals the existence of an unmistakable relationship between fares, traffic, and revenue. A fare reduction of $33\frac{1}{3}$ per cent, for example, from 3 to 2 cents per mile, was, on the average, associated with the following percentage increases in passenger-miles and revenue:

	Winter Months	Summer Months	Annual
Passenger-miles......87	87	117	103
Revenue............24	24	45	35

The survey noted that, on the graph for the summer months, the observation for 1936 was below the curve of relationship because there is a time lag of about two months after a fare change before traffic reaches the level it would ordinarily have at that fare. As fares were lowered on June 1, 1936, two of the three summer months were experiencing this lag. Both 1936 and 1940 are generally low

Exhibit 4

AVERAGE FARES, PASSENGER-MILES, AND REVENUES FOR LOCAL
TRAFFIC ON SHORE LINE OF NEW HAVEN RAILROAD, 1935–40

YEAR	WINTER (JANUARY, FEBRUARY, MARCH)			SUMMER (JUNE, JULY, AUGUST)			ENTIRE YEAR		
	Fare (Cents per Mile)	Pas- senger- Miles (Millions)	Revenue (Millions of Dollars)	Fare (Cents per Mile)	Pas- senger- Miles (Millions)	Revenue (Millions of Dollars)	Fare (Cents per Mile)	Pas- senger- Miles (Millions)	Revenue (Millions of Dollars)
1935.......	2.75	48	$1.32	3.10	38	$1.18	3.10	180	$5.58
1936.......	2.95	56	1.65	2.25	70	1.58	2.45	275	6.74
1937.......	2.25	84	1.89	2.20	82	1.80	2.25	345	7.76
1938.......	2.25	83	1.87	2.35	69	1.62	2.35	315	7.40
1939.......	2.65	70	1.86	2.50	74	1.85	2.55	310	7.90
1940.......	2.50	73	1.83	2.20	81	1.78	2.25	330	7.43

Source: William J. Dixon, *The Elasticity of Demand for Railroad Passenger Transportation* (New Haven: Yale University Press, 1941), p. 24.

on the graph of annual figures, and fare changes probably contributed to this. On the basis of this evidence, it was tentatively concluded that traffic volume was strongly influenced by the changes of fares and that, within the actual ranges of rate change, revenues would increase appreciably at lower fares.

Some improvements in equipment were introduced in the period 1935–40. On June 5, 1935, the streamlined "Comet" began mile-a-minute operation between Providence and Boston. The first of some 200 new air-conditioned, streamlined coaches went into service late in 1934, and the remainder at irregular intervals thereafter up to the fall of 1938, although most Shore Line trains had been assigned this type of equipment by the end of 1936. In addition, many of the older cars in through-service, including the de luxe coaches purchased in 1931, were air-conditioned.

The number of trains serving Shore Line points remained essentially the same until April, 1940, when frequency of service was materially

Exhibit 5

GRAPHIC RELATIONSHIPS OF AVERAGE FARES, PASSENGER-MILES, AND
REVENUES FOR LOCAL TRAFFIC ON SHORE LINE OF NEW HAVEN
RAILROAD, 1935–40

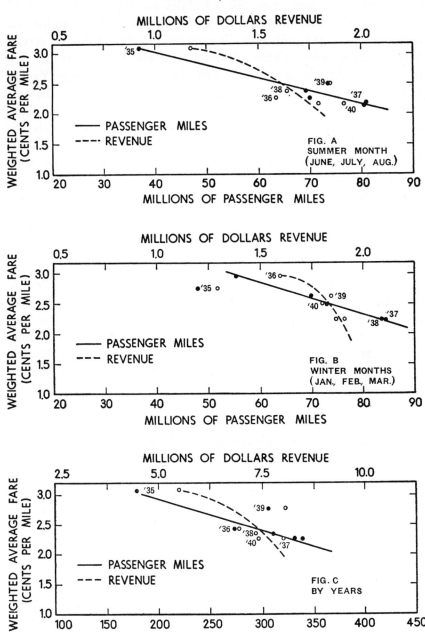

Source: William J. Dixon, *The Elasticity of Demand for Railroad Passenger Transportation* (New Haven:
Yale University Press, 1941), p. 24.

improved. An hourly-on-the-hour leaving time between 8:00 A.M. and 6:00 P.M. was established from Boston and New York for trains connecting these two cities, and schedules for the run were cut 15 to 30 minutes. The number of New York–New Haven trains was increased by 11 per cent, providing approximately half-hourly service between these points. Other schedules were also rearranged and new trains added. At this time, too, the extra fare for travel on the "Yankee Clipper" was abolished, leaving the "Merchants' Limited" as the only extra-fare train in the system. Minor adjustments in the running times of Shore Line trains were made throughout the period under study, the only general change aside from that of April, 1940, occurring in July, 1935, when the schedules of most New York–Boston trains were speeded 10 to 15 minutes.

Aside from the influence of rate changes on volume of passenger traffic, it was possible that shifts in the level of business activity and in consumer income might have had some effect on travel. The Dixon survey, therefore, examined various indicators of business activity such as the Dun's Regional Trade Barometers for New York City and for Boston, department store sales in New York and Boston, employment and payroll statistics, and volume of toll calls. In order to learn whether business activity caused the deviations from the lines of relationship shown in Exhibit 5, actual passenger traffic volumes for each year were plotted as deviations against various series showing business activity. It was discovered from these studies that business activity "does have some effect on passenger traffic, but a tremendous increase or decrease in such activity is required to produce a noticeable change in the regular fare traffic taken as a whole."[9] In a similar manner, deviations were plotted against changes in consumer income as shown by data on family buying power published by *Sales Management* magazine. Again, the conclusion was that passenger traffic "variations with income level are not too striking."[10]

The Shore Line of the New Haven was faced with competition from four sources: private automobiles, buses, airplanes, and steamship lines. The short-haul character of the New Haven's traffic made it exceedingly vulnerable to highway competition, especially that of private automobiles. A comparison of automobile registrations in the three New England states through which the Shore Line passes with Boston–New York rail travel is presented in Exhibit 6.

---

[9] *Ibid.*, p. 39.
[10] *Ibid.*, p. 40.

Monthly figures for private automobile traffic on the Merritt Parkway, which extends from a few miles west of New Haven to the New York state line, parallel to U.S. Route 1 and the New Haven Shore Line, were available from electric-eye counts and toll-payment records of the Connecticut State Highway Department. The counts were started in March, 1939, 20 months after the first section of the parkway opened. Traffic along the parkway showed a 14.7 per cent

Exhibit 6

PASSENGER CAR REGISTRATIONS FOR CONNECTICUT, RHODE ISLAND, AND MASSACHUSETTS; AND PASSENGER TRAVEL, BOSTON–NEW YORK, ON NEW HAVEN RAILROAD, 1929-40

YEAR	PASSENGER CAR REGISTRATIONS			RAIL TRAVEL, BOSTON–NEW YORK
	Conn.	R.I.	Mass.	
1929	278,057	114,010	719,436	1,276,024
1930	279,830	116,792	743,288	1,179,091
1931	302,594	118,313	736,302	971,178
1932	270,192	114,992	698,358	740,913
1933	285,563	118,296	689,934	623,095
1934	295,548	124,062	686,884	728,271
1935	308,402	130,169	684,973	803,463
1936	338,196	140,417	714,081	1,080,114
1937	368,473	148,583	742,521	1,206,599
1938	369,693	149,634	739,323	1,062,080
1939	387,299	155,369	765,656	1,125,581
1940	417,828	166,792	795,201	1,192,175

Sources: Car registrations from *Automobile Facts and Figures*. Rail travel from New Haven Railroad.

increase in 10 months of 1940 over 1939, while railroad traffic to New York in and out of New Haven and Bridgeport, adjusted to a 2-cent-fare level, would have dropped 9.3 per cent.

In Exhibits 7 and 8 are presented data for passenger traffic and fares, Boston–New York, on highway bus lines, air lines, and railroad. Some effect of reductions in rail fares in 1936 is evident in the decline of bus travel the following year. It is also possible that the rail rate increase in 1938 promoted the larger volume of bus travel shown for that year. No decline in bus travel followed the rail rate reduction of 1940.

Although the relatively high price of air travel made comparison with total regular-fare rail traffic of little significance, the volume of air travel had an important bearing on Pullman traffic. Pullman traffic accounted for 14 per cent of the New Haven's total passenger travel and for an even larger share of revenue. About 80 per cent of this

Exhibit 7

BOSTON–NEW YORK PASSENGER TRAFFIC ON
BUSES, AIR LINES, AND RAILROADS, 1929–40

Year	Buses	Air Lines	Railroad
1929.........	156,000	3,986	1,276,024
1930.........	229,000	12,279	1,179,091
1931.........	268,000	15,750	971,178
1932.........	295,000	15,286	740,913
1933.........	325,000	14,543	623,095
1934.........	289,000	18,417	728,271
1935.........	260,000	31,497	803,463
1936.........	220,000	45,139	1,080,114
1937.........	185,000	56,700	1,206,599
1938.........	205,500	81,012	1,062,080
1939.........	215,180	122,315	1,125,581
1940.........	233,796	168,994	1,192,175

Sources: Air-line traffic from American Airlines. Bus and railroad
traffic from New Haven Railroad.

Exhibit 8

BOSTON–NEW YORK ONE-WAY PASSENGER FARES FOR BUSES, AIR
LINES, AND RAILROAD, 1929–40

YEAR	BUSES	AIR LINES	RAILROAD		
			Limited	Coach	Pullman
1929..........	a	$25.00 / 34.55[k] / 17.43[l]	$10.96	$8.26	$12.01
1930..........	a	18.68[m]	10.96	8.26	12.01
1931..........	a	15.85[n]	10.96	8.26	12.01
1932..........	a	13.90[o]	10.96	8.26	12.01
1933..........	a	13.90	10.96	8.26	12.01
1934..........	a	13.90	10.96	8.26	12.01
1935..........	$4.25[b]	13.90	10.96	8.26	12.01
1936..........	3.50[c] / 3.00[d] / 2.95[e]	13.90	10.00[c]	4.60[c]	9.40[c]
1937..........	2.95	13.90	10.00	4.60	9.40
1938..........	3.60[h]	11.95[p]	10.00	5.73[f]	9.55[g]
1939..........	3.60	11.95	10.00	5.73	9.55
1940..........	2.95[i]	11.95	9.00[j]	4.60[i]	9.55

a Not available.
b Effective June 12, 1935.
c Effective June 1, 1936.
d Effective August 16, 1936.
e Effective September 15, 1936.
f Effective July 25, 1938.
g Effective August 1, 1938.
h Effective August 25, 1938.

i Effective March 25, 1940.
j Effective April 28, 1940.
k Effective July 1, 1929.
l Effective August 1, 1930.
m Effective October 1, 1930.
n Effective January 1, 1931.
o Effective March 1, 1932.
p Effective June 1, 1938.

traffic was between New York and Boston, and New York and Providence. The survey showed a marked downtrend in Pullman travel
over the period 1937–40. Although comparison of variations in coach
travel and Pullman travel showed little relationship between these

variables, comparisons of air travel and Pullman travel showed significant relationships. An increase in the former was clearly associated with a decrease in the latter. Likewise, Pullman traffic was found to be influenced appreciably by the level of business activity and total buying income.

In the period covered by this survey, four steamship lines competed with the Shore Line of the New Haven (see Exhibit 9). The

Exhibit 9

RAIL AND STEAMSHIP PASSENGER TRAFFIC,
NEW YORK–BOSTON

Year	Local New Haven Railroad	Eastern Steamship	Colonial Line	New England Steamship
1935	395,854	168,399	14,680	39,514
1936	585,054	183,887	15,700	32,689
1937	710,664	206,221	23,020	13,139

Source: William J. Dixon, *The Elasticity of Demand for Railroad Passenger Transportation* (New Haven: Yale University Press, 1941), p. 43.

railroad's subsidiary, the New England Steamship Company, operated two lines, one of which engaged in service between New York and Providence; and the other between New York and Fall River, with boat-train connection to Boston. The Providence Line abandoned service in May, 1937, and the Fall River Line discontinued operations in July of that year. The independently owned lines, the Eastern Steamship Company and the Colonial Line, operated between New York and Boston over the entire period of the survey. Monthly figures of New York–Providence rail tickets sold showed no gain when the Providence Line discontinued operation in May, 1937. Officials of the New Haven were doubtful, however, whether the small volume of the Providence Line's traffic, averaging only 500 or 600 passengers a month, would have influenced railroad traffic, which was over 20,000 a month at that time. An increase in New York–Boston rail traffic in July over June of 1937, which ran contrary to the normal seasonal pattern, suggested that some of the Fall River Line traffic might have shifted to the railroad when that line abandoned service early in July. Company officials noted, however, that increases in traffic of the two remaining steamship lines, Colonial and Eastern, more than accounted for the passengers lost by the New England Steamship Company. It was also evident that reductions in rail fares had not resulted in taking business from the water carriers; in both 1936 and 1937 the Eastern Steamship Company and the Colonial Line experienced increases in traffic.

In addition to the external competition of other forms of transportation, regular-fare traffic on the Shore Line was influenced by two types of internal competition: limited-train service and excursion traffic. Limited trains competed exclusively with Pullman traffic, excursions with regular-fare coach traffic.

Two limited or extra-fare trains operated on the New Haven's Shore Line during the period under study until April 28, 1940, when one of them, the "Yankee Clipper," was taken out of that class of service. The principal feature of limited trains was their short schedule time between New York and Boston. Prior to April 28, 1940, this was 4 hours and 30 minutes; thereafter it was reduced to 4 hours and 15 minutes. The equipment of extra-fare trains was not materially changed during these years except for remodeled diners; the Pullman, parlor, club, and observation cars were of standard design. The "Yankee Clipper" served all points except Bridgeport; the "Merchants' Limited" did not stop at Bridgeport or New London. During the period when both trains were operated, the "Merchants' Limited" always carried about 50 per cent more passengers than the "Clipper," possibly because of its 5:00 o'clock leaving time from New York and Boston compared to the 1:00 o'clock departure of the "Clipper." Prior to April 28, 1940, New York–Boston and New York–Providence passengers made up more than 90 per cent of the limited-train users. During this period, about one fourth of the Pullman traffic between these cities was limited-train traffic; after the "Clipper" was removed from extra-fare service, this proportion dropped somewhat.

There were two principal changes in limited-train fares in the period 1935–40. The first occurred in 1936, when the Pullman rate was reduced to 3 cents a mile. At that time, *extra* fares were increased, although the *total* fare on limited trains between Boston and New York was reduced from $11.95 to $10.00. In 1940 the total New York–Boston rate was further reduced to $9.00, with proportional reductions in the rates between other points. There was no increase in the New York–Boston and New York–Providence traffic on the "Merchant" because of this change. In fact, it did not even absorb any passengers from the "Clipper" when this train was removed from the extra-fare class. With the exception of July, during the entire year of 1940 until December the "Merchants'" monthly traffic was less than in 1939, when both trains were operating.

Several kinds of excursions were operated by the New Haven during the years 1935–40: Sunday and one-day holiday excursions, two- and three-day holiday excursions, weekday World's Fair excursions, and football excursions. The bulk of this traffic, however, was confined to the Sunday and one-day holiday excursions which were continuously in effect over this period. Excursion tickets, being at reduced rates, were valid only on certain trains, which were usually operated only for excursion passengers.

During most of this period the principal excursion rates approximated 1 cent a mile. In the period from April 30 to August 6, 1939,

Exhibit 10

EXCURSION PASSENGERS AND AVERAGE REGULAR FARES, NEW YORK AND BOSTON-PROVIDENCE, 1935–40

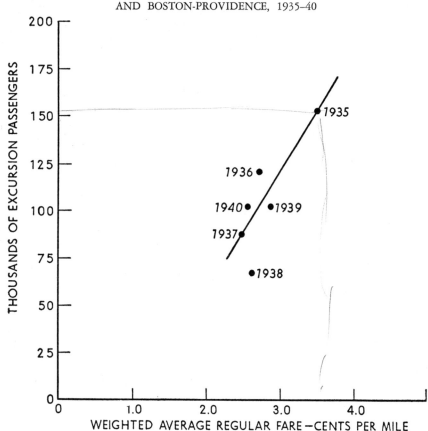

Source: William J. Dixon, *The Elasticity of Demand for Railroad Passenger Transportation* (New Haven: Yale University Press, 1941), p. 58.

they were temporarily raised somewhat above this level. From 1935 to 1940, total excursion traffic between New York and Bridgeport, New York and New Haven, and New York and Providence-Boston declined from 400,000 passengers per annum to about 260,000. In this same period, of course, regular coach fares were reduced drastically. Exhibit 10 shows the graphic relationship of excursion travel and average *regular* fares, New York and Boston-Providence.

QUESTIONS

1. Was the demand for regular-fare passenger transportation on the Shore Line of the New Haven Railroad elastic or inelastic? Why?

2. From the standpoint of the New Haven management, was the reduction on March 25, 1940, in the basic rate for coach travel a desirable move?

3. In the light of the Dixon report, is the result of this reduction, shown in Exhibit 1, one you would have anticipated? Why or why not? ⁀ⱳ

4. What bearing have factors other than prices on the results shown?

5. Using the figures in Exhibit 4 for the entire year, plot passenger-miles against fares. Fit a freehand demand curve to these data. Using the geometrical technique, estimate the elasticity of demand at a fare of 2.45 cents per mile.

APPENDIX TO CASE 3–2: DISSENTING OPINION OF COMMISSIONER MEYER OF INTERSTATE COMMERCE COMMISSION[11]

It is said that the reduced fares will increase both gross and net revenues because of the increased volume of traffic which the railroads will secure through them. The crucial point in the entire report, therefore, is the prospective increase in the volume of traffic.

That the reduced fares will result in some increase in the volume of traffic may be admitted. The extent of that increase is a matter of speculation. That it will be sufficient, as found in this report, not only to offset the losses resulting from the reduction in the basic fares but sufficient to increase both the gross and the net revenue and correspondingly to improve the financial condition of the carriers is open to grave question. In fact, to me it seems almost a certainty that the expected result cannot be realized.

In my judgment the future of the passenger business of the railroads lies in the day coach. Basic fares of 2 cents and 3 cents, respectively, cannot attract to the railroads enough additional business to keep them whole, at least so far as the eastern district is concerned. I agree with the report that experiments which the railroads have been making for several years past must be continued, as pointed out in detail in the text. On what basis the equilibrium between competitive forces represented by competing transportation agencies will or can be established no one can now know. In my opinion it will not be on a basis of 2 cents and 3 cents, respectively, per passenger-mile on the railroads. A straight fare of 2 cents in coaches and 3 cents in Pullmans will not recover to the railroads the volume of traffic which this report asserts will result from the reduction and which must result to avoid confiscation.

The report apportions the existing passenger mileage performed by the traveling public in the entire country as follows: Buses 3 per cent, railroads 7 per cent, private automobiles 90 per cent. This is the best estimate available. The report further assumes that the increased volume of passenger traffic for

---

[11] *Interstate Commerce Commission Reports*, Vol. CCXIV, No. 26550 (February 28, 1936), pp. 259–61.

the railroads must come chiefly from the private automobile. I believe the latter also to be correct. However, in my judgment the basic fares of 2 cents and 3 cents can never recover from the private automobile the volume of traffic which this report assumes they will recover, and which they must recover in order to prevent outright confiscation under the order. The soundness of this analysis can be tested anywhere by any private automobile owner. Let me illustrate, using only the proposed basic fares in the comparisons.

It is a notorious fact that private automobiles generally are not nearly used to the extent of their service life. The chief factor which enters into the decision on the part of the private automobile owner when he is confronted by the choice between using his automobile and riding on a railroad train is the cost of gasoline and oil. Depreciation does not enter because he has his automobile anyhow and he will not exhaust its service life. Everyone knows that the higher-priced heavy automobiles travel only 10 miles or less on 1 gallon of gasoline, while the lighter and lower-priced ones travel from 15 to 20 miles and more on a gallon. Where only one person travels the cost by train and by automobile may approximate each other rather closely, depending chiefly upon the cost of a railroad ticket compared with the cost of gasoline consumed by that particular automobile. When two or more travel, the set-up is radically different. For two persons the alternative presented is that of 4 cents or 6 cents per mile for both together by rail, compared with from 1 cent to 2 cents per mile for both in a private automobile. Where three persons travel the comparison is between 6 cents and 9 cents per mile for the three together by rail, compared with from 1 cent to 2 cents for the three together by private automobile. As the number of persons in the group becomes still greater the decision against the railroad becomes more decisive. As I have stated before, anyone owning an automobile can test this line of reasoning for himself anywhere where there are railroads and highways competing with one another. It is unnecessary to go into many minor factors such as weather, personal convenience, train schedules, location of railroads compared with highways, differences in time on the way, hours of departure or arrival, etc.

Facts like these demonstrate to my mind that much lower fares are needed than 2 cents and 3 cents respectively, in order to recover a large volume of business from the private automobile. Highly profitable trains falling into the class of so-called excursion trains, are being operated at fares much less than 2 cents per passenger-mile and even at less than 1 cent.

By reaching into pools of traffic of this kind and establishing fares which will attract that traffic at a profit, the railroads may reestablish themselves in the passenger business. No one claims that we can issue orders which will require such low fares on all traffic. That is a problem which is distinctly one for the management. The location of such pools of traffic must be discovered and developed by the individual railroads or groups of railroads. By application of commercial sales methods, with reasonable experimentation the railroads should be able to determine the extent to which low fares will be financially advantageous, just as a clothing merchant decides whether to sell suits that cost his customer $5 and less, or higher-priced suits.

CASE 3–3: FORECAST OF TRUCK SALES IN 1950

The entire text of this case is reproduced, by permission, from the *Wall Street Journal* of February 23, 1950.

Truck makers advance a theory that the industry generally will sell far fewer trucks this year than last. But almost every important producer behaves as if he expects to sell more—by scheduling big production.

Perhaps the optimism springs from the fact truck makers have been sprucing up their models, paring some prices and teaching salesmanship to their dealers. This seems to have paid off in January, with some makers reporting record sales.

The pessimism comes from the very best people, however. That semiofficial industry oracle, Ward's Automotive Reports, thinks only 850,000 trucks will be made in the U.S. this year. That would be a 25 per cent drop from last year, a 37 per cent decline from the peak production of 1948.

Sales officials of leading manufacturers generally go along with this. Both J. W. Burke, Chevrolet's truck sales manager, and E. C. Quinn, general sales manager of Dodge division of Chrysler Corporation, think total domestic sales will be down about 800,000 units, and exports will be even smaller than last year, when they made up only 11.2 per cent of production. (Before the war they ran 20 per cent or higher.) J. C. Ball, Ford's manager of product sales and services, suggests his colleagues may be a little too gloomy, but agrees the statistics will record a slide. Yet each of these three gentlemen insists his own company's outlook is very good indeed, at least if the dealers really go after the business.

Chevvy, biggest of the lot, has stepped up the horsepower of its engines and is making the most of it by splashing ads proclaiming the "most powerful trucks in Chevrolet history." Unless prevented by some outside influence such as a prolonged coal strike, it aims to top 1949 output in each of the first six months of 1950.

Ford, which has made a score of improvements and changes in its 1950 trucks, and cut prices $20 to $80 on all but its largest models, is about to launch an intensive truck sales training program for its dealers. With additional wheelbase options, it is proclaiming in ads the "broadest selection" ever. It is scheduling output of 180,000 trucks in the first six months of this year, which would be the biggest such period in its history.

Dodge has trimmed its prices, too, by as much as $125, and is plugging the slogan: "Priced with the lowest." After adding a four-ton truck to its line it is also heralding "more basic models" than ever. This does little good at the moment, with assembly lines idled by a strike, but when that is over Dodge expects to come back with a manufacturing rush that will carry its output for this full year up to equal 1949.

International Harvester, fourth of the "big four," aims to beat its production of last year. It spent $30 million preparing its current models, which feature more powerful engines, cabs that are more comfortable and easier to see out of, new styling and mechanical changes. Its line includes new intermediate sizes.

If the big producers are correct in their pessimism about industry sales, and are right in their optimism about their own sales, it means they will be seizing a larger share of a shrinking market. That trend was noticeable last year, when they accounted for 78.7 per cent of the industry's production, compared to 75.3 per cent in 1948. It could be that the big four are gradually regaining the 82.2 per cent of the market they held back in 1939, before wartime military orders and post-war scarcity of trucks for civilians gave the smaller companies a glittering opportunity.

But at least some of the smaller truck manufacturers refuse to feel depressed. They've got ambitious plans of their own. A spokesman for White Motor Company, for instance, which has added a new lighter truck to its line, looks forward to an increase in sales volume. Autocar says sales of its heavy models "have been improving at a slow but steady rate" after weakness in 1949.

The forecast of a diminishing market for all trucks in 1950 is based on three ideas: The export market will contract because foreigners haven't conquered their dollar difficulties. The deferred domestic demand of war years has now been satisfied. Lower agricultural income means less buying by farmers, who now own almost 30 per cent of all trucks in the United States.

Statistics can be used in more cheerful fashion, of course. There are still about 2,500,000 trucks 10 years or more in age, and these should be replaced, auto makers figure. That alone would take a couple of years at last year's rate of production.

Brightest spot in the picture is the increasing use of trucks. Registrations jumped from 4,875,000 in 1941 to 7,670,000 at the end of 1949, according to the Automobile Manufacturers Association, and one company official argues that the average truck is piling up more mileage nowadays, so will have a shorter life.

Well, how has truck production actually been running thus far in 1950? It started out with a rush that belied the experts' fears. Chevrolet, Ford and Dodge all reported the best January sales in their histories, and truck production by all U.S. factories from January 1 through February 4, rose to 110,000, an increase of 4,000 from the similar period of 1949. By February 18, however, the total for the year to date had mounted only to 156,136; it was lagging nearly 30,000 behind last year's pace. But this was apparently more the result of the strike at Dodge plants and a suspension of assemblies at Willys than evidence of any general weakening in demand.

In February last year dealers all over the country were reported cutting prices on medium and light-heavy trucks because those sizes were accumulating unsold. Word now is there is much less price cutting. Dealer inventories are better balanced, in part because in 1949 manufacturers shifted about 70 per cent of production to light duty models, compared with only 55 per cent in 1948, and a pre-war average of about 50 per cent.

The major companies fell short of recapturing their pre-war share of the market last year mainly because of the larger-than-pre-war share held by the top three of the smaller producers. These are GMC Truck & Coach Division (second entry of General Motors Corporation, the first being Chevrolet), Studebaker and Willys-Overland. GMC was the industry's fifth ranking truck maker before the war, but the other two were far down the list. Last year the three did 17.4 per cent of the nation's truck producing business. In 1939, they accounted for only 7.8 per cent. While the small producers, as a group, were slipping in percentage of total output from 1948 to 1949, GMC and Studebaker actually showed an increase.

Studebaker's ability to hang on in the developing buyer's market of the last year or so has been one of the big post-war surprises in the truck industry. Another was the unexpectedly large number of Jeeps sold by Willys up to the middle of last year. These vehicles are classified by the Government as

Exhibit 1

PRODUCER	1949		1948		1939	
	Number	Per Cent of Total	Number	Per Cent of Total	Number	Per Cent of Total
Chevrolet.........	383,543	33.9	389,690	28.5	244,709	35.6
Ford..............	244,613	21.6	301,791	22.0	153,981	22.4
Dodge...........	151,513	13.4	172,020	12.6	85,557	12.5
Int. Harvester......	110,572	9.8	166,784	12.2	80,260	11.7
GMC.............	83,840	7.4	92,677	6.8	44,036	6.4
Studebaker........	63,473	5.6	67,983	5.0	7,100	1.0
Willys...........	49,973	4.4	104,989	7.7	2,800	0.4
Mack............	9,025	0.8	11,570	0.8	10,060	1.5
White............	8,707	0.8	12,507	0.9	9,258	1.3
Diamond T........	5,545	0.5	12,684	0.9	8,930	1.3
Reo..............	3,600	0.3	11,425	0.8	1,812	0.3
Pontiac...........	2,490	0.2	....	....	....	....
Federal...........	1,649	0.15	3,898	0.3	3,255	0.5
Nash.............	676	0.06	1,051	0.1	....	....
Plymouth.........	....	.....	....	....	14,500	2.1
Crosley...........	375	0.03	2,673	0.2	....	....
Hudson...........	....	.....	....	....	850	0.1
Miscellaneous......	12,544	1.1	17,703	1.3	19,727	2.9
Total.........	1,132,138		1,369,472		686,835	

Source: *Ward's Automotive Reports.*

trucks and were responsible for bringing Willys into fifth place among truck producers in 1946, 1947, and 1948. Last year, however, Willys fell to seventh place, with its output of Jeeps and light trucks less than half the 1948 figure. But it was still far ahead of pre-war.

Most of the other small producers—firms like Mack, Diamond T., White, Reo, Federal, Divco, Autocar and Brockway—were also squeezed into a smaller share of the nation's truck output last year. This year the competition of the big companies promises to be even tougher, but industry men say the three middle bracket makers—GMC, Studebaker and Willys—may feel the pressure most. The small makers have all been getting ready for the sales fight. GMC stepped up the horsepower of its light and medium duty truck engines in December, made a number of cab and chassis improvements and added several new models.

Reo is counting on its new "Gold Comet" engine and an expanded model line to keep it in the running. It is about to begin shipments on a $31 million military order obtained last summer.

Federal Motor Truck Company is planning to introduce new models this year and its application for a $1 million loan to cover tooling expense has been approved by the Reconstruction Finance Corporation.

Mack Truck will spend three times as much as last year to push sales of its heavy-duty trucks. It plans to step up advertising in trade publications, popular magazines and direct mail. The company is also offering free courses for mechanics in diesel truck and bus maintenance. In the New York City area the classes were so popular Mack had to hire the huge Manhattan Center to handle applicants.

Exhibit 1 compares 1949 output by the various truck makers with 1948 and prewar 1939 figures. It also includes each company's percentage of total production.

QUESTIONS

1. How would you explain the fact that, while the demand for the truck industry apparently is expected to be lower in 1950 than in 1949, almost all the truck producers are planning a higher output in 1950? Would this not indicate that there may be excess capacity in the industry before the end of 1950?
2. What is the nature of demand for trucks? Does the fact that they are durable goods play any part in forecasting production for the coming year?
3. Would you, as one of the smaller producers listed in Exhibit 1, have any reasons for increasing output in the face of declining demand for the industry? What additional data or facts would you desire in making such a decision?
4. Are there any indications that the truck industry may be afflicted with overinvestment? Would you, as a truck producer, enter upon a program of expansion of capacity at this time?
5. What are some of the factors affecting the demand for trucks?

CASE 3–4: MARSHALL FIELD & COMPANY

In the spring of 1941, Marshall Field & Company faced a problem of internal competition between the basement division and the upstairs division of its main retail department store in Chicago. This competition caused duplicate investment in inventories, uncertainty of aims within the organization, and confusion among customers of the store. As a result, actual sales of the company fell short of the volume which management believed should be attained.

Marshall Field & Company began business as a retail store in Chicago in 1852. The company grew rapidly and attained a position of national pre-eminence by the turn of the century. A privately controlled corporation, it expanded into manufacturing, wholesaling, and real estate. It also extended retail operations by increasing the number of store units in the Chicago area and elsewhere. Its large Chicago department store continued, however, to produce a very important part of the firm's total revenues and net profit. Until 1931 the basement division of the Chicago store had accounted for about 25 per cent of the total sales of the store. This share of total store business was well above the national average for department stores.

During the decade 1930–40, important changes took place in department store retailing, and these changes had their effect on the operations of Marshall Field & Company. A primary factor was the progressive decline in the general price level after 1920, a movement which was accelerated by the business depression beginning in 1929. This decline was reflected also in retail prices, as is shown in Exhibit 1. Technical as well as cyclical factors contributed to the general price decline. In 1921, for example, a heavy, crudely styled leather jacket sold for from $25 to $30. By 1941, manufacturers were producing highly styled, precision-tailored jackets, with dress-clothing refinements, in a wide variety of high-quality leathers, to retail at $10. As another example, in 1921 a man's lightweight wool sweater for sportswear retailed at $10. By 1941, through economies of mass production, sports sweaters of equal quality retailed at $5. This qualitative improvement was not generally reflected in statistical measures such as those shown in Exhibit 1. A second factor changing the distributive position of the department store was a marked decline, after 1929, in consumer incomes. More than a decade later the level of incomes was still below that of 1929. Retail customers with less money insisted on low-priced merchandise.

As a result of the foregoing changes, the structure of retail trade was believed by many marketing experts to have shifted substantially over the ten years preceding 1940. Department stores found it difficult to maintain sales volume through the traditional methods of operation, and relatively low-cost distributors made inroads into the department store market (see Exhibit 2). Among the latter, mail-order houses which had opened retail store units began making important competitive advances and were attracting from established department stores many customers, especially those who bought low-priced merchandise. Conventional department stores began to place more emphasis on goods bought by the middle and lower-middle income groups. Marshall Field & Company was one of the last stores in the country to be affected by these changes, largely because the upstairs divisions of the Chicago store had developed an extensive following in the finest lines of domestic and imported merchandise. Despite its loyal clientele, however, the store felt under pressure to compete for business in the lower-priced lines.

Prior to 1930 the Chicago store of Marshall Field & Company had divided its retail market between the upstairs and the basement

Exhibit 1

COST OF GOODS PURCHASED BY WAGE EARNERS AND LOWER-SALARIED WORKERS IN 34 LARGE CITIES, 1920–40; NATIONAL INCOME, UNITED STATES, 1929–40

(1935–39 = 100)

Year	All Items	Clothing	House Furnishings	National Income (Millions of Dollars)
1920	143.2	201.0	164.6	......
1921	127.7	154.8	138.5	......
1922	119.7	125.6	117.5	......
1923	121.9	125.9	126.1	......
1924	122.2	124.9	124.0	......
1925	125.4	122.4	121.5	......
1926	126.4	120.6	118.8	......
1927	124.0	118.3	115.9	......
1928	122.6	116.5	113.1	......
1929	122.5	115.3	111.7	$83,326
1930	119.4	112.7	108.9	68,858
1931	108.7	102.6	98.0	54,479
1932	97.6	90.8	85.4	39,963
1933	92.4	87.9	84.2	42,322
1934	95.7	96.1	92.8	49,455
1935	98.1	96.8	94.8	55,719
1936	99.1	97.6	96.3	64,924
1937	102.7	102.8	104.3	71,513
1938	100.8	102.2	103.3	64,200
1939	99.4	100.5	101.3	70,829
1940	100.2	101.7	100.5	77,809

Source: *Statistical Abstract of the United States.*

divisions. Under this policy the price lines of the basement division went up to a certain point, and the price lines of the upstairs division generally began at a point a little above where the basement store left off. This was particularly evident in price lines which were featured in newspaper advertising.

With the decline in prices and with other changes in the structure of retail trade, the upstairs division after 1930 began competing more and more directly with the basement division. The upstairs and basement divisions soon found themselves making bids for the same group of customers. This resulted in duplicate investments in inventory, in the maintenance of two buying organizations which were shopping the same wholesale markets, and in other undesirable forms of duplication and competition. The outcome of this competition was that the upper-floor sections became much more important in the moderate-price field and took a large amount of sales volume out of the basement division.

In order to recover sales losses caused by the competitive situation within the company, the basement division gradually began to put

Exhibit 2

SALES OF MARSHALL FIELD & COMPANY, AND OF
SEARS, ROEBUCK AND COMPANY, 1930–40

Year	Marshall Field, Total Operating Revenues	Basement Sales as Percentage of Total Store Sales, All Department Stores*	Sears Roebuck, Sales
1930	$150,698,967	†	$390,382,107
1931	114,348,692	15.4	347,209,054
1932	78,267,829	16.0	280,061,229
1933	90,445,699	17.4	274,707,651
1934	102,623,568	20.6	273,249,494
1935	110,810,658‡	19.4	318,060,563
1936	106,135,693	18.9	392,097,720
1937	100,044,813	18.5	494,968,022
1938	82,279,916§	18.4	537,242,403
1939	86,773,921	†	501,676,644
1940	92,773,220	18.4	617,414,267

* Based on department stores with annual sales volumes in excess of $10 million, reporting to National Retail Dry Goods Association.
† Not reported.
‡ The wholesale division, which accounted for $18 million in annual sales volume, was abandoned in November, 1935.
§ Departments in the manufacturing division, accounting for $10.5 million annual volume, were closed.
Sources: Marshall Field & Company sales from company's annual reports. Basement sales from National Retail Dry Goods Association, *Departmental Merchandising and Operating Results, 1931–1940*. Sears, Roebuck sales from *Moody's Industrials*.

more and more emphasis on a highly promotional type of business, which minimized the importance of regular lines and which put a premium on sale goods. As a result, the basement division planned and executed huge special sales, such as the annual "May Celebration," the "Harvest Festival," and the "Twin Dollar Days." These basement-wide sales brought in immediate sales volume, but this business came mainly from customers who followed special sales events and who bought only when a sale price was being offered. Very few of them became regular customers of any one store.

The results of this type of promotional effort, which was so foreign to the old way of operating, were particularly evident as the nation was coming out of the depression in the late thirties. Increases in sales volume of the basement division remained below those of moderate-priced stores throughout the country. There was, therefore, a constant drive each year to make promotions larger, in order to increase sales volume over the year before. As each year's sales budget was being planned, however, there could never be any reliance on cumulative business because of the nature of the previous year's promotional sales volume. Each year an effort was made on a short-run appeal, designed to bring in immediate sales and not to develop consumer response which had lasting, long-run value. Each year's sales volume had to be produced by increased advertising expenditures or by high-pressure sales methods. This, in turn, raised new problems in the form of dangerously low markup on the goods offered for sale, greatly increased operating costs, and complicated personnel problems caused by the thousands of extra salespeople who had to be brought in from time to time to conduct these great sales. These promotions caused such variation in sales volume between the days of the week that efficiency and economy of operation had to be sacrificed. Fourteen or fifteen times during the year, it was common to find Monday's sales running four and five times heavier than those of the next day, Tuesday.

Thus, in the spring of 1941, Marshall Field & Company faced four alternatives with regard to maintenance of an adequate volume of retail sales in its Chicago store:

1. Continuance of the promotional operation in the basement, with a concerted attempt to reduce expense by leveling out fluctuations in daily and seasonal sales. This course appealed to management because of the advantage there would be in having the basement carry a large share of total store overhead.

2. Conversion of the basement division into a bargain basement, such as that operated by the E. A. Filene Company of Boston. If this plan were followed, upstairs stocks could be cleared into the basement, where prices would be drastically cut on an automatic turnover basis. The basement would be known as a cut-rate operation. This course would have the advantage of reducing competition with the upstairs store, thereby permitting a considerable reduction in investment and inventory and in the size of the organization.

3. Abandonment of the basement division and use of the space for expansion of the housewares and appliances departments. This policy had been followed by R. H. Macy & Company of New York.

4. Reorientation of the merchandising policy of the basement division so as to cover the low-price ranges on terms which would be directly competitive with other low-priced department store and chain store competitors. At the

same time, some more or less regular sharing of the retail market by upstairs and basement divisions could be reinstituted. Some members of the management believed that the increase in national income in 1940 indicated this alternative as the soundest policy for the company.

QUESTIONS

1. What effect did changes in consumer income after 1930 have on the demand for goods sold by department stores? On the demand for goods sold in Marshall Field's basement store? In the upstairs store?
2. What was the effect of the basement division's promotional policy after 1930 on the demand for its goods? On the demand for goods of the upstairs divisions?
3. Evaluate the effects on total store demand of each of the four policies proposed in the spring of 1941, using the assumption that the United States would not enter World War II. If United States entry had been anticipated, would this change your recommendation?
4. Which policy would produce the greatest total revenue for the store?

APPENDIX TO CHAPTER 3: STATISTICAL MEASUREMENT
OF DEMAND

PART A: SOME THEORETICAL CONSIDERATIONS

A French mathematician, Augustin Cournot, writing in 1838,[12] is generally credited with having first clearly expressed the "law of demand" (sales as a function of price), both mathematically and graphically. More than half a century later, Alfred Marshall,[13] a famous British economist, greatly extended the application of the concept and popularized its use. Economists did not, however, seriously attempt to derive demand curves from actual statistical information until about 1910.[14] Most of the published results have been for commodities analyzed at the producer-manufacturer level or at the wholesale level. A smaller number of published studies pertain to demand at the retail level, although a great many more or less successful attempts have undoubtedly been made privately by businessmen and economists for all levels of selling activity.[15] Agricultural products have proved to be especially adaptable to this type of empirical analysis; but such items as automobiles, tin plate, wool, fish, and railroad travel have also been treated in this way. Some federal agencies, such as the Department of Agriculture, are regularly involved in statistical studies of demand. Trade associations, marketing co-operatives, and large individual firms are also frequently interested in measurement of market demand. It should

---

[12] *Researches into the Mathematical Principles of the Theory of Wealth,* translated by Nathaniel T. Bacon (New York: Macmillan Co., 1929), chap. iv.

[13] *Principles of Economics* (8th ed.; London: Macmillan Co., Ltd., 1920), Book III.

[14] A history of statistical measurement of demand is given by Henry Schultz, *The Theory and Measurement of Demand* (Chicago: University of Chicago Press, 1938), chap. ii. This book is itself a classic in the field.

[15] Werner Z. Hirsch, "On the Phenomenon of Inelastic Demand," *Southern Economic Journal,* July, 1951, pp. 30–45, sets forth the results of 34 demand studies at the producer-manufacturer level, 16 studies at the wholesale level, and 14 at the retail level. Hirsch made a comprehensive survey of the field.

be kept in mind, however, that a statistical demand curve for an entire commodity may have little importance for the individual firm in a competitive situation where it supplies only a small fraction of the total output and where its control over price is negligible.

The benefits of accurate measurement of demand to the individual sellers or associations which are able to exercise control over price are quite obvious. As noted in Chapter 3, total revenue from sales can be derived readily from a demand schedule or curve. If these have been measured, the seller can determine whether his price is too high or too low to bring maximum monetary returns. (As already mentioned, maximum revenue does not, however, necessarily mean maximum profit, since cost of production is also a factor.)

Because of the key role attributed by economists to price as the determinant of sales of any commodity, it is customary to consider the price-quantity relationship as the end product of a statistical demand study. Other important factors such as population, income, advertising, and prices of substitutes are treated as causes of shifts in the demand curve. This procedure has the merit of being closely related to economic theorizing and of facilitating comparisons between commodities by placing them on similar bases. It is possible, however, to place price on the same basis as other variables in a statistical study of sales determination and perhaps even to leave it out of consideration as being relatively unimportant in some cases.

Shifts in Demand and Supply

The most common method of deriving statistical demand curves involves the use of time series data on prices, sales, and other relevant variables.[16] The first step is usually to plot all of the price-sales data on a chart where price is measured vertically and quantity sold is measured horizontally. (This has become conventional although, theoretically, it would be preferable to plot price, the independent variable, against the horizontal scale [X-axis] and sales against the Y-axis.) If the investigator is unusually fortunate, he can immediately draw the statistical demand curve merely by fitting a "regression" line to the price-sales data.[17] Usually, however, it is necessary to consider additional factors.

In the case of a competitively produced commodity, each price-sales point can be considered to have been determined by the intersection of a supply and a demand curve. This is illustrated in Exhibit 1 for a hypothetical situation in which both the demand and the supply curves have shifted over a period of time. Each of the intersections (D_1 and S_1, D_2 and S_2, etc.) indicates a short-run equilibrium price which existed at one time during the period studied. It is clear that if the demand and supply curves have both shifted rapidly to the right, as suggested by Exhibit 1, the price-quantity data plotted by the statistician

---

[16] Family budget data have been used by statisticians to derive demand curves for some consumer goods. This method will not be considered in the present Appendix.

[17] Such a line of "best" fit may simply be drawn freehand in such a way as to minimize, approximately, the sum of the deviations of the plotted points from the regression line. Or mathematical methods such as the "least-squares" method may be employed. The least-squares method may minimize the sum of the squared vertical distances, squared horizontal distances, or squared perpendicular distances from the regression line.

would not trace out a demand curve, a supply curve, or any other of the curves of economic theory.

On the other hand, if the situation has been that of Exhibit 2, in which the demand curve was stable over the period while the supply curve shifted to several different positions (due, for example, to different crop yields in successive years), the price-sales data would trace out the demand curve which the statistician was seeking.[18] If the demand curve shifted only slightly while the supply curve shifted substantially, the intersections would come close to showing the path of an "average" demand curve for the period. It is not difficult, similarly, to see that if the supply curve were unchanged while the demand curve shifted, the price-sales data would trace out a supply curve.

Exhibit 1

SUPPLY-DEMAND INTERSECTIONS DETERMINE PRICE-QUANTITY DATA

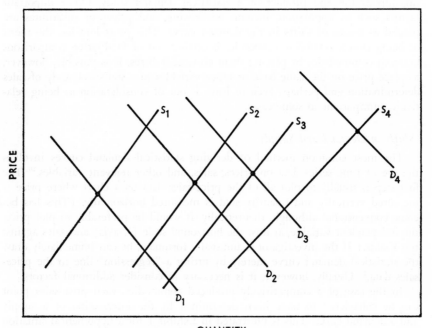

QUANTITY

In practice, unfortunately, the demand curve usually shifts a good deal over the period for which the statistician has price-sales data. Numerous statistical devices are available for removing the shift and coming out with an approximation to the static demand curve of economic theory. A simple graphical method for accomplishing this end may be illustrated by its application to the hypothetical price-sales data of Exhibit 3. The "period" referred to is usually a year, but may be a shorter span of time. "Price" must refer to a weighted average for the period unless, of course, a single price persisted throughout the time interval.

---

[18] The various possibilities are shown by E. J. Working, "What Do Statistical Demand Curves Show?" *Quarterly Journal of Economics,* February, 1927, pp. 212–35.

Exhibit 2

SHIFTING SUPPLY AND STEADY DEMAND—INTERSECTIONS TRACE
DEMAND CURVE

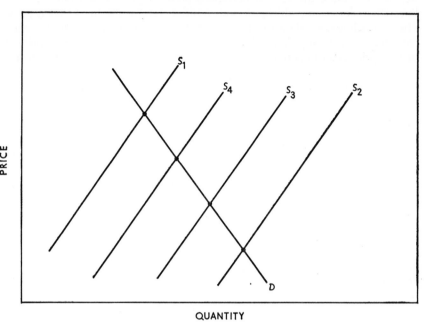

QUANTITY

As a first step in finding the influence of price on quantity sold, the analyst would probably plot these data as in Exhibit 4. At this point, he might be discouraged, because the plotted points do not even come close to falling along a negatively declining demand curve such as would be expected from a knowledge of the economist's "law of demand." An examination of the original data reveals clearly, however, that there has been an upward trend in sales over the seven periods. This is easily seen by reference to the fact that in Period 1 a price of $9.00 was associated with sales of 50 units, while in Period 7 the

Exhibit 3

HYPOTHETICAL PRICE-SALES
DATA

Period	Quantity Sold	Price per Unit
1...............	50	$ 9
2...............	75	8
3...............	65	15
4...............	110	10
5...............	150	7
6...............	150	14
7...............	200	9

same price was coupled with sales of 200 units. One way of eliminating the trend in order to isolate the influence of price is to fit a trend line to the time series of sales.[19] Such a line has been fitted to the data in Exhibit 5. The next step is to measure the vertical deviations of the observations from the trend line. These deviations, which are both positive (above the line) and negative (below the line), are shown in Exhibit 6.[20] Since the trend has been eliminated from the sales, the remaining fluctuations should be closely related to price if, in fact, price is an important determinant of the quantity sold. In order to test

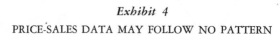

Exhibit 4

PRICE-SALES DATA MAY FOLLOW NO PATTERN

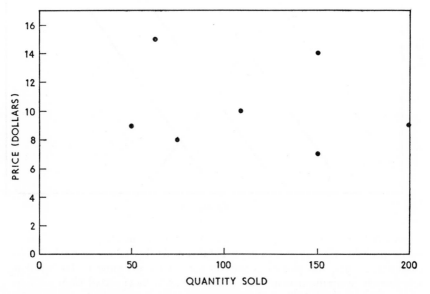

the latter hypothesis, the statistician can plot deviations of sales from trend against price for the corresponding time period. This step is shown in Exhibit 7. A rather close correlation of sales and price is apparent in Exhibit 7, and a freehand regression line has been drawn to fit the points. In order to convert this line into an "average" demand curve for the period, it is only necessary to add to the quantity measurements along this line the quantity read off the trend line of Exhibit 5 for the mid-period (No. 4). (This value is about 115.) And to get a picture of the demand curve as it was at the end of the period studied, it is only necessary to add instead a quantity of 188, taken from the trend line for Period 7. A demand curve as of Period 1 can be derived in a similar

---

[19] This trend may be fitted freehand or by the method of least squares. In order to save time, it is often advisable to use freehand methods as a means of discovering the basic relationships and later, if it appears worth while, to rework the problem, using the more complex techniques.

[20] Instead of using deviations from the trend line, it is also feasible to compute "trend ratios" by dividing each observation by the value of the trend line for the same date. The trend-ratio method is used extensively by Schultz, *op. cit.*

Exhibit 5

QUANTITY SOLD SHOWS SHARP UPWARD TREND

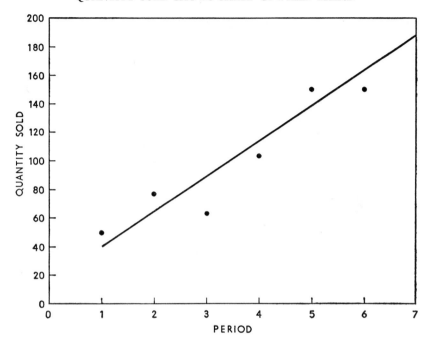

Exhibit 6

DEVIATIONS OF SALES FROM
TREND

Period	Deviations
1.	+$ 9
2.	+ 10
3.	− 25
4.	− 5
5.	+ 11
6.	− 13
7.	+ 12

manner. This process yields the three demand curves of Exhibit 8. The upward shifting of demand is clearly apparent, and the analyst would have to take this shift into account in any attempt to use the demand curve for purposes of sales forecasting.

PART B: DEMAND FOR FROZEN ORANGE CONCENTRATE[21]

The problem of deriving a statistical demand curve for frozen orange concentrate is much like that which has been treated for a hypothetical situation.

---

[21] This part is based largely on a Master's thesis written by Eugene C. Holshouser, *The Frozen Orange Concentrate Industry: An Analysis of Consumer Demand,* deposited in the library of Florida State University, August, 1953.

Exhibit 7

EFFECT OF PRICE APPEARS WHEN TREND IS REMOVED

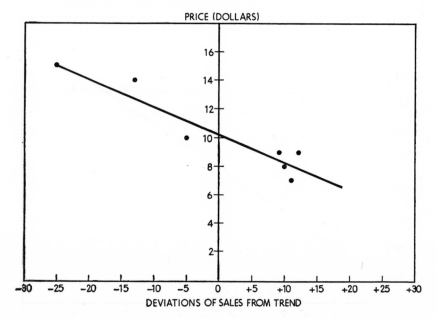

Exhibit 8

SHIFTING DEMAND CURVE APPEARS AS END PRODUCT

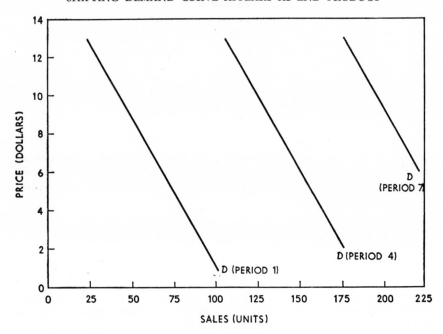

Demand for this good has increased rapidly as consumers have become acquainted with it and as grocery stores in all parts of the country have installed the necessary refrigerated cabinets.[22] At the same time, prices have fluctuated quite sharply with changes in supply, which in turn are traceable to changes

Exhibit 9

FROZEN ORANGE CONCENTRATE—PRICES
AND SALES

Month	Retail Price (Cents per Can)	Retail Sales (Thousands of Gallons)
1950:		
September	25.5	1,470
October	22.1	1,865
November	21.7	1,762
December	21.6	1,638
1951:		
January	21.6	1,716
February	21.5	1,917
March	22.1	1,872
April	21.9	1,892
May	21.9	1,768
June	21.6	1,775
July	21.8	1,756
August	21.3	2,022
September	20.7	2,470
October	20.4	2,608
November	19.7	2,600
December	19.1	2,619
1952:		
January	18.2	3,060
February	16.7	3,358
March	16.3	3,314
April	16.5	3,350
May	14.8	3,812
June	15.3	3,811
July	15.6	3,970
August	16.1	3,859
September	16.2	3,904
October	16.1	3,871
November	16.3	3,929
December	16.1	3,836

Source: Market Research Corporation of America, as shown in Eugene C. Holshouser, *The Frozen Orange Concentrate Industry: An Analysis of Consumer Demand*, Master's thesis deposited in the library of Florida State University, August, 1953, p. 75.

in the orange crop; and there has been a general downward trend of price. Exhibit 9 gives retail price and sales data for the six-ounce can of frozen orange concentrate. In order to make the monthly sales totals comparable, a period of four weeks only in each month was used.

[22] In 1946 and 1947, however, when the industry was just getting started, the producers had serious financial difficulties, especially because concentrate moved very slowlv at the grocery stores.

An examination of the price-sales data shows that the rapid increase in month-to-month sales was associated with a substantial decline in price. If quantity were plotted against price, the apparent influence of price would be great, and the demand would appear highly elastic. This would be an improper analysis of the effect of price, however, since much of the increase in purchases would have occurred even if price had not declined; that is, demand shifted rapidly to the right during the period under consideration. It would be equally mis-

Exhibit 10

LINK RELATIVES OF PRICES AND SALES

Month	Price Relatives	Sales Relatives
1950:		
October..................	86.7%	126.9%
November................	98.2	94.5
December................	99.5	93.0
1951:		
January.................	100.0	104.8
February................	99.5	111.7
March...................	102.8	97.7
April...................	99.1	101.1
May.....................	100.0	93.4
June....................	98.6	100.4
July....................	100.9	98.9
August..................	97.7	115.1
September...............	97.2	122.2
October.................	98.6	105.6
November................	96.6	99.7
December................	97.0	100.7
1952:		
January.................	95.3	116.8
February................	91.8	109.7
March...................	97.6	98.7
April...................	101.2	101.1
May.....................	89.7	113.8
June....................	103.4	100.0
July....................	102.0	104.2
August..................	103.2	97.2
September...............	100.6	101.2
October.................	99.4	99.2
November................	101.2	101.5
December................	98.8	97.6

leading, however, to conclude that price changes had no effect on sales of frozen orange concentrate.

One way to isolate the effect of price changes would be to fit a trend line to the sales data and correlate price with deviations from trend. This is the procedure illustrated earlier for a hypothetical situation. When the number of observations is large, this technique is rather time-consuming, however; and a general picture may be secured more speedily through the use of "first differences." This involves finding the month-to-month changes in price and in sales, and examining the relation between these changes. This method eliminates most of the trend in both series, permitting the analyst to see whether a decrease in price actually stimulated sales to go up more than they were already increasing. A closely related method is that of "link relatives." In this procedure, each sales figure is expressed as a percentage of the sales for the preceding month, and each price is similarly related to the previous month's price. This method eliminates much of the trend and may be somewhat more accurate than the first-difference method if consumers react more strongly, for example, to a 1-cent cut from a 15-cent level than to a 1-cent cut from a 25-cent

Exhibit 11

FROZEN ORANGE CONCENTRATE SALES RELATIVES ARE CORRELATED WITH PRICE RELATIVES

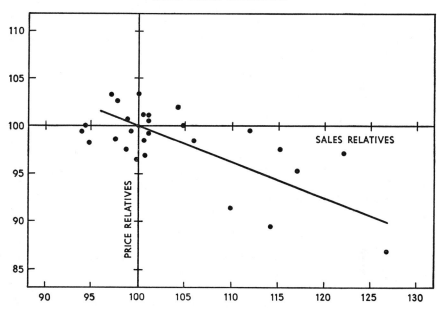

level. The former cut would produce a larger change in the series of link relatives than would the latter cut.

Link relatives for the monthly data on frozen orange concentrate prices and sales are shown in Exhibit 10. These are plotted against one another in Exhibit 11. While the scatter of points about the freehand regression line is considerable, it is apparent that the large gains in sales were achieved in the months when price cuts were sharp. It is not clear how great a dampening effect on sales would have been exerted by sharp price increases, since there were no large price increases in the period studied. It appears probable that there would be a strong effect of this sort, however, since no large sales gains were made in the nine months during which moderate price increases took place.

Least-Squares Analysis

The advantage of using graphic methods to discover price-sales relationships lies in the speed with which results may be obtained. And, frequently, the statistician feels that it is irrational to spend very much time in finding a precise fit to the very imprecise data with which he may have to work. (It is *not* true that "anything worth doing is worth doing well.") However, where the graphical analysis indicates that a satisfactory demand curve can be obtained, and where the results may affect a managerial decision, it is often desirable to use the more accurate method of least squares in order to find a regression equation from which sales can be estimated.

One useful way of handling a situation in which demand has been shifting steadily upward is to use "time" as one of the variables which is considered to affect sales. The time variable will then take care of such factors as population growth, income changes, and changes in tastes, so far as these cause demand to shift in a regular fashion.[23] If this procedure is adopted, the quantity sold will appear in the final equation as a function of price and of time—that is, a larger quantity can be sold at the same price at later dates than at earlier dates; and at any date the lower the price, the larger the quantity which can be sold. Mathematically, this can be written:

$$(1) \quad q = f(p,t),$$

where q is quantity demanded, p is price, and t is time.

In order to secure the regression line showing consumer purchases as a function of price and time, it is necessary to assign values to t—e.g., October, 1950, as 1; November, 1950, as 2; and so on, through December, 1952, as 27. Assuming a straight-line relationship to exist between the dependent variable (q) and the independent variables (p and t), the problem can readily be worked by means of the least-squares method (which is explained in most statistics textbooks). The regression equation which appears as an end product of this statistical process[24] is:

$$(2) \quad q = -217.1p + 40.0t + 6,320.$$

To turn this equation into a relationship between price and quantity as of any particular month, it is only necessary to substitute the t-value for that month in the equation. To get an "average" demand curve for the period, one should use a t-value of 14 (which is the average of the t-values). This gives the following equation:

$$(3) \quad q = -217.1p + 6,880.$$

In order to estimate sales for this central month at 15 cents per can, for example, one substitutes this value for p and solves for q (which turns out to be 3,623,000 gallons). This would be interpreted as follows: *If* the price had been 15 cents per can in November, 1951, sales of frozen orange concentrate would have been about 3,623,000 gallons. (Actually, the price was nearly 20 cents per can, and sales were 2,600,000 gallons.) The relation between price and quantity can similarly be measured for any other month of the period by substituting the appropriate value for t.

---

[23] Schultz, *op. cit.*, chap. 4, discusses this use of time as a variable in least-squares analysis. Schultz found this to be the most useful method of dealing with the demand for many agricultural commodities.

[24] As computed by Holshouser, *op. cit.*, p. 78. He found a coefficient of multiple correlation of $-.978$.

The coefficient of p (-217.1) indicates that a 1-cent change in the retail price per can of frozen orange concentrate was associated with a change in the opposite direction of about 217,000 gallons per month in consumer purchases. The coefficient of t ($+40.0$) indicates that purchases increased at a rate of 40,000 gallons a month due to changes in such factors as tastes, availability, population, and income. If study of the industry indicated no sudden change in these factors, the regression equation could be used for forecasting the volume of sales. This would be done by inserting the anticipated price and the numerical

Exhibit 12

STATISTICAL DEMAND CURVE FOR FROZEN ORANGE CONCENTRATE AS OF DECEMBER, 1952

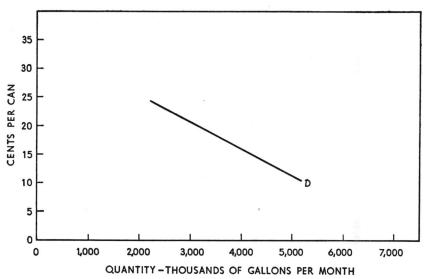

value of the month, counting from October, 1950, as 1. It should be emphasized that a close correlation for the period studied does not guarantee a close correlation for the future. However, analysis of the sort described is more likely to lead to a useful forecast of sales than would be obtained by a mere extrapolation of the trend of sales, because of the explicit recognition and measurement of the force exerted by changes in price.

A demand equation for frozen orange concentrate as of the end of the period studied (December, 1952) can easily be obtained by substituting 27 for t in Equation 2. This gives:

$$(4) \quad q = -217.1p + 7,400.$$

Equation 4 can easily be turned into a demand curve. If p is zero, q will be 7,400; therefore, the line will intersect the quantity axis at 7,400,000 gallons. If q is zero, p will be 34.1 cents per can. These points determine the location of the demand curve, which is plotted in Exhibit 12.

Elasticity of Demand

The simple geometrical technique described in Chapter 3 for measuring elasticity of demand can be applied to the demand curve of Exhibit 12 to determine the elasticity of demand at any chosen price. It may be of particular importance to a businessman to make this calculation at the price actually prevailing. A finding of elastic demand would indicate that a price cut would bring in more revenue to the industry; a finding of inelastic demand would indicate that a price cut would reduce industry revenue. If price is taken as 16.1 cents per can, this price is divided by the difference between this price and the intersection of the extended demand curve with the vertical axis. The intersection is at 34.1 cents.[25] Consequently, the elasticity is 16.1 ÷ (34.1 − 16.1), which is equal approximately to 0.9, an inelastic demand. In addition to suggesting that a further price reduction would decrease total revenue, this measurement indicates that the frozen orange concentrate industry is a competitive one. A monopolistically controlled industry is not likely to sell in the region of inelastic demand, since total revenue could be increased by an increase in price and, in addition, the smaller quantity produced would have a lower total cost. It should not be inferred, of course, that monopoly is desirable from a social point of view, since consumers gain from the superior allocation of resources and productive efficiency which are engendered by competition.

PROBLEM

1. From governmental or private sources, secure price-sales data by years for some commodity, and attempt to construct a statistical demand curve using the short-cut procedure described in the text.

    It is suggested that an agricultural product be used and that data for the post-World War II years only be utilized.

    Give reasons why your statistical procedure should logically be expected to yield a demand curve. If no suitable demand curve can be secured, tell why you think this happened.

---

[25] This intersection is found only for convenience in measuring elasticity of demand and should not be thought of as actually lying on the demand curve. It is not true, of course, that a price of 34.1 cents a can would completely eliminate the sale of frozen orange concentrate. A statistical demand curve should not be drawn to cover points outside the range of experience.

Chapter 4

~~~~~~

COST AND OUTPUT IN THE SHORT RUN

IT IS common in economic analysis of price to distinguish between the "short run" and the "long run." The former is defined as a period which is long enough to permit changes to be made in the rate of use of existing capacity but not long enough to permit a change in the amount of productive capacity itself. When a change is made in amount of capacity, the action is termed a "long-run" adjustment. While useful, the distinction is quite arbitrary, and the businessman might often have trouble in deciding whether a particular action was of a short-run or long-run nature. This is because a great many changes in the rate of production involve some modification of, and some addition to, the existing capital equipment, so that while the principal action may be of a short-run nature, certain long-run adjustments are apt to be involved.

Measurement of cost plays several different roles in a business firm: (1) It is a necessary measurement in the determination of net income; (2) it is an instrument of control of efficiency of operation within the firm; (3) it is an important factor affecting the pricing of products; and (4) it is related to certain types of governmental regulation of business activity. These roles will be briefly surveyed in turn.

Income Determination

As it bears on the determination of income, cost is a necessary basis for numerous actions of management. Some of these, such as tax payments, bonuses, and dividend declarations, rely largely on income results of the current period. Other actions, such as wage increases and plant expansion, are usually based on the sustained results of several accounting periods. Costs, as used in determining income, appear as part of the accounting statement of profit and loss. They are the aggregate of accounting charges pertaining to a given period for the entire operations of the firm. Some costs, such as direct labor and materials, offer no difficulty of allocation to the current period. Others, such as outlays on machinery and on research and development, are undertaken not only with a view to present benefits in the current accounting period but for benefits in subsequent periods. There arises the problem of allocation of these expenses over several time periods—that is, the determination of depreciation and other charges attributable to given fiscal periods. The accountant's distinction between current and capital expenditures is as arbitrary as the economist's parallel distinction between the short and the long run. This is well illustrated by the following quotation: "If the accounting period were increased from the customary year to a decade, most of what is now treated as capital expenditure would become chargeable to income; while if the period were reduced to a day, much of what is now treated as current maintenance would become capital expenditure."[1]

It should be recognized that many accounting measurements are merely estimates rather than "firm" figures. Depreciation charges are an outstanding example. For tax calculations, depreciation may be charged off at the maximum permissible rate, in order to reduce taxable income. For general financial reporting a slower rate of depreciation may be appropriate. Thus, even in the well-defined area of income accounting, the meaning of costs depends somewhat on the uses to which they are to be put.

Control

A different type of cost information is required for purposes of control of the firm's operations. Here, the problem is that of isolating the particular costs bearing on that segment of the firm's operations in which the controller's interest centers. This may be a department, a process, a product, or other cost "center." How to reduce costs of certain operations, whether to adopt a new technique, what sales channels to use—these are decisions in which cost information of a specific sort can be useful. In dealing with these issues, the focus of the businessman's interest is frequently the cost of producing or selling a *unit* of product. Cost accounting, as distinguished from financial accounting, develops cost information related to the production and distribution of *each unit* of product. To the direct costs, such as labor and materials, associated with each unit of product are added prorated amounts of overhead burden—representing the general charges for

[1] George O. May, *Improvements in Financial Accounts* (Lecture on the G. Lowes Dickinson Foundation, Graduate School of Business Administration, Harvard University, April 12–14, 1937), p. 4; quoted in Conference on Price Research, *Cost Behavior and Price Policy* (New York: National Bureau of Economic Research, 1943), p. 23.

indirect labor, depreciation, taxes, maintenance, and such other items as are not directly traceable to the unit of product. This gives the "actual" unit costs of making and selling the product. However, since a fluctuation in the volume of production would result in greater or less *per unit* charge for overhead, a rise or fall in unit cost under this scheme is not necessarily attributable to greater or less efficiency of plant management. To impound the effect of changing volume of production on unit costs, accountants have devised *standard cost* systems, which establish normal or standard amounts of overhead to be charged against each unit of product.[2] If actual production exceeds or falls short of this standard volume, the resulting difference between actual and standard costs is carried directly to a "Variance" account (which is closed periodically to the Profit and Loss account). But the standard unit cost remains unchanged by variation in output. It constitutes a yardstick by which management measures the internal efficiency of performance.

Pricing

A third use of cost analysis relates to pricing. Obviously, the aggregate costs shown on the statement of profit and loss afford little direct assistance in setting prices for a company's products. This is especially true where numerous lines and conditions of sales are involved. Unit costs determined by cost accountants come closer to the mark. There are many situations, however, in which businessmen are forced to abandon accounting costs and to determine prices by other methods. In general, the cost information needed for pricing is distinctly different from that required for income determination or for internal management control. "Sunk" costs, while affecting net income, should be disregarded by the businessman when he determines price and current output policy. This has led accountants to modify formal cost accounting information in the direction of determining the additional or incremental costs involved in changing output. These methods, while they have to do with the accounting records of the company, embody some of the concepts of cost employed by economists, especially the marginal cost concept.[3] It is in the field of cost determination and pricing that economic analysis

---

[2] Standard cost systems also establish standard charges for variable costs, such as labor and materials. Departures of actual unit variable cost from standards are usually attributable to causes other than variation in volume of production.

[3] An interesting article which shows the importance of the economist's cost concepts to recent developments in cost accounting is J. S. Earley, "Recent Developments in Cost Accounting and the 'Marginal Analysis,' " *Journal of Political Economy,* June, 1955, pp. 227–42.

can make one of the greatest contributions to business practice. The economic analysis of cost will be discussed further below.

Government Regulation

Finally, the growth of government activity in economic life has led to an increased use of cost information to justify prices. Business firms have found it necessary and desirable to justify their action on the basis of cost under such laws as the "Unfair Practices" acts (which are in effect in many states and which prohibit certain sales "below cost"), and the federal Robinson-Patman Act (which permits price discrimination only to the extent that "costs" differ). Public-utility firms, railroads, truckers, taxicab operators, and others whose rates are subject to regulation frequently appeal to costs in seeking to justify rate increases. And in periods of emergency government control over a great many prices, petitions for increases in ceiling prices are usually based on showings of increased cost.

Fixed and Variable Costs

In short-run analysis, it is extremely useful to distinguish between fixed ("constant," "sunk") costs and variable costs. The former are those which can be considered to be unaffected in their total by variations in the rate of use of existing plant capacity. The latter are those which vary with the rate of output from the fixed plant. In the former classification fall such items as depreciation on buildings which the firm owns, taxes and insurance on these buildings, and the minimum amount of maintenance expenditure which is necessary to keep them from deteriorating unduly. Machinery normally outlasts a single accounting period, and its life may not be greatly affected by short-term fluctuations in the rate at which it is used. Under these conditions, depreciation on machinery would be classified as a fixed cost. And this would be true for purposes of correct business decisions, even though cost accounting conventions might cause depreciation to be associated with each unit of output. Salaries, especially those paid to company officials, are unlikely to vary—in the short run, at least—with the rate of production; hence, they can be considered as fixed costs. Interest paid on bonded indebtedness, license fees, and rental charges on land are other examples of fixed costs.

On the other hand, direct labor costs, social security taxes, material costs, depreciation which is closely related to use, and cost of gas, coal, and electric power are examples of variable costs. Interest paid on working capital needed to finance current production would probably fall in this category also, since its amount would vary with output, even though the relation might be less precise than it would be for other variable costs.

Union activity in recent years has been directed quite heavily toward stabilizing the incomes of nonsalaried workers through securing guaranteed wage plans—the employer guaranteeing two thirds of regular pay for a half-year period, for example, regardless of the amount of time actually worked. This has the effect of converting direct labor costs into semifixed costs. Although wage payments will still be related to the rate of production, the relation between the two may be much less close than in the situation where the firm pays only for hours spent in productive activity. Other costs, such as advertising and salesmen's compensation, may be difficult to classify as either wholly fixed or wholly variable in nature.

The analytical importance of the distinction between fixed and variable costs is related to a general philosophical principle of rational behavior suggested by such sayings as "Don't cry over spilled milk" and "That's water over the dam." That is, rational behavior in general requires neglect of past actions about which nothing can be done and concentration on making the most of future opportunities. If, for example, one has unwisely wasted ten minutes by standing in a line at the bank and has made little progress, this investment of time should not deter one from switching to any other line where the *additional* time required promises to be less. Similarly, a man who has bought a security at 100 and has watched it fall to 60 should not buy an equal amount at the lower price in order to bring his "average" to 80 unless he finds after careful study that no better investment opportunity is then open to him. That is to say, the money previously sunk into the stock at a high price is irrelevant to further investment decisions.

The principle just illustrated is of great importance to the businessman in making rational short-run decisions as to output and price. It indicates that *marginal* cost rather than *average* cost should guide such decisions. Average cost is affected by the amount of investment which has been made in capital equipment, and by insurance, interest, and other fixed expenses. Marginal cost, however, is *additional* variable cost and, as such, can either be incurred or be avoided in the short run. Consequently, it is comparable to the additional time in the bank line and constitutes the proper cost to be regarded in making output decisions.

A hypothetical short-run cost schedule for a small factory is shown in Exhibit 1. Output is assumed to be capable of variation between zero and 20 units per day.

Attention will first be directed to the "total" columns of the table—i.e., columns 2, 4, and 6—and to the Marginal Cost column (8). Total fixed costs remain at $32, regardless of output. Total variable costs rise continually as output increases, rising at first by decreasing increments and later by increasing additions as output is stepped up. These increments are shown in Column 8 as "marginal

Exhibit 1

DAILY COST SCHEDULE FOR A SMALL FACTORY

(1) Output (No. of Units)	(2) Total Fixed Costs	(3) Average Fixed Costs	(4) Total Variable Costs	(5) Average Variable Costs	(6) Total of All Costs	(7) Average Total Cost	(8) Marginal Cost
1.........	$32.00	$32.00	$ 7.20	$ 7.20	$ 39.20	$39.20	$ 7.20
2.........	32.00	16.00	12.90	6.45	44.90	22.45	5.70
3.........	32.00	10.67	17.40	5.80	49.40	16.47	4.50
4.........	32.00	8.00	21.00	5.25	53.00	13.25	3.60
5.........	32.00	6.40	24.00	4.80	56.00	11.20	3.00
6.........	32.00	5.33	36.70	4.45	58.70	9.78	2.70
7.	32.00	4.57	29.40	4.20	61.40	8.77	2.70
8.........	32.00	4.00	32.40	4.05	64.40	8.05	3.00
9.........	32.00	3.55	36.00	4.00	68.00	7.55	3.60
10.........	32.00	3.20	40.50	4.05	72.50	7.25	4.50
11.........	32.00	2 91	46.20	4.20	78.20	7.11	5.70
12.........	32.00	2.67	53.40	4.45	85.40	7.12	7.20
13.........	32.00	2.46	62.40	4.80	94.40	7.26	9.00
14.........	32.00	2.28	73.50	5.25	105.50	7.53	11.10
15.........	32.00	2.13	87.00	5.80	119.00	7.93	13.50
16.........	32.00	2.00	103.20	6.45	135.20	8.45	16.20
17.........	32.00	1.88	122.40	7.20	154.40	9.08	19.20
18.........	32.00	1.78	144.90	8.05	176.90	9.83	22.50
19.........	32.00	1.68	171.00	9.00	203.00	10.68	26.10
20.........	32.00	1.60	201.00	10.05	233.00	11.65	30.00

Source: Albert L. Meyers, *Elements of Modern Economics* (3d ed.; New York: Prentice-Hall, Inc., 1948), p. 158. Reproduced by permission.

cost"—the cost added by one more unit of output. (Marginal cost can be measured either as additional total variable costs or as additional total costs, since the only changes in total costs are those caused by changes in variable costs.) This pattern of total variable costs and, consequently, of marginal cost is traceable to operation of the famous law of diminishing returns. In the low-output range (1 to 6 units) the efficiency of organization of production increases as more labor, materials, and other variable inputs are used in conjunction with the fixed plant. That is, a better proportion is attained between fixed and variable inputs, and this shows up the declining rate of increase in total variable costs. Above a daily output of 7 units the factory is operating in the stage of diminishing marginal returns, which causes marginal cost to rise or, in other words, causes total variable costs and total costs to increase at an increasing rate. This is because each additional input (e.g., each additional worker) adds less to output but must be paid the same amount (e.g., the same wage rate). Each output unit is consequently producible only at a higher additional expense.

While marginal or incremental cost is rising, however, average variable costs (Column 5) may be declining. This is apparent at outputs of 8 and 9 units. Also, average total cost per unit continues to decline even after average variable costs rise. This is apparent at outputs of 10 and 11. Average total cost is the sum of average fixed cost and average variable cost; it is possible, therefore, for an increase in the latter to be more than offset by a decrease in the former in its effect on average total cost. The effect of "spreading the overhead" is directly observable in Column 3, where average fixed costs decline continuously as the rate of output is stepped up.

It should be kept in mind that price and output decisions are made by the management of the company (firm) rather than by the officials in charge of a factory (plant). A single firm may own dozens or even hundreds of plants; and many costs, such as advertising, research, and selling costs which are borne by the firm, might not appear in the simplified sort of cost table which has been examined. To keep the problem manageable, however, and to bring basic principles into sharp relief, it will be assumed that the cost table used is for a firm rather than for a plant. (If the firm has only a single plant, the costs of the firm will probably not differ greatly from those of the plant.)

Break-Even Analysis

Businessmen often prefer to think in terms of total costs and total revenues rather than in terms of average and marginal cost and revenue. As a consequence, "break-even" charts are common in the business world. The name is something of a misnomer, however, since more interest is likely to attach to the maximization of profits than to merely breaking even. A break-even chart which utilizes the cost data of Exhibit 1 is shown in Exhibit 2. These data are assumed to pertain to a perfectly competitive firm which can sell any quantity it wishes at $10 per unit. Total cost starts at $32 (the fixed cost) and rises at a decreasing rate, and then at an increasing rate. The first break-even point comes at an output of just under 6 units per day. If fewer than this number of units are produced, total cost will exceed total revenue; if more than 18 units are produced daily, total cost will again exceed total revenue. A net profit can be made at outputs between these break-even points, the greatest profit coming at an output a little above 13 units, where the excess of revenue

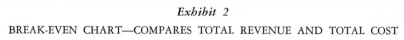

Exhibit 2

BREAK-EVEN CHART—COMPARES TOTAL REVENUE AND TOTAL COST

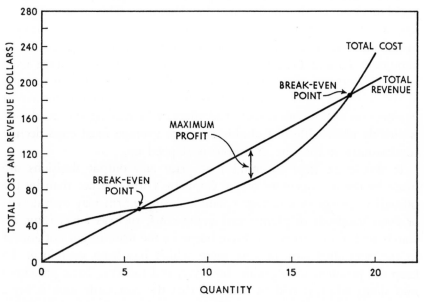

above cost is at a maximum.[4] This is the output which the firm will normally attempt to attain.

Break-even analysis is also useful to a firm which possesses some price-making power. Management is then forced to consider different prices as well as different outputs. The total revenue curve becomes a parabola similar to that of Exhibit 3 of Chapter 3 (p. 82), its shape depending on the nature of the demand curve. Break-even points and maximum profit are found in a similar way. Frequently, break-even charts are drawn up *before* an article is put into production. From

---

[4] In drawing a break-even chart of this form, one implicitly assumes that output units are completely divisible—that the firm could turn out 13.45 units, for example, if it wished. This may or may not be the case. If it is not the case, the best output is simply the attainable output at which the positive difference between total revenue and total cost is maximized—13 units in Exhibit 1. It should also be kept in mind that it is implicitly assumed that all output is sold currently.

engineers' and accountants' estimates a total cost curve can be drawn for an item which is being considered, while statistical study or executive experience can be drawn upon to arrive at an estimate of revenue possibilities. These calculations may help the firm to decide whether or not to produce the article. If the item is not yet in production, the estimated costs and revenues may, however, be so subject to error that the top executive will instead decide the issue on the basis of his general experience with similar situations, a general belief in the desirability of innovation and growth, or other grounds.

Average and Marginal Cost Curves

Economists usually prefer to work with average and marginal costs and revenues rather than with total costs and revenues. Cost accountants usually have average cost per unit as their principal end measurement although, to an increasing extent, they are interested in measuring marginal cost.[5] One reason for this preference lies in the fact that the break-even point of view may be misleading. A break-even chart seems to imply that the firm should not produce in the short run unless it can at least break even. Actually, this is only correct from a long-run point of view—that is, when management is considering whether or not to invest in plant. In the short run the firm should produce if it can at least break even on its variable costs rather than its total costs.

The four principal short-run cost curves of economic theory are shown in Exhibit 3, the data being plotted from the figures in Exhibit 1. Average fixed cost (AFC) is of little importance except as a reminder of the source of high cost per unit when fixed capacity is lightly utilized. Average variable cost (AVC) is of limited use, being important chiefly as a means of identifying the "shutdown" price —the lowest price at which it is worth operating rather than suspending operations. This shutdown price is found at the lowest point on the average variable cost curve and is equal to a little less than $4.00 per unit.[6] At any lower price, it would pay to close shop, since variable costs (which are avoidable costs) could not be covered. Minimum average total cost is much higher—slightly above $7.00 per unit. This means that there exists a substantial range of prices (about $4.00

---

[5] Earley, op. cit., p. 239, points out that accountants are increasingly finding the measurement of marginal cost important in the pricing of multiple products. Most firms are actually multiple- rather than single-product firms.

[6] If total variable cost were plotted in a break-even chart (Exhibit 2) and price were set below the shutdown price, the two curves would not intersect—i.e., the firm could not find any output at which it could break even on its variable costs.

to $7.00) where it is better to produce at a loss than to shut down. The average total cost (*ATC*) curve is a handy one if used in conjunction with price, since profit per unit is the difference between price and average total cost. For purposes of making short-run operational decisions, however, it is the marginal cost (*MC*) curve which is important. If price cannot be changed—as is true for the perfectly

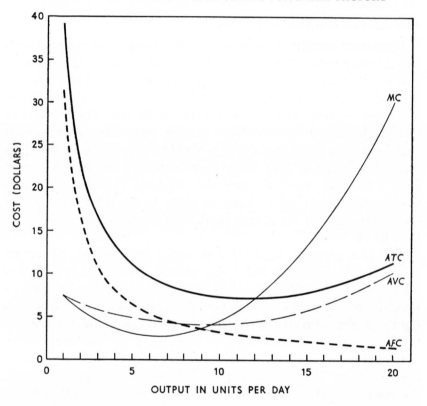

Exhibit 3

AVERAGE AND MARGINAL COST CURVES FOR SMALL FACTORY

competitive seller—output should be expanded to the point of equality between marginal cost and price.

The logic of using marginal cost as a guide to short-run output decisions is not difficult to follow if it is kept clearly in mind that marginal cost is *additional* cost per unit. As long as price (the additional income per unit) exceeds marginal cost, output is too low, because further units of output will add more to revenue than they add to cost. But if marginal cost exceeds price, output is too large— some units are adding more to cost than to income. Consequently, optimum output occurs when marginal cost is equal to price.[7] This rule, however, implies perfect divisibility of output units. If such divisibility does not exist, the rule of profit-maximizing, short-run behavior must be slightly modified as follows: Produce all units for which price exceeds marginal cost, but none for which marginal cost exceeds price. If price is $10 per unit, for example, this rule would require production by the small factory of Exhibit 1 at a daily rate of 13 units. The thirteenth unit would be worth producing, because it would add $10 to income and would add $9.00 to cost. The fourteenth unit would not be worth producing, since its sale would add $10 to income but its production would add $11.10 to cost. An optimum output of 13 units is, of course, the same as that arrived at by means of the break-even chart, except for the problem of divisibility of units.

A somewhat more confusing question of divisibility is involved when the manager of the firm must make an "all-or-nothing" decision rather than being able to choose the particular rate of output which he wants. Suppose that our same small factory must accept or reject an order for 12 units at a price of $5.00 per unit, and that no other sales opportunities are presently open to the firm due, for example, to its being the slack season of the year. The marginal cost relevant to this decision is not $7.20, but $4.45 (which is the average variable cost). This is because the choice must be between either zero or 12 units of output. The entire variable cost of $53.40 is the additional cost which taking the order would involve. This amounts to $4.45 per unit. It would, therefore, be better to accept the order than to turn it down. Even though the order would not yield a profit over *total* costs, the income would more than cover total *variable* costs. Examination of Exhibit 1 shows that the loss on the order would be $25.40. However, if the order were turned down, the loss would be $32, the entire amount of the fixed costs. Even though filling the order would not yield enough income to cover all costs, it would cover all variable costs and contribute *something* toward meeting the "overhead." When a profit cannot be made, it is, of course, wise to minimize the loss.

Optimum Output under Monopoly

The profit-maximizing, short-run output under monopoly is determined according to principles which are identical to those just de-

---

[7] Marginal cost must be rising, rather than declining. If marginal cost were declining but equal to price, an equilibrium would not exist, because additional units could be turned out which would add more to income than to cost.

scribed for a competitive firm, although the calculations on the price side are somewhat more complicated. For both the competitive and monopolistic firm the best profit position obtains when marginal cost is equal to marginal revenue. Marginal revenue is identical with price for the competitive firm, because each unit can be sold at the prevailing market price and consequently adds that amount to the firm's revenue. Marginal revenue is less than price under monopoly, because a greater quantity can be sold only by lowering price, as described in Chapter 3.

The use of the marginal cost–marginal revenue comparison in the analysis of optimum price and output under monopoly can be illustrated by the simple data of Exhibit 4. In this table the output and

Exhibit 4

MONOPOLIST'S MARGINAL REVENUE AND MARGINAL COST

Quantity	Price	Total Revenue	Marginal Revenue	Marginal Cost
1.	$20	$ 20	$20	$7.20
2.	19	38	18	5.70
3.	18	54	16	4.50
4.	17	68	14	3.60
5.	16	80	12	3.00
6.	15	90	10	2.70
7.	14	98	8	2.70
8.	13	104	6	3.00
9.	12	108	4	3.60
10.	11	110	2	4.50
11.	10	110	0	5.70
12.	9	108	− 2	7.20

marginal cost figures are taken from Exhibit 1. A demand schedule has been added; and from the price-sales data, total revenue and marginal revenue are computed.

An examination of Exhibit 4 shows that the most profitable output is 9 units per day; these can be sold for $12 per unit. This is true because this is the largest revenue at which marginal revenue exceeds marginal cost. If the output rate were raised to 10 units a day, the extra unit would add $4.50 to the cost but only $2.00 to the revenue. The reader can verify the fact that the largest profit ($40 per day) is made at 9 units by taking differences between the total revenues of Exhibit 4 and the total costs of Exhibit 1. This example should make it clear, however, that for a monopolistic firm as well as for a competitive firm the best short-run output can be found without regard to the fixed costs, since marginal costs are affected only by those costs which vary with output.

Graphical determination of optimum output and price for a monopolist is illustrated in Exhibit 5, which is based on the data of Exhibit 4. The marginal revenue and marginal cost curves intersect at an output slightly in excess of 9 units per day. This is the most profitable output, and the price at which it can be disposed of is found directly above on the demand curve. It should again be noted that complete divisibility of output units and of prices is implied by the drawing of continuous curves. If such divisibility were not actually

Exhibit 5

MARGINAL REVENUE EQUALS MARGINAL COST—
AT MOST PROFITABLE OUTPUT

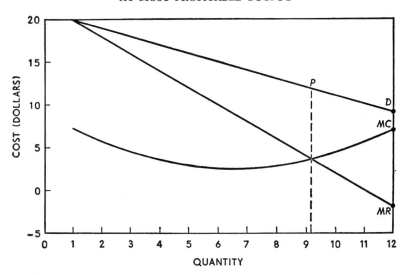

attainable, the best output would be exactly 9 units rather than a little more than this number.

Adaptability and Divisibility of Plant

As a matter of convenience in drawing, average variable, average total, and marginal cost curves are usually made quite markedly U-shaped.[8] While this does occur in actual practice, many other shapes are possible. It is frequently claimed, for example, that marginal costs are approximately constant over a wide range of output. This would clearly be the case for a firm which purchases and resells commodities

---

[8] This also helps emphasize the mathematical rule that the marginal cost curve must intersect both the average variable cost and average total cost curves at their lowest points.

instead of manufacturing them. If all additional quantities of a good (say TV sets) could be bought at the same price from the manufacturer, the retailer's marginal costs would be nearly the same, regardless of the volume which he bought and resold. The added cost of handling each additional set would consist chiefly of the manufacturer's price.

If attention is concentrated on the producers of goods, it is useful to examine the concepts of "adaptability" and "divisibility" as they apply to plant capacity.[9] A plant may be said to be "adaptable" to the extent that it is capable of being used with changing amounts of variable inputs. A piece of farm land, for example, is quite adaptable to different amounts of fertilizer and labor, while a steam shovel is highly unadaptable in the sense that it can be used with only one operator at a time. Plant capacity is highly "divisible" when it contains a large number of identical machines—for example, 20 identical machines for producing concrete blocks, 20 nailmaking machines, or 20 printing presses within a single manufacturing establishment. Complete indivisibility exists, for example, when the plant consists of one long assembly line, each station of which is wholly dependent on the previous ones.

Divisible but unadaptable plants are common in manufacturing, since many machines are built to operate at only one rate, and require a fixed number of operators and specific amounts of material per time period. In this case, marginal costs are horizontal over a wide range of output. In order to secure more output, a greater number of machines is utilized, and each requires a fixed complement of labor, power, and materials; consequently, each one adds the same amount to cost as the previous ones. Reduced output in this case is attained by the shutting-down of a number of machines, and each one which is shut down reduces total variable cost by the same amount.

If plant capacity is indivisible but highly adaptable, a saucer-shaped marginal cost curve will result. Marginal costs will at first fall, as a better proportion is attained between the indivisible fixed plant and the variable inputs; but eventually, the proportions will become less compatible, and marginal costs will rise. The high degree of adaptability of the plant would cause both the decline and the increase of marginal costs to be gradual.[10]

---

[9] See George J. Stigler, "Production and Distribution in the Short Run," *Journal of Political Economy*, June, 1939, pp. 305–27.

[10] Several other combinations of adaptability and divisibility are described by Stigler, *op. cit.*

Marginal costs are likely to be approximately horizontal in activities which require much labor but little or no capital equipment. Shops which sell sea shells along the Florida coast hire unskilled workers to pick up the best specimens on the beaches before the tourists have awakened. The capital of each worker consists of no more than a bucket in which to carry the shells. Since the shell gatherers are paid according to the quality and quantity of their harvest, the marginal cost to the firm which hires them is constant for any given type of shell. Total variable cost of the shell-gathering operation is practically equal to total cost because of the unimportance of the capital equipment.

In summary, it should be recognized that short-run marginal cost curves may take various shapes according to the divisibility and adaptability of the fixed plant employed, and according to the relative importance of fixed and variable costs. Variable costs may constitute virtually the entire costs in certain simple productive activities or a fairly small part of the total in highly mechanized activities such as the production of portland cement. If most costs are variable, a small drop in the price of output may compel the abandonment of operations. Where investment in plant has been heavy, however, it is frequently better to operate in the short run, even at a sharply reduced price, as long as all variable costs can be covered and some amount is available to apply against the high fixed costs.

CASE 4–1: AIR-FREIGHT RATES

On October 15, 1944, American Airlines inaugurated an air-freight service in addition to its carriage of passengers, mail, and express. By January, 1946, several other air lines engaged in the transportation of passengers, mail, and express had also entered the field. These carriers were licensed by the Civil Aeronautics Board to fly regularly scheduled trips between designated points and were known as "certificated carriers." Initially, they carried freight only in the same aircraft as passengers, mail, and express; but subsequently, the larger lines, such as American Airlines, United Air Lines, TWA, and Pennsylvania Central Airlines, instituted the use of all-cargo planes in which no passengers were carried. These aircraft made regularly scheduled flights, as permitted in the certificate of the carrier, and frequently carried mail and express as well as freight cargo.

After July, 1945, a number of noncertificated carriers was organized and began to compete with the certificated carriers for air-freight traffic.[11] On August 1, 1947, the Civil Aeronautics Board set up a classification of noncertificated cargo carriers which permitted these new air-freight companies to operate on a scheduled basis as common carriers. The C.A.B. also required them to file tariffs and reports. Slick Airways, Inc., California Eastern Airways, Air Cargo Transport, Inc., and the Flying Tiger Line transported the largest share of the total volume of traffic carried by this group.

The rates set up by American Airlines on October 15, 1944, established a system of class and specific commodity rates, and applied

Exhibit 1

GRADUATED RATES QUOTED BY UNITED AIR LINES, INC., EFFECTIVE FEBRUARY 1, 1946

Weight Group (Pounds)	Rate Basis per Ton-Mile (Cents)	Percentage of 100-Lb. Rate
100–499	26.5	100.0
500–999	25.6	96.6
1,000–1,999	24.7	93.2
2,000–2,999	23.0	86.8
3,000 and over	21.2	80.0

Source: H. W. Torgerson, "History of Air Freight Tariffs," *Journal of Air Law and Commerce* (Winter, 1948), p. 50. All rates are on an airport-to-airport basis.

these rates on a mileage-block basis. For the four classes of commodities, A, B, C, and D, the distance charges were 50, 43, 36.5, and 30 cents per ton-mile, respectively, all rates including pickup and delivery service. With minor variations, the other certificated carriers followed the same system of tariffs, except that some tariffs were lower than that of the American Airlines. Upon the entry of the United Air Lines into the air-freight business on February 1, 1946, its tariff eliminated the four classes of commodities and set up instead a single general commodity class with graduated rates according to weight classification, to which the rates shown in Exhibit 1 applied. Other carriers soon made adjustments to meet the rates and terms of United Air Lines. Effective July 15, 1946, Pennsylvania Central Airlines filed a tariff quoting lower rates than competitors except on quantity shipments. TWA followed shortly in a partial rate adjustment to meet the competition of Pennsylvania Central Airlines.

---

[11] Prior to August 1, 1947, noncertificated carriers were not required to file tariffs with the Civil Aeronautics Board. They were not certificated to fly on a scheduled basis but made irregular flights at rates negotiated with each individual shipper.

The noncertificated carriers soon began to compete vigorously in the air-freight market. In February, 1946, Air Cargo Transport announced a schedule of rates which varied with the weight of shipments. The ton-mile rates, as advertised, were 22 cents for shipments of 1,000 pounds, 21 cents for 4,000 pounds, and 20 cents for 5,000 pounds. As the number of companies in the noncertificated group increased, rates were gradually reduced. The average revenue per ton-mile flown by Slick Airways in the months of March, April, May, and June, 1946, was 20.1, 16.1, 17.5, and 13.6 cents, respectively.[12]

The certificated carriers made adjustments to meet the competition of the noncertificated carriers; and on August 1, 1947, a consolidated tariff was filed on behalf of all the certificated trunk-line carriers.[13] In this tariff the basic ton-mile rate was again lowered, the 100-pound rates being constructed on a basis of 20 cents per ton-mile, as compared to 26.5 cents per ton-mile in earlier tariffs. This tariff, with minor exceptions, brought about lower rates on all commodities. On the same date, Slick Airways, a noncertificated carrier, filed a tariff with rates between New York and other principal cities served by it from 12 to 39 per cent lower, according to weight, than rates shown in the consolidated tariff of the certificated carriers. Other noncertificated carriers filed tariffs early in August similar to that of Slick Airways. On October 5, 1947, American Airlines, PCA, and United Air Lines, which competed actively with the noncertificated carriers, filed specific commodity tariffs which were not on a uniform basis but approximated 13.8 cents per ton-mile on shipments from New York to Chicago and 12.8 cents per ton-mile from New York to Los Angeles. These rates were lower than those of the noncertificated carriers on shipments weighing between 100 and 999 pounds. TWA met this reduction of rates in part. United also filed a new tariff, effective October 25, 1947, giving substantial reductions; in this, it was joined by some of its competitors among the certificated carriers.

Upon petition of Slick Airways and the Independent Air Freight Association, Inc., the C.A.B. halted these rate reductions by suspending the supplemental tariffs of United, Inland, Southwest, Western, and TWA, and also the specific commodity rates of PCA, TWA, and

---

[12] H. W. Torgerson, "History of Air Freight Tariffs," *Journal of Air Law and Commerce* (Winter, 1948), p. 52.

[13] This tariff consisted of three parts: (1) a rules tariff, (2) a pickup and delivery tariff, and (3) a rate tariff. This tariff had the effect of making the tariffs of the various participating certificated carriers more uniform.

American, with some qualifications. The C.A.B. then ordered an investigation of these tariffs and the tariffs filed by ten noncertificated cargo carriers. The board stated that the purpose of this investigation was "to attempt to develop some national principles for tariff-making

Exhibit 2

ESTIMATED ANNUAL TRAFFIC VOLUME (NOW
PRIMARILY SURFACE-BORNE) WHICH WOULD
BECOME AVAILABLE AT RATES INDICATED

Rate per Ton-Mile (Cents)	Ton-Miles (Millions)	Rate per Ton-Mile (Cents)	Ton-Miles (Millions)
35	30	15	800
30	60	12	3,550
25	100	10	5,000
20	200	8	7,400

Source: *Exhibit SA–4B, Exhibits of Slick Airways, Inc.* (C.A.B. Docket No. 1705 *et al.*), p. 13.

in air transportation as well as to inquire into the validity of the tariffs that have been filed."[14] To carry out its inquiry, the board required all carriers of both types to submit briefs and exhibits supporting their tariffs.

Although the arguments presented in these briefs indicated a sharp difference of opinion over the question of costs for the purpose of

Exhibit 3

ESTIMATES OF FRESH FRUITS AND VEGETABLES
WHICH WOULD BE MOVED BY AIR FREIGHT
AT RATES INDICATED

Rate per Ton-Mile (Cents)	Ton-Miles	Rate per Ton-Mile (Cents)	Ton-Miles
15	24,419,000	5	967,711,000
10	63,714,000	3	4,018,743,000
7	333,127,000		

Source: Spencer O. Larsen, *Wayne University Studies in Air Transport*, No. 1, p. 5; based on historical movements of 1941.

rate making, the revenue aspects of the problem were not neglected. Exhibits 2 and 3 show estimates of the relationship between rates and volume of traffic as air-freight rates approach the level of surface rates. "Expert economic witnesses who appeared for the various parties generally agreed that in transportation history, each new form of

[14] Torgerson, *op. cit.*, p. 61.

transportation which has persisted offered services and rates which were able to (1) divert some traffic from older transportation systems, and (2) create new traffic. Air freight, in its genesis, has shown such propensities."[15] In addition, representatives of several carriers pointed out that it might be necessary at times to quote rates below cost in order to develop traffic.

The certificated carriers tended to treat the transportation of freight as a by-product of their main operations in the transport of passengers, mail, and express. The noncertificated carriers, on the other hand, transported freight as their main and only product. Although all certificated carriers were requested to present an exhibit showing both revenues and expenditures pertaining individually to passenger, mail, express, and freight service, only one carrier, Braniff Airways, submitted such an exhibit. The remaining companies stated that lack of information and time prevented them from presenting an accurate statement. The statement of Braniff Airways is shown in Exhibit 4.

The noncertificated carriers served primarily a few large cities on the East and West coasts. Slick Airways served regularly 11 principal points; California Eastern, 7; and the Flying Tigers, 8. The certificated carriers, on the other hand, served a substantially larger number of cities; American Airlines, for example, provided all four of its services to 65 cities broadly distributed over the United States. United Air Lines, similarly, covered a wide geographic area. PCA and TWA served a smaller number of cities over a somewhat more restricted geographical area. The distance factor was greater for the noncertificated than for the certificated carriers. Average load was also greater in the noncertificated carriers than in the certificated. Both distance and weight factors are shown in Exhibit 5. These factors, which affected the costs of carrying freight, became one of the principal points of dispute between the two groups of carriers as to the nature of certain costs.

The certificated carriers based their main argument upon the principle of "out-of-pocket" costs directly attributable to the provision of air-freight service. In their arguments before the C.A.B., they pointed out that, because their aircraft provided regularly scheduled flights for the carriage of passengers, mail, and express, and because there was adequate unused capacity in these carriers, it was not necessary to include as costs of freight service any expenses for flying operations, depreciation of flying equipment, and ground operations, which would

---

[15] *Examiner's Report* (C.A.B. Docket No. 810 *et al.*), p. 236.

Exhibit 4

BRANIFF AIRWAYS, INC., REVENUES AND EXPENSES FOR QUARTER-YEAR ENDED SEPTEMBER 30, 1947

Showing Direct Distribution to Services Affected and to Proration "Pools"

Description	Total	Passenger	Mail	Express	Freight	Allocable to All Cargo	Balance Allocable to All Services
Operating revenues:							
Passenger	$2,779,168	$2,779,168					......
Mail	112,832		$112,832				......
Express	78,495			$78,495			......
Freight	26,299				$26,299		......
Excess baggage	25,875	25,875					......
Other (including charter)	40,739	24,661			8,673		$ 7,405
Totals	$3,063,408	$2,829,704	$112,832	$78,495	$34,972		$ 7,405
Operating expenses:							
Flying operations	$ 746,259	$ 4,648			$ 2,426		$ 739,185
Flying maintenance	366,911	2,400			1,453		363,058
Flying depreciation	370,432	3,301			1,483		365,648
Total Direct Flying	$1,483,602	$ 10,349			$ 5,362		$1,467,891
Ground operations	$ 464,601	$ 2,017	$ 933		$ 523	$66,631	$ 394,497
Ground indirect maintenance	245,502						245,502
Passenger service	246,030	246,030					......
Traffic and sales	357,463	307,361	684		1,102		48,316
Advertising and publicity	73,442						73,442
General and administrative	218,469	15,826	852		1,436	1,178	199,177
Ground equipment, depreciation	42,615	14,038	305		622	657	26,993
Total Operating Expense	$3,131,724	$ 595,621	$ 2,774		$ 9,045	$68,466	$2,455,818
Net Operating Profit or Loss	$ 68,316*	$2,234,083	$110,058	$78,495	$25,927	$68,466*	$2,448,413*

* Loss.

Source: *Exhibit No. B-4*, p. 1, *Exhibits of Braniff Airways, Inc.* (C.A.B. Docket No. 1705 *et al.*).

Exhibit 5

AVERAGE WEIGHT, AVERAGE LENGTH OF HOP, AND
AVERAGE LENGTH OF SHIPMENT FOR SELECTED
CERTIFICATED AND NONCERTIFICATED
CARRIERS

Carrier	Average Weight per Shipment (Tons), Week of Sept. 7, 1947	Average Length of Hop in Miles, Week of Sept. 7, 1947	Average Length of Shipment in Miles, Third Quarter, 1947
Certificated:			
American.............	0.0736	*	900†
United..............	0.0776	291.9	1,030†
PCA................	0.1179	140.5	345
Braniff.............	0.0443	161.2	557
TWA...............	0.0820	265.4	1,178
Noncertificated:			
Slick...............	0.1361	740.2	2,069.1
Flying Tiger.........	0.4431	1,341.8	1,837.7
California-Eastern.....	0.1767	742.9	2,101.0
Air Cargo...........	1.5284	*	564.2

* Not available.
† Estimates.

Source: *Average Weight per Shipment, Exhibit PC 226A* (C.A.B. Docket No. 1705 *et al.*, January 20, 1948). *Average Length of Hop, Exhibit PC 235* (C.A.B. Docket No. 1705 *et al.*, February 20, 1948). *Average Length of Shipment, Exhibit PC 227A* (C.A.B. Docket No. 1705 *et al.*, January 20, 1948).

Exhibit 6

AVAILABLE FREIGHT SPACE AND PERCENTAGE UTILIZA-
TION ON COMBINATION AIRCRAFT FOR AMERICAN
AIRLINES, UNITED AIR LINES, AND TWA FOR
THE FIRST 10 MONTHS OF 1947

Carrier	Available Space (Ton-Miles)	Ton-Miles of Freight Carried	Percentage Utilized
American..........	76,692,230	6,870,096	8.95
United..............	60,828,015	3,351,723	5.51
TWA...............	40,374,432	2,009,152	4.97
Average........			6.87

Source: *Brief of Public Counsel to C.A.B.* (C.A.B. Docket No. 1705 *et al.*, March 22, 1948), p. 30.

be carried on even if there were no freight service. Exhibit 6 shows the average monthly utilization of this space by American, United, and TWA, for the ten-month period ended October 31, 1947.

Several factors were emphasized which affected the percentage utilization of this space.

Since [freight] cargo moves primarily between 9 P.M. and 9 A.M., most available space on combination planes during the period 9 A.M. to 9 P.M. is not commercially usable. . . . During the period between 9 P.M. and 9 A.M. United originated 65 per cent of its freight from its major stations. . . . Since cargo moves primarily on week days, a large proportion of the space flown on week ends is not commercially usable. The testimony of PCA shows that 70 per cent of its cargo is carried Tuesday through Friday. . . . United's calculations do not relate the available space to the place where the cargo demand exists. If there is a cargo demand at Chicago, tonnage available on com-

Exhibit 7

COMPARATIVE COSTS OF FREIGHT SERVICE IN CENTS PER AVAILABLE
TON-MILE AND PER ADJUSTED REVENUE TON-MILE FOR SELECTED
CERTIFICATED AND NONCERTIFICATED CARRIERS

CARRIER	AVAILABLE TON-MILES			ADJUSTED REVENUE TON-MILES			CARRIERS' ESTIMATE: OTHER GROUND AND INDIRECT EXPENSE APPLICABLE TO FREIGHT
	Air Operating Expense	Ground and Indirect Maintenance Expense	Other Ground and Indirect Expense	Air Operating Expense	Ground and Indirect Maintenance Expense	Other Ground and Indirect Expense	
Certificated:							
American........	11.98	2.50	9.40	19.30	4.03	15.15	5.44
Braniff..........	14.91	2.47	9.47	24.40	4.04	15.50	2.46
PCA............	13.26	2.12	10.00	25.41	4.06	19.14	5.67
TWA...........	13.14	3.07	9.82	20.71	4.83	15.48	5.91
United..........	11.56	1.85	9.61	18.26	2.93	18.27	9.80
Average.......	12.74	2.35	9.29	21.72	4.01	15.83	
Noncertificated:							
Air Cargo.......	10.67	0.79	5.75	15.65	1.16	8.43	
California-Eastern........	5.89	0.13	3.66	10.71	0.24	6.65	
Flying Tiger.....	9.30	0.40	3.85	12.78	0.56	5.29	
Slick...........	5.81	0.74	4.86	7.26	0.92	6.06	
Willis..........	6.82	1.30	2.69	16.95	3.24	6.69	
Average.......	6.67	0.55	4.21	9.92	0.82	6.27	

Source: *Exhibits PC 433A, 433B, Public Counsel's Exhibits* (C.A.B. Docket No. 1705 *et al.*, January 20, 1948).

bination planes at Reno is not commercially usable space. . . . When the directional flow of cargo is considered, a large proportion of cargo space on combination planes is not commercially usable. Exhibits of United show that 82 per cent of United's cargo is westbound and only 18 per cent eastbound. . . . For the certificated carriers as a whole the eastbound traffic was only 37.6 per cent of the westbound.[16]

There are shown in Exhibit 7 comparative costs of freight service for selected certificated and noncertificated carriers. The column

[16] *Brief of United Airlines, Inc., before the Civil Aeronautics Board, March 22, 1948,* pp. 33-36, *passim.*

headed "Carriers' Estimate" is the approximate out-of-pocket cost to the certificated carriers for the transportation of air freight. These estimates do not include an allocation of expenditures for personnel, facilities, and equipment at stations where passenger, mail, express, and freight traffic are handled jointly. It was noted in the hearings:

> These added cost arguments appear valid with respect to station personnel, facilities and equipment at any point where traffic volume is low, that is, where all traffic can be handled by the minimum staff, and even where greater volume would require additional clerks and handlers, some economy might conceivably be realized by having the station manager take on the added supervisory work. But when the larger traffic points are considered, the argument loses force— as freight traffic grows in volume the relative amount that can move in combination as opposed to all-cargo equipment will become less. A considerable all-cargo operation at any point will make necessary separate freight terminal handling and loading facilities, perhaps at a different airport than is used for passenger flights. Rather than acquire additional space for freight reservation employees at the relatively expensive locations used for passenger sales, they will doubtless be located in less costly space, probably at the freight terminal. As traffic grows, a fairly complete segregation of passenger and freight operations will follow. Any appreciable physical separation of passenger and freight loading points would tend to reduce the practicability of using passenger-plane space for air freight. Thus, while there is found some merit in the added cost presentation of the carriers, as traffic increases it is foreseen that the operations at major points will closely resemble those of an independent all-cargo operator. As to station costs at relatively small traffic points the argument will probably remain valid as against a conventional operation serving property only.[17]

In one instance, American Airlines estimated the cost of carrying freight in combination planes at 2.1 cents per ton-mile,[18] while National Airlines estimated its total cost of freight transportation at $6.54, the cost of printing waybills.[19] It was the use of these costs as the lower limit to air-freight rates to which the noncertificated carriers objected.[20] They claimed that the certificated carriers, on the

---

[17] *Examiner's Report* (C.A.B. Docket No. 810 *et al.*), pp. 245–46.

[18] *Examiner's Report* (C.A.B. Docket No. 1705 *et al.*), p. 252.

[19] Note 66, p. 48, *Brief of Public Counsel to C.A.B.* (C.A.B. Docket No. 1705), pp. 32–48.

[20] For the quarter ended September 30, 1947, Capital Airlines reported that the total revenues per ton-mile for its all-cargo operations was 65.19 cents. For this same quarter, direct flying costs were 68.38 cents per ton-mile, and indirect costs were 6.3 cents per ton-mile, making a total of 75.49 cents total cost per ton-mile. The total loss on operations of all cargo equipment amounted to $10,958, based on the 106,393 miles flown. Capital Airlines had operating revenues of $110,503 from carrying freight on its combination airplanes, on the basis of 437,840 ton-miles of freight on combination planes at a cost of 6.3 cents per mile; total cost of freight on combination aircraft amounted to

basis of out-of-pocket costs, were charging rates below the cost of service and were engaging in unfair competition. The noncertificated carriers contended that some of the flying, depreciation, and maintenance costs should be charged to the carriage of freight. They further claimed that, because of air-mail payments, the certificated carriers could fly freight at lower rates and compensate themselves for any deficits by petitioning for an increase in mail payments.[21] The certificated carriers denied this and in their defense argued that any such revenue from air-freight service over and above their out-of-pocket costs *reduced* their need for air-mail subsidy.

Public counsel of the C.A.B. raised the question of the future of the air-freight business. It was pointed out that in the first nine months of 1947, 70 per cent of all revenue ton-miles of freight was carried in all-cargo planes. Only 31.7 per cent of the revenue ton-miles of freight carried by certificated carriers was, however, carried in all-cargo planes.[22] Witnesses for both certificated and noncertificated carriers were confident that the air-freight industry was at the beginning of a long period of great growth. All parties concerned were asked to estimate their 1948 freight ton-miles. The total of these estimates, compared to the actual experience of previous years, is shown in Exhibit 8. In determining the future relative importance of the all-cargo plane and the combination plane, it was recognized that the important element was not the growth of freight traffic per se but its growth relative to passenger traffic. If the freight traffic in the future were to grow much more than the passenger business, then the trend would be toward a proportionately greater use of all-cargo planes.[23] Exhibit 9 shows the growth of property traffic compared to passenger traffic since 1938.

$27,585, leaving a profit of $82,918 from freight operations on combination planes. Subtracting the loss on all-cargo freight operations leaves a net profit of $71,960 for all freight operations of Capital Airlines. Owing to a substantial increase in volume, attributed to lower rates, Capital Airlines showed a net profit on its all-cargo operations as well as its combination operations of freight service for the months of October and November, 1947.

[21] "In determining the [air-mail] rate in each case, the Authority shall take into consideration among other factors . . . the need of each such carrier for compensation for the transportation of mail sufficient to insure the performance of such service, and together with all other revenue of the air carrier, to enable such carrier under honest, economical and efficient management, to maintain and continue the development of air transportation to the extent and of the character and quality required for the commerce of the United States, the Postal Service, and the National Defense" (Civil Aeronautics Act of 1938, Sec. 406 [b]).

[22] *Brief of Public Counsel to C.A.B.,* (C.A.B. Docket No. 1705 *et al.,* March 22, 1948), pp. 22–23.

[23] Testimony of Mr. C. R. Smith, Chairman of the Board, American Airlines, Inc.:

Exhibit 8

AIR FREIGHT CARRIED, 1945–47, AND ESTI-
MATES FOR 1948, ALL CARRIERS

Year	Freight Carried, Revenue Ton-Miles	Percentage Increase over Previous Year
1945....................	3,189,106	.....
1946....................	41,451,956	1,200
1947....................	82,739,186	100
1948 (estimated)........	208,705,703	152

Exhibit 9

GROWTH OF PROPERTY TRAFFIC* COMPARED
TO PASSENGER TRAFFIC, 1938–47†

YEAR	COMPARISON BY REVENUE TON-MILES		COMPARISON BY PERCENTAGE (1938 = 100)	
	Property‡	Passengers§	Property	Passengers
1938.........	2,173,134	47,560,000	100.00	100.00
1939.........	2,704,837	67,975,600	124.47	142.93
1940.........	3,464,684	104,713,100	159.43	220.17
1941.........	5,240,867	137,715,200	241.17	289.56
1942.........	11,728,747	140,583,500	539.72	295.59
1943.........	15,139,359	161,713,000	696.66	340.02
1944.........	16,411,299	216,713,000	755.19	454.38
1945.........	22,104,306	333,627,800	1,017.16	701.49
1946.........	65,103,622	572,963,194	2,995.84	1,204.72
1947.........	111,209,749	579,621,516	5,117.48	1,218.72

* Includes both freight and express. Prior to July, 1945, freight and express statistics were reported together. Although reported separately since then, they have been combined to make the data comparable.

† Includes 16 certificated carriers from 1938 to date, plus 9 all-freight carriers from the time of their entrance into service during 1945–46.

‡ Converted from pound-miles to ton-miles for period 1938 to June, 1945.

§ Converted from passenger-miles to ton-miles on basis of 200 pounds per passenger for years 1938–45.

Sources: *Annual Airline Statistics, Domestic Carriers, and Recurrent Reports*, Appendix D, p. 2 (*Brief of Public Counsel to C.A.B.* [C.A.B. Docket 1705 *et al.*, March 22, 1948]).

Public counsel of the C.A.B., however, stated that "the combination plane has a definite place in the freight field. It enables combination

"*Question:* Mr. Smith, in American's future thinking about air freight, do you antici-pate that most of the freight in the future will be carried in combination aircraft or in all-cargo type?

"*Answer:* I think the trend will be toward carrying a higher proportion than now in all-freight planes. In other words, we are definitely proposing to add additional all-freight planes to our service . . . and the bulk of the tonnage will be carried in all-freight planes."

Testimony of Mr. Moore of United Air Lines:

"*Question:* In view of this trend [toward all-cargo planes] on United's system, would it be fair to say that the all-cargo plane will assume an increasing importance in the carriage of freight by United?

"*Answer:* If you are looking into the ultimate future, I think yes." *Brief of Public Counsel to C.A.B.* (C.A.B. Docket No. 1705 *et al.*, March 22, 1948), p. 28.

carriers to provide an expedited around-the-clock service which benefits some shippers. It also enables the carriers to serve small towns
where the operation of all cargo planes would not be economically
feasible."[24]

QUESTIONS

1. Do you agree with the position of the certificated carriers concerning costs
   of carrying air freight in combination planes?
2. Exhibit 4 shows that only a small share of total expenses is attributable directly to passenger traffic. Would the reasoning of the certificated carriers
   with regard to air freight apply with equal force to passenger traffic?
3. Does the cost structure of the noncertificated carriers make them more
   sensitive than the certificated carriers to rate changes?
4. From the standpoint of the national interest in developing improved transportation, what costs presented in this case are significant?

CASE 4–2: HOMELAND TAILORING COMPANY

The Homeland Tailoring Company manufactured men's woolen
suits, topcoats, and overcoats. A small part of the total output was
sold under its own brand name; the remainder was sold to men's
furnishings stores, department stores, and wholesalers, all of whom
distributed the merchandise under their respective brand names. The
company did no direct retail selling. Clothing produced under its
own brand name was sold in men's clothing stores catering to individuals of higher-than-average income. The small number of salaried
salesmen who constituted the sales force were under the direct supervision of Mr. Abrams, president of the company, who had founded
the business in 1924. From its origin as a tailor shop, the company
had grown to a firm producing approximately 200,000 suits and
coats per year.

Actual production of clothing in the company's plant was concentrated in a period of about nine months each year. Since the company produced no line of summer clothing, there was a period of
about three months from January 1 to April 1 when idle capacity frequently reached 90 per cent. During this period, vacations without
pay were granted to as many employees as practicable, and needed
repairs and renovations were made in plant and equipment.

Mr. Abrams normally sold his own brand of suits and coats at an
average price of $29.50 each, and suits and coats produced under the

---
[24] *Ibid.*, p. 36.

brand names of others at an average price of $28.50 each. The price of $28.50 was arrived at by adding approximately 10 per cent to total cost per suit as the profit margin, as follows:

Labor	$10.00
Material	9.50
Depreciation	1.414
Overhead	1.93
Administration and selling expense	1.153
Repairs and supplies	1.825
Total Cost	$25.822
Plus 10% for profit	2.60
Total Cost and Profit	$28.422

In October, 1947, Mr. Abrams received an inquiry from the manager of a large chain of department stores operating in the southwestern part of the United States, expressing interest in placing an order for 50,000 men's suits of various sizes as specified, for delivery between April 1 and April 15, 1948. It was stated that the order would be confirmed if the price did not exceed $18.75 per suit.

Although in the past the company had taken small orders for a few hundred suits during slack periods, it had never handled such a large order or sold at a price less than $24.50 per suit at such times. There was no system of standard costs in the plant, and the accounting system was somewhat crude. Mr. Abrams, because of his familiarity with all operations, relied primarily upon his own experience in estimating costs of orders.

The chief accountant recommended that the order be rejected. Mr. Abrams, unwilling to lose this business if it could be handled profitably, sought the help of a business management counsel, who prepared a new statement of costs per suit, as follows:

Direct labor	$7.23	
Material	9.11	
Spoilage	0.39	
Total Direct Costs		$16.73
Indirect labor	$2.77	
General factory burden	1.93	
Depreciation	1.764	
Repairs and supplies	1.475	
Administrative and selling expense	1.153	9.092
Total Costs		$25.822

In addition to the costs shown above, it was estimated that, because of vacations, overtime would have to be paid in the amount of 20 per cent of direct labor per unit. Inability of regular sources of supply to provide the full amount of the woolen goods required for this order forced Mr. Abrams to use other suppliers. One woolen mill was found which was willing to supply the full amount, but the mill refused to grant the usual cutters' discount of 2 per cent, net 30.

The fee of the management counseling firm was $2,000.

QUESTIONS

1. Should the company have accepted the order for 50,000 suits?
2. Explain the principle involved.
3. Does average variable cost per unit differ from marginal cost per unit? Why or why not?
4. Cite some factors which might make an opposite decision wise.

CASE 4–3: AUTO SPECIALTY PRODUCTS, INC.

Auto Specialty Products, Inc., of Kansas City, Kansas, manufactured a wide line of automobile accessories such as spotlights, rear-view mirrors, hub caps, wheel covers, continental tire kits, bumper guards, gasoline-tank and radiator caps, automobile trim, and floor mats. In addition to its main plant in Kansas City, the company owned and operated a plant in Birmingham, Michigan. Hub caps, wheel covers, continental tire kits, and bumper guards were produced in the Michigan plant. All other products were produced in Kansas City.

The firm served a national market. A large share of the hub caps, trim, wheel covers, and bumper guards were produced for two automobile manufacturers. All items produced by the company were sold in the replacement market through garages, service stations, and automobile parts chain stores, and, in some areas, through department stores. The company maintained five warehouses in various parts of the United States and one in Toronto, Ontario. Company salesmen, employed on a salary and commission basis, served jobbers, wholesalers, and department stores. Sales to automobile manufacturers and chain stores were usually handled by the president or vice-president of the firm. Several of the items, such as hub caps, wheel covers, trim, and bumper guards, required a new design each year as automobile models changed. Other items in the line were not modified so frequently.

In the decade following the close of World War II the company had expanded with the growth of automobile production. In the period immediately following the war, replacement demand had been rather heavy; but as new cars became more available, replacement demand declined noticeably. To a large extent, this was offset by increasing demand for those items sold to automobile manufacturers. The Korean War restricted supply on some items, such as trim, hub caps, and wheel covers. In 1955 the automobile industry had its largest year since 1950.

With the decline in replacement demand, price competition among the items in these lines increased. Further decline in demand was anticipated in this market. Furthermore, the forecast for new-car production in 1956 was about 1 million units less than in 1955. The greatest competition in the replacement market was appearing in hub caps and wheel covers. The automobile parts chain stores were the largest single customers for these items other than the automobile manufacturers. The items were sold in case lots, consisting of five dozen to the case. Each was marked with the brand name of the make of car or bore a design with no name.

Hub caps, until 1955, had sold at $28.75 per case, while wheel covers were priced at $67.50 per case. In May, 1955, to meet competition, prices were reduced to $25.50 and $61.50 per case, respectively. In October, 1955, the president of the company, Mr. Wallace, began negotiations with one of the larger automobile parts chain stores on several items. On one item, wheel covers, he learned that a competitor had offered a price of $49.75 per case. Mr. Wallace met the price and obtained the order for 1,125 cases of wheel covers. Upon his return to Kansas City, he learned from other sources that some competitors were offering even lower prices. He called a meeting with Mr. Kemp, the sales manager, Mr. Waxman, the production manager, and Mr. Ollen, the controller, to discuss price policy on wheel covers.

Exhibit 1 shows the cost of producing wheel covers per case. This item passed through six departments in process of manufacture: stamping, welding, buffing, painting, polishing, and packing. Total sales in 1954 were 14,176 cases, of which 6,731 were in the replacement market. In view of the competitive situation, Mr. Kemp believed that in order to maintain sales in the replacement market, the company would have to offer a price of $47.50 per case. If the price were kept at $61.50, he estimated 1956 replacement sales would be approximately 5,000 cases. If the price were lowered to $42.50, he estimated replacement sales at 7,500 cases. Mr. Waxman said that he could not produce the covers at costs any lower than shown in Exhibit 1. Mr. Ollen recommended that the line be discontinued if the price were less than $61.50, since it would involve the company in further losses. He pointed out that on the basis of the costs shown in Exhibit 1, the price Mr. Wallace quoted to the chain would result in a loss. He suggested that the line of wheel covers be dropped immediately and that efforts be devoted toward the development of a product which would be more profitable. Mr. Wallace pointed out

Exhibit 1

STANDARD COSTS, CHROME-PLATE WHEEL COVERS, PER CASE

Material*...	$16.61
Direct labor...	19.52
Packaging and crating...	1.14
Equipment repairs..	0.71
Depreciation..	1.37
Indirect labor†...	6.26
Factory overhead‡..	4.89
Administrative and selling costs§..............................	2.93
	$53.43

* Steel prices were expected to rise 5–10 per cent as a result of a new wage agreement in the steel industry.
† Allocated on the basis of 30 per cent of direct labor.
‡ Allocated on the basis of 25 per cent of direct labor.
§ Allocated on the basis of 15 per cent of direct labor.

that the development of a new product which could be produced with the same equipment would probably require many months. He further stated that the decline in sales of new cars would result in an improvement in replacement sales within a year or two.

QUESTIONS

1. Was Mr. Wallace wise in meeting the competitive price of $49.75 per case? Explain.
2. In view of Mr. Kemp's sales estimates, which price would you find most profitable? Why?
3. Do you agree with Mr. Ollen that the line should be dropped immediately? Why?
4. What effect will the anticipated rise in the price of steel have upon prices in the short run? In the long run?

CASE 4–4: DRYBAK CORPORATION

The Drybak Corporation manufactured men's trousers, coats, and vests for hunting, work, and other uses. Its production was about equally divided between goods made for stock and those made to order for customers. Its output included about 250 different items, but constant changes in design meant that the line as a whole was continuously shifting. Individual production orders were small; and at any one time, there were many different orders in process. For this reason the company used the job-lot method of manufacturing. The company operated only one plant, which normally required a force of 350 employees.[25]

Originally, the company used a costing system which accumulated historical costs by job orders. Subsequently, it developed a standard cost system for purposes of pricing, production planning, cost control, budgeting, and valuation of inventory. The latter system had been developed gradually over a period of fourteen years.

The standard costs were based on an analysis of material requirements, labor operations performed, and the overhead applicable. Since the garments to be made for any one order usually differed in some respects from any made previously, a different combination and sequence of manufacturing operations were required for each product. But these processes were widely used in many types of garment manufacture, and the operating characteristics of the equipment used were known. Consequently, it was usually possible to set reliable costs, based on past experience, for the particular combination of operations involved in making any specific garment.

In determining standard costs for a garment, the company based its calculations on an average size. Thus, coats ranging in size from 37 to 49 would have a standard cost based on the average size, which might be Size 43. Variations in costs might occur on individual orders because of a heavier demand for larger or smaller sizes, but in the long run the company believed these variations would average out.

When the company received an order, the manufacturing data sheet (Exhibit 1), based on a dozen garments, was made up. The description and the material quantity standards were shown on the front of the sheet, and on the back were listed the operations to be performed and the standard allowed hours required. The information on this sheet was then carried over to the standard cost record sheet (Exhibit 2), on which the standard cost was developed by costing the materials and labor at standard rates.

The material quantity standards for the major materials of the garment were determined by the use of templets or patterns designed for the average size chosen. These templets were arranged to give the best usage of the material, and the standard yardage was determined

[25] This case is adapted from the *N.A.C.A. Bulletin*, Vol. XXX (December 15, 1948) (Research Series No. 15, "A Standard Cost Case Study").

Exhibit 1

MANUFACTURING DATA SHEET

COATS   LOT NO.

MANUFACTURING DATA SHEET

COAT DESCRIPTION Hunting		DATE		PCD.	PATTERN NO.

Regular corduroy

4 Buttons - setting on face

Plain shoulders

Hinge adjustable - W/B and B Hole

2 Stitch down muff pockets

COLLAR	4501
UNDER COLLAR	
FRONT	5016
FRONT FACING	
BACK	6091
SLEEVE	7350
POCKET	8540
POCKET	
POCKET	
POCKET	
FLAPS	
FLAPS	
FLAPS	
FLAP LINING	
FLAP LINING	
FLAP LINING	
CUFFS	
CUFF LINING	
SLEEVE LINING	
BODY LINING	
SHO. PADS	
SHELL LOOPS	
GAME PRT.	
ENT. FLAPS	
ENT. LININGS	

BARTACKS

CODE NO.	MATERIALS	WIDTH	QUANTITY	CODE NO.	MATERIALS	UNIT	QUANTITY
23	11 oz. Army Duck	40"	40	610	Size ticket	M	12
					36/E Br. buttons	G	108

OUR NO.	CUSTOMER	LOT NO.	LABELS	PACKAGING	P.R. CHANGES

Reproduced by permission of the National Association of Cost Accountants.

from these areas plus an allowance for end pieces and lappings.[26] Standard quantities for the miscellaneous items of material, such as buttons, zippers, tags, purchased pockets, etc., were obtained by inspection of the garment.[27] The standard material quantities were transferred from the manufacturing data sheet to the standard cost sheet (Exhibit 2), where they were multiplied by standard prices. Standard

[26] This standard is shown on the lower left-hand side of Exhibit 1.

[27] These were listed on the lower right-hand side of the data sheet (Exhibit 1).

Exhibit 2

STANDARD COST RECORD SHEET

STANDARD COST RECORD									
DESCRIPTION				**DATE**		**CUSTOMER**		**STYLE NO.**	
Hunting Coat				**SIZE SCALE** 37-49		**SIMILAR TO**		**CODE NO.**	
DIRECT MATERIALS				**STANDARD COST PER DOZ.**		**ESTIMATED**		**ESTIMATED**	
CODE	DESCRIPTION	WIDTH	QUANTITY	PRICE	EXTENSION	PRICE	EXTENSION	PRICE	EXTENSION
	BODY MATERIALS			$	$	$	$	$	$
23	11 oz. Army Duck	40"	40	0.65	26.00				
	TOTAL				26.00				
	TRIM	UNIT							
610	Thread				0.93				
610	Size Ticket	M	12	0.80	0.01				
420	36/E Br. Buttons	G	108	0.60	0.45				
	TOTAL				4.00				
	TOTAL MATERIALS				30.00				
	TRANSPORTATION IN			%		%		%	
	LABOR & EXPENSE	COST CENTER	RATE	SAN	EXTENSION	SAN	EXTENSION	SAN	EXTENSION
	CUTTING		2.00	1.00	2.00		$		$
	SEWING	51	1.50	12.00	18.00				
	INSPECTION		1.50	0.50	0.75				
	TOTAL LABOR & EXPENSE				20.75				
	STANDARD MANUFACTURING COST				50.75				
	ADMINISTRATION SELLING - CHAIN - JOBBER - RETAIL								
	PROFIT & LOSS				9.00				
	TOTAL STANDARD COST				59.75				
	COMMISSION % DISCOUNT % MARK-UP % STANDARD SELLING PRICE				5.30 65.05				

Reproduced by permission of the National Association of Cost Accountants.

material prices were determined by an annual forecast of the cost of material to be purchased, tempered by the inventory on hand at the time that the forecast was made.

The labor operations to be performed on the garment were determined by careful analysis of the laying-out of templets, the material cutting and trimming, and the sewing, pressing, inspecting, etc.

By studying these operations in the light of recorded motion and time study data, standard times could be determined and entered on the standard cost record sheet. Standards set by this method for pricing purposes were temporary but were used until additional orders were received. Then they were revised by a study of the actual time on the previous order.

Operation time standards were summarized in standard hours for each of three departments: cutting, sewing, and inspection. The time to process a dozen garments of the specified design in each department was then entered on the standard cost record (Exhibit 2) and multiplied by the standard hourly rate for labor and overhead expense combined. The standard labor rate was the average rate being paid at the time the standard was set.

Standard hourly overhead rates for each department were determined by dividing the standard allowed hours at the practical production capacity[28] of the department into the budgeted overhead expense for the department at capacity. Overhead costs were computed through the use of flexible budgets. The budget for each department contained only those expenses which were controllable by the executive in charge of the department. These expenses were composed principally of labor, machine parts, and materials, which were accounted for as indirect charges to the product but which were directly chargeable to the specific department. These amounts constituted the *departmental* overhead charge.

To the departmental overhead was added prorated general plant overhead. This included such items as power, light, office expense, vacation pay, depreciation, etc. These were separately budgeted.

Finally, selling, administrative, and other expenses were applied to the job, by means of standard rate multiplied by the manufacturing cost. This rate was derived from another flexible budget similar to those for departmental and general overheads. In this budget, sales dollars instead of standard allowed hours were used to measure activity.

The standard cost sheet was completed by adding the markup to the cost to determine the selling price.

QUESTIONS

1. Discuss the conditions which might make standard costs depart from "actual" unit costs of any one order.
2. As a basis for pricing, would the standard cost system of the Drybak Corporation be more satisfactory in periods when there were large backlogs

---

[28] That is, the total number of hours which *could* be worked by the department in a given period if there were enough orders to keep it busy.

of unfilled orders or in periods when the plant was operating at less than full capacity?

CASE 4–5: WARING GOLF AND COUNTRY CLUB

The Waring Golf Club was organized in 1929 to operate a public golf links. Its facilities included an eighteen-hole golf course, a riding academy run by a concessionaire, and 150 acres of woodland, which had been developed with bridle paths. The owners of the Waring Club entrusted the actual operation of the enterprise to a hired manager.

The club was located at the eastern edge of an industrial community of 250,000 population, about 1,000 feet beyond the city limits, and was easily accessible by both automobile and public transportation. The city parks department operated two municipally owned golf links, which were fairly well maintained but which were constantly overcrowded. There was a golf links open to the public 4 miles north of the city, one 2 miles west, another 9 miles south, and still another whose entrance was approximately 1,500 feet distant from that of the Waring Club. At some points, this latter club was separated from the Waring Club only by a county highway. The adjoining club, which had been in operation since 1924, offered, in addition to a public gold links, dining and dancing facilities, winter sports such as skating and skiing, and—in good weather—tennis. Patrons of the adjoining club were drawn primarily from professional and middle-income white-collar groups.

The owners of the Waring Club believed there was a good business opportunity in providing golf facilities for industrial workers and lower-income white-collar groups. They believed it was not to their advantage to compete directly with the adjoining club. A preliminary survey convinced them that the provision of good-quality golf facilities for this group at moderate rates not only would draw players from the municipal links and from more distant links but also would reach persons who were not now playing because of lack of facilities at moderate prices. Rates for the Waring Club and the adjoining club in the summer of 1929 were as shown in Exhibit 1. Fees for the Waring Club were for the entire day, with no limit to number of holes played. Fees for the adjoining club were for eighteen holes, with additional fees for further play.

The rates for the Waring Club remained in effect until July, 1933, when they were reduced by 15 cents in each classification. This change in rates was prompted by a decrease in the number of players, as shown in Exhibit 2. The decline in income following the crisis of 1929 had not seriously affected the Waring Club until 1933. In April of that year the fees on the municipal links, which were already lower than Waring's rates, were decreased still further, in spite of the fact that the links were heavily used. The club adjoining Waring

Exhibit 1

RATES, WARING CLUB AND ADJOINING CLUB

Time	Waring Club	Adjoining Club
Weekdays (until 5 P.M.) and Saturday mornings....	$0.50	$0.75
Weekdays after 5 P.M.............................	0.50	1.00
Saturdays after 1 P.M............................	0.75	1.25
Sundays until 1 P.M..............................	1.00	1.50
Sundays after 1 P.M..............................	0.75	1.00

had reduced its rates approximately 10 per cent on June 1, 1933. After the reduction in rates in July, 1933, growth in the Waring Club's business continued as before. The rates were restored to their original level in April, 1937.

In May, 1937, the manager of the Waring Club noted that the club's facilities were not being fully used at all hours of the day. The

Exhibit 2

WARING GOLF AND COUNTRY CLUB,
NUMBER OF PLAYERS BY MONTHS, 1929–36

Month	1929	1930	1931	1932	1933	1934	1935	1936
April........	257	211	403	527	297	487	593	521
May.........	781	943	1,091	981	891	1,001	1,457	1,875
June.........	1,254	1,652	2,057	1,649	982	1,895	2,581	2,643
July.........	1,209	2,147	2,612	2,004	2,493	2,569	2,957	3,102
August.......	1,057	1,822	2,561	1,823	2,291	2,542	2,900	2,989
September....	995	1,565	2,219	1,251	2,273	2,114	2,542	2,659
October......	886	1,204	1,533	729	2,051	2,027	2,083	1,921
November....	218	761	644	453	519	652	1,104	925

bulk of the players on weekdays appeared after 5 P.M. The average number of players per day during July and August, 1936, was as shown in Exhibit 3.

Increased industrial activity led the manager to propose that the club offer group rates to various enterprises employing large numbers of workers. Under these group rates, employees of the participating companies would use the golf course, or at least begin their play, before 5 P.M. each day except Saturdays and Sundays, when no players on group rates would be accepted. It was the manager's belief that an influx of players on a weekday as a group playing a tournament would not greatly reduce the number of players at regular rates on Saturdays and Sundays, when most players formed their own personal groups.

One company which the manager had approached tentatively agreed to guarantee a minimum of 100 players each Tuesday, under the

Exhibit 3
NUMBER OF PLAYERS PER DAY, JULY–AUGUST, 1936

Day	Before 5 P.M.	After 5 P.M.	Total
Monday	10	30	40
Tuesday	20	50	70
Wednesday	25	65	90
Thursday	15	35	50
Friday	10	50	60
Saturday	135	15	150
Sunday	245	5	250

conditions offered, provided that the rate was not more than 15 cents per player. The owners were not certain whether it was desirable to accept this proposal. One director, after inspecting the operating costs shown in Exhibit 4, objected to a rate of 15 cents and proposed, instead, a rate of 25 cents. The manager pointed out that the facilities were capable of handling an additional 200 players per day without

Exhibit 4
AVERAGE COST PER PLAYER, 1935–36

Depreciation (buildings, machinery, etc.)	$0.0527
Labor (5 maintenance employees)	0.0833
Labor (golf professional, mechanics, administrative)	0.0151
Taxes and insurance (property, compensation, liability)	0.0092
Material and supplies (including water)	0.0517
Occasional labor	0.0017
Total	$0.2137

any changes except the hiring of an additional starter on Tuesdays. The daily rate for a starter was $2.00. After some debate the owners concluded a group contract with the industrial company at a rate of 15 cents per player.

Not long afterward, four other companies indicated a willingness to sign similar group contracts for other days of the week, but at a rate of 10 cents per player. Each of these proposed contracts would provide a minimum guarantee of 150 players.

The manager believed that, when the average number of players using the course rose much above 1,000 per week, an additional full-time maintenance worker would be required, and that additional expenses for materials and supplies would be encountered. He estimated these additional expenses at $55 per week.

QUESTIONS

1. Was the director justified in objecting to a rate of 15 cents per player for the group contract accepted by the Waring Club?
2. Should the owners have entered into additional group contracts with the four other companies at 10 cents per player?
3. If competing clubs reduced *regular* weekday rates to 15 cents, could the Waring Golf Club profitably accept *regular* business at this price?

Chapter 5

LONG-RUN COST OF PRODUCTION

PART I. THEORETICAL CONSIDERATIONS

MOST FIRMS are regularly confronted with the problem of whether to change the short-run rate of output of the commodities which they handle. For the manufacturing firm the meaning of "changing the rate of output" is quite clear. In the case of wholesalers and retailers the concept is less obvious, especially because such firms are almost invariably multiple-product firms, and because the notion of "output" is somewhat vague. If a retailer adds clerks to his staff within a given store, it is clear that he has made a short-run adjustment. If he adds a new line of canned goods or drops an item previously carried, he is similarly making a short-run change if the adjustment does not require an addition to, or subtraction from, the amount of fixed capital which he has invested in his store. If, however, he is forced to increase this investment in order to accommodate added personnel or merchandise, his action is "long run" in nature. While an aggressive enterpriser is likely to give thought quite often to the profit possibilities which might be open through expansion of his scale of activity, actual implementation of long-run plans is more difficult than that of short-run desires because such matters as additional financing, construction, product alterations, and new advertising are usually involved.

Economic theory considers long-run changes to consist primarily of changes in the amount of plant capacity. Such adjustments are then considered to carry along with them the necessary increases or decreases in such variable inputs as labor, materials, fuel, and supplies. In practice, it is often necessary that additional executive talent be hired when plant capacity is expanded. And occasionally, it is necessary to replace most of the top executives of a corporation in order to make a substantial change in the nature of the operations.

The Long-Run Cost Curve

It is useful to think of long-run cost curves as "planning curves" for plant and firm size. That is, they are useful as planning devices rather than in an operating sense, since output which is actually produced is turned out with some particular scale of plant (operated at some short-run rate). The long-run cost curve, to the extent that its form is known to the businessman, is useful in helping him plan the best scale of plant, or the best size of firm, for his purposes. If he anticipates that sales will be sufficient to justify that amount of investment, and if he is able to raise the necessary capital, the entrepreneur will want to build plants of a size which will minimize average production costs. If he cannot secure the needed capital or does not anticipate sufficient demand, he will settle for smaller-scale operations.

Exhibit 1

SHORT-RUN AVERAGE COST FROM A PLANNING VIEWPOINT—
COST DEPENDS ON SCALE OF OPERATIONS

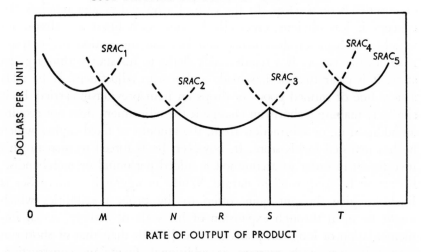

The relation between short-run average cost curves for plants of various sizes and long-run average cost can be seen in Exhibit 1. Only five alternative sizes of plant are assumed to be technically possible due, for example, to the need to use some type of machine which is available only in one (large) size. The five possible plants may be assumed to utilize one to five of these indivisible units of equipment. If the anticipated rate of output during the life of the plant is less than OM, it will be most economical to have the smallest-size plant (for which $SRAC_1$ is the expected short-run average cost curve). If the expected output rate is just a little more than OM, it would be possible to use the smallest-size plant; but the next larger-size plant, utilized at a relatively low rate, would give lower average cost. If anticipated output is between ON and OS, it will be desirable to build a plant of "optimum" size, associated with curve $SRAC_3$. A larger plant may encounter problems of co-ordination which will increase average costs. It is easy to conceive of a food-retailing store, for example, which is so large that clerks and customers would have to spend an undue amount of time in stocking shelves and finding items. A manufacturing plant may be so large as to create unusually severe automobile, truck, and railroad congestion. Curves $SRAC_4$ and $SRAC_5$ reflect the diseconomy of having excessively large plants. The

Exhibit 2

LONG-RUN AVERAGE COST—WITH COMPLETE DIVISIBILITY

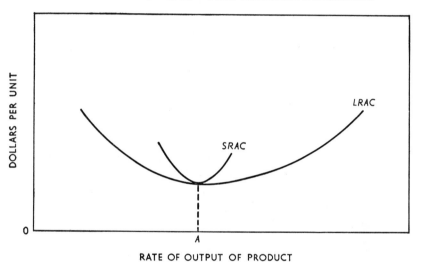

problem of high costs due to undersized plants which are unable to make sufficient use of some types of specialized machinery, skilled management, and optimal organization of processes is in practice, however, much more common than that of the plant which is oversized. This is true especially because a shortage of capital funds frequently compels enterprisers to build smaller plants than they would otherwise build.

In drawing Exhibit 1, it was assumed that some sort of indivisibility of equipment permitted the plant to be built in only five alternative sizes. As a consequence, long-run average cost is shown by the wavy solid line in that diagram. However, it may instead be possible to build a plant of any desired size; and the long-run average cost curve then becomes a smooth, saucer-shaped curve, such as $LRAC$ of Exhibit 2. This curve can be conceived of as being the one which is tangent to all of the possible alternative short-run average cost curves when an unlimited number of sizes of plant is technically possible. It touches the *minimum* point of only one of these curves—*SRAC* in Exhibit 2.

Typically, in manufacturing and trade, anticipated sales per period are much greater than *OA,* the rate at which output can be produced at the lowest average cost by building plant to an optimal scale. In this situation a large number of plants, each of the best size, will be built if the situation is properly anticipated. Generally, many firms will participate in the ownership of these plants, but any or all firms may control many plants. If, however, the advantages of large-scale production are such that the output of one plant of efficient size is a large fraction of the sales of the product in the entire market, it is clear that there will be room for only a small number of plants and, consequently, only a small number of companies. A small city usually has only a few brickyards and a few "ten-cent" stores, for example.

An Empirical Study of Scale

This situation is illustrated by an interesting statistical study carried out by a well-known economist.[1] From engineering data the percentage of the national capacity in various industries accounted for by one plant of the most efficient size was estimated. These percentages are shown in Exhibit 3.

It can be seen in Exhibit 3 that an efficient typewriter factory has to include from 10 to 30 per cent of the national capacity for this commodity, while an efficient tractor plant must include 10 to 15 per cent of the total, according to these estimates.[2] This would leave room for approximately 3 to 10 efficient typewriter plants and 7 to 10 tractor plants in the country. Somewhat smaller-scale production in relation to total demand is possible in the industries listed in Category 2. Around 20 efficient plants could exist in each of the following fields: cigarettes, farm machines apart from tractors, soap, and rayon. In flour milling, shoe manufacturing, and canning of fruits and vegetables, the advantages of scale in relation to market are such that 200 to 1,000 plants of efficient size can exist.

---

[1] Joe S. Bain, "Economies of Scale, Concentration, and the Condition of Entry in Twenty Manufacturing Industries," *American Economic Review,* March, 1954, pp. 15–39.

[2] The difficulty of getting unbiased information on this subject should not, however, be underestimated. Personnel connected with industries featuring high concentration of production would be inclined to attempt to justify such concentration as technically necessary.

The same statistical study gives estimated capital requirements for one efficient plant. An automobile plant requires an outlay of between $250 and $500 million; a tractor plant, about $125 million. A steel plant costs $265 to $665 million, while a fountain pen factory runs about $6 million. Shoe factories are relatively cheap—$0.5 to $2 million each. These figures show forcibly why it is so much easier to set

Exhibit 3

SCALE OF EFFICIENT PRODUCTION IN
VARIOUS INDUSTRIES

Industry	Percentage of National Industry Capacity Provided by One Efficient Plant, circa 1951
Category 1:	
Flour milling	$\frac{1}{10}$–$\frac{1}{2}$
Shoes	$\frac{1}{7}$–$\frac{1}{2}$
Canned fruits and vegetables	$\frac{1}{4}$–$\frac{1}{2}$
Cement	$\frac{4}{5}$–1
Distilled liquor	$1\frac{1}{4}$–$1\frac{3}{4}$
Petroleum refining	$1\frac{3}{4}$
Meat packing, fresh	$\frac{1}{50}$–$\frac{1}{8}$
Tires and tubes	3
Category 2:	
Steel	1–$2\frac{1}{2}$
Metal containers	$\frac{1}{2}$–3
Rayon	4–6
Soap	4–6
Farm machines, except tractors	4–6
Cigarettes	5–6
Category 3:	
Gypsum products	$2\frac{1}{2}$–3
Automobiles	5–10
Fountain pens	5–10
Copper	10
Tractors	10–15
Typewriters	10–30

Source: Joe S. Bain, "Economies of Scale, Concentration, and the Condition of Entry in Twenty Manufacturing Industries," *American Economic Review*, March, 1954, p. 36.

up such businesses as filling stations, plants for production of concrete block, repair shops, and haberdasheries than to enter the industries covered by the survey. An exception among the listed industries was meat packing, where capital requirements for an efficient plant were reported as "very small."

Flexibility of Plant

From a planning viewpoint the plant associated with curve *SRAC* in Exhibit 2 is the one which is constructed to such a size as to take full advantage of the "economies of scale" without being so large as to encounter diseconomies. Exhibit 2 is drawn on the assumption that the planner can anticipate with complete certainty the output rate at which he will want to operate the plant over its useful life. Actually, there may be considerable uncertainty in the planner's mind as to the rate at which he will subsequently find it desirable to operate. As a type of hedge against this uncertainty, he may decide to build a plant which incorporates more "flexibility," in the sense that it can be operated at nonoptimum rates of output without greatly increasing the short-run average cost. Hedging usually involves cost,

Exhibit 4

BUILT-IN FLEXIBILITY—A HEDGE AGAINST UNCERTAINTY

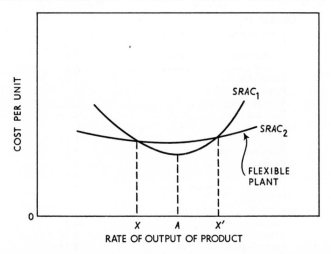

however, and in this case the building of a more flexible plant is likely to mean that minimum average cost will be higher than if the output rate could be perfectly foreseen and the plant designed specifically for that rate.

The meaning of building flexibility into a plant is illustrated graphically in Exhibit 4. $SRAC_1$ is the short-run cost curve applicable to a plant of optimum size built specifically to operate at the least-cost output rate OA. The other curve, $SRAC_2$, is associated with a plant of about the same size which has been built to give more flexibility of operation in the sense that nonoptimum outputs can be turned out without greatly increasing the average cost. At outputs below OX and above OX' the more flexible plant can be operated more cheaply. At outputs between X and X', however, the less flexible plant operates more economically. If the planner expects with sufficient confidence that it will usually be desirable to operate between X and X', he will prefer the plant associated with $SRAC_1$. If he believes output will fluctuate sharply from period to period, or if he is highly uncertain as to what output rates will prove consistent with demand, he may decide in favor of the more flexible setup.

Flexibility of operation may be attained by making the plant highly divisible. As pointed out in Chapter 3, a divisible plant may contain a large number of identical machines. In order to reduce output, a smaller number of machines is used, but each of these can be operated efficiently. If the plant had only one or a few machines, a reduction in the rate of output would probably raise unit cost more sharply, as in $SRAC_1$. Flexibility can also be obtained by some substitution of labor for capital equipment. If the ratio of labor to capital is kept relatively high, a reduction in output can be effected without much increase in average cost by laying off workers or reducing hours of employment. (A machine which is owned or rented by the firm on a long-term contract canot be "laid off" in order to reduce fixed costs.) To the extent that guaranteed wage plans are put into effect, however, the achievement of flexibility through the maintenance of a high ratio of labor to equipment is less feasible.

Size of Firm and Cost

The "planning curves" shown in Exhibit 1 pertain to the variation in average costs as the scale of plant is altered. If the firm has only one plant, and if most of its costs are production costs, the best size of firm will be governed almost entirely by the optimum size of plant. If the firm is a multiplant organization, its optimum size may have little relation to the optimum scale of plant. (Large food-retailing companies, for example, are probably somewhat more efficient than smaller firms in this field, although individual plants [stores] are of moderate size.)

It may be necessary for a firm to be large in order to secure the efficient operation of its plants when the efficiency of each plant is related to the operation of the others. This seems to be the situation in the interstate bus business, for example, where plants (buses and terminals) are small, but where a large number of buses is needed in order to maintain regular schedules and where the terminals must be numerous if adequate common carrier service is to be furnished. Up to a point, at least, a larger firm enjoys advantages in raising capital, in purchasing, in carrying on research, and in selling. These activities require for their most efficient performance certain specialized personnel, equipment, or procedures which a small firm may be unable to afford. (The possibility of hiring the services of experts who also serve other firms somewhat reduces the diseconomy of small size, however.) A large, integrated firm—one which owns plants at different stages in the production process—will probably have lower costs than a nonintegrated company if there is an important degree of monopoly power at some of the earlier stages, since integration will make it possible to avoid paying monopolistic prices for materials. Unless the firm uses enough materials to make possible their production on an optimum scale, however, integration may be unprofitable. Use of part of the output and sale of the rest may afford the integrated firm a chance both to avoid high-priced materials and components, and to secure an adequate scale of output at all levels.

Most economists believe that a firm, as well as a plant, may be too large, as well as too small. This makes a saucer-shaped, long-run average cost curve appropriate for the firm also. The diseconomy from excessive size is usually considered to arise from the managerial problem of guiding very large operations efficiently. Considerable authority must be delegated to the various branches in order that they may carry on their part effectively. The central management must, however, keep close track of many activities, and this means a great deal of paper work and duplicate record keeping as well as expenditure of time and money on conferences between company officials. In a large company, it may be difficult to find the degree of delegation of authority which is optimal in that it permits adequate leeway to subordinate officials, without so much leeway that operations within the firm become poorly co-ordinated.

An advantage of large size from a private—but not from a social—point of view may consist in the monopoly power thereby secured by the firm. This power may make it possible for the firm both to charge prices for output in excess of those that could be charged under competitive conditions and to pay lower prices for certain inputs than could be obtained with thoroughgoing competition in effect. Monopoly in the purchase of inputs is frequently called "monopsony" by economists. A firm may have monopoly power in the sale of output at the same time that it purchases in fully competitive markets. Or it may have monopsony power while it lacks monopoly power. In general, however, large size is conducive to both. The effect of the exercise of monopsony power is a lowering of costs, while monopoly is profitable because it permits the establishment of a more favorable relation between price and cost.

PART II. STATISTICAL STUDY OF COST

The following excerpts are derived from a case study of a retail shoe chain by Joel Dean and R. Warren James.[3] They illustrate an interesting attempt to determine the nature of long-run costs by means of statistical investigation of a group of retail shoestores. This sort of analysis parallels the statistical measurement of demand as an attempt to give empirical content to economic theories.

A. Nature of the Sample

From the several hundred stores operated by the parent shoe corporation, a sample of 55 stores was selected for the purposes of this analysis. Annual data on the retail operations of each store were made available for the two years 1937 and 1938.[4] The sample of stores was selected in such a way as to provide a fairly uniform coverage of various operating conditions. An attempt was made, therefore, to choose a group of stores selling different proportions of the various types of shoes which were, at the same time, representative of the sales volume of the stores in the chain as a whole.

In order to secure as high a degree of comparability as possible, the sample was further restricted on the basis of the following considerations. First, only those stores situated in the metropolitan area of a large city were included. It was thus possible to minimize regional variations in wages, rentals, and public-utility rates. Moreover, since this area is under the control of one supervisor, differences in managerial efficiency attributable to supervisory skill were eliminated. Second, although the parent shoe corporation operates several shoe chains, each of a different price class, stores from only one of these chains were included in this sample, in order to obtain the homogeneity of sales service associated with uniformity of selling price. Third, the sample was restricted to those stores selling men's, boys', and girls' shoes only, stores selling women's shoes being excluded. Fourth, stores recently opened were excluded from the sample, on the grounds that they might exhibit marked peculiarities because of immaturity. "Immaturity" in this case signifies not only that systematic underutilization may exist but also that sufficient time has not

---

[3] *The Long-Run Behavior of Costs in a Chain of Shoe Stores: A Statistical Analysis* (University of Chicago Studies in Business Administration, Vol. XII, No. 3) (Chicago: University of Chicago Press, 1942).

[4] These two years were selected both because of their recency and because of their occurrence in markedly different phases of the business cycle.

elapsed to allow the store to adapt its merchandise to the special characteristics of its market. Fifth, some attempt was made to select the sample on the basis of a uniform time distribution of sales, but it cannot be claimed that this was rewarded with any success.

. . . .

As far as the factor market which confronts the firm is concerned, it appears that the demand of the individual stores is such a small proportion of the total that the prices of input factors are independent of the action of the individual store. Even though there is centralized purchasing by the shoe corporation of some supplies, and some centralized hiring, which may affect factor prices, the influence of any one store can be neglected.

B. The Measurement of Size

The concept of the size of the individual firm is not a simple one. Size, however measured, cannot be dissociated from capacity in some sense. It is necessary to make a primary distinction between "technical" and "economic" capacity. Technical capacity refers to a maximum rate of operations, an upper limit set by the technical character of the plant and equipment. Economic capacity, on the other hand, refers to some rate of operations which is optimal from the point of view of cost—i.e., the rate at which average cost is a minimum. "Normal" capacity, in addition, may refer to some average or modal rate of operations which is not associated with either technical or economic capacity.[5]

Of the many size concepts possible, it is necessary to select one which is practically measurable, which is relevant to cost, and which at the same time permits comparisons of the sizes of different firms. There are available several concepts of size which can be measured and which are not without significance for cost. The choice can be narrowed to the following three types of measure: (1) physical size of plant and equipment, (2) input capacity, and (3) output capacity.

1. *The Amount of Fixed Equipment.* Size may refer to the aggregate of productive resources that are not alterable in the "short run." The amount of fixed equipment, however, is difficult to measure in terms that permit interfirm comparison, unless the equipment is highly standardized and in homogeneous units. If equipment is standardized, significant aspects of size for comparative purposes could be obtained —for example, by counting the number of spindles in a cotton mill,

---

[5] E.g., in Chamberlin's treatment of the individual firm under monopolistic competition, output is established at some level less than the "economic" capacity.

the number of beds in a hospital, the number of knitting machines in a hosiery mill, or some such similar units.[6] In the case of shoe-stores, one can obtain physical measures of plant size from the number of seats in a store, the area of floor space, or the number of standard lighting units (if electrical fixtures are sufficiently standard-ized). All these measures are subject to such a high degree of acci-dental variation, however, that none of them gives a trustworthy meas-ure of size which permits interstore comparability.

2. *Input Capacity.* It may be possible in some instances to devise a measure of size based on input capacity. A commonly used index of size is the number of employees in an enterprise (in census classifications, for example). Raw-material inputs may also serve this purpose—for example, the crude-oil input of a refinery, the size of the charge of a blast furnace, or the number of tons of ore per day a crushing machine can handle. It may, however, often be extremely difficult to select from the complex of inputs that aspect which is most relevant. Especially when human services are involved, the concept of input capacity lacks the precision which is desirable when measure-ment is required. In the case of retailing, where the dominant input is labor service, measurement presents special difficulties, so that input measures were rejected as a possible index of size.

3. *Output Capacity.* Another alternative is to look on the size of a firm as defined by its output. Here again, however, some important difficulties are encountered. First, when output consists of variegated products, a complex measurement problem is introduced.[7] It may, therefore, be necessary to employ index numbers to deal with cases of multiple products. Second, it is necessary in this case, as well as in the case of input capacity, to distinguish whether output represents the maximum possible rate of production, the optimum rate (for a given body of fixed plant), or some modal rate. In one of these cases the measure of size by output is clearly superior to any other. This occurs under the circumstances in which each output is produced at the minimum total cost for that output. Here, there is a one-to-one correspondence between output and size, although it is true that this case may represent idealized behavior. Despite the fact that firms rarely operate under these minimum-cost conditions, the use of actual

[6] The use of value measures, while it has the advantage of comparing heterogeneous physical units, raises complex problems of valuation which need not be considered here.

[7] The superiority of an input measure arises when the degree of input homogeneity is greater than the degree of output homogeneity—e.g., in oil refining, it is simpler to use the input of crude oil rather than the complex of end products.

output as representative of size is the most satisfactory measurement device obtainable.

The next question to be considered is the information which is available concerning the output of the shoestores. The total sales of each retail outlet in the sample are composed of the following types of merchandise: (a) men's shoes; (b) boys' shoes; (c) girls' shoes; (d) hosiery (men's, boys', and girls'); (e) rubbers; and (f) sundries. These categories are self-explanatory except for sundries, which include bedroom slippers, shoelaces, shoe polish, and other small accessories. The dollar volume of sales of each category was available for 1937 and 1938, and information concerning the physical volume of sales of men's and children's shoes was also provided.[8] The assortment of shoe styles stocked differed somewhat from store to store, but information concerning the composition of shoe sales with respect to the various types and styles was not available.[9]

With this information at hand, the next step was to derive from it some satisfactory index of output. Retail selling output is best considered as the production of sales service. Sales service is the contribution of the shoe salesman to the prospective purchaser in the form of help, advice, and expert knowledge. Without too much violence to the facts, this sales service can be treated as a homogeneous product. Although the quantity and quality of sales service per transaction may differ somewhat from type to type, from style to style, from store to store, and from time to time in the same store, the variability of sales service is nevertheless limited. There are several influences making for uniformity of service standards. For example, all the stores in the sample are in one city, are under the same supervisor, and have standardized recruiting and training policies. Moreover, the employment of extra salesmen drawn from a trained reserve force tends to prevent serious impairment of service standards during rush periods. Since marked deterioration of service would result in loss of customer goodwill and patronage, it may be presumed that, with good management, efforts will be made to confine variations in service quality within narrow limits. The assumption is probably correct that the intangible output of sales service is highly correlated with some aspect

---

[8] The lack of data concerning the physical volume of sales of hosiery, rubbers, and sundries constituted an important gap in the data, which prevented examination of the effect on cost behavior of varying the proportion of total *physical* sales composed of these miscellaneous items.

[9] Since the styles and sizes stocked were adapted to the peculiarities of the individual store's clientele within the limits of the standard styles carried by the chain, it appeared unlikely that important heterogeneity in the sales-service unit resulted from the relatively minor store-to-store variations in assortment of styles.

of retail transactions which is capable of measurement. The immediate problem is to select some one composite measure of the volume of shoe sales, in either physical or value terms, which will most reliably reflect output in terms of sales service.

. . . .

Despite the omission of sundry sales, it was decided to employ number of pairs of shoes sold, including both men's and children's shoes, as the best available index of output. This choice was made on grounds of convenience and because a more satisfactory measure was lacking.

. . . .

C. The Measurement of Cost

The primary cost data made available by the shoe corporation show the details of the annual expenditures of each store in the sample. The total operating cost is broken down into 23 accounts, for each of which the annual total is known for the two years 1937 and 1938.

Two of the elements of cost listed deserve special mention, however. These are general indirect expense (which is an allocation to each store of its share of the expenses of the chain as a whole which cannot be accurately charged to one account) and administrative expense (which is the share of the corporation's central administrative expenses charged to each store). In view of the arbitrary method of allocation, it was considered that the inclusion of these two elements might obscure the relations which it was desired to investigate. Consequently, in the calculation of operating cost, these two elements were omitted.

In order to obtain an insight into the behavior of broader categories of cost, the elements of cost were classified into the following groups:

1. Selling expense
    a) Salaries
    b) Reserve salaries
    c) Employees' discount
    d) Hosiery award
    e) Shoe bonus
    f) Advertising
    g) Taxes
2. Handling expense
    h) Delivery (including inbound, outbound, and interstore)
    i) Insurance
    j) Postage

k) Supplies
l) Miscellaneous
3. Building expense
   m) Rent
   n) Light
   o) Heat
   p) Window display[10]
   q) Repairs
   r) Depreciation
   s) Water, ice

. . . .

D. Statistical Findings

As pointed out already, a separate analysis of the relation of cost to input in the 55 shoestores was undertaken for each of the years 1937 and 1938. This was advisable not only because of the lack of precise comparability in the data for the two years but also because of the additional confirmation that would be afforded by agreement in the two sets of results. Preliminary examination of the relation between cost and output indicated that the pattern of cost behavior was essentially the same in both years.

This preliminary analysis of the data by means of scatter diagrams showed the observations to be distributed in a fashion which indicated logarithmic dispersion. This was substantiated by the appearance of the scatter diagrams when plotted on double logarithmic paper. Consequently, except in the analysis of average cost behavior, the logarithms of the cost and output variables were employed in the calculations throughout the investigation.

Correlation analysis was used as the basic statistical technique, either linear or curvilinear functions being fitted to the data by the method of least squares. The fitting procedure was carried through, first, for total cost, which is the aggregate of reported expenditures of the store, excluding allocated administrative expense and general indirect expense. Second, the behavior of average cost, derived directly from the data, was examined by means of correlation analysis.

. . . .

1. *Total Cost.* The relation of total cost to physical volume of shoe sales for 1937 and for 1938 is shown in the scatter diagrams in the upper and lower panels of Exhibit 5. A detailed examination

[10] The inclusion of window display under building expense rather than under selling expense may be questioned. It is classed as it is mainly because of its similiarity to interior displays. On the other hand, almost the whole of a store is devoted to display and advertising, so that if the window display were classified as advertising, so should much of the other building expense. Its inclusion in one or the other category is, however, not an important matter.

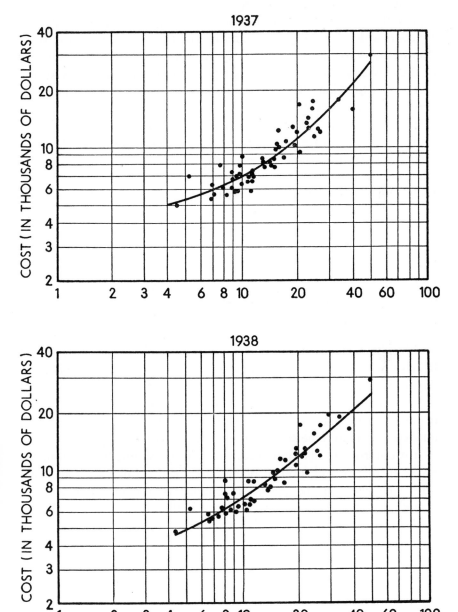

Exhibit 5

SHOESTORE CHAIN

Simple Regressions of Total Cost on Output Measured by Shoe Sales in Pairs

1937

COST (IN THOUSANDS OF DOLLARS)

1938

COST (IN THOUSANDS OF DOLLARS)

OUTPUT (IN THOUSANDS OF PAIRS OF SHOES)

of the position of the individual stores indicated that the relation between cost and output remains fairly stable during these two years.
The principal virtue of logarithmic analysis is that changes in the
magnitude of the logarithms of the variables in which interest lies
represent relative changes in the variables. Consequently, the slope of a
function which is in logarithmic terms gives the elasticity of the function of the variables themselves. From a knowledge of the behavior
of the elasticities, it is immediately possible to deduce the shape of the
cost-output functions. The parabolic shape of the fitted regression lines
shows that the relative change in cost is increasing, compared to the
relative change in output. In other words, since the slope of the regression line is always becoming steeper, the elasticity of total cost is
increasing over the whole range of output. On the basis of this knowledge of the behavior of total cost elasticity, it is easily possible to
translate the relations portrayed on the double logarithmic scatter diagram into arithmetic terms.

For example, in order to analyze the behavior of average cost, it is
necessary only to make use of the proposition that average cost elasticity is equal to total cost elasticity minus one. It is, therefore, apparent that unitary elasticity of total cost corresponds to zero elasticity
of average cost. If total cost elasticity moves from values less than
unity to values greater than unity, it is seen that the corresponding
elasticity of average cost is at first negative, then zero, and finally
positive. This means that the average cost curve displays the familiar
U-shape with a minimum point where average cost elasticity is zero.
An inspection of Exhibit 5 indicates that for both 1937 and 1938
the minimum point of the average cost curve is reached at an output
of approximately 33,000 pairs, since it is at this level of output that
total cost elasticity (the slope of the regression curve) is unity.

It is unfortunate that only three stores in the sample have outputs in
excess of this critical level of operations, for one can, therefore, have
little confidence in the precise magnitude of the optimum rate of
operations. This does not mean, however, that the significant change
in the elasticity of total cost is attributable only to the influence of
the large stores. Even if they are excluded from the analysis, an upward bend occurs in the regression line—in fact, it becomes more
marked, and the parabolic shape of the average cost curve is even
more clearly defined.

There are, indeed, some grounds for the exclusion of the three
largest stores from the sample. Those stores which sell more than
30,000 pairs of shoes annually may have special characteristics which

set them apart from the smaller stores in the sample. The three large stores are located in the downtown area and therefore are faced with selling conditions which are different from those of the stores in the outlying regions. While downtown stores generally have marked daily peak loads at noon and in the late afternoon, peripheral stores are more likely to be subject to heavy peak loads on different days of the week—e.g., Saturdays. This influence, which depends on location, may be sufficient to explain the atypical behavior of these stores. If one could be sure that these stores are not homogeneous, they could be omitted from the analysis altogether. If this were done, there would be stronger confirmation of the existence of an optimum-size shoestore for outlying metropolitan markets. However, since even without the retention of these large stores the existence of an optimum size is clearly shown, it was decided to retain the large stores in the statistical analysis.

. . . .

2. *Average Cost.* Apart from the information concerning average cost derived from the regression functions fitted to the logarithms of the cost and output data, supplementary confirmation was obtained directly by the analysis of average cost behavior. Scatter diagrams were made of average cost per 100 pairs of shoes sold for the two years, the pictorial representation of this being shown in Exhibit 6. Regression functions were also fitted to the average cost data. The scatter of the extreme observations is so wide that the behavior of average cost is not well defined in that region where the optimum output was found to be by other methods. Consequently, the upward trend of average cost is not apparent when the three large stores are excluded.

E. The Nature and Measurement of Retail Output

A primary difficulty is encountered in attempting to define precisely the character of the output of a retail enterprise. The traditional theory of the individual firm considers the output produced by the firm to be units of physical commodities—gallons, bushels, tons, etc.

. . . .

Physically, retail commodities as a rule undergo no change in being placed in the hands of consumers. Therefore, the treatment of production as a physical process of transformation is not appropriate to retail selling. Nevertheless, the retail store makes an essential contribution to the completion of this transformation.

. . . .

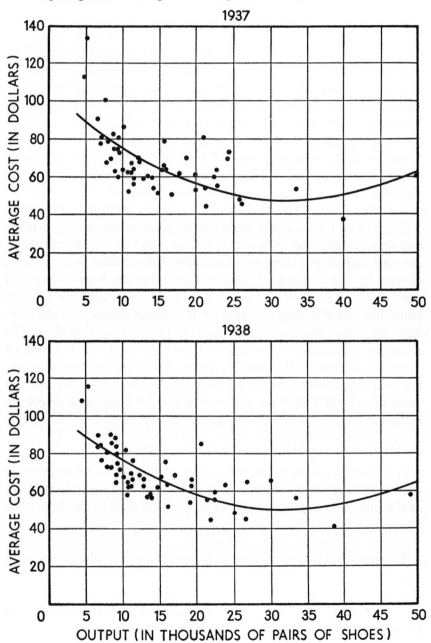

Exhibit 6

SHOESTORE CHAIN

Simple Regression of Average Cost on Output Measured by Shoe Sales in Pairs

The assumption upon which this study is based is that the output of a retail enterprise consists of the services which it renders to purchasers. These services place the physical commodities conveniently at the disposal of the consumer, widen his range of choice, and add to his knowledge of quality, grades, and prices.

. . . .

It is necessary now to consider the assumptions underlying the measurement of size by rate of output and to investigate the bearing of the special features of the type of retail enterprise under discussion on this identification. The simplest case is the representation of size by "normal" or planned output, where the technical equipment of the enterprise is adjusted ideally to the originally planned output. The rate of output is assumed to be uniform and synchronized to a repetitive demand situation for each future period or "week." Moreover, equipment is assumed to be at all times utilized at its planned capacity. This is, however, an idealized case; and some account must be taken of the fact that all firms subject to daily, seasonal, and cyclical fluctuations in demand and using, none the less, equipment which outlasts successive waves of high and low demand, face a recurrent problem of unused capacity. It is not a question of errors of planning in many cases; rather, it is foreseen by the entrepreneur that the existing demand situation gives rise to marked peaks and troughs. It will be essential for the entrepreneur to secure some degree of flexibility in operations.

. . . .

When the extreme variability of output which characterizes retail selling is introduced, there is no longer any clear-cut relation between output and size. Plants will be constructed so that peak loads can be handled in some manner, but it may well be true that under such circumstances the minimum-cost combination cannot be achieved for any output. Rather, the fixed plant may be designed to achieve sufficient flexibility so that it is possible to produce for demand in both the peaks and the troughs. As a result of such an uneven time distribution of demand, therefore, the precise correspondence of output and size which is relevant in the case of uniform and repetitive demand does not exist.

CASE 5–1: EAST-WEST AIR LINES, INC.

In 1947, East-West Air Lines, Inc., was operating a main-line fleet of 22 prewar, twin-engine air liners. With the reduction in air traffic following the war, the company was losing money each month. Mr. Henry L. Avion, president of East-West Air Lines, had had conferences with representatives of the Glenn L. Martin Company, airplane manufacturers, who suggested to him the desirability of replacing the company's main-line fleet of prewar planes with Martin 2–0–2's. The Martin Company claimed that replacement of the old equipment would put East-West in a profit position again.

East-West Air Lines was a domestic carrier, operating passenger planes from Washington and Baltimore to Miami, and westward to New Orleans and Houston. Its three main routes described a triangle, with the northwestern side of the triangle bounded by alternate routes from Houston and New Orleans to Nashville and thence, as one route, to Washington and Baltimore. Feeder lines were maintaineed to deliver traffic to points on the main lines.

The capital structure of the air-line company was considered strong. Adequate financial backing made it possible to add to its capital equipment, either through borrowing or through issuance of additional securities, if that seemed desirable.

The twin-engine air liners averaged 400 miles per trip. Because of the inflexibility of schedules, no change in average trip mileage would be expected even if equipment were replaced. There was also no change anticipated in average numbers of hours of utilization per plane per year; this remained at 3,650. The Martin 2–0–2's, however, were capable of maintaining a cruising speed of 253 miles per hour as against an average speed of 191 miles per hour for the prewar planes. Block speed of the Martins was also higher—219 miles per hour as against 168 for the prewar planes. The Martin air liners seated 36 passengers, while the existing planes seated only 24. As a result of the greater speed and greater seating capacity, therefore, 12 Martin 2–0–2's in the course of a year could produce more passenger seat-miles than could the larger fleet of 22 prewar planes. The estimated capacities of the two types of planes were as follows:

	12 Martin 2–0–2's	22 Prewar Planes
Available seat-miles per year	345,000,000	335,000,000
Seat-miles at 60 per cent load factor	207,000,000	201,000,000

Despite the reduction in number of planes contemplated with the new equipment, improved speed and turnabout time indicated that the same number of flights could be maintained as formerly.

The original cost of East-West Air Lines' prewar air liners was approximately $115,000 per plane, although some were purchased for as much as $125,000. On the accounts of the company, these capital values had been reduced to an average, after depreciation, of $50,000. The new Martin 2–0–2's were available at a capital expenditure of $380,000 per plane. This figure included engines, radio equipment, and other equipment. It was regarded as sound accounting practice to depreciate new airplanes such as the Martin 2–0–2 over a five-year period with a 10 per cent residual. Most air lines with

Exhibit 1

OPERATING EXPENSES, EAST-WEST AIR LINES, INC.

Operating Expenses	Expense per Airplane Hour	
	Martin 2–0–2	Prewar Plane
Direct:		
Fuel cost	$ 28.20	$ 14.11
Oil cost	1.56	0.91
Airplane depreciation	13.24	4.93
Engine depreciation	6.25	2.00
Engine overhaul and repair	8.59	4.05
Airplane overhaul and repair	9.50	4.36
Airplane and engine ground service	7.54	6.87
First pilot cost	10.90	10.19
Co-pilot cost	5.45	4.77
Cabin attendant cost	2.23	1.97
Crew expenses:		
Cockpit	0.97	0.76
Cabin	0.70	0.58
Airplane insurance cost	7.78	2.58
Total Direct Expense	$102.91	$ 58.08
Indirect*	128.64	72.60
Total Operating Expense	$231.55	$130.68

* Includes ground operations, ground and indirect maintenance, passenger service, traffic and sales, advertising and publicity, general administration, and depreciation of ground equipment. These expenses were regarded as fixed within the usual limits of plane operation. In minor degree, however, some of these expenses fluctuated with numbers of passengers handled, but not with airplane-miles flown. Indirect expenses were calculated at 125 per cent of direct expenses.

prewar equipment planned to write it off over one or two years because of obsolescence. In the opinion of the East-West Air Lines maintenance department, however, the prewar equipment could be kept up to C.A.B. standards for about five years without excessive maintenance charges.

To demonstrate the desirability of replacing East-West's prewar equipment with Martin 2–0–2's, representatives of the Glenn L. Martin Company prepared two operating cost schedules, one for the present fleet of 22 twin-engine planes and one for the reduced fleet of 12 new air liners which could replace it. These costs are shown in Exhibit 1. On the basis of these figures, Martin representatives claimed that the total cost of flying 345 million seat-miles would be almost $500,000 less than the cost which East-West incurred in 1946, when it flew 335 million seat-miles.

The average annual load factor experienced by air lines in the United States after the war was 65 per cent. Martin Company representatives, in making revenue estimates on which to base their arguments, used a conservative load factor of 60 per cent. In many operating periods, East-West had been well above the national average, and on some sections of line had approached 80 per cent load factors for short periods.

QUESTIONS

1. Should the East-West Air Lines replace its main-line fleet of 22 prewar planes with 12 Martin 2–0–2's?
2. If conditions of demand indicated a probable decline of substantial proportions in the volume of passenger traffic, would your answer be the same?
3. How would changes in demand for the products of the airplane manufacturing industry differ, over a period of year, from changes in demand for air transportation?
4. What effect do cost calculations made by the air transport industry have on demand calculations made by the airplane manufacturing industry?

CASE 5–2: THE COMMONWEALTH EDISON COMPANY

The Commonwealth Edison Company is a public utility providing electrical energy to more than 1.8 million customers in the Chicago area. Since the company is a public utility, the rates charged its customers are regulated by the Public Service Commission of the State of Illinois so as to yield net earnings of approximately 6 per cent on total capital investment. Rate changes are not frequently made. A change in customer rates ordinarily involves a public hearing, so that there is usually some delay between an application for a rate change and a decision by the Public Service Commission approving, denying, or modifying the request. As a result of regulation of rates, earnings of the company have not fluctuated in the same manner or with the same intensity as with a business not subject to public regulation.

The company generated all of its electricity in coal-fired steam plants located in the Chicago area. The topography of the surrounding territory was such that no hydroelectric installations were possible. Almost all the coal was transported by rail from the Illinois-Indiana area. In May, 1951, the company entered into an agreement with the Peabody Coal Company of Taylorville, Illinois, to purchase at least 50 per cent of its coal requirements from Peabody at cost plus 15 cents per ton. This agreement expires in 1982.

Subsequent to the discovery of atomic energy and its potential use as a source of power production, the Commonwealth Edison Company, in May, 1951, entered into an agreement with the Atomic Energy Commission to study the practicability of applying atomic energy to the production of electric power. As a result of these studies, the company made application to the Atomic Energy Commission, in March, 1956, for a permit to construct a full-scale nuclear power plant about 47 miles southwest of Chicago.

This nuclear plant would be the largest all-nuclear power plant yet proposed. It would be a boiling water reactor type and have a capacity of 180,000 kilowatts. An agreement was entered into with the General Electric Company to build the plant at a cost of $45 million.

The costs involved in erecting such a plant presented several problems for a regulated company. It was felt that present customers could not be expected to bear a large burden for the benefit of future customers. Neither could the stockholders be expected to bear large development costs because, if a cheaper way were found to produce electricity, the regulatory body would pass the benefits to the customers rather than the stockholders. After much study the following financing proposal was made.

Commonwealth Edison will own and operate the plant and will pay $30 million toward the $45 million contract price. This $30 million, plus the cost of the site and overhead costs, will be included in the Utility Plant account. On this basis (which leaves out $15 million of the total cost), it is estimated that the nuclear plant will produce electricity at an over-all cost of three fourths of a cent per kilowatt-hour—a cost approximately competitive with new coal-fired plants in the company's service area. The $15 million remainder of the contract will be paid as a research and development expense over a period of five years by a research group. Were the $15 million research item to be capitalized, the estimated over-all power cost would be one third higher, or about 1 cent per kilowatt-hour.

By not including the research expense, the charges to the cost of generating electricity in the nuclear plant will be about the same as the cost of electricity supplied from present company coal-fired plants. The $15 million is to be considered a research and development expense—a cost incurred to learn how to build and operate a competitive nuclear plant.

It has long been established that a utility can properly charge to its current operating expenses a reasonable amount for research and development. Although today's customers gain little from today's research expenditures, they benefit from the research expenditures of the past. However, it was felt that $15 million of research and development cost in connection with this "demonstration plant" was too large an expense for Commonwealth Edison alone. It was proposed that this expense be shared with seven other companies in the industry which would benefit from the experience of the demonstration plant, and such an agreement was worked out. When shared with these other companies and spread over a five-year period, the extra cost was considered a reasonable research and development expense for each company.

The $15 million will be paid through Nuclear Power Group, Inc., a nonprofit corporation which is also conducting continuing nuclear research. The group is making studies of other promising types of power reactors as well as following the design and construction of the Commonwealth Edison reactor. The companies associated in Nuclear Power Group, Inc., and their contributions to the research cost of the proposed Commonwealth Edison plant, are as follows:

Commonwealth Edison Company	$ 2,833,334
American Gas and Electric Service Corporation	2,833,333
Pacific Gas and Electric Company	2,833,333
Union Electric Company of Missouri	2,000,000
Illinois Power Company	1,500,000
Kansas City Power and Light Company	1,500,000
Bechtel Corporation	1,000,000
Central Illinois Light Company	500,000
	$15,000,000

In addition to the costs of construction, there were additional costs not yet known. The insurance industry proposed to make available, at a premium yet to be disclosed, a coverage of $50 million to $60 million third-party liability insurance. It was expected that the cost of this insurance will not upset the economic basis of the proposed plant; thus, it posed no major problem.

Because of the lack of experience with atomic reactors, there was the possibility of a major nuclear catastrophe. The likelihood of a major nuclear accident was considered rather remote; but if one should occur, the potential damage might be extreme. The designers of the proposed plant had specified every known safeguard against a nuclear accident, each of which was to be checked by the Atomic Energy Commission. In spite of these precautions, no expert in atomic energy

Exhibit 1

COMMONWEALTH EDISON COMPANY AND SUBSIDIARY COMPANIES
Statements of Consolidated Income for the Period Ended December 31, 1955

Electric operating revenues			$336,268,695
Electric operating expenses and taxes:			
Production fuel		$64,623,697	
Other operations		77,250,701	
Maintenance		20,533,181	
Provision for depreciation		35,002,168	
Provision for taxes:			
State, local, and miscellaneous federal		38,205,848	
Federal income		39,812,000	
Deferred federal income		1,800,000	277,227,595
Electric net operating income			$ 59,041,100
Other income, miscellaneous (net)			1,365,871
Gross income			$ 60,406,971
Deductions:			
Interest on long-term debt		$17,803,349	
Amortization of net premium on debt		287,562	
Other deductions		58,750	
		$17,574,537	
Less: Interest charged to construction		3,628,300	
Net deductions			13,946,237
Net Income			$ 46,460,734
Shares of common stock outstanding at end of year			17,764,921
Earnings per share			$2.62

could be found who would say that without a period of years of actual experience the hazard, although remote, could be ignored. It was proposed that the federal government assume liability for a major nuclear accident; but to date, no decision had been made. In the meantime, Commonwealth Edison, together with the other companies in the group, was paying the General Electric Company at the rate of one sixtieth of the contract price of the plant each month. These payments began on January 1, 1956.

Exhibits 1 and 2 show the balance sheet and profit-and-loss statement, respectively, for Commonwealth Edison for 1955.

Exhibit 2

COMMONWEALTH EDISON COMPANY AND SUBSIDIARY COMPANIES

Consolidated Balance Sheets, December 31, 1955

ASSETS

Utility plant—at original cost or less		$1,448,963,941
Less: Provision for accrued depreciation		351,765,253
		$1,097,198,688
Investments—at cost or less:		
Subsidiary companies not consolidated:		
Chicago & Illinois Midland Railway Company	9,458,500	
Heating subsidiaries	2,150,000	
Nonoperating real estate	500,974	
		$ 12,109,474
Current assets:		
Cash	42,921,450	
Deposit for bond interest	650,000	
U.S. government obligations, at cost	33,989,073	
Receivables	25,267,267	
Less: Provision for uncollectible accounts	1,382,071	
Materials and supplies, at average cost:		
Production fuel	21,026,306	
Other	15,874,336	
Prepaid insurance, taxes, and other items	1,410,884	
		$ 139,757,245
Deferred charges		1,131,634
		$1,250,197,041

LIABIILTIES

Capital stock—$25 par value per share:		
Common stock:		
Outstanding—17,764,921 shares at the end of 1955		$ 444,123,025
Premium on common stock—after deducting expenses of		
$547,054 in 1955		31,315,008
Retained earnings		65,461,930
		$ 540,899,963
Long-term debt:		
First-mortgage bonds, 3%, due 1977 to 1985		380,000,000
First-mortgage bonds, 3¼%, due 1982		40,000,000
Sinking fund debentures, 3%, due 1999		41,895,000
Sinking fund debentures, 2¾%, due 1999		41,885,000
Sinking fund debentures, 2⅞%, due 2001		44,000,000
Sinking fund debentures, 3⅛%, due 2004		48,000,000
		$ 595,780,000
Current liabilities:		
Accounts payable		17,139,274
Accrued and matured interest		5,441,623
Accrued taxes (subject to final determination)		64,550,411
Dividends		8,882,460
Sundry current liabilities		4,309,698
		$ 100,323,466
Deferred liabilities:		
Reserve for deferred federal income taxes		2,200,000
Other		8,538,342
		$ 10,738,342
Unamortized net premium on debt		2,455,270
		$1,250,197,041

Rental obligations: At December 31, 1955, rentals under 91 leases extending beyond 1956 approximated $600,000 annually.

Contingent liabilities: At December 31, 1955, construction commitments approximated $111 million.

QUESTIONS

1. What costs are involved in the construction of the nuclear plant?

2. Do you believe the company is economically justified in proceeding with this building program under the arrangements outlined in the case?

3. Would you, as an officer of the company, recommend approval of this project if all of the $15 million research cost had to be borne by Commonwealth Edison alone? Why?

4. If the anticipated costs, without the research costs, are three fourths of a cent per kilowatt-hour, and the existing rate structure allowed a maximum of three fourths of a cent per kilowatt-hour, would you proceed with the construction of the atomic power plant? Why?

5. Do you believe the company should have begun construction before all of its costs were known? Why?

6. Are any social costs involved in this project? Explain.

CASE 5–3: PENNSYLVANIA RAILROAD COMPANY

In the winter of 1946–47, the Pennsylvania Railroad faced the problem of possible replacement and supplementing of its fleet of locomotives. If new motive power were to be acquired, the choice lay between improved types of steam locomotives, on the one hand, and Diesel-electric locomotives, on the other.

The new locomotives would serve on that part of the Pennsylvania's main line which extended from Harrisburg to St. Louis on the southwest and to Chicago on the northwest. From Harrisburg west to Altoona the line rose steadily in elevation. Between Altoona and Pittsburgh, it encountered the Allegheny Mountains, with grades up to 1.75 per cent. West of Pittsburgh the terrain became undulating to Columbus and Crestline, beyond which the roadbed was practically level.

The application of the Diesel principal to railroad motive power had its practical inception at the beginning of the 1930's. It was not immediately apparent, from the early record of Diesel power, that these units were destined to become reliable instruments for the movement of freight and passenger trains. In the late 1920's the Pennsylvania Railroad began the major task of completing its electrification between New York and Washington. Electric energy from a central power source had long demonstrated its utility as a form of railroad motive power. The eastern seaboard, with its great, closely spaced passenger terminals and its tunnels, seemed to be better adapted to electric power than to Diesel, with its noise and fumes. Furthermore, the frequent use of trains of eighteen cars and more in length required tremendous concentrations of power for rapid acceleration in pulling out of the numerous terminals. Electric engines energized through catenary systems were particularly well adapted to this purpose.

Thus, while some other roads were looking more closely into the Diesel field, the Pennsylvania Railroad electrified its main lines along the Atlantic seaboard. The substitution of electric for steam power in this area eliminated use of coal for fuel at its most expensive point, so far as the Pennsylvania was concerned. It had been necessary to pull company coal for this area over the Allegheny Mountains into the numerous large eastern terminals. Because of the great volume of high-speed passenger business between New York, Philadelphia, and Washington, and because of the tonnage of perishable and other important freight moving between Potomac Yard and New York, the steam power then utilized in that territory was of the highest quality and efficiency. Electrification thus released a fleet of excellent steam engines for use in the other regions of the Pennsylvania Railroad. This made possible the retirement of hundreds of older and less efficient steam engines, thereby lowering the average age and raising the efficiency of the steam power generally. If any substantial Dieselization had been undertaken in the late 1930's, it would have been in substitution for highly efficient forms of steam power.

Nevertheless, the Pennsylvania Railroad looked closely into the possibilities of Diesel power. At that time (1939), new steam engines could have been acquired for half of what was to be their postwar prices, while the cost of Diesels held at about $110 per horsepower before and after the war. Thus, on an investment cost basis, the Diesel was, by 1946, much more attractive than before the war.

One of the principal considerations affecting replacement of the existing equipment of the Pennsylvania Railroad was the remaining service life of its fleet of locomotives. The age distribution of this motive equipment was as indicated in Exhibit 1.[11] Of the 4,692 locomotives in the fleet, 282 were electric, 38 were Diesel locomotives and gasoline switching engines, and 4,372 were steam. The usual replacement period for steam locomotives was 30 years; for Diesels and electrics, it was 27 years.[12] In the 11-year period from 1935 to

---

[11] One official of the Pennsylvania Railroad stated: "During the war our steam locomotives had taken a terrific beating from being almost continually in service and many were in need of extensive repairs and hundreds were facing immediate obsolescence. This was a further incentive for quick replacement by Diesel-electric power."

[12] Interstate Commerce Commission, *Statistics of Railways in the United States* (Washington, D.C., published annually).

1946 the Pennsylvania Railroad had purchased 331 new electric locomotives. Thus, in view of the usual service life, most of the 282
electric locomotives in its service on December 31, 1946, were relatively new.

Maintenance policy also played a part in the company's decision
on replacement of equipment. During the war, railroads brought out
of retirement all available equipment. This fact accounted for the
relatively large number of old locomotives shown in Exhibit 1. It had

Exhibit 1

AGE DISTRIBUTION OF LOCOMOTIVES OPERATED BY
PENNSYLVANIA RAILROAD, DECEMBER 31, 1946

Year Built	Number	Percentage of Total	Average Age in 1946 (Years)
1919 and prior..............	2,858	60.9	27 or over
1920–24...................	761	16.2	24
1925–29...................	473	10.1	19
1930–34...................	189	4.0	14
1935–39...................	122	2.6	9
1940–45...................	242	5.2	4
1946.....................	47	1.0	Less than 1
Total...............	4,692	100.0	

Source: *Moody's Manual for Railroads, 1947.*

long been company policy, however, for the Pennsylvania Railroad to
maintain its equipment in good repair in order to insure efficiency in
use and satisfactory length of life. A "full maintenance" policy had the
effect of reducing the rate of replacement.

Certain company officials believed that investment in new locomotives should be determined in large measure by the anticipated trend
of rail traffic. Exhibit 2 gives freight revenues and tonnage carried
by the Pennsylvania Railroad for the years 1921–46. Exhibit 3 presents passenger revenues and train-miles for these years. The management estimated that revenue freight ton-miles in the 10 years following
the war would fluctuate between 50 and 60 billion per annum, while
revenue passenger train-miles in this period were expected to average
between 40 and 46 million per annum. It was recognized, however,
that the general adoption of improved motive power by competing
railroads would have an adverse effect on the Pennsylvania's revenues
unless the company also replaced some of its obsolete equipment.

A further consideration in determining the desirability of replacements was the operating cost of Diesels and of new types of steam

Exhibit 2

FREIGHT TONNAGE, REVENUES, AND MOTIVE POWER,
PENNSYLVANIA RAILROAD, 1921–46

Year	Freight Revenue Ton-Miles (Thousands)	Freight Locomotives, Dec. 31	Freight Ton-Miles per Locomotive	Freight Revenue
1921	34,341,733	4,220	8,137,800	$405,210,980
1924	41,587,072	5,022	8,281,000	440,567,310
1928	44,989,625	4,353	10,342,500	457,294,397
1932	25,222,172	3,559	7,084,900	235,347,937
1936	35,706,781	3,222	11,082,100	333,350,239
1940	39,755,555	3,069	12,949,700	363,510,306
1942	67,028,327	3,086	21,692,000	608,598,902
1943	71,261,015	3,198	22,269,100	658,767,266
1944	71,262,339	3,217	22,132,000	674,395,308
1945	63,688,834	3,237	19,657,100	603,561,529
1946	56,741,355	3,187	17,787,300	551,296,168

Source: Revenues and tonnage data from Interstate Commerce Commission, *Statistics of Railways in the United States* (Washington, D.C., published annually). Motive-power data from *Moody's Manual for Railroads, 1947.*

Exhibit 3

PASSENGER-MILEAGE, REVENUES, AND MOTIVE POWER,
PENNSYLVANIA RAILROAD, 1921–46

Year	Revenue Passenger Train-Miles (Thousands)	Passengr Locomotives (Steam, Electric)	Passenger Train-Miles per Locomotive	Passenger Revenue
1921	47,701	1,117*	42,705	$155,065,297
1924	60,430	1,330*	45,436	147,523,905
1928	60,110	1,152*	52,179	131,179,771
1932	44,353	942	47,084	59,738,930
1936	42,638	884	48,233	67,552,238
1940	41,613	807	51,565	71,623,220
1942	48,803	794	61,465	169,122,194
1943	54,105	799	67,635	245,537,445
1944	56,104	795	70,571	260,804,982
1945	57,248	807	70,940	258,864,371
1946	53,650	839	63,870	207,023,702

* Estimate, based on 1936–46 division between freight passenger and switching locomotives.

Source: Revenues and tonnage data from Interstate Commerce Commission, *Statistics of Railways in the United States* (Washington, D.C., published annually). Motive-power data from *Moody's Manual for Railroads, 1947.*

locomotives, and a comparison of these costs with those for operating present equipment. Although the Pennsylvania Railroad had had no opportunity within its own system to compare operating costs of Diesels with those for steam, an experiment with new types of steam and Diesel passenger locomotives, conducted by the New York Central Railroad in the fall of 1944 and spring of 1945, threw some light on relative operating costs. These are shown in Exhibit 4. In these tests the New York Central used six 4,000-horsepower, double-end Diesels and six 4–8–4, S1 Niagara steam locomotives, which were comparable to the Diesels.

The steam locomotives in the New York Central experiment were used in passenger traffic for an average monthly distance of 25,168 miles. The Diesels averaged 29,021 miles per month. The lower mileage for steam locomotives in the test was traceable to an average time out for repairs of 28 days per annum. With Diesels, repair time was reduced to 12 days per annum. Steam locomotives also were

Exhibit 4

OPERATING COSTS PER MILE FOR STEAM, DIESEL, PASSENGER LOCOMOTIVES, NEW YORK CENTRAL RAILROAD, 1945

Item	Steam	Diesel
Repairs	$0.356	$0.352
Fuel	0.410	0.280
Water	0.031	0.004
Lubrication	0.011	0.030
Other supplies	0.005	0.002
Engine-house expenses	0.100	0.100
Vacations and social security	0.0233	0.0237
Crew wages (2 men)	0.1944	0.1979
Depreciation, interest, insurance	0.0853	0.1194
Total	$1.2160	$1.1090

Source: P. W. Kiefer, "An Evaluation of Railroad Motive Power," *Railway Age*, August 23, 30, 1947. Costs for steam locomotives based on 288,000 miles per annum. Costs for Diesel locomotives based on 324,000 miles per annum.

more affected by adverse weather than were Diesels. Exhibit 4, there-fore, is constructed to show a service availability of 8 hours for steam for every 9 hours for Diesel. This service availability ratio is reflected in the 324,000 miles per annum for Diesels as compared with 228,000 miles for steam. Based on these mileages, the New York Central ex-perience indicated that costs for operating Diesels were 10.7 cents per mile less than for improved types of steam locomotives.

A substantial part of the operating cost of a locomotive was made up of fixed charges—depreciation, interest, and insurance. Because of the lower initial cost of steam locomotives ($270,000 for a 4–8–4-wheel-arrangement steam locomotive as against $395,000 for a com-parable 4,000-horsepower Diesel locomotive), annual fixed charges for steam locomotives in the New York Central test were only $24,453 as against $38,841 for Diesels. The effect of these lower fixed costs on total operating costs per mile for steam locomotives can be seen in Exhibit 4. With lower annual mileages the differential in favor of Diesel locomotives declines, as shown in Exhibit 5.

In applying the New York Central experience to the operating conditions of their own system, Pennsylvania officials noted that the average mileage operated by their serviceable passenger locomotives was somewhat lower than mileages on which the costs of Exhibit 4 were based. Average mileage per passenger locomotive in the Pennsylvania system was estimated at 75,000 per annum.[13] This estimated rate, however, included all types and ages of passenger locomotives

Exhibit 5

ESTIMATED OPERATING COSTS PER MILE FOR STEAM LOCOMOTIVES AND DIESEL LOCOMOTIVES FOR SELECTED ANNUAL MILEAGES

Annual Mileage		Operating Costs per Mile		Savings by Diesel
Steam	Diesel	Steam	Diesel	
160,000................	180,000	$1.284	$1.205	$0.079
222,000................	250,000	1.241	1.145	0.096
288,000................	324,000	1.216	1.109	0.107

Source: Based on data from P. W. Kiefer, "An Evaluation of Railroad Motive Power," *Railway Age,* August 23, 30, 1947. Annual charges for depreciation, taxes, and insurance: $24,453 for steam locomotives; $38,841 for Diesel.

and consequently was lower than would be expected from new locomotives. The company's actual experience with new passenger Diesels averaged 240,000 miles per annum. The New York Central experiment, moreover, was for passenger locomotives only; annual mileages for freight locomotives were much lower. For Diesels used by Class I railroads, annual mileage was estimated at 120,000; and for new 5,400-horsepower steam locomotives, it was 102,000.[14] Thus, company officials believed that mileages, shown in Exhibit 5, of 160,000 for steam and 180,000 for Diesel would be closer than the higher base mileages of the New York Central test to the experience of Pennsylvania main-line locomotives. Aside from depreciation charges, executives of the Pennsylvania Railroad believed that operating costs of main-line steam locomotives were not greatly different from those of the new types used in the New York Central experiment.

---

[13] This is slightly in excess of the "passenger train-miles per locomotive" shown in Exhibit 3, because of double-heading and light locomotive movements.

[14] P. W. Kiefer, "An Evaluation of Railroad Motive Power," *Railway Age,* August 30, 1947.

In examining the New York Central experience, officials of the Pennsylvania were impressed with the lower fuel costs of Diesels. While Diesel locomotives used relatively high-cost fuel in terms of B.T.U. content, actual fuel costs for Diesel locomotives were substantially less than those for steam locomotives because of the much greater efficiency of Diesels. A survey of the Interstate Commerce Commission[15] indicated that steam passenger locomotives of the Eastern District roads used an average of 170 pounds of coal per locomotive mile, while Diesels required 2.7 gallons of Diesel fuel to accomplish the same work. In recent years, prices of both coal and Diesel fuel had been going up, although the rate of increase of coal was substantially more than that of fuel oil, as shown in the following tabulation:

	Cost in 1940	Cost in 1946	Per Cent Increase over 1940
Coal per ton (mine purchases)............	$1.88	$3.25	72.9
Diesel fuel, per gallon..................	0.0442	0.0613	38.7

Based on 1946 fuel prices, the New York Central study arrived at the following fuel costs per mile:

Coal: 170 lbs. @ $3.25 per ton..........................	$0.276	
Transportation & storage...........................	0.134	
Diesel fuel: 2.7 gal. @ $0.0613 per gal....................		$0.166
Transportation & storage..........................		0.144
	$0.410	$0.310

It seemed to the Pennsylvania officials that a cost of $0.134 per mile for transportation and storage of coal was somewhat high, in view of the company's proximity to coal deposits. On the other hand, transportation and storage charges for fuel oil would probably be as high as the New York Central figures indicated, since it would be necessary to transport the oil from the Southwest, outside the Pennsylvania Railroad's network and with consequent outpayment for transportation expense.

Special processing of water for steam locomotives was necessary at practically all water stations west of Harrisburg. These facilities consisted of large overhead tanks, equipment for chemical treatment, and pumping machinery where gravity flow was not available. For Diesels, on the other hand, no special facilities were required, as water was treated on the locomotives. No abandonment of main-line water sta-

---

[15] Statement M–230, December 1946.

tions was contemplated, as it was recognized that operation of some steam power would continue for many years.

Fueling facilities, because of the greater operating span of the Diesel, could be reduced in number, although new facilities would be required to handle liquid fuel, if Diesels were used. The Pennsylvania Railroad estimated that approximately $2.5 million would be adequate for installation of fueling facilities necessary to inaugurate Diesels, should they be used.

Moreover, Diesel locomotives, being very intricate pieces of machinery in contrast with the relatively simple steam locomotives, would require the establishment of extensive shop facilities. Here, however, because of the greatly expanded range of the Diesel, not so many shops would be maintained as would be required for steam locomotives. In converting to Diesel, the Pennsylvania officials estimated that a large passenger Diesel repair shop would be needed, at a cost of approximately $4.2 million, and a freight Diesel shop, estimated at about $3 million. It was probable that these repair shops would be located near the lines of heaviest traffic, preferably at Harrisburg.

In addition, smaller repair and storage facilities would be necessary if Diesel power were used. Such shops would be located over the western end of the system, at such places as Chicago, St. Louis, and Crestline, Ohio. It was contemplated that space in existing engine houses would be used and that modifications of such space would require an outlay of $500,000 for each of six shops. Facilities of this sort were usually amortized in 20 years.

One of the most difficult problems which the management foresaw for the road, in converting to Diesel power, was the retraining of operating and repair personnel. Because of the seniority system enforced by the railway brotherhoods, engineers of steam locomotives were generally older men who had attained their positions only after many years of service with the road. This made retraining difficult. To a lesser extent, these obstacles would be encountered in the repair departments. The personnel department estimated costs of retraining personnel and pensioning superannuated employees at about $500,000, to be spread over three years.

Eventual replacement of the 4,372 steam locomotives of the Pennsylvania system by Diesels, if accomplished, would involve a substantial cash outlay by the company, but it was anticipated that conversion could be undertaken gradually as funds for reinvestment became available. The company's financial position was extremely strong;

and until 1946, there had been an unbroken record of net earnings for 100 years. In 1946 the deficit was attributable largely to the disproportionately high volume of commuter service, short-haul L.C.L., express, and mail handled by the Pennsylvania Railroad at relatively low rates. It was impossible in the short run for the Pennsylvania system to reduce its expenses in proportion to the decrease in its revenue. The management believed, however, that after a year of readjustment to more normal operation, a more favorable balance between revenue and expense would again be established.

To assist the roads in postwar readjustment, the Interstate Commerce Commission granted certain rate increases. The Pennsylvania Railroad had received a 6 per cent temporary freight rate increase in July, 1946. As of January 1, 1947, this increase was raised to about 17.6 per cent on freight rates. Effective on June 1, 1947, there was an increase in passenger fares for coaches from 2.2 to 2.5 cents per mile, and in Pullmans from 3.3 to 3.5 cents per mile.

With the tremendous volume of freight and passenger traffic handled during the war years, revenues of the Pennsylvania system increased greatly, as may be noted from Exhibits 2 and 3. Both revenues and earnings dropped off markedly after the war to new postwar levels—which, however, were well above prewar levels. Since the Pennsylvania Railroad system was located in the primary industrial area of the nation, the management believed that its revenues would not materially decline in the near future. But it was noted that 32 per cent of the company's revenue and 58 per cent of total weight in 1946 came from hauling mineral products, chiefly coal. Possible declines in the production of coal as industry and transportation agencies converted to the use of other fuels suggested a decline in one source of revenue. It was not believed that the company's change from steam to Diesel power would have any marked effect in accelerating the general movement of industry to abandon coal as a fuel.

Related to this problem was the supply of coal as compared with that of fuel oil. Rapid conversion of industrial and domestic consumers from coal to petroleum products had created a shortage of oil in the years immediately following the war. While this condition was regarded by some executives as likely to be of short duration, certain leaders in the rail industry were extremely wary of the dangers inherent in an uncertain supply of oil.

By the end of 1946 the Pennsylvania Railroad had not yet adopted a definite policy of conversion to Diesels. In his annual report for 1946 the president of the road, Mr. M. W. Clement, stated:

During the year, thirty-seven steam locomotives and tenders were received. . . . These are the most powerful passenger steam locomotives in our service. . . . There were on order at the close of the year twenty 6,000 horsepower passenger and two 7,500 horsepower freight Diesel-electric locomotives, scheduled for delivery in 1947. Since the close of the year, nineteen additional 6,000 horsepower passenger and six 7,500 horsepower freight Diesel-electric locomotives were placed on order.

Further Diesel orders were placed during 1947, and in the *Chicago Tribune* on March 25, 1948, there appeared the following:

The Pennsylvania railroad has placed orders for 114 additional Diesel-electric locomotives . . . in connection with its 157 million dollar improvement program, M. W. Clement, president, announced yesterday. These orders bring the road's total since the war to 374 diesels.

We are well under way, said Mr. Clement, on one of the largest Diesel locomotive installations in the country. By May of this year we expect all of our important east-west through passenger trains will be handled by diesel power in the non-electrified territory west of Harrisburg, Pa. Our Diesel switcher program also is extensive.

QUESTIONS

1. Was the Pennsylvania Railroad justified, on the basis of operating costs, in converting from steam power to Diesel power in the postwar period of 1946–48?

2. How would the prospect of a substantial delcine in traffic affect calculations to convert to Diesel locomotives?

Chapter 6

PRICE POLICY WHEN SELLERS ARE FEW

A very common situation in production, wholesaling, and retailing is that of "oligopoly," where the number of sellers of a particular item is small enough so that each seller must consider his rivals' reactions to his own actions. It was pointed out in Chapter 3 that the oligopolist is not faced by a single demand curve but rather that his demand can assume a great variety of shapes (and even a positive slope), depending on the nature and extent of rivals' reactions. Oligopoly thus differs sharply on the demand side from both monopoly and pure competition, in both of which the demand can be considered to "stay put" while the firm adjusts itself to the demand-cost situation.

Oligopoly is common in local markets throughout the country. Many towns and cities are large enough to support only a few drugstores, variety stores, department stores, massage parlors, building materials producers and suppliers, etc. Especially where there is considerable geographic separation between cities, each such seller serves a substantial percentage of the local market and usually is highly sensitive to attempts of competitors to capture larger shares of the market by price cuts or other means.

The larger the market in which a product is sold, the more opportunity there is for a large number of firms (of efficient size) to participate. Nevertheless, oligopoly is common also in industries which serve national and international markets. Here, the situation is usually not literally one of only a "few" sellers; but frequently, there are only a few large firms plus a number of small firms, with the dominant firms accounting for a large percentage of total sales. An oligopolistic situation then exists between the large firms, each being highly sensitive to the actions of the others. Usually, the small firms in the field are reluctant to follow price policies which put them in sharp conflict with the industry leaders. (Many interesting exceptions occur, however, where small companies with aggressive management consistently follow policies of their own choosing.)

Concentration of American Industry

One statistical device for disclosing the existence of oligopolistic situations is the "concentration ratio," where the percentage of total output or employment accounted for by the largest firms is computed. Exhibit 1 shows concentration ratios for industries in which the four largest firms accounted for over 75 per cent of the value of the entire industry output in 1947, according to a comprehensive study by the Federal Trade Commission. The list is incomplete, however, since value of product was considered to be an unsatisfactory measure of concentration in a number of industries, including the automobile industry, which would otherwise easily have made the list.

Primary aluminum heads the list of highly concentrated industries, since three companies—Aluminum Company of America, Reynolds Metals Company, and Permanente Metals Corporation (later renamed Kaiser Aluminum and Chemical Corporation)—turned out all of this product.[1] Concentration ratios above 95 per cent are also evident for small-arms ammunition, aircraft propellers, and telephone and telegraph equipment. The cigarette industry shows a concentration ratio above 90 per cent, especially because of the dominance of the American Tobacco Company, the Liggett and Myers Company, and the R. J. Reynolds Company. The gypsum industry, with a concentration ratio of 84.6 per cent, has two large firms—U.S. Gypsum and National Gypsum. The American Can Company and the Continental Can Company contribute largely to the concentration ratio of 77.8 per cent for tin cans and other tinwear, while the Corn Products Refining Company accounts heavily for the high concentration ratio (77.2 per cent) in the corn products industry. The reader will be familiar with many other large corporations within the industries listed in Exhibit 1.[2]

While concentration ratios are useful in disclosing industries in which sellers (at least large sellers) are few in number, some of their shortcomings for this purpose should not be overlooked. First, it is assumed, in compiling the ratios, that all of the industries sell in national markets. Actually, such firms as brick producers sell in local markets, and one or two such firms may dominate in many local markets at the same time that the national concentration ratio is low; that

---

[1] There are, however, some 17,000 independent aluminum fabricators turning out a large number of semifinished and finished products. John V. Krutilla, "Aluminum—A Dilemma for Antitrust Aims?" *Southern Economic Journal*, October, 1955, p. 168.

[2] Very low concentration exists, of course, in many industries. Concentration ratios below 10 per cent are common in such fields as apparel manufacturing, lumber and lumber products, printing and publishing, and stone, clay, and glass products.

Exhibit 1

INDUSTRIES WITH CONCENTRATION RATIOS
ABOVE 75 PER CENT, 1947

Industry	Concentration Ratio*
Primary aluminum	100.0
Small-arms ammunition	99.9
Aircraft propellers	98.0
Telephone and telegraph equipment	95.7
Aluminum rolling and drawing	94.2
Botanical products	92.1
Electric lamps	91.8
Files	91.6
Locomotives and parts	90.7
Cyclic (coal tar) products	90.6
Cigarettes	90.4
Electrometallurgical products	88.3
Flat glass	88.1
Tobacco stemming and drying	88.0
Steam engines and turbines	87.6
Carbon and graphite products	87.1
Softwood distillation	85.8
Pulp goods, pressed and molded	85.5
Gypsum products	84.6
Leavening compounds	83.4
Matches	82.7
Compressed and liquefied gas	82.6
Safes and vaults	82.4
Cork products	81.9
Rubber footwear	80.7
Salt	80.5
Explosives	80.4
Hard-surface floor coverings	80.3
Primary copper	80.0
Typewriters	79.4
Soap and glycerin	79.0
Phonograph records	78.8
Synthetic fibers	78.4
Carbon black	78.3
Tin cans and other tinwear	77.8
Organs	77.6
Graphite, ground or blended	77.4
Corn products	77.2
Sewing machines	77.1
Tires and inner tubes	76.6
Primary batteries, dry and wet	76.4
Wool-felt hats and hat bodies	76.3

* Percentage of value of each industry's output accounted for by four largest firms, according to Federal Trade Commission, *Report on Changes in Concentration in Manufacturing, 1935 to 1947 and 1950* (Washington, D.C.: U.S. Government Printing Office, 1954), pp. 138–48. The list is not complete, because value of product was not considered an appropriate measure of concentration in some industries. In some cases, data were withheld to avoid disclosing information for individual companies.

is, oligopolistic situations in local or regional markets do not show up in the ratios for items which are usually not transported over long distances. Second, the narrowness or breadth of industry classifications has a great deal of effect on the size of concentration ratios. The "file" industry, for example, with a ratio of 91.6 per cent is defined narrowly, and some broader classification of toolmakers would have reduced the ratio. Third, the Federal Trade Commission, in compiling the data, has left imports out of account. Some industries, such as the sewing machine industry, would show lower concentration if imports—which actually compete for domestic sales—were included. And fourth, concentration ratios are computed "horizontally." They consequently tend to understate economic power when that power is derived from vertical integration.

It is not safe to assume that high concentration is necessarily associated with a low degree of competition between firms or that low concentration ratios are necessarily associated with active competition. High concentration does suggest a high degree of demand interdependence, which makes thoroughgoing competition less likely. But even in industries where concentration is low, competition is often curtailed by means of price agreements between sellers of similar commodities. In short, concentration ratios are not in themselves measures of monopoly power, but must be used in conjunction with other information.

Plant Concentration and Company Concentration

The Federal Trade Commission has also studied the matter of plant concentration in relation to company concentration for 1947. Plant concentration measures the percentage of industry output turned out by a designated number of plants. Thus, an industry in which both plant concentration and company concentration are high is one which has both a small number of plants and a small number of firms. It is also possible for plant concentration to be low while company concentration is high. This situation would mean ownership of a large number of plants per firm. It is also common, of course, for both plant concentration and firm concentration to be low.

Exhibit 2 lists industries in two groups: (1) On the left are those with the greatest difference between plant and company concentration; (2) on the right are those in which company concentration is only slightly above plant concentration. In general, it can be said that the number of firms existing in the industries on the right is based in large measure on economies of scale in the manufacturing process. Most of the firms in these fields have only one plant, so that firm size is closely correlated with plant size. Firms within the industries shown on the left are mainly multiplant organizations, so that there is little relation between firm size and plant size. The size of the larger firms in this left-hand list must be explained in terms of economies of large firms (in financing, buying, advertising, research, etc.), or else large size is due to mergers or other actions which may have been designed to increase monopoly power.

The compressed and liquefied gas industry constitutes a striking example of low plant concentration and high company concentration, even though it did not make the left-hand list in Exhibit 2. The 20 largest plants accounted for only about 20 per cent of the industry's value of product, whereas the 20 largest companies accounted for 94 per cent of the industry total.[3] Another example of the same sort of

Exhibit 2

INDUSTRIES WITH LARGEST AND SMALLEST DIVERGENCES
BETWEEN COMPANY AND PLANT CONCENTRATION

Largest Divergence	*Smallest Divergence*
Petroleum and coal products	Electrical motors
Transportation equipment	Fabricated metal products
Primary metals	Apparel and related products
Leather and leather products	Printing and publishing
Food and kindred products	Instruments and related products
Paper and allied products	Machinery, except electrical
Chemicals and allied products	Lumber, except furniture
Stone, glass, and clay products	Miscellaneous manufactures
Textile mill products	Furniture and fixtures

Source: *Study of Monopoly Power* (Hearings before the Subcommittee of the Judiciary, House of Representatives, 82d Congress, 1st Session), Serial 1, Part 2, p. 3.

situation is the distilling industry. The four large distillers—National Distillers, Schenley Distillers, Seagram Distillers, and Hiram Walker —operate a total of 54 plants.[4]

If company concentration is high and plant concentration is also high, antitrust action is unlikely, because there is a presumption that large firms are needed to secure low production costs. If, however, company concentration ratios are high while plant concentration is low, there is more likelihood that unnecessary monopoly power exists. (The concentration ratios alone do not *prove* this, of course.) As mentioned earlier, concentration ratios do not measure the important matter of the degree of vertical integration (control of successive stages of production) which exists, and this must be kept in mind when the possible antitrust implications of such ratios are assessed. And even where company concentration is low, price conspiracy and monopolistic mergers must be watched by the Federal Trade Commission.

---

[3] *Study of Monopoly Power* (Hearings before the Subcommittee of the Judiciary, House of Representatives, 82d Congress, 1st Session), Serial 1, Part 2, p. 13.

[4] *Ibid.*, p. 19.

Pure and Differentiated Oligopoly

Pure oligopoly may be said to exist when sellers of a homogeneous commodity are few in number. This situation is more common among producers of industrial materials than in the consumers' goods fields. Most consumers' goods are differentiated from one another by means of brand names, trade-marks, and packaging, and usually by some differences in physical characteristics. Materials and components turned out by different companies for use as inputs into production processes are more frequently identical. Even if the name of the producer is stamped on the good, this is not apt to influence an experienced industrial buyer if the product is, in fact, identical with that of another firm. Consumers of finished products, on the other hand, are often influenced by brand names and advertising, even where no difference in the commodity actually exists. (Aspirin is a famous example.) As a consequence, "pure oligopoly" may be said to be present in such fields as the manufacture of primary aluminum, primary copper, aluminum rolling and drawing, and certain gypsum products, whereas "differentiated oligopoly" exists for automobiles, cigarettes, hard-surface floor coverings, typewriters, sewing machines, and a great many other commodities.

When oligopolistic firms are few in number and have identical products, their demands are highly interdependent. As concentration of production diminishes, and as products are more differentiated, demands are less closely interdependent. If the number of firms selling in a market becomes large enough so that each can disregard the reactions of his rivals to his own price-output actions, the market situation is often designated by economists as "monopolistic competition" or "pure competition," depending on whether differentiated or nondifferentiated products are sold. In each case a single demand curve confronts the firm; in the former case, this is a downsloping monopoly demand curve, (Exhibit 5, Chapter 3, p. 85), while in the latter case, it is a horizontal line (Exhibit 6, Chapter 3). If there are *no* rivals selling the same commodity in the same market, the situation is designated as monopoly. The distinction between "monopoly" and "monopolistic competition" is not a clear one, however, since it encounters the same difficulty of classifying industries as is involved in compiling statistics on concentration. If "industry" is defined very narrowly and products are differentiated, there is only one firm in each industry (e.g., the "Campbell soup industry"). If the industry is defined more broadly, the Campbell Soup Company becomes instead one firm of a number in the "canned soup industry." On a still broader basis, it is one of a very large number of firms in the "food and food products industry." Whether the company is "oligopolistic" or not depends on whether, in fact, its price adjustments will cause speedy reactions on the part of the other companies. If such reactions would occur, the company can be classified as a "differentiated oligopolist."

Graphic Comparison of Oligopoly Positions

The distinction between an oligopolistic and a monopolistic firm can be made clearer by the use of a chart. The firm for which demand is represented on the left side of Exhibit 3 is in a position where its

Exhibit 3

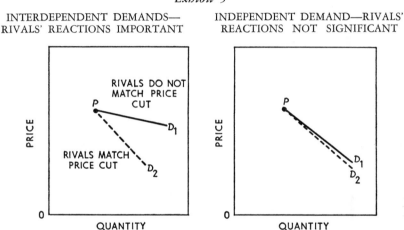

INTERDEPENDENT DEMANDS—
RIVALS' REACTIONS IMPORTANT

INDEPENDENT DEMAND—RIVALS'
REACTIONS NOT SIGNIFICANT

sales depend strongly on the reactions of its close rivals to a price cut from the prevailing level indicated by point P. If rivals do not match a price cut, sales will expand along the highly elastic curve D_1. This may be called its *ceteris paribus* demand curve,[5] since it is drawn on the assumption that other things (especially the prices charged by rival sellers) remain constant. If, however, rivals match the price cut, sales will expand less substantially along the less elastic curve D_2. In the right-hand diagram the *ceteris paribus* and "rivals match" demand curves are very close together. Consequently, the firm is nearly in a position to disregard the reactions of other sellers to its own price adjustments; the firm is almost in a monopoly position, where there is a single demand curve to which it can adjust. If the two demand curves

---

[5] This terminology is used by J. S. Bain, *Pricing, Distribution, and Employment* (New York: Henry Holt & Co., 1953). This work contains an excellent discussion of price and output decisions under oligopoly.

were entirely coincident, rather than just close together, the firm would be monopolistic rather than oligopolistic and could be independent in its policies. Monopoly can thus be considered to be a limiting case of oligopoly in which rivals' reactions are of negligible importance.

The Incentive for Making and Breaking Agreements

The demand situation portrayed on the left side of Exhibit 3 is an underlying cause of conservative pricing practices and outright collusive action on the part of sellers in oligopolistic markets. If price is at the level indicated by point *P,* the firm in question may be reluctant to "rock the boat" by lowering price, because the sales result of the cut will depend so greatly on what competitors do in response. It was pointed out in Chapter 3 that the firm may even lose physical sales by cutting price, in the event that rivals cut even more. In the more likely event of a matching cut on their part, an oligopolist's sales may expand only along an inelastic demand curve, so that dollar volume of sales will be lower after the price cut. (In addition, costs will be larger because physical sales volume will be up.) The uncertainties inherent in the situation are conducive to "letting well enough alone" or making outright price agreements to which all sellers promise to adhere. At the same time, the sharp gain in sales which any one oligopolist can make by lowering price while others hew to the line offers a constant temptation to cut price openly or in a less overt manner. Small firms are often troublesome to the larger ones in this regard, since they may be able to cut price a bit without making it worth while for the larger firms to retaliate in any way. A small firm accounts for such a small percentage of total sales that it may get away with a price cut even when the industry practice is to agree on price. Should the manager of the small firm miscalculate, however, he may precipitate a price war in the industry—a war in which he may well be a casualty.

Price-fixing agreements for commodities sold in interstate commerce are illegal under the federal antitrust laws. (These laws will be examined in a later chapter.) The federal government, through the Federal Trade Commission and the Department of Justice, has brought a substantial number of such agreements to light.[6] Collusion on price

---

[6] From 1920 to 1940 the Federal Trade Commission issued "cease and desist" orders involving price agreements in the following industries: viscose rayon yarn, pin tickets, flannel shirts, turbine generators and condensers, liquid chlorine, medical cotton goods, calcium chloride, corn cribs and silos, certain types of waterworks and gas-system fittings, fire-fighting equipment, pulverized iron, rubber heels, music rolls, lithographed labels, plumbing supplies, fertilizer, metal lath, gasoline, and brushes (Clair Wilcox, *Competition and Monopoly* [T.N.E.C. Monograph No. 21] [Washington, D.C.: U.S. Government Printing Office, 1940], p. 132).

is always difficult to prove, however. In part, this difficulty springs from the fact that under perfect competition the prices charged for a particular commodity are identical. It is not always clear whether identical prices are the result of competition or monopoly. The antitrust job of the federal authorities is made more difficult when products are differentiated rather than homogeneous, since prices are then unlikely to be identical even where a price agreement has been entered into. Costlier varieties of the product are apt to be priced somewhat higher, even when all prices are arrived at collusively. It should also be kept in mind that price agreements are not illegal in intrastate commerce. In fact, they are often actively encouraged by state and local governments. Also, while the right hand of the federal government is attempting to discourage price fixing, the left hand is encouraging it and supplying the machinery for enforcing the agreements.

A striking example of governmentally induced price fixing was found under the National Recovery Administration (N.R.A.) codes of the New Deal era. "Soon after he took office in 1933 the Administrator announced that, although conduct in accordance with approved codes was exempted from prosecution under the anti-trust acts, it was not intended to authorize price agreements. Nevertheless, 560 of the first 677 codes contained some provision relating to minimum prices or costs."[7] The most important codes permitting direct setting of prices were those in the bituminous coal, lumber, and petroleum industries. The immediate result was an abrupt rise in prices in these industries. Because of the difficulties of enforcement and lack of general agreement as to the desirability of prices set by the code authority, there was widespread evasion. In the case of the coal industry, subsequent legislation attempted to carry on industry-wide price making after the N.R.A. had been declared unconstitutional by the Supreme Court.

Similarly, price agreements between firms, as well as individual price fixing, have been fostered by the federal and state "fair-trade" laws and by the state "unfair practices" acts. Marketing co-operatives, with their power over sales and prices, have been encouraged by legislation; and extensive governmental and private price determination is involved in the federal farm programs. Governmental encouragement of labor unions has tended to cause wage rates (labor prices) to be determined by collective agreements rather than through competitive market forces. In addition, interest rates (prices for the use of capital) are subject to a good deal of government control. Some of these mat-

---

[7] Arthur R. Burns, *Decline of Competition* (New York: McGraw-Hill Book Co., Inc., 1936), pp. 471–72.

ters will be examined in more detail at a later point. Their inclusion here is to remind the reader that industrial, labor, and financial price determination is frequently removed from the arena of open competition by means of deliberate legislative action. Once sellers have been brought together by government action, as occurred under the N.R.A., they are apt to continue to act in collusion even after the legislation has ceased to be in effect.

When sellers decide to collude rather than to compete in price and other matters, their action can take various forms, some of which are much more rigid than others. The principal forms may be classified as (1) a cartel arrangement, (2) overt price agreement without cartellization, (3) tacit agreement on price, and (4) follow-the-leader pricing. These will be discussed in turn.

Cartels

Although the word "cartel" attained popularity (or notoriety) in reference to associations of firms trading internationally in such commodities as sulfur, explosives, magnesium, and rubber, its use is appropriate for any combination of sellers who turn over to a central authority their power to determine price. Frequently, the authority also is given power to allot exclusive sales territories, to control entry into the industry, and to control production. Cartels are common in such fields of intrastate commerce as dry cleaning and haircutting, where antitrust laws do not apply. Fluid milk prices in most parts of the country are controlled by commissions established under either state or federal law, thus cartellizing the sale of this important commodity. Cartels may operate either in oligopolistic industries or in fields where the number of competing sellers would otherwise be large. International cartel arrangements in which American firms participate very often take the form of patent-licensing agreements.[8]

When price is determined centrally for all sellers in an industry, an attempt may be made to maximize profit for the group as a whole. In this case, price-output policy would be the same as that of a single-firm monopoly (Exhibit 5, Chapter 4, p. 143), the demand curve to which adjustment is made being the demand facing the industry as a whole. A difficulty involved in such central price determination is the unlike cost situation for different firms. This may make the price which is optimal for the group as a whole differ from that which some firm or firms would like to have in force. A solution may be the establishment

---

[8] See Dudley F. Pegrum, *The Regulation of Industry* (Chicago: Richard D. Irwin, Inc., 1950), p. 396, for a discussion of this matter.

of two or more different prices to be charged by two or more subgroups or firms. For example, downtown cleaners may charge one uniform price per garment while cleaners in outlying areas are permitted to charge a somewhat lower price. Where the central policy is clearly detrimental to the interests of a particular seller, there is always a chance that he will leave the association. If he then lowers the price and the cartel decides not to retaliate, his own sales are likely to increase sharply. Similarly, if the cartel makes sales territory, output, or other assignments which are not to the liking of a particular firm, there may be a possibility of its withdrawal from the association. Where the power of government is behind the cartel arrangement, however (as in the case of milk price fixing), firms cannot cut price without invoking legal penalties.

Price Agreements without Cartellization

Frequently, businessmen enter into definite price agreements without the mechanism of a formal cartel arrangement. Trade associations, chambers of commerce, and other organizations often afford the necessary opportunities for sellers to meet and agree on price. Unlike cartel-determined price agreements, these are usually of a *sub rosa* nature; and frequently, great care is taken to destroy any written evidence of such agreements.

Interlocking directorates may also provide a useful instrument for preventing genuine price competition. The Federal Trade Commission, which looks with suspicion at such multicompany use of a single official, has compiled a table dealing with this matter for the 200 largest nonfinancial and 50 largest financial corporations in 1935. Exhibit 4 summarizes this information. It can be seen that most of the large corporations had at least one director who did not devote his time entirely to the corporation. More often than not, directors of the large corporations also helped to direct three or more other companies. Opportunity for collusive action of many kinds is suggested by the data.

Noncartel price agreements are less likely than cartel agreements to have as their goal the approximate maximization of profits for the group as a whole. Stronger companies are likely to have especially great influence in determining price. As a consequence, agreements are more likely to be quite unsatisfactory to some firms and are more apt to be broken by disgruntled sellers than where the association is a more formal one. A decline in business activity is especially likely to strain a price agreement, since excess capacity will then appear and this will provide firms with a special incentive to cut price in order to gain volume. Similarly, the establishment of an excessive number of firms in a particular field, even in a period of general prosperity and expansion, may lead to the breaking of price agreements and to price wars. Price wars frequently occur in the retailing of gasoline, for example, due to the erection of too many filling stations in an area.

Often, agreements to charge identical prices, to charge "manufacturers' suggested prices," or to avoid head-on price competition are tacit

Exhibit 4

INTERLOCKING OF CORPORATE DIRECTORSHIPS*

TYPE OF CORPORATION	ALL CORPORATIONS	CORPORATIONS INTERLOCKING WITH:		
		One or More Other Companies	Two or More Other Companies	Three or More Other Companies
Industrial........................	107	91	71	60
Utilities.........................	54	46	34	26
Railroads........................	39	38	36	31
Banks...........................	30	30	28	22
Other financial...................	20	20	18	12
	250	225	187	151

* Source: *Study of Monopoly Power* (Hearings before the Subcommittee of the Judiciary, House of Representatives, 82d Congress, 1st Session), Serial 1, Part 2, p. 76.

(unspoken) rather than overt. There may simply be a general understanding among sellers that the welfare of each is promoted by non-aggressive price policies. This form of agreement is the most tenuous of all and the most likely to be broken when it appears advantageous to a seller to do so.

Price Leadership

An effective method of avoiding price competition in oligopolistic industries is often found in the practice of price leadership. (This practice may, however, run afoul of the antitrust laws; and it has done so in recent years, as will be described in a subsequent chapter.) Under this system of collusive pricing an important firm is usually the one to decide upon and initiate a price change, which is then automatically followed by the other companies. It is, of course, difficult to generalize with respect to how much consultation takes place between industry officials prior to the initiation of a price change by the leader. If a great deal of interchange occurs, the system may not differ basically from that of overt agreement on price. If, however, the leader initiates the change after little or no advice from others in the industry, the form of collusion is quite different in nature. It is then primarily an "agree-ment to agree" on price rather than an agreement as to what the ac-tual price should be.

Frequently, the largest firm in the industry acts as price leader. If the product is sold in interstate commerce, there is danger in this practice, however, since the pattern may be too obvious to any inter-ested antitrust investigator. For this reason, it may be safer to have other firms initiate the price change from time to time, with the "leader" a temporary follower. To carry out this sort of rotation of

Exhibit 5

RIVALS' REACTIONS HAVE GREAT   RIVALS' REACTIONS NOT HIGHLY
            IMPORTANCE   IMPORTANT

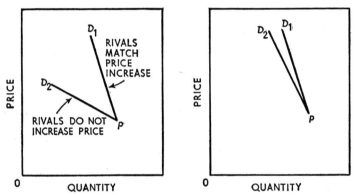

leadership, however, may require so much co-operation that the col-lusion is really of the price-agreement variety rather than one of actual price leadership.

Some light can be cast on the phenomenon of oligopolistic price leadership by means of a chart similar to Exhibit 3 of this chapter. In Exhibit 5, both sides of the diagram show the demand curve which would obtain if (1) rivals match a price increase or (2) rivals do not match a price increase.[9] On the left-hand side, sales by the price-raising firm will fall off sharply if rivals do not increase their prices. On the right side, however, it does not make a great deal of difference to the price-raising firm whether or not rivals go along with the change. This may be the situation because the firm represented on the right accounts for a large percentage of the sale of the commodity. This firm is in a

---

[9] Exhibit 3 was based on reactions following a price cut rather than an increase in price. For purposes of analyzing price leadership, it is more convenient to assume an in-crease in price.

better position to be the industry price leader than the firm on the left, because in the event of a rebellion on the part of the other companies with respect to following its lead, it will not lose heavily in sales. The more vulnerable firm on the left would find its volume badly reduced if it attempted to lead a price increase and others did not follow. If there is an understanding that the large firm will let the smaller one lead, this danger is, of course, diminished.

Possession of the power of price leadership places a firm in an enviable position. It is much easier to calculate the probable effect on sales when there is assurance that others will follow a price change. The "rivals match" demand curve becomes the one which the leader can count on in its attempt to set price and output in such a way as to maximize its own profits; that is, it can attempt to equate marginal cost with marginal revenue computed from this demand. A price leader which is anxious to insure industry co-operation on a long-run basis may, however, set a price which it does not consider optimal for itself if its own optimum price would be quite unsatisfactory to other companies.

Nonprice Competition

Even where it is the industry practice not to compete in price, firms are usually in vigorous competition for sales—"nonprice competition" then exists. There are three principal forms of nonprice competition: (1) variation in quality and style, (2) sales promotion, and (3) extension of services and other terms of trade. These methods of competition are sometimes alternatives; frequently, they supplement one another.

Quality and Style Competition

In relatively few markets today are firms engaged in selling competing standardized products. This is especially true of final consumer goods, as was pointed out earlier. Competition in quality, style, and design is the most common form of nonprice competition.

The concept of "quality" is by no means simple. It involves numerous variables, some of which can be measured; others are incapable of measurement. Any one product can involve several quality variables. An automobile, for example, can be appraised as to horsepower, durability, gasoline consumption, probable frequency and cost of repairs, comfort, riding qualities, safety, and ease of handling.

Competition in some industries has served to give the consumer substantial improvements over the years, with part of the gain reflected in lower prices and the rest in better quality. For example, since World War I, automobile tires have been both improved greatly in quality and lowered in price. Economy of operation is another aspect of quality competition which can be measured approximately. According to tests made by the Procurement Division of the United States Treasury in 1931, the average consumption of 5 makes of 6-cubic-foot refrigerators was 44 kilowatt-hours per month. A test based on 14 makes in 1938 showed average electricity consumption to have declined to 35 kilowatt-hours per month.[10] By 1954, this amount of current was sufficient to operate the average 8.3- to 9.6-cubic-foot refrigerators for a month, according to tests by Consumers Union.[11] Improvements such as these afford successive occasions for firms to engage in nonprice competition.

Although many quality changes are physically measurable in terms of performance, as a rule it is impossible to translate these changes into price equivalents.[12] Where quality changes are of the intangible sort involving design, taste, and style, not even measures of physical performance are available. Yet these intangible elements are often the chief determinants of consumer choice. In women's clothing, for example, the indefinable element of style is far more important than are thread count, tensile strength of the cloth, or quality of workmanship. The success of a new model of automobile is determined more by the design of the hood than by the efficiency of the motor.

The degree to which quality competition emphasizes measurable elements of the product varies with commodities. Where industrial buyers constitute the chief market, there is a tendency to stress such features as operating economy, tensile strength, and durability. In consumer goods markets, sellers find it desirable to emphasize the intangible elements of quality, style, and design because these are less easily copied. Sellers of food products seldom mention their conformity with government standards of quality; sellers of dresses do not usually emphasize fiber content; and distributors of cosmetics do not ordinarily refer to the quality of ingredients of their products. Flavor, style, and attractive containers are more important selling features.

The practice of selling goods at generally adopted price lines is a

---

[10] T.N.E.C. Monograph No. 1 (76th Congress, 3rd Session), *Price Behavior and Business Policy* (Washington, D.C.: U.S. Government Printing Office, 1940), p. 64.

[11] Calculated from data given in *Consumer Reports,* September, 1954, p. 403.

[12] Andrew T. Court made an interesting attempt to develop a price index for automobiles which would reflect changes not only in price but also in weight, wheelbase, and horsepower, expressed in terms of price (cf. A. T. Court, *Dynamics of Automobile Demand* [New York: General Motors Corporation, 1939], pp. 99–117).

reflection of the basic competition in quality, rather than price, which prevails in some industries. Although price lining extends to many markets at wholesale and retail, it is almost universal in the apparel industry. In women's dresses, for example, the following wholesale prices have become established through habit and tradition:

$1.875 each..........$10.75 each		$4.75 each........$19.75 each	
2.25 " .... 12.75 "		6.75 " .... 22.75 "	
2.875 " .... 14.75 "		7.75 " .... 29.75 "	
3.75 " .... 16.75 "		8.75 " .... 39.75 and over	

Rarely, if ever, are these prices subject to modification by bargaining. Competition among manufacturers producing for the $6.75 dress market centers not on price but upon quality of materials, workmanship, and especially upon style. Buyers, in turn, accept these price lines and concentrate attention on getting the best values at each of the recognized price levels. In retail markets, there is a similar, if less defined, clustering of prices at certain major price lines. The United States Bureau of Labor Statistics, in reporting 114 quotations from 32 cities for women's medium-quality, woven elastic girdles, showed distribution of price frequencies on June 15, 1938, as in Exhibit 6. Similar concen-

Exhibit 6

Price	Number of Quotations	Price	Number of Quotations
$2.95..................	4	$4.00................	1
2.98..................	2	4.69................	1
3.39..................	1	5.00................	67
3.50..................	32	5.50................	2
3.59.................	1		
3.95..................	2	Total............	114
3.98.................	1		

tration of retail prices at a few price lines is evident in other types of merchandise. Prior to the war the retail prices of vacuum cleaners, for example, were usually spaced at intervals of $10 from $39.95 to $79.95.[13] For some products, price lines are preserved by modifying quantity rather than quality of the product. The usual price lines, dictated by customer convenience, of 5 and 10 cents for chocolate candy bars has led manufacturers to make frequent adjustments in the weight of their products. Quantity adjustments of this sort actually amount to price changes, since price per ounce is altered.

[13] T.N.E.C. Monograph No. 1, pp 70–71.

Sales Promotion

As an alternative to varying the product, many business companies compete by incurring selling expenses which are directed primarily at creating demand. Collectively, these expenditures can be called "sales promotion." Among the most spectacular is advertising, which involves outlays for newspaper and magazine publicity, direct mail, catalogues, television and radio programs, window displays, and packaging. The basic characteristic of these expenditures is that they are undertaken with a view to influencing the buyer, though some changes of the physical form of the product, as in packaging, may also be involved. Obviously, in some cases, it is difficult to distinguish changes in the product expressly designed for their effect on the consumer from those which have substantive utility. Who is to say whether a catsup bottle which is conveniently designed for table use may not also be the one whose contours catch the consumer's eye on the supermarket shelf?

Related to advertising is the use of trade-marks and brand names. The purpose of these is to furnish an easy means of identifying a particular seller's product. It is conceivable that brands might be employed merely to enable the buyer to identify products embodying certain measurable quality differences. But usually, sellers combine the use of brands with advertising which attempts to persuade buyers that the product has certain desirable intangible characteristics which are unique or which it possesses in greater degree than competing goods. The brand is built into a limited monopoly, with a regular following created by advertising.

The effectiveness with which trade-marks and brands can protect a product against price competition varies with different lines of goods. In fields in which comparisons are relatively simple, or in markets where buyers are well equipped technically (as in many industrial goods markets), there is a strong tendency for buyers to switch to competing brands as soon as substantial price differences appear. On the other hand, where the consumer is unable to compare rival brands intelligently, the effective use of brands and trade-marks frequently permits wide price differentials to be maintained between virtually identical products. A lack of correspondence between price and United States Department of Agriculture grade for particular food products often exists. In the case of grocery products, the element of taste is so subjective that comparisons among brands are very difficult; and, as a result, sellers are presented with an opportunity to create demand through nonprice competition. Similar situations exist in many other lines. A

Federal Trade Commission investigation revealed that the Goodyear Tire and Rubber Company sold tires to Sears Roebuck under the brand name "All State" which were of the same quality as those marketed by Goodyear under its own "All Weather" brand. The difference in wholesale prices between these two brands ranged from 29 to 40 per cent in the period 1927–33. At retail, All State tires were sold at prices 20 to 25 per cent below those of All Weather tires.[14] The most striking illustrations of the insulation from price competition afforded by brand names are in the drug and cosmetic field. The consumer is almost completely uninformed as to the merits of rival products; few are aware of the significance of specifications of the United States Pharmacopoeia. Here, patent-medicine advertising has free rein.

Where brands are "fair-traded" under the resale price-maintenance laws, retail price competition is effectively ruled out. In these situations, competition must necessarily be in advertising, service, and other nonprice forms. To some extent, private brands supply alternatives on which price competition can take place; but these are not universally available, nor do they constitute complete substitutes for well-advertised brands which have been "fair-traded."

Other devices of sales promotion include personal selling, free distribution of samples of the product, give-away contests (which have gained such great popularity in recent years, especially on nationally televised programs), and other methods, such as the use of coupons exchangeable for other products. With regard to personal selling, it should be noted that some use of salesmen's time is for "production," such as making estimates, giving instruction in the use of the product, handling complaints, and making collections. But it cannot be doubted that the chief use of salesmen is for promotion of demand for the product. As such, personal selling is an alternative or a supplement to other means of sales promotion.

Competition in Services and Other Terms of Trade

Such concessions as freight allowances, discounts, and coupons with definite cash value can be translated in terms of price. There are many terms of trade and collateral services, however, which cannot easily be commuted into price differences. The increased resort to nonprice competition has led many sellers to use "escape devices" in order to attract trade. A comprehensive list of these methods of modifying the terms

---

[14] Federal Trade Commission, Docket No. 2116.

of sale is presented in the Appendix to this introduction.[15] It will be observed that a few of these concessions, especially those in the first group, can be directly expressed in price terms.

The inability of businessmen to compete in price because of legal barriers or because of private price agreements or cartel arrangements has frequently led to ingenious methods of nonprice competition. Under the N.R.A., when prices were controlled by code provisions, a retail druggist in California, unable to cut prices, employed a medium to give free psychic readings to his customers! An automobile dealer was accused of price cutting because he bought six suits of clothes from a tailor to whom he sold a car.[16] In many cases, of course, the services form an integral and necessary part of the sales transaction. The purchaser of an automobile or household appliance reasonably looks to the manufacturer to maintain adequate facilities for repair and replacement of parts. The conscientious effort made by many sellers of technical goods to supply continuing service for their products bespeaks the importance of this form of nonprice competition. It is to be clearly distinguished from the proliferation of unwanted services which exists in some fields.

Effects of Nonprice Competition

The results of competition through other means than price can be considered from the standpoint of (1) the business company which employs these methods and (2) the consumer whose welfare is affected by the shift to nonprice competition. The point of view of this book is primarily that of the business company; however, no business policies can be adjudged sound in the long run if they are basically detrimental to the interest of the consumer—hence the need for considering the effect of business policies on the latter.

The use of nonprice competition protects the seller to some extent against price cuts made by competitors. Nonprice competition can bring direct benefits to the firm in larger volume of sales. Under many circumstances, this greater output can be produced at lower unit costs, which increase profits more than proportionally on the additional units. As a defensive measure, nonprice competition may also be preferable to price cuts, because customers who might be attracted to competitors by price cuts are more likely to remain securely with a seller who differentiates his product either by qualitative differences or by service or

---

[15] Cf. pp. 226–31 ff.
[16] T.N.E.C. Monograph No. 1, p. 56.

advertising nonprice competition; in other words, nonprice competition is a superior method of retaining customer goodwill. Where sales promotion is used skillfully, it is capable of reducing seasonal fluctuations in sales and stabilizing production and employment. The Proctor and Gamble Company claims that its operations have been stabilized in this way. On the other hand, some retail sales promotion appears to accentuate sales peaks, as in the case of department store trade at Christmas and Easter. Companies which have become well known through sales promotion also find certain collateral advantages of operation, such as easier procurement of personnel and facilitated sale of securities.

Sales promotion is not without disadvantages to the company employing it. Large advertising budgets are in the nature of recurring cash outlays which must be sustained to prevent sales from falling. A substantial amount of advertising must be looked on as the competitive burden of maintaining a share of the market, not of enlarging it. The institution of style cycles and annual model changes in some industries leaves firms in a precarious position where each new season presents a gamble. In the automobile industry, for example, there have been marked differences in the competitive success of yearly models. Companies which resort to nonprice competition expose themselves frequently to nonassessable risks. On the whole, however, businessmen appear to prefer these risks to those of price competition.

Effects on the Consumer

Much of the foregoing discussion has indicated the effects of nonprice competition on the consumer. In some cases, there seems to be little doubt that he has been benefited by competition in quality. The improvements in many technical products—such as automobiles, television and radio sets, and home appliances—over the last three decades are obviously advantageous to the consumer, and these changes have been brought about chiefly by competition in quality. Although less evident, the improvement of industrial goods—such as structural steel, chemicals, and electronic devices—has also contributed materially to improving production processes and products. The focusing of style competition on a relatively small number of price lines in the apparel trades has likewise had many advantages, reducing the costs of carrying inventories, reducing selling time at wholesale and retail levels, and simplifying the problem of selection for the final consumer. In some cases, but not all, sales promotion has stimulated demand to such an extent that, with declining costs of production due to economies of scale, the product has become available at a lower price to consumers. (The exact results of sales promotion depend on the shape of the demand and cost curves, and on the effects of transference of demand and resources from other industries.) It is possible, moreover, to count as benefits the incidental advantages which sales promotion offers, such as radio and television entertainment, a cheap press, and certain "free" services. None of them, of course, is to be regarded as a *net* gain, and all could probably be more cheaply gotten by direct rather than by indirect expenditure by consumers.

Conclusion

The disadvantages of nonprice competition have been strongly emphasized, if not overemphasized, by many critics. If the cost of securing a product which is sold through nonprice competition (such as advertising) be compared with the cost of producing it under pure competition—where, by definition, there would need to be no advertising—it may be more costly to produce the product under nonprice competition. But, as has been indicated in earlier parts of this volume, the rarity of pure competition among actual market structures makes this comparison of little practical importance. Given the degree of imperfection which seems an essential characteristic of most markets, the question is: Does nonprice competition necessarily increase prices to the consumer? Where there is no net expansion of market demand, and where firms are engaged in competitive advertising, it seems clear that prices will be increased by nonprice competition. This result certainly follows where nonprice competition takes the form of sales promotion. The judgment on quality and style competition is more difficult, because it involves some determination of how many styles and how much differentiation of product consumers really want. In the absence of more objective criteria, it must be concluded that they want as much as they are willing to pay for under conditions of adequate information about alternatives (e.g., under these conditions, a consumer might choose between a brand-name tomato juice at 15 cents per can and United States Grade A tomato juice at 13 cents per can).

Perhaps the strongest objection to nonprice competition is that, as more expensive, improved products are placed on the market, the lower-priced, stripped models frequently disappear. The "low-priced" automobiles, for example, have virtually all of the costly refinements of the larger cars. A partial answer to this objection is that—in durable goods, at least—the secondhand market satisfies the needs of those who want lower-priced products. Another objection is that advertising has in some cases been used to mislead consumers; but in accuracy, it must be acknowledged that the standards of most large advertisers are above reproach. The difficulty seems to lie more, not in deliberate deception, but in failure to give more objective information about the product. In large part, this is traceable to the nature of the typical consumer, who is more likely to be swayed by fancy names attached to automobiles and their motors, or by the picture of a pretty girl standing by the car, than by the technical description of the characteristics of the motor and body.

APPENDIX

Under the N.R.A. codes, businessmen were frequently forbidden to cut prices. As a result, numerous forms of evasion sprang up. The following list of concessions designed to influence sales was prepared by the Division of Industrial Economics of the National Recovery Administration:

1. Concessions primarily related to time of buyer's payment:
   Discounts.
   "Terms" and "conditions" of sale or payment.
   Credit practices.
   Credit terms.
   Cash discounts.
   Periods of free credit.
   Interest rate beyond free-credit period.
   Datings.
   Seasonal datings.
   Installment sales.
   Deferred payment.
   Anticipation of bills.
   Sales to delinquent accounts.
   Sales not contingent upon buyer's credit standing.
   Payment due when money received from other sources.
   Retained percentages.
2. Concessions primarily related to risks of buyer:
   Guarantees.
   Price guarantees.
   Contracts for deferred delivery not subject to price change.
   Price offer not subject to change.
   Advance notification of price change.
   Delaying acceptance of order.
   Options.
   Agreements indefinite as to time or quantity.
   Offers without time limit.
   Offers not expiring within specified period of time.
   Offers without withdrawal provisions.
   Guarantees against defective goods.
   Product guarantees.

Product guarantees against other than defective merchandise.

Uniform product guarantees specified in code.

Guarantees in excess of manufacturer's warranty (distributing and fabricating codes).

Maintenance guarantees.

Adjusting incorrect shipments.

Accepting return of merchandise.

Accepting return of obsolete, discontinued, or "unsalable" merchandise.

Exchanging merchandise.

Accepting return of other than defective merchandise.

Repurchase agreements.

"Money-back" agreements.

Sales subject to trial.

Sales on approval.

Shipments without order.

Sales on consignment or memorandum.

Storing goods with customer.

Display for direct sale in customer's store.

Renting or leasing industry products.

Resale guarantees.

Agreeing that payment be governed by sales of secondary product.

Accepting orders for specific jobs before customer secures award.

Guaranteeing accounts due customer.

"Compensation of customer for business losses."

Unilateral agreements (buyer not bound).

Contracts containing penalty clauses.

Contracts not subject to adjustment necessitated by noncontrollable factors.

Assuming liability for nonperformance caused by noncontrollable factors.

Assuming liability for damage to buyer's drawings or equipment caused by noncontrollable factors.

Assuming liability for errors in plans or specifications furnished or approved by buyer.

Assuming liability for consequential damages.

Assuming liability for patent infringement.

Failure to give advance notice of discontinued lines.

3. Concessions primarily related to supplying additional goods:

Any gratuities.

Free deals.

Premiums.

Sales of other or additional goods at reduced prices.

Combination sales.

Combination offers.

Coupons.

Samples.

Scrip books.

Prices.

Sales promotion awards.
Containers.
Special containers.
Labels.
Special labels.
Special equipment.
Accessories.
Certain advertising material.
Display materials.
Printed matter (other than advertising material).

4. Concessions rendered buyer through use of seller's employees or property:
Any unusual service.
Providing sales help.
Demonstrating.
Estimating.
Furnishing drawings.
Furnishing plans and specifications.
Furnishing surveys and formulas.
Installation and erection.
Inspections.
Furnishing unusual processing services specified in codes.
Stampings or markings.
Repair and maintenance.
Reconditioning.
Engineering services.
Handling.
Crating or packing.
Repacking.
Delivery service by seller's trucks.
Warehousing and storage.
Lending of equipment.
Permitting retention of trade-in equipment.

5. Concessions rendered buyer through financial assistance or favors:
Favors.
Entertaining.
Patronizing publications in which buyer is interested.
Participating in group showing.
Gifts.
Gifts to organizations (in which buyer is interested).
Paying buyer's personal expenses.
Paying permit or inspection fees of buyers.
Paying customer's insurance.
Paying customer's advertising expenses for products other than member's.
Assuming reversed telephone or telegraph charges.
Assisting customer to obtain used products for trade-ins.
Assisting customer to find purchaser for used products.
Subsidizing or financing buyer.
Employing customers, employees, relatives, associates.

Purchase of buyer's capital stock.

Financing payments due customers.

6. Concessions related to manner and/or time of shipment:

Split shipments.

Shipments smaller than specified minimum.

Tolerance in time of shipment.

Deferred delivery.

7. Concessions through payment or diversion of commissions or fees to customer:

Payment of commissions or fees by members to buyers.

Payment of commissions or fees by members to other than bona fide or controlled sales representatives.

Payment of commissions or fees by members to purchasing agents compensated by buyers.

Payments of commissions or fees by agents of members to buyers.

Splitting of commissions or fees by agents of members with agents of buyers without buyer's knowledge.

Splitting of commissions or fees by members or their agents with buyers or their agents.

Payment of brokerage to other than bona fide brokers.

8. Concessions through allowances or payments for value rendered by buyer:

Allowances.

Trade-in allowances.

Advertising allowances.

Catalogue allowances.

Distribution service allowances.

Container allowances.

Installation allowances.

Allowance for further processing.

Maintenance or repair allowance.

Rental allowances for space hired.

Allowances on supplies furnished by purchaser for production of product ordered.

Cartage allowances when buyer receives goods at factory.

Allowance for special service.

Label allowances.

Purchasing from buyer.

Renting from buyer.

9. Concessions through acceptance of competitor's materials from buyers:

Exchange of own for competitor's products.

Purchase of competitor's products from customer.

10. Concessions through sale of substandard or obsolete goods:

Sale of seconds.

Sale of used goods.

Sale of damaged goods.

Sale of rebuilt or overhauled goods.

Sale of demonstrators.

Sale of obsolete goods.

Sale of discontinued lines.
Willful manufacture of substandard products.
Sale of returns.
Sale of scrap.
Sale of chaff.
Sale of culled goods.
Sale of surplus stock.

11. Concessions granted during performance contrary to provisions of agreement:
    Rebates.
    Departure from credit of contract.
    Settlement of old accounts at less than full value.
    Permitting improper deductions when buyer remits.
    Permitting buyer's cancellation or repudiation.
    Substitution of higher quality or greater quantity of goods.
    Substitution of new contract at lower price.
    Receipting bills before payment.
    Extending or exceeding contract.
    Collateral agreement not to enforce part of contract.
    Departure from delivery date of contract.
    Retroactive settlement or adjustments.

12. Acceptance of forms of payment in which concessions may be concealed:
    Accepting securities.
    Accepting buyer's capital stock.
    Accepting goods from buyer.
    Accepting real or personal property.
    Accepting negotiable instruments.
    Accepting other than lawful money.
    Accepting credit transferred from one buyer to another.
    Selling for customer account and accepting proceeds for credit.
    Accepting form of payment other than specified in code.
    Accepting rental payments as part payment on purchases.
    Accepting deposit made to another manufacturer.
    Assignments (of receivables, etc.).

13. Types of agreements, offers, invoicing, etc., by means of which concessions may be concealed:
    Oral agreements.
    Oral offers.
    Oral appraisals.
    Oral orders.
    False billing.
    False orders.
    False receipts.
    False agreements.
    False offers.
    Delayed billing.
    Misdated invoices.
    Misdated contracts.

Misdated orders.
Misdated offers.
Misdated receipts.
Invoices omitting terms of sale.
Invoices omitting date of shipment.
Invoices omitting specifications.
Invoices omitting other specified detail.
Agreements omitting terms of sale.
Agreements omitting date of shipment.
Agreements omitting specifications.
Agreements omitting other specified detail.
Offers omitting terms of sale.
Offers omitting date of shipment.
Offers omitting specifications.
Offers omitting other specified detail.
Orders omitting terms of sale.
Orders omitting date of shipment.
Orders omitting specifications.
Orders omitting other specified detail.
Split billing.
Lump-sum offers.
Unitemized billing.
Orders not subject to member's acceptance.
Auction sales.
14. Types of agreements, offers, invoicing, etc., primarily designed to prevent
    the concealing of concessions:
Uniform contract form.
Uniform order form.
Uniform bid or quotation form.
Standard invoice form.
Standard leasing form.
Form of contract.

CASE 6–1: ACME-WESTERN MACHINERY COMPANY

Mr. Paul Bigelow, president of the Acme-Western Machinery Company, in reviewing the company's operations for 1949, noted that there was a decline in the production of heavy tools and equipment. The company manufactured heavy machinery for the construction industry. Its chief products were trucks, bulldozers, power shovels, and loading machinery. In addition, it produced heavy concrete-mixing machinery and builders' concrete-handling equipment. None of the trucks were of less than eight-ton capacity, and they were usually built to order. While the bulldozers and power shovels were more standardized, they were of a very heavy type and were manufactured by only two other firms in the United States. About 65 per cent of the company's business consisted of building equipment to specifications. The company maintained a staff of engineers who either visited jobs where such equipment was needed or assisted contractors in drawing up equipment specifications for their particular type of work.

The company was organized in 1925, for the purpose of building road-maintenance machinery. In that year, Mr. Bigelow produced a machine designed for the upkeep of dirt and gravel roads. By 1930 the company had built some road-construction machinery and ditch-digging equipment. It was not until the second World War that the company began to build heavy-duty equipment on a large scale. To meet the increase in demand for its equipment, the company had about doubled its capacity as of 1940. The company operated its own foundry and machine shops. Motors for the trucks and other power equipment were purchased from other firms and usually were standardized. The motor manufacturers and the Acme-Western Machinery Company often engaged in joint research for the purpose of designing more powerful engines as larger and heavier equipment was demanded.

The price policy of the company had always been one of cost of labor and materials plus a percentage for overhead and profit. The accounting department had developed a system of standard costs which was frequently checked and revised in an attempt to keep in line with actual costs. The company had shown an annual profit from its organization through 1930, when the impact of the depression caused a sharp curtailment of operations. Prior to 1930, production had been at an average of 90 per cent of capacity. During the early thirties, operations dropped as low as 5 per cent of capacity; as a result, the company suffered deficits from 1931 to 1935, inclusive. Practically all the operations during that time consisted of the production of parts, with occasional orders for a new piece of equipment. The company entered the depression with a sizable inventory of parts, so that little production of these was undertaken early in that period. In an effort to keep costs at a minimum, the company purchased parts and sublet jobs to other firms if the price quoted was lower than the company was able to meet in its own plant. In 1936 the company showed a small profit, but a heavy loss was incurred in 1937, with the sharp recession of that year. Subsequent to that year the company had shown an annual profit.

The main products of the company were relatively expensive and of high durability. A 10-ton earth-mover truck, for example, sold in 1949 for about $30,000–$40,000, depending upon specifications. A concrete-mixing and -loading plant, which could be assembled and dis-assembled for movement from job to job, with a capacity of 425 yards per eight hours, sold for about $60,000–$75,000, according to specifications. The first 10-ton truck built by the firm in 1934 was still in operation, as was the first gravel loader, built in 1927. Some of this equipment had been modernized by rebuilding. There was also the problem of used equipment, especially in periods of low construction activity.

In February, 1950, Mr. Bigelow attended the convention of the Associated General Contractors of America, Inc., at San Francisco, California. The attitude which prevailed at the convention, and which was shared by Mr. Bigelow, is described in the following column which appeared in the *Wall Street Journal* of March 2, 1950:

This country in 1950 will probably see the biggest volume of building in its history—but, brother, will the competition be fierce!

That's the chorus coming from 1,500 building contractors meeting here this week for the annual convention of the Associated General Contractors of America, Inc. They're the men who lay the nation's roads, build the dams and factories, the skyscrapers and apartment houses. You'd think they'd be singing a hymn of rejoicing. They are wailing the blues.

The reason is simple: Too many builders. A good index to their mush-rooming growth is the membership roster of the Associated General Contractors. In 1939, members numbered 2,300. By January, 1945, the roll call had expanded to 3,161, and four years later, on January 1, 1949, there were 5,009. Another 502 firms joined last year; the total now is 5,511. This figure takes in almost all the big building firms, and the trade association says its members do 80 per cent of all U.S. contract construction. But there are thousands of other small contractors, and their ranks have swelled, too. The A.G.C. estimates there are more than 32,000 contract builders in the country today.

But building volume hasn't increased recently at that pace. This year, estimate statistical experts of the Associated General Contractors, total U.S. construction will hit $30 billion—$20 billion in new building and about $10 billion in maintenance and repair work. That $20 billion guess—should it come to pass—would be a slight $700 million more than the 1949 record of $19,300 million of new building. At the wartime peak, where there were only a little more than half as many contractors as now, new construction totaled $18 billion.

That discrepancy means contractors are at each other's throats on almost every job that comes on the market. Nearly all non-residential building is awarded on a bid basis. Result: they've had to trim profit margins, often to loss levels, to beat out the other fellow. That trend, which began last year, is certain to grow in 1950, say builders from coast to coast.

In San Diego, for instance, where a 10 per cent increase in construction is expected this year, as many as 30 bidders for medium-sized highway jobs are reported. "Up to last year the average public project would draw five to eight bidders," says John A. Volpe, of the Volpe Construction Co. of Malden, Mass. "We recently bid against 19 others for a high school job."

In Spokane, Washington, 13 to 15 bidders are reported as "average" these days and a lot of contracts attract as many as 25 to 30. In Los Angeles, where 1950 construction is expected to set a new peak, competition has reached a frantic stage John MacLeod, president of the Macco Corporation there, reports, "One project in the million dollar class recently had 33 bidders."

New York's F. H. McGraw & Company—not a member of the Associated General Contractors—agrees there are "too many contractors bidding for each job." Relates an official: "We submitted a bid for an industrial plant, believing we were one of three bidders. We later discovered there were 30 bids submitted. If we had known there were going to be that many, we wouldn't have bothered."

Adds Gayle Armstrong, of Armstrong & Armstrong, located in Roswell, New Mexico: "I bid on a dam job in Texas about two weeks ago. There were more than 20 bidders. Our bid was about $3 million. I figured we'd get beat by $300,000 to $400,000. Actually the low bid was around $2 million and the average was around $2,700,000."

Bidding for contracts can be expensive. One company estimates the cost of preparing a bid for constructing a $2 million industrial plant might run from $2,000 to $5,000—with all the odds against its acceptance. An executive tells of another firm that submitted bids on 85 jobs before it was awarded one. In Kentucky, a month ago, the low bid on a piece of highway construction was $836,087. Before the bidding, state road engineers had estimated it would cost $1,012,887 to do the job.

Another problem that general contractors have to contend with is the growing practice of contract splitting. An industrial firm, for instance, planning to put up a new plant, asks for one set of bids for excavation work, another batch for plumbing and heating, and still a third for installation of machinery. Contracts are awarded separately for each type of work to the low bidder in that field.

How do builders feel about this trend? A Portland, Oregon contractor, Donald W. Hall of E. C. Hall & Company, sums up the mood: "We're doing more work, but on much smaller margins than ever before. Our capital investment is a great deal larger than ever and, frankly, many of us are beginning to worry about the future." But there's also a bright side to this picture. "At least the customer should be happy—he's getting more for his money than he has in years," remarks a midwestern contractor.

The bidding battle has already resulted in building "prices" dipping an average of 10 per cent from the peak reached late in 1948. Costs of some kinds of work have come down more than others; some fees are still declining, others have more or less stabilized. The contractors' association has just completed a poll of its members on cost trends. This survey, covering all parts of the nation, shows the cost of building new factories, stores and big apartment houses now averages 8.5 per cent under the 1948 high. Contractors think that figure will stay steady through 1950. Heavier construction—dams, bridges, railroads and large public works projects—now cost 10 per cent less and builders look for some "stability" in that division. But the "price" of highly competitive highway work is still sliding, with the average decline nearly 13 per cent.

Of this year's looked-for $20 billion in new building, about $2 billion is expected to go into road projects (1949 road work cost $1,700 million); some $6,500 million for one-family type houses ($500 million more than last year; another $6,500 million (about the same amount as in 1949) for heavy construction, such as big public works, pipelines, railroads, dams and the like; and the remaining $5 billion for factories, stores, apartment houses and smaller public works, such as schools or hospitals, is expected to be some $300 million below last year.

The contractors foresee a shift this year toward less private construction. Based on their survey, they predict a decline in industrial building, such as new factories, will more than offset an expected increase in new housing. They estimate $13,500 million of the year's anticipated $20 billion in new work will be for private construction and the other $6,500 million for public works. Last year the ratio was $14 billion private and $5,500 million public.

Except in the housing field, building men believe construction volume will hold at a high level for several years. But how long can the present intense competition continue without undermining the industry? There'll be a natural readjustment, some prophesy, during this year. "It looks," says an East Coast contractor, "like the start of the battle to weed out the weak ones." Some weak ones, it would appear, are already dropping by the wayside. Dun & Bradstreet counted 65 building contractor failures during January, up from 53 in the similar month last year. The number laying aside hammers and hods during all of 1949 was 838—91 per cent over the 1948 casualty list. This mortality increase was more striking than for industry as a whole which last year ran 76.1 per cent over the 1948 figure.

Many builders trace the roots of their troubles back to wartime. Then, many building organizations grew to huge size to meet the demand for swift-paced construction of airports, army camps and other defense needs. Now many of these firms are reluctant to shrink in size or to reduce their key personnel. Consequently, they have too much plant, men and equipment for the work available. They have to keep bidding to keep their machinery busy. "The whole construction industry is out of kilter," claims a southwestern contractor. "The tendency is to put more equipment on a job and do it faster. That's what is eating up the volume so fast. Some outfits take jobs when they know they haven't a chance to make a profit. They've got equipment on which they have to meet payments so they take the cheap jobs." Adds Walter L. Couse of Detroit: "There are a large number of firms which have entered the field during and since the war and not yet reached stability. They take anything to keep busy, and, in a lot of cases, have only gotten in deeper. Some large firms doing the same thing can stand the losses better, but their lower bids force others out."

Some old-timers in the business are trying to "wait out" the situation by bidding only on a profitable basis. Says F. W. Parrott, president of C. F. Lytle Company of Sioux City, Iowa: "When we bid on a job we do it on a conservative basis in the hope that some day bids will be let that way again. That means that right now only half our plant and top personnel is occupied.

The overhead is eating into our reserves. We went through the same kind of a cycle in the middle 30's." One of the West Coast's biggest building firms has stopped bidding on highway work. "It's too competitive for us," declares an official. "The people who are bidding are losing their shirts."

Often firms which have decided to submit low bids find ex-employees competing with them. In New England, reports an eastern builder: "There are still more contractors coming into the field than going out. The newcomers are mostly men who worked as estimators, managers, or superintendents for other contractors. Some are finding the pasture is not as green as they expected."

If a contractor wants to stay in the bidding against the pressure of sharp competition, he has to do so, say builders, against costs that have not dropped nearly as fast as the bid in prices. "There's no sign of labor costs coming down this year," reports Paul Frederickson, of Seattle. Adds M. C. Harrison, of Pittsburgh: "When we see excavation work going on for as much as 30 per cent below our cost estimates in a territory where wages are unionized and holding stable, we know the pinch is tight." Other builders say a greater efficiency on the part of workers is helping offset only a part of high wage costs. Some materials prices have eased, contractors report, but most building equipment "is not down a dime" according to one contractor who says his investment in machinery is more than double the pre-war cost. L. M. Denton, of Detroit, concurs: "That amount you have to have in order to keep yourself in a strong competitive position means at least 25 to 30 per cent more machines than were necessary before the war." C. P. Street of McDevitt & Street Company, located in Charlotte, North Carolina, comments: "There haven't been sufficient decreases in labor or material costs to justify the price decreases since October, 1948. Some of the latter decline has come about through increased efficiency of labor and lower sub-contract prices, but lower general contract prices have mainly stemmed from over-eagerness."

In some parts of the country, contractors are also worrying over a downtrend in private industrial and commercial construction, offset only by a corresponding uptrend in public works. Says an East Coast builder: "Only work involving public funds has kept the market up at all in our area lately. So far the situation is not alarming. Private postwar construction has more or less caught up and institutional and public building that's held back is now going ahead. At the moment, the proportion is distorted in favor of public building. But if this trend continues it will worry us." A Long Beach, California, builder adds: "If municipal construction were to stop, the construction industry would be in a very serious condition. This prospect is ominous."

Upon his return from the convention, Mr. Bigelow called a meeting of his board of directors and outlined the situation to them. Two of the directors proposed that the company immediately make a general reduction in prices, so that volume of output might be maintained. Mr. Bigelow pointed out that to do this would mean a reduction in the profit margin, since there was no indication of a decrease in the company's labor costs and there was considerable rumor that there would be an increase in the price of steel. Mr. Bigelow had advised the directors at an earlier meeting that a decline in output was to be expected in 1950; but since attending the convention, he was more pessimistic as to reaching the level earlier proposed. This meant that unit costs would necessarily rise somewhat. To this, the same two directors favored an immediate price reduction to increase the volume of sales.

QUESTIONS

1. Do you agree with the two directors who proposed a price reduction?
2. What is the nature of demand for heavy equipment in the building industry?
3. Is there any information in the newspaper account which would indicate that the market for heavy builders' equipment is about saturated? Is there anything in the account to indicate that the "acceleration principle" operated in this industry during and following the war years? What effect would this have upon the outlook for the Acme-Western Machinery Company?
4. How does the expected decline in the number of builders affect the Acme-Western Machinery Company? Would the situation be any different if, instead of two competitors, the Acme-Western Machinery Company had a dozen competitors?
5. What recommendations would you make, as president of the company?
6. Why does the number of building contractors fluctuate so sharply from year to year?

CASE 6–2: THE BERYLLIUM ALLOY INDUSTRY[17]

On May 9, 1939, Mr. H. L. Randall, president of the Riverside Metal Company, of Riverside, New Jersey, submitted the following statement of price policies to the Temporary National Economic Committee:

The price schedules issued by the Riverside Metal Company are contingent upon the prices published by the larger units of the industry. From time to time these larger units publish their scale of prices, and our company has no alternative except to meet such published prices in order to compete.

Beryllium is an element which can be combined with copper, nickel, and certain other metals to produce alloys which possess great qualities of hardness, lightness, and strength. The principal industrial form in which this metal is used is in the alloy, beryllium copper, which con-

---

[17] Material for this case was derived largely from *T.N.E.C. Hearings,* Part 5 (76th Congress, 1st Session) (Washington, D.C.: U.S. Government Printing Office, 1939).

sists of about 2 per cent beryllium and 98 per cent copper. The chief advantages of beryllium copper are the combination of extraordinary high-fatigue properties with good electrical conductivity. Beryllium alloys have many industrial uses, such as parts for electric motors, telephone instruments, diamond drills, and airplanes. Altimeters used in airplanes have beryllium copper diaphragms because these are more sensitive than other materials. Beryllium alloys are also used in bushings on machine parts.

Beryllium metal is derived from beryl oxide-bearing ores, which are refined by a relatively simple process. For technical reasons, refiners sell beryllium in the form of a master alloy, which contains 3.5–5 per cent beryllium, with the remainder copper. Fabricators melt the master alloy and add copper to bring the final beryllium copper alloy to the desired weight, frequently 2 per cent in beryllium content.

In 1939, beryllium master alloy was being produced from ore by two principal companies, the Beryllium Corporation of Reading, Pennsylvania, and the Brush Beryllium Company, of Cleveland, Ohio. These companies also fabricated the master alloy into sheets, strips, castings, and other products. Both companies sold master alloy to fabricators of beryllium alloy products. The largest of these fabricators was the American Brass Company, of Waterbury, Connecticut. The Riverside Metal Company was one of the smallest fabricating firms in the beryllium alloy industry.

The following testimony from the *Hearings* of the Temporary National Economic Committee[18] describes some aspects of price policies used in the industry (see also Exhibits 1, 2, and 3).

MR. COX: You are the president of the Riverside Brass Co.?

MR. RANDALL: Riverside Metal Co.

MR. COX: What is the business of that company?

MR. RANDALL: The business of the Riverside Metal Co. is the fabrication of nonferrous alloys into rod, wire, sheet, and strip. We supply the manufacturer with a raw product.

MR. COX: You buy the master alloy and fabricate the material?

MR. RANDALL: That is correct.

. . . .

We make nickel silvers, phosphor bronzes, some brass; I think altogether we have an alloy list of over 80 different alloys.

MR. COX: Are all of the alloys which your company makes alloys which are also made and sold by The American Brass Co.?

MR. RANDALL: I think that would be true.

MR. COX: How large a company is your company? Will you give us your capitalization?

---

[18] *Ibid.,* pp. 2084 ff.

Exhibit 1

BERYLLIUM COPPER BASE PRICES, 1935–39

RIVERSIDE METAL CO.				AMERICAN BRASS CO.			
Date	Sheet	Wire	Rods	Date	Sheet	Wire	Rods
Feb. 25, 1935....	0.97	1.25	0.97	Feb. 6, 1935....	0.97	1.25	0.97
June 28, 1935....	0.96	1.24	0.96	June 27, 1935....	0.96	1.24	0.96
Aug. 22, 1935....	0.96½	1.24½	0.96½	Aug. 20, 1935....	0.96½	1.24½	0.96½
Sept. 19, 1935....	0.97	1.25	0.97	Sept. 17, 1935....	0.97	1.25	0.97
Oct. 27, 1936....	0.98	1.26	0.98	Oct. 27, 1936....	0.98	1.26	0.98
Nov. 7, 1936....	0.98½	1.26½	0.98½	Nov. 7, 1936....	0.98½	1.26½	0.98½
Dec. 15, 1936....	0.99	1.27	0.99	Dec. 15, 1936....	0.99	1.27	0.99
Dec. 31, 1936....	1.00	1.28	1.00	Dec. 31, 1936....	1.00	1.28	1.00
Jan. 14, 1937....	1.01	1.29	1.00	Jan. 14, 1937....	1.01	1.29	1.01
Feb. 16, 1937....	1.02	1.30	1.02	Feb. 16, 1937....	1.02	1.30	1.02
Feb. 22, 1937....	1.03	1.31	1.03	Feb. 22, 1937....	1.03	1.31	1.03
Mar. 8, 1937....	1.05	1.33	1.05	Mar. 8, 1937....	1.05	1.33	1.05
Mar. 31, 1937....	1.06	1.34	1.06	Mar. 31, 1937....	1.06	1.34	1.06
Apr. 6, 1937....	1.05	1.33	1.05	Apr. 6, 1937....	1.05	1.33	1.05
Apr. 20, 1937....	1.04	1.32	1.04	Apr. 20, 1937....	1.04	1.32	1.04
Oct. 26, 1937....	1.03	1.31	1.03	Oct. 26, 1937....	1.03	1.31	1.03
Nov. 23, 1937....	1.02	1.30	1.02	Nov. 23, 1937....	1.02	1.30	1.02
Jan. 20, 1938....	1.12	1.30	1.12	Jan. 20, 1938....	1.12	1.30	1.12
Jan. 28, 1938....	1.11½	1.29½	1.11½	Jan. 28, 1938....	1.11½	1.29½	1.11½
May 20, 1938....	1.10½	1.28½	1.10½	May 20, 1938....	1.10½	1.28½	1.10½
July 5, 1938....	1.11	1.29	1.11	July 5, 1938....	1.11	1.29	1.11
July 25, 1938....	1.11¼	1.29¼	1.11¼	July 25, 1938....	1.11¼	1.29¼	1.11¼
Sept. 19, 1938....	1.11½	1.29½	1.115	Sept. 19, 1938....	1.11½	1.29½	1.11½
Oct. 10, 1938....	1.118¾	1.298¾	1.118¾	Oct. 10, 1938....	1.11⅞	1.29⅞	1.11⅞
Oct. 13, 1938....	1.12	1.30	1.12	Oct. 13, 1938....	1.12	1.30	1.12
Apr. 20, 1939....	1.11	1.29	1.11	Apr. 20, 1939....	1.11	1.29	1.11

Source: *T.N.E.C., Hearings,* Part 5 (76th Congress, 1st Session) (Washington, D.C.: U.S. Government Printing Office, 1939), pp. 2284, 2287–88.

Exhibit 2

PRICES OF BERYLLIUM COPPER PRODUCTS, RIVERSIDE METAL CO.,
1933–39

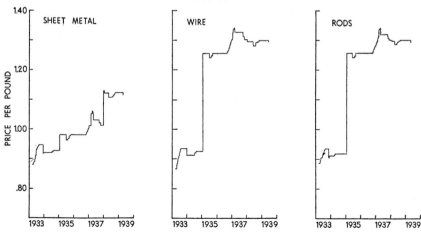

Source: *T.N.E.C. Hearings,* Part 5 (76th Congress, 1st Session) (Washington, D.C.: U.S. Government Printing Office, 1939), p. 2285.

Exhibit 3

PRICES OF BERYLLIUM COPPER PRODUCTS, AMERICAN BRASS CO.,
1932–39

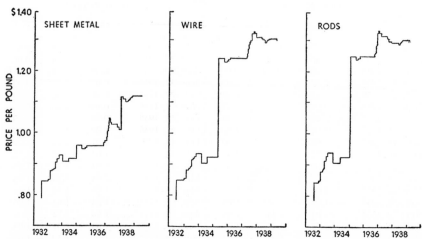

Source: *T.N.E.C. Hearings*, Part 5 (76th Congress, 1st Session) (Washington, D.C.: U.S. Government Printing Office, 1939), p. 2289.

MR. RANDALL: Our capitalization is one and a half million dollars, and we are almost the smallest unit in the industry; there may be one or two smaller, but I think we are almost the smallest.

MR. COX: Can you give us any approximate figure to indicate what percentage of the industry your company controls?

MR. RANDALL: Less than one and a half per cent.

. . . .

MR. COX: From whom do you buy the master alloys?

MR. RANDALL: We buy the master alloys from the Beryllium Products Corporation.

MR. COX: That is Mr. Gahagan?

MR. RANDALL: Mr. Gahagan.

MR. COX: Have you always bought all of your master alloy from that company?

MR. RANDALL: Practically all; yes.

. . . .

MR. COX: Mr. Randall, would it be correct to say that there is a well crystallized practice of price leadership in the industry in which you are engaged?

MR. RANDALL: I would say so.

MR. COX: And what company is the price leader?

MR. RANDALL: I would say the American Brass Co. holds that position.

MR. COX: And your company follows the prices which are announced by The American Brass?

MR. RANDALL: That is correct.

MR. COX: So that when they reduce the price you have to reduce it, too. Is that correct?

MR. RANDALL: Well, we don't have to, but we do.

MR. COX: And when they raise the price you raise the price.

MR. RANDALL: That is correct.

MR. COX: Do you remember that in February 1937, Mr. Gahagan's company reduced the price of the master alloy from $30 to $23 a pound?

MR. RANDALL: I didn't know it at that time.

MR. COX: You did know there was a price decrease.

MR. RANDALL: I do now.

MR. COX: Weren't you buying any from Mr. Gahagan?

MR. RANDALL: I think we were buying from them but it was quite some time after that I got the information that the price had gone down.

MR. COX: After that decrease in the price of the master alloy, it is a fact, isn't it, that there was no decrease in price of the fabricated product which you made?

MR. RANDALL: I don't remember about that, I don't know, because I don't know when that decrease took place.

MR. COX: Looking at your sheet prices for the year 1937, you started at $1.01 a pound on January 14, 1937, and rose progressively until you reached $1.06 on March 31, and then on April 6, 1937, they dropped to $1.05. You remember those.

MR. RANDALL: Yes; I remember those. That was copper.

. . . .

MR. COX: But you do know there was about that time a decrease of $7 a pound in the price which you were paying to Mr. Gahagan.

MR. RANDALL: Yes; I do know that.

MR. COX: I will put this question to you, Mr. Randall. Why didn't you reduce the price of the fabricated product following that decrease in the price of the master alloy?

MR. RANDALL: Well, of course I would not make a reduction in the base price of beryllium copper unless The American Brass made a price reduction in beryllium copper.

MR. COX: And The American Brass Co. made no reduction at that time?

MR. RANDALL: If they did, we did, as indicated on that sheet.

MR. COX: Assuming you didn't make a price change then, the reason you didn't was because The American Brass Co. didn't.

MR. RANDALL: That is correct.

MR. ARNOLD: You exercise no individual judgment as to the price you charged for your product, then, in a situation?

MR. RANDALL: Well, I think that is about what it amounts to; yes, sir.

MR. ARNOLD: When you say you have to follow, you don't mean anybody told you you had to follow?

MR. RANDALL: No sir; I don't mean that at all.

MR. ARNOLD: But you have a feeling something might happen if you didn't?

MR. RANDALL: I don't know what would happen.

MR. COX: You don't want to find out, do you?

THE CHAIRMAN: Well, as a matter of fact, Mr. Randall, if The American Brass Co. raised the price would the Brass Co. consult you about raising it?

MR. RANDALL: No, sir; not at all.

THE CHAIRMAN: You would, however, follow them without exercising any independent judgment as to whether or not it was desirable.

MR. RANDALL: That is correct.

THE CHAIRMAN: Suppose The American Brass Co. raises its price, but you are satisfied with your output and with the profit that you are making at the old price. Why is it necessary for you to increase your price to your customers, who are already paying you a price sufficient to give you a profit that is satisfactory to you?

MR. RANDALL: I don't know that it is necessary; as a practical matter, if we didn't raise our prices The American Brass Co. or other companies, whoever they might be, would put their price back to where it was.

MR. CHAIRMAN: That wouldn't bother you, because you were making a profit at the old price.

MR. RANDALL: Not on beryllium copper.

THE CHAIRMAN: Why do you do it?

MR. RANDALL: It is the custom of the industry, at least of the smaller companies, to do that.

THE CHAIRMAN: And other small companies do the same thing?

MR. RANDALL: Yes, sir.

THE CHAIRMAN: Is there any reason outside of custom for it?

MR. RANDALL: No, sir.

THE CHAIRMAN: Isn't it likely to reduce the amount of business that you can obtain?

MR. RANDALL: I don't think so.

THE CHAIRMAN: Well, if a competitor raises the price for an identical product, isn't it likely to believe that the producer who does not raise the price would get more business?

MR. RANDALL: I imagine it would, if the other price stayed where it had been raised to. I think that might work out over a period of time.

THE CHAIRMAN: You see, I am trying to get some understanding of the exact reasons why this price policy is followed, and it is not an answer—understand me, I am not criticizing your answer—that carries conviction merely to say it is the custom of the industry. There is a reason for customs. What, in your opinion, is the reason for this custom to follow the leader?

MR. RANDALL: Well, of course, that is a custom which has been prevalent, I think, in the industry for many, many years prior to my entry into it.

THE CHAIRMAN: Oh, yes; we hear a lot about price leadership, but I am trying to get the picture of this practice as you see it, and why you follow it.

MR. RANDALL: Well, I don't think I have ever given the matter very much consideration. We simply, when the new prices come out, print them just as they are. We don't give the matter any consideration. The prices are published and we print those prices.

THE CHAIRMAN: Is there any sort of compulsion, moral or otherwise?

MR. RANDALL: Absolutely none.

THE CHAIRMAN: Do you think it is a good practice?

MR. RANDALL: Well, I have never given the subject very much consideration.

THE CHAIRMAN: Now, of course, it is one of the most important subjects in your business.

MR. RANDALL: Yes; it is, of course.

THE CHAIRMAN: The price that you get for your product.

MR. RANDALL: I can't answer that question. I don't know whether it is a good practice or whether it isn't a good practice. I know that it has been the custom of the industry for years on end, and I know that is what we do, that's all.

THE CHAIRMAN: A moment ago, in response to either Mr. Cox's question or my question, you answered that if you did not follow the price up, then The American Brass Co. or some other company would come down again.

MR. RANDALL: I don't think I said they would. I said they probably would or they might. I don't know what they would do.

THE CHAIRMAN: Then I made the comment that that would not be a disturbing result, because it would mean merely the restoration of the old price. I could imagine, however, that you might start a price war, and that the other companies might go below you. Is there a possibility that that is what you have in mind?

MR. RANDALL: I didn't have it in mind until this moment. That is a possibility; yes.

THE CHAIRMAN: So you want the committee to understand that so far as you and your company are concerned, this price-leadership question is one to which you have never given any real consideration, and you have boosted your prices along with The American Brass Co. just as a matter of custom?

MR. RANDALL: Yes.

. . . .

MR. ARNOLD: . . . but if this policy is continued, you will continue to follow the American Brass regardless of what your costs are, won't you, so that won't be an element in the picture?

MR. RANDALL: Of course, to be perfectly frank, on that subject we don't know what our costs are on beryllium.

MR. ARNOLD: It wouldn't make any difference if you did, so far as the present prices are concerned, would it?

MR. RANDALL: No, sir; I don't think it would.

MR. ARNOLD: In other words, there is a situation here where there is a lot of competitors and no competition.

MR. RANDALL: Well, we simply, as I said before, follow the prices that are published, and that is what we have been doing for a good many years.

. . . .

At the conclusion of Mr. Randall's testimony, Mr. John A. Coe, Jr., general sales manager of the American Brass Company, was called to the stand. His testimony follows:

MR. COX: What is the nature of the business of The American Brass Co.?

MR. COE: The American Brass Co. is engaged in the production of copper, brass, bronze, and nickel silver in wrought forms, including sheet, wire, rods and tubes and other fabricated forms.

MR. COX: What is the capitalization of the company?

MR. COE: The American Brass Co. is a wholly owned fabricating subsidiary of the Anaconda Copper Mining Co.

MR. COX: Can you tell us what the capitalization of the company is?

MR. COE: I do not know what it is.

MR. COX: You heard Mr. Randall testify that his company did less than $1\frac{1}{2}$ per cent of the business in which he was engaged. Can you give us any approximate figure as to the percentage of the business which your company does.

MR. COE: Approximately 25 per cent.

. . . .

MR. COX: You heard Mr. Randall's testimony with respect to the system of price leadership which prevails.

MR. COE: Yes.

MR. COX: Would you agree with his description of that system insofar as it denoted your company as the price leader?

MR. COE: I wouldn't agree with that statement.

MR. COX: You wouldn't agree with the statement?

MR. COE: No.

MR. COX: In other words, it is your position that your company is not the price leader in the industry?

MR. COE: We are not the price leader of the industry.

MR. COX: It is a fact, is it not, that your prices for beryllium copper have been substantially the same as those of Mr. Randall for a period between 1934 and the present time?

MR. COX: So far as I know, they have been practically the same.

MR. COX: Practically the same prices. Now, you say you are not the price leader. Is there any price leader in the industry?

MR. COE: There is none.

MR. COX: Then how do you explain the fact that the prices are the same?

MR. COE: We publish our prices; they are public information; anybody who wishes to, may follow those prices at his own discretion.

MR. ARNOLD: They all wish to apparently, don't they?

MR. COE: They do not, sir.

MR. ARNOLD: You mean they have not been following those prices?

MR. COE: On our product they have not, sir.

MR. ARNOLD: I got the impression, I may be wrong, that the prices of competitors and your prices have been substantially identical.

MR. COE: To some extent they have been identical. There are always variations in many prices.

MR. ARNOLD: You said that anyone who wished to might follow. Some of them certainly wish to.

MR. COE: Some of them do wish to.

MR. ARNOLD: And some of them did follow.

MR. COE: That is correct.

MR. ARNOLD: And therefore to that extent you have been the leader.

MR. COE: To some extent we have been the leader in that we have put out our prices. However, others have put out prices and we have followed them at times.

MR. ARNOLD: What other companies would you put in the position of price leadership aside from your own?

MR. COE: Practically any member of the industry.

MR. COX: Including Mr. Randall?

MR. COE: Including Mr. Randall.

. . . .

MR. ARNOLD: I take it that the prices are fixed generally by someone following someone else, and that sometimes they follow you and other times you follow others.

MR. COE: May I ask what you mean by "fixed"? We publish our prices; they become our prices; they are public information. In that way the prices of The American Brass Co. are fixed by us.

MR. ARNOLD: Then you understand what we mean by "fixed" and I repeat my question: Is it true that prices are fixed in this industry either by someone following you or by your following others?

MR. COE: Not in all respects. Many times we do not follow others in all respects; many times they do not follow us in all respects.

MR. ARNOLD: But there is a following on the part of the various companies in the industry?

MR. COE: A general following; yes, sir.

THE CHAIRMAN: Not that you impose your ideas as to what the price should be upon anybody else, or that anybody else imposes it upon you, but when any company makes a change in price, the tendency is for all to follow that change?

MR. COE: That is the tendency.

THE CHAIRMAN: And how long has that been the system?

MR. COE: As far back as I have been with the company that has been in vogue; water seeking its own level.

. . . .

THE CHAIRMAN: What factors go into the determination of the price?

MR. COE: The cost of our raw metals going into the alloys, plus our manufacturing differentials. The latter is determined by our price committee.

THE CHAIRMAN: And if the price of the raw material should go down, then one would naturally expect the price of the finished product to go down, unless there was some countervailing change in some other factor?

MR. COE: There are other factors to be taken into consideration; yes, sir.

THE CHAIRMAN: Well, now, would you say that the price fluctuates in the same degree that the price of these countervailing or these other factors fluctuate?

MR. COE: That is a difficult question to answer. I don't quite know what you mean by that.

THE CHAIRMAN: Well, I tried to make it simple. The price of the finished product would naturally, one would suppose, depend upon the cost of the various factors which go into making the finished product?

MR. COE: That is correct.

THE CHAIRMAN: Well, now, do you want the committee to understand that always the price of the finished product is determined by these other factors and by no other consideration?

MR. COE: The price is determined by the price of raw materials going into those products, plus our cost of manufacturing.

THE CHAIRMAN: Yes; those are the other factors?

MR. COE: Those are the other factors.

THE CHAIRMAN: And there is no other consideration that goes into the determination of the price?

MR. COE: That is correct.

THE CHAIRMAN: And how about this leadership, why do you follow somebody else's lead sometimes?

MR. COE: We can get no more for our product than other people can get for theirs; will charge for theirs.

THE CHAIRMAN: Here is another outfit which is supposedly competing with you, which is not as efficient as you are, and therefore which finds for example that there is a much heavier plant charge, let us say; therefore, it is not able to produce this finished product at as low a price as you, and because it doesn't produce it at as low a price as you, it has to raise the price, but according to your testimony when such a company raises the price, then you follow and raise your price, although your costs have not changed.

MR. COE: We have not necessarily raised our price.

THE CHAIRMAN: Oh, now, let's drop the word "necessarily." You have just said that you have done that and that other companies follow you occasionally. Now, Mr. Coe, we are merely trying to get the facts here; we are not laying the basis for a case against The American Brass Co. I am trying to get through my mind this picture of price leadership in industry.

Now, you have told us as explicitly as it can be told that in some cases other companies in the same business as you follow the price that you fix, and you have told us how you determine that price, and then you say in other instances you followed the price of other companies, and when you do that necessarily you do it upon factors that are not reflected in your business, but on factors that are reflected in the business of the company which raises the price. Now why do you do it?

MR. COE: We can get as much for our product as any competitor can get for his product.

THE CHAIRMAN: Now we are getting somewhere. If some other company raises the price and is getting that price, then you think you had better come up and equalize it?

MR. COE: I feel that our product is as good as any made by the industry.

THE CHAIRMAN: It may be better.

MR. COE: I hope it is.

THE CHAIRMAN: But the point in determining the price thing is that you base it not upon the actual costs of manufacture in your plant, but upon the highest charge that anybody in the industry makes by and large, isn't that the effect of this price leadership policy?

MR. COE: It is usually predicated on the lowest price that anybody makes.

THE CHAIRMAN: Well, of course, there was an old familiar saying that the price the companies charge is what the traffic will bear. Now isn't that the motto which guides those who follow the practice of price leadership?

MR. COE: It depends on what you mean by "traffic." Of course we have to compete with many other things besides brass and copper.

THE CHAIRMAN: Well, would you say The American Brass Co. puts its product out at the lowest possible price, bearing in mind all of these factors of cost?

MR. COE: It is necessary when we get our products to the ultimate consumer as low as we reasonably can, and still at a fair margin of profit, in order that we will not be—that our products will not be supplanted by substitutes.

THE CHAIRMAN: But under this plan of price leadership, is it not inevitable that the tendency would be to raise the price so as to cover the cost of the less efficient member of the industry?

MR. COE: The tendency has been just the opposite. The tendency has been to lower the price.

QUESTIONS

1. Was the price policy of the Riverside Metal Company based on sound economic reasoning?
2. What was the effect of changes in raw-material prices on the prices set by the Riverside Metal Company?
3. What were the chief factors influencing the price policy of the American Brass Company? What effect did changes in prices of raw materials and other cost factors have on the prices set by this company?

CASE 6–3: THE BITUMINOUS COAL INDUSTRY

In April, 1937, Congress passed the Bituminous Coal Act, which provided for industry-wide price fixing. The actual setting of prices was to be accomplished by joint action of a national Bituminous Coal Commission of seven members and twenty-three district boards located in each of the regions into which the industry had been divided for administrative purposes. Price schedules covering each type, size, and quality of coal were established for each of ten minimum-price areas and were to yield a net return equal to the weighted average of total costs for each area.[19] The act also provided for a Bituminous Coal Code governing marketing practices, including pricing, and all producers were required by law to accept the code or to pay a tax of 19.5 per cent of the sale price of coal not produced under the code.

The number of producers in the bituminous coal industry was large. In 1936, there were 6,875 mines producing more than a thousand tons

---

[19] Each minimum-price area consisted of from one to nine districts.

a year,[20] but this figure failed to include a large number of small producers, such as truck and wagon mines, "snowbirds," and "fly-by-nights." The 6,875 listed mines were operated by more than 4,000 separate companies, but the total number of operators was well in excess of this—11,500 having accepted the Bituminous Coal Code by November 15, 1938. Only a few hundred of the larger mines were "captive," i.e., owned by railroad, steel, or other industrial companies which consumed all or a large part of their output.[21] Most of the companies and most of the mines were small. In 1937, three fifths of the mines produced less than 10,000 tons, three quarters less than 50,000

Exhibit 1

CONSUMPTION OF BITUMINOUS COAL AND LIGNITE,
BY CONSUMER CLASS, 1936
(In Thousands of Short Tons)

Consumer Class	Consumption	Per Cent of Total
Colliery fuel	3,227	0.7
Electric power utilities	40,029	9.8
Bunker, foreign trade	1,622	0.4
Railroads, Class I	86,391	20.9
Coke, beehive ovens	2,698	0.7
Coke, by-product ovens	63,244	15.4
Steel and rolling mills	13,471	3.2
Coal-gas retorts	1,945	0.5
Cement mills	4,771	1.1
Other industries	108,620	26.6
Retail dealer deliveries	84,200	20.7
Total	410,218	100.0

Source: *Statistical Abstract of the United States* (1947), p. 754.

tons, and nine tenths less than 200,000 tons; only 3 per cent of them produced more than 500,000 tons. Although the bulk of the output came from larger mines—over a third of it came from the 3 per cent of mines that produced more than 500,000 tons each—even these were numerous, there being 212 mines in the top 3 per cent.[22] Moreover, there was no large degree of concentration of control of output in the hands of a few. In 1929 the forty-eight largest producers con-

[20] *Minerals Yearbook* (1938), p. 713.

[21] Captive mines, however, produced one fifth of the total output. Cf. Fred E. Berquist and Associates, *Economic Survey of the Bituminous Coal Industry under Free Competition and Code Regulation* (N.R.A., Division of Review, Work Material No. 69, mimeo., 1936), p. 32. Quoted by Wilcox, *op. cit.*, p. 25.

[22] *Ibid.*, p. 24.

trolled only 43 per cent of the output. The largest producer controlled only about 3 per cent; the four largest between 8 and 10 per cent.[23]

The buyers of coal were, for the most part, large and well informed. Railroads accounted for one fifth to one fourth of all purchases, utilities 10 per cent, and coking plants over 16 per cent (see Exhibit 1). Domestic consumers bought a relatively small part of the total output. As a result, rational buying motives predominated, and price played an important part in purchase negotiations.

In the period after 1923, there was a progressive shift from coal to other fuels. The extent of this substitution is shown in Exhibit 2. De-

Exhibit 2

CONSUMPTION OF BITUMINOUS COAL, COAL EQUIVALENT OF FUEL OIL AND NATURAL GAS, AND OUTPUT OF HYDROELECTRIC POWER REDUCED TO COAL EQUIVALENT, 1923–38

(Thousands of Net Tons)

Year	Bituminous Coal Consumed (Net Tons)	Per Cent of Total	Fuel Oil Consumed in Coal Equivalent (Net Tons)	Per Cent of Total	Natural Gas Consumed in Coal Equivalent (Net Tons)	Per Cent of Total	Output of Hydroelectric Power Reduced to Coal Equivalent on Basis of Current Efficiency Rate for Steam Generation (Net Tons)	Per Cent of Total	Total
1923....	518,993	81.5	66,599	10.5	27,740	4.4	23,212	3.6	636,544
1924....	484,004	79.4	74,038	12.2	29,577	4.8	21,666	3.6	609,285
1925....	499,193	78.1	85,287	13.3	31,227	4.9	23,474	3.7	639,181
1926....	532,581	78.5	85,319	12.6	35,217	5.2	25,534	3.7	678,651
1927....	499,801	76.5	88,450	13.5	37,585	5.8	27,485	4.2	653,321
1928....	498,828	74.7	97,519	14.6	40,957	6.1	30,532	4.6	667,836
1929....	519,555	74.3	102,403	14.7	47,563	6.8	29,262	4.2	698,783
1930....	454,990	73.4	90,532	14.6	47,593	7.7	26,747	4.3	619,862
1931....	371,869	70.8	83,667	15.9	45,874	8.8	23,717	4.5	525,127
1932....	306,917	67.8	77,039	17.0	42,836	9.5	25,574	5.7	452,366
1933....	321,617	68.5	79,086	16.8	43,608	9.3	25,524	5.4	469,835
1934....	347,043	68.6	85,093	16.8	49,029	9.7	25,033	4.9	506,198
1935....	360,292	67.3	91,681	17.1	54,395	10.2	29,177	5.4	535,545
1936....	422,796	68.4	102,660	16.6	62,931	10.2	29,475	4.8	617,862
1937....	428,496	66.9	110,589	17.3	70,532	11.0	31,028	4.8	640,645
1938....	340,735	63.1	102,304	18.9	65,814	12.2	31,295	5.8	540,148
Total.	6,907,710		1,422,266		732,478		428,735		9,491,189

Source: *T.N.E.C. Hearings*, Part 30, Exhibit 2737, Table 5. Reproduced in T.N.E.C. Monograph No. 22, p. 101.

[23] John P. Miller, "The Pricing of Bituminous Coal: Some International Comparisons," *Public Policy* (Yearbook of the Graduate School of Public Administration, Harvard Uni-

clining demand for coal was attributed also to improved efficiency in the use of fuel.

In the short run, there was little possibility for most industrial users to substitute other fuels, so short-run changes in the relationship between coal prices and those of other fuels did not materially affect the amount of coal demanded. Under these conditions the amount of coal consumed depended principally on the rate of activity of the coal-using industries. Much of the demand, moreover, came from railroads, public utilities, steel, and other industries whose prices were relatively stable. For many industrial users the cost of coal was but a small part of their total costs.

The costs of distribution, which included transportation and middlemen's margins, were large in relation to the price of coal and were quite inflexible. A large percentage decline in the price of coal at the mine caused a relatively small percentage decline in the price of coal at the point of consumption.

The cost structure of the industry reflected the great importance of labor costs, which accounted for almost 60 per cent of the total (see Exhibit 3). Because of the geographic isolation of many coal-mining

Exhibit 3

MINING COSTS: APPALACHIAN REGION (DIVISION I),
NOVEMBER, 1933

Item	Cost per Ton	Percentage of Total Cost
Mine labor...............................	$0.93	59.0
Mine supplies.............................	0.22	13.9
Other mine expenses........................	0.03	1.8
Royalties, dues, compensation insurance, and depletion.......................................	0.15	9.5
Depreciation, taxes, insurance.................	0.11	7.0
Sales and administration.....................	0.14	8.8
Total................................	$1.58	100.0

Source: W. C. Trapnell and R. Ilsley, *The Bituminous Coal Industry, with a Survey of Competing Fuels* (Washington, D.C.: Federal Emergency Relief Administration, 1935), p. 73; quoted by John P. Miller, "The Pricing of Bituminous Coal: Some International Comparisons," *Public Policy* (Cambridge, Mass.: Harvard University Press, 1940), p. 148.

communities, miners had few alternative employment opportunities; the supply of labor, therefore, was inelastic and did not vary much, in the short run, with changes in wage rates. In the absence of strong union organization prior to 1933, changes in price of the final product

versity, 1940, ed. C. J. Friedrich and Edward S. Mason) (Cambridge, Mass.: Harvard University Press, 1940), pp. 145–46. Professor Miller's article offers an excellent discussion of the issues considered in this case.

had a direct impact on wages. Other production costs were, like those for labor, largely out-of-pocket expenses to the mine operators.

The bituminous coal industry was one in which supply could be readily expanded. There was a large amount of underutilized capacity, partly attributable to seasonal and cyclical fluctuations of demand. Because storage of coal is expensive, fluctuations in demand were met largely by changes in the rate of production rather than by changes in inventories. It was customary to run mines with a full crew when they were in operation and to adjust the output of individual mines by varying the number of days worked per month. In 1923, with the industry at a high rate of output, the theoretical capacity was only 58 per cent in use; in 1929, only 71 per cent; in 1932, only 47 per cent; and in the years from 1934 through 1937, about 60 per cent.[24] New concerns entered the business easily. The supply of coal in the United States was widely distributed, and title to workable seams was held by thousands of owners. Much of the supply was so readily accessible that mines could be opened quickly and at small expense. Groups of miners who could command a small amount of capital, chiefly for trucks, were free to enter the field. A slight rise in prices would encourage operators to increase output of existing mines, to reopen abandoned mines, and to bring new areas into production.

Although the industry was quick to expand, it was slow to contract. Describing this condition, one observer commented:

Falling prices do not result in a proportionate reduction in the number of operators or the volume of output. A mine once opened cannot be closed without expense. It must be ventilated to prevent accumulation of dangerous gases, pumped to prevent flooding, and timbered to prevent the loss of working places. Maintenance of idle properties may be more costly than operations at a loss. Bankruptcy eliminates mining companies but does not affect their mines; new owners, with a lighter burden of fixed charges, continue to produce. Enterprises that might otherwise have disappeared were kept alive during the twenties by the establishment of wage differentials in union contracts, a significant concession since labor constitutes two-thirds of the cost of mining coal. Producers who might otherwise have failed to reach the market have been enabled to do so by the inclusion of similar differentials in the structure of freight rates, another significant arrangement since the cost of transportation represents three fifths of the value of delivered coal. Although the price realized at the mine in 1929 was 52 per cent below that received in 1920, production was only 6 per cent below the level established in the earlier year.[25]

---

[24] U.S. Department of the Interior, Bituminous Coal Division, *Bituminous Coal Tables, 1937–38*, p. 5; quoted by Wilcox, *op. cit.*, p. 24.

[25] Wilcox, *op. cit.*, p. 25.

As a result of these conditions, there was chronic long-term excess capacity in the industry.[26] Only by a slow process of attrition was capacity gradually reduced in the ten years following 1923 (see Exhibit 4).

Exhibit 4

PRODUCTION, PRICES, CAPACITY, AND MINERS' WAGES, BITUMINOUS COAL INDUSTRY, 1920–40

(1) Year	(2) Production (Thousands of Short Tons)	(3) Average Value per Ton at Mines*	(4) Number of Mines	(5) Average Number of Men Employed	(6) Capacity of Mines† (Millions of Tons)	(7) Average Spot Price per Ton	(8) Miners' Weekly Wages
1920	568,667	$3.75	8,907	639,547	798	$5.64	‡
1921	415,922	2.89	8,038	663,754	860	2.55	‡
1922	422,268	3.02	9,299	687,958	917	3.64	‡
1923	564,565	2.68	9,331	705,000	970	2.77	$25.60
1924	483,687	2.20	7,586	619,604	871	2.08	23.59
1925	520,053	2.04	7,144	588,493	823	2.06	26.47
1926	573,367	2.06	7,177	593,647	821	2.21	28.63
1927	517,763	1.99	7,011	593,918	835	1.99	24.33
1928	500,745	1.86	6,450	522,150	760	1.80	24.66
1929	534,989	1.78	6,057	503,000	752	1.79	25.72
1930	467,526	1.70	5,891	493,202	770	1.75	22.21
1931	382,089	1.54	5,642	450,213	736	‡	17.69
1932	309,710	1.31	5,427	406,000	653	‡	13.91
1933	333,631	1.34	5,555	418,703	615	‡	14.47
1934	359,368	1.75	6,258	458,011	622	‡	18.10
1935	372,373	1.77	6,315	462,403	640	2.04	19.58
1936	439,088	1.76	6,875	477,204	680	‡	22.71
1937	445,531	1.94	6,548	491,864	710	2.10	23.84
1938	348,545	1.95	5,777	441,333	663	2.04	20.80
1939	394,855	1.85	5,820	421,788	676	2.02	23.88
1940	460,772	1.91	6,324	439,075	703	‡	24.71

* Average value per ton less selling expenses (Bureau of Mines series) prior to 1937; thereafter, average gross realization, including selling expense (Bituminous Coal Division series).
† Calculated at 308 working days per annum.
‡ Not available.

Source: Col. 2, *Statistical Abstract of the United States*. Cols. 3–7, *Mineral Resources of the U.S.* (1920–30); *Minerals Yearbook* (1931–40). Col. 8, *Historical Statistics of the United States, 1789–1945* (U.S. Department of Commerce, Bureau of the Census).

The history of the industry since World War I was one of almost steady recession of prices and wages. Market forces determined prices and output until, in 1933, the establishment of a code for the industry under the National Recovery Administration. Even before the N.R.A. was declared unconstitutional, the bituminous coal industry had come

---

[26] "To characterize a market as having excess capacity means . . . that there is momentarily a greater willingness to supply product over a certain price range than there would be if time were allowed to make all equilibrium adjustments. There is excess capacity if the quantity of factors associated with the industry would have been less if present prospects of future demand and costs had been foreseen; or if in view of the present prospects fixed factors and labor show a desire and intent to withdraw from the industry with the passage of time" (Miller, *op. cit.*, p. 151).

under the National Coal Conservation Act of 1935, which regulated prices and labor relations; but this, in turn, was declared unconstitutional.[27] Shortly thereafter, Congress passed the Bituminous Coal Act of 1937, the pricing provisions of which were described in the opening paragraph of this case.

QUESTIONS

1. Analyze the conditions of supply and demand which, from the standpoint of the individual mine operator, made price agreement under the Bituminous Coal Act a desirable price policy.

2. Would price agreements be equally desirable from the standpoint of an individual producer in a competitive industry such as cotton textiles?

3. Is governmental sponsorship of price agreements socially desirable in the bituminous coal industry?

CASE 6–4: CIGARETTE ADVERTISING[28]

Advertising expenditures by manufacturers of tobacco products have for many years been among the highest of any industry. Much of the total has been devoted to the advertising of cigarettes. In 1939, cigarettes accounted for three fourths of the estimated total advertising expenditure of $60 million on tobacco products. In 1931 the Association of National Advertisers reported the expenditures of four large tobacco companies as averaging 8.23 per cent of sales. In recent years, advertising expense of individual companies has ranged from 6 to 30 per cent.

Approximately three quarters of all advertising expenditures on cigarettes and about the same share of total sales were made by these companies: the American Tobacco Company, with its Lucky Strike brand; the Liggett and Myers Company, with the Chesterfield brand; and the R. J. Reynolds Company, with the Camel brand (see Exhibit 1). The dominance of the cigarette market by these three companies, combined with their heavy advertising outlays, led certain critics to charge that other companies had been prevented from getting a large share of the market because they could not match these expenditures.

The R. J. Reynolds Company began the practice of concentrating advertising on one brand of cigarette with the introduction of Camels in 1913. Reynolds' share of the cigarette market rose from 0.2 per

---

[27] *Carter* v. *Carter Coal Co.*, 298 U.S. 238 (1936).

[28] This case is based on materials contained in Professor Neil H. Borden's volume, *The Economic Effects of Advertising* (Chicago: Richard D. Irwin, Inc., 1942), chap. viii.

Exhibit 1

CIGARETTE CONSUMPTION BY BRAND AND TRACEABLE ADVERTISING EXPENDITURE IN NEWSPAPERS, MAGAZINES, FARM PUBLICATIONS, AND CHAIN RADIO, 1929–39

YEAR	CAMEL Consumption (Billions of Cigarettes)	CAMEL Traceable Advertising Expenditure (Thousands of Dollars)	CHESTERFIELD Consumption (Billions of Cigarettes)	CHESTERFIELD Traceable Advertising Expenditure (Thousands of Dollars)	LUCKY STRIKE Consumption (Billions of Cigarettes)	LUCKY STRIKE Traceable Advertising Expenditure (Thousands of Dollars)	TEN-CENT BRANDS Consumption (Billions of Cigarettes)	TEN-CENT BRANDS Traceable Advertising Expenditure (Thousands of Dollars)	ALL OTHER Consumption (Billions of Cigarettes)	ALL OTHER Traceable Advertising Expenditure (Thousands of Dollars)	GRAND TOTAL Consumption (Billions of Cigarettes)	GRAND TOTAL Traceable Advertising Expenditure (Thousands of Dollars)
1929	40.0	$ 1,942	26.0	$ 5,254	36.4	$ 6,589	.....	.....	16.6	$7,022	119.0	$20,806
1930	38.0	4,813	25.0	5,968	42.6	10,095	.....	.....	14.0	5,142	119.6	26,018
1931	33.0	10,006	24.6	9,130	44.6	13,649	.....	.....	11.2	5,210	113.4	37,996
1932	24.6	2,389	21.0	11,138	37.0	10,850	12.0	$ 26	9.0	4,058	103.6	28,461
1933	26.5	10,248	29.0	7,590	37.5	7,192	8.5	100	10.3	2,340	111.8	27,471
1934	32.0	10,382	33.5	9,575	33.5	8,120	13.0	143	13.6	3,441	125.6	31,661
1935	37.0	9,265	36.0	9,443	32.5	5,588	13.1	68	16.0	4,852	134.6	29,216
1936	43.0	9,042	38.0	8,909	37.0	6,846	16.0	827	19.2	6,848	153.2	32,472
1937	45.0	8,529	38.0	8,949	38.5	5,617	19.0	470	22.1	7,191	162.6	30,755
1938	41.0	8,362	37.4	9,279	38.3	4,095	24.0	483	23.0	4,866	163.7	27,085
1939	40.0	7,367	36.5	7,776	39.5	4,214	30.0	1,157	26.4	4,442	172.4	24,956
Average...	36.4	$ 7,486	31.4	$ 8,455	37.9	$ 7,532	17.0	$ 409	16.5	$5,037	134.5	$28,809

Source: Neil H. Borden, *The Economic Effects of Advertising* (Chicago: Richard D. Irwin, Inc., 1942), p. 229.

cent in 1913 to 40 per cent in 1917 and 45 per cent in 1925. Noting the success of Camels, the Liggett and Myers Company similarly concentrated advertising on its brand, Chesterfield, which had been launched in 1912. American Tobacco Company followed with the Lucky Strike brand in 1917. In 1926 the P. Lorillard Company attempted to enter the field with its Old Gold brand. It embarked on an ambitious advertising campaign, financed by the flotation of a $15 million issue of debenture bonds in 1927. Despite large advertising expenditures, which exceeded $1.5 million by 1938, the Old Gold brand failed to increase its share of the market, as is indicated in Exhibit 2.

Exhibit 2

ESTIMATED DOMESTIC CONSUMPTION OF LEADING BRANDS IN
BILLIONS OF CIGARETTES AND PERCENTAGE OF TOTAL
CONSUMPTION BY BRANDS, 1929–39

YEAR	CAMEL		CHESTERFIELD		LUCKY STRIKE		OLD GOLD	
	Cigarettes (Billions)	% of Total	Cigarettes (Billions)	% of Total	Cigarettes (Billions)	% of Total	Cigarettes (Billions)	% of Total
1929...	40.0	33.6	26.0	21.8	36.4	30.6	8.0	6.7
1930...	38.0	31.8	25.0	20.9	42.6	35.6	8.0	6.7
1931...	33.0	29.1	24.6	21.7	44.6	39.3	7.6	6.7
1932...	24.6	23.7	21.0	20.7	37.0	35.7	5.7	5.5
1933...	26.5	23.7	29.0	25.9	37.5	33.1	5.5	4.9
1934...	32.0	25.5	33.5	26.7	33.5	26.7	5.0	4.0
1935...	37.0	27.4	36.0	26.7	32.5	24.1	5.3	3.9
1936...	43.0	28.1	38.0	24.8	37.0	24.2	6.8	4.4
1937...	45.0	27.7	38.0	23.4	38.5	23.7	7.9	5.0
1938...	41.0	25.0	37.4	22.8	38.3	23.4	6.3	3.8
1939...	40.0	23.2	36.5	21.2	39.5	22.9	5.3	3.1

YEAR	PHILIP MORRIS		MENTHOLATED BRANDS		COMBINED TEN-CENT BRANDS		ALL OTHER BRANDS		TOTAL BILLIONS	% OF TOTAL REPRESENTED BY THREE LEADING BRANDS
	Cigarettes (Billions)	% of Total	Cigarettes (Billions)	% of Total	Cigarettes (Billions)	% of Total	Cigarettes (Billions)	% of Total		
1929......	...	...	...	...	....	....	8.6	7.2	119.0	86.0
1930......	...	...	...	...	....	....	6.0	5.0	119.6	88.3
1931......	...	...	*	...	*	....	3.6	3.2	113.4	90.1
1932......	*	...	*	...	12.0	11.6	3.3	3.2	103.6	80.1
1933......	*	...	*	...	8.5	7.6	4.8	4.3	111.8	82.7
1934......	2.8	2.2	3.3	2.6	13.0	10.4	2.5	2.0	125.6	78.9
1935......	3.8	2.8	4.1	3.0	13.1	9.7	2.8	2.1	134.6	78.2
1936......	5.0	3.3	3.7	2.4	16.0	10.4	3.7	2.4	153.2	77.1
1937......	7.5	4.9	2.6	1.6	19.0	11.7	4.1	2.5	162.6	74.8
1938......	9.2	5.6	1.9	1.2	24.0	14.7	5.6	3.4	163.7	71.2
1939......	11.0	6.4	2.0	1.2	30.0	17.4	8.1	4.7	172.4	67.3

* Included in "All Other Brands."

Source: "Basic Survey—Tobacco," *Standard Trade and Securities*, Vol. XCVI, No. 20 (June 7, 1940), Sec. 3.

In January, 1933, the Philip Morris Company launched a new blend of 15-cent cigarettes under the brand name Philip Morris. The new brand was first tried experimentally in certain large cities, where it met with such success that the company began an extensive advertising campaign financed out of earnings. By 1939, expenditures for advertising exceeded $1.5 million, and the company was firmly intrenched in fourth place.

Relying on an inelastic demand for the product, the leading tobacco companies raised the wholesale price of cigarettes from $6.00 per thousand to $6.40 in October, 1929, and to $6.85 in June, 1931. These wholesale prices resulted in retail prices on the more popular brands of 14 and 15 cents per package. The maintained high prices of the leading brands encouraged transference of demand, particularly after June, 1931, to 10-cent cigarettes, as indicated by Exhibit 3. Prior to

Exhibit 3

PERCENTAGE OF TOTAL CIGARETTE SALES SECURED BY THE
10-CENT BRANDS BY MONTHS FROM JANUARY, 1931, TO
FEBRUARY, 1936, INCLUSIVE

Month	1931	1932	1933	1934	1935	1936
January	0.26	2.33	16.76	10.00	10.85	10.59
February	0.27	3.30	11.60	9.96	11.71	10.51
March	0.28	3.26	7.07	10.43	11.25	.....
April	0.27	6.13	8.55	11.11	11.70	.....
May	0.23	6.59	6.43	10.37	11.72	.....
June	0.28	9.12	7.03	10.01	11.36	.....
July	0.57	12.46	9.58	12.09	11.87	.....
August	1.82	17.76	8.67	12.38	13.72	.....
September	2.00	19.57	9.78	11.62	13.53	.....
October	2.41	19.00	9.54	12.46	11.01	.....
November	2.39	22.78	11.21	13.13	12.15	.....
December	2.88	21.31	9.26	12.28	12.54	.....

Source: *Report of the Federal Trade Commission on Agricultural Income Inquiry*, Part I: "Principal Farm Products" (Washington, D.C.: U.S. Government Printing Office, 1938), p. 462.

1931, there were only two 10-cent brands of significance—Coupon, sold by Liggett and Myers, and Paul Jones, sold by Continental Tobacco Company. After June, 1931, several "other companies entered the field: in September, Larus & Brothers, Inc.; in March, 1932, Brown & Williamson Tobacco Company reduced the price on its Wings brand to put it in the 10-cent class; in May, 1932, Sunshines, manufactured by the Pinkerton Tobacco Company, were put in the 10-cent class; in June, 1932, Axton-Fisher entered its new brand, Twenty Grand; during the same month, Scott & Dill came into the scramble; and in September, Stephano Brothers brought out Marvels.

The rise in sales of the 10-cent brands during the depression was phenomenal. Starting almost from nothing in 1931 they accounted for over 20% of the domestic cigarette market for a few months during the fall of 1932."[29] On January 3, 1933, the Big Three reduced wholesale prices to $6.00 per thousand, and a month later to $5.50. Retail prices fell to 12.5 cents, then to 10 and 11 cents. With the price differential for the leading brands practically removed, sales of 10-cent cigarettes fell from 21.3 per cent of total sales in December, 1932, to 6.4 per cent in May, 1933. During all this period, retail prices of Philip Morris cigarettes were maintained at 15 cents. In January, 1934, the Big Three increased wholesale prices to $6.10 per thousand and in January, 1936, to $6.25, with resulting increases in retail prices to 12.5 and then 13.5 cents a package. The 10-cent brands responded by increasing to a share of the total market which ranged from 10 to 12 per cent. By 1939, however, this share had increased to over 17 per cent.

In 1936, most of the companies producing 10-cent cigarettes swung over to advertising, as indicated in Exhibit 1. Although it was clear that their margins could not permit the extensive advertising employed by the standard brands, they thought that a limited amount was desirable to build volume.

A survey by *Fortune* magazine in 1935 indicated that cigarette smokers did not frequently shift brands. In response to the question, "How many years have you been smoking this brand?" the survey reported the following replies:

Years	Per Cent	Years	Per Cent
1	12.6	5	10.1
2	12.9	Over 5	44.3
3	10.0	Don't know	4.2
4	5.9		

Managements of tobacco companies believed, however, that the stability of demand for their respective products was based largely on subjective valuations created by continued advertising outlays. Blindfold tests carried on experimentally among fifty-one subjects, all of whom smoked regularly and generally stuck to one brand, indicated the difficulty which consumers experienced in identifying brands. Each subject was tested with four cigarettes, three leading brands and one other. Each was told that his own brand would be among the four

---

[29] *Ibid.*, p. 234.

which were presented in random order. Adequate time was allowed between smokes to compensate for taste confusion and fatigue. Although chance alone would have resulted in a 20 per cent identification, only 31 per cent of the smokers guessed their own brand. The results are shown in Exhibit 4.

Exhibit 4

IDENTIFICATION OF DIFFERENT CIGARETTE BRANDS IN
BLINDFOLD TEST, 51 SUBJECTS

BRAND	PER CENT OF SUBJECTS IDENTIFYING BRAND IN COLUMN 1 AS:					
	Camel	Lucky Strike	Chester-field	Twenty Grand	Spud	Miscel-laneous
Camel.............	31	14	38	6	2	10
Lucky Strike........	19	41	21	4	0	14
Chesterfield.........	27	23	33	2	0	15
Twenty Grand......	38	26	3	17	0	15
Spud..............	0	6	6	0	76	11

Source: R. W. Husband and Jane Godfrey, "An Experimental Study of Cigarette Identification," *Journal of Applied Psychology*, Vol. XVIII, No. 2 (April, 1934), p. 222.

Although consumers found it difficult to identify brands, there were some indications that they discriminated among different brands of cigarettes as to blending and flavor. When the R. J. Reynolds Company introduced Camel cigarettes in 1913, the product was based on a domestic blend of bright-leaf tobacco. This proved so popular that Camels quickly rose to first place. Competition thereupon followed with the promotion of domestic blends. In the opinion of executives of the major companies the success of any cigarette was determined to a considerable extent by the flavor or blend of the product. The failure of one brand of cigarettes, which was supported by large advertising expenditures, was attributed to the lack of success in finding an acceptable blend. In the first three months that the cigarette was on the market, it enjoyed a large sales volume, but soon it became evident to company executives that it had failed to win lasting consumer acceptance. Sales dropped. Investigation showed that many consumers, after once trying the new cigarette, did not repurchase. Executives believed that, although the blend approximated those of the leading brands, it had failed basically because consumers did not like it. The importance of blend led the Philip Morris Company, before placing the cigarette of that name on the market in 1933, to work out a large number of blends. The blenders then chose what they regarded as the twenty best blends from this group and forwarded them to company executives for final selection. The executives, after careful consideration, finally selected the blend which later met with great consumer favor. Another illustration of the importance of blend was the transference of demand from the inferior tobaccos of the 10-cent cigarettes to the standard brands in 1933, when differentials between these two groups were virtually eliminated. Consumers were evidently sensitive to quality differences where price differentials were not great.

Although advertising expenditures of each of the Big Three were vastly in excess of those of other companies in the field in the period 1930–39, the three leaders did not hold the same relative positions throughout the period. Moreover, as is indicated in Exhibits 5 and 6,

Exhibit 5

BILLIONS OF CIGARETTES SOLD AND TRACEABLE ADVERTISING EXPENDITURE IN NEWSPAPERS, MAGAZINES, FARM JOURNALS, AND CHAIN RADIO OF CIGARETTE BRANDS, IN THOUSANDS OF DOLLARS FOR EACH BILLION OF CIGARETTES SOLD, 1929–39

YEAR	CAMEL		CHESTER-FIELD		LUCKY STRIKE		TEN-CENT BRANDS		ALL OTHERS	
	Advertising, Thousands of Dollars per Billion Cigarettes	Billions of Cigarettes Sold	Advertising, Thousands of Dollars per Billion Cigarettes	Billions of Cigarettes Sold	Advertising, Thousands of Dollars per Billion Cigarettes	Billions of Cigarettes Sold	Advertising, Thousands of Dollars per Billion Cigarettes	Billions of Cigarettes Sold	Advertising, Thousands of Dollars per Billion Cigarettes	Billions of Cigarettes Sold
1929	48.5	40.0	202.1	26.0	180.2	36.4	....	....	413.0	16.6
1930	126.7	38.0	238.7	25.0	237.0	42.6	....	....	367.3	14.0
1931	303.2	33.0	371.1	24.6	306.0	44.6	....	....	473.7	11.2
1932	97.1	24.6	530.4	21.0	293.3	37.0	2.4	12.0	450.9	9.0
1933	386.7	26.5	261.7	29.0	191.8	37.5	11.8	8.5	227.2	10.3
1934	324.4	32.0	285.8	33.5	242.4	33.5	11.0	13.0	253.0	13.6
1935	250.4	37.0	262.3	36.0	171.9	32.5	5.2	13.1	303.3	16.0
1936	210.3	43.0	234.4	38.0	185.0	37.0	51.6	16.0	230.3	19.2
1937	189.5	45.0	235.5	38.0	145.9	38.5	24.7	19.0	309.8	22.1
1938	203.9	41.0	248.1	37.4	106.9	38.3	20.1	24.0	211.6	23.0
1939	184.2	40.0	213.1	36.5	106.7	39.5	38.6	30.0	168.3	26.4
Average	211.4	36.4	280.3	31.4	199.0	37.9	20.7	17.0	309.8	16.5

Source: Neil H. Borden, *The Economic Effects of Advertising* (Chicago: Richard D. Irwin, Inc., 1942), p. 243.

the advertising outlays of these companies varied in effectiveness. Over this ten-year period, Chesterfield spent an average of $280,000 in advertising for each billion cigarettes sold; Camel spent $211,000; and Lucky Strike, $199,000. By contrast, the 10-cent brands spent less than $30,000 per billion cigarettes sold.

Exhibit 6

TRACEABLE ADVERTISING EXPENDITURES PER BILLION CIGARETTES,
AND SALES IN BILLIONS, BY BRANDS, 1929–39

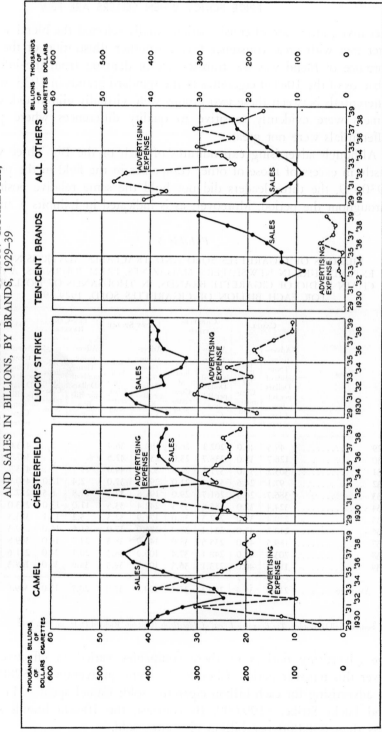

Source: Neil H. Borden, *The Economic Effects of Advertising* (Chicago: Richard D. Irwin, Inc., 1942), p. 244.

QUESTIONS

1. Was the over-all demand for cigarettes elastic or inelastic in the relevant price range during the depression of the 1930's?
2. What could you say about the demand for the product of any one of the large cigarette companies if it had cut price while the other large companies held the line on price?
3. What happened to demand in 1932?
4. Were the makers of 10-cent cigarettes well advised to use advertising?
5. Were the Big Three wise in raising prices in 1931?
6. Is cigarette advertising socially wasteful?

CASE 6–5: NASH-KELVINATOR CORPORATION[30]

During the early months of 1940 a major change in price structure occurred in the electric refrigerator industry. In the second week of January the Nash-Kelvinator Corporation presented its 1940 models at prices which were substantially lower than its 1939 quotations. In the announcement accompanying these reductions, prominence was given to a 6-foot stripped model offered at a retail price of $119.95, delivered east of the Rocky Mountains. This was the lowest price ever quoted for a comparable model by any leading manufacturer utilizing the traditional wholesaler-retailer system of distribution. The other leading companies had earlier announced prices of $129–$134 for competing lines, and the large mail-order companies quoted prices only slightly below $119.95 for their 6-foot stripped models.

This action by the Nash-Kelvinator Corporation precipitated a wave of similar reductions by competitors. General Motors, General Electric, and Westinghouse cut prices on comparable 6-foot stripped models to $114.75, delivered in the zone nearest their respective plants. In each case, this involved substantial reductions below the prices which had been previously announced for 1940.

Companies which had been selling at levels below those of the Big Five also lowered prices. The Crosley Corporation reduced the price of its 6-foot stripped model and also cut the prices of its other models. Sears Roebuck offered its 6-foot stripped model at $89.95 and reduced the price of its de luxe 6-foot model from $139.50 to $129.50.

To meet these new reductions, Nash-Kelvinator in turn announced

---

[30] Materials for this case are derived from T.N.E.C. Monograph No. 1, pp. 109–64.

another 6-foot stripped model for $114.75. Some of the other leading companies thereupon cut prices further to $112.75.

Changes in price structure were made simultaneously. The Nash-Kelvinator Corporation discarded its former zone system and sold refrigerators on a delivered basis anywhere east of the Rocky Mountains. The Norge division of the Borg-Warner Corporation offered an all-porcelain refrigerator at $159.95, a price which was considerably below that of other all-porcelain models. The Philco Corporation presented a 7-foot refrigerator retailing at $119.95, instead of the usual 6-foot model. For most companies the widest price reductions were for the 6-foot model, which sold for between $112.75 and $114.75. On other 6-foot models and on 5-foot models, reductions from 1939 prices were considerably less.

The electric refrigerator industry experienced its major growth in the two decades prior to 1940. In the experimental period, while the product was being developed, costs were high because of lack of standardization, coupled with a low aggregate volume of output. Prices were correspondingly high, and sales were confined to the limited group which could afford the luxury of experimentation. Gradually, the product became relatively satisfactory; manufacturing methods were standardized; and prices fell in anticipation of, and partly as a result of, the introduction of mass production. The product passed out of the class of curiosity and obtained a wider market. Sales expanded rapidly as more and more consumers realized the convenience and desirability of electric refrigeration.

Exhibit 1 indicates that the period of most rapid price decline

Exhibit 1

AVERAGE RETAIL VALUE AND SALES OF ELECTRIC
REFRIGERATORS, 1927–37

Year	Average Retail Value	Sales (Units)	Year	Average Retail Value	Sales (Units)
1927........	$350	375,000	1932........	$195	798,000
1929........	292	778,000	1937........	171	2,310,000

Source: T.N.E.C. Monograph No. 1, p. 112.

was from 1927 to 1932. The period of most rapid sales expansions, on the other hand, came from 1932 to 1937. Evidently, the stimulus to sales caused by the decline in price was somewhat delayed by the depression of 1929–32. After 1932, prices of refrigerators remained fairly stable to 1940.

Distribution of the product among families in the upper- and middle-income brackets reached a high level by 1937. Although the number of wired homes was also increasing in this period, the percentage of wired homes having electric refrigerators showed a marked rise. The market for refrigerators, as shown in Exhibit 2, was becoming

Exhibit 2

PERCENTAGE OF WIRED HOMES
OWNING ELECTRIC
REFRIGERATORS, 1925–38

Year	Per Cent	Year	Per Cent
1925............	*	1932............	22
1926............	2	1933............	25
1927............	4	1934............	29
1928............	6	1935............	34
1929............	9	1936............	41
1930............	13	1937............	49
1931............	17	1938............	52

* Less than 1 per cent.
Source: T.N.E.C. Monograph No. 1, p. 118.

saturated. One result of market saturation was evident in the different effects on sales volume experienced in two periods of business decline. The average number of units sold in 1932–33 was 17 per cent above the number sold in 1929, when saturation was only 9 per cent. Between 1937 and 1938, on the other hand, sales declined 46 per cent, starting from a saturation level in 1937 of 49 per cent.

In the downswing of the cycle from 1929 to 1932, price competition was especially severe. In 1931–32 a price war carried the retail price of some boxes to under $100 retail. From 1932 on, less attention was given to price, and more stress was placed upon the development of efficient, modern equipment. Prices among companies were fairly uniform, and, in general, price competition was not emphasized. By 1938, prices quoted by the leading electric refrigerator manufacturers, with one important exception, had approached a degree of almost complete uniformity, as is shown by Exhibit 3. Altogether, the concerns listed in this exhibit controlled 80 per cent of the total sales of electric refrigerators. The one important exception to the pattern of price uniformity was the Coldspot refrigerator, produced by Sears, Roebuck.

In the early period of expansion of the refrigerator industry, new concerns entered the business freely. In the depression of 1929–32, which followed this period, high mortality occurred among the smaller

Exhibit 3

LIST PRICES OF ELECTRIC REFRIGERATORS, PRINCIPAL COMPANIES, 1938*

Size (Cubic Feet)	Frigidaire	General Electric	Westinghouse	Kelvinator	Crosley	Leonard	Norge	Stewart-Warner	Universal Cooler	Coldspot
3.0–3.9:										
Size	3.1	......	3.2	3.16	3.16	3.14	3.12	......	......	......
Model	D3	......	HDS-32	K3-38	KB5-31	L3-38	R32-8	......	......	......
Price	$119.50	......	$119.50	$118.95	$117.50	$118.95	$117.50	......	......	......
4.0–4.9:										
Size	4.1	4	4.2	4.15	4.3	4.1	4.14	4.5	......	4.2
Model	N4-38	B-4	HDS-42	K4-38	KB5-43	L4-38	R41-8	458	......	3804
Price	$144.50	$144.50	$144.50	$142.95	$142.50	$142.95	$142.50	$144.75	......	$114.50
5.0–5.9:										
Size	5.1	5	5.2	5.16	5.07	5.12	5.15	5.64	5.25	......
Model	Sp. 5-38	JB-5	HS-52	K5-38	KB5-50	LS5-38	S52-8	550	AD-538	......
Price	$164.50	$164.95	$169.50	$162.95	$162.50	$162.95	$162.50	$164.75	$164.95	......
6.0–6.9:										
Size	6.1	6.1	6.2	6.13	6.0	6.09	6.15	6.3	6.51	6.3
Model	Sp. 6-38	JB-6	HS-62	KS6-38	KB5-60	LS6-38	S62-8	770	AD-658	3816
Price	$184.75	$184.75	$189.50	$182.95	$182.50	$182.95	$182.50	$179.75	$184.95	$169.50
7.0–7.9:										
Size	7.2	7.1	7.2	7.19	7.1	7.3	7.14	......	7.45	......
Model	Sp. 7-38	JB-7	HS-72	KS7-38	KB5-71	LS7-38	S71-B	......	AD-758	......
Price	$204.75	$204.75	$209.50	$202.95	$202.00	$202.95	$202.50	......	$204.95	......
8.0–8.9:										
Size	8.25	8.1	......	......	......	......	8.11	......	......	8.6
Model	M8-38	B-8	......	......	......	......	R81-8	......	......	3838
Price	$264.50	$264.50	......	......	......	......	$259.50	......	......	$179.50

* Prices are for lowest-priced comparable model in each size group.

Source: *Air Conditioning and Refrigeration News*, March 9, 1938; reprinted in T.N.E.C. Monograph No. 1, p. 162.

companies. *The Electric Refrigerator News,* in May, 1933, published a list of concerns which had ceased manufacturing electric refrigerators. Of 250 producers in the industry in 1932, only 75 remained in 1933: 110 had gone out of business, 41 could not be reached by mail, and 24 had been absorbed by other manufacturers. This high mortality reflected in part the stress of the depression for all business companies; but more particularly, it foreshadowed the approaching maturity of the electric refrigerator industry, with a weeding-out of weaker firms. By 1937 the industry's production was concentrated largely in four companies, as indicated by Exhibit 4.

Exhibit 4

CONCENTRATION OF CONTROL OF MARKET FOR DOMESTIC
ELECTRIC REFRIGERATORS, 1937

CAPACITY	FIRST 4 COMPANIES		INDUSTRY	
	Production	Per Cent of Total	Production	No. Companies
Under 6 feet:				
Number.................	754,130	69	1,093,026	21
Value...................	$48,464,364	69	$84,458,077	
6–10 feet:				
Number.................	728,660	74	991,022	25
Value...................	$73,739,375	77	$95,985,895	
10 feet and over:				
Number.................	*	*	....	14
Value...................	$ 2,406,123	77	$ 3,130,046	

* Data not available.
Source: T.N.E.C. Monograph No. 1, p. 163.

The corporations surviving the depression—especially the large firms—invested heavily in research and experimental activities. Modern sealed units for the refrigerant were introduced by the majority of manufacturers, streamlined refrigerator cabinets were perfected, economical methods of insulation were devised, and great advances were made in improving internal features of refrigerators.

At the same time, sales effort was intensified, not only by manufacturers and dealers but also by public utilities, which sought to expand the demand for electric current. House-to-house canvassing and demonstrations of the product became a common practice. Manufacturers sought for and developed new markets. This required new distributors and more outlets. This movement toward the extension and expansion of distributive outlets was aided by established retail stores of various kinds. Furniture stores, hardware stores, music stores, automobile accessories shops, and department stores seized the opportunity to handle refrigerators. The largest group of outlets, however, was the electrical specialty stores.

Prior to 1931, most manufacturers presented relatively few models and styles. After business recovery began in the spring of 1933, the number of price lines increased. Instead of showing only three or four refrigerators, as was the case in 1929, by 1935 the average dealer was able to present to the prospective customer eight or ten distinct lines. After 1932, when efforts to expand the market were intensified, small 4-foot refrigerators were introduced to attract low-income consumers. Later, the stripped model in the 6-foot box became the most popular size. This model was used especially in leader selling, where stores attempted to influence the consumer to buy de luxe models at higher prices.

Throughout this period, dealers' margins, as indicated in Exhibit 5, remained fairly constant percentagewise; but, with the decline in

Exhibit 5

DISTRIBUTIVE MARGIN FOR ELECTRIC REFRIGERATORS, 1928–37

YEAR	ESTIMATED AVERAGE FACTORY PRICE	ESTIMATED AVERAGE RETAIL PRICE	MARGIN		YEAR	ESTIMATED AVERAGE FACTORY PRICE	ESTIMATED AVERAGE RETAIL PRICE	MARGIN	
			Actual (on Retail)	Per Cent				Actual (on Retail)	Per Cent
1928......	$166	$334	$168	50	1933......	$83	$170	$87	51
1929......	134	292	158	54	1934......	84	172	88	51
1930......	132	275	143	52	1935......	78	166	88	53
1931......	129	258	129	50	1936......	81	164	83	51
1932......	101	195	94	48	1937......	85	173	88	51

Source: Factory price, National Electrical Manufacturers' Association; retail price, *Air Conditioning and Refrigeration News*. Both sources quoted in T.N.E.C. Monograph No. 1, p. 144.

retail prices, the dollar margin dropped. But costs of distributing electric refrigerators remained at high levels. The one important exception to these high costs of distribution was marketing through mass distributors. In Exhibit 6 the distributive margins of regular channels and mass distributors are compared.

Up to 1938, replacement sales accounted for less than one fifth of the total market. As sales expansion and market saturation proceeded, however, it became evident that the demand for electric refrigerators was coming increasingly from replacement (see Exhibit 7). Under these conditions, sales were influenced strongly by three factors: durability, obsolescence, and trade-in allowances. In Exhibit 8 the increasing

Exhibit 6

DISTRIBUTIVE MARGINS OF STANDARD BRAND SALES
ORGANIZATION AND OF MASS DISTRIBUTOR,
ELECTRIC REFRIGERATORS, 1938

Type of Distribution	Retail Price	Manu-facturer's Cost	Cost of Distribution	
			Actual	Per Cent of Retail Price
Typical standard brand sales organization...............	$207.50	$ 93.34	$114.16	55.0
Mass distributor.................	158.00	100.00	58.00	36.7

Source: John F. Thomas, "Varying Functions in Distribution: Their Costs and Influences on Retail Prices," *Journal of Marketing*, July, 1938, p. 56; quoted in T.N.E.C. Monograph No 1, p. 145.

Exhibit 7

REPLACEMENT SALES AS A PERCENTAGE OF TOTAL SALES
OF ELECTRIC REFRIGERATORS, TWO COMPANIES, 1929–38

Year	Company A	Company B	Year	Company A	Company B
1929..........	3	..	1934..........	9	7
1930..........	2	..	1935..........	10	10
1931..........	3	..	1936..........	13	14
1932..........	1	1	1937..........	15	16
1933..........	3	2	1938..........	19	18

Source: T.N.E.C. Monograph No. 1, p. 148.

Exhibit 8

ESTIMATED DURABILITY OF ELECTRIC
REFRIGERATORS, 1920–38

Year of Manufacture	Life Expect-ancy (Years)	Year of Manufacture	Life Expect-ancy (Years)
1920..........	6	1930..........	13
1921..........	7	1931..........	13
1922..........	8	1932..........	13
1923..........	9	1933..........	13
1924..........	10	1934..........	14
1925..........	11	1935..........	14
1926..........	11	1936..........	14
1927..........	12	1937..........	15
1928..........	12	1938..........	15
1929..........	12		

Source: T.N.E.C. Monograph No. 1, p. 149. The life expectancy for each year is an average of data compiled from a sample study which was made by a large manufacturer of refrigerators.

durability of refrigerators is shown. Obsolescence as well as absolute durability was a determining factor in replacements; to some extent, owners of refrigerators were influenced to buy new models which had technical improvements, but the effect of this factor was much less than in the case of automobiles. Finally, the cost of making a replacement was determined not only by the price of a new product but also by the trade-in allowance granted by the dealer on the old piece of equipment. While the acceptance of trade-ins in the refrigerator market became increasingly common up to 1938, it had not reached the proportions found in the automobile market. Exhibit 9

Exhibit 9

CASH VALUE OF TRADE-INS, AS A PERCENTAGE OF
LIST PRICE OF ELECTRIC REFRIGERATORS, 1933–37*

Year	7-Foot	6-Foot	5-Foot	4-Foot
1933.........	10.0	13.8	10.3	16.5
1934.........	11.0	17.9	16.6	18.5
1935.........	21.0	22.2	21.3	24.1
1936.........	23.0	24.2	24.7	25.5
1937.........	32.0	32.4	31.6	34.8

* Manufacturers' suggested retail delivered price, northeast zone.
Source: *National Market Index*, published by National Refrigerator Index Publishing Co., Inc.; quoted in T.N.E.C. Monograph No. 1, p. 163.

shows the growth of trade-ins up to 1938.

It was clear by 1940 that the electric refrigerator industry had come to a critical turning point as a result of the increasing saturation of a substantial portion of its market, particularly in the more prosperous sector of the population. There was abundant evidence that the initial period of rapid technologic development, aggressive price reductions, and vigorous growth was rapidly approaching an end. The decision by Nash-Kelvinator to cut prices in January, 1940, however, led to immediate resumption of price competition by the industry. Sales of electric refrigerators during the first quarter of 1940 totaled 814,000 boxes, as compared with 611,000 for the same period in 1939.

Accompanying the price reduction on the stripped model was a policy adopted by Nash-Kelvinator, advocating the sale of higher-priced models wherever possible. On March 27, 1940, the company addressed the following communication to its dealers:

Yes; the evidence is pouring in—and it proves the soundness of Kelvinator's 1940 program. Look at the chart showing the percentage of Kelvinator's sales by models and prices, and then compare these facts with your own sales. The evidence shows clearly that Kelvinator dealers are selling higher-priced merchandise.

Those who sell Kelvinator have more than a selling plan . . . they have a working selling plan. And it is working because it was carefully planned months ago with logical and easy-to-sell step-ups between models. There are low-priced models for the vast low-income market . . . and beautiful, full-featured models (including the new "Moist-Master" controlled humidity system) specifically designed to get the rapidly growing replacement business. Throughout Kelvinator's line of sixes and eights the salesman can step up sales because plus features in each step offer visible and provable added value to the customer.

79.8 per cent of the Kelvinator volume is in refrigerators with the greatest margin, the greatest gross dollar sale. The average unit sales price is better than $160.00.

According to this advertisement, field reports received by the company up to March 19 showed that actual sales of the various models were in the ratio shown in Exhibit 10.

Exhibit 10

Price	Model	Per Cent	Price	Model	Per Cent
$114.75..........	CSX–6	6.4	$179.95..........	S–8	7.3
124.95..........	SS–6	13.8	209.95..........	HD–6	8.1
139.95..........	S–6	30.3	209.95..........	R–8	4.1
169.95..........	HS–6	13.5	239.95..........	HD–8	4.0
179.95..........	R–6	12.5			
					100.0

QUESTIONS

1. Was the policy of price cutting adopted by Nash-Kelvinator in the spring of 1940 a desirable one?
2. Would it have been desirable to make equal price reductions for all models in the line?
3. What effect did the other sales policies of the company have?
4. In what way would the price policies appropriate to 1929 require adjustment to meet the conditions of 1940?

CASE 6–6: THE SULFUR INDUSTRY

The following excerpts are from the testimony of Dr. R. H. Montgomery, of the University of Texas, presented before the Temporary National Economic Committee on March 14, 1939.[31]

IMPORTANCE OF SULFUR AND SULFURIC ACID

DR. MONTGOMERY: The best authority that I know in this field in the United States has made this simple statement, which I should like to read into the record, just one paragraph, and very short: "Sulfuric acid is the most basic of all chemical products. There is scarcely a manufactured product

[31] *T.N.E.C. Hearings*, Part 5, pp. 1986 ff.

known in the preparation of which either of the raw material or in the actual process of making the article sulfuric acid does not play a part."

ACTING CHAIRMAN LUBIN: Will you quote the source of that statement, please?

DR. MONTGOMERY: From Theodore J. Kreps' book on sulfuric acid:[32] "Sulfuric acid, I believe, is the narrowest and at the same time most vital bottle neck of modern industry. I have a list here, which will be extended in the tables just submitted, indicating the importance in some of our basic industries." [See Exhibit 1.]

Exhibit 1

SULFURIC ACID (EXPRESSED AS 50° B.) CONSUMED IN THE
UNITED STATES, 1937, BY INDUSTRIES, IN SHORT TONS

Industry	Tons	Industry	Tons
Fertilizer	1,943,000	Paints and pigments	525,000
Petroleum refining	1,210,000	Explosives	230,000
Chemicals	1,060,000	Rayon and cellulose	380,000
Coal products	860,000	Textiles	112,000
Iron and steel	780,000	Miscellaneous	406,000
Other metallurgical	640,000		
			8,146,000

COLONEL CHANTLAND: Doctor, you have spoken of sulfuric acid, and we are talking about a sulfur study. Please relate those.

DR. MONTGOMERY: Over 70 per cent of the sulfuric acid of the United States is produced from natural sulfur or brimstone. Approximately 85 per cent of all of the sulfur produced in the United States is used in the manufacture of sulfuric acid.

ACTING CHAIRMAN LUBIN: Do you have any figures showing the trend of production of sulfuric acid from various sources, namely, whether or not more or less of sulfuric acid is being produced from sulfur direct?

DR. MONTGOMERY: Yes. The fertilizer industry took approximately 2,000,-000 tons of sulfuric acid in 1937; petroleum refining, 1,200,000; chemicals, over 1,000,000 tons; coal products, iron and steel, metallurgical, paints and pigments each took over 500,000 tons. There are many others including the refining of gasoline, the manufacture of rayon, of cellulose film, most cotton textiles, explosives, which use large amounts, usually between 100,000 and 500,000 tons per year.

Sulfuric acid, and back of that brimstone, is probably the most vital single military product, or product to be used in war for war purposes. Every pound of smokeless powder manufactured requires 2.3 pounds of sulfuric acid; every pound of TNT requires 2.2 pounds of the acid, and every pound of picric acid requires 6.5 pounds of sulfuric acid.

. . . .

THE CHAIRMAN: Have you testified as to how this sulfur is used, Dr. Montgomery?

[32] *Economics of the Sulfuric Acid Industry* (Stanford, California: Stanford University Press, 1938).

DR. MONTGOMERY: I have. I entered an exhibit showing the entire, at least the major uses.

THE CHAIRMAN: Is it used in its raw state? It has to be transposed into acid first.

DR. MONTGOMERY: I believe it is never used in its raw state. About 85 per cent of it is used as sulfuric acid. The other in various minor uses such as for medicinal purposes, but so far as the sulfur companies are concerned the sulfur is sold as it comes out of the ground; no processing whatever is involved to the sulfur company.

THE CHAIRMAN: But so far as its commercial use is concerned, the sulfur content of commodities which are put upon the general market is comparatively small, is it not?

DR. MONTGOMERY: It depends on the commodity.

THE CHAIRMAN: We will take fertilizer, for example.

DR. MONTGOMERY: In the case of superphosphate fertilizer almost 50 per cent of it is sulfuric acid. To 1,000 pounds of phosphate rock is added 900 pounds of sulfuric acid, and then a few minor factors, water, for instance, about 30 pounds, to make a ton of fertilizer. Now in some other cases, for instance in the production of steel and in the production of gasoline and in the production of cellulose film, much smaller amounts of sulfur are used.

THE CHAIRMAN: Have you any idea as to what generalization could be made with respect to the over-all uses of sulfur?

DR. MONTGOMERY: Well, Senator, I do not believe any such average could be made at all, because certainly it would run from almost 50 per cent in the case of superphosphate fertilizer to almost zero in other cases.

COLONEL CHANTLAND: While in fertilizer the sulfuric acid is 50 per cent, or 1,000 pounds of phosphate rock to 900 pounds of sulfuric acid, how as to the matter of costs of the two, the rock and the sulfuric acid?

DR. MONTGOMERY: Of course, phosphate rock is very, very cheap, if stated in terms of tonnage, as contrasted with sulfuric acid.

COLONEL CHANTLAND: So that in the superphosphate fertilizer the sulfuric acid is a big element of cost?

DR. MONTGOMERY: It is so far as the materials going into the fertilizer are concerned; it is by far the most important. For instance, the phosphate rock sold on an average last year at $3.28 per ton.

． ． ． ． ． ． ．

SOURCES, PRODUCTION, AND METHODS OF PRODUCING SULFUR

THE CHAIRMAN: What are the sources of the production of sulfur in its natural state?

DR. MONTGOMERY: There are primarily, throughout the past 40 years, two sources, one of them the Sicilian sulfur mines, where sulfur is mined very much as coal or iron is mined in this country, and deposits along the Gulf coast in Texas and Louisiana, where the sulfur is mined by the Frasch process, which I shall describe in just a moment.

． ． ． ． ． ．

Now, to answer your question as to the source of American production, all of that comes from two States, Texas and Louisiana.

THE CHAIRMAN: What is the extent of the deposits, the physical deposits?

DR. MONTGOMERY: That is very difficult to answer. Sulfur is found in its natural state in connection with what we know as the salt domes. There seem to be some 60 or 70 of those on the Gulf Coast. How many of them contain sulfur in commercial quantities is not known at present. At present there are only 6 plants producing sulfur.

. . . .

The Frasch process, patented by Mr. Herman Frasch, a chemist for the Standard Oil Co. in 1891, involves the forcing of superheated steam, steam at approximately 220° and under tremendous pressure, approximately 6 atmospheres, into an inert deposit of natural sulfur or brimstone. The sulfur is melted and then is pumped out of the ground in a liquid form. The process was not immediately put into use when discovered by Mr. Frasch because of the difficulty of securing fuel for heating water and operating pumps.

In 1902 the discovery of oil at Spindle Top, Tex., near the then known sulfur deposit, gave him a cheap fuel. In 1903 the Union Sulphur Co. was reorganized to exploit that deposit, using the Frasch process, using crude oil as its fuel.

Until 1903 Union Sulphur Co. produced 85,000 tons. The next year 200,000 tons were produced. By 1908 about 800,000 tons per year were produced by that one company, and their production stayed at approximately that figure, sometimes going as high as 1,000,000 tons per year, until the dome was exhausted in 1924.

In 1906 the Anglo-Sicilian monopoly became tremendously excited about this new process of producing sulfur.

THE CHAIRMAN: Were the deposits in Sicily concentrated as they are in the United States?

DR. MONTGOMERY: Not by any means, Senator, and the Frasch process cannot be employed in Sicily at all on their deposits. The use of this process is determined by certain physical characteristics of the deposits. All of the known deposits which have been exploited by this method have been between 400 and 1,400 feet under the surface of the ground. In the Gulf coast area the sulfur deposit being found is a porous limestone rock formation with an overlay of several hundred feet of what we call sea mud. Essentially in using this process the surrounding ground must collapse the rock structure in order to permit the extraction of the melted sulfur in liquid form.

In 1906 the Italian Government sent a commission to Louisiana to study the process of extraction. That commission reported that Union Sulphur Co. could supply the American market at a cost of approximately 40 lire per long ton or about $7.72. In 1906 the Italian Government organized a consorzio, a pool of all the sulfur producers in Sicily, and the next year an agreement was made by it with Union Sulphur Co., known as the Consortium of 1907.

. . . .

Between this Sicilian trust and the Union Sulphur an agreement as to European and American markets was made early in 1907.

. . . .

The substance of that contract is that the Export Corporation was given the North American market with the outlying islands and 50 per cent of the

European market. The price at which sulfur was to be sold in the European market was determined by agreement between Consorzio and the Corporation.

. . . .

THE CHAIRMAN: Under the Webb-Pomerene Export Trade Act?

DR. MONTGOMERY: Yes.

. . . .

THE CHAIRMAN: Of course, the Webb-Pomerene Act was a statute passed by Congress which in effect repealed the antitrust law so far as foreign trade is concerned. In other words, corporations or persons were given the authority to make combinations in restraint of trade so far as export trade was concerned.

. . . .

COLONEL CHANTLAND: It was a question of meeting what they called the foreign cartels, where the Government did back them up, and the plea was that we couldn't do much against them unless we did something of that sort.

. . . .

DR. MONTGOMERY: From 1906 until 1913, the original Frasch patents apparently prohibited or prevented any other company from entering the field. The Freeport Sulphur Co. was organized in 1908. The Union Sulphur Co. immediately sued for infringement of patent. That suit was ultimately decided in 1919, at which time all of the patents were declared null and void by the Federal circuit court, Judge Buffington's decision, in the Philadelphia circuit.

In 1913 the Freeport Sulphur Co. began to produce. Within 2 or 3 years it was producing approximately half a million tons per year, a large enough volume to furnish real competition for Union in the American market. However, the war created a tremendous demand for sulfur. The use of sulfuric acid in the manufacture of explosives increased from approximately 150,000 tons pre-war to 2,700,000 in 1 year, 1918. The War Industries Board and the military authorities became interested in 1917 for fear we wouldn't have an adequate supply of sulfuric acid for war purposes. In 1918 they allocated the uses of sulfur, requiring both companies to keep at least half a million tons of sulfur above ground at their mines. In 1918 the Texas Gulf Sulphur Co. was organized, and in 1919 began production at Bryan Mound, which is one of the richest deposits that has been discovered up to the present time.

SULFUR PRICES

DR. MONTGOMERY: At the end of the war America's capacity to produce had been trebled. The depression, the slight depression of 1919 and the larger depression of 1920–21, reduced the demand for sulfur by more than 50 per cent.

Apparently a price war developed for approximately 1 year. The price of sulfur was reduced from $22 a ton, f.o.b. the mines, where it had been set by the War Industries Board in 1918, to $16.50 a ton, then $14.50, then $12.50 per ton. In that situation in 1922 the Sulphur Export Corporation was formed by the three companies then engaged in producing sulfur, Union Sulphur Co., of Louisiana; the Texas Gulf Sulphur Co., of Texas; and the Freeport Sulphur Co., of Texas.

. . . .

In 1924 Union Sulphur quit producing, having exhausted their deposits, but having a tremendous inventory of sulfur above ground continued to ship until 1928, at which time Union withdrew from the production of sulfur and from the Sulphur Export Corporation, selling its stock in the Sulphur Export Corporation to the other two companies on a 50–50 basis.

COLONEL CHANTLAND: What companies were those?

DR. MONTGOMERY: Freeport Sulphur Co. and the Texas Gulf Sulphur Co., the two companies agreeing to divide export business in the ratio of 50–50, where it has remained with minor exceptions to the present time.

Since 1924 Freeport Sulphur Co. and Texas Gulf Sulphur Co. have produced on an average over 94 per cent of the total production in the United States.

MR. BALLINGER: What happened to the price of sulfur at the time this corporation was formed; I mean, this export agreement was entered into?

DR. MONTGOMERY: The price of sulfur, which had declined very sharply, was raised to approximately $18 per ton f.o.b. the mines, and it has remained at approximately that figure—at exactly that figure—for some 10 years down to the present time. [See Exhibit 2.]

Exhibit 2

SULFUR AND PYRITE PRICES, 1922–37

Year	Sulfur Price at Mine	Import Pyrites, Cents per Unit f.a.f. U.S. Ports	Year	Sulfur Price at Mine	Import Pyrites, Cents per Unit f.a.f. U.S. Ports
1922	$16.37	13	1930	$17.98	13
1923	16.06	12.25	1931	18.00	12
1924	16.26	12	1932	18.00	12
1925	15.61	11.5	1933	18.00	12
1926	17.99	12	1934	18.00	12
1927	18.48	12.75	1935	18.00	12
1928	18.00	13	1936	18.00	12
1929	17.97	13	1937	18.00	12

COLONEL CHANTLAND: You mean for the prime grade. There have been reductions for off-color and off-grade sulfur.

MR. BALLINGER: You mean $18 a ton for sulfur sold domestically in the United States?

DR. MONTGOMERY: Yes.

MR. BALLINGER: How about the price of sulfur sold abroad?

DR. MONTGOMERY: It has been figured apparently on the price of $18 per ton f.o.b. the mines plus freight, insurance, and other costs of shipment.

I should like to amend that statement in this way: It might be better to say that the export price of sulfur has been set, as it has, by agreement with the Sicilian producers.

(Dr. Lubin assumed the Chair)

ACTING CHAIRMAN LUBIN: You said a minute ago that under the agreement with the Sicilian producers, the markets of the world have been allocated between the American export group and the Sicilian producers, which means in effect, then, that this export price is applicable only in those limited markets, namely the North American continent and certain islands contiguous to the continent.

DR. MONTGOMERY: You mean that $18 per ton f.o.b. the mine? Yes. The prices to the foreign markets are, of course, affected by distance, difficulty of shipment, and things of that sort.

ACTING CHAIRMAN LUBIN: Under this agreement we have no foreign markets. I understood you to say the territory has been divided in such a way that the American producers have only the North American Continent and certain contiguous islands.

DR. MONTGOMERY: Not at all. We have supplied approximately 75 per cent of the world market outside of the North American continent. The North American Continent and the outlying islands are retained for the American producers exclusively, and most of the time, I believe with the exception of 1 year, the Italian market has been retained by the Sicilian producers, but the rest of the world market has been divided with the American producers supplying some 75 per cent of the world market.

. . . .

DR. MONTGOMERY: In addition there has been developed within the past 10 years a new process for extracting raw sulfur from pyrites. The patents on that process were obtained by a Norwegian company. For the past 5 years the Sulphur Export Corporation of the United States has allotted to the Norwegian company, Orkla Grube, A.B., usually referred to as Orkla, approximately 70,000 tons per year of its part of export or world-market sulfur.

ACTING CHAIRMAN LUBIN: May I interrupt at that point? Is that sulfur being produced under Norwegian patents being produced in the United States?

DR. MONTGOMERY: Not at all. The Texas Gulf Sulphur Co. holds the patent on that process for the United States, and I believe for the whole Western Hemisphere. The Texas Gulf Sulphur Co. has secured options on and leases on deposits from which sulfur may be produced, or which they think sulfur may be produced in both Newfoundland and Peru. I assume from that that they hold the patents on the process for the entire Western Hemisphere.

By this contract with Orkla, Orkla is effectively prevented from either expanding its own production or leasing patent rights to anyone else in the world outside of the Western Hemisphere.

ACTING CHAIRMAN LUBIN: This proportion of the output that has been allocated to Orkla, where is it being produced?

DR. MONTGOMERY: In Norway, and the allocation specifies that the sulfur is to be sold only in Scandinavia and Finland by Orkla.

MR. BALLINGER: Doctor, I would like to go back a little bit to the picture you have been drawing here for the committee. Following a rather vigorous price war in the sulfur industry, the companies entered into this export agreement?

DR. MONTGOMERY: That is correct.

MR. BALLINGER: And then the price of domestic sulfur was immediately raised—

DR. MONTGOMERY (*interposing*): That is correct.

MR. BALLINGER: And it stood stationary for how many years?

DR. MONTGOMERY: According to my records, for the past 17 years it has varied slightly for about 2 of those 17 years, being from 1926 down to October 1938. The price remained absolutely stationary at $18 per ton except for 2 years. In one of those years the price varied by 3 cents per ton from $18; in the other year it varied by 2 cents per ton.

MR. DAVIS: Well, now, you stated that there has been a break in the price, or a sharp decline. What was the extent of that decline, and in what year did it occur?

DR. MONTGOMERY: In 1919 the price declined, the average price, for the best grade of sulfur, at the mine, about $2.50 per ton.

COLONEL CHANTLAND: The war price had been what?

DR. MONTGOMERY: Twenty-two dollars per ton. In 1925 the price again declined by approximately $2.50 per ton.

MR. DAVIS: Declined from what price?

DR. MONTGOMERY: From $18 per ton f.o.b. the mine.

MR. DAVIS: Well, now, that was subsequent to the approval of the original export trade agreement, was it not?

DR. MONTGOMERY: Yes; it was.

MR. DAVIS: To what do you attribute that decline in 1925, if you have any knowledge or information?

DR. MONTGOMERY: I do not have knowledge from which I could state positively at all.

MR. DAVIS: Well, now, when you refer to the price at the mine in different years mentioned, do you refer to the price to everybody, including American buyers as well as foreign buyers?

DR. MONTGOMERY: Whether foreign buyers get their sulfur at $18 f.o.b. the mine or not is impossible to state from the records. The price, however, does apply to their first quality of sulfur, the true yellow, pure sulfur, to all American buyers, regardless, apparently, of quantity or distance from the mine.

MR. TUPPER: Have we ever imported any sulfur?

DR. MONTGOMERY: We imported approximately one-third of world production until the opening of the Union Sulphur Co.'s mine in Louisiana. We were at that time importing approximately one-third of the total Sicilian production. Since 1906 our sulfur imports dropped, of course, immediately, to zero, or almost zero, where they have remained during the past 32 years.

MR. TUPPER: In this price war of 1921 there wasn't any problem of competition from abroad?

DR. MONTGOMERY: None whatever, so far as one can tell from the records.

. . . .

MR. BLAISDELL: As I understand it, there was a date shortly after the war when there was a severe price war in the industry.

DR. MONTGOMERY: Yes.

MR. BLAISDELL: At that time an agreement was made with the foreign producers which had the effect of stabilizing the price.

DR. MONTGOMERY: Yes; in my opinion, that is entirely correct.

MR. BLAISDELL: In 1925 again a similar situation arose in spite of the agreement.

DR. MONTGOMERY: Yes.

MR. BLAISDELL: A new agreement was then entered into which had essentially the same effect of reestablishing new terms of agreement.

DR. MONTGOMERY: So far as I know, there was no new agreement made in 1925 either between the Sulphur Export Corporation and the Sicilian producers or between the producers in this country. I consequently cannot state as of my own knowledge the reason for the stability of prices from 1925 to the present time. For some reason, the price of sulfur after that break in '25 became absolutely stationary. According to the report made by the Texas Gulf Sulphur Co. to the Federal Trade Commission on their request, during this investigation it has not varied a penny since '26.

MR. DAVIS: Dr. Montgomery, how long did the variation in prices in 1925 continue?

DR. MONTGOMERY: Apparently for 1 year only. During 1 year the break was great enough to pull the average for that year down by some $2.50 per ton.

MR. DAVIS: Do you not think that there was a natural fluctuation more or less following the World War of prices in this industry, just as there was in nearly all industries—becoming readjusted from war prices to a peacetime basis?

DR. MONTGOMERY: Yes; certainly; plus the fact that this industry, because of the entrance of a new company, Texas Gulf Sulphur Co., with the largest plant in the industry, with the largest plant the industry had ever known, plus the fact that the Freeport Sulphur Co. had more than doubled its production by opening a new mine, gave us a trebled production of sulfur as against pre-war years. That plus the business depression of 1920, '21, and the slight recession of '25 may be entirely responsible for the break in price which is indicated.

On the other hand, it might be pointed out that the business depression from 1929 down to 1939 has not had that effect. The price of sulfur has not been depressed during the past 10 years.

MR. DAVIS: Has it varied any during the past 10 years?

DR. MONTGOMERY: None whatsoever except 3 cents apparently 1 year and 2 cents 1 year.

COLONEL CHANTLAND: Up to what time?

DR. MONTGOMERY: Up to October 1938.

. . . .

COMPETING PRODUCTS

COLONEL CHANTLAND: Will the chairman bear with me while I bring out one other point that I think will be informative to the committee? That is this: Pyrite sulfur is spoken of sometimes as competitive. Will you express a judgment as to when, at what price level, it becomes competitive, and as to the matter of countries producing enough pyrites?

DR. MONTGOMERY: Sulfuric acid is produced from three, basically three, sources: The brimstone or raw sulfur, which accounts for approximately 70 per cent of the total; pyrites, iron pyrites usually, from which 15 to 20 per cent of the total—I mean within the United States—is produced; and 10 to 15 per cent produced from mining operations in zinc and copper. The price rigidity in pyrites parallels exactly the price rigidity in sulfur. In other words, during those 12 years in which there is no variation in price of sulfur there is no variation in the price of pyrites. Pyrites have to be approximately 12 cents per unit, a unit I believe is 22.4 pounds of 48 to 52 per cent sulfur pyrites, to compete with sulfur at $18 per ton in the manufacture of sulfuric acid. A price of $18 per ton for sulfur f.o.b. the mines is equivalent in competitive terms to a price of approximately 12 cents per unit for pyrites. This relationship in prices has been maintained for many years. Just how low the price of sulfur would have to be to induce the acid producers to change over from pyrites to sulfur I do not know. I should think it would be more accurate to say that the price of pyrites is determined by the price of sulfur.

.   .   .   .

COST OF PRODUCING SULFUR

DR. MONTGOMERY: I was asked earlier about the cost of producing sulfur in the United States under the Frasch process. [See Exhibit 3.] In 1917,

Exhibit 3

SULFUR—COST OF PRODUCTION

Year	Freeport Sulphur Company	Texas Gulf Sulphur Company	Union Sulphur Company
1906	. . . . .	. . . . .	$7.72
1917	$6.15	. . . . .	5.71
1927	6.07	. . . . .	. . . . .
1928	5.71	. . . . .	. . . . .
1929	5.98	$5.27	. . . . .
1930	6.79	5.77	. . . . .
1931	6.17	5.75	. . . . .
1932	6.15	6.11	. . . . .
1933	5.64	6.22	. . . . .
1934	6.51	5.52	. . . . .
1935	6.23	5.54	. . . . .
1936	5.77	5.43	. . . . .
1937	5.93	5.18	. . . . .

the Federal Trade Commission made two studies on cost of production. According to their study it was then costing Freeport Sulphur Co., $6.15 per ton; and Union Sulphur Co., $5.71 per ton. In 1927 and 1928, Freeport Sulphur Co. reported to Moody's Manual that their costs of production were $6.07 and $5.71 per ton. In their annual balance sheets, as reported in Moody's Manual, both Freeport and Texas Gulf from 1929 to 1938 have carried their inventory of sulfur above ground "at cost." I have divided this figure by the companies' reports of their sulfur inventory as of December 31 for each of the 10 years. According to this computation Freeport Sulphur Co.'s costs have varied from $5.64 to $6.79; a 10-year average of $6.13 per ton. Texas Gulf

Sulphur's costs have varied by this computation from $5.18 per ton in 1937 to $6.22 per ton in 1933; for a 10-year average of $5.64 per ton. In my opinion these represent the best figures we have available on cost of production.

QUESTIONS

1. By what name would you designate the market situation in sulfur around 1936?

2. Was the demand for sulfur relatively elastic or inelastic at prices of about $6.00 per ton? Why do you believe this to be the case? How do you explain this by referring to the principal use of sulfur?

3. Was the stability of the price of sulfur in the 1930's a contribution to over-all economic stability?

Chapter 7

~~~~~~

GAME THEORY AND
BUSINESS DECISIONS

SUPPOSE YOU are invited to be a spectator at a meeting of the board of directors of a large corporation. And suppose that, soon after the meeting is called to order, each director, at the request of the chairman, begins to toss a coin into the air, and to record the resulting heads and tails on a piece of paper. You will probably conclude that the assembled officials have suddenly felt an irresistible urge to gamble or else that the hectic pace of modern business has finally proved to be too much for the human mind. Actually, however, the directors may be engaging in a new and quite rational method of decision making according to the theory of games developed principally by a famous mathematician, the late John von Neumann.[1] As will be explained later, the purpose of the coin tossing may be to secure guidance of a pure chance (hence, unpredictable) nature as to an important business move. They may be taking the steps necessary to minimize the likelihood that their opponents will be able to guess their next move, since they themselves will not know what they are going to do until the coin-tossing ceremony is over. In the words of von Neumann and Morgenstern, "Ignorance is obviously a very good safeguard against disclosing information directly or indirectly."[2] The executive coin tossing is carried out, however, as only a part of a carefully calculated process of making a decision and differs sharply from the action of the motorist who tosses a coin to decide which fork of the road to take when he is completely lost.

Since its original promulgation the theory of games has attracted much attention in military planning circles because of its implications for certain situations encountered in war. Theoretically, it can also be useful to the gambler in guiding his play in such games as poker and in

---

[1] The theory is set forth in most complete form in John von Neumann and Oskar Morgenstern, *Theory of Games and Economic Behavior* (Princeton: Princeton University Press, 1944).

[2] *Ibid.*, p. 146.

the more purely intellectual activity of chess playing. However, its actual application to such complicated games is extremely difficult and not likely to prove of practical help to the players.[3] It is especially difficult to visualize the tough, gun-toting poker player of the western movies sitting patiently while one of the players is running off on his portable electronic computer the calculations necessary to decide whether to raise, call, or drop out.

Certain simple games, however (which might conceivably be suitable for gambling), can readily be handled by means of the theory of games. The player who uses the system indicated by game theory is playing conservatively. He assumes that his opponent is skilled rather than stupid. In the words of J. D. Williams of the RAND Corporation, game theory "refers to a kind of mathematical morality, or at least frugality, which claims that the sensible object of the player is to gain as much from the game as he can, safely, in the face of a skillful opponent who is pursuing an antithetical goal."[4]

Often, the business situation in which an executive decision is required is so complex that application of the theory of games is not likely to be considered feasible. When there is a clean-cut conflict of interests between one firm and another, however, or between one firm and all other close rivals taken as a group, an optimal sort of business behavior may be calculable by the use of game theory. Even where an actual solution cannot be reached, the "way of thinking" about a problem which is suggested by game theory may be useful to the business executive. And as was suggested earlier, some knowledge of game theory should at least cause one to appreciate the possible virtue of basing an important decision on the outcome of some apparently frivolous action such as the toss of a coin or the throw of a pair of dice or a single die.

The Game of Hul Gul

The present chapter will not attempt to give any systematic or comprehensive explanation of the elements of game theory (such as is given in mathematical terms by von Neumann and Morgenstern, and more simply by J. D. Williams), but will instead apply the

---

[3] Von Neumann and Morgenstern devote a considerable amount of space to analysis of a simplified version of poker and conclude that "the mathematical problem of real poker is difficult but probably not beyond the reach of techniques which are available" (*ibid.*, p. 219).

[4] J. D. Williams, *The Compleat Strategyst* (New York: McGraw-Hill Book Co., Inc., 1954), p. 23. This book gives a simple and humorous exposition of the elements of the theory of games. The present chapter is heavily indebted to this work.

theory to certain simple conflict situations in such a way as to enable the reader (it is hoped) to analyze some simple business cases by this method.[5] This simple introduction may (it is also hoped) kindle some interest in further study of the theory and its possible business applications. An old game called Hul Gul, which is reputedly played by children, will first be investigated. By using the results of the analysis, one should be able to win a considerable amount of candy from even an extremely intelligent child, unless the child is too bright to stake his sweets on the outcome of the game.

The game of Hul Gul is played with beans or other small objects. In the simplest version, only two beans are used. One player holds his hands behind his back, then brings forth one fist in which he holds either one or two beans. The other player must attempt to guess the number of beans. If he does so correctly, he gets the beans or other remuneration—otherwise, he pays an amount equal to the difference between what he guessed and the actual number of beans held. It is quite obvious that the first player will wish to hold one bean more often than two beans, since when he holds only one, that is all he can lose; whereas when he holds two beans, he may lose two. He cannot hold one bean each time, however, for his strategy would quickly be figured out. To find out what proportion of the time he should hold one bean and what proportion of the time he should hold two beans in order to lose the smallest amount to a clever opponent is a suitable task for the theory of games. The holder of the beans is at a disadvantage compared with the guesser, since part of the time he will lose two beans on a particular play, whereas the guesser cannot lose more than one bean on a play. Consequently, a realistic objective of the holder is to minimize his loss, and a proper objective of the guesser is to maximize his gain by means of scientific play. The proportion of the time that the guesser should call "one bean" and "two beans" can also be determined by game theory.

Payoff Matrix

The first step is to arrange gains and losses (payoffs) in matrix form, showing who pays how much to whom under various possible circumstances. The holder of beans will be called "North," and the guesser will be called "West." Exhibit 1 shows this matrix, with

[5] We shall be concerned only with "two-person zero-sum games." In such a game the interests of the players are diametrically opposed, and one player gains only at the expense of the other. The fact that collusion is unprofitable simplifies the game. On this point see D. Blackwell and M. A. Girshick, *Theory of Games and Statistical Decisions* (New York: John Wiley & Sons, Inc., 1954), p. 10.

positive numbers indicating payments by North to West and negative numbers denoting payments by West to North. For example, if North holds two beans and West guesses two, West receives the two beans from North. Consequently, the number $+2$ is in the box corresponding to "North holds 2" and "West guesses 2." The propriety of the other payoffs can as readily be seen.

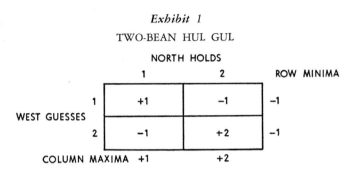

Exhibit 1

TWO-BEAN HUL GUL

NORTH HOLDS

		1	2	ROW MINIMA
WEST GUESSES	1	+1	−1	−1
	2	−1	+2	−1
COLUMN MAXIMA		+1	+2	

Solution of the Game

The first step in finding the solution to the game, once the payoff matrix has been set up, is to find the minimum figure in each row and the maximum figure in each column. These are entered alongside and under the table, respectively. If the larger of the row minima were equal to the smaller of the column maxima, the game would have a "saddle point" which would immediately indicate the best strategy for each participant. (This will be explained later.) In the game of two-bean Hul Gul, however, the larger row minimum is −1, while the smaller column maximum is +1, so the game does not have a saddle point, and further calculations are necessary.

In a "two-by-two" zero-sum game, these further calculations are simple. First, subtract each figure in Row 2 from the number immediately above. This gives $+2$ and $−3$. Signs are then disregarded, and these numbers are switched so that the 3 is associated with the left-hand column and the 2 is associated with the right-hand column. This solves the game for North, the bean holder. He should hold one bean three times and two beans two times out of five plays, on the average. In order to avoid falling into any sort of predictable pattern, he should ideally use a chance device of some suitable sort. For example, if North owned a miniature of the Pentagon Building in Washington, D.C., he could mark three of the sides with a 1 and two of the sides with a 2, and roll the replica on its side before each play. Each time a 1 came up, he would hold one bean;

and each time a 2 came up, he would hold two beans. (It would be important, of course, to roll the building behind his back, so that his opponent would not also know the answer.)

It is also simple to find the relative use which West should make of his two alternative guesses. Subtract each figure in Column 2 from the figure just to the left in Column 1 to get $+2$ and -3. Disregard signs, and switch the numbers, so that the former is associated with the second row and the latter with the first row. This indicates that West should guess "one bean" three times out of five plays and "two beans" two times out of five plays, preferably using a suitable chance device to guide his calls also. It will be noted that this appeals quite readily to one's reason. Since North is going to hold one bean three times out of five, West should have the greatest success in guessing by using the same proportions. This helps one see how game theory is based on the assumption that each participant is intelligent. It is, of course, possible to devise a strategy superior to that suggested by this theory if one is playing with someone who "tips his hand" in any way.

Value of the Game

Even if both players follow the rules of good play as determined by game theory, the game may be biased in favor of one player or the other. The game of two-bean Hul Gul is disadvantageous to the holder and is stacked to favor the guesser, as was observed earlier. The value of the game is found by a calculation which uses the best mixture of either player against the results of either alternative action of the other player and involves an averaging process.

North's best mixture is three of "hold 1" to two of "hold 2." Used in conjunction with "West guesses 1," this gives the following calculation of average payoff:

$$\frac{3(1) + 2(-1)}{3 + 2} = +\frac{1}{5}.$$

Alternatively, the value of the game could be calculated by using North's best mixture with the "West guesses 2" alternative, as follows:

$$\frac{3(-1) + 2(+2)}{3 + 2} = +\frac{1}{5}.$$

Or the value of the game can be calculated by using West's best mixture against either of North's alternatives:

$$\frac{3(+1) + 2(-1)}{3 + 2} = +\frac{1}{5},$$

or

$$\frac{3(-1) + 2(+2)}{3 + 2} = +\frac{1}{5}.$$

The value of the game comes out $+\frac{1}{5}$ in each of the four alternative calculations.[6] A positive value denotes that the game is unfair to North. If both players play "correctly," West will gain an average of $\frac{1}{5}$ (of whatever the unit of payoff may be) per play. In 20 guesses, for example, West will win an average of four units, and North will lose this amount.[7]

Saddle-Point Solution

As already mentioned, the game of two-bean Hul Gul does not have a saddle point—the maximum of the row minima does not equal the minimum of the column maxima. However, the matrix shown in Exhibit 2, which is not related to any particular game, meets these requirements. Here, 3 is both the maximum of the figures to the

Exhibit 2

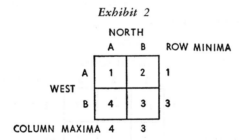

right of the matrix and the minimum of those below the matrix. Payoffs are from North to West, so North wants to keep the payoff as low as possible, and West wants to make it as high as possible. West will always select Alternative B, since both of the possible payoffs are superior to those in Row 1. North will also always select Alternative B, since he assumes West to be intelligent and is therefore convinced that West would choose Alternative B and gain 4 if North used Alternative A. The solution of the game is, therefore, that North always uses B, and West always uses B. It would do North

---

[6] Actually, the first and third equations are the same, and the second and fourth are the same, but each of the four equations is derived in a different way.

[7] It is, of course, possible (but extremely improbable) that all guesses will be wrong in a series of 20 guesses. In that case, West's loss would be 20 units. But the longer they play, the more likely it is that West will come out ahead.

no good to mix his choices between A and B because, since West will stick to B, this would merely result in West's gaining more than 3 on some plays. The value of the game is 3, since that is the payoff to West each time; 3 is called the "saddle value."

Three-Bean Hul Gul

The solution of a simple "three-by-three" zero-sum game by means of game theory can also be illustrated by reference to Hul Gul if three beans are used rather than two. The holder is permitted to have one, two, or three beans in his fist; and the guesser gets the beans (or some more interesting payoff) if he guesses the right number. Otherwise, he pays the difference between what he guesses and the number actually held. It is at once obvious that this version is much less favorable to the guesser than is the two-bean variety, since there are two ways to miss and only one way to hit each time. Also, it is by no means apparent how the game should be played against a wise opponent until one utilizes game theory. Unfortunately, the solution takes longer than that of a two-by-two game.

The payoff matrix, with positive numbers again denoting gains by West and negative numbers gains by North, can readily be determined as shown in Exhibit 3.

Exhibit 3

NORTH HOLDS

		1	2	3	ROW MINIMA
	1	+1	−1	−2	−2
WEST GUESSES	2	−1	+2	−1	−1
	3	−2	−1	+3	−2
COLUMN MAXIMA		+1	+2	+3	

There is no saddle point, and the matrix must be solved in order to find the best "mixed strategy" for each player. The calculations are as follows:

First, subtract each row from the one above to get:

	1	2	3
(ROW 1 MINUS ROW 2)	+2	−3	−1
(ROW 2 MINUS ROW 3)	+1	+3	−4

Then, strike Column 1, and the following two-by-two matrix will remain:

2	3
–3	–1
+3	–4

Take the difference in diagonal products, as follows:

$$(-3)(-4) - (+3)(-1) = +15.$$

This number (15) indicates the relative frequency with which one bean should be held. To find the relative frequency with which two beans should be held by North, strike Column 2 instead of Column 1. This leaves:

1	2
+2	–1
+1	–4

The same sort of cross-multiplication and subtraction yields:

$$(+2)(-4) - (+1)(-1) = -7.$$

(The negative sign is to be disregarded.)

Similarly, by striking Column 3, one gets:

1	2
+2	–3
+1	+3

This gives:

$$(+2)(+3) - (+1)(-3) = +9.$$

It has been determined that North should hold one bean 15 times out of 31 plays, two beans seven times out of 31, and three beans nine times out of 31 plays, on the average. A chance device should be used to determine each particular play but should be devised so as to secure this mixture of probabilities.

From the results of the two-bean version, one can now guess that West should also use the mixture 15:7:9 for guessing one, two, and three beans, respectively. This can be verified by a similar sort of calculation.

First, subtract each figure in each column from the figure just to the left:

1	+2	+1
2	−3	+3
3	−1	−4

Strike Row 1, and there remains:

2	−3	+3
3	−1	−4

The difference in diagonal cross-products is found as follows:

$$(-3)(-4) - (-1)(+3) = +15.$$

Next, strike Row 2, leaving:

1	+2	+1
3	−1	−4

And get, by cross-multiplying and subtracting:

$$(+2)(-4) - (-1)(+1) = -7.$$

Then, strike Row 3:

1	+2	+1
2	−3	+3

And subtract one cross-product from the other:

$$(+2)(+3) - (-3)(+1) = +9.$$

This verifies that West as well as North should use the mixture
15:7:9 for alternatives 1, 2, and 3, respectively.

Value of the Game

As before, the value of the game can be calculated by using the
optimal mixture of either player against any of the alternative strategies of the other. For example, West's 15:7:9 mixture can be
used against North's "hold 1" strategy:

$$\frac{15(+1) + 7(-1) + 9(-2)}{15 + 7 + 9} = -\frac{10}{31}.$$

Or, as one of the other five ways of calculating this value, try
North's best mixture against West's "guess 3" strategy:

$$\frac{15(-2) + 7(-1) + 9(+3)}{15 + 7 + 9} = -\frac{10}{31}.$$

The reader can easily satisfy himself that the other four calculations
yield the same answer.

A negative value shows that the game is unfair to West. If both
players play well, West will be more certain to lose, and to lose
more, the longer they play. The game could be made fair to West
by payment to him of $\frac{10}{31}$ of a payoff unit before each guess. If the
payoff unit were 31 cents, North should pay West a dime before
each play of the game.

A Loss-Leader Problem

Unfortunately, it is easier to apply game theory to games than to
business. Nevertheless, there are certain types of conflict situations between firms where the theory may be helpful, provided the businessman is able to set up a reasonably accurate payoff matrix relating
to the situation. (If he has no idea of payoffs under various courses
of action open to him, he cannot make a rational decision by any
other method, either.)

Suppose that two firms, which we shall rather unimaginatively
call North and West, are grocery stores located in the same area
but well isolated from other sellers. This makes them close rivals who
watch each other's prices and selling activities warily. Every Thursday
evening, each entrepreneur turns over his advertising copy to the
local newspaper; included in the advertising items is a loss leader
designed to attract customers to his store and away from the rival

store. Experience has shown, we will assume, that coffee and butter
are the most satisfactory loss leaders; each Thursday, each manager
chooses one of these to be the special bargain during the Friday-
Saturday period. Suppose further that historical experience has taught
each seller that the gains and losses from various possible actions
are as shown in Exhibit 4, positive payoffs being gains in total dollar
sales by West and losses of sales by North, and negative payoffs
being gains in dollar sales by North at the expense of his rival, West.[8]

Exhibit 4

A LOSS LEADER GAME

NORTH USES AS LOSS LEADER

		BUTTER	COFFEE	ROW MINIMA
WEST USES AS LOSS LEADER	BUTTER	0	+100	0
	COFFEE	+150	− 50	−50
COLUMN MAXIMA		+150	+100	

It is apparent that the whole practice of using loss leaders is more
favorable to West than to North. However, experience has shown
North that it is not wise to run no loss leader at all, in view of West's
consistent policy of using leaders.[9] A glance at the row minima and
column maxima shows that there is no saddle point. It is clear that it
would not be desirable for West to use butter each week as the loss
leader, because North would do the same and no sales advantage
would accrue to West. It would be undesirable for West to use
coffee as the leader each week, because North would also do so and
would take $50 in sales away from West. Similarly, it would be
foolish for North to settle on a policy of using butter each week as
the leader, because West would use coffee as the leader and gain $150
in sales at North's expense. It can similarly be seen that a constant
strategy of using coffee as the leader would be unwise for North.
Clearly, a mixture of strategies by each grocer is called for, with

[8] This assumption makes it a zero-sum game. Actually, it is quite possible that total
sales will be somewhat increased by the loss leaders for the two stores taken together
and that the gain of one will not be entirely at the expense of the other. If the assumption is close to the truth, however, the game-theory solution may be of practical utility.

[9] The strategy on North's part of using either butter or coffee as a leader may be said
to be "dominant" over a strategy on his part of using no leader at all. If a third column
labeled "No Leader" were added to the matrix, the payoffs might be, for example, +80
and +200 in rows 1 and 2, respectively. This strategy is clearly so inferior from North's
viewpoint that it should never be followed. Therefore, it can be eliminated from the
matrix.

the loss-leader special for each week being kept a secret until it is too late for the rival firm to change its advertising copy in the newspaper. The optimal mixture of the two alternative actions can be calculated as in two-bean Hul Gul, since this too is a two-by-two matrix without a saddle point.

Subtracting each figure in Row 2 from the figure just above it, we get −150 and +150, which means that North should use each loss leader half of the time, perhaps tossing a coin once a week and using butter as the leader when heads turns up and coffee when tails turns up.

To obtain West's optimal mixture, subtract each figure in Column 2 from the figure just to the left. This gives −100 and +200. Disregarding sign and switching the numbers, it turns out that West should use butter twice for each time he uses coffee as a loss leader. His choice on any particular Thursday should be determined by using a chance device which has twice as great a probability of indicating butter as it has of indicating coffee. He might, for example, shake a cocktail shaker containing two yellow marbles and one brown marble of equal size, close his eyes and withdraw one—and then use butter as the loss leader if he comes up with a yellow marble and coffee if he picks out the brown one.

The value of the loss-leader "game" can be calculated by using the best mixture of either seller against the results of either alternative strategy of the other. The average payoff according to the four methods of calculation is as follows:

$$1) \quad \frac{1(0) + 1(+100)}{2} = +50.$$

$$2) \quad \frac{1(+150) + 1(-50)}{2} = +50.$$

$$3) \quad \frac{2(0) + 1(+150)}{3} = +50.$$

$$4) \quad \frac{2(+100) + 1(-50)}{3} = +50.$$

Since the value of the game is positive, it is "unfair" to North and favorable to West. West should continue to use loss leaders, and this forces North to do so also. North should try to convince West that it would be better to discontinue these special bargains and even offer West some valuable consideration if he will discontinue using loss leaders (so long as this consideration is not more damaging to his net profits than the loss of $50 a week in sales).

Business Situation with a Saddle Point

The theory of games seems to hold more promise of being useful in guiding executive decisions in repetitive situations like the weekly choice of a loss leader than in one-time decisions. It may, however, logically be applied to the latter type of decisions also. Suppose that there are two large—but not entirely modern—motels so located between a mountain range on one side and a national park on the other that, while they are in vigorous competition with one another, they are well isolated from other accommodations for motorists. (This assumption makes a zero-sum game solution quite plausible, since the gains made by each will be mainly at the expense of the other.) The motels will again be named North and West.

Exhibit 5

THE MOTEL GAME

		NORTH INSTALLS				
		TV	POOL	BOTH	NEITHER	ROW MINIMA
	TV	+2	−10	−20	+10	−20
	POOL	+10	+4	−10	+15	−10
WEST INSTALLS	BOTH	+15	+5	+6	+20	+5
	NEITHER	−5	−10	−15	0	−15
	COLUMN MAXIMA	+15	+5	+6	+20	

Aware of the luxury demanded by American motorists, both motel owners begin to ponder the desirability of installing free television in all rooms and/or building a swimming pool on the premises in order to take business away from the rival firm. By chance, both hire the same management consultant who, after considerable study, furnishes each manager with estimated payoffs from various combinations of actions. Payoffs are estimated increases and decreases of weekly net profits, positive figures being profit gains by West, and negative figures being profit gains by North. Each entrepreneur learns that the other has access to the same payoff information, and each regards the other as an astute businessman. (See Exhibit 5.)

It will be noted that the installation of TV, a swimming pool, or both is somewhat more favorable to West than to North. This may be because North's location is somewhat lower and shadier than West's location, which will force North to erect higher antennas, and which will make swimming somewhat less attractive to the guests. Nevertheless, it will not pay North to abstain entirely from these improvements. The matrix has a saddle point at "install both" for West and "install pool" for North.[10] North's weekly loss of net profits (after costs, including the new maintenance, repair, and depreciation) will be $5.00, because of the new investment by the two motels. However, if West installed both TV and a pool while his rival did nothing, he could deprive North of an estimated $20 a week in net profits.

General Observations on Game Theory and Business

A main practical difficulty in applying game theory to business decisions is that of getting reasonably accurate estimates of payoffs under various sets of conditions. These estimates need not be perfectly accurate, of course; but it is clear that if they err too greatly, they may lead to incorrect action. In this respect the estimates do not differ, however, from calculations made to guide executive decisions in nongame situations—e.g., whether or not to build an additional plant when the actions and reactions of rivals need not be considered. Any decision based on inadequate work on the part of statisticians, accountants, and engineers is apt to be nonoptimal.

Another problem is that of choosing the best payoff criterion. In business, this is usually assumed to be net profits to the firm. Sometimes, however, the maximization of short-run profits is not consistent with maximization of long-term profits—if, for example, such earnings attract new competitors who would otherwise not enter the field, or if they bring on a union demand for a wage increase. In the case of the loss-leader problem examined earlier, the payoffs were measured in terms of gains and losses of sales in the two stores. This tacitly assumed that profits are positively correlated with storewide sales. Otherwise, sales do not constitute a rational payoff criterion (unless short-run sales are considered to be positively correlated with long-run progress and profitability of the enterprise through their power to mold consumers' buying habits).

Another major problem in the application of reasonably simple game theory is the need to find situations in which the gains of one businessman are entirely, or at least almost entirely, at the expense of another. This is needed to make their competitive struggle a "zero-sum game"—one in which the gains are exactly equal to the losses.

---

[10] The saddle value is $5.00, because this figure is both the maximum of the row minima and the minimum of the column maxima.

Most of the development of the theory of games refers to zero-sum games, although a chapter of von Neumann and Morgenstern's book contains a discussion of game theory for situations where this condition is not present. Most business decisions involve actions which are designed to increase the net income of the particular firm without necessarily affecting other firms in any clearly discernible manner. This is especially true in a growing economy where total dollar and physical sales are increasing in volume. Where businessmen are sharply in conflict with one another, however, simple applications of two-person zero-sum game theory may improve the quality of certain business decisions.

According to J. C. C. McKinsey,[11] the most "crying need" in game theory is development of a more satisfactory theory of nonzero sum games and games where the number of players exceeds two. This development would be of great aid in solving certain types of economic and business problems. Nevertheless, game theory in its present state has been characterized as an important "intellectual breakthrough."

QUESTIONS

1. Solve the game of two-bean Hul Gul where holding no beans, holding one bean, and holding two beans are the permitted alternatives.
2. Change *one* of the payoffs in the loss-leader example in such a way as to make the best mixture of strategies for West 1 to 1.
3. In the motel example, change *one* payoff in such a way as to make it desirable for each motel to install both TV and a swimming pool.
4. Describe a business situation in which the theory of games may be useful to executive decision making. Try to make it entirely different from those used in the text. (It is not necessary to set up the matrixes or to solve the problem.)

---

[11] *Introduction to the Theory of Games* (New York: McGraw-Hill Book Co., Inc., 1952), p. 358.

Chapter 8

~~~~~~

PRODUCT DIVERSIFICATION

MOST OF the discussion thus far has been concerned with demand, output, and cost for a single commodity produced by a firm or industry. This is obviously an unrealistic assumption for virtually all firms engaged in the wholesaling, retailing, or transporting of goods. Manufacturing establishments more frequently specialize in only one good (e.g., bricks, portland cement, a soft drink, airplanes, wheat, or tobacco), but even so, usually produce the good in various sizes, models, packages, and qualities, so that it is not entirely clear whether they should be called single-product or multiple-product firms. In recent years, there seems to have been a particular emphasis on product diversification on the part of manufacturers—single-product firms becoming multiple-product producers and those already handling multiple products adding even more lines.[1]

The assumption of one product to a firm is a simplifying abstraction which is useful in developing numerous principles applicable to multiproduct companies as well. For the most part, it is true that the entrepreneur handling many commodities should make short-run and long-run calculations in the same way as is suggested by economic theory for the single-commodity firm; he should equate marginal cost and marginal revenue in short-run operational decisions with respect to every product, and should anticipate at least covering average costs (including normal returns to self-employed factors) when making new investment pertaining to any product.

The multiproduct firm is often a member of several industries when "industry" is classified according to the federal government's statistical procedure (as indicated, for example, in Exhibit 3 of Chapter 5). It is equally appropriate, though usually less useful, to consider the firm to be a member of as many industries as it produces distinct commodities. Competitive conditions may differ greatly from good to good for any particular firm. Some commodities may be turned out under conditions approaching pure competition, where price is set

---

[1] This trend is interestingly described by Gilbert Burck in "The Rush to Diversify," *Fortune,* September, 1955, p. 91.

by market forces outside the control of any individual company. Others may be turned out under monopolistic conditions, where the firm can choose its price, within limits, without regard to rivals' reactions. Other goods may be supplied to oligopolistic markets, where the power to set price exists, but where rivals' reactions are of prime importance (and where the conflict of interests may sometimes be usefully viewed as a "game" between firms).

Growth through Diversification

Alert management is usually in constant search of ways to promote the growth of the firm.[2] Very often, such growth is effected by adding new products; and frequently, this is accomplished by the acquisition of entire companies. It is apparent that a systematic search for new investment opportunities will usually indicate the best opportunities to be associated with commodities other than those already being produced, rather than with current products, simply because there are so many more items in the former category. This is especially true because new goods are constantly being developed through research. The scope for useful diversification is usually somewhat limited, however, by the desirability of having the new products of a firm related in some way to the old ones. The types of relationship making for compatibility are many; and often, more than one type of relationship exists at the same time. Goods may be (1) cost-related, (2) related in demand, (3) related in advertising and distribution, or (4) related in research. (Other relations conducive to multiple products might be named, but these appear to be the most important.)

Joint Costs

The most obvious cost relationship which brings about multiple products within the firm is the situation of joint costs. These exist when two or more products are turned out in fixed proportions by the same production process. Often, proportions are variable in the long run but fixed in the short run, since it may be necessary to alter the amount of capital equipment used in order to change proportions. Fixed proportions are especially common in the chemical industry. The cracking of petroleum, for example, yields gasoline, kerosene, and other joint products. Joint products are also quite common in the processing of agricultural and fishery output. A famous example

---

[2] Many corporations now employ a vice-president who is primarily in charge of growth and development. While greater size often leads to larger and more dependable profits, part of the urge to grow is undoubtedly based on bigness as a goal in itself.

is the ginning of cotton, where cottonseed and cotton linters are produced in a weight ratio of about two to one. In processing frozen orange concentrate, the concentrated juice, orange peel and pulp (used as cattle feed), molasses (also used in cattle feed), essential oils (used in flavoring extracts), and seed (used in plastics and animal feed) appear in approximately fixed proportions. In the processing of a shark of a given variety, there are secured, in approximately fixed proportions, liver oil (rich in Vitamin A), skins for leather, meat for dog food, bones for novelties, and fins for shipment to the Orient for use in soup.

If joint products are sold in perfectly competitive markets, their prices are determined by total demand and supply, and the individual firm has only the problem of deciding upon its own rate of output. The firm's short-run adjustment may be shown most simply if output units are defined in such a way as to keep the quantity of each product turned out always equal. If, for example, X and Y are joint products, and three pounds of X are secured simultaneously with two pounds of Y, we can usefully define three pounds of X as one unit of X and two pounds of Y as one unit of Y. Thus defined, the output of each, measured in the new units, would always be the same. If, for example, 300 pounds of X and 200 pounds of Y were produced during a given day, we could say that the output was 100 units of each good.

In Exhibit 1, units of output of two joint products are defined in this special way. One marginal cost curve and one average cost curve serve for both goods, but separate demand curves are drawn for each of the joint products, since they are sold separately. Demand curves are horizontal lines, since the individual firm can sell all it wishes at the prevailing market prices. In addition, a line (D_{x+y}) which represents the sum of the two prices has been drawn.

The optimum output of the firm is OA units of each product per time period, since at this production rate the price OP received for the two goods regarded as one is equal to the marginal joint cost. Any higher rate of output would be unwise, because additional cost to the firm would exceed additional revenue from the sale of both goods; any smaller output would be nonoptimal, because if less than OA were being produced, additional units could be turned out which would add more to revenue than to cost. Since average cost (which is total cost divided by the quantity of either good) is below OP, the operation is yielding economic profit to the firm; that is, more than the usual returns are accruing to those receiving income on a noncontractual basis. If this situation is expected to persist, additional firms will enter the industry, gradually eliminating economic (but not accounting) profit.

From the point of view of an industry (rather than an individual firm), an increase in the demand for one of two joint products increases the price of that good but lowers the price of the other joint product, provided demand for the latter does not also rise. This is because

Exhibit 1

JOINT PRODUCTS UNDER COMPETITION—FIRM
REGARDS TWO AS ONE

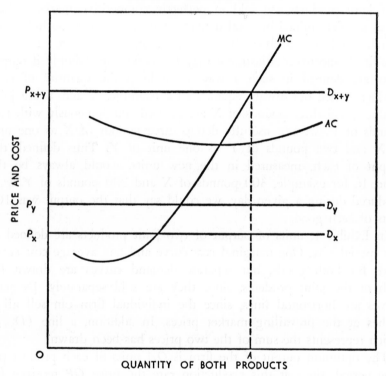

the output of both goods will necessarily be stepped up in order to take advantage of a better demand for one good, and this will necessitate a lower price on the other in order to clear the market. Under perfect competition the price of any joint product can easily remain far below average cost of production, since as a long-run matter, average cost is covered by the *sum* of the prices of the joint products. As long as any positive price can be obtained for a good, a competitive firm has no incentive to withhold any output from the market, inasmuch as its own sales will not depress price. If the price of a joint product falls to zero, it becomes a "waste product."[3]

Joint Costs and Monopoly

When two or more joint products are produced for sale under monopolistic rather than competitive conditions, profit-maximizing be-

Exhibit 2

MONOPOLIZED JOINT PRODUCTS—ENTIRE OUTPUT SOLD

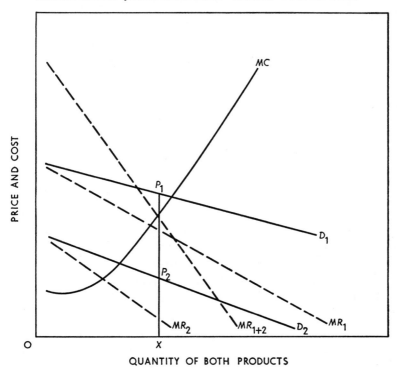

QUANTITY OF BOTH PRODUCTS

havior on the part of the firm is somewhat different. Assume again, for the sake of simplicity, that only two joint products are turned out by a monopolistic firm and that units are again so defined as to keep their outputs the same. If the demand for both of these is sufficiently strong in relation to productive capacity, the determination of optimum price and output is much like that of the single-product monopolist. In Exhibit 2 the separate demands are represented by D_1 and D_2,

---

[3] A waste product may also have a negative value in the sense that additional costs must be incurred in order to get rid of it. Orange peel, pulp, and seed were formerly in this category but now constitute valuable by-products.

marginal joint cost is MC, and MR_1 and MR_2 are marginal revenue curves corresponding to D_1 and D_2, respectively. Combined marginal revenue, MR_{1+2}, is derived by adding MR_1 and MR_2 for each output. The best output (of both) joint products is OX, determined by the intersection of MC and MR_{1+2}. The separate prices P_1 and P_2 are found on demand curves D_1 and D_2, respectively, and represent the prices at which quantity OX can be disposed of. It is worth while for the firm to sell all of both products, because marginal revenue from each is above zero at the optimum output. The "last" unit of each good makes a positive contribution to revenue, and the sum of the contributions of the last unit of good 1 and the last unit of good 2 is just equal to the addition to cost which their production entails.[4]

If the demand for one of two joint products is substantially lower than the demand for the other, profit-maximizing behavior on the part of the monopolistic firm is somewhat different. This behavior can be analyzed most clearly by means of Exhibit 3. The curves have the same meaning as before, the difference between Exhibits 2 and 3 being that in the latter the intersection of MC and one of the separate marginal revenue curves (MR_1) lies to the right of the intersection of MC and MR_{1+2}. Optimum output OX in Exhibit 3 is determined by the interesection of MC and MR_1, and this is necessarily the output of both joint products, in view of the way units of quantity are defined. Marginal revenue from the sale of OX units of good 1 is positive, but marginal revenue from OX units of good 2 is negative (below the horizontal axis). It is necessary for the firm to produce OX units of good 2 in order to exploit fully the demand for good 1, but the monopolist is under no compulsion to sell all that he produces. He should sell OX of good 1 but only OA of good 2, since selling more of the latter would reduce his total revenue and reduce his profit. He will discard AX units of good 2 each period unless he anticipates a change in cost-demand conditions which will make it worth while to incur storage costs for this commodity.

If a monopolistic firm produces joint products which it then processes further, the graphical exposition becomes quite complex and will not be presented here.[5] It is not difficult to see, however, that the entre-

---

[4] Actually, any unit can be considered to be the "last" unit turned out, and this terminology has only the merit of convenience. The quantity axis measures rate of output per time period, and any particular unit can be considered marginal during that period just as well as any other one.

[5] The interested reader is referred to M. R. Colberg, "Monopoly Prices under Joint Costs: Fixed Proportions," *Journal of Political Economy*, February, 1941, p. 109.

Exhibit 3

MONOPOLIZED JOINT PRODUCTS—PART OF OUTPUT DESTROYED

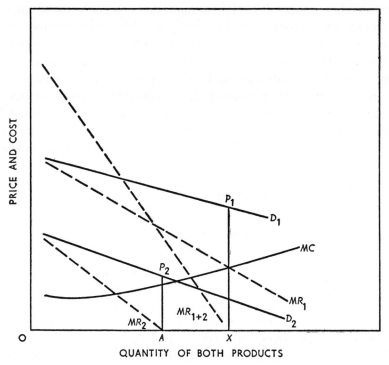

preneur may find it worth while to "work up" only part of the output of one or more jointly produced raw materials, since further processing of all the output of some joint products may add more to conversion costs than sale of the associated final product would add to the firm's revenue.

Often, multiple products are turned out by a given process but in proportions which are readily variable or which vary in ways which are beyond the control of the firm. In this situation the less important products may be designated as "by-products" of the manufacture of the most valuable product. Natural pearls are a by-product of the shelling of oysters, clams, and certain other mollusks; gas is a by-product in the manufacture of coke; and public recreational facilities are a by-product of power and flood-control projects. The dividing line between a joint product and a by-product is usually not sharp in practice, since absolute fixity of proportions is rare, especially in the long run.[6]

---

[6] It is also clear that the accuracy with which quantity is measured affects one's opinion as to whether proportions are fixed. If measurement is extremely accurate and utilizes very small units of weight or volume, fixed proportions become extremely unlikely.

It should be apparent from the analysis of joint products that the amount of competition which exists may be a determinant of whether a commodity produced in fairly rigid proportions with another is considered by a producer to be wholly a salable joint product or in part a waste product.[7] A monopolist will often find it advantageous to discard some units of output which would be marketed under more competitive conditions. As long as a positive price can be secured for any joint product or by-product, the competitive producer has no incentive to withhold any of it from the market, since by himself he cannot affect price; the monopolist, however, may find such withholding profitable inasmuch as the quantity which he markets does clearly affect price.

Multiple Products to Utilize Capacity

Frequently, goods can be turned out more cheaply together than in separate facilities, even though they do not necessarily appear as the simultaneous product of the same process. For example, unless the available volume of one commodity is sufficient for a full trainload, it is obviously more economical to transport a number of goods at once than to have a separate train for each good. This advantage of transporting multiple products derives from the indivisibility of such resources as locomotives, engineers, and cars. If the capacity of any indivisible resource is not being fully utilized (because the train is too short, for example, or cars are not fully loaded), additional products can be hauled at a very low marginal cost. Additional revenue in prospect need not be great to induce the railroad company to carry extra items when excess capacity is present.

Similarly, a manufacturing plant which has excess capacity may have a strong incentive to add another product or products. Excess capacity may be due to a variety of causes. A decline in the demand for the product for which the plant was originally designed is clearly a possible cause. Or a plant may have been built purposely too large for present needs in anticipation of future requirements, and this may make at least the temporary installation of another product advantageous. Excess capacity may exist for a substantial period of time even under highly competitive conditions where inefficient firms tend to be driven

---

[7] If proportions of product are variable but unpredictable, a monopolistic firm may also find it profitable from time to time to withhold some output from the market, since a commodity may accidentally be secured in excessive amount. (The same can be true of single-product production when output is difficult to predict.)

out of the field. But excess capacity is more likely to be chronic when collusive pricing or a cartel arrangement among sellers (e.g., motel owners) both restricts total sales and attracts additional investment because of the temporary profitability of the high prices to those already in the field.

Industry Development and Integration

It has sometimes been observed by economists that firms in relatively new industries produce multiple products simply because the demand for any one of the products is insufficient to make it possible to produce it in a volume sufficient to secure the advantages of scale. In this situation, some of these advantages can be secured by utilizing a large plant and producing several commodities.[8] However, if the demand for the principal commodity expands sufficiently, it may become more economical to cease producing the others and to specialize in this main good. This is because the indivisible factors are seldom equally adapted to all of the goods being produced, so that it pays to specialize output further if sufficient volume can be secured in one or a few goods.

Young industries are often forced to be vertically integrated (to produce at several stages) because the economic system is not geared to produce specialized raw materials and components which they require. As an industry grows, it is often both possible and profitable to turn over the production of these special raw materials and components to other firms. For example, a few years ago the frozen orange concentrate industry "disintegrated" its operations as it grew larger by turning over to trucking firms the transportation of the finished product, which had previously been handled by its own trucks. (On the other side, though, there has been a recent tendency for concentrators to acquire orange groves.) Another example: As transactions on the New York Stock Exchange have grown in volume, brokers who do not wish to engage in extensive analysis of securities have been able to omit most of this work because of the growth of specialized market advisory services.[9]

The tendency toward vertical disintegration as an industry grows

---

[8] N. Kaldor, "Market Imperfections and Excess Capacity," *Economica*, N.S., Vol. II, No. 5 (1935), p. 47.

[9] On the other hand, the volume of "put" and "call" options on stocks has not been sufficient to support a trade journal or specialized advisory services. The individual brokers publish separate informational pamphlets regarding options trading.

depends, however, on the existence, or potential existence, of thoroughgoing competition at all stages of production. If it is necessary for a firm to pay monopolistic prices for materials or components, it may be better to undertake their manufacture itself, even if great efficiency cannot be secured in such production. Most raw-material cartels have experienced trouble with customers who wish to integrate backward in order to avoid paying monopoly prices.[10]

During periods of war or postwar emergency, when the federal government allocates certain "scarce" materials in furtherance of its preferred programs (aircraft, atomic bombs, housing, etc.), a special advantage is inherent in integration in that the output of "captive" facilities producing in earlier stages is unlikely to be subject to allocation. Instead, such production will probably go automatically to the owning firms, just as the early items on a plant's assembly line go automatically to the later stages on the line. Raw-material shortages under emergency conditions may have their impact mainly on the nonintegrated producers. Thus, vertical integration constitutes something of a hedge against emergency shortage of materials.

Integration in the Food Industries

Grocery chains in the United States are outstanding examples of integrated operations; and in this case, there does not appear to be a tendency toward disintegration as the industry grows. A & P, Kroger, and other food chains operate such facilities as warehouses, bakeries, milk-condensing plants, coffee-roasting plants, salmon and tuna fish canneries, and plants for processing many special products such as mayonnaise, spices, jellies, and beverages.[11] Reasons which have been cited for the growth of integration in this field are several. Probably the most important pertain to the savings of costs of transfer of ownership of goods from company to company. This saving can easily be exaggerated, however, since much intracompany bookkeeping with respect to such transfers is still required in an integrated operation. Certain advertising and other selling expenses can be eliminated by means of integration, since one stage does not have to "sell" the next. Freight and cartage costs may be lower when a number of products are shipped from the company warehouse to retail outlets. Faster

---

[10] G. J. Stigler, "The Division of Labor Is Limited by the Extent of the Market," *Journal of Political Economy*, June, 1951, p. 191. Stigler gives historical examples of cartels which have encountered this difficulty.

[11] A. C. Hoffman, *Large Scale Organization in the Food Industries* (T.N.E.C. Monograph No. 35) (Washington, D.C.: U.S. Government Printing Office, 1941), p. 12.

handling due to uniformity of distribution channels under integrated operations may be especially important for fresh fruits and vegetables.

Pitfalls in Integration

It has been noted that disintegration of operations has frequently been observed, especially as industries grow in size. In part, this is to permit management to devote its time to the production and sale of the principal end product, which is apt to be very different in nature from the raw materials and transportation which are required in the production-distribution process. That is to say, the multiple products turned out at different stages by a vertically integrated firm are especially likely to be incompatible from a managerial standpoint. Capital which can be obtained by selling facilities used in the earlier stages can often be better invested in the final stage, where the chief interest of the company is likely to lie.

A leading danger in integration is that demand at the earlier levels provided by the firm's end-product operations may not be sufficient to justify production of the earlier commodities on a scale large enough to secure the full advantages of size.[12] Fixed costs are especially high in transportation and in some types of mining. Consequently, a decline in demand for these items due to a decrease in output at the final-product stage will raise unit costs sharply for the firm. Unless quite a steady rate of output of the final good can be foreseen, it is usually better for a firm to purchase inputs from other firms in order to avoid this hazard. It may, of course, be possible to sell some of the output of the earlier stages to other firms; but this is not always feasible, since selling and advertising facilities are not likely to be well developed at these levels because, typically, only an intracompany transfer is required.

There is often danger of inefficiency in the earlier stages of an integrated firm, since these stages do not have the usual competitive check of having to cover costs by their sales revenues. As a means of preventing this inefficiency, some integrated companies have made their earlier stages compete on a price basis with outside suppliers for the business of the parent firm, thus in part treating the earlier stages like separate companies. The Ford Motor Company is reported to follow this practice.[13]

---

[12] For convenience, we are referring to the "earlier" stages in an integrated operation. Actually, some of the stages may instead be "later." Transportation of bottled beer is a case in point.

[13] Burck, *op. cit.*, p. 206.

Demand-Related Goods

Often, multiple products are turned out by a firm because they are related on the demand side instead of the cost side. (Or they may be related in both respects.) The motorist who buys gasoline is obviously a likely customer for oil, grease, tires, and soft drinks. The housewife who buys groceries is an excellent prospect for meat and fish, and the man who buys fire insurance on a home is a likely buyer of burglary or liability insurance. Usually, it pays the firm—once it has established contact with a customer—to be in a position to sell him other products. The Mexican peddler, for example, is well aware of this possibility. Once he has secured a degree of attention from the tourist, he is usually prepared to present several types of jewelry or other goods rather than only one variety. Generally, he keeps his other wares hidden until he has sealed a sale on the principal item or has been definitely turned down on that item. The more difficult it is to secure contact with a customer, the greater the gain from handling a multiplicity of products is likely to be. Thus, traffic and parking congestion cause it to be difficult for the motorist to make several stops on a shopping trip. This factor leads a great many retailers to run something approaching a "general" store, where the customer can engage in satisfactory one-stop shopping. The "shopping center," however, permits stores to specialize to a greater degree by providing common parking with easy access on foot to a variety of shops.

Where parking is a municipal problem and the store is not located in a comprehensive shopping center, there is an especially strong incentive for a supermarket to carry nonfood items. This saves the customer the difficulty of going elsewhere for such items of frequent need as magazines, hair tonic, toothpaste, children's socks, and everyday glassware. It is important, however, that the nonfood items be easy to carry to the car, be difficult to steal, and have a rapid turnover, so that they do not tie up valuable space unduly. The high percentage markups on many nonfood items have been an important factor in the trend toward handling more of this merchandise in the chain grocery stores.[14]

Seasonal Demand

Frequently, multiple products are carried by the firm because they have opposite seasonal demand patterns. Coal and ice are famous ex-

---

[14] "Shifting Shelves: Some Big Supermarkets Stop Adding Non-Food Items," *Wall Street Journal*, November 25, 1955, p. 1.

amples of this demand situation. In the past, most firms which delivered coal in the winter used the same wagons or trucks for delivering ice in the summer, and this is still done to a lesser degree. Commodities which are demand-related in this way are at the same time cost-related, since the purpose of handling multiple products is to utilize capacity which would otherwise be seasonally idle. Numerous other examples of such seasonal demand relationships can be found. An athletic stadium may be used for baseball in the spring and summer months, and for football in the fall. A clothing manufacturer changes the nature of his output from season to season in anticipation of temperature changes. The appliance dealer who stocks air conditioners in the summer may switch to heaters in the winter. In general, it is usually good business for the firm which has a seasonally fluctuating demand to install some item with an opposite seasonal demand pattern to take up the slack. This may not be desirable, however, if the commodity is storable, since it can then be produced in the off-season for sale later. The portland cement industry typically builds up inventories during the winter, to be drawn down during the spring and summer when construction is heavy. This policy is traceable to the ready storability of cement and to the desirability of limiting industry capacity, for the cement-manufacturing process uses a very high ratio of capital equipment to labor. Also, cement-producing equipment is highly specialized to that use instead of being adaptable also to other kinds of production. The industry finds the annual shutdown valuable for cleaning up the plants and making repairs.

A firm producing articles subject to sharp seasonal swings in demand sometimes finds it desirable to diversify by adding items which are stable in demand rather than opposite in seasonal demand pattern. This prevents the percentage decline in total business from being so sharp at any season. That is, a 30 per cent seasonal decline in demand for one item can be converted into approximately a 15 per cent decline for the company as a whole by adding an item of equal sales importance but with no seasonal demand pattern. An example of this sort of diversification was the addition in 1949 and 1952 of utility-company equipment such as transformers and circuit breakers by McGraw Electric Company. This helped offset the seasonal fluctuations in the Toastmaster and other home appliance lines.[15] While such diversification may help only moderately in utilizing seasonally idle plant capacity, because of the specialization of machinery to certain

---

[15] Burck, *op. cit.*, p. 92.

products, it may provide fuller utilization of labor, management, sales facilities, and other more adaptable factors. This is especially true if the items of relatively stable demand are readily storable, since labor, for example, which is seasonally idle in one line can temporarily be added to the regular working force in the more stable lines. This may make it possible to carry a smaller regular labor force in the stable lines. Management as well as labor tends to gain if employment can be regularized in seasonal industries, because labor turnover is reduced; consequently, the problem of training new workers is made less difficult.

Brand-Name Carry-Over

An important force making for multiplicity of products in such fields as the manufacture of home appliances is sometimes referred to as "brand-name carry-over." That is, a customer who is satisfied with a Westinghouse, General Electric, or Philco refrigerator, for example, is quite likely to buy such items as a washing machine, range, and television receiver from the same company. Opportunity is especially great in supplying "package kitchens" of particularly compatible appliances, all turned out by the same firm. In economic terminology the demands for such items are "complementary"; an increase in the rate of sale (and home inventories) of one appliance bearing a given brand name tends to increase the demand for other appliances with the same brand name.

Numerous examples of a rapid trend toward "full-line production can be cited. Westinghouse has introduced 27 new kinds of appliances since World War II.[16] General Electric (Hotpoint appliances), Philco, General Motors' Frigidaire division, Borg-Warner's Norge division, and American Motors' Kelvinator division have all steadily expanded their lines in recent years. The full-line trend has brought on a wave of mergers of appliance makers. For example, a laundry equipment maker, a refrigerator producer, and the stove and air-conditioning division of the Radio Corporation of America have recently merged under the name Whirlpool-Seeger.

Internal Brand Competition[17]

Another force which frequently promotes multiple products within the firm is, in a sense, just the opposite of "brand-name carry-over."

---

[16] "Full-Line Fever," *Wall Street Journal*, December 6, 1955, p. 1.

[17] This section is based in part on Lowell C. Yoder, *Internal Brand Competition* ("Economic Leaflets") (Gainesville, Fla.: Bureau of Economic and Business Research, University of Florida, July, 1955).

It consists in submerging the name of the company and using different brand names for two or more varieties of a product which are sold to the same group of customers. For example, two different qualities of canned corn may be turned out by a given firm under different labels. One brand may be so much poorer than the other that it is better not to emphasize that it is produced by the same company. To do so would be to run the same risk of unfavorable association as would a full-line producer of appliances who sold a decidedly inferior washing machine. When the quality of the product is not wholly under the control of the firm, as in the case of fruits and vegetables, there is likely to be especially good reason to avoid publicizing the company name. While the firm which cans tomatoes, for example, can choose to process only the best portion of its purchases, this may necessitate discarding large quantities which can instead be marketed under another brand name without greatly reducing sales of the top-quality product.

The phenomenon of internal brand competition is especially interesting when a given firm sells two or more varieties of a single product under different brand names to the same set of customers and when, further, the quality of the varieties is very much the same.[18] The following appear to be among the leading reasons for this practice on the part of some of the larger firms:

1. Mergers or amalgamations of firms producing a given product may have occurred. Previous brand names are likely to be retained by the new company, at least in part, because of the customer following which might otherwise be lost.

2. Often, a sizable segment of the consuming public prefers one variety of a product, even though a larger segment prefers another variety. To concentrate on the latter alone would deprive the firm of large sales which could be secured by carrying both varieties. A case in point is the production of both standard and filter cigarettes by a given cigarette company.

3. The struggle between companies for display space in the supermarkets is a keen one. A given soap company, for example, is likely to be able to capture a larger portion of such space by producing more than one variety of soap for use in washing clothes or dishes. The various brands produced by a firm may be promoted as vigorously as if they were turned out by competing companies. It is generally felt that more sales are taken away from competitors than from other products of the company by such internal brand competition. Also, the various divisions of a firm are forced by both internal and external

---

[18] Yoder, *ibid.*, prefers to limit use of the term "internal brand competition" to this situation rather than including the case of the vegetable canner or other seller of two or more quite different qualities of a product. However, no sharp dividing line can be drawn between the cases, since it is only a matter of the degree of difference of the products. Similarly, it is never possible to say that two different brands of a consumer good are sold to *exactly* the same set of customers.

competition to be efficient in their operations. Proctor and Gamble is an outstanding example of a firm which engages in vigorous internal brand competition.

4. By installing products very similar to those already being produced, a firm may be able to secure better distribution of its product than through exclusive dealerships. Regular dealers may receive only one variety of the product, while another variety is sold through discount houses or other channels. (This practice is, of course, unpopular with the "exclusive" dealers.) A manufacturer may in this way take advantage of high prices on "fair-traded" items and lower prices on much the same items in order to promote volume.

5. Under some circumstances, a firm's advertising may be more effective when it is distributed over two or more quite similar products than when it is concentrated on one brand. Two or more types of advertising appeal can be used simultaneously, and this may have greater total effect than an equal expenditure devoted to one product. Further, one product of the company can effectively be advertised on the package in which a rather similar product is sold. Armour-produced soapflakes, for example, are advertised on the can in which an Armour liquid detergent is sold.

Commodities Related in Advertising and Distribution

Frequently, firms find it advantageous to handle multiple products at least in part because they are related in advertising, even if the situation is not one of internal brand competition. The various items advertised individually by the roadside gift shop have a cumulative appeal which may cause the driver to pause in his headlong dash. A full-page advertisement may be optimal in attracting the attention of the newspaper reader; but once his attention has been gained, he is likely to be willing to read about a number of items carried by a firm rather than just one. (In fact, the housewife may be anxious to check many items at once, in order to see whether a particular store is worth visiting on a particular week end.) Also, a multiple-product firm is in a position to use coupons attached to one product to help sell another product. The coupons provide both a means of advertising and a direct financial incentive to the customer to buy the indicated commodity.

Multiple products are frequently carried by a firm largely because they are related in distribution. This factor may not be clearly separate from the relationship through advertising. For example, the salesman-driver who delivers coffee, tea, or eggs to the door can easily "advertise" (orally) all sorts of other products handled by his firm. In recent years, there has been a trend away from the specialized, motorized vendor of such commodities as coffee and toward the traveling variety store, in order to take fuller advantage of the contacts which are made with customers.

Salesmen who regularly call on drugstores, for example, can often quite easily supply these stores with other products of the same firm for which delivery facilities are suitable. The Gillette Company recently diversified its operations by entering the ball-point pen field, buying the companies which made and distributed Paper Mate pens.[19] The production and distribution facilities of Gillette were both considered by its management to be well suited to ball-point pens. Similarly, Standard Brands, Inc., is able to use a common system of distribution for a variety of products bought by bakeries and grocers, including yeast, baking powder, desserts, coffee, and tea.

Commodities Related in Research

A firm which has a strong research department is obviously apt to be frequently adding new products as these are developed. To the extent that new items can be patented, the legal system is likely to make possible substantial monopoly gains for a period of time. Even if other firms can readily add the same product or very similar items, the firm which first enters the field may reap substantial innovation profits before others are tooled up and otherwise adapted to turn out the good. Once qualified chemists, engineers, and others are hired and trained to work as a research department, a firm is likely to be making inadequate use of such a department unless it is ready to produce and distribute any promising new products which are developed. This is similar to the principle noted earlier that available unused capacity of any kind—in plant, management, or skilled labor —may lead to opportunities for product diversification on the part of the alert firm.

CASE 8–1: L & M PRODUCTS CORPORATION

The L & M Products Corporation manufactured and marketed a wide line of both industrial and consumer electrical products on a nationwide basis. The main office and central plant were located in Minneapolis, Minnesota, but manufacturing of various items was carried on in plants in Newark, New Jersey; Atlanta, Georgia; and Los Angeles, California. Industrial products were sold directly to users by company salesmen. Consumer items were sold through company sales-

---

[19] "Gillette President Says Paper Mate Companies Cost Firm $15 Million," *Wall Street Journal*, November 22, 1955, p. 1.

men to jobbers and distributors, although some chain and department store accounts were handled directly.

The entire line produced by L & M was of high quality. On several items, both industrial and consumer, the company had long maintained prices above those of competing products. Quality and service had been emphasized as selling points. The company engaged in an extensive advertising program annually. Institutional-type advertisements were carried in several trade journals serving the firm's industrial customers. In the consumer field, advertisements featuring specific articles were regularly supported in several national magazines and in selected urban newspapers in co-operation with local dealers. Spot announcements on radio and television were made at various times.

In 1952, one of L & M's competitors introduced a heat-controlled electric frying pan. Shortly thereafter, the largest electrical company in the nation introduced an electric frying pan of its own. Both of these items were priced identically at $29.95. Early in 1953, the originator of this item reduced his price to $24.95, which was almost immediately followed by the other company.

By rearranging some manufacturing operations in its Atlanta plant, L & M began the production and sale of an electric frying pan in June, 1953. It contained several features not possessed by competing frying pans. Among them was the fact that it was completely submersible in water for cleaning; it could even be placed in electric dishwashers. Another feature was free lifetime repair service when returned to the factory with a small handling charge. The pan was initially priced at $26.95. By the end of 1953, there were several brands of electric frying pans on the market ranging in price from $13.95 to $26.95, L & M being the highest priced. The company felt that because of its reputation for service and quality, it could command a premium price, as it had done on other items in the past.

At the beginning of the Christmas shopping season in 1953 the originating company reduced its price to $21.95. One week later the largest company met this price. L & M maintained its price of $26.95. As a result of rather disappointing sales during the Christmas season, and this in spite of an intensive seasonal promotion, the company reduced its price to $23.95 on January 15, 1954. It had been learned that the two large competitors had enjoyed most satisfactory Christmas sales.

In May, 1954, the originating company reduced its price to $19.95 and introduced an identical electric frying pan, but somewhat larger in size, at $23.95. The other large competitor reduced its price to $19.95, but did not introduce a larger pan. L & M reduced its price to $21.95, and launched an advertising campaign featuring the usefulness and convenience of the pan as ideal for summer cottages as well as generating less heat in the home kitchen during the summer season.

In preparation for the 1954 Christmas season, L & M reduced its price to $19.95, the same as that of its competitors. Sales showed an increase following this price reduction. Early in 1955, it was ap-

Exhibit 1

L & M PRODUCTS CORPORATION

Monthly Factory Shipments, Electric Frying Pans, June, 1953, to May, 1956

Month	1953	1954	1955	1956
January	......	15,985[a]	15,330	20,005[e]
February	......	17,630	19,880[d]	19,765
March	......	18,315	23,525	19,755
April	......	17,990	24,690	19,960
May	......	18,050[b]	25,070	19,870
June	7,400	19,455	24,155	......
July	11,150	17,360	23,650	......
August	11,775	16,990	21,385	......
September	15,160	16,340	22,100	......
October	17,180	17,920[e]	23,455	......
November	15,730	20,115	23,210	......
December	14,825	16,340	21,645	......

[a] January, 1954, price reduced to $23.95.
[b] May, 1954, price reduced to $21.95.
[e] October, 1954, price reduced to $19.95.
[d] February, 1955, price reduced to $14.95.
[e] January, 1956, price increased to $17.95.

parent that sales needed another stimulus, since it was felt that the company was not getting its share of the market. A more drastic reduction in price, to $14.95, was ordered. Neither of the larger competitors met this price. As indicated in Exhibit 1, there was an almost immediate increase in sales until August, 1955, when a decline appeared. Following another disappointing Christmas season in 1955, the company increased its price in January, 1956, to $17.95. The two large competitors continued their price of $19.95.

The vice-president in charge of production suggested that the company discontinue the line of electric frying pans. He pointed out that capacity production had been designed for 35,000 units per month, a level which had never been reached. At an output of 20,000 units per month, labor, material, and packaging amounted to $6.83, and overhead averaged $1.31 per unit. Prices to dealers and distributors averaged $9.27 per unit. This same officer noted that the small electric motor division was working two shifts and had a backlog of approximately five months. He recommended that the space currently used for frying pan production be converted to small motors. These motors were now produced at a cost of $4.01 each, including overhead, and were sold at an average price of $6.10 each. He estimated that the conversion of this space would permit the manufacture of an additional 30,000 motors per month.

The president of the company, as well as the vice-president in charge of sales, did not agree with this proposal. The president felt that the company should not drop a line which was showing a profit. He further believed that the company had made a mistake in lowering the price of its frying pan to that of the average popular price of competitive makes. This, he said, was contrary to the long-established price policy of the company of maintaining a higher differential price over competitive products. He suggested that the poor performance in sales was due to a departure from this policy which he stated had destroyed the preference of customers for L & M products because of their superior quality. He proposed that the price be increased to $21.95 immediately. This, he believed, would result in larger profits, although the volume might decline slightly.

The vice-president in charge of sales felt that the product needed some improvement in design and construction to improve sales. He believed that the product had not yet been on the market long enough to conclude that it had reached its maximum potential of sales. Rather than discontinue the line and convert the space to small motors, he proposed that two new products, which the research department already had in the pilot-model stage, be added to the line. One was a two-quart electric saucepan, and the other was a rectangular electric grill suitable for pancakes, eggs, etc. The introduction of these products would give the company a more complete line of portable cooking equipment. It seemed to him that the conversion of existing facilities to small motors would quickly eliminate the backlog now in the department, and the company would then be faced with the same problem as now confronted it in the frying pan department. He could see no particular advantage in exchanging one problem for the other.

QUESTIONS

1. Do you think the company made a mistake by adding the electric frying pans to its line? Why?
2. Do you agree with the proposal to discontinue the line? Why?

3. What is your reaction to the proposal that the line be expanded by the addition of new products? Explain.

4. Do you subscribe to the company's policy of pricing its products slightly above the competitive price and promoting them on the basis of superior quality? Why?

5. Is product diversification always the best policy in the face of declining sales? Explain.

CASE 8–2: STANDARD PROCESSED FOODS, INC.

From its beginning as a small cannery in 1923, Standard Processed Foods, Inc., had grown to a large, integrated canned foods firm serving a national market by 1940. About 10 per cent of its output was sold in Canada, Mexico, Central America, and the West Indies. Originally, the company had canned only vegetables; but in 1928, canned fruit was added to its line. In this same year, it had shifted from selling only through brokers and wholesalers to a combination of food brokers and direct selling. In 1934 the firm entered the infant-food market with a line of strained vegetables and fruits. In 1937, canned pulverized meats were added to the infant-food line. With the growth of chain groceries in the decade of the thirties, the company soon found itself selling more than three fourths of its output through its own sales organization.

By 1940 the infant-food division accounted for more than 70 per cent of total sales. The rapid growth of this division was attributed to the wide acceptance of strained and pulverized baby foods by mothers throughout the country. To meet this demand, the company had built or purchased four plants for the processing of infant foods. Each was located in an area suitable for the growing of fruits and vegetables. Contracts for vegetables were made with farmers at the beginning of the growing season. Seed was furnished by Standard Processed Foods, Inc., and planting time was scheduled so as to control delivery of fresh vegetables to the plants during the harvest season. Fruits were purchased in season from commission houses. Both fruits and vegetables received in excess of a plant's daily operating capacity were canned in fifty-gallon barrels for later processing. This permitted operation of the plants on a more regular schedule. All foods containing meat were prepared in the Iowa plant.

During World War II the infant-food division experienced another period of rapid expansion. The sharp increase in the marriage rate during this time was accompanied by an even higher increase in the birth rate. The company experienced difficulty in meeting demand. Because of wartime restrictions, containers were more of a problem than the contents. In addition, the firm enjoyed a large increase in its sales of canned goods to military establishments. All of its products sold at retail were subject to O.P.A. rationing controls. Upon the cessation of hostilities the company began the construction of additional facilities at three of its plants. These were completed in 1946.

Demand for infant foods continued to grow until 1948, when there was a leveling of sales. In 1949 the company reduced operations in this division because of an absolute decline in demand. In view of the apparently increasing prosperity of the nation, an investigation was initiated by the sales manager to determine the reasons for such a decline. His report contained, among other observations, the following:

1. The decline was industry-wide.

2. Infants usually begin the use of processed foods early in their first year. They consume the maximum amount of such foods during their second year. By their third year, they have begun the consumption of home-prepared foods. Usually, after their fourth year, they eat little, if any, strained food.

3. The birth rate, which reached its peak in 1943–44, declined thereafter until 1946, when it leveled at a rate substantially above the prewar rate. The leveling-off and decline in infant-food sales by 1948 could be attributed to a decrease in the number of infants under two years of age and an increase in the number over four years of age.

4. The birth rate for 1948, projected through the decade of the fifties, indicated that the number of infants under two years of age would remain level for a few years and actually decline somewhat before moving upward. This was because the new parents of this period were born during the thirties, when the birth rate was very low. This also indicated that the rate of new marriages would actually decline during the middle and late 1950's. This forebode a further decline in the sale of infant foods.

The results of the sales manager's study were presented at a meeting of the board of directors. The decline in sales had now reached approximately 15 per cent and was considered serious. Along with the report, the president of Standard Processed Foods, Inc., presented several alternative courses of action, as follows:

1. The company could attempt to secure a larger share of the market. It now supplied about 30 per cent of the infant-food market, a proportion which had remained fairly stable since 1940. An aggressive but expensive promotional campaign might enlarge its share of the market, but the president was skeptical of such an outcome. There were only three other major companies in the field, one of which also supplied approximately 30 per cent of the market.

2. The company could expand its present line. In its effort to meet the constantly increasing demand for infant foods during the thirties, the president felt that three areas of the market had been neglected: (*a*) processing and canning of low-calorie fruits and vegetables for dietetics, (*b*) promotion of the use of strained and pulverized foods by hospitals and convalescent homes, and (*c*) some means of retaining infants as consumers of the company's products beyond their third and fourth birthdays.

a) The first of these areas (dietetic foods) had already been entered by several small canneries with fairly satisfactory results. With the current popularity of and emphasis upon individual weight control, the president believed there were profitable possibilities in this line. Furthermore, there would be no major problems of production and distribution, since existing canning facilities and equipment, warehouses, and selling organization could be used. Capacity could easily be increased by 10 per cent without strain on resources.

b) The second area (strained and pulverized foods for institutional use) was as yet untouched. For many years, Standard Processed Foods, Inc., had packed fruits and vegetables in two- and five-gallon containers for institutional use. In the development of infant foods the company had solicited and obtained the co-operation and endorsement of pediatricians as well as several medical organizations. Preliminary research had disclosed that considerable chopping and straining of foods is done in hospital kitchens. Little or nothing is done with the pulverizing of meats. If the foods now prepared for infants were packaged in containers of convenient size, the president believed that potential sales here would more than offset the decline in sales of infant foods at retail. Also, in this case, production and distribution could be handled by existing facilities and organization.

c) The third possible area of expansion was the addition of a line of junior foods for children from three to six years of age. The firm's experimental kitchen had developed a method of chopping certain vegetables and fruits which made them "bite size" and attractive. These could be packaged in slightly larger containers than those of the infant foods. These foods had been tried with selected families, more than 90 per cent of whom had approved of them. If the junior food line could be successfully promoted, it would add materially to the market. Infants who began on infant foods would probably continue with junior foods. If this line proved successful, it could conceivably raise total sales above their original level.

3. Another possibility for strengthening the company's position was entry into the frozen food business. This would be an entirely new experience for the company. Although the popularity of frozen foods was increasing, there were several companies already in the field. If Standard Processed Foods, Inc., were to enter this market, additional capital in the amount of $10 million would be required. The company would have to build at least two frozen food processing plants and arrange for adequate cold-storage space in several cities, as well as provide for frozen food delivery to retail outlets. Because of the backlog for machinery, it would be approximately fourteen months before plants could be built and equipped. An alternative was the purchase or acquisition of an existing frozen food business. The latter would have the

advantage of an established market. Whether a plant were built or purchased, the president stated that initial expenses would rule out profits for at least two years. Beyond that period, however, he was very optimistic. The president had made some preliminary inquiries as to the possibility of purchasing a frozen food business located in New Jersey. This business could be acquired for $14.5 million. Standard Processed Foods, Inc., had approximately $1 million in liquid resources above its present working capital requirements. If the company expanded its present line as suggested above, working capital requirements would increase by $1 million.

QUESTIONS

1. Which course of action would you recommend? Why?
2. One of the directors recommended that the company ride out the present downward trend in sales. Do you agree? Why?
3. What do you think of the proposal of attempting to increase the company's existing share of the market?
4. Under what conditions would you recommend entering the frozen food market? What are the disadvantages of this proposal?

CASE 8–3: DIAMOND ELECTRIC COMPANY

The Diamond Electric Company manufactured a line of radios, television sets, and industrial electrical products. The company was established in 1927, and through merger and expansion of its markets had grown to serve a national market. It operated seven different plants, located in California, New Jersey, Georgia, and Illinois. Of the four plants in Illinois, one was used for radio production, one for television manufacture, and two for industrial products. In addition, the firm maintained twenty-two sales and service offices in various parts of the United States.

The company organized its activities in four divisions on a product basis. These were the radio, television, light industrial, and heavy industrial divisions. The company began as a radio manufacturing company. Light industrial products were added in 1936, heavy industrial products in 1942, and television in 1946. Research had always been carried on rather extensively, and the company was considered one of the leaders in all of its fields. It was the Diamond Electric Company which had led in the production of radios for installation in automobiles. Many of the improvements in automobile radios resulted from research in its laboratories.

From the initial introduction of automobile radios until about 1940, the Diamond Electric Company was the chief supplier of sets to the automobile industry. In the mid-thirties, several companies entered the field; some supplied automobile radios as original equipment, while others produced for sale to the public. Some companies, including Diamond Electric Company, produced for both markets. The automobile radios produced for public sale by Diamond were under its own brand name. With one exception, this was done by all companies who served both markets. In 1940 the company supplied approximately 40 per cent of automobile radios used as original equipment. One of the large automobile manufacturers, which had begun its own production of radios in 1938, supplied 10 per cent, and the remainder was supplied by several other companies.

During World War II, both automobile and radio production was suspended. In the reconversion period following the war, a major automobile manufacturer undertook the production of more than one half of its own automobile radio requirements. This reduced the proportion of the Diamond Electric Company to approximately 30 per cent of the total market. Although the proportion supplied was smaller, the total number of automobile sets produced exceeded that of 1941. This was attributed to the backlog of demand for automobiles in the first year of postwar production.

The company began the production of television sets in 1946. A great deal of research on television had been undertaken just prior to World War II, plus experiments with electronic equipment during the war. Facilities which had been expanded to meet the demands for military equipment were available for television production. Output of television sets by the company in 1946 was 7,292, but production was hindered by material and labor shortages. The 1947 output was 47,-574, an increase of almost sevenfold. By 1948 the company was producing at the rate of approximately 55,000 sets per year. This rate was the maximum capacity of the television plant. This level of output, however, was insufficient to meet demand. Attempts to purchase or lease additional space had been unsuccessful. Consideration had been given to the construction of additional facilities, but the backlog in construction was so large that a new building could not be ready for occupancy for at least eighteen months. The problem of equipment for a new plant was equally acute. While the company could build much of its own equipment, it had a backlog of ten months in both the light and the heavy equipment divisions. Efforts had also been made to subcontract television production to other companies; but they, like Diamond Electric Company, were struggling to meet their own demands and were unable to provide delivery at specified dates. It was feared that much business in the television market would be lost unless output was increased.

By July, 1948, output of automobile radios had declined. The largest customer, an automobile manufacturer, was now supplying practically all of his own requirements. With the growth of television, sales of other model radios had also declined. Exhibit 1 shows production of automobile radios and television sets by months from April, 1946, to July, 1948. Automobile radios, as original equipment,

Exhibit 1

DIAMOND ELECTRIC COMPANY, MONTHLY PRODUCTION OF AUTOMOBILE
RADIOS AND TELEVISION SETS, APRIL, 1946—JULY, 1948

Month	1946		1947		1948	
	Automobile Radios	Television	Automobile Radios	Television	Automobile Radios	Television
January	....	......	20,834	2,469	15,104	5,971
February	....	......	20,692	2,704	15,432	6,004
March	....	......	20,654	3,011	15,071	6,435
April	17,119	184	20,619	3,841	14,938	7,013
May	18,375	293	20,435	3,938	14,973	8,009
June	19,104	401	20,109	3,994	15,007	10,408
July	19,273	547	19,231	4,005	14,981	11,652
August	20,421	628	18,414	4,119	....	......
September	20,592	752	17,192	4,633	....	......
October	20,672	1,097	16,452	4,821	....	......
November	20,686	1,451	15,785	4,937	....	......
December	20,921	1,939	15,134	5,102	....	......
Total	177,163	7,292	225,551	47,574	105,506	55,492

now accounted for slightly less than 15 per cent of the total market. The radio division occupied a plant of its own. Exhibit 2 shows the costs of production of radio and television sets.

At the August, 1948, meeting of the board of directors, the president of Diamond Electric Company proposed that the automobile radio line be dropped entirely and that the space in the radio plant be converted to the production of television sets. This would permit an increase in television output of approximately 5,000 sets per month. Radio manufacturing equipment could be easily and quickly converted by some modifications and additions. The labor problem would be minor, since radio workers could be easily and rapidly trained to assemble television sets. Output of the light industrial division could provide all the additional parts by reducing only slightly the output of such parts for a few small television manufacturers. Two directors objected, pointing out that it was poor business to abandon a profitable line. The president stated that he believed the television market had excellent potential for growth, while the demand for automobile radios would probably shrink further as the supply of automobiles approached the level of demand. There appeared to be little possibility of addi-

Exhibit 2

DIAMOND ELECTRIC COMPANY, COSTS AND FACTORY SELLING PRICES, TELEVISION SETS AND AUTOMOBILE RADIOS

(Per Unit)

ITEM	TELEVISION SETS			AUTOMOBILE RADIOS		
	1946	1947	1948	1946	1947	1948
Materials................	$31.72	$32.04	$31.04	$ 9.31	$ 9.82	$10.01
Direct labor..............	17.37	17.62	16.14	7.43	7.96	8.02
Depreciation.............	2.14	1.89	1.23	1.12	1.17	1.21
Factory overhead.........	8.90	8.41	8.05	1.62	1.65	1.72
Indirect labor............	6.51	6.43	5.72	2.19	2.23	2.28
Administration and selling expense............	3.03	2.83	2.54	0.24	0.33	0.35
Total................	$69.67	$69.22	$64.72	$21.91	$23.16	$23.59
Factory selling prices.......	$96.50	$97.25	$96.50	$27.00	$29.00	$29.50

tional sales to the automobile manufacturers, since most of them presently had well-established sources of supply.

QUESTIONS

1. Do you agree with the president of the company? Why?
2. In what sense is the automobile radio operation profitable?
3. What is the nature of demand for automobile radios? For television receivers?
4. Do you believe a company should always add new products rather than discontinue a current item? Why?
5. Do you believe the Diamond Electric Company should have expanded its total operations? Why?

Chapter 9

~~~~~~

PRICE DISCRIMINATION

IN THE previous chapter, it was pointed out that most firms handle multiple products and that there seems to be a marked trend toward further diversification on the part of American industry. In part, the urge to add products reflects a desire to increase profits through "price discrimination"—the practice of selling essentially the same product at different prices in different markets. While the handling of multiple products is not always necessary to price discrimination (since *exactly* the same product can sometimes be sold at different prices), the discriminating monopolist usually finds it worth while to build certain technical differences into two or more versions of a product (e.g., soap) and to apply distinguishing names to the various versions.[1] That is, the practice which is sometimes designated as "internal brand competition" may be followed, in order to charge quite different prices for very much the same thing. Sometimes, the difference is only one of packaging—for example, precisely the same cornstarch may be packaged under different labels by a firm and sold at different prices.

As already suggested, multiple-product production is not always necessary to the practice of price discrimination. A surgeon may sell the same quality of tonsillectomy or a lawyer the same legal opinion for different fees to persons who are clearly in different income brackets. A magazine is often sold at a lower price to new subscribers and to those who are slow to renew than to the habitual and eager subscriber whose name can easily be gotten on the dotted line each year at regular rates. (Hint: Let the magazine publishers coax you.)

Price discrimination often occurs in monopolistic markets but does not exist under "perfect competition," if the latter is defined to include complete knowledge and mobility on the part of buyers in addition to the presence of a large number of sellers of a homogeneous commodity. From the point of view of economic analysis, price discrimination may be said to exist when a different markup

---

[1] The similarity of price discrimination and multiple products is emphasized by Eli W. Clemens, "Price Discrimination and the Multiple Products Firm," *Review of Economic Studies,* Vol. XIX (1951–52), p. 1. In fact, Clemens seems to overemphasize the similarity. The handling of a great many items by a chain food store, for example, bears only a relatively minor relation to the desire to earn greater profits by discriminating in price.

above marginal cost is made for different units of the same, or much the same, commodity. This unlike markup may occur in that customers who can be served only at different marginal costs are charged the same price—as is the case whenever a commodity which is produced only in one locality is sold throughout the country at a uniform price (in spite of unlike freight or postage costs). Or it may occur through imposition of unlike prices when marginal costs of serving customers are the same. An approximate example is the charging of a higher price upstairs than in the basement of a department store when precisely the same commodity is sold on both floors.[2] Still another possibility exists. Marginal costs of serving different customers may be dissimilar, and prices may also differ, but not in such a way as to provide a uniform markup for all buyers. An example is the provision of standard and de luxe models of many commodities such as automobiles, refrigerators, and fountain pens, where sellers' margins above marginal cost are usually higher on the fancier versions.

Sometimes, a commodity like aspirin, which is clearly definable technically, is sold by different firms at very different prices. In a sense the consumers who pay the higher prices are discriminated against compared with those who buy the low-priced brands. This situation does not fall within the usual meaning of "price discrimination," however, because it is not accomplished by a single firm. On the other hand, sale of a given company's product under different brand names and through separate channels of distribution involving another firm can probably be usefully designated as price discrimination. For example, a Federal Trade Commission investigation some years ago revealed that the Goodyear Tire and Rubber Company sold tires to Sears Roebuck under the brand name "All State" which were of the same quality as those marketed by Goodyear under its own "All Weather" brand. The difference in wholesale prices between these two brands ranged from 29 to 40 per cent in the period 1927–33. At retail, All State tires were sold at prices 20 to 25 per cent below those of All Weather tires.[3]

Separation of Markets Essential

Whether price discrimination is practiced with respect either to precisely the same commodity or to different versions of a commodity,

---

[2] The example may be only approximate, because it may well add somewhat more to cost to sell a unit in the upstairs store. However, the main element in marginal cost—the wholesale price at which the store buys the good—would be the same whether it was sold upstairs or in the basement.

[3] Federal Trade Commission, Docket No. 2116.

a necessary condition is that customers be somehow segregated for different treatment. When the versions of the commodity are differentiated by means of minor technical differences, trade-marks, packaging, or other means, customers are segregated on the basis of their own preferences (their preferences being heavily influenced, however, by sellers through the forces of advertising and salesmanship). When precisely the same commodity is sold at different prices, numerous bases of separation which are under the control of the seller may be feasible. The following appear to be among the most important:

1. *Apparent income or wealth of the buyer.* The man who drives a large car is often charged more for an identical repair job than the owner of a more modest vehicle. The sale of a larger house typically involves a larger commission to the real estate agent, since these fees are usually computed as a percentage of sales price, and probably the effort involved on his part does not increase so rapidly as price. Discrimination by surgeons and lawyers on the basis of income and wealth has already been mentioned.

2. *Convenience to the buyer.* A reserved seat may sell at a higher price than an unreserved seat which is equally well located, the difference being a premium paid by the buyer in order to avoid uncertainty and possible inconvenience.

3. *Quantity purchased by individual buyer.* The practice of granting "quantity discounts" is a common one which takes several forms. The buyer of the large "economy size" tube of toothpaste, box of soap powder, or package of ice cream usually gets a better price in relation to cost than the buyer of a smaller amount. A large firm may get a lower price than a smaller one on a like purchase, and the large buyer of electricity usually gets a lower average price per kilowatt-hour than the small consumer.[4]

4. *Newness of customer's business.* The favoritism often shown to new subscribers to magazines has already been mentioned. Similarly, graduate students often receive lower subscription rates on professional journals than regular buyers.[5] In other fields the established customer, however, may receive better treatment than the new buyer. Price discrimination on either basis is motivated more by long-run profit considerations than simply by a desire to maximize immediate profits.

5. *Location of buyers.* Geographic separation of buyers often provides a convenient basis for price discrimination. When "blanket" freight rates bring about equal transportation charges over wide areas irrespective of distance, the buyers located relatively near the source of shipment are discriminated against compared with distant customers. Also, the device known as "basing-

---

[4] The relation between marginal and average rates per kilowatt-hour is another illustration of a mathematical relationship which is common in economics and other sciences. Decreasing marginal rates as usage is increased occasion declining average rates for greater purchases; that is, the average curve declines continually because the marginal curve lies below it.

[5] This illustration is given by A. G. Papandreou and J. T. Wheeler in *Competition and Its Regulation* (New York: Prentice-Hall, Inc., 1954), p. 95.

point pricing" (which will be discussed in some detail later in this chapter) discriminates against the buyer located near a source of supply which is not a basing point, since he must pay for more freight than is actually involved in the delivery.

6. *Time of purchase.* Frequently, price is different to those who buy at various times of the day or at different seasons of the year. A motion-picture theater on 42nd Street may vary its price several times during the day, charging the highest rates at night. Or a department store may charge more for the same item before Christmas or Easter than after these holidays. This basis of separation emphasizes the fact that price discrimination and multiple products may be indistinguishable from one another, since it is an arbitrary matter whether one considers an afternoon and evening showing of a given film to constitute the same or different commodities. Similarly, long-distance telephone and telegraph rates are lower at night than during the day. The monopolistic seller of such services has an incentive to lower the rates at night in order to make better use of existing capacity, just as the firm has an incentive to add new products when it has unused managerial or plant capacity.

7. *Age of buyer.* Youthful and aged persons sometimes receive lower prices than those of intermediate ages. In part, this is a way of discriminating according to purchasing power, since incomes tend to be lower among the young and the old. The pricing of motion pictures and rides in amusement parks exemplifies discrimination in favor of children. Aged persons sometimes receive such concessions as free or cheaper hunting and fishing licenses. Group life insurance plans, when they provide for payment of the same premium by persons of all ages, discriminate in favor of the older participants, for whom mortality rates are higher. When children are charged lower prices than adults (at theaters, for example), this is in part an effort to build up habits which will sustain long-run demand.

8. *Prestige of buyer.* The influential person, such as a senior executive in a corporation, may be given an especially favorable price on property in a new real estate subdivision in order to attract ambitious junior executives to the area. Similarly, a well-known motion-picture actress may be invited to dine "on the house," whereas an unknown nonpayer would have to wash dishes. Price discrimination on this basis somewhat resembles the practice of using "loss leaders" to attract customers who will buy other items.

Resale Must Be Difficult

If buyers can somehow be segregated, services often lend themselves readily to the practice of price discrimination, because they usually cannot be resold. The tonsillectomy already referred to is an obvious example. Commodities, however, can often be resold by those who receive lower prices to those who qualify only for higher prices, thus ruining the latter market for the would-be discriminatory monopolist. That is to say, activities of an arbitrage nature may interfere with effective price discrimination. Where transportation costs constitute a substantial barrier between markets, however, resale is unprofitable so long as the price differential which is imposed does not exceed the cost of transport between the markets.[6] This is why goods can often be "dumped" abroad at prices substantially below those charged at home. Any tariff on imports then becomes an additional impediment to resale in the producing country. Similarly, a highly perishable commodity cannot readily be resold, because suitable refrigerated delivery facilities are likely to be lacking, and thus may lend itself to discriminatory pricing. Also, commodities such as electricity and gas, which for technical reasons cannot readily be redistributed, are well suited for this purpose.

Even when resale is not practicable, price discrimination may not be feasible if it causes resentment on the part of those who are charged the higher prices. Such resentment may cause buyers either to demand the more favorable rates or to take their custom elsewhere. Consequently, price discrimination is apt to be more feasible when customers are geographically or temporally separated. There obviously may also be an advantage in keeping price lists secret. Similarly, technical complexity makes it difficult for the buyer to judge the propriety of price and hence favors discrimination. This is one reason for the confusing array of policies offered by insurance companies. It also helps explain the aversion which most life insurance companies have to selling pure insurance (term insurance), which is simplest in form and for which an appropriate selling price can most easily be judged by reference to mortality tables.

Perfect Discrimination

It is instructive to consider the extreme case of "perfect" price discrimination in order to understand the motivation behind more practicable schemes of discrimination. Whereas the usual assumption employed in the economic theory of monopoly is that the *single* most profitable price is charged, the theory of perfect discrimination requires that every unit be sold at a *different* price and that this be the highest price at which that unit would be taken off the market. If each customer buys only one unit per time period, this means a different price to each customer; otherwise, it involves lower prices on successive units purchased by a given buyer—i.e., "quantity discounts."

Under perfect price discrimination the demand curve facing the firm is also its marginal revenue curve. This is true because each unit sold is independent of the others; that is, to sell an additional unit,

---

[6] This point is elaborated on by C. G. F. Simkin, "Aspects of the Theory of Discrimination," *Review of Economic Studies,* Vol. XV (1), No. 37 (1947–48), p. 5.

the monopolist does not have to take a lower price on the earlier units. Whatever price he gets for a particular unit adds exactly that amount to his revenue. (Under the single-price assumption, he *does* have to accept a lower price on earlier units in order to sell later units, and this causes marginal revenue to be below price.) The average revenue curve lies above the demand curve, since whatever quantity is considered along the horizontal axis, the earlier units in this "batch" will bring a higher price than the later ones and hence .will hold the average price above the price at the margin.

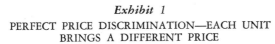

Exhibit 1
PERFECT PRICE DISCRIMINATION—EACH UNIT
BRINGS A DIFFERENT PRICE

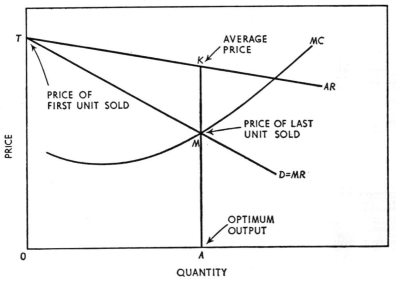

The perfectly discriminating firm, if it sought to maximize profit, would produce and sell quantity *OA* in Exhibit 1. Prices would range between *OT* and *OM* for the various units sold. Total revenue would amount to *OA* times *AK,* and this is the largest revenue which can possibly be secured when output is subject to the restriction that no unit should be produced which does not add at least as much to income as it does to cost. Full advantage of the demand has been taken by the seller, in that every unit has been sold at the highest price which it individually can bring.

Imperfect Discrimination

In practice, a much lower degree of price discrimination is feasible. Even an electric power company, whose product is unusually well

suited to price discrimination, uses "blocks" of substantial size when it
gives quantity discounts. When the monopolistic seller is able somehow to divide the market into two or more segments for unequal
treatment, he secures maximum profit by pricing in such a way as to
equalize the marginal revenue received in each submarket.[7] Unless this
equalization is attained, he can increase profits by switching units from
submarkets where marginal revenues are lower and selling them instead where they are higher. This rule alone does not, however, tell
at what *level* marginal revenues should be equated or what total
quantity should be produced and sold. Marginal cost enters into these
determinations. Optimum output is the one at which marginal cost is
equal to aggregate marginal revenue, and the level at which these are
equated is the level to which marginal revenue must be brought in
each submarket. This construction, which was originated by a well-
known British economist, Joan Robinson,[8] is shown in Exhibit 2.

Demand in one submarket has been labelled D_1 and demand in
the other submarket, D_2; corresponding marginal revenues are MR_1
and MR_2. Aggregate marginal revenue, AMR, is obtained by the
horizontal summation of these marginal revenue curves. Aggregate
marginal revenue coincides with MR_1 between T and K, since there
is no quantity corresponding to MR_2 between these points. The MR_2
curve begins at point K, so that AMR branches off to the right of
MR_2 below this point. The marginal cost of production is shown by
MC. Optimum output is OA, determined by the equality of MC and
AMR. If the rate of production were above OA, it would be too high,
because units above OA would add more to the firm's cost than to its
revenue, even if units were properly allocated in sale between the
two submarkets (that is, allocated so as to equate marginal revenue
from each).

Buyers in Market 2 receive a substantially lower price (OP_2) than
buyers in Market 1 (who pay OP_1). Optimum sales in Market 2
are OA_2, determined by the intersection of MR_2 with a horizontal
line drawn at the level at which MC equals AMR. Optimum sales in
Market 1 are determined by the intersection of MR_1 and the same
horizontal line. (As a consequence, marginal revenues are equated in

[7] Except if units sold in a submarket are indivisible, since this will usually make
exact equalization impossible. In the case of perfect price discrimination, units sold
within every submarket are indivisible because each is infinitesimally small; consequently,
marginal revenues are not equalized.

[8] *The Economics of Imperfect Competition* (London: Macmillan Co., Ltd., 1938),
p. 183.

the two submarkets.) Prices in the two submarkets are those at which the optimum quantities can be sold; consequently, the prices are found on the demand curves directly above the optimum sales quantities.

Discrimination when One Market Is Competitive

In Exhibit 2, demand at any price which is chosen for consideration is considerably more elastic in Market 2 than in Market 1. This is the reason for the profitability of charging less in Market 2 than in the other market. Customers who make up Market 2 would desert the

Exhibit 2

DISCRIMINATION BETWEEN TWO SUBMARKETS—TWO PRICES
FOR ONE GOOD

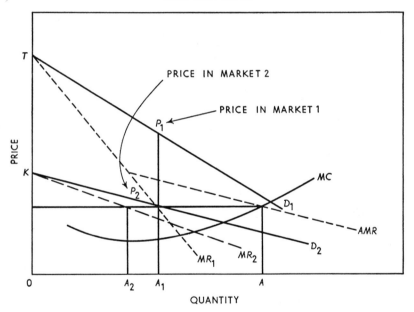

firm much more drastically than those in the other submarket if confronted by a high price. If price were *OK*, for example, none of the commodity could be sold to the potential customers in Market 2, whereas sales would be substantial at this price in Market 1.

Sometimes, a firm divides its sales of a given commodity between a monopolistic market and a highly competitive market. In this case the price is, of course, considerably higher in the former. Marginal revenue is equated in both markets, since the firm will not sell any units in the monopolistic market which will add less to revenue than they would have added if they had been sold in the purely competitive market.[9] This situation frequently occurs for commodities which are traded internationally. As already mentioned, transportation costs create a natural barrier between foreign and domestic markets, and resale by foreigners in the United States may be further impeded by tariffs and quotas imposed by this country. This creates a situation favorable to price discrimination and frequently results in the "dumping" of a product abroad at a relatively low, competitive price while at the same time price is maintained at a monopolistic level at home. Recently, an attempt has been made by cotton growers in the United States to induce the Commodity Credit Corporation to sell large quantities of stored cotton abroad at competitive prices while the domestic price is artifically maintained by the government's price-support program. The purpose of this proposed "dumping" would be to get rid of stored cotton which might otherwise eventually depress domestic prices. The State Department has pointed out the danger of harming friendly nations who have cotton to sell by this policy.[10] In such a case, where sales are made out of stocks accumulated by a government agency over time, the price which is charged in the world market might well be considerably below its marginal cost of production in this country. Under the theory of price discrimination outlined above, which considers current production to be sold currently, no units of product are sold below marginal cost.

Discrimination when Products Are Dissimilar

The theory of price discrimination, which has been briefly described, is based on the assumption that a firm may find it possible to sell exactly the same commodity to two or more groups of buyers at different prices. More frequently, however, companies which are in a position to increase profits by means of price discrimination find it necessary or desirable to differentiate products from one another, so that similar—but not quite the same—goods are sold at two or more prices. This does much to prevent those who pay the higher price from being dissatisfied and switching their custom to other firms. When products are not quite the same, it is often very difficult for a buyer to know what a proper price differential would be. It is also impossible analytically to say whether the firm is practicing "price discrimination" or is merely a multiple-product firm.

---

[9] The student is advised to draw this chart for himself; this is usually the best way to make a diagram and the underlying principles "sink in."

[10] "Government Should Export Cotton at Competitive Prices, Group Says," *Wall Street Journal*, February 7, 1956, p. 5.

The essence of price discrimination which is motivated by a desire to maximize short-run profit, as can be inferred from Exhibit 2, is that the excess of price over marginal cost differs in the various markets in which a good is sold. In that diagram the price in Market 1 is well above marginal cost, while the price in Market 2 is only a little above marginal cost. (No reference need be made to average cost.) Where products are somewhat dissimilar, separate marginal cost curves are applicable to the various products (so long as they are not joint products produced in fixed proportions). The firm may find it possible to charge a substantially higher price in relation to marginal cost for one commodity than for the other(s); this can be considered to be price discrimination. But, as already mentioned, it is not possible to say definitely where "price discrimination" ceases and the ordinary production and sale of unlike multiple products begin. The situation which was designated in the previous chapter as "internal brand competition" can be considered to be one of price discrimination if, in fact, the markup above marginal cost is not the same for each of the versions of a commodity.

Geographic Price Discrimination

Frequently, markets which are subjected to unlike treatment by a firm are separated on a geographic basis—that is, transportation costs impose an economic barrier between the markets. The case of "dumping" a commodity abroad at a low price while the domestic price is maintained has already been mentioned. Geographic price discrimination makes its appearance in numerous other forms also. For example, "blanket" freight rates are sometimes charged by the railroads which result in the same charge for transporting a unit of commodity over a wide geographic range irrespective of the actual length of the haul. An outstanding example is the movement of California oranges in carload lots from all points of origin in that state to any point between Denver and the North Atlantic seaboard at the same rate.[11] This means, for example, that buyers in Chicago are discriminated against compared with those in New York, in that the former are charged the same price despite the lower marginal cost of production plus transportation involved in placing California oranges in Chicago. More resources are used up in delivering a box of California oranges to New York, but price does not reflect this fact.

The same sort of price discrimination occurs whenever a commodity

---

[11] Kent T. Healy, *The Economics of Transportation in America* (New York: Ronald Press, 1940), p. 250.

is "fair-traded" at the same price throughout the country (so far as the law permits), especially when the transportation cost per unit is substantial. Points close to the plant or plants in which the good is made are charged a higher markup above marginal cost, including transportation, than are more distant points. Frequently, mail-order houses do not make an explicit charge for postage to the buyer, at least on lightweight items. This, again, is a form of discrimination, though not a very serious one, against the buyers who are close to the origin of shipments. A more serious, though understandable, form of geographic price discrimination occurs through the practice of the railroads of charging lower freight rates to seaports and other places where water competition is present than to near-by cities where such competition does not prevail.

Basing-Point Pricing in Steel

A historically important, and still significant, form of geographic price discrimination is known as "basing-point pricing." The most famous example of the practice was the "Pittsburgh-plus" system of pricing used by the steel industry prior to 1924.[12] Under this system, mills all over the United States calculated prices not by reference to their own costs and shipping charges but by reference to the single set of basing-point prices at Pittsburgh, plus rail freight from Pittsburgh to the buyer's location.[13] Thus, steel delivered to Washington, D.C., for example, was priced as if it came from Pittsburgh even if, in fact, it came by boat from near-by Baltimore. The steel industry changed to a multiple basing-point system in 1924 after the United States Steel Corporation was ordered by the Federal Trade Commission to "cease and desist" from the Pittsburgh-plus system. Under the amended system the delivered price at any city was calculated by adding to the mill price the freight from the *applicable* basing point. This was done by calculating the lowest combination of mill price and rail freight for any given buyer. The "applicable basing point" would always be the one from which rail freight was lowest if mill prices were the same but might not be if mill prices were dissimilar. Any steel mill which wished to sell in a particular locality could offer its product at the

---

[12] Steel beams were sold on this basis as early as 1880. Frank A. Fetter, *The Masquerade of Monopoly* (New York: Harcourt, Brace & Co., 1931), p. 147.

[13] A few exceptions were permitted for particular locations. One of these locations was Detroit, Michigan, where the automobile industry used tremendous quantities of steel. Also, part of the Alabama output of the U.S. Steel Corporation was sold on a "Birmingham-plus" basis after 1908. Fritz Machlup, *The Basing-Point System* (Philadelphia: Blakiston Co., 1949), p. 65.

delivered price thus computed.[14] This required the absorption of part of the freight charge by more distant steel mills, however.

Under a multiple basing-point system, there is less collection of "phantom freight" than with a single basing point. Under the "Pittsburgh-plus" arrangement, steel buyers all over the country, except those in the area served by the Pittsburgh mills, had to pay fictitious freight charges equal to the difference between rail freight from Pittsburgh and actual freight from the source of the shipment. Even under a multiple basing-point system, a buyer in the same city as a steel mill which was not designated as a basing point would have to pay phantom freight from the nearest basing point. Use of a cheaper means of transportation than rail freight also led at times to receipt of phantom freight by the seller. However, the larger the number of sources designated as basing points, the less the importance of phantom freight.

If *all* of the sources of supply of a product were designated as basing points, the system would approximate an f.o.b. mill system (in which actual freight is paid from the actual source of supply). It would still not be precisely the same, however. For example, the basing-point system might still specify the use of *rail* freight from the nearest mill, whether or not this was the actual mode of shipment. Also, there would be a single delivered price in each city, regardless of the actual origin, instead of unlike prices for shipments from different sources. Probably the most serious objection to a multiple basing-point system with every source a basing point would derive from the interfirm collusion necessary to establish and police such a pricing system. A basing-point system of any kind, with published lists of delivered prices in each locality, serves as a strong deterrent to overt price cutting to gain additional sales.

Other Basing-Point Industries

The portland cement industry was also a well-known practitioner of the multiple basing-point system of pricing; and historically, this system was second only to that of the steel industry in importance to the American economy. Cement prices charged by different companies

---

[14] It should be remembered that geographic distance and economic distance are often quite different. Mountains, for example, raise transportation costs, so that a short distance may actually be a considerable economic obstacle to the movement of goods. On the other hand, the possibility of water transportation renders distance less costly. The latter possibility did not, however, affect delivered prices, since *rail* freight was made a part of price.

were thus identical at any point of delivery.[15] During the 1930's, about half of the cement mills were basing points, and about half were not. Buyers located near the nonbasing-point mills were forced to pay some "phantom freight," while those near basing points were not at this disadvantage. In 1948 the Supreme Court upheld a Federal Trade Commission order that the portland cement industry "cease and desist" from selling cement at prices calculated in accordance with a multiple basing-point system or using other means to secure identical price quotations for the product of the various companies.[16] Shortly after this decision, both the portland cement and the steel industries abandoned the basing-point method of pricing and adopted systems of f.o.b. mill pricing.

The corn refining industry and the pulp, sugar, copper, zinc, gasoline, lead, asphalt roofing, maple and oak flooring, and other industries have also made use of basing-point systems, temporarily or permanently.[17] While some of the most important systems from a historical viewpoint have been abandoned, the system continues to be in effect for some products.

Recently, the Ford Motor Company and General Motors have taken action to abandon a modified version of basing-point pricing.[18] Since about 1915, it had been the industry practice to charge dealers for full transportation charges, as though the car were shipped from the home plant, when it may actually have been assembled at a near-by facility. This had the effect of overpricing cars in the more distant cities compared with their prices in the Detroit area. As a result, it was often worth while for "car bootleggers" to buy new cars in or close to Detroit and to tow or haul them to the Southwest or Far West and sell them at lower prices than the authorized dealers were permitted to charge. Also, a great many individual customers living on the West Coast found it worth while to fly or take the train or bus to Detroit in order to buy and drive home a new car; this at least provided a very cheap vacation. The automobile manufacturers other than General Motors and Ford have fewer assembly plants

---

[15] This resulted in identical bids on government contracts. For example, eleven companies bid exactly $3.286854 per barrel of cement on a contract for delivery of 6,000 barrels for a federal project at Tucumcari, New Mexico (Machlup, op. cit., p. 99).

[16] The wording of the order may be found in Dudley F. Pegrum, The Regulation of Industry (Chicago: Richard D. Irwin, Inc., 1950), p. 337.

[17] Machlup, op. cit., p. 17.

[18] "GM Says It, Too, Is Abandoning Use of Phantom Freight Charges," Wall Street Journal, February 27, 1956, p. 1.

located away from the home area and have participated less fully in the collection of phantom freight.[19]

Market Penetration

Advocates of basing-point pricing usually claim that the system is highly competitive because each seller can offer his product at the same price in any locality—that is, firms may compete freely for sales but may not compete in price. Any plant which has unused capacity, and whose owners are therefore anxious to increase sales, can offer its wares at the same price as others in any locality, although this may be possible only through "freight absorption," which means a reduction in the "mill net" price realized. Although this may help utilize the excess capacity of the mill which penetrates the usual territory of another mill, it clearly tends to cause excess capacity in the plant whose market is being penetrated. If such freight absorption were not practiced and buyers were instead given prices equivalently lower, the resulting increase in total sales would help avoid excess capacity in both plants.

Market penetration, phantom freight, and freight absorption can perhaps be more easily understood from Exhibit 3. In this chart, *A* and *B* are mills producing the same commodity; but *B* is a basing point (the "applicable" one in the region considered), while *A* is not. Circles are drawn around *B* to reflect transportation costs from *B;* at each point on a circle the delivered price is the same. These delivered prices are shown by the numbers attached to each circle, and are calculated by assuming the mill price at *B* to be $45 and the transportation cost from one circle to the next to be $1.00 per unit.[20]

If we assume that freight costs are the same in either direction and that equal distances represent equal freight costs, it is clear that Mill A has a very favorable mill net price in selling near home. If Mill A sells at point *H,* for example, the price will be $50, which includes a $5.00 freight charge from the basing point. Since actual freight from *A* to *H* is $1.00, the "phantom freight" collected by

---

[19] L. L. Colbert, president of the Chrysler Corporation, declared in a hearing before Chairman Monroney's Senate Commerce Subcommittee that his company in 1955 paid out more than it took in for transportation of automobiles. "President of Chrysler Is against Any Law to Bar 'Phantom Freight,'" *Wall Street Journal,* March 2, 1956, p. 18.

[20] The use of circles assumes that transportation costs are uniform in all directions. Actually, they would be affected by the availability of railroads, highways, and waterways, and by mountains, etc.; this would cause the isoprice lines to be irregular in shape.

Mill A is $4.00. On the other hand, if Mill A sells at point *F*, the price will be $47, which includes $2.00 of freight. Since actual freight from *A* to *F* is $4.00, Mill A must absorb $2.00 in freight costs in order to make the sale. On sales anywhere between *A* and the vertical line *XY*, Mill A will realize phantom freight; while

Exhibit 3

MILL A COLLECTS PHANTOM FREIGHT TO LEFT OF *XY* BUT ABSORBS
FREIGHT TO RIGHT OF *XY*

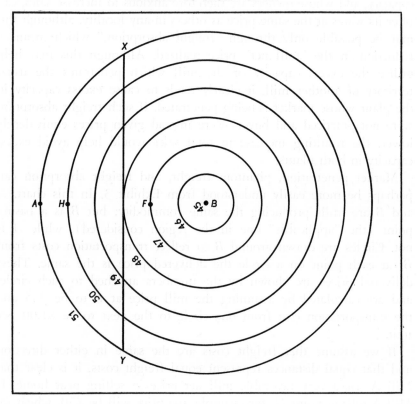

to penetrate beyond line *XY*, it will have to absorb freight. Line *XY* is drawn so as to be equidistant between the two mills.

It is also apparent from the chart that the basing-point Mill B can penetrate the territory of Mill A without penalty. If Mill B sold at point *H*, for example, it would secure the same mill net as on a sale at point *F*, because the delivered price always includes full freight cost from point *B*. Under the "Pittsburgh-plus" plan the Pittsburgh mills could sell anywhere in the country without reducing their mill net. This system was well adapted to minimizing unused capacity at Pittsburgh but tended to promote excess capacity in other districts.[21] On the other hand, mills located at the basing point do not have an opportunity to collect phantom freight, as do nonbasing-point plants.[22]

Cross-Hauling

Under any system of pricing a certain amount of "cross-hauling" is bound to occur—that is, one mill shipping the same commodity into the natural territory of another mill at the same time the other mill is delivering in the territory of the first mill. This occurs even if the term "cross-hauling" is defined strictly so as to require that a mill in City A be shipping a given commodity to a buyer in City B at the same time a mill at City B is shipping to a buyer at City A. The shipments are likely even to pass one another on freight trains headed in opposite directions. Under a basing-point pricing system, cross-hauling is especially likely to occur, because the delivered price at any destination is the same regardless of origin of shipment. If shape, size, quality, and finish of the product are precisely the same, there is an obvious waste of transportation resources when this occurs.

Some data on cross-hauling in the steel industry were collected by the Temporary National Economic Committee for 1939 (when the industry was operating under a multiple basing-point system). Detroit is a very large user of both cold-rolled and hot-rolled sheets because of its automobile plants. In February, 1939, the Detroit area received 43,671 tons of cold-rolled sheets and 46,153 tons of hot-rolled sheets. Although these quantities exceed the amounts which can be produced in Detroit, the Detroit mills shipped out of the area 5,253 tons of cold-rolled steel sheets and 11,357 tons of hot-rolled sheets.[23] Detroit mills were shipping large tonnages to Chicago, especially, at the same time the Chicago mills were shipping to Detroit. In part, this type of persistent cross-hauling can be explained as a sort of hedge against a decline in demand. It may be useful for Detroit mills, for example,

---

[21] In 1920 the Chicago mills, which had much unused capacity, broke away from the "Pittsburgh-plus" plan and established Chicago as a basing point. At about the same time the Federal Trade Commission began investigations which eventually led to abandonment of the single basing-point system in the steel industry.

[22] Except when a basing-point mill is able to use a cheaper mode of transport than the railroads.

[23] George W. Stocking, *Basing Point Pricing and Regional Development* (Chapel Hill: University of North Carolina Press, 1954), p. 113.

to have some regular customers who are not members of the automobile industry in the event of a severe drop in automobile production.

Basing-Point Pricing and Location of Plants

Under an f.o.b. mill system of pricing, there is an obvious cost advantage, other things equal, in being located near a mill which supplies a principal raw material. When a basing-point system is employed, however, it is necessary to be near a basing point in order to hold down the freight charge which is included in the price of the raw material. Proximity to a nonbasing-point mill does not help when freight on the raw material is calculated as if it came from another source. The "Pittsburgh-plus" single basing-point system thus favored the location of steel-using plants in the Pittsburgh area. A well-known economist, after an extensive study of basing-point pricing, concluded that the "Pittsburgh-plus" system undoubtedly handicapped the South in developing a steel fabrication business.[24] A *multiple* basing-point system also tends to impede the development of fabricating industry in the vicinity of nonbasing-point mills, although effects are less serious than under a single basing-point system.[25]

The basing-point system can also be used by a strongly led industry to discourage the construction of new capacity in the industry itself. Referring to Exhibit 3, suppose that the mill at point A is extremely prosperous and that a new firm is considering building a plant there to produce the same product. The industry may then threaten to make point A a basing point if the new plant is built there. This would immediately lower the mill net price which could be realized by sales in the area to the left of line XY, since phantom freight would be eliminated. This threat might be sufficient to keep out the new mill. Alternatively, Mill B might threaten to conduct an especially aggressive selling campaign in the natural area of Mill A. This it could do because it can sell as profitably in the natural market area of Mill A as in its own market area. This sort of sales concentration by Mill B would leave additional customers in the territory of Mill B who might be served by mills at point A, but they could do so only by absorbing freight, and this prospect would not be attractive to the men considering the erection of new capacity at point A.

---

[24] *Ibid.,* p. 74.

[25] As was noted earlier, the "Detroit-plus" system of pricing automobiles by some companies tended to curtail sales of cars in the Southwest and Far West. This effect is similar in nature to the handicapping of nonbasing-point regions, described above.

Price Discrimination and the Law

Section 2 of the Clayton Act (1914) prohibited discrimination in price between different purchasers of commodities "where the effect of such discrimination may be to substantially lessen competition or tend to create a monopoly in any line of commerce." This prohibition was, however, greatly weakened by the proviso "that nothing herein contained shall prevent discrimination in price between purchasers of commodities on account of differences in grade, quality or quantity of the commodity sold, or that makes only due allowance for difference in the cost of selling or transportation, or discrimination in price in the same or different communities made in good faith to meet competition. . . ."

This provision was completely rewritten in 1936, when Congress passed the Robinson-Patman Anti-Discrimination Act, an amendment to the Clayton Act. This act prohibited discrimination in price between different purchasers of commodities of like grade and quality, where the effects of such discrimination might be substantially to lessen competition or create a monopoly in any line of interstate commerce. Price differentials were permitted, however, if they made only due allowance for differences in the cost of manufacture, sale, or delivery. Certain other less important provisions were also included. The Federal Trade Commission was empowered to limit quantity discounts, even where they could be shown to be consistent with differences in cost, if it concluded that differentials based on cost would give an undue advantage to large-scale marketing.

The Robinson-Patman Act has often been called an "antichain store law" because of the last-mentioned provision. This was clearly an attempt to make it possible for the federal government to protect small business from competition from large, well-organized firms. As such, it is socially undesirable, unless one feels that small business has social merit which cannot be measured exclusively in terms of price to the consumer or the efficiency of resource allocation.

Basing-point pricing quite clearly is vulnerable under the Robinson-Patman Act, since different net prices are received by nonbasing-point mills on sales to buyers in different locations. Nongeographic price discrimination is, of course, also covered to the extent that it takes place in interstate commerce. (There are practically no laws against either monopoly or price discrimination in intrastate commerce.)

Average or Marginal Cost?

A serious defect of the Robinson-Patman Act is that it does not specify whether "cost" means average cost or marginal cost. The theory of price discrimination as developed by Joan Robinson (not related to the legislator) indicates that an unlike markup over marginal cost constitutes the essence of price discrimination. Since this is a "short-run" solution, no attention need be paid to average cost in order to arrive at the most profitable sales and prices. It would theoretically be better if "cost" were clearly defined as marginal cost rather than being left indefinite, because this would plainly obviate the need to allocate the fixed costs of the firm among different groups of customers. Such allocation is likely either to be arbitrary or to be purposely made by a firm in such a way as to attempt to justify any price system which is in effect. Marginal short-run costs exclude all fixed costs, being determined by considering only expenses which are variable in the short period. Legislators tend to think only in terms of average cost; hence, when they legislate on economic matters, they are likely to cause considerable confusion in circumstances where they should actually be framing laws in terms of marginal cost. On the other hand, so many businessmen and accountants are unaware of the meaning of "marginal cost" that they would have difficulty in complying with a properly framed law even if they wanted to do so.

CASE 9–1: STANDARD BRANDS, INC.[26]

On November 21, 1936, the Federal Trade Commission issued a complaint against Standard Brands, alleging that the respondent's scale of differential prices for bakers' yeast constituted illegal discrimination in price. The complaint was brought under Section 2 [a] of the Clayton Act, as amended (i.e., the Robinson-Patman Act).

Standard Brands was a consolidation of the former Fleischmann Company and a number of other companies in the food field. In 1936, it was the largest manufacturer of yeast in the United States, enjoying between 55 and 65 per cent of the total yeast business. It produced approximately 120 million pounds annually, of which 10–12 per cent was foil yeast and the remainder was bakers' yeast.

---

[26] The facts contained in this case have been drawn chiefly from 29 F.T.C. 121 (1939).

Among the largest competitors of the company were Anheuser-Busch Co., St. Louis; National Grain Yeast Co., New York; Red Star Yeast Co., Milwaukee; Consumers' Yeast Co., San Francisco; and Federal Yeast Co., Baltimore. Standard Brands operated six factories, located at Peekskill, New York; Chicago; Pekin, Illinois; San Francisco; Sumner, Washington; and Washington, D.C.

Yeast, as used in baking bread, is a necessary leavening ingredient. A pound of yeast is required in the manufacture of from 75 to 125 pounds of bread, depending upon the particular type of dough.

The yeast, all of which was of like grade and quality, was manufactured daily at the company's six factories. Bakers' yeast was molded into 1-pound and $\frac{1}{2}$-pound cakes, wrapped, and then packed in 50-pound cartons. Because of the perishable nature of the product, prompt delivery was essential; to accomplish this, the company maintained 444 agencies so located geographically throughout the country that the yeast would reach these agencies by common carrier within 24 hours after its manufacture. At the agencies, there were refrigerated warehouses maintained exclusively for the storage of yeast. Here, the yeast—still in 50-pound cartons—was placed upon company-owned trucks. Operating over 1,300 routes, this wagon distribution system brought the yeast to some 25,000 customers in all parts of the country. In addition to the so-called "personal delivery" sales of yeast to bakers, a small amount of bakers' yeast was shipped to customers by common carrier, and still smaller amount was sold to grocers for resale.

In the delivery of the yeast, the driver-salesman was accustomed to take daily route sheets made up at the agency headquarters, call on customers named therein, leave the amount of yeast they required, and either collect the cash or take the customer's receipt according to his instructions. Charge customers who receipted for the yeast were billed directly by the agency at the end of the month. Driver-salesmen solicited business from new and reclaimed prospects, but other salesmen were employed by the company as solicitors to sell its products. Where the quantity to be delivered to a customer was less than 50 pounds, the original cartons were broken by the driver-salesman. With the exception of a few wholesale routes, yeast was delivered from the same truck to both large and small customers. Many of the routes operated from the agencies were exclusively bakery routes, while others, so-called "unified routes," covered yeast and other products sold by the company. There were also a number of routes devoted solely to grocery products.

In addition to bakers' yeast the company sold many other products which were grouped into two principal classes—bakery products and grocery products—as follows:

Bakery Products	Grocery Products
Bakers' yeast	Foil yeast
Bulk products (including arkedy, diamalt, frozen eggs and fermaloid)	Bulk products—tea
	Package products (including Royal Baking Powder, Dr. Price Baking Powder, desserts, coffee, and tea)
Package products (including Fleischmann Baking Powder and other leaveners)	

The company required no written contracts with its customers, and there were no commitments which could not be terminated by either party at will. However, as a general practice, customers who paid less than 25 cents per pound for yeast and who purchased all their requirements from the company were obligated to purchase definite quantities monthly, in order to secure the yeast at more favorable prices.

To assist customers in improving products made from yeast, the company maintained a research laboratory, where experiments were conducted. A corps of experts was also maintained for the purpose of visiting bakeries and rendering assistance to customers in overcoming difficulties encountered in the manufacture of bread and other bakery products. Merchandising counselors from the company instructed customers in methods of displaying and selling goods. The company also conducted national advertising campaigns in periodicals and by radio to promote the increased consumption of bakers' bread, and it furnished advertising material to local bakers at cost to enable them to tie in with national advertising campaigns. The company maintained a school for bakers, giving free instruction to all customers interested. No extra charge was made by the company for any of these technical and promotional services.

Because of the company's large number of customers, its products were sold in practically every community in the United States. Among the customers of the company was the Great Atlantic and Pacific Tea Company, with 38 bakeries located east of the Rocky Mountains and with 14,000 retail stores located chiefly east of the Rocky Mountains. The annual output of bread by the A & P amounted to 446 million pounds, and its yeast consumption approximated 5 million pounds per year. Another customer of Standard Brands was the Continental Baking Co., with 78 bakeries located throughout the United States, whose yeast requirements also approximated 5 million pounds per year. Other large customers included the General Baking Company, whose annual requirements were 4 million pounds; Hathaway Bakeries, Inc., whose products were distributed throughout New England; and First National Stores, with 2,400 stores located in New England. There were also thousands of customers whose operations were entirely local.

For many years prior to the issuance of the Federal Trade Commission complaint, Standard Brands had employed a scale of prices based on the number of pounds of yeast used per month by the purchaser. This scale is presented in Exhibit 1. The poundages on

Exhibit 1

PRICES OF BAKERS' YEAST SOLD BY STANDARD
BRANDS, INC., 1936

Price Bracket	Pounds per Month	Price per Pound (Cents)	Effective Discount in Terms of 25¢/Lb. Base Price (Per Cent)
1...................	1–149	25	..
2...................	150–299	23	8
3...................	300–499	22	12
4...................	500–999	21	16
5...................	1,000–1,499	20	20
6...................	1,500–2,999	19	24
7...................	3,000–4,999	18	28
8...................	5,000–7,999	17	32
9...................	8,000–9,999	16	36
10..................	10,000–49,999	14½	42
11..................	50,000 and up	14	44

which the discount structure was based represented the *total* usage of yeast by the customer, which was not necessarily the same as the amount purchased from Standard Brands. Thus, a bakery using 2,000 pounds of yeast per month, but purchasing only 1,000 pounds from Standard Brands, would nonetheless pay the 2,000-pound rate of 19 cents per pound for the 1,000 pounds rather than 20 cents per pound, which would be the 1,000-pound rate. The basing of quantity discounts on total consumption rather than on quantities actually purchased was claimed to be a custom in the trade, from which Standard Brands could not easily depart.

The company did not publish its price lists, and customers were not acquainted with the discount structure. Before any price was quoted at which a customer might purchase bakers' yeast from the company, the customer first was required to indicate what his monthly requirements would be.

Standard Brands followed the practice of selling to some customers at "off-scale" prices, when a customer's yeast requirements had dropped enough to place him in a higher bracket but when the company continued to sell at the former price. The largest customers, who purchased yeast off-scale at the 14-cent price, were granted this concession by the central office. Divisional managers were authorized to sell off-scale to smaller customers, but never more than 2 or 3 cents off. About 16 per cent of the customers served by the company's agency at Minneapolis purchased at off-scale prices; while in the New York City area, about 35 per cent of the customers in the 3,000–5,000-pound class paid less than the price scale of 18 cents per pound. The company continued this practice because, where a customer had been granted a certain price on the basis of a certain consumption, he might desert Standard Brands for another supplier if, when his volume dropped off, Standard Brands insisted on putting him into a higher-price bracket.

The company also determined prices of bakers' yeast to its customers on the basis of total consumption, irrespective of the number of individual deliveries. The A & P, for example, had a total national consumption per month of the company's yeast ranging from 451,000 pounds for July, 1936, to 403,625 pounds for January, 1937. These amounts were delivered from the company's various agencies to 37 bakeries in locations from Louisiana to Iowa and Maine, in quantities ranging from 30,400 pounds delivered at Pittsburgh in July, 1936, to 2,200 pounds delivered at New Orleans in September, 1936. At no individual bakery of this customer was as much as 50,000 pounds delivered in one month. For the quantities delivered to the respective bakeries, according to the scale shown in Exhibit 1, the prices to 23 of the bakeries would have been $14\frac{1}{2}$ cents; to eight, prices would have been 16 cents; to four, 17 cents; to one, 18 cents; and to one, 19 cents. However, the A & P paid 15 cents per pound for all its yeast. Federal Bakeries, Inc., with 78 branches located over the entire country, consumed nationally in excess of 10,000 pounds and also purchased this yeast at a price of 15 cents per pound, although monthly deliveries to its respective branches did not exceed 200 pounds. Individual customers purchasing only 200 pounds per month would have been required to pay 23 cents per pound.

In order to justify the price differentials before the Federal Trade Commission, Standard Brands made certain studies of the costs of distribution and sale of bakers' yeast. These studies were based on the company's experience during the months of January, February, and March, 1937.

Average actual monthly costs of sale and delivery of all products in this period are shown in Exhibit 2. Average monthly sales, by products, for this same period are shown in the first column of Exhibit 3. The *known* factors, therefore, were actual total costs for all products and sales by products. The company's methods of determining costs of sale and delivery for each price bracket of bakers' yeast

Exhibit 2

AVERAGE MONTHLY COSTS OF SALE AND DELIVERY
OF ALL PRODUCTS, STANDARD BRANDS,
JANUARY–MARCH, 1937

Group Classification	Average Monthly Costs
Agency stockrooms	$ 34,295
Automobiles:	
Route selling and delivery	119,551
Solicitation	24,055
Service	107
Other usage at divisions and agencies	858
Agency delivery	323,386
Agency bakery merchandising	23,504
Agency grocery merchandising	32,162
Agency administration	182,507
Division stockrooms	17,404
Division bakery merchandising:	
Solicitation	32,108
Service	12,848
Division grocery merchandising	28,366
Division administration	147,346
Foreign commissions	298
Total	$978,795

involved two principal points of procedure—namely, (1) allocation of costs to separate products; and (2) allocation of the various elements of cost, apportioned to bakers' yeast, to the separate quantity-price brackets.

Allocation of costs to separate products, shown in Exhibit 3, was accomplished by applying certain predetermined percentages to average monthly dollar sales. The percentages thus applied were: yeast, 23 per cent; bulk products, 7.25 per cent; and package products, 11.3 per cent. This constituted the method for the apportionment and allocation of sales and delivery expenses to products which had been in actual use by the company since 1932, several years prior to the enactment of the Robinson-Patman Act. The company stated that these percentages were "based, in part, on the company's experiences and, in part, on generally recognized costs of distribution of grocery and other products and, in the opinion of its financial officers, they provide for a fair and reasonable allocation of such costs." The commission noted that "nowhere in the respondent's cost study does it appear that any factual study has been made to determine the correctness of the percentages that have been applied to the dollar sales of the respective products whereby the costs of sale and delivery of these products have been determined in the form of lump-sum estimates." As a result of the allocation of costs shown in Exhibit 3, it was determined that total average monthly costs of sale and delivery of bakers' yeast were $330,792. This was for sales by personal delivery, which was the chief method of sale. This total was separated into the following components of direct and indirect costs:

Direct costs:
Route selling and delivery.................................$ 78,140.38
Solicitation... 103,366.39
Service... 10,951.18
    Total Direct Costs...................................$192,457.95
Indirect costs.. 138,334.27
    Total Costs Applicable to Sale and Delivery of Bakers' Yeast...$330,792.22

The company's next step was to allocate the above costs to the groups of customers whose monthly purchases of bakers' yeast fell in the respective quantity-price brackets. The results are shown in Exhibit 4. Items of direct costs making up the total of $192,457.95 were allocated and applied to the respective quantity-price brackets by time studies and call studies. Route selling and delivery costs were apportioned according to the time for stops of the driver-salesmen and trucks at customers' premises, as determined by stop-watch studies and collected data for six days. Solicitation costs were apportioned according to number of calls on customers by solicitors, foremen, and managers. Service costs were apportioned according to actual time spent in calling on customers by servicemen. Indirect costs were allocated to quantity-price brackets in the same proportions as total direct cost. Before transforming total direct and indirect costs into costs per pound, the company apportioned $3,316.26, representing bakery consultants' salaries and expenses, to the quantity-price brackets on the basis of a time study. Total costs applied to each price bracket were then converted to costs per pound, as indicated in Exhibit 5, on the basis of a tabulation of all sales of bakers' yeast throughout the United States during January, 1937, in each price bracket.

Exhibit 3

STANDARD BRANDS, ALLOCATION OF TOTAL FIELD COSTS OF
SALE AND DELIVERY TO PRODUCTS

Products	Dollar Sales	Percentages Applied to Dollar Sales	Estimated Costs	Adjustment Factor (1.78 per Cent of Estimated Costs)	Final Allocation to Products of Total Average Monthly Costs
Bakery products:					
Pound yeast:					
Personal delivery...............	$1,413,095	23.00	$325,012	$ 5,780	$330,792
Shipping sales.................	35,369	23.00	8,135	145	8,280
Sales to grocers................	26,277	23.00	6,044	107	6,151
Bulk products.....................	749,368	7.25	54,329	996	55,295
Package products..................	68,505	11.30	7,741	138	7,879
Total.........................	$2,292,614		$401,261	$ 7,166	$408,397
Grocery products:					
Foil yeast.......................	$ 710,391	23.00	$163,390	$ 2,906	$166,296
Bulk products...................	3,878	7.25	281	5	286
Package products................	3,511,133	11.30	396,758	7,056	403,814
Total.........................	$4,225,402		$560,429	$ 9,967	$570,396
Grand Total................	$6,518,016		$961,690	$17,133	$978,793

Exhibit 4

STANDARD BRANDS, ALLOCATIONS OF COSTS TO
QUANTITY-PRICE BRACKETS

Bracket No.	Route Selling and Delivery Costs	Solicitation Costs	Service Costs	Indirect Costs	Total Field Costs of Sale and Delivery	Bakery Consultants' Costs	Total Costs Applied to Bakers' Yeast
1..........	$25,366	$ 32,570	$ 854	$ 42,256	$101,046	$ 45	$101,091
2..........	10,644	22,848	1,293	25,002	59,787	67	59,854
3..........	6,539	13,918	1,407	15,715	37,579	73	37,652
4..........	6,828	11,582	2,305	14,890	35,605	158	35,763
5..........	3,526	5,391	1,193	7,267	17,377	167	17,544
6..........	5,793	5,141	1,770	9,132	21,836	338	22,174
7..........	5,322	4,432	842	7,617	18,213	643	18,856
8..........	4,148	2,812	503	5,364	12,827	418	13,245
9..........	4,155	1,950	447	4,709	11,261	247	11,508
10..........	5,819	2,722	338	6,382	15,261	1,160	16,421
11..........	....	....	....	....	....	......	....
Total...	$78,140	$103,366	$10,952	$138,334	$330,792	$3,316	$334,108

It will be noted that the cost differentials per pound roughly parallel the price differentials. Exhibit 5 shows that, after the first step down in price, the cumulative decrease in cost per pound exceeded the cumulative decrease in price.

Exhibit 5

STANDARD BRANDS, DETERMINATION OF COST PER POUND
BY QUANTITY-PRICE BRACKETS

BRACKET No.	PRICE PER POUND (CENTS)	TOTAL COSTS APPLIED TO BAKERS' YEAST	POUNDS OF BAKERS' YEAST SOLD THROUGH PERSONAL DE- LIVERY SERVICE*	COST PER POUND (CENTS)	REDUCTIONS In Cost from Cost for 25- Cent Bracket (Cents)	In Price from Price for 25- Cent Bracket (Cents)
1...........	25	$101,091	859,226	11.765	......	....
2...........	23	59,854	597,049	10.025	1.740	2.0
3...........	22	37,652	488,146	7.713	4.052	3.0
4...........	21	35,763	625,842	5.714	6.051	4.0
5...........	20	17,544	358,457	4.894	6.871	5.0
6...........	19	22,174	872,442	2.542	9.223	6.0
7...........	18	18,856	905,271	2.083	9.682	7.0
8...........	17	13,245	921,843	1.437	10.328	8.0
9...........	16	11,508	781,025	1.474	10.292	9.0
10...........	14½	16,421	1,782,121	0.921	10.844	10.5
11...........	14	....	....	......	......	....
Total....		$334,108	8,191,422			

* Sales during month of January, 1937.

In determining unit costs of sale and delivery of bakers' yeast for each price bracket, Standard Brands excluded manufacturing costs, transportation costs, and home-office general administrative costs (including advertising).

QUESTIONS

1. From the viewpoint of Standard Brands, Inc., what factors made the differential price system shown in Exhibit 1 a desirable price policy?
2. Are there any reasons which might make the scale of differentials an undesirable price policy—aside from aspects of governmental regulation?
3. What characteristics of the market for bakers' yeast made it possible for Standard Brands to maintain a differential price structure? Do you believe it rested primarily on cost differentials?
4. Was the price scale of Exhibit 1 socially undesirable?

CASE 9–2: MARTIN-TURNER TOOL COMPANY

For many years the Martin-Turner Tool Company produced a wide line of small industrial tools such as saws, grinders, jigs, drills, and die cutters. In 1940 the firm introduced a number of portable power tools for distribution through retail outlets. The line of industrial tools had been sold directly to industrial users through the company's own salesmen. The distribution of portable tools at retail was established through dealers and distributors. During World War II, all production of tools for retail sale was suspended.

In the years immediately following the close of the war, there developed a rapid growth of the "do-it-yourself" idea. The movement provided a huge demand for power tools, and the Martin-Turner Company capitalized upon this development. By 1949 the firm had well established itself in this market as a producer of high-quality,

Exhibit 1

COMPARATIVE RETAIL PRICES OF SELECTED TURNER TOOLS AND
LEADING COMPETING BRANDS

Item	Turner Tools	Brand A	Brand B	Brand C	Brand D*
Circular saws (6")	$79.95	$79.95	$74.95	$79.95	$51.95
Drills ($\frac{1}{4}$")	59.95	56.95	49.95	54.95	32.95
Jig saws (21")	59.95	54.95	54.95	52.50	36.95
Band saws (18")	63.95	64.95	69.95	67.50	44.95

* Median price of the five most popular lower-priced brands.

precision power tools for home use. These were sold under the brand name of "Turner Tools." The line included circular saws, jig saws, drills, lathes, band saws, grinders, sanders, polishers, and planer-joiners. The drills, grinders, and lathes were made for both metal and wood. The remainder of the line was for woodworking only. The principal retail outlets were hardware stores, lumber yards, and department stores.

As early as mid-1948 the sales manager had observed that the sales of Turner Tools were not expanding as rapidly as the sales of the entire portable tool industry. Sales were at a satisfactory level in so far as profits were concerned, but the fact that the line was not maintaining its relative share of the market was disturbing to the officers of the company.

Since the introduction of the line of Turner Tools, there began to appear, during 1946 and 1947 especially, an increasing number of competing brands of tools. There were three other brands of high-quality tools comparable to the Turner line. Like Turner Tools, they sold at a price somewhat higher than many of the other competing lines. This is indicated in Exhibit 1. It was the lower-priced lines which were enjoying an increasing share of the total market. These developments prompted a series of discussions among the company's executives which centered around the possibility of adjusting prices downward so as to retain at least the firm's share of the market, if not increase it.

One of the chief obstacles to a price reduction of any substance was production costs. These costs, for selected portable tools, are shown in Exhibit 2. Sales of these selected items are shown in Exhibit 3.

Exhibit 2

COSTS, PER UNIT, OF SELECTED TURNER TOOLS

Item	Circular Saws (6″)	Drills (¼″)	Jig Saws (21″)	Band Saws (18″)
Direct labor.......................	$12.53	$ 7.87	$ 9.01	$ 9.71
Materials........................	11.36	10.62	9.19	11.55
Spoilage.........................	0.34	0.15	0.12	0.23
Indirect labor....................	2.19	0.46	0.44	1.00
Factory overhead..................	1.22	1.01	0.82	0.92
Administrative and selling expense...	0.61	0.31	0.56	0.59
Total Cost...................	$28.25	$20.42	$20.14	$24.00
Profit...........................	7.75	5.50	5.50	5.00
Factory Selling Price.........	$36.00	$25.92	$25.64	$29.00

Exhibit 3

NET SALES OF SELECTED TURNER TOOLS,
JANUARY 1 TO DECEMBER 31, 1948

Circular saws (6″)........................... 9,371
Drills (¼″)................................21,426
Jig saws (21″)............................. 5,211
Band saws (18″)........................... 3,608

After several discussions the president and sales manager proposed the following plan of action, which the executive committee presented to the board of directors:

1. The Martin-Turner Tool Company should enter the lower-priced tool market. Since the company had acquired a reputation for high-quality products which it was successfully selling at premium prices, the present line of Turner Tools should be retained. It was believed that any cheapening of the line by lowering its quality would result in a loss of this particular segment of the market.

   At the current volume of output of these various tools, it was more economical to assemble them by bench work rather than by an assembly line with more and simpler operations. Under the bench-work system, one employee was required to perform several operations, including some sub-assembly work. Some of these operations were rather complex and required some skill. This method of assembly frequently resulted in an irregular flow of products through the manufacturing process. All gears were machined. No stamped gears were used, as in the case of some of the lower-priced lines. The housings of most of the line consisted of two or three steel parts which were bolted together in the assembly process. Redesign of these housings to cast them as a single piece would reduce the cost of both materials and assembly. Other than the proposed change in housing design the line would remain as presently designed.

2. The Martin-Turner Tool Company should set up a wholly-owned subsidiary to market a lower-priced line of tools under the brand name of "Chieftain." The use of a subsidiary with a different brand name was recommended, so that the general public would not associate the lower-priced tools with Turner Tools. This would protect the Turner line from suspicion of lowering quality.

This subsidiary would contract for all of its production with Martin-Turner Tool Company. It was estimated that the Chieftain Tools would, within two years, have a market at least twice the current volume of Turner Tools. If total output of the two brands reached approximately 50 per cent of this estimate, the bench method of assembly could be replaced by the line. This, it was estimated, would reduce assembly costs by at least 30 per cent, or more. In addition, the purchase of raw materials in larger quantities would result in lower unit material costs.

Materials in the Chieftain line would be of the same quality as used in Turner Tools. There would be a difference in the housings of the Chieftain Tools. Not only would the designs differ somewhat, but they would be made of aluminum and plastic. All working parts of Chieftain Tools would be identical with Turner Tools. There would be no distinction between the two brands in the assembly of the chassis. Only when the chassis were mounted in the housings would there be separate assembly lines.

3. In order to obtain an immediate market for the Chieftain line, it was proposed that the subsidiary acquire ownership of a division of a firm currently producing and marketing a line of power tools. Such a purchase was available and could be obtained on a stock-exchange basis, which would minimize the need for a large amount of cash. The manufacturing facilities of this acquired plant would be transferred to Martin-Turner Tool Company.

The company to be acquired was presently engaged in the production of several private brands of tools, as well as its own brand. These private brands were produced according to purchasers' specifications and were inferior in quality and performance to Turner Tools, yet were considered satisfactory at their prices. This acquisition would give Martin-Turner a third line of power tools which could also be produced on the proposed new assembly line, using less expensive materials.

Exhibit 4 shows the estimated costs of selected Turner Tools and Chieftain Tools when produced under the projected assembly method.

Exhibit 4

PROJECTED COSTS OF SELECTED TURNER TOOLS AND CHIEFTAIN
TOOLS UNDER PROPOSED ASSEMBLY-LINE
METHOD OF PRODUCTION

ITEM	TURNER TOOLS		CHIEFTAIN TOOLS	
	Circular Saws (6")	Drills ($\frac{1}{4}$")	Circular Saws (6")	Drills ($\frac{1}{4}$")
Direct labor	$ 7.51	$ 4.73	$ 7.03	$ 4.46
Materials	9.09	8.50	8.61	7.64
Spoilage	.19	0.08	0.19	0.08
Indirect labor*	1.96	0.42	0.70	0.10
Factory overhead*	1.01	0.83	0.71	0.53
Administrative and selling expense...	.60	0.27	0.37	0.19
Total Cost	$20.36	$14.83	$17.61	$13.00
Profit	15.64	11.09	6.90	5.50
Factory Selling Price	$36.00	$25.92	$24.51	$18.50
Suggested retail price	$79.95	$59.95	$51.95	$36.95

* Includes amortization of the acquired plant; these amounts allocated between Turner Tools and Chieftain Tools on basis of projected volume of each.

QUESTIONS

1. Which of the proposed policies would you recommend? Why?
2. One of the Martin-Turner officers objected on the grounds that this was a scheme of price discrimination which was unfair to purchasers of Turner Tools. Comment.
3. Is price discrimination an effective means of contributing to profit? Explain.

CASE 9–3: NATIONWIDE AIRWAYS

At a meeting of the board of directors of Nationwide Airways on January 20, 1954, the president reported that some pronounced changes had occurred in the company's traffic pattern during the past six months. These changes were seriously affecting the company's operations.

Nationwide Airways was authorized by the Civil Aeronautics Administration to provide air transportation between New York City and Los Angeles, serving a specified number of cities en route. In addition, the line was certificated to provide service from Boston to Miami, with certain intermediate stops. Both runs provided nonstop as well as local service. To serve these routes, the company operated a fleet of 83 aircraft, composed of Convair types for local service, and DC–6 and DC–7 types for both nonstop and intermediate service.

Except for 11 aircraft which were used exclusively for air freight, all craft carried combination cargoes of passengers, express, mail, and freight. The New York–Los Angeles run was served by four other competing air lines, while three air lines in addition to Nationwide Airways provided service between New York and Miami. The competing lines did not, however, serve the same intermediate cities on these routes as did Nationwide Airways.

Throughout 1952 the company had operated with a fleet of 52 aircraft. Schedules had been set up to make the most efficient use of this equipment over the various routes. In spite of constant schedule revision the firm had been hard pressed to meet its total traffic demand, primarily because of lack of equipment. With the delivery of 31 additional aircraft during 1953, the company had added a number of flights and had overcome the traffic problem to a major extent.

Five nonstop flights were scheduled daily between New York and Los Angeles. Except on Tuesdays, Wednesdays, and Thursdays, flights departing at 8:30, 10:30, and 11:30 A.M. were always booked to capacity. Flights departing at 4:30 and 7:00 P.M. were usually booked at 60 to 90 per cent of capacity. The lowest load factor was on Tuesdays, Wednesdays, and Thursdays.

On nonstop flights between Los Angeles and New York, the 6:00 A.M. flight normally operated at 40 to 60 per cent of capacity; the 7:00 A.M. flight, at 45 to 70 per cent of capacity; the 12:00 M. and 3:00 P.M. flights, at or near full capacity; and the 7:10 P.M. flight, at about 50 per cent of capacity. On Mondays, Fridays, Saturdays, and Sundays, these flights operated at the higher capacities shown. During the remaining days of the week the lower level tended to prevail. These schedules were initially organized and filed so that incoming equipment at both terminals could be serviced and made ready for departure with a minimum investment in ground facilities and crew. When these nonstop flights were originally established, they had operated at or near capacity on all runs. Since their introduction, several competing air lines had added similar service.

In 1952, when the decline in traffic on Tuesdays, Wednesdays, and Thursdays became appreciable, the company had put into operation a family-fare plan, in an effort to increase the load factor on those days. This plan was in effect from 1:00 P.M. on Mondays through 11:00 A.M. on Thursdays. Under this arrangement, one adult member of a family (husband or wife) purchased a full-fare ticket, and the remaining adult member and all children from ages 12 through 21 purchased tickets at one half the regular fare. Children under 12 traveled at one-half fare on any day of the week. This plan had not produced the results originally estimated. Under this arrangement, many morning flights frequently operated with a load factor as low as 40 per cent.

A rearrangement of schedules to permit more flights during late morning and early afternoon was considered but was rejected for several reasons. There was objection from the Civil Aeronautics Administration as well as from civic and business organizations in the two cities served. Such a change would also necessitate an increase in the physical and staff service facilities. On the basis of costs alone, this was a major obstacle. Another difficulty was the lack of adequate airport facilities in both cities to accommodate more flights at the hours desired.

A similar load factor situation existed in the nonstop flights between Washington and Los Angeles, and between Memphis and Los Angeles. It was also noted that flights which originated in New York, Washington, and Memphis, with scheduled stops before arrival in Los Angeles, carried few through-passengers. This same condition prevailed also on flights originating in Los Angeles for Memphis, Washington, and New York with intermediate stops en route. These flights operated at an average of 70 per cent of capacity. The lapsed time of such flights from New York to Los Angeles was $4\frac{1}{2}$ hours longer than nonstop flights; from Washington to Los Angeles, $3\frac{1}{2}$ hours longer; and from Memphis, $2\frac{1}{2}$ hours longer.

Capacity of the Convair aircraft was 40 passengers. These planes were used on all flights with intermediate stops, except for two flights daily which employed a DC–6 type. The Convair flights, except on Mondays, Fridays, and Saturdays, operated at an average load factor of 60 per cent. The break-even passenger-load factor for the Convair was 60 per cent. Capacity of the DC–6 was 54 persons, and its break-even load factor was 68 per cent. The DC–7 carried 60 passengers and also had a break-even load factor of 68 per cent. The one-way, first-class fare from New York to Los Angeles was $158.85; from Washington to Los Angeles, $149.35; and from Memphis to Los Angeles, $104.95. All fares were subject to a federal tax. On all first-class flights, meals were served at appropriate hours at no extra charge.

In an attempt to correct the load factor on the nonstop flights, it was suggested that the 4:30 and 7:30 P.M. flights from New York to Los Angeles be changed to departure times of 5:30 and 9:00 P.M., respectively, and designated as air-coach flights. It was also recommended that the 6:00 A.M., 7:00 A.M., and 7:10 P.M. flights from Los

Angeles to New York be changed to air-coach flights. All air-coach flights used the same crews and equipment as first-class flights, except that no meals were served. The company currently operated three air-coach flights daily on its New York–Miami run. On such flights, DC–6 equipment was used, but it was modified by the installation of an extra row of seats, increasing capacity from 54 to 80. The change from first-class flights to air-coach flights on this run had resulted in an increase in passenger revenues.

It was also suggested that the 8:30 and 10:30 A.M. flights from New York to Los Angeles, and the 7:00 A.M. and 12:00 M. flights from Los Angeles to New York, be converted to coach flights on Tuesdays, Wednesdays, and Thursdays. This would still provide two first-class flights between these two cities.

It was proposed that the following air-coach rates be established and submitted to the Civil Aeronautics Board:

New York–Los Angeles.................$99.00
Washington–Los Angeles................ 98.00
Memphis–Los Angeles................... 78.80

In addition, it was recommended that through-passengers between these points who purchase tickets for flights with intermediate stops be granted a reduction of 20 per cent on one-way fares and 25 per cent on round trips.

If the above changes were put into effect, it was estimated that the air-coach flights would operate at an average load factor of 90 per cent. It would require some modification of the routine of equipment handling and servicing, but the maintenance department believed it could be handled with existing facilities. The installation and removal of the third row of seats for coach flights would reduce the number of pieces of stand-by equipment on Mondays and Thursdays, but recent experience had indicated that this would not seriously hamper operations, except in extreme emergency. The total additional cost of maintenance per week was estimated at $300 for each of the New York and Los Angeles terminal facilities.

QUESTIONS

1. Do you concur with the above recommendations? Why?
2. Would you propose a general price reduction for all fares instead of the proposed plan? Why?
3. Is the proposed plan a case of price discrimination? Do you think it is fair to charge one person more than another for the same service?
4. What are some of the conditions essential to successful price discrimination?

CASE 9-4: THE STEEL INDUSTRY

In April, 1948, the United States Supreme Court declared the basing-point system of pricing in the cement industry to be a form of unfair competition and therefore illegal.[27] Shortly thereafter, the steel industry abandoned the basing-point method of pricing, which it had followed for over half a century, and adopted a system of uniform f.o.b. mill pricing. Under the latter system, each seller quoted the same price to every potential or actual buyer at the seller's mill.

The basing-point system, as it had been applied in the steel industry, permitted sale only at the delivered price. This was calculated by adopting as a base price that at the basing point nearest the buyer. To this amount was added rail freight from the basing point to the place of actual delivery. This method of calculating delivered prices is shown in Exhibit 1. As the system developed prior to 1924, there was only

Exhibit 1

THE BASING-POINT METHOD: HOW THE DELIVERED PRICE IS
COMPUTED

(Most Steel Products Are Sold on a Delivered-Price Basis)

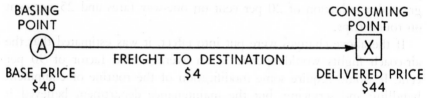

BASING
POINT

CONSUMING
POINT

Ⓐ ——————— FREIGHT TO DESTINATION ———————▶ X

BASE PRICE $4   DELIVERED PRICE
$40 $44

Source: United States Steel Corporation, *T.N.E.C. Papers* (New York, 1940), Vol. III, p. 2.

one basing point for all steel products—Pittsburgh. Under the "Pittsburgh-plus" practice, mills all over the United States calculated prices, not by reference to their own costs and shipping charges, but by reference to the single set of basing-point prices at Pittsburgh, plus rail freight from Pittsburgh to the buyer's location. When, in 1924, the Federal Trade Commission ordered certain subsidiaries of the United States Steel Corporation to "cease and desist" from this practice, the industry changed to a multiple basing-point system, in which several basing points were established for each product. With more than one basing point in existence, it became necessary for mills to calculate delivered prices by figuring rail freight from the *applicable* basing point. This was done by calculating the lowest combination of base price and freight for any given buyer.

---

[27] *F.T.C.* v. *The Cement Institute,* 333 U.S. 683 (1948).

With common delivered prices quoted to any given buyer, mills closer to the buyer gained an advantage over mills at a distance. Nonetheless, the more distant mills, by absorbing freight charges, still sold at the same delivered prices as those offered by the closer mills. The effect of freight absorption is illustrated in Exhibit 2. By absorbing freight, mills found it possible to penetrate the "natural" market territory of other mills. Under some circumstances, where the seller was

Exhibit 2

THE BASING-POINT METHOD: EXPLANATION OF FREIGHT
DISADVANTAGE AND FREIGHT ABSORPTION

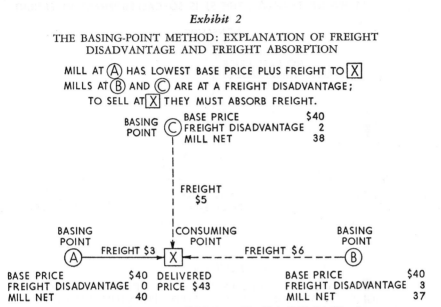

MILL AT Ⓐ HAS LOWEST BASE PRICE PLUS FREIGHT TO ☒
MILLS AT Ⓑ AND Ⓒ ARE AT A FREIGHT DISADVANTAGE;
TO SELL AT ☒ THEY MUST ABSORB FREIGHT.

Source: United States Steel Corporation, *T.N.E.C. Papers* (New York, 1940), Vol. III, p. 2.

not located at a basing point, the delivered price was higher than the combination of base price and actual freight. Exhibit 3 indicates how "phantom freight" could arise. Phantom freight also arose in some cases from the use by the seller of cheaper means of transportation than rail freight, on which delivered prices were calculated[28] (see Exhibit 4). As a result of freight absorption on some sales and the realization of phantom freight on others, steel mills experienced varying mill net prices after deduction of actual transportation costs from the delivered prices at which products were sold.

---

[28] There were, however, some circumstances when other forms of transportation, such as water shipment, were not more advantageous because (1) a barge shipment had to be much larger than a rail shipment before it could be carried economically; (2) water transport was much slower than rail; (3) handling facilities for water shipment might be lacking; (4) extra handling costs were usually incurred, both at the mill and at the destination; and (5) seasonal closure of navigation limited the availability of water transport.

358 BUSINESS ECONOMICS

Exhibit 3

THE BASING-POINT METHOD: EXPLANATION OF FIRST TYPE OF
FREIGHT ADVANTAGE AND SO-CALLED "PHANTOM FREIGHT"

MILL AT (A) HAS LOWEST BASE PRICE PLUS FREIGHT TO [X]

MILL AT (C) CHARGES THE SAME DELIVERED PRICE. HAVING A FREIGHT

ADVANTAGE OF $1 OVER (A), (C) REALIZES A MILL NET

$1 HIGHER THAN (A). THIS $1 IS SO-CALLED "PHANTOM FREIGHT"

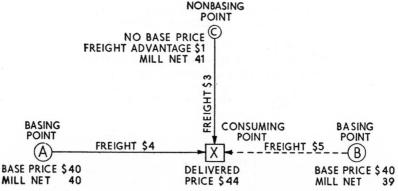

Source: United States Steel Corporation, *T.N.E.C. Papers* (New York, 1940), Vol. III, p. 6.

Exhibit 4

THE BASING-POINT METHOD: EXPLANATION OF SECOND TYPE OF
FREIGHT ADVANTAGE AND SO-CALLED "PHANTOM FREIGHT"

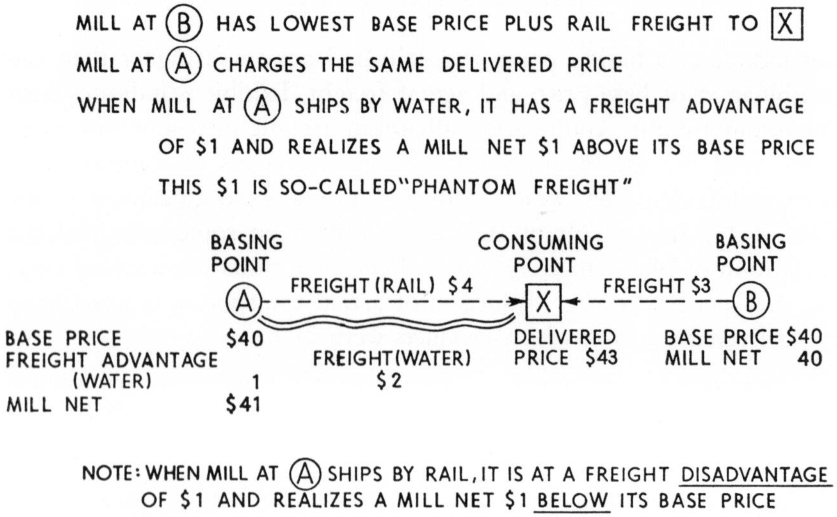

MILL AT (B) HAS LOWEST BASE PRICE PLUS RAIL FREIGHT TO [X]

MILL AT (A) CHARGES THE SAME DELIVERED PRICE

WHEN MILL AT (A) SHIPS BY WATER, IT HAS A FREIGHT ADVANTAGE

OF $1 AND REALIZES A MILL NET $1 ABOVE ITS BASE PRICE

THIS $1 IS SO-CALLED "PHANTOM FREIGHT"

NOTE: WHEN MILL AT (A) SHIPS BY RAIL, IT IS AT A FREIGHT DISADVANTAGE
OF $1 AND REALIZES A MILL NET $1 BELOW ITS BASE PRICE

Source: United States Steel Corporation, *T.N.E.C. Papers* (New York, 1940), Vol. III, p. 8.

Critics of the basing-point system asserted that it rested on agreement among members of the industry.

The basing point system of pricing steel comprises the following features: (1) leadership by United States Steel in announcing the base prices of standard products and adoption of its announcements by the other firms, (2) agreement upon the extras that are to be charged and the deductions that are to be allowed for variations in size and quality in the pricing of nonstandard products, (3) refusal by all sellers to quote prices on any but a delivered basis or to ship steel to any place other than the one where it is to be used, (4) agreement, in the case of each product, as to the cities that are to be employed as basing points, each seller, wherever located, charging freight from these points, and (5) agreement concerning the method to be used in calculating the delivery charge.[29]

. . . .

The system is thus essentially noncompetitive. When a producer makes a shipment by a cheaper method of transportation than that assumed in the computation of his price and when he makes a charge for delivery from a basing point which is farther from the buyer than is his own establishment, he collects "phantom freight." His ability to do so arises from the fact that other producers employing the cheaper means of transportation and those located closer to the buyer make no attempt to undercut his price. When he makes a charge for delivery from a basing point which is nearer to the buyer than is his own establishment, he "absorbs" freight. His ability to do this must be attributed to the fact that the whole level of prices established by the system is high. When a producer is not located at the basing point from which he quotes his prices, his "mill net realization" varies with the amount of "phantom freight" and "freight absorption" involved in different sales. This variation, again, results from the fact that distant producers do not undercut the prices which he quotes on sales made in the area adjacent to their mills, while he sets his own prices at figures which enable them to sell in the area which would otherwise belong to him. "Cross-hauling" and the "inter-penetration of market territories" show that each seller is voluntarily foregoing his competitive advantages in order to support the system as a whole. Sellers who are close to consumers do not underbid those who are far away. Sellers who are located on waterways charge an all-rail freight. Sellers whose efficiency is high ask prices which enable the less efficient to survive. Such behavior cannot be said to be competitive.[30]

Industry spokesmen, on the other hand, claimed that the delivered-price system of the steel industry was highly competitive because any seller could enter the market of any other (by absorbing freight). Interpenetration of markets, it was stated, prevented the development of local monopolies.

When the steel industry abandoned the basing-point system in favor of the uniform f.o.b. mill pricing method, steel fabricators all over

---

[29] T.N.E.C. Monograph No. 21, p. 148.

[30] *Ibid.,* p. 150.

the country, especially those distant from their steel suppliers, became greatly concerned. Much confusion attended the change. Under these circumstances, the Maryland State Planning Commission undertook to study the effects of f.o.b. mill pricing on the iron and steel industry of Maryland.[31]

By far the largest producer of iron and steel in Maryland was the Sparrows Point plant of the Bethlehem Steel Company. This plant, the second largest steel mill in the world, produced all the state's pig iron and 97 per cent of the ingots and steel for casting.

In order to determine the effects of f.o.b. mill pricing, the commission studied the market for hot-rolled sheets. In July, 1947, this product was sold through a multiple basing-point system with eleven

Exhibit 5

From:	Price per Net Ton	From:	Price per Net Ton
Pittsburgh	$65.00	Youngstown	$65.00
Chicago	65.00	Sparrows Point	65.00
Gary	65.00	Granite City	72.50
Cleveland	65.00	Middletown, Ohio	65.00
Birmingham	65.00	San Francisco, Los	
Buffalo	65.00	Angeles, Seattle	79.00

published bases. These bases, together with prices for July, 1949, were as shown in Exhibit 5. On the basis of rail freight rates and water-shipment rates as of August 1, 1949, the natural market of Sparrows Point was as indicated in Exhibit 6.[32]

The commission's report continued:

---

[31] *Survey of the Impact of F.O.B. Mill Pricing on Maryland Manufacturers* (Publication No. 61) (Baltimore, 1949), chap. v. This study investigated the effects of f.o.b. mill pricing on all classes of manufacturers in Maryland, including iron and steel producers.

[32] Example of calculation of delivered prices of hot-rolled sheets at Greensboro, North Carolina:

From:	F.O.B. Mill Price	Actual Rail Freight Cost	Delivered Price
Pittsburgh, Pa.	$65.00	$16.40	$81.40
Middletown, Ohio	65.00	14.00	79.00
Birmingham, Ala.	65.00	13.00	78.00
Sparrows Point, Md.	65.00	12.00	77.20

The delivered price at Greensboro, therefore, was $77.20, regardless of the origin of the steel. Greensboro, under a uniform f.o.b. mill price system, would be in the natural market of Sparrows Point.

Exhibit 6

SPARROWS POINT NATURAL MARKET FOR HOT-ROLLED SHEETS

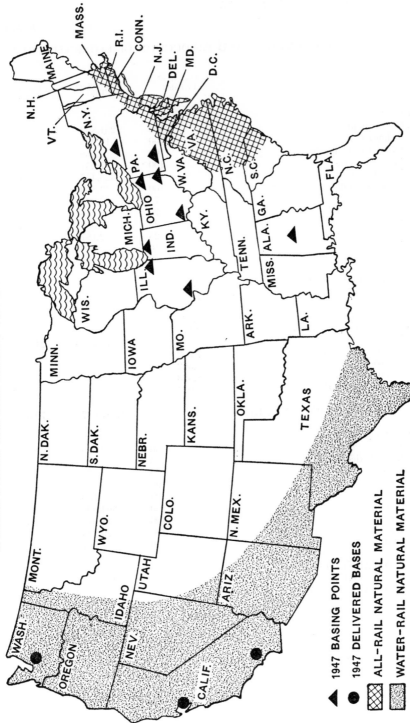

1947 BASING POINTS

● 1947 DELIVERED BASES

ALL-RAIL NATURAL MATERIAL

WATER-RAIL NATURAL MATERIAL

Reproduced by permission from Maryland State Planning Commission, *Survey of the Impact of F.O.B. Mill Pricing on Maryland Manufacturers* (Publication No. 61) (Baltimore, 1949), p. 55.

CONSUMPTION AND PRODUCTION OF HOT-ROLLED SHEETS

	Per Cent of State Included	(1) Consumption in Tons	(2) Per Cent of Total Rail-Water Market
All-rail states:			
Connecticut	100	251,832	10.72
Delaware	100	12,291	0.52
District of Columbia	100	2,488	Neg.[4]
Massachusetts	100	287,051	12.22
New Jersey	100	325,447	13.86
Rhode Island	100	23,839	1.01
Virginia[1]	75	22,394	0.95
North Carolina[1]	75	8,938	Neg.
South Carolina[1]	25	559	Neg.
New Hampshire[1]	25	2,187	Neg.
Maine[1]	10	456	Neg.
West Virginia[1]	10	4,686	Neg.
Maryland	98	146,565	6.24
100% Baltimore City	142,827		
50% Other Maryland[1]	3,738		
New York	33	227,873	9.70
100% New York City	207,101		
20% Other New York[1,2]	20,772		
Pennsylvania	57	570,431	24.29
100% Lancaster-York	47,292		
100% Philadelphia	335,562		
100% Reading	128,523		
50% Other Penn.[1,3]	59,054		
TOTAL ALL-RAIL MARKET		1,887,037	79.51
Rail-Water Market			
Texas[1]	50	49,629	2.13
New Mexico[1]	40	125	Neg.
Arizona[1]	70	2,670	Neg.
Nevada	95	99	Neg.
Idaho	20	160	Neg.
California	100	364,900	15.54
Oregon	100	14,172	.60
Washington	100	29,245	1.25
Utah	10	397	Neg.
TOTAL RAIL-WATER MARKET		461,397	19.52
TOTAL ALL-RAIL AND RAIL-WATER MARKET		2,348,434	100.00[5]

[1] Estimated from Map I.
[2] Excluding Albany, Binghamton, Elmira, Buffalo, Rochester, Syracuse, Utica, and New York City.
[3] Excluding Erie, Pittsburgh, Sharon, New Castle, as well as those listed.
[4] Neg. means less than 0.05 per cent.

Source: Report by *Iron Age* to the metalworking industry, "Steel Consumption in 1948." Reproduced *Maryland Manufacturers* (Publication No. 61) (Baltimore, 1949), p. 57.
Note: If Sparrows Point had only 60.53% of market, it would sell 1,421,420 tons, which is over 100 per

7

AND STRIP IN SPARROWS POINT NATURAL MARKET, 1948

	(3) Capacity in Tons (1948)[6]	(4) Per Cent of Total Capacity	(5) Excess Demand	(6) Excess Supply
All-rail states:				
Connecticut	150,000	6.54	101,832	
Delaware				
District of Columbia				
Massachusetts	172,000	7.50	153,447	
New Jersey	31,200	1.36		7,361
Rhode Island				
Virginia[1]				
North Carolina[1]				
South Carolina[1]				
New Hampshire[1]				
Maine[1]				
West Virginia[1]				1,241,435
Maryland	1,388,000	60.53		
100% Baltimore City				
50% Other Maryland[1]				
New York				
100% New York City				
20% Other New York[1, 2]	88,100	3.84	482,331	
Pennsylvania				
100% Lancaster-York				
100% Philadelphia				
100% Reading				
50% Other Penn.[1, 3]				
TOTAL ALL-RAIL MARKET	1,829,300	79.77	57,737	
Rail-Water Market	9,000	0.39	40,629	
Texas[1]				
New Mexico[1]				
Arizona[1]				
Nevada				
Idaho				89,830
California	454,730	19.83		
Oregon				
Washington				
Utah				
TOTAL RAIL-WATER MARKET	463,730	20.22		2,477
TOTAL ALL-RAIL AND RAIL-WATER MARKET	2,293,030	100.00[7]	55,260	

[5] Negligible difference, 0.97 per cent of total.
[6] Taken from *Directory of Iron and Steel Works of the United States and Canada* (1948).
[7] Figures will not necessarily total 100% because of rounding.

by permission from Maryland State Planning Commission, *Survey of the Impact of F.O.B. Mill Pricing on*

cent of capacity.

Exhibit

1948 MARKETS UNDER F.O.B. AND BASING-POINT SYSTEM

	(1) Total Consumption 1948	(2) Per Cent Received from East Pennsylvania and Delaware	(3) Tons Received from East Pennsylvania and Delaware	(4) Per Cent Received from Baltimore	(5) Tons Received from Baltimore
Maine	4,557	2.5	114	11.0	501
New Hampshire	8,749	. . . .	. . . .	0.2	17
Vermont	8,447			3.5	296
Massachusetts	287,051	5.2	14,927	4.9	14,066
Rhode Island	23,839	0.2	48	8.0	1,907
Connecticut	251,832	0.9	2,266	2.3	5,792
New Jersey	325,447	0.8	2,604	37.6	122,368
New York	681,742	0.7	4,770	13.7	93,361
Pennsylvania	997,057	0.9	8,974	22.9	228,326
West Virginia	46,859	Neg.*		0.3	141
Delaware	12,291	29.8	3,663	16.6	2,040
Maryland	150,304	5.5	8,267	34.5	51,855
District of Columbia	2,488			15.5	386
Virginia	29,859	0.9	269	20.4	6,091
Ohio	1,383,791	Neg.		0.1	1,384
Kentucky	77,224			0.4	309
Indiana	708,255			Neg.	
Illinois	1,090,245			0.2	2,180
Michigan	1,967,594			Neg.	
Wisconsin	803,297			0.1	803
Missouri	198,432				
Iowa	129,149			0.1	1,292
Minnesota	82,289			0.1	823
Kansas	25,028			0.4	100
Nebraska	29,828			0.1	298
South Dakota	2,266				
North Dakota	802				
Montana	1,153				
Idaho	802			27.1	217
Wyoming	339				
Colorado	14,905				
Alabama	54,380				
Georgia	47,854	0.4	191	7.1	3,398
Florida	18,000	3.1	558	5.5	990
Mississippi	2,521			1.8	45
North Carolina	11,918	0.5	60	4.3	512
South Carolina	2,235			1.2	27
Tennessee	63,538	Neg.		0.2	127
Arkansas	3,369				
Oklahoma	19,775			0.1	20
Louisiana	32,790			2.1	689
Texas	99,257	0.2	198	11.7	11,613
New Mexico	312				
Utah	3,969			5.5	183
Nevada	104			4.4	5
Washington	29,245	6.0	1,755	46.8	13,687
Oregon	14,172	2.1	298	35.7	5,059
California	364,900	0.5	1,824	39.0	142,311
Arizona	3,814	11.9	454	8.3	317
Total	10,118,074	0.3	51,240	7.2	713,536

* Neg. means less than 0.05%.

Sources: Report by *Iron Age* to the metalworking industry, "Steel Consumption in 1948." (81st Congress, Senate Report No. 44.) *Changes in Distribution of Steel 1940–47*, 1949, Table 6, pp. 27–28. Reproduced

8

ASSUMING DISTRIBUTION PROPORTIONAL TO 1938

	(6) Per Cent Received from West Coast	(7) Tons Received from West Coast	(8) Natural Market (Tons)	(9) If Changed to F.O.B. Mill Pricing Gain (Tons)	(10) If Changed to F.O.B. Mill Pricing Loss (Tons)
Maine................	....	....	456		159
New Hampshire.....	....	....	2,187	2,170	
Vermont............					296
Massachusetts......			287,051	258,058	
Rhode Island........			23,839	21,884	
Connecticut.........			251,832	243,774	
New Jersey.........			325,447	200,475	
New York..........			227,873	129,742	
Pennsylvania.......			570,431	333,131	
West Virginia.......			4,686	4,545	
Delaware...........			12,291	6,588	
Maryland...........			146,565	86,443	
District of Columbia..			2,488	2,102	
Virginia............			22,394	16,034	
Ohio...............					1,384
Kentucky...........					309
Indiana.............					
Illinois.............					2,180
Michigan...........					
Wisconsin...........					803
Missouri............					
Iowa...............					1,292
Minnesota..........					823
Kansas.............					100
Nebraska...........					298
South Dakota.......					
North Dakota.......					
Montana............					
Idaho..............	16.3	131	160		188
Wyoming...........					
Colorado............					
Alabama............					
Georgia.............					3,589
Florida.............					1,548
Mississippi.........					45
North Carolina......			8,938	8,366	
South Carolina......			558	531	
Tennessee...........					127
Arkansas...........					
Oklahoma..........					20
Louisiana...........					689
Texas..............	Neg.		49,629	37,818	
New Mexico.........			125	125	
Utah...............	11.5	456	397		242
Nevada.............	84.2	88	99	6	
Washington.........	28.9	8,452	29,245	5,351	
Oregon.............	27.5	3,897	14,172	4,918	
California..........	35.2	128,445	364,900	92,320	
Arizona............	19.1	728	2,670	1,171	
Total..........	1.8	142,197	2,348,433	1,455,552	14,092
				NET GAIN 1,441,460	

by permission, from Maryland State Planning Commission, *Survey of the Impact of F.O.B. Mill Pricing on Maryland Manufacturers* (Publication No. 61) (Baltimore, 1949), p. 60.

What are the implications of this natural market? Is the Sparrows Point plant, as well as other Maryland producers, in a favorable position? That is, will she gain or lose sales by being limited to the Sparrows Point natural market? Exhibit 7 describes the natural market for Sparrows Point, assuming prices of July, 1949, and bases of 1947. Column (1) lists the estimated consumption by the metalworking industry for each state wholly or partly inside the natural market for hot-rolled sheets. The consumption figures were calculated on a 1948 basis, and in some instances were estimated percentages of a state's total consumption. If the figures included all consumption they would be approximately 30% higher, but they include only the consumption by metalworking industries. The total consumption for the United States of finished steel products was about 66 million tons in 1948. The metalworking industry consumed about 46 million tons.

Column (2) gives the percentage of the total rail-water natural market consumption for each district. Pennsylvania is the largest consumer on the East Coast, while California is the big purchaser on the West Coast.

Column (3) shows the rated capacity for each competing district. Column (4) lists the percentage of the total market capacity each district represents. Note that the Sparrows Point capacity is over 60% of the total. Columns (5) and (6) show the excess demand or supply for each producing area assuming production at 100% capacity. Maryland is shown to have an excess supply of 1¼ million tons. Consequently it must sell the larger proportion of its production outside Maryland.

Now if the assumption is made that all competitors of Sparrows Point, located inside the natural market, produce at 100% capacity, and sell all they produce, Sparrows Point could still sell over 100% of its rated capacity, as shown in Exhibit 7. Obviously, using these assumptions, Sparrows Point will be very favorably affected, as far as hot-rolled sheets are concerned, by a shift to f.o.b. mill pricing. It could sell all it could produce, and even expand existing capacity without suffering from unused plant capacity.

. . . .

Under a basing-point system what would sales be for Maryland's steel industry? Unfortunately, sufficient information was not obtainable to make our discussion more realistic. However, some past results may be used to draw tentative conclusions.

First, assume consumption in the metalworking industry in various states as of 1948. Second, assume that sales under a continuing basing-point system would be made more or less in proportion to the 1938 distribution. For example, in 1938 Baltimore supplied Massachusetts with 4.9% of Massachusetts purchases. Now, if proportional distribution is assumed, Baltimore would, under a continuing basing-point system, still supply Massachusetts with 4.9% of her purchases. In 1948 Massachusetts consumed 287,051 tons of hot-rolled sheets and strip. Consequently it is assumed that under a basing-point system Maryland would supply this state with 4.9% of 287,051, or 14,066 tons. Now, by calculating in a similar fashion for each state, Baltimore's total sales to the metalworking industry under a basing-point system may be calculated. It should be remembered that these estimates may be fairly close, for under a continuing basing-point system steel mills would tend to retain old customers except during peak years of production or during war periods. There would of course be changes in distribution in a growing economy because of new customers entering the steel market.

Now examine Exhibit 8. Column (1) contains the consumption figures in the metalworking industry for various states in 1948. Column (2) lists the percentage of sales to each state by Eastern Pennsylvania and Delaware mills. Column (3) is the actual sales made by Eastern Pennsylvania and Delaware firms using our assumption. This as calculated by multiplying columns (1) and (2).

Column (4) gives the percentage of sales made by Baltimore firms to various consuming districts, and column (5) shows the sales in tons (column (1) times column (4)). Columns (6) and (7) are the percentage and actual sales by West Coast firms under our assumptions.

Column (8) is the natural market sales taken from Exhibit 7. Columns (9) and (10) show the change in sales that result if there were a shift from the basing-point system to a system of uniform f.o.b. mill pricing, with all previous base prices becoming f.o.b. mill prices, i.e., without increases of Baltimore prices or decreases of f.o.b. prices of competing mills.

The results are amazing. Under a basing-point system mills in the Sparrows Point natural market area could sell 906,973 tons of hot-rolled sheets and strip to the metalworking industry, while under an f.o.b. mill system sales would be 2,348,434. This would represent a 1,441,460-ton gain in sales.

If the limiting assumptions are removed, the results might be different. Nonetheless, as far as hot-rolled sheets are concerned, Maryland stands to be in a far better competitive position under f.o.b. mill pricing in the steel industry.[33]

QUESTIONS

1. How do you account for the expansion of the Sparrows Point market under f.o.b. mill pricing?
2. Would the expansion of the Sparrows Point market have been the same if, instead of the adoption of an f.o.b. pricing system, the multiple basing-point system had been retained and Sparrows Point had been made a basing point?
3. In view of the expansion of the Sparrows Point market under f.o.b. mill pricing, does it appear that the previous policy of basing-point pricing was unsound *from the standpoint of the industry?*
4. Against what customers did the basing-point system in steel discriminate? What were the probable effects of basing-point pricing on plant location?

[33] *Survey of the Impact of F.O.B. Mill Pricing on Maryland Manufacturers,* pp. 54–61.

Chapter 10

~~~~~~

EMPLOYMENT OF MEN
AND MACHINES

IN EARLIER chapters the relations between price and cost were described for both the short run and the long run. The description ran in terms of the output of products; for example, the optimum short-run rate of output requires that marginal cost of production be equated with the marginal revenue from the sale of this output. The firm must, of course, hire inputs in order to produce outputs. Once the appropriate rate of output has been determined, management's task can be considered to be that of minimizing the total cost of inputs required to turn out this volume of product. This requires, among other things, using the most efficient available production processes and using labor, executives, and capital in the best proportions. Actually, decisions as to what outputs to produce and what inputs to hire are not independent of one another. A decision to build a plant of a particular size implies an expectation of turning out the product within its economical output range, and a decision to step up the rate of production carries with it a decision to acquire the necessary additional inputs. It is useful analytically, however, to concentrate attention at any one time on either output or input. The latter will be examined in the present chapter. Separate attention will be devoted to the employment of labor, executives, and capital equipment; but exhaustive treatment cannot, of course, be given to this broad area of economic theory. Rather, emphasis will be on some of the fundamentals of the problem.

Marginal Productivity of Labor

In the short run the capital equipment of the firm and the executive staff can be considered to be fixed, but the number of workers hired and the quantity of materials and supplies utilized are subject to variation by the firm. Additional output requires that an increased amount of these variable factors be applied to a fixed quantity of "plant."

In Exhibit 1 the total number of units of a product which would result from the employment of successive workers in a small hypothetical plant is shown in Column 2. Outputs and inputs should be considered to pertain to some specified time period. This is assumed to be one month. Column 3 shows the "marginal product" of labor per month—the additional physical product secured by the employment of an additional worker for that length of time. Column 3 is, therefore, derived by finding the difference between successive total outputs. This process is known as "imputation." The only way to measure the importance of one man to the firm is to observe how much total output would be diminished if he were not employed—or how much total output is increased because he is employed. Since the amount of capital

Exhibit 1

MARGINAL PRODUCTIVITY OF LABOR IN A
HYPOTHETICAL PLANT

(1) Labor Input per Month	(2) Total Output per Month	(3) Marginal Product	(4) Price per Unit	(5) Value of Marginal Product
1.	25	25	$10	$250
2.	53	28	10	280
3.	84	31	10	310
4.	118	34	10	340
5.	155	37	10	370
6.	191	36	10	360
7.	226	35	10	350
8.	259	33	10	330
9.	285	26	10	260
10.	305	20	10	200

utilized is held constant, the output changes can be attributed to labor alone.

The firm is assumed to be able to sell any output at a price of $10 per unit. This would occur if the company were too small to affect the price by its own output—that is, if the firm sold in a purely competitive market.[1] If the firm is considered to be in some line of manufacturing, it would need additional materials, supplies, fuel, etc., as well as additional labor, in order to increase the rate of output. The additional cost of these ancillary inputs could be deducted in each row from Column 5 in order to arrive at a net value of the marginal product of labor.[2] For the sake of simplicity, however, it is

---

[1] If the firm were a monopolistic seller of the commodity, the price at which the product could be disposed of would be lower for higher rates of output. The additional revenue imputable to labor is then derived by multiplying each total output by the price at which it will sell, and finding the increments in total revenue as workers are added. The same method could be used for the purely competitive firm instead of the slightly different calculation involved in Exhibit 1.

[2] Alternatively, the "capital" factor which is held constant can be considered to include the "working capital" necessary for maintaining the needed inventories of materials and supplies. Viewed in this way, no deduction for materials and supplies is necessary.

assumed in Exhibit 1 that there are only two required inputs—labor and fixed capital.

Under these assumptions, how many workers should the firm hire? This depends on the monthly wage rate which it must pay. Suppose the prevailing wage is $355 per month. The firm should then hire six workers. The sixth man employed would add $360 to the monthly value of the firm's output, whereas he would receive $355 in wages. Consequently, it is worth while for the firm to hire six men but not a seventh, since the additional product of a seventh man would be only $350. (He would have to be paid $355.) It may be difficult, of course, for management to compute the marginal productivity of labor precisely; but somehow, a decision must be made as to how many workers to employ, and the comparison of the marginal productivity of labor and the wage rate indicates a correct approach.

The general rule is that workers should be hired by the firm (which is assumed to be a competitor both in the sale of output and in the hiring of labor) until the value of the marginal product of labor is equal to the wage rate which must be paid. This equalization must take place in the region of diminishing, rather than increasing, value of the marginal product; otherwise, additional men could be hired who would add more to income than to cost. A separate calculation must, of course, be made for each type of labor hired. In Exhibit 1 (as in any table), it was necessary to proceed by finite steps, and this prevented an exact equalization of the value of the marginal product and the wage rate.[3]

If labor inputs are considered to be perfectly divisible, rather than coming in "lumps," a smooth marginal productivity curve can be drawn for labor, as in Exhibit 2. This curve tacitly assumes that the plant is indivisible, because there is a stage of increasing marginal returns as the input of labor is increased to OA units. That is, a better combination of labor and capital is obtained as labor input is increased up to this point. If the plant were highly divisible, utilizing many small, independent machines, it would be possible to secure even at low labor inputs the combination of labor and capital which would maximize the value of the marginal product of labor. This would be done simply by not utilizing many of the machines. Exhibit 2 is based on the assumption that plant is indivisible but adaptable to different

---

[3] This is true unless the wage rate happens to be exactly equal to one of the values of the marginal product. In that case, it would not matter whether or not the last man was hired. If the wage rate were $350 per month, for example, it would not make any difference to profits whether six or seven men were hired.

labor inputs. It also assumes that labor is perfectly divisible; otherwise, the marginal productivity curve would not be continuous. It should be noted that these concepts are the same as those discussed in Chapter 4 in connection with short-run cost of production.[4] A U-shaped marginal cost curve exists when the marginal productivity curve for the variable input has the inverted U-shape shown in Exhibit 2.

If the prevailing wage rate is assumed to be OW, the firm will find it profitable to hire OX units of labor. If it stopped short of this input,

Exhibit 2

MARGINAL PRODUCT OF LABOR—INDIVISIBLE BUT ADAPTABLE PLANT

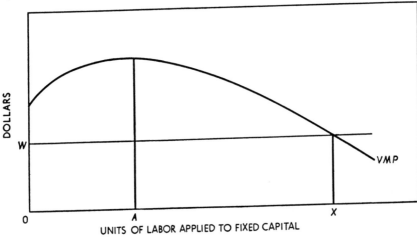

the number of workers would not be optimal, because additional men could be hired whose product would bring in more revenue than they would be paid. If more than OX men were hired, employment would be nonoptimal, because some men would add less to the firm's revenue than they were being paid.

It was pointed out in Chapter 4 that marginal cost curves in manufacturing are frequently horizontal over a wide range of output. On the input side, this means that the curve showing the value of the marginal product is horizontal over the corresponding range. This occurs when the plant is divisible but not adaptable. That is, the plant may have many independent machines, each of which requires a fixed complement of labor for its operation. (A trucking firm with a large number of trucks, each requiring one driver, is an example.) In this

[4] The concept of adaptability is explained in detail by George J. Stigler, *The Theory of Price* (New York: Macmillan Co., 1949), p. 122.

case, each unit of labor is combined with a definite additional amount of capital and adds the same amount to the product of the firm as the preceding and succeeding units of labor.

Exhibit 3 illustrates this case, the *VMP* curve being horizontal up to labor input *OA;* immediately after that input, it falls to zero, since the full capacity of the plant is assumed to have been reached. (Additional truck drivers would have no trucks to drive, and hence would not bring in additional revenue.) In this case the number of workers employed in the short run would be independent of the prevailing

Exhibit 3

MARGINAL PRODUCT OF LABOR—DIVISIBLE BUT UNADAPTABLE PLANT

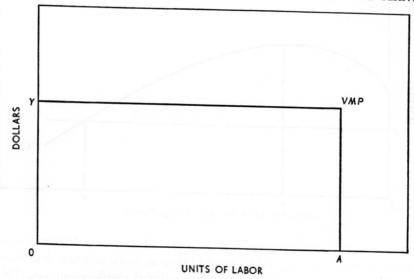

wage rate, so long as the wage rate did not exceed *OY*. (Once the trucking firm had purchased the trucks, it would probably employ the same number of drivers even if the drivers secured a substantial wage boost through union negotiations.) If, however, the wage rate rose to such a level that the typical firm could not secure a normal rate of return on its investment in capital goods, there would be a tendency for capital to be withdrawn from this industry and invested elsewhere.[5]

---

[5] The total return to the firm is represented by the area under the *VMP* curve out to the optimum input of the variable factor. The total income left to remunerate the owners of capital is that part of the total area which lies above the line drawn in at the prevailing wage. If this area is too small, capital will not receive a normal return. If the prevailing wage is above the *VMP* curve, it would be cheaper to shut down the plant than to operate. This is equivalent to saying that the firm should shut down if it cannot cover even its variable costs.

A plant may be both indivisible and unadaptable, and this makes the marginal productivity of labor quite different from the curves of either Exhibit 1 or Exhibit 2. This situation might exist if the plant contained a single assembly line, with each station requiring a definite complement of labor for its operation. Since every operation depends on the previous ones, there is no output at all until the employment of labor is sufficient to man all stations, but further labor input would not add to the product. The value of the marginal product of labor would then be a single point rather than a curve. This point would also

Exhibit 4

MARGINAL PRODUCT EQUALS TOTAL PRODUCT—INDIVISIBLE AND
UNADAPTABLE PLANT

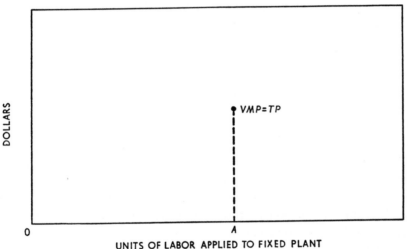

represent the total product, since the addition of the last essential man brings forth the entire product, and the withdrawal of any one man would eliminate the entire product. Exhibit 4 shows this marginal productivity "curve" for labor.

In this case the firm should employ OA workers as long as the wage rate does not exceed the average product of labor. (Average product would equal the vertical value of the single point on the chart divided by its horizontal value.) If the wage rate were any higher, it would be cheaper to shut down the plant, since the wage bill would more than exhaust the total product. If the prevailing wage is less than the average product of labor, there will be some income to apply against the fixed costs. Whether or not a "profit" (in the economic sense) is earned depends on whether the return to capital exceeds or falls short of a "normal" return.

It can be seen from the foregoing analysis that the probable reaction of a firm to a change in the prevailing competitive wage rate or to a union demand for higher pay may depend a great deal on the technical conditions of production and on the nature of the demand for its output. If plant capacity is highly divisible but unadaptable (Exhibit 3) and the firm in question sells its output competitively, an increase in the wage rate will not cause it to lay off labor unless the wage rate becomes so high as to make it undesirable to operate at all. This would not be the case if its output were sold monopolistically, however, because a negative slope would be imparted to the marginal revenue productivity of labor by the need to cut price as the output rate expands. In this case an increase in the wage rate would occasion a decrease in employment, but the divisibility and unadaptability of plant would tend to reduce the extent of the layoffs.

If plant capacity is indivisible and unadaptable (Exhibit 4), an increase in the wage rate will again not affect the number of workers employed (it is still necessary to man all of the stations along the assembly line)—unless it becomes necessary to shut down entirely. On the other hand, if plant is adaptable to various numbers of workers (Exhibit 2), an increase in wages tends to reduce the number of workers hired. An example of this situation is a department store, where it is possible to vary the number of employees within certain limits and still operate effectively.

It should be recognized clearly that the above analysis is of a "short-run" nature. In the longer run, it is generally possible to substitute capital for labor to some extent if this is made desirable from management's point of view by an increase in the wage rate which must be paid. That is, the long-run demand curve of the firm for labor is generally downsloping, so that a given volume of output will be produced by more laborsaving methods at higher wage rates. If demand for a product is increasing, however, there may be no absolute decrease in employment even if more capital-using processes are introduced. It should also be noted that new inventions can make the substitution of capital for labor profitable even when there is no change in the wage rate.

Productivity of Executives

The classical economists (who held sway mainly in the first half of the nineteenth century) considered the entrepreneur to be at once the owner and the manager of the firm. While they discussed the determination of wages and profits (the latter including interest as well as what is now termed "economic profit"), they did not see a need to develop a separate theory of executive remuneration. Although the separation of ownership and management through the device of the corporation was increasingly recognized in the latter half of the century—especially by Thorstein Veblen—little theorizing has been done on the subject.[6] In the modern corporation the hired executives are usually substantial stockholders but seldom own a controlling interest. The great mass of stockholders take little or no interest in management except, on occasion, to sign and mail back a proxy request sent out by the hired officers in actual charge of corporate affairs.

One difficulty inherent in measuring the marginal revenue productivity of labor to the firm is the lack of homogeneity of this factor of production. The firm may hire many different types of labor, and the measurement must be made separately for each variety. Measuring the marginal productivity of executives is obviously even more difficult. Different executives have unlike duties as a matter of policy and are apt to differ greatly in type of education and experience. Their basic function is decision making in the face of uncertainties of many kinds, and the quality of their judgment greatly affects the prosperity of the firm.[7] However, even when viewed historically, the quality of executive decisions is difficult to assess. The company may have prospered, may have declined, or may have been about an average performer; but it is usually hard to know just how this performance was related to the particular decisions which were made. If a firm possesses a good deal of monopoly power, it may prosper with only fair management, whereas management may have to be extremely capable to cause the firm to do well in the more competitive areas of the economy.

---

[6] A recent exception is David R. Roberts, "A General Theory of Executive Compensation Based on Statistically Tested Propositions," *Quarterly Journal of Economics,* May, 1956, p. 270.

[7] Perrin Stryker, "Who Is an Executive?" *Fortune,* December, 1955, p. 108, lists five basic functions of the executive, based on a survey of the opinions of executives themselves: (1) He directly helps to set his company's objectives and over-all policies; (2) he is required to make or approve decisions that significantly affect profits and future plans; (3) he co-ordinates several major corporate functions, or those of a major division or department; (4) he maintains and develops an organization of trained subordinates to achieve the company's objectives; and (5) he delegates responsibility and authority to the organization, and controls performance and results through at least one level of supervision. Of these, the first two are clearly decision making. To the extent that the last three are not merely routine matters of communication and record keeping, they too involve the making of decisions (e.g., deciding how much authority should be delegated to subordinates).

The hiring of an executive obviously presents an even greater problem than assessment of his past performance, since it is necessary to anticipate in some rough way what the quality of his actions will be in the inscrutable future. Most executives are brought up through the ranks rather than being hired after they are already recognized as experienced and competent managers. This places on personnel officers the difficult job of trying to assess the executive potential of college graduates.

It is possible to define in marginal productivity terms the upper limit to the amount which a firm will theoretically pay an executive. Since his job is to produce profits for the firm by making decisions of high quality, the maximum which he will be paid can be stated in terms of profit differentials. That is, the executive's marginal revenue productivity is the excess of the firm's total profit under his direction over the total profit which would have been earned under the best alternative executive plus the amount which would have been necessary to secure the latter's services.[8] Suppose it is estimated that under Mr. X the corporation can earn $5 million a year, while under the presidency of Mr. Y, it could earn $50,000 less. The maximum which the firm could afford to pay Mr. X would be $50,000 plus the salary necessary to attract Mr. Y—say, $40,000 a year. (Mr. X thus is worth a maximum of $90,000 a year, which can be called his marginal revenue productivity.) While some sort of calculation of this sort is essential to good management—lest executive compensation get completely out of line with its worth—the difficulties inherent in making the necessary estimates are quite obvious. It is difficult to know how much it would take to hire Mr. Y away from his present employer, especially since most executives are not mobile.[9] It is even more difficult to know that Mr. X's decision-making capacity is such as to bring in $50,000 more in profits than could have been garnered by Mr. Y. Since no one else is really trained to do Mr. X's job (except, perhaps, his assistant), the concept of the next best alternative executive is a vague one.

Actually, those who determine the compensation of an executive are often motivated by considerations other than maximizing the profits of the firm. The executive at the top may raise the pay of subordinate officers in order to make his own compensation appear to be in need of a boost. Or executives as a closely knit group may be in a

[8] Roberts, op. cit., p. 290. He found size of firm to be the most important determinant of the income of the top executive officer.

[9] According to Roberts, ibid., p. 291, 87 per cent of the sample of 500 executives studied worked for only one employer after becoming corporate officers.

position to exact a sort of monopoly tribute from stockholders by paying all executives unnecessarily large salaries. This is less likely to happen if there are important and active stockholders who are not themselves in managerial positions.

The importance of securing competent executive decisions clearly increases with the size of the firm. The officials of a large firm may, through incompetence, inflict losses on a larger group of stockholders than equally incompetent executives of a small firm. Or the former may, if capable, bring large dividends and/or capital gains to a larger body of stockholders. The number of executives per dollar of sales tends to decrease as the company increases its size.[10] Thus, the financial importance of managerial decisions relating to prices, products, advertising, etc., increases with firm size. Similarly, the importance of investment decisions increases with the size of the firm, and it is appropriate that executive salaries also increase with firm size.

The Remarriage of Ownership and Management

Although, historically, the corporation has been the device by which management has been separated from ownership, there has been a tendency to bring the two partially together again by means of compensating executives in part by granting them stock options. Such options give the right to buy a specified total of the corporation's stock at a specified price during a specified period of years. If the stock rises in market price, the holder can still purchase it at the price stated in the option. If it falls in price, he will not exercise the option. Thus, the executive is given the possibility of securing a large speculative return without risk to himself (unless he chooses to hold the stock after buying it, in which case a capital loss might result from a sufficient price decline). In the event of a profit on a stock option deal, the compensation is better than straight salary from the executive's point of view because it is taxed only at the capital gains rate, meaning a maximum of 25 per cent if the gain qualifies as "long term." A much higher income tax rate applies to straight salary income received by key executives.

The stock option device of compensating executives tends to improve the efficiency of such employees. Not only does an executive have the

---

[10] Arch Patton, "Current Practices in Executive Compensation," *Harvard Business Review,* Vol. XXIX, January, 1951, p. 62, states that, in a sample of firms studied, the number of executives per $1 million of profit varied from 10.3 for firms earning less than $2 million per year to 1.5 for those earning over $7 million per year. Since profits and sales are positively correlated, the same sort of relationship could be found for executives per dollar of sales.

prospect of a higher salary if his work is of high quality, but he can also help himself obtain a greater capital gain by being efficient. Management and ownership tend to be rejoined to a degree. Similarly, some corporations have stock purchase plans for all employees, based on the theory that workers will be more loyal and more efficient if they participate in company ownership. These plans are quite different from stock option plans for executives, however, in that the workers pay for securities out of their regular wages or salaries. They are often alike, however, in that the specified purchase price is below the market price which prevails when the plan is established.[11]

As already mentioned, the turnover of key executives is very low. Fringe benefits of various kinds are an aid in keeping down turnover at the top. For example, retirement programs are often so liberal that the executive is very reluctant to change companies after building up a substantial stake in one firm's retirement system. Some contracts have provisions for the executive to remain on salary as a consultant after 65 or other retirement age. Similarly, life insurance contracts of impressive size, some of which pledge a lifetime income to the wife, constitute an important fringe benefit and a detriment to executive mobility.

Executive compensation plans are usually based not only on reducing the temptation of the key man to leave the company, but also on reducing his personal income tax liability. As already mentioned, this is partly responsible for the popularity of stock option plans. Since the federal income tax is not really a tax on all income but only on money income, any device to give the executive benefits in nonpecuniary form or to substitute long-term capital gains for direct payment is likely to be seriously considered. Expense accounts which permit him to indulge in expensive entertaining and travel for the company usually bring him a great deal of untaxed satisfaction. Country club memberships, health examinations and programs, and vacations at company-owned resorts contribute to real income. Spreading out money income more evenly over the lifetime of the executive also reduces his lifetime income tax liability. This is an important reason for the popularity of deferred bonus arrangements in which a company votes an officer a bonus payable over a number of years rather than all at once. Also, the income tax favors the establishment of retirement

---

[11] Stock purchase plans for employees are popular in a rising stock market but can bring discontent in the event of a sustained downturn in security prices. In that event, employees would be paying more than the market price. If the company adjusts the purchase price to bring it below the new market price, there will be grumbles from those employees who paid the higher price. Stock option plans avoid this risk, since the options need not be exercised if they are unprofitable.

systems, so that the executive need not save out of his salary the bulk of the funds which he will require after retirement. It should be noted, however, that income tax savings from this source can be largely or wholly lost to the executive in the long run if sufficient price inflation occurs. The real income loss due to inflation can exceed the real income gain due to the spreading-out of income over time.

Nature of Capital Equipment

When an executive is hired, his worth—in the sense of his marginal revenue productivity to the firm—is difficult to anticipate. This is less true of a piece of capital equipment, since technical performance specifications are apt to be quite dependable. However, decisions regarding the purchases of equipment are among the more difficult ones which management must make. This is because a machine represents a stock of productive services which will be utilized over a considerable period of time, usually many years, but which must be contracted for at a specific price at the time of purchase. This long-time commitment can sometimes be avoided by renting the equipment, but careful calculation is required in order to make a wise decision as to whether it is more economical to buy or to rent. While the *volume* of services which will be forthcoming from a given piece of equipment is usually quite predictable, the *value* of those services is more uncertain, since this depends on the price of the product turned out by the machine. Output prices may change a great deal over the life of the equipment, and such changes may, of course, be unfavorable in direction. The invention of an improved machine to do the same sort of job is a particular hazard, since this can quickly lower the value of output by cutting competitors' costs of producing the same product and permitting them to lower their selling prices. Decisions in this field are hard to make, at best; but they are more likely to be correct if use is made of the relevant theory, since this pinpoints some of the basic considerations which should not be neglected.

Capitalization

The concept of capitalization is extremely important to the calculations which enter into a rational decision with respect to the purchase of any capital good. Capitalization is the mathematical process of finding the present value of a future stream of income. The calculation is simplest if this income stream is one without end—an income in perpetuity. Suppose a public-utility company has paid a dividend of $5.00 per year per share on its common stock for many years, and will—so far as can be seen—continue to do so indefinitely. The market price of the stock should then depend almost entirely on the interest rate which is considered appropriate for this sort of investment.[12] (This percentage yield will be lower than on most stocks, because of the relatively low risk of loss of interest or principal due to the stable nature of the company.) Suppose that the appropriate interest rate is 5 per cent per year. The stock would then sell at about $100 per share. This is determined by the capitalization formula for a perpetual income, where V is the present value of a share, I is the anticipated

$$V = \frac{I}{r}$$

yearly income from a share, and r is the market interest rate on investments of this quality. The formula is appropriate only if no change is anticipated in either I or r. Suppose that I is expected to remain at $5.00 per year, but that most buyers anticipate that interest rates in general will rise slightly in the near future. They would then be unwilling to pay quite as much as $100 per share, since they believe that, by waiting awhile, they can secure a little more than $5.00 a year on $100 invested in a security of this grade (or even in this same security). On the other hand, if there is a general expectation of a *decline* in interest rates, the stock should now sell at a little more than $100 a share. This simple capitalization formula is also applicable to evaluation of a piece of land which is expected to yield a steady and perpetual income above taxes and all other costs. For example, the value of a piece of city land recently rented on a 99-year lease to a dependable firm which pays the owner a yearly rental of $10,000 would be $200,000 if, again, 5 per cent were considered the appropriate rate of interest on such an investment. If the land changed hands at this price, the new buyer would, of course, receive a 5 per cent return on his investment of $200,000, since this is just another view of the same problem.

The capitalization calculation is somewhat more complicated when the income will be received only for a finite number of years instead of in perpetuity. Income received today is more valuable than the same amount of income received a year from now because, if it is received today, it can begin immediately to earn interest for the owner. Therefore, its additional worth is just the amount of interest which it will

---

[12] The market price is also affected by the number of dividends paid per year and by brokerage fees and transfer taxes, but these will have a relatively minor effect on market price and are disregarded for purposes of simplification.

earn in a year. By the same token, income which is still a year away must be discounted—a year's interest must be taken away—in order to find its present value. If the income is more than a year away, it must be discounted more heavily.

Suppose that a merchant has a claim to three $1,000 payments which are due to him one year, two years, and three years from today, respectively. He may wish to sell this claim in order to secure all of the cash immediately (from someone else who will look upon the claim as a suitable investment). The amount for which he can sell the claim depends on the risk which is deemed by potential buyers to be associated with the claim—that is, by the apparent degree of danger of non-payment or slow payment of an installment when due.

The present value of this claim can be found from the formula:

$$V = \frac{1,000}{1+r} + \frac{1,000}{(1+r)^2} + \frac{1,000}{(1+r)^3}.$$

This formula discounts each successive payment more heavily. The first payment is now worth the sum which will build up to $1,000 in one year, without compounding the interest. The second payment is now worth the sum which will build up to $1,000 in two years, with interest compounded at the end of the first year; while the third payment is now worth the amount which would build up to $1,000 in three years if compounded at the end of the first and second years. Suppose r is 6 per cent. The first $1,000 installment is now worth $943.40, the second installment is worth $890.00, and the third is worth $839.62. The entire claim is worth the sum of these amounts, or $2,673.02. This worth would, of course, be greater if the relevant interest rate were deemed to be less than 6 per cent, and it would be lower if a higher discount rate were used.

The same sort of calculation is involved in finding the present value of a machine. In this case the annual income is the "quasi rent"[13] derived from its productive contribution. Annual quasi rent is found by deducting from the value of the annual product of the machine all variable costs (labor, materials, fuel, etc.) incurred in the same process. No deduction is made, however, for depreciation on the machine or for interest on its cost.

Suppose a machine has three years of productive life remaining and that, at the end of that time, it will have no scrap value. Assume

---

[13] This name was given by Alfred Marshall to the "income derived from machines or other appliances for production made by man" (*Principles of Economics* [8th ed.; London: Macmillan & Co., Ltd., 1930], p. 74).

also that (like an electric light bulb or, perhaps, a TV picture tube) it gives satisfactory service until it expires, rather than gradually running down or requiring ever-increasing maintenance expenditures. If the product turned out by the machine is worth $4,000 a year and variable expenses of $3,000 a year are incurred in its operation, the machine has a present value of $2,673.02, if a 6 per cent rate is used in discounting. (This is the same calculation as made previously—a trick which saves the writers a considerable amount of time.)

Usually, a machine will have scrap value or trade-in value at the end of its productive life. This requires only the modification of adding in the discounted value of this last-ditch contribution of the machine. The scrap value is assumed to be realized as soon as the last output is sold (at the end of the nth year). Letting Q stand for quasi rent received at the end of each year and S for scrap value, the formula for the present value of a machine is:

$$V = \frac{Q_1}{1+r} + \frac{Q_2}{(1+r)^2} + \frac{Q_3}{(1+r)^3} + \cdots + \frac{Q_n}{(1+r)^n} + \frac{S}{(1+r)^n}.$$

It is not necessary that the quasi rent be the same each year. Normally, it will decrease with time as maintenance and repair expenses connected with the aging machine increase. It is implicitly assumed, however, that quasi rent is maximized each year by the operation of the machine at the output rate where marginal cost equals marginal revenue. In Chapter 4, it was pointed out that a plant is operated optimally only when marginal revenue and marginal cost are equated, and the same is true of an individual machine. The correct present value of the machine can only be derived on the assumption that its earnings will be maximized through correct management.

It should be realized that regardless of the arithmetical care with which the present value of a machine is calculated, much uncertainty is present in the calculation. The stream of quasi rents will be affected by the price of the output; by prices which will be paid for materials, labor, etc., in the future; and by possible breakdowns of the machine itself. Its scrap or trade-in value is probably not definitely ascertainable if the machine has a number of years of life remaining. Also, the selection of the interest rate to be used in discounting requires much information concerning the structure of interest rates and judgment as to the riskiness of the particular business operation. This is not surprising, however, when one considers that a great many of the entries made by an accountant—entries which affect reported net profits—are matters of judgment. Accumulated depreciation, reserves for bad debts, and inventory evaluations—to give a few examples—

are all only estimates. Also, cost accountants constantly use arbitrary rules for allocating certain types of costs (such as overhead) to particular products.

Decision to Purchase a Machine

Estimating the worth of a machine involves difficulties but must somehow be accomplished, at least roughly, if a rational decision to purchase or not to purchase a machine is to be made. Once the present value (V) has been determined, it is only necessary to compare this with the cost of the machine. If its value is greater than its cost, it should be purchased; if its value is less than its cost, it should not be purchased; if its value is just equal to its cost, it is a matter of indifference whether it is purchased, since funds invested in the machine will bring the same return as they could earn in an alternative investment.[14]

If V exceeds the cost of the machine, it means that, according to the best calculation which can be made, the returns from the machine will more than cover all variable costs, depreciation on the machine, and a normal interest return on the capital tied up in the machine. The investment opportunity then appears to be a good one, and management is likely to buy the machine (unless a still better one is available for the job). Sales opportunities may be such that additional machines would also be expected to have a present worth greater than their cost. In this event, management should purchase additional machines as long as the value added by another machine to the present value of the whole stock of machines exceeds the cost of the machine. In this calculation, account must be taken of the fact that each machine which is added may lower the present value of the earlier machines by lowering the market price at which the output can be disposed of. It is also possible that "quantity discounts" can be secured on larger orders for machines, and this further complicates the calculation. These complications are greater than we wish to enter into in this elementary and partial treatment.[15]

---

[14] This may not be strictly true, since the possession of the machine may permit some other factor of production in which the owner of the machine has an interest to earn an income. For example, a man may be able to put his wife to work by buying her a washing machine, whereas she would otherwise send out the laundry and spend the time playing bridge. The present value of the machine to the husband would exceed its discounted stream of quasi rents plus its discounted trade-in value. This is because the wife's labor is "gravy" to him.

[15] An excellent book which should be consulted by the reader desiring a thorough training in this subject is F. A. and V. C. Lutz, *The Theory of Investment of the Firm* (Princeton: Princeton University Press, 1951). Such problems as optimum productive techniques, optimum size of firm, optimum length of life of equipment, and optimum method of finance are treated mathematically.

Should a New Model Be Purchased?

Management faces a slightly different sort of investment decision when confronted with the problem of whether to replace machinery which is still usable with a new, improved model. The problem is similar to that of the fairly opulent family which has to decide each year whether to buy a new model automobile or to continue to drive the old car. (The firm is more likely than the household to make a rational decision, however.) The development of a dramatically altered model, such as a jet-propelled air liner or an atom-powered ocean liner, can bring this question forcibly before a great many firms at the same time.

It would seem at first glance that a new type of machine which becomes available should be purchased if it will lower the unit cost of production. Comparison of the average cost of production using different machines is valid, however, only if neither is already owned by the firm. In that case, all costs (including depreciation) should be counted. If investment has already been made in one machine, however, it is often correct to compare the *variable operating costs* per unit using the old machine to the *total cost* per unit using the new machine. This is the principle which was emphasized in Chapter 4—namely, that costs which are already sunk should not enter into decisions regarding new steps to be taken or avoided. They are bygones which should remain bygones.

This comparison is not entirely correct, however, because the sunk costs are really not lost, to the extent that they can be partially recovered through the sale or trade-in of the old machine. As long as variable operating costs using the old machine are below the selling price of the product, it can continue to yield quasi rent. If this quasi rent is sufficient to cover interest on its own scrap value plus interest on the difference between the value and cost of a new machine, use of the old machine should be continued.[16]

Like most calculations involving interest, the appropriateness of this formulation is not easy to see. The following may help. If the old machine is continued in use, the firm sacrifices during each time period the interest which could otherwise be earned on its market value. This is one cost of keeping the old machine. Also, by retaining the old machine, the firm sacrifices interest income on the difference between the present value and the cost of the new machine. This interest would actually be secured from the quasi rents which would

---

[16] This formulation is given by Lutz, *ibid.*, pp. 113–14.

be returned by the new machine over time. If the new machine is markedly superior to the old one, this will be a large item and will make it desirable to replace the old machine with the new one immediately. If, however, the new machine is only a slight improvement over the old one, this will not be a large amount. In that event, it is quite possible that, for some years yet to come, the annual quasi rent returned by the old machine will exceed the sum of the annual interest on its disposal value and the annual interest on the difference between value and cost of a new machine. Eventually, of course, the old machine should be replaced, but premature replacement by a model which is only slightly better is both common and uneconomical.

Alternative Formulation of Replacement Criterion

The rather complex-sounding considerations which have been set forth for deciding rationally between retaining and replacing old machinery can be restated in a somewhat simpler way if "average cost" is redefined for purposes of this sort of decision. Ordinarily, average cost is made up of variable cost per unit and fixed cost per unit, including in the latter depreciation based on the original cost of the asset. However, it will seldom happen that the market value of an old machine will exactly equal its original cost less depreciation as charged off on the books from the time of acquisition to the time at which a decision to keep or replace is to be made. Most frequently, the book value will exceed what could be secured in an actual sale of the machine.

A direct comparison of the average cost of production using the new machine and using the old machine is appropriate if three things are done: (1) Average cost of producing with the old equipment must include depreciation based not on original cost but on present market value less estimated scrap value; (2) interest must be added in as a cost, with its amount being computed on the cost and market value, respectively, of the new and the old equipment; and (3) the average cost calculation using both old and new equipment must be made in each case for the expected optimum output—i.e., where marginal cost equals marginal revenue. This may not be the same output in both cases. If it is expected that demand will fall off, replacement of the old machinery becomes less desirable, since a reduction in output will raise average cost of output more sharply for the new machinery than for the old. This is due to the higher fixed costs which will be associated with the new equipment.

In summary, the decision whether to replace existing machinery with new machinery usually cannot be made simply by comparing expected average cost of production by the two methods. Capital will have been "sunk" in the old equipment, but this historical event is irrelevant to a present decision except to the extent that capital could now be recovered by selling or trading in the old machinery. This requires an amended calculation of average cost of production using old machinery. In addition, interest must be included as a cost of production. This is normal procedure for the economist but not for the accountant, except where the interest payment is explicit. Also, the average cost of production using either old or new equipment will depend on the rate of production; consequently, not a single average cost but instead an average cost *curve* should be computed for output from both old and new machinery. The optimum rate of output which is anticipated for each of the two productive processes then determines an average cost for each, and these averages can be directly compared to judge whether replacement is desirable. If *none* of the capital sunk in the old machinery can be recovered by its sale or trade-in, the relevant comparison is simply average cost at the expected output with the new machine versus average variable cost at the expected rate of output using the old machine. Interest is an element in the former but not in the latter.

CASE 10–1: C. C. WOODLEY (1)

For many years, it has been the practice of the United States Post Office Department to contract with private carriers for transportation of the mails between the main post-office building, substation post offices, and the railroad stations in various cities. Bids for performance of these services are usually invited by the local postmaster through newspaper advertisements and notices posted on bulletin boards in post-office buildings. These announcements solicit sealed bids from interested parties and describe the character of the services in such matters as duration of contract, distance to be covered, frequency and timing of trips, type of equipment, bonding requirements of personnel, and provisions for modifying the contract during its lifetime. These contracts are usually awarded for a period of four years. The successful contractor is required to furnish equipment conforming to specifications in the announcement, personnel, bonds guaranteeing performance of service, and all materials and supplies necessary to fulfill the contract. In the larger cities the equipment is so specified as to prohibit its use for any other purpose without some alterations. Frequently, schedules do not permit a vehicle to be idle long enough to be useful for other purposes.

In September, 1929, Mr. C. C. Woodley was successful in securing a four-year contract of this type in a large city in northern New York. His contract called for the provision of fourteen trucks varying in capacity from one-half ton to two tons. They were to be painted olive green in color and bear in gold lettering the inscription "United States Post Office," followed by a serial number to be assigned to each truck. Bodies were to be constructed of wood or steel and provide protection from the elements. All bodies were to be equipped with doors and locks. Mr. Woodley purchased eight of the trucks from the previous contractor, and six he purchased new. The terms of the contract provided for a compensation of $28,550 per year for four years. The contract also provided for additional compensation for mileage covered in excess of that stated and penalties for failure to perform the required mileage where such failure was not beyond the control of the contractor.

Mr. Woodley personally supervised the operations under this contract. During rush hours and when drivers were absent, he acted as a driver. He retained several drivers employed by the former contractor, so that he had a crew of five full-time drivers, who worked twelve-hour shifts, and seven part-time drivers. One of the part-time drivers also served as a garage man and mechanic. Operations began on January 1, 1930.

In September, 1933, Mr. Woodley was again the successful bidder for a second four-year period beginning January 1, 1934. The terms of this contract were identical with the contract executed in September, 1929, with the exception of compensation. The new contract called for annual compensation of $27,200, although several miles per day had been added to the total distance traveled because of relocation of one of the railroad stations.

At the time of renewal of the contract, Mr. Woodley, reviewing his expenses of operation, noted that he had been paying a premium of $4,700 per year for liability insurance on his fleet of trucks. This insurance was written by a large and reputable insurance company. During the period of contract from January 1, 1930, to December 31, 1933, total claims had amounted to $1,783.25, all of which had been promptly paid by the insurance company. None of the claims had involved a personal injury, and the largest single claim amounted to $356.75. This claim had resulted from the collision of one of the two-ton trucks with another truck carrying several large pieces of plate glass, which were broken. The average claim was about $25, and almost all the damage involved the repairing or replacement of fenders, headlights, or doors. All Mr. Woodley's trucks were equipped with governors, which permitted a top speed of twenty-five miles per hour, the official speed limit of the city. None of the operations extended beyond the city limits. All trucks were kept in good mechanical condition and were inspected semiannually by the Accident Division of the Department of Public Safety. Commercial vehicles which

Exhibit 1

C. C. WOODLEY

Statement of Profit and Loss, 1930–32

Item	1930		1931		1932	
Receipts............		$28,550.00		$28,673.00		$28,579.00
Expenses:						
Salaries............	$11,880.00		$11,430.00		$11,290.00	
Liability insurance..	4,700.00		4,700.00		4,700.00	
Comprehensive fire						
and theft.........	1,300.00		1,300.00		1,300.00	
Garage rent........	1,400.00		1,400.00		1,400.00	
Gas and oil........	552.00		519.00		507.00	
Depreciation.......	1,700.00		1,700.00		1,700.00	
License fees........	183.00		229.00		229.00	
Repairs............	638.00		629.00		955.00	
Bond expense.......	175.00		175.00		175.00	
Total Expense....		22,528.00		22,082.00		22,256.00
Net Profit......		$ 6,022.00		$ 6,591.00		$ 6,323.00

passed such tests were insurable at standard rates, regardless of age. Of the eight trucks purchased from the previous contractor, six were new in 1927 and two in 1928. All other trucks in the fleet were purchased new in 1929 by Mr. Woodley. There had been an annual turnover of about 50 per cent in the crew of drivers until about the end of 1931, after which the rate had dropped to about 10 per cent. This was attributed to the scarcity of jobs because of depressed economic conditions.

Effective January 1, 1934, the insurance company increased the annual premium on Mr. Woodley's liability insurance to $5,100 per year. In addition, the rate on his performance bond was increased to $285 per year because of an increase in the number of business failures. The automobile accident rate had increased in this city in the previous two years, and the rate of deaths per thousand attributable to automobile accidents had increased about 25 per cent in the first six months of 1933 compared to the same period of 1932. The agent of the insurance company suggested an increase in Mr. Woodley's liability limits because of the increasing tendency on the part of juries to grant larger awards in cases involving personal injuries. Several recent decisions had been in excess of $5,000 for personal injuries where the victim was not totally incapacitated.

Mr. Woodley was of the opinion that he would be better off if he canceled his insurance and set up a reserve of $3,000 the first year, and $1,000 to $2,000 each year thereafter. Exhibit 1 shows a condensed statement of profit and loss for the years 1930 through 1932.

QUESTIONS

1. Would you recommend that Mr. Woodley cancel his insurance and assume his own underwriting? Why? What effect would this have upon his profits?
2. Did the profits of Mr. Woodley arise from risk bearing?

CASE 10–2: C. C. WOODLEY (2)

In September, 1929, Mr. C. C. Woodley was awarded the contract to transport the mails between the main post office and the railroad stations, and between the main post office and substation post offices in a large city in northern New York. This contract covered the period from January 1, 1930, to December 31, 1933. The contracts were awarded on the basis of sealed bids, which were submitted under conditions prescribed by the Post Office Department. Under the terms of the contract the contractor agreed to provide all equipment, personnel, and supplies necessary to render the required service. Equipment complied with specifications as to size, weight, and color of trucks and provisions for safety of the mails. Personnel was bonded and made available to meet whatever schedule local conditions demanded. For this service, Mr. Woodley received $28,550 per year. In September, 1933, Mr. Woodley was again awarded the contract for another four-year period ending December 31, 1937, for an annual payment of $27,200. Under the terms of the contract, the contractor would be compensated, on a pro rata basis, for any service demanded above that outlined in the contract.

In July, 1937, Mr. Woodley prepared estimates preliminary to submitting a sealed bid for the renewal of his contract, which expired on

December 31, 1937. Although the terms of the proposed contract were almost identical to those of the existing contract, several factors had changed to the extent that they had to be reconsidered. The most important of these factors was wages. Mr. Woodley was not experiencing any current labor difficulties, but the occurrence of several events prompted a survey of the future labor picture.

For several years, Mr. Woodley had been aware of the increasing organization of labor in his city, and particularly clear in his memory was a violent strike in relation to the organization of the steel workers by the Steel Workers Organizing Committee at a local plant of the United States Steel Corporation. His own employees were not organized. Early in 1937 a moderately successful drive had been made to organize the drivers of the larger cross-country trucking lines, and there had been some reports in the local papers of proposals of the local unit of the Teamsters Union to organize local truck drivers. Up to that time, no definite steps had been taken in this direction. Since the passage of the National Labor Relations Act in July, 1935, there had been an increased tempo in the organization of labor. Mr. Woodley also noted that with each successful organization of a group of workers a rise in wages usually followed, in spite of the fact that there were currently about 17,000 unemployed persons in his city in June, 1937.

In September, 1936, Mr. Woodley had purchased three five-ton trucks which he used to operate an intercity freight trucking business. These operations were kept separate from those of the transportation of the mails, although he occasionally used one of his intercity drivers to drive a mail truck when he was not otherwise occupied. A proper charge was made against the mail contract whenever a freight driver was used. The three trucks used in the freight business were kept and serviced in the same garage with the mail trucks. Drivers of the freight trucks were organized, and their wages were $40 per week on a straight-time basis. The use of a higher-paid freight driver had caused dissatisfaction among the regular mail drivers on a few occasions.

Mr. Woodley had learned that a Mr. Connally, as well as several others, proposed to submit bids for the contract beginning January 1, 1938. Mr. Connally had submitted a bid in 1933, which was $10 less than that of Mr. Woodley. It was the policy of the Post Office Department to accept the lowest bid unless there were good reasons for doing otherwise. Owing to the small difference in amounts and the problems accompanying the breaking-in of a new contractor, Mr. Woodley was awarded the contract in 1933. In July, 1937, Mr. Woodley was considering a voluntary increase in wages for his mail drivers and the submission of a bid to cover the increased wages. The fact that Mr. Connally intended to submit a bid at this time, however, led him to fear a loss of the contract if such action were taken. Mr. Woodley had shown a net profit in his statements of mail contract operations of $6,317, $5,938, $6,035, and $5,123 for the years 1933, 1934, 1935, and 1936, respectively.

When Mr. Woodley began service on January 1, 1930, he retained several drivers employed by the preceding contractor and paid them the going rate of $25 per week for full-time drivers and 35 cents per hour for part-time drivers. No change was made in this rate following the economic collapse of 1929 and the subsequent sharp decline in prices, wages, and employment. He had given serious thought, however, to a reduction in wages in 1932, when the prevailing rate for truck drivers in the city was about $15 per week. Such a reduction would have increased his profits considerably, but he decided against such a move. From 1929 to 1932, his labor turnover declined considerably, and so did his accident rate. By 1937, there had been some recovery in the price level and wage rates, but the prevailing rate for drivers was still somewhat under that paid by Mr. Woodley, but until this time he had given no further thought to a revision of his wage rates. He believed, however, that if the upward movement continued, a revision of his wage rate would be necessary.

In September, 1937, he submitted a bid in the amount of $29,300, and was declared the successful bidder. In May, 1938, he voluntarily increased the wages of his drivers from $25 to $30 per week and adjusted the hourly rate accordingly. There was no pressure directly from his drivers, although they had joined the local unit of the Teamsters Union in December, 1937. In 1936 the twelve-hour shift had been reduced to an eight-hour shift. This had been accomplished voluntarily when a rearrangement of railroad schedules made it possible to use only one driver between the hours of 12:30 A.M. and 5:00 A.M. Such a shift had increased the use of part-time drivers, but the increased expense had been nominal.

In July, 1938, the business agent of the local Teamsters Union approached Mr. Woodley with a demand that he increase the weekly rate of his regular drivers to $40. Mr. Woodley replied that he could not afford to pay this increased rate and refused to meet the demand. Shortly thereafter, he was informed by mail, over the signature of the business agent, that unless the demands were met, Mr. Woodley's drivers would go on strike fifteen days from the date of the letter. There was a rapid increase in wage rates in the city, but the changes were so frequent that Mr. Woodley was not aware of the exact amount of the going wage rate for truck drivers. He discovered there were sharp differentials throughout the city but believed that the going rate was substantially higher than in 1937.

On July 1, 1938, Mr. Woodley had in his employ five full-time drivers who worked an eight-hour shift within ten hours, and nine part-time drivers who were employed an average of six hours per day. One of the part-time drivers also served as garage man and mechanic, which, in effect, made him a full-time employee.

QUESTIONS

1. Should Mr. Woodley grant the wage demand in July, 1938?
2. Should he have reduced wages in 1932?
3. Do you think Mr. Woodley was wise to increase wages voluntarily in May, 1938?
4. What is the relationship between Mr. Woodley's "ability to pay" and the demands made by the business agent of the Teamsters Union?
5. Suppose that Mr. Woodley's intercity freight operations produced a net profit of $5,000 per year. Would this affect the amount of the bid Mr. Woodley submitted in September, 1937? Would it affect his "ability to pay" in the case of his mail contract? How?

CASE 10-3: KELSO HEATING AND SHEET METAL COMPANY, INC.

In the spring of 1941 the Kelso Heating and Sheet Metal Company was experiencing difficulty in obtaining an adequate supply of oil- and gas-burning furnaces and boilers. The company had been operating at capacity for about two years, primarily engaged in the installation of heating systems in new homes. There had also been a marked trend toward the substitution of gas-fired furnaces in place of coal, and the company was also active in this line. In addition, the company had developed a reputation in its region as expert installers of sheet-metal work of all kinds.

The company was established in 1932, as a furnace repair business, by four brothers whose father had long been engaged in the sheet-metal business. In spite of depressed economic conditions the firm had prospered and grown. It obtained business, to a considerable extent, on a price basis. On sheet-metal work the firm underbid most of the other companies in the area, but its work was of only the best quality. The brothers were willing to sacrifice profit for the sake of obtaining business during the early years of the firm. The business was built upon the theory that the customer must always be satisfied both as to quality of work and as to price charged.

By 1938 the company owned a new building, in which operations were housed. The building was free of encumbrance and had cost $44,000. The company also had a stock of sheet metal and furnaces worth about $35,000, which was paid for. It was the practice of the firm to pay cash upon receipt and inspection of all materials. All four brothers worked on estimates, performed the actual work with the help of laborers, and, when time permitted, manufactured stovepipe and elbows in their own shop. The pipe and elbow manufacturing operations were the only ones of the kind within a radius of 200 miles. Both pipe and elbows were sold through jobbers in several states. The balance of the company's operations was primarily local.

During the calendar year 1940 the company installed complete heating systems in 527 of approximately 1,100 new homes built in the area. In addition, it installed 381 gas furnaces in place of coal furnaces. This was done with a crew of 21 men in addition to the owners of the business. Some of the electrical work and steam-fitting operations were performed on subcontracts to other firms. The company handled a nationally known oil furnace and boiler, and two equally well-known gas furnaces and boilers. It also handled conversion units of both kinds. Shipments were received by rail direct from the factories in carload lots. The company had adequate space in its building and carried inventories so that it could keep itself continuously occupied. Toward the end of 1940, however, as defense operations began to get under way throughout the nation, the shipments became less regular. Occasionally, the intervals between shipments were so long that lack of supplies caused the company to have idle time and resulted in upset schedules. This was causing some dissatisfaction among local contractors with whom the company did a great deal of business.

In a near-by city was located a company—the Apex Furnace Manufacturing Company—which had been engaged in the manufacture of coal furnaces for a number of years. It had three models which were produced in different sizes, and all were designed for use of coal only. The company had enjoyed an excellent reputation as a producer of quality furnaces during the twenties; but since that time, its business had continually declined. The best-known furnace of its line was the "Heatgenerator," which was made in both a commercial and a residential model. It worked on the hot-air principle and was hand-fired but easily adaptable to stoker firing. It was designed about 1917 and patented a few years later. It was a rather large piece of equipment and was assembled from over 175 parts, but had been highly rated for efficiency by the Anthracite Coal Institute. It had not been redesigned since the original patent, and one reason for its decline in use was the expense of maintenance. Because of so many parts, dealers were required to carry a considerable inventory, and it required a trained mechanic to take such a furnace apart for repairs and assemble it again. This resulted in high labor costs. Its original cost was somewhat higher than furnaces of similar heating capacity, but its fuel consumption was less. Apparently, the high cost of maintenance, together with other factors, caused the downward trend in sales of this model.

A second model produced by the Apex Company was exclusively for residential use. It was also designed early in the 1920's and had not been modified since. It was considerably lower in price than the "Heatgenerator" of similar size and was known as the "Airtube." It was much more simply constructed than the "Heatgenerator," in that it was composed of seven castings and a sheet-metal cabinet which sat on top of the castings. This cabinet was filled with a number of tubes through which the exhaust from the firebox passed, and the heat was transmitted to an air chamber and then into ducts. The outside of the furnace was covered with a round sheet-metal jacket which permitted the entrace of cold air at the bottom and upward into the air chamber for reheating. It was designed as a gravity system and usually installed as such. This model was the largest-selling item in the Apex line and was competitively priced.

The third model in the Apex line was a simple cast-iron furnace similar to the "Airtube" except for the air chamber above the firebox. It was the cheapest and least efficient furnace made by the company and was priced to compete with similar furnaces in the market. Like the other two models, it also suffered from lack of improvement in appearance and efficiency.

During the 1920's the Apex Company owned its foundry and machine shop, and confined itself exclusively to the manufacture and sale of furnaces. It operated primarily in the New England and Middle Atlantic states, although it made some sales in the Great Lakes area. It maintained branches in seventeen of the larger cities in that area at the peak of its operations. It sold through jobbers and retailers. Branch offices carried a large inventory of both furnaces and repair parts in order to maintain prompt and efficient service, although the company itself performed no service operations. The two higher-priced models in its line were well known in the heating business in the territory served and enjoyed an excellent reputation.

During the depression of the thirties the Apex Company lost its foundry through default of bonds and sold its machine shop to avoid foreclosure by creditors. The company managed to retain ownership of its patents, much of its inventory, and the patterns from which the castings were made. It reduced its operations to the maintenance of only two branch offices and had its castings made on a contract basis at a foundry in a near-by city. The machining of parts was handled in a similar manner. The company also engaged in direct selling, and concentrated its attention more upon replacement business and the sale of parts than on an attempt to obtain new business. In the city in

Exhibit 1

APEX FURNACE MANUFACTURING COMPANY
Condensed Balance Sheet, December 31, 1940

Assets:		Liabilities:	
Cash	$ 1,121.23	Accounts payable*	$13,125.71
Accounts receivable	2,276.38	Notes payable	3,611.08
Parts inventory	8,233.94	Accrued taxes†	6,141.29
Furnace inventory	5,123.18	Capital stock	15,000.00
Land and buildings	6,259.45	Surplus	136.10
Goodwill and patents	15,000.00		
Total Assets	$38,014.18	Total Liabilities	$38,014.18

* Includes $4,239.73 due foundry for casting; foundry has a lien on patterns as security.
† Includes $2,862.41 in social security taxes and income taxes which are past due, plus interest and penalties to date.

which the company had its home office, it even went into the business of installation of new and replacement business. At no time during the thirties did the company attempt to adapt its furnaces to either gas or oil. The president of the company was an elderly person who had difficulty getting along with people. As a result, relations with jobbers and retailers tended to deteriorate.

The Kelso Heating and Sheet Metal Company had installed some of the furnaces of the Apex Company in the past and was aware of the decline of the Apex Company. The Kelso Company learned through its attorney that the Apex Company might possibly be purchased if the purchaser would assume the liabilities of the company. Investigation revealed that the company was on the verge of bankruptcy. Exhibit 1 shows a condensed balance sheet of the Apex Company as of December 31, 1940.

Arrangements were made with the Apex Company for an inspection of its operations, and the following was determined:

1. The chief assets of the company were its inventory of parts, patterns (subject to liens by the foundry), patents upon its furnaces, and some unassessable amount of goodwill.

2. The "Heatgenerator" model was unsuitable for the present market without considerable redesign, but the outcome of even such attempts was quite uncertain. It was completely out of date and should be continued only to take care of old customers who were unwilling to accept a substitute. Profit from this model had come primarily from the sale of parts rather than the sale of the furnace. Considerable research expense was necessary on this model.

3. The "Airtube" model furnished an excellent opportunity for adaptation to either gas or oil fuel with a minimum of expense. It could be easily adapted to a boiler by appropriate modification of the castings. A slight change in the firebox and redesign of the outer jacket would give this furnace a modern and streamlined appearance. The air chamber above the firebox was easily adapted to either forced warm-air circulation or air conditioning. The redesign of the patterns for casting the firebox would cost approximately $5,000. New patterns would be required to convert it to a boiler, at a cost of approximately $8,500. The new outer jacket could be made in the plant of the Kelso Company from sheet metal and painted any desired color by spray equipment. Stokers could be easily adapted to this model also, at low cost.

4. The cheap model in the line could be carried in its present state by the Kelso Company to meet whatever demand the company might have for a standard hand-fired coal furnace. Some streamlining of its appearance and the adaptation of a forced-air mechanism would perhaps help this model.

5. The chief problem presented was the capacity of the Apex Company, even in its present state, in relation to the demand of the Kelso Company. Currently, the Kelso Company sold about 900 to 1,000 furnaces per year. By continued use of the contracting of foundry and machinery operations, the Apex Company had a capacity of about 7,500 to 8,500 furnaces per year. At this level of operations the Kelso Company could enjoy a profit margin of about 55 to 60 per cent on the sale of furnaces, compared to its present 25 per cent. The present distribution system of the Apex Company disposed of only 1,500 to 1,800 furnaces per year. To dispose of capacity output of the Apex Company would necessitate the building of new outlets and a decision as to whether sales should be handled by company salesmen or through agents and distributors. If the Kelso Company acquired the Apex Company at this time and made no attempt to produce more than its own needs, the profit margin per furnace would be about 8 to 10 per cent, but the Kelso Company would be assured of a steady supply of furnaces. This margin was computed on the basis of the modifications suggested above and the purchase of oil and gas burners from outside sources, since neither the Apex nor the Kelso Company was currently set up to produce them. In short, the acquisition of the Apex Company would mean moving into a larger and wider market for the Kelso Company. The Kelso Company had never had experience in handling a sales force.

6. In addition to the foregoing, there was the problem of maintaining demand of the Kelso Company at the present level. A large share of the company's present sales was dependent upon the construction of new houses. A decline in this area would force the company to increase its efforts to sell more furnaces in a wider market. If the decline in building were widespread, this problem would become acute.

The owners of the Apex Company asked $50,000 for the business, the purchaser to assume all liabilities. The attorney for the Kelso Company believed that an offer of $10,000 would be accepted. Working capital of approximately $50,000 cash would be required immediately to handle an output of 4,000 to 5,000 furnaces during the first year of operations by a new owner. Additional personnel would be required to handle both production and sales of the Apex Company in the event of purchase.

The Kelso Company had approximately $40,000 cash on hand, plus an excellent credit standing at all local banks.

QUESTIONS

1. Would you recommend that the Kelso Company purchase the Apex Company?
2. At a price of $10,000, with all liabilities assumed by the Kelso Company, how much would the Apex stockholders lose?
3. What effect would the imminence of World War II have on the decision?
4. Were goodwill and patents worth $15,000?

CASE 10–4: MID-SOUTH PRODUCTS CORPORATION

In 1901 the Mid-South Wholesale Grocery Company was formed by the merger of two small wholesale firms. The company acted as a wholesale firm only until the first World War, at which time it acquired a small fish-packing plant in New Orleans, Louisiana. Shortly after the war a small company in Texas which milled flour and processed dry cereals was purchased. In 1923 the firm was reorganized into the Mid-South Products Corporation, with the main office and warehouse in Memphis, Tennessee. A subsidiary corporation, wholly owned, was organized to handle all food manufacturing and processing. In 1926 the company purchased a commission house dealing in fresh fruits and produce. Another wholly owned subsidiary was organized to direct this division. The parent company concentrated its efforts on the distribution of these various products to brokers, wholesalers, retailers, and other manufacturing firms such as bakers, confectioners, and specialty food processors.

Among the products handled by the company were pecans, which were sold both in the shell and as shelled kernels. Pecans were purchased from individual growers by the commission division, and transferred for shelling and packaging to the manufacturing division, which turned them over to the parent company for distribution. About 90 per cent of all nuts handled were shelled. Shipments were made from the home office and also direct from the processing plants, as described below. Purchasers of pecans were located in various parts of the United States. The company had no retail outlets of its own. Pecans were processed and packaged for several grocery chains under their respective labels, as well as under the brand name of the Mid-South Products Corporation.

Prior to 1932 the company had purchased pecans in the shell through its commission division and resold about 60 per cent of them without further processing. Those that were processed were shipped by truck or train from the chief growing areas in southern Mississippi, northern and central Florida, Georgia, and eastern and southern Texas. Processing was done by hand, except that shells were cracked by hand-operated machines. Since highest prices were obtained for whole kernels, efforts were made to crack the shells without damaging the kernel. Kernels which were broken were sold ungraded, primarily to bakers and confectioners. Hand-processing was a high-cost operation; but, up to 1932, the price had been high enough to cover this high labor cost and show a profit.

In 1932, however, the price of shelled pecans dropped sharply in relation to costs of processing. Although labor was relatively cheap in Memphis at the time, the prevailing wage was still such that the company could barely cover variable costs in the processing of pecans. On a total cost basis the operations were carried on at a loss for the years 1931 and 1932. In an effort to cut costs, the company decided to decentralize the processing operations. It was observed that the wage level in smaller towns and villages in the South was lower than in Memphis. As a result of several investigations, the company moved its pecan processing to three different locations—one in Quitman, Georgia; another in Crockett, Texas; and the third in Picayune, Mississippi. All locations were in pecan-growing areas, and all were towns of a few thousand population. In these small towns, it was possible to secure a considerable amount of part-time labor at very low wages. In Picayune, Mississippi, for example, all the employees were women who worked as domestics part of each day and could be secured for 20 cents per hour for three to four hours each afternoon to shell and clean pecans. The rate of turnover was high, but the nature of the labor was unskilled, so that this factor was not serious. About 300 part-time workers were used in this plant for six or seven months each year.

Since pecans are harvested in the autumn season within a period of about two months, they must be stored in warehouses and withdrawn as needed. Prior to decentralization of operations, this necessitated the use of expensive warehouse space in Memphis, until the nuts were processed and again stored. Since substantially less space is required to store the shelled kernels, there was considerable pressure upon the manufacturing division to process the pecan stocks as rapidly as possible. Frequently, it was necessary to employ overtime to hasten the processing. In the new locations the company was able to acquire satisfactory existing structures for storing the newly harvested pecans which were less expensive than the urban location in Memphis. In addition, the net freight charges were less on shelled pecans, plus the fact that the shells were more easily disposed of in the rural locations. In the latter places the processing could be spread over a much longer period of time. Pecans were shelled and shipped in 50-pound containers to the main plant in Memphis, where they were graded and repacked for distribution.

This decentralization permitted the company to show a profit on a total cost basis. In 1933 the company processed approximately 16,-000 pounds of shelled pecans at a net profit of 21 cents per pound. By 1937 the company was processing about 24,000 pounds of shelled pecans annually at a profit of 20 cents per pound. The largest item of cost in the processing was labor. A good worker could shell about $1\frac{1}{2}$ pounds of whole kernels per hour and about $\frac{3}{4}$ pound of broken kernels. In view of hand operations the rate of broken kernels was not considered too high.

In 1938 the President of the United States signed the Fair Labor Standards Act, which required, among other things, a minimum wage of 40 cents per hour for labor engaged in or affecting interstate commerce. In addition, the act contained provisions for payment of overtime in excess of 40 hours per week. Upon recommendation of legal counsel the company decided to comply with the provisions of the act. In the pecan-processing operations, this would require a wage increase in excess of 100 per cent.

Coincident with the passage of this act, there was a sharp decline in economic activity and prices. Coupled with an unusually large walnut and almond crop in California, the price of pecans declined so that the profit per pound decreased to 4 cents. The price of pecans tends to conform in movement to the prices of nuts which are fairly good substitutes, such as walnuts, almonds, cashews, Brazil nuts, etc. The Mid-South Products Corporation distributed all kinds of nuts, but processed and packaged none other than pecans.

The executive committee called a meeting of the board of directors to consider the status of the pecan-processing operations. To pay the required minimum wages and overtime would involve the company in a substantial loss at the existing market prices of shelled pecans. There was divided sentiment among the directors as to what should be done. One suggestion was to abandon the pecan business entirely, since it constituted such a small part of the business, although it was growing in size. Another was to deal only in pecans in the shell. One director suggested raising the price to cover the new labor costs.

Early in 1937 the vice-president of the company had investigated the possibilities of mechanical processing of pecans. There was little standard equipment available which the company did not already possess. However, a large eastern electrical manufacturing company had, at the request of the vice-president, drawn up plans for a machine which would crack, shell, grade, and package pecans in containers of various sizes. It was designed to operate by means of a battery of electric "eyes." Since the machine was a specially designed affair and many parts would have to be made by hand, it was estimated to cost approximately $35,000. It would, however, have a capacity of 10,000 pounds of shelled pecans per week and would require two highly skilled operators in addition to several laborers to close the containers as they were filled. The cost of constructing a machine of half that capacity was estimated to be only $2,000 less. The idea was rejected at the time because of the high cost. The cost accounting department had calculated that, with the current volume of operations, the installation of such a machine in any one of the three locations would result in a cost per pound higher than that incurred by hand operations.

The Mid-South Products Corporation competed with five other similar food processing and distributing companies in the sale of shelled pecans. Two of these companies were much larger than the Mid-South Corporation. In addition, there were numerous smaller companies who also sold small quantities of shelled pecans. These companies "farmed out" their shelling operations to individuals who performed the work in their homes. The Mid-South Corporation had experimented with this method at one time but had found it unsatisfactory for large-scale operations. The vice-president of the company had discussed the labor problems occasioned by the new law with three of his larger competitors and found that they faced the same problems. The two larger competitors each sold about 40,000 pounds of shelled pecans annually, while the third sold about the same volume as the Mid-South Corporation.

The cost accounting division of the Mid-South Corporation reported in 1938 that if a volume of 75,000 pounds of shelled pecans could be sold annually, the company could reduce labor costs to approximately 8 cents per pound for the entire pecan operations if the machine were purchased. This included amortization of the purchase price, a special building to house the equipment, and wages of the skilled operators. At the price of pecans in 1938, this would produce a profit of about 16 cents per pound on a total cost basis.

QUESTIONS

1. What action would you recommend for the company? State your reasons.
2. If the machine were purchased, what considerations would affect your choice of its location?
3. If the machine were purchased, should the book value of the three existing processing plants be added to the cost of the machine?
4. Does this case introduce any relationship between size of market and unit cost? Explain.
5. Adam Smith said, "Specialization is limited by the extent of the market." Can you apply this principle to the present case?
6. What is the present minimum wage? On what sections of the country do you believe the latest increase had its greatest effects? Give arguments both for and against the minimum wage.

CASE 10–5: THE PAPER INDUSTRY[17]

INTRODUCTION

Two paper companies co-operated in this inquiry by making available their cost records for the years 1936–38 and by discussing their wage, price, and technological-change policies.

During the 1936–38 period, wage rate changes were made by these two paper companies after careful consideration of their profit and cash position. In the case of company A, the action of other paper companies and of industry generally was also watched by those responsible for wage policy, and in company B decisions on wage changes were influenced by negotiations with the union to which its employees belonged.

Changes in wage rates have affected the hourly earnings of company A's employees about proportionately, although changes in the volume of employment and in the proportion of women workers have also had some effect on the average for the plant. No data on hourly earnings in company B were available. Changes in wage rates have been followed by proportionate changes in labor costs per unit in company A, although here again fluctuations in the volume of output have been a factor. In company B both the volume of output

---

[17] This case is drawn entirely from Temporary National Economic Committee, *Industrial Wage Rates, Labor Costs, and Price Policies* (T.N.E.C. Monograph No. 5) (Washington, D.C.: U.S. Government Printing Office, 1940), pp. 26–42.

and labor-saving technological improvements have affected labor costs, and there has been no close relationship between wage rate changes and movements in the company's labor costs per unit. By the end of 1938 direct labor costs per unit were only a little over 5 per cent above the early 1936 level, although wage rates had been increased nearly 20 per cent.

Labor costs are not so important as raw-material costs and fixed expenses in the total costs per unit of either company, nor do they fluctuate so widely. Costs and realizations have been closely related during this period, largely because of the flexibility of raw-material costs rather than through any attempt to fix prices on the basis of costs. Prices are, to a large extent, market-determined and not subject to administrative control by the company's management. These circumstances have combined to minimize the importance of labor costs in the prices at which paper is sold. Wage policy is almost unrelated to price policy, although it is important to the profits and to the general financial position of both companies.

Technological changes are made more or less as a matter of routine to reduce costs and to improve quality. Reduction in overhead costs has been a more important consideration in recent years than prospective savings in labor costs. The level of wage rates is not considered by officials to be of any importance in deciding on technological improvements.

According to the Census of Manufactures, in 1937 there were 841 establishments engaged in the production of paper and pulp, employing 137,803 wage earners and paying approximately $175,000,000 in wages. The total value of product for this industry was in excess of $1,200,000,000, and value added by manufacture was $484,000,000. The paper industry proper, with which this study is primarily concerned, comprised 647 establishments having 110,000 wage earners and a total wage bill of $142,000,000. Value of product was $958,000,000, and value added was $390,000,000.[18]

Two companies were requested to co-operate in this survey, and data were secured for one of the plants operated by each company for the period 1936–38 inclusive. Company A is a large producer of paper, with plants located at various points in the eastern part of the United States. It is engaged in the manufacture and sale of four chief types of product: (a) wood pulp, almost all of which is absorbed by its own paper mills; (b) book and other white papers; (c) other paper products; and (d) commercial by-products of the pulp-making processes.

The present study is concerned only with the company's largest mill, which in recent years has accounted for approximately half the total net sales of the company as a whole. The principal products of this mill are publication grades of book paper. Production of these grades comprised from 60 to 75 per cent of the total tonnage for the plant during the period studied.[19] They are sold either direct to publishers or through a sales agency on a flat commission basis.

---

[18] U.S. Department of Commerce, Bureau of the Census, *Biennial Census of Manufactures, 1937,* Part I, pp. 556 and 563.

[19] The fluctuation in the percentages was mainly due to variations in the output of other grades. The volume of production of the publication grades was fairly steady throughout the period.

Other products of this mill include the lower grades of bond and envelope papers and certain similar specialties.

The mill has a full line of equipment. There are nine paper machines, as well as coating machines, supercalenders, rewinders, etc. There is a soda pulp plant which produces about 30 per cent of the requirements of the paper machines, using softwoods, most of which are grown in the vicinity by farmers and others. There is also a de-inking plant for the production of pulp from old magazines, etc. The balance of the pulp requirements is purchased in the open market.

The mill is well located from the point of view of access to raw materials. Although it is at a slight disadvantage in comparison with some of its competitors with respect to that portion of its pulp which it must purchase on the open market, this disadvantage is probably offset when the other sources of its pulp are taken into account. Fuel costs are likewise low. The company as a whole has an excellent reputation in the industry for progressiveness and efficiency.

While the present survey was confined to the operations of the one plant as a unit, its position as part of a large organization must be kept in mind, since certain corporate policies are determined by the needs of the company as a whole and affect all its plants.

Company B, located in the eastern part of the country, is a much smaller concern than company A and is also smaller than its more important competitors. Four paper machines are housed in three mills, which are near to one another. The company has no equipment for the production of wood pulp, but de-inked book stock is made from old magazines and used in the production of certain grades of paper.

In technical equipment and operating efficiency the company has been at something of a disadvantage. Most of its machinery was installed many years ago, and the funds necessary for maintaining and improving their efficiency were not available during the depression. Since 1934, however, the equipment has been substantially modernized. The company's raw-material costs are probably close to the average of those of its competitors. Freight costs to the major eastern markets are low.

The production and sales policy of the company has been radically altered in recent years. Prior to 1930, large contract orders formed a major portion of total sales. Most of these contracts were lost or given up during the depression years when prices were falling rapidly. In recent years, smaller specialty orders have been substituted for these earlier contracts. This policy required heavy expenditures for research and experimentation, but it has resulted in greater diversification and less price competition. The larger companies are less likely to underbid on small and specialized orders. The consumer, moreover, is less likely to shift in order to make a small saving in price, since the papers have been designed to meet his particular specifications.

WAGE POLICIES

The wage policies of both companies studied are influenced greatly by their individual financial positions, although other factors, such as wage trends in industry in general and in the paper industry in particular, have provided broad guides to wage policy, particularly in the case of company A. Collective bargaining has played a role in the wage policy of company B but not in that of company A, which was not organized during the period covered by the study.

Company A. The wage structure of the company A plant surveyed was established about 1920 as the result of a job-evaluation study. The wage differentials set at that time have been changed somewhat in recent years, though no single outside influence has been of great importance in determining the present differentials. The going rate in the community is considered in establishing the base labor rates, and the rates paid by both near-by and distant competitors are used in establishing rates for the skilled and semiskilled papermaking jobs. Since the abandonment of a bonus system in December, 1936, substantially all employees have been paid on a straight hourly basis.

During the period covered in this study, the employees of company A's mill were unorganized. Some years ago the Brotherhood of Papermakers organized a large proportion of the workers, but negotiations for an agreement broke down and have not since been resumed. In recent years there has been no collective bargaining machinery, and changes in wages, hours, and working conditions have been made without consultation with the workers.

Final decisions with respect to general wage changes rest with the executive committee, composed of the president and two vice-presidents. According to company officials, wage changes are usually not discussed until the need for them has become apparent to all the executives. Consequently, discussion is usually confined to the extent, form, and timing of the change. The policy of the company is to make similar wage changes in all its mills simultaneously.

During the years 1936–38 three general wage changes were put into effect. On December 13, 1936, a basic increase of 10 per cent was granted, accompanied by additional increases of 1–5 per cent on individual jobs to compensate for the loss of bonus accompanying the concurrent discontinuance of an incentive system. While it is impossible to determine the precise extent of the average change in wage rates, it was probably substantially less than 10 per cent when full allowance is made for the elimination of the bonus. Wages were further increased by 5 per cent on August 8, 1937, and then decreased by 7 per cent on September 4, 1938.

According to officials of the company, these wage changes were made after consideration of the course of wage changes in other firms, both inside and outside the paper industry, and of the financial condition of the company. Trends in wages paid by other paper producers and by industry generally are watched closely by those responsible for wage policy. Naturally, the actions of paper producers located near the company's principal plant, which is the one here described, exert the most immediate effect. The company exchanges information regarding general wage rates with a number of its competitors, but, even in the absence of such a formal arrangement, wage changes made by any of its important competitors quickly become known. While it is not the policy of the company to lead in making wage changes, it avoids being the last to follow.

Although the decision to make a change is guided by conditions in industry generally and among other paper firms in particular, the amount and exact timing of wage changes are largely determined by the financial position of the company itself.[20] Wage increases are usually made after relatively long periods of increasing volume and profits. When volume is sustained at a level high enough to insure good profits, wage rates are likely to be raised; and when lower volume has reduced profits or resulted in losses, wage cuts become likely, although the pressure to reduce rates may not be great until the cash balance of the company becomes low. It is conceivable that these guides might on some occasion point in different directions. In actual practice, such conflicts have apparently been rare, primarily because all important mills in the country, even those making somewhat different grades of paper, are affected to a great degree by the same external conditions.

However, when most of the industry is reducing wages, officials of this company feel it important to take similar action, even though its profit position may not seem to officials to require a wage reduction. This policy is based upon the belief that failure to reduce wages during a downturn would not avert pressure to increase wages during the ensuing upswing. The same reason is given for the policy of changing wages simultaneously in all the company's mills regardless of the conditions prevailing in any one mill.

Exhibit 1, listing the wage changes made by company A and three leading competitors from 1932 to 1939, reveals the broad similarity in direction and magnitude without any consistent pattern of closely grouped changes which the foregoing statement of the basis of wage policy might lead one to expect.[21] On the whole, the wage changes made by company A have been fewer and smaller in extent than those of its competitors. According to company officials, this is largely due to their large contracts, which have given them a more uniform volume of business and steadier employment than most of their competitors.

Company B. In general, wage changes made by company B have been determined independently of the action of the other paper companies or of industry generally, according to company officials. The company has been largely guided by its own financial position and has paid little attention to the general trends of the industry. Exhibit 2 shows the changes in wage rates made by company B and by four other paper firms located in the same general area in the period between 1930 and 1939. There is little uniformity apparent between these mills in the timing or extent of wage changes. This may be due partly to the fact that only one of the other mills produces paper which is strictly competitive with company B, although all have at least some similar operations and compete to some extent in the same labor market.

During the last few years, the employees of company B, as well as those of other mills in the area, have become organized in a union affiliated with the American Federation of Labor, and the union has thus become a factor in its wage policy. This union was not formally recognized by company B until 1937, though many of its workers had been members for several years preceding that time. Since the advent of the union, there has been a tendency for wage changes in firms in the vicinity to be more closely related. Fairly uniform mini-

---

[20] It is only natural that company-wide changes should be based on company-wide profits rather than on the condition of individual plants.

[21] None of these companies is a competitor with company A for labor.

mum rates prevail, but there remain material differences between mills with respect to rates paid for the more skilled operations. The persistence of these differences may be due to the fact that skilled workers have little opportunity to shift from one of these plants to another.

Over the period 1936–38 there were three general increases in wages put

Exhibit 1

TIMING AND APPROXIMATE AMOUNT OF WAGE CHANGES, 1932–39, SELECTED COMPANIES IN THE PAPER INDUSTRY* (IN PERCENTAGES)

	Company A	Competitor X	Competitor Y	Competitor Z
June 1, 1932		−10		
June 5, 1932			−10	
July 1, 1932				−3 to −6
August 1, 1932	−10			
January 22, 1933			−10	
April 2, 1933		−10		
July 1, 1933		+11.1		
July 24, 1933	+11			
July, 1933				+10
July 30, 1933			+11	
August 1, 1933				+15
August 7, 1933		+12.5		
October 15, 1933			+12	
May 15, 1934		+5		
July 9, 1934	+4			
October 1, 1934				+2.5
November 1, 1934			+5	
December 1, 1936			+5	+10
December 13, 1936	+10			
January 3, 1937		+10		
February 28, 1937			+5	
April 15, 1937				+5
June 1, 1937			+10	
July 19, 1937		+5		
August 8, 1937	+5			
August 7, 1938		−10		
September 4, 1938	−7		−5	
November 1, 1938				−10
January 1, 1939		+5		
March 1, 1939				+5

* It should be understood that most of the figures shown in the above table are only approximate, since many readjustments in differentials were made at the time of most of the changes.

Source: These statistics were compiled for a study of wage changes in the paper industry from 1929 to 1939 made by W. R. Maclaurin and J. A. Brownell.

into effect by company B. The volume of production had increased substantially during 1935, and this fact, coupled with the growing activity of the union, largely explains the 10 per cent increase of January, 1936. Production continued to rise, and a second increase was made in January, 1937, with many other mills increasing wages at approximately the same time. In July, 1937, after 8 months of near-capacity production, the union was officially recognized

Exhibit 2

TIMING AND APPROXIMATE AMOUNT OF WAGE CHANGES,
1930–39, SELECTED COMPANIES IN THE PAPER
INDUSTRY* (IN PERCENTAGES)

	Company B	Mill M	Mill N	Mill O	Mill P
December 1, 1930................			−10		
February 25, 1931...............	−5				
August 31, 1931................			−5		
October 4, 1931................	−5				
May 16, 1932..................				−10	
August 18, 1932................			−10		
September 12, 1932..............	−15				
November 14, 1932..............				−15	
December 2, 1932...............					−10
January 1, 1933................	−10				
January, 1933..................		−10			
January 23, 1933...............			−25		
July 24, 1933..................	+10				
August 1, 1933................				+10	
August 16, 1933...............					+10
August 28, 1933...............			+15		
December 1, 1933...............				+10	
May 13, 1934..................	+10				
May 14, 1934..................				+10	
November 7, 1934..............					+10
August 26, 1935................			+10		
January 19, 1936...............	+10				
June 7, 1936..................			+5		
November, 1936................		+11			
December 13, 1936..............			+10		
January 4, 1937................	+8				
March 10, 1937................					+10
March 29, 1937................				+7	
July 4, 1937...................	+10				
July 5, 1937...................					
July 20, 1937..................					+10
July 25, 1937..................			+8		
September 13, 1937..............				+5	
November 16, 1937..............					+10
October 16, 1938...............			−7		

* It should be understood that most of the figures shown in the above table are only approximate, since many readjustments in differentials were made at the time of most of the changes.
Source: These statistics were compiled for a study of wage changes in the paper industry from 1929 to 1939 made by W. R. Maclaurin and J. A. Brownell.

and wages increased by another 10 per cent. As in the case of company A, wage increases are made when volume is large.

It is interesting to note that, although wage decreases were general throughout the paper industry in 1938, only one of the mills in this area followed the trend, and this was a mill which was controlled by a company having various plants in other parts of the country. There seems to have been a general reluctance on the part of each of these companies to take the lead in seeking a cut; it was probably believed that a reduction would cause more difficulties than the savings would warrant.

WAGE RATES AND AVERAGE HOURLY EARNINGS

The relation in company A between changes in wage rates and in average hourly earnings has been examined for the period 1936–38 (figures for company B were not available). Hourly earnings for company A are reported for 4-week accounting periods, with 13 such periods in each year.

In general, the average hourly earnings of employees of company A varied in close relation to changes in the level of wage rates. Exhibit 3 shows that each change in wage rates was followed by almost an exactly proportionate change in average hourly earnings in the succeeding accounting period.

Average hourly earnings are also affected somewhat by changes in the volume of employment, and to a lesser extent, by the ratio of women employees to total employees. This is illustrated in Exhibit 3. The largest fluctuations in average hourly earnings without a general change in wage rates were in the year 1936, when major variations in the volume of employment and in the proportion of women workers resulted in changes of as much as 4 per cent. Earnings declined as employment expanded and the ratio of women workers rose, and increased as these trends were reversed. This relation is partially explained by the policy of the company in starting new employees, or old employees transferred to new jobs, at the beginning rate for the particular job. These rates are increased automatically by 2 cents an hour every 3 months until the full rate for the job is reached. It requires 9 months for the lower-paid jobs and as long as 18 months for more highly paid work to reach full-time rates.

A significant exception to this relation between earnings and employment is provided by the thirteenth period in 1938, when employment rose about one-fourth without any appreciable change in average hourly earnings. A complete explanation of this exception is not available, but it is known that the increase in employment was attributable to the Fair Labor Standards Act. It may be that the additional employees required by the act, unlike those added when business expands, were of about the same average skill as those already on the job.

WAGE RATES, LABOR COSTS, TOTAL COSTS, AND PRICES

Although employees are primarily interested in wage rate changes as they affect hourly earnings, to the employer their chief importance lies in their influence on labor costs and, through them, on total costs and prices. As in the case of the other industries included in the present study, these questions can be approached only through an understanding of the accounting procedures used by each company.

ACCOUNTING PROCEDURES

The system of cost accounting used by company A has the reputation of being one of the best in the paper industry, and it is unquestionably thorough and detailed. However, it is not designed in such a fashion as to provide ready answers to the questions toward which the present inquiry is primarily directed.

The chief objective of the accounting systems of both companies is departmental control. Both standard and actual costs are computed, but only standard costs are available for particular grades of paper. Comparisons of the sort made in this inquiry are wholly satisfactory only when they can be made for a single,

Exhibit 3

EMPLOYMENT AND EARNINGS, COMPANY A
(1936–38 Average = 100)

Year and Period (Number)	Total Number of Employees	Ratio of Women to Total Employees	Average Hourly Earnings
1936			
1............	88	6.3	102.1
2............	94	7.2	101.0
3............	102	8.5	98.4
4............	107	8.9	98.2
5............	109	8.7	98.4
6............	101	6.5	99.6
7............	96	4.9	101.4
8............	95	4.5	101.7
9............	95	4.7	101.2
10............	100	4.7	101.4
11............	105	5.8	99.8
12............	110	6.0	85.5
13*............	....	....	....
1937			
1............	112	6.3	106.2
2............	115	6.4	105.5
3............	116	6.7	106.0
4............	117	7.4	105.5
5............	117	7.4	106.2
6............	116	7.5	106.5
7............	116	7.9	107.1
8†............	116	7.2	107.1
9............	116	7.6	112.0
10............	116	8.3	111.8
11............	116	7.9	112.2
12............	115	8.0	113.3
13............	113	8.2	114.1
1938			
1............	111	7.8	113.8
2............	111	7.6	114.1
3............	111	7.6	114.1
4............	110	7.4	115.0
5............	109	7.2	115.2
6............	107	6.6	114.7
7............	107	6.5	114.3
8............	105	6.4	114.9
9‡............	104	6.5	114.9
10............	104	6.5	106.9
11............	106	7.3	106.5
12............	107	7.4	106.3
13............	132	7.3	106.5

* Figures for thirteenth period of 1936 were not available. Wage rates were increased 7–10 per cent on December 13, 1936.
† Wage rates were increased 5 per cent on August 8, 1937.
‡ Wage rates were decreased 7 per cent on September 4, 1938.

reasonably homogeneous product, such as a single grade of paper. In this instance the standard costs for one grade of paper could not be used, however, as they are not broken down by functions, such as labor, materials, overhead, etc. Hence actual cost figures have had to be used, though they are available only for the entire output of the selected plant rather than for single grades of paper.

Both company A and company B compile their accounting records for thirteen 4-week periods in each year. The data presented below are either for these periods or for averages of a group of consecutive periods with similar characteristics.

Company A. Actual aggregate costs for all grades are computed by 4-week accounting periods, and are broken down into their most important components. These data are, of course, not entirely satisfactory for analysis of changing total costs in relation to wages and prices, the chief difficulties arising from the variation in the proportions of the various grades of paper in the total output. There is no way in which the effect on costs of this variation can be measured. For example, if labor costs per unit of output have risen, the rise may have been due to an increase in wages, to lowered efficiency, to the production of a larger share of grades of paper requiring proportionately more man-hours of labor, or to a combination of all these factors. The difficulties of interpretation thus imposed are real and, for the present inquiry, insurmountable.

Another major problem arises from the fact that administrative, selling, and interest expenses are not allocated to individual mills. Only manufacturing costs are computed for each mill, all other expenses and all income merely being lumped together for the company as a whole. In order to get an indication of the actual net profit for the particular mill, it was necessary to make an *ad hoc* allocation of these expense items. Net administrative expense was allocated on the basis of tonnage sold by each mill. Commission expenses were distributed on an actual basis, other selling expenses in proportion to tonnage sold. Interest charges were allocated on the basis of the book value of plant and equipment in the various mills.

Total costs, as presented in the subsequent discussion, are thus a composite of actual manufacturing costs and a hypothetical allocation of administrative, selling, and interest expense made especially for this inquiry. The results are expressed in terms of costs per ton. Since the number of tons produced in a given period does not coincide with the number sold, the more appropriate of these two items has been chosen as the divisor in each case. All the items included in manufacturing costs have been divided by the number of tons produced; the other items have been divided by the number of tons sold.

These total cost and net profit figures have all been calculated for the specific purposes of this inquiry. Since they were not computed in the course of the ordinary business practice of the company, they could not have been used by executives as a guide to the determination of policies. They do, however, afford an indication of the changes in profitability of operations for the particular mill over the 3-year period.

One further point should be mentioned in connection with the accounting procedures of the company. Certain items, notably social security taxes, which obviously bear a direct relation to expenditures for labor, are not included in the "labor" components of manufacturing costs. In the summaries of actual manufacturing costs which are regularly compiled for each 4-week period, these taxes are included under the general heading for "Depreciation, etc." A similar disposition is made of charges for workmen's compensation and group insurance. In 1938 these three charges taken together amounted to approximately 6 per cent of total payroll. In Exhibit 6 they have been included under item 11, "Insurance, taxes, and miscellaneous."

Company B. In the case of company B, the accounting methods are of more than ordinary interest. "Actual" costs are compiled for each 4-week period for all grades of paper combined. These same costs, broken down by departments, are used for purposes of cost control. Actual costs are divided into three groups —raw materials; controllable (or variable) mill expense, such as direct labor, most of the indirect labor, supplies, fuel, social security taxes, etc.; and fixed expense, including depreciation, taxes, insurance, repair materials, labor for maintenance of the outside of buildings, administration, and selling expense other than commissions. The data presented below refer to these actual costs and have the same limitations as the actual cost figures used for company A.

Both the standard and the actual cost figures of company B are set up to indicate readily what portion, if any, of the fixed expenses have been covered. Thus they both emphasize the fact that the mill cannot afford to turn down any order on which the price will cover all the variable expenses and some of the fixed charges unless other orders can be secured at higher prices.

WAGE RATES AND LABOR COSTS

In general, direct labor costs in the two companies studied rose when wage rates were increased and fell when rates were cut. However, the relation between wage changes and changes in labor costs per unit of output in the plants of companies A and B has been neither simple nor direct but has been affected by a number of factors, two of which deserve special emphasis. In the first place, labor costs per unit depend to a considerable degree upon the volume of production of the mill as a whole. With a larger volume, longer runs are possible, and the time required for starting and stopping operations is reduced.[22]

In the second place, technological improvements were made in the 1936–38 period, particularly in company B's plant, which reduced labor costs materially. A 19 per cent increase in wage rates over this period in company B's plant was accompanied by an increase of only 6.4 per cent in direct labor costs.

---

[22] When business is scarce, orders will be put on the machines almost as they come in, and almost every change in the grade being turned out is costly. But when a mill has a large backlog of orders, longer runs of a single grade can be made at a considerable saving. When business is scarce, most mills will take orders for grades which cannot be run as efficiently as their regular grades or which require costly experimentation before a satisfactory sheet of paper is produced. A third factor is that a certain amount of time is lost each week in starting up and shutting down the continuous operations in a paper mill, but this time is no greater in a 6-day than in a 4-day week, so that production per hour tends to increase as the operating time per week increases. If a mill can run 7 days a week, the start-up and shut-down time are eliminated entirely, but this cannot be done for more than a few weeks in succession, as shut-downs for repairs are required.

These conclusions must be expressed in general terms, since they are not based on labor costs for a homogeneous product but for all grades of paper produced. Labor costs per ton of production will obviously vary with the type of product. When a larger proportion of the output of the mill consists of grades which require the use of more labor in finishing operations, unit labor costs naturally tend to increase. In similar fashion these costs depend upon the size of the paper machines, different grades of paper being produced on machines of different sizes; in general, they are lower for grades produced on the larger machines. If grade labor costs had been available, this difficulty would have been avoided.

Since it was necessary to use costs for the entire plant output of all grades, changes in labor cost figures from month to month may be due to changes in the proportions of different grades of paper made. In order to diminish the importance of fluctuations of this character, the labor cost figures are presented

Exhibit 4

WAGE RATES AND LABOR COSTS PER UNIT, COMPANY A

(Average of First 12 Periods of 1936 = 100)

Date	Amount of Wage Change (Per Cent)	Operating Labor Costs	Repair Labor Costs	Total Labor Costs	Average Production per Period
1936 (first 12 periods)* December 13, 1936..........................	+7 to +10	100.0	100.0	100.0	100.0
1937 (first 8 periods) August 8, 1937....	+5	104.4	110.8	105.0	129.1
1937 (last 5 periods)...................	....	112.4	133.3	114.1	115.9
1938 (first 9 periods) September 4, 1938.	−7	109.8	123.5	110.9	102.7
1938 (last 4 periods).................	....	106.2	129.4	108.2	102.2

* No data were available for the thirteenth period.

as averages of a group of periods usually separated by a wage change. This procedure assumes that monthly variations in the importance of different grades of paper in the output of each plant will tend to balance out in the course of several periods.

It is clear from Exhibit 4 that general changes in wage rates were accompanied in this plant of company A by changes of unit labor costs in the same direction. There was, however, no precise correspondence in the extent of the changes. Between 1936 and the first eight periods of the following year, wages were increased by something less than 10 per cent, but labor costs increased by only 5 per cent. Undoubtedly the explanation of this divergence lies largely in the fact that the volume of production had increased by almost 30 per cent. During the last five periods of 1937, after a further 5 per cent increase in wages, labor costs advanced 8.8 per cent. Again, the variation in production seems to account for the discrepancy; the volume of production fell off by more than 10 per cent between the two parts of the year. During the first nine periods of 1938, unit labor costs were 2.8 per cent lower than during the latter part of 1937, in spite of the fact that no general change in wages had been made and that production had decreased. The change in labor costs between these two periods of time is probably explainable in terms of the changing composition of the output. Publication grades of paper, which require less labor per ton, accounted in the earlier months for approximately 63 per cent of total tonnage; this proportion increased to more than 70 per cent in the later months.

The explanation of the change in labor costs which occurred between the two parts of 1938 is not so clear. Following the general 7 per cent reduction in wages, labor costs fell by only 2.3 per cent. Operating labor costs fell by 3.2 per cent. Changes in the volume and nature of production were insignificant and would not account for the differences. The fact that labor costs failed to decline as much as wage rates is probably connected with the increase in employment, following the adoption of the Fair Labor Standards Act, which has already been noted. It is probable that the addition of new employees, to the extent of almost 25 per cent of the existing force, brought down the average level of efficiency by an amount sufficient to account for the discrepancy. If the last four periods of the year are considered separately, added weight is

Exhibit 5

WAGE RATES AND LABOR COSTS PER UNIT, COMPANY B

(1936 Average = 100)

Date	Amount of Wage Change (Per Cent)	Direct Labor Costs	Indirect Labor Costs	Tonnage Production per Period	Average Production per Machine-Hour
1936 (13 periods) January 4, 1937* .	+8	100.0	100.0	100.0	100.0
1937 (first 6 periods) July 4, 1937...	+10	102.5	97.1	128.7	105.3
1937 (last 6 periods)...............	....	105.5	121.6	95.0	110.2
1938 (13 periods).................	....	106.4	114.5	91.9	109.2

* Approximately.

given to this hypothesis. For the tenth and eleventh periods, operating labor costs were almost 6 per cent lower than in preceding months; during the last two periods when the act was in effect, they were almost exactly the same as they had been during the early part of the year.

In summary, it may be said that the movements in unit labor costs have had a tendency to parallel those in wage rates, except for variations in the volume and nature of production. There is no evidence that systematic changes in labor policy or production methods were made to compensate for the changes in wage rates. This conclusion is consistent with the history of technical changes over the period.

Company B. For company B, the relation between general changes in wage rates and in labor costs is indicated in Exhibit 5. In each instance the 4-week accounting periods are divided into groups. The grouping conforms primarily with the dates of the general wage changes, although no change in wages intervened between the last half of 1937 and the year 1938.

It is quickly apparent that the variations in direct and indirect labor costs bore little relation to the wage changes. The 8 per cent wage increase of January, 1937, was followed by a rise of only 2.5 per cent in direct labor costs per ton and by an actual fall in indirect labor costs. The second wage increase, 10 per cent, was followed by a rise of 2.9 per cent in direct and of more than

25 per cent in indirect labor costs. With no intervening wage change, direct labor costs rose slightly in 1938, while indirect labor costs fell by almost 6 per cent.

Most of these differences in rate of change are probably explained by variations in the volume of production and by the gradual increase in "production per machine per hour" through technical improvements over the 3-year period. In general, indirect labor costs tended to vary inversely with the volume of production, when allowance is made for the general wage changes. This is not true, however, when a comparison is made between 1937 and 1938; from the data at hand, it is not possible to explain the decline which took place in these costs during the latter year. Direct labor costs tended to vary inversely with the average "production per machine per hour," again making allowance for the general increase in wages.

Neither direct nor indirect labor costs advanced as much as wage rates over the period as a whole. As a result of the two increases, wages were approximately 19 per cent higher in 1938 than they had been in 1936. Direct labor costs were only 6.4 per cent higher and indirect labor costs 14.5 per cent higher. Had the volume of production been as great in 1938 as in 1936, it is probable that indirect labor costs per ton would have been even lower in the latter year. The basic reason for the smaller increase in costs is undoubtedly to be found in the larger production per machine per hour, this being, in turn, primarily due to technological improvements which permitted the machine to be run at a more rapid pace.

LABOR COSTS, TOTAL COSTS, AND PRICES

It is difficult to obtain a clear picture of the relation between the wage and price policies of company A and company B during a business cycle from the data secured in this survey. The impact of a prolonged period of low volume on wage and price policies is not disclosed in such a brief period as 1936–38. Moreover, the data assembled have certain limitations, already indicated. The cost and price information available is for the entire output of each mill rather than for a single product, and hence changes in cost-price relationships are in part attributable to shifting proportions of different grades of paper in the total output. This difficulty, together with the practice of selling most of their paper on a contract basis with the possibility of a different price for each sale, makes it difficult to identify turning points in price trends for companies A and B. The statistics describe the effect of executive action on prices only indirectly. It is possible that one result is an overemphasis on the role of the market in paper prices as contrasted with company policy.

Nevertheless, it is clear that cost structure and the competitive situations of these companies put definite limits on the importance of wages in determining prices. The cost structure of the paper industry not only relegates wage policy to a secondary position but also influences greatly the reaction of each company to market and competitive pressures.

Between 1936 and 1938 labor costs per unit of output ranged from 13.3 to 14.2 per cent of total unit cost in company A and from 11.5 to 12.4 per cent in company B, taking the averages for the group of accounting periods shown in Exhibits 6 and 7. It is apparent that during this period they have represented a remarkably stable proportion of total costs, despite the fact that wage rates in company A were increased by 16 per cent and in company B by 19 per cent. These increases were not fully reflected in the unit labor costs of the two companies, partly because increased volume made possible the more efficient

Exhibit 6

COST COMPONENTS AS A PERCENTAGE OF NET PRICE PER TON, COMPANY A

	1936	1937		1938	
	First 12 Periods*	First 8 Periods*	Last 5 Periods*	First 9 Periods*	Last 4 Periods*
1. Average net price per ton.....	100.0	100.0	100.0	100.0	100.0
2. Raw materials, fibers........	34.51	29.82	28.39	35.26	36.35
3. Raw materials, others........	13.96	21.96	22.96	11.14	10.15
4. Total raw materials..........	48.47	51.78	51.35	46.40	46.50
5. Operating labor.............	12.68	12.08	12.41	12.71	12.76
6. Repair labor................	1.17	1.18	1.36	1.32	1.43
7. Total labor.................	13.85	13.26	13.77	14.03	14.19
8. Supervision.................	2.25	1.77	1.96	2.44	2.26
9. Clerical....................	1.43	1.26	1.39	1.42	1.28
10. Supplies...................	6.31	5.29	5.96	5.45	6.49
11. Insurance, taxes, and miscellaneous.................	2.20	1.97	1.99	2.70	2.23
12. Fuel and water.............	3.70	3.26	3.26	3.83	3.88
13. Total manufacturing cost (items 4, 7, 8, 9, 10, 11, 12).	78.21	78.59	79.68	76.27	76.83
14. Selling expense.............	3.09	3.20	3.02	2.98	3.04
15. Administrative expense......	4.90	4.03	4.11	5.19	5.32
16. Interest...................	2.15	1.68	1.72	1.79	2.18
17. Depreciation...............	6.51	5.30	5.63	7.12	7.45
18. Balance, profit.............	5.14	7.20	5.84	6.65	5.21
Total fixed expenses (items 8, 15, 16, 17).............	15.81	12.78	13.42	16.54	17.21

* Accounting periods of 4 weeks each.

utilization of labor and also, especially in the case of company B, because of the installation of laborsaving machinery.

Labor costs as a factor in total costs are overshadowed both in absolute magnitude and in the extent of their fluctuations by raw-material costs and by fixed expenses. Raw-material costs, primarily pulp, averaged a little less than 50 per cent of total costs in company A and a little more than 50 per cent in company B. Fixed expenses for these plants (supervision, administration, selling expense, interest, and depreciation) ranged from 12.8 to 17.2 per cent of total costs in company A and from 13.3 to 20.1 per cent in company B (see Exhibits 6 and 7). Fixed expenses per unit decline when volume is expanding and increase when less paper is being produced. Even in so short a period as the three years 1936–38, volume changes were great enough to cause wide swings in fixed charges per unit.

Exhibit 7

COST COMPONENTS AS PERCENTAGES OF NET PRICE PER TON, COMPANY B

	1936 13 Periods*	1937		1938 13 Periods*
		First 6 Periods*	Last 6 Periods*	
1. Net price per ton produced..........	100.0	100.0	100.0	100.0
2. Book pulp.......................	16.8	18.4	19.5	16.3
3. Other raw materials...............	39.7	41.3	40.1	39.4
4. Total raw materials................	56.5	59.7	59.6	55.7
5. Direct labor......................	6.0	5.9	5.7	6.0
6. Controllable indirect and repair labor.	6.0†	5.6	6.5	6.4
7. Total labor......................	12.0	11.5	12.2	12.4
8. Controllable mill expense...........	11.3	10.0	11.2	10.2
9. Total controllable cost (items 4 + 7 + 8)........................	79.8	81.2	83.0	78.3
10. Gross profit (item 1 minus item 9).....	20.2	18.8	17.0	21.7
11. Fixed mill expense.................	5.0	4.1	6.2	7.2
12. Administrative expense.............	5.0	3.9	4.4	5.0
13. Selling expense...................	4.7	2.9	3.7	4.4
14. Depreciation.....................	3.1	2.4	3.1	3.5
15. Total fixed expenses...............	17.8	13.3	17.4	20.1
16. Operating profit (item 10 minus item 15).......................	2.4	5.5	−0.4	1.6
17. Other income less other charges......	0.1	0.2	0.4	0.4
18. Loss on rejected paper.............	−1.1	−0.2	−0.2	−0.4
19. Net profit or loss per ton............	1.4	5.5	−0.2	1.6

* Accounting periods of 4 weeks each.
† Approximate figure only for 1936, as the breakdown was changed after the fifth period.

The movements of unit raw-material costs have been, in general, opposite to those in fixed expenses per unit, rising when business is good and falling when business is poor. Yet raw materials are such a large proportion of total costs that the latter figures have followed closely the changes in raw-material costs. Labor cost changes have in nearly every case been in the same direction as the changes in raw-material costs, but too small in size to influence appreciably the total cost figures.

Not only have changes in labor costs played a minor part in each company's costs, but total unit costs have not been an important factor in price policy. The officials of these two companies can play only a limited role in determining the prices of their products. In fact, prices are spoken of by company officials as fixed for them "by the market." However, the fact that company B has recently concentrated primarily on specialty grades of paper permits that concern a somewhat greater degree of freedom from price competition than company A, whose major product is publication grades of paper.

Despite the importance of the market in determining prices, costs and realizations for both those companies have been closely related during the period 1936–38. This is due largely to the importance of raw materials in total costs, a fact to which reference has been made above. Pulp prices fluctuate widely; the average raw-material cost per ton for company A was over 20 per cent larger for the last five periods of 1937 than it was during the year 1936. When shorter periods are compared, the differences are much greater. Changes in raw-material prices are generally similar for all producers and vary in rough correspondence with activity in the paper industry. Consequently, when business is good, the prices of both raw materials and paper tend to rise, while, when volume is declining, both raw-material prices and paper prices decline. Thus costs and realizations for those companies have moved together, more because both were under similar industry-wide pressures than because prices were fixed on the basis of costs.

This tendency for prices of the finished product and the principal raw material to move together makes profits dependent primarily on changes in other manufacturing costs, largely labor and overhead costs. The situation is similar to that in the cotton textile industry, which puts great emphasis on changes in mill margins. In the paper industry, overhead costs represent more than half these "other manufacturing costs." This fact, together with the dependence of unit overhead costs on the volume of production, accounts for the attitude of paper company officials toward volume and for the common slogans in the industry, "keep the machines running" and "get the volume."

This situation also explains the price policies followed by these companies during severe depressions. According to officials of both companies, the pressure of fixed charges is sufficient to require that every effort be made to sustain volume. To do this, prices are cut in periods of severe and prolonged depression to a level which may just cover variable costs, i.e., materials and labor, and some part of fixed expenses. It is at such times, according to company officials, that costs play an important part in price policy, fixing a lower limit below which prices will not be cut. This function of costs is clearly recognized by company B, which breaks down all its cost figures into fixed and variable costs.

The importance which company B attaches to this distinction between fixed and variable expenses may be illustrated by a concrete example. During a period when the volume of production was low, the firm had an opportunity to secure a large order from a concern whose credit rating was low. After some deliberation, the company finally accepted the order on the basis of (1) cash on delivery for an amount carefully calculated to cover all the variable expenses and (2) long-term notes for the balance of the price. The notes were never paid, since the purchasing company went out of business before they fell due. Officials feel that no real loss was sustained, inasmuch as no other orders were obtainable at the time, and this order permitted them to maintain their organization and provide employment.

Only under these rather exceptional circumstances are changes in labor costs of any considerable importance in price policy. At such a time a reduction in wage rates will reduce variable costs and permit lower prices than would otherwise be possible. At no time during the 1937–38 recession did such a situation arise, although volume declined rather sharply.

Changes in labor costs are important in the view of both companies to their cash position and to their profits. When business is depressed, the cash position of the company becomes an important management problem. Capital expenditures may be curtailed, raw-material inventories reduced, and dividends suspended. The largest cash item remaining within the control of the company is the labor bill. The management of both companies feel that in such a situation even a small percentage reduction in wage rates is a substantial help.

TECHNOLOGICAL CHANGES

In both company A and company B, technological improvements reduced labor costs during the relatively short 1936–38 period, and in one of them the reduction was very substantial. In these two well-established paper companies, technological changes are made under a constant pressure for improvement in product and reduction in costs, and their effectiveness in limiting the influence of recent wage rate increases on labor costs has played only a minor role. Improvements in quality and reduction in overhead and material costs were even more important objectives of technological improvements than were savings in labor costs.

During the years 1936–38, company A spent substantial sums for new equipment and for improvements on older equipment. In the mill which has been the particular subject of this inquiry, the major changes were not such as to produce radical alterations in techniques or costs. In 1936, for example, when capital expenditures were approximately twice as great as in either of the other two years, the bulk of the money was spent for additional equipment of the same type as that already in use. The major consideration in deciding on capital expenditures is the rapidity of return expected from the investment. On all large investments the development engineers or the officials of the operating department discuss the proposal with the plant manager. If he approves, estimates of its cost and of its expected effect on paper costs and quality are submitted to the vice-president in charge of operation of all mills. If he indorses the proposal, a request for an appropriation is made to the quarterly meeting of the board of directors, which makes the final decision.

The chief reason for the technological changes which were made is described by company officials as a desire to improve the quality or uniformity of the product or, in more general terms, to keep abreast or ahead of the technical procession in the industry. A substantial proportion of the changes made in this mill, as elsewhere throughout the industry, brought this about primarily by improvements which increased the speed of the machines. These developments brought about some saving in labor costs, but they resulted in even greater savings in overhead costs, and this appears to have been the more fundamental reason for their introduction. It must be borne in mind, however, that machine speed is less important in a mill making many small orders than in a mill running for long periods on one grade. In the former case start-up and wash-up time constitute a substantial part of the total machine time per order. Company B has one large modern machine, installed in 1926, which is not considered suitable for small runs because of the high fixed charges that it carries, though it is more economical for large tonnage orders.

An examination was made of all the technical changes proposed or put into effect during the 3-year period by company A in the mill selected for study. There is no indication that the increases in wage rates exerted any influence on the amount or nature of the capital expenditures. Nor is there any indication that the desire to reduce labor costs was an important factor in bringing about capital expenditures. In only one instance was a prospective saving in labor costs emphasized as a reason for making a change, and this particular suggestion was not adopted.

Most of the major capital expenditures made by company B over the 3-year period 1936–38 were also for the primary purpose of improving the quality and uniformity of the product. As in the case of company A, a related objective was to run the machines at higher speeds. One of the largest projects, for instance, increased the drying capacity of one of the paper machines. Since this had been the factor limiting the speed of this particular machine, higher machine speed resulted, with a consequent reduction of all important costs except raw materials. There were many other improvements of a similar nature.

From a survey of the technical changes actually introduced and from information supplied by officials of the company, it is clear that there was little or no causal connection between increased labor costs and the introduction of improvements. Only one change during the entire period could be attributed mainly to an expected reduction in labor costs, and this was a minor purchase of equipment. To be sure, the increase in the speed of machines tended to lower labor costs, but this was not the most important effect of the changes, and it was not the primary reason for making them.

QUESTIONS

1. What is the effect of changes in wage rates upon paper prices? How is this explained?

2. What is the relationship between changes in wage rates and changes in unit costs?

3. Does the over-all cost structure of the paper industry have any relationship to the effects of changes in wage rates?

4. Did the fact that Company A employed nonunion labor while Company B employed union labor cause a significant difference in the effects of wage changes upon total costs of both companies? How would you explain this?

5. It was concluded that in the paper industry, changes in wage rates had little effect upon technological improvement. Under what conditions would you expect changes in wage rates to affect the rate of technological improvement?

6. How does accounting procedure affect labor costs in the paper industry? Would you expect this condition to be found in other industries?

7. On the basis of the information shown in Exhibits 6 and 7 for the year 1938, could both companies afford to pay a wage increase of 10 per cent? Why?

Chapter 11

~~~~~~

THE FINANCING OF INVESTMENT

IN THE previous chapter, it was pointed out that investment in capital equipment can rationally be made if its calculated present value exceeds its present cost. It is obvious that fairly long-term forecasting is required in order to compute the present value, since, it will be remembered, this is the discounted value of quasi rents expected to accrue over the entire useful life of the machine (or other form of capital good). If the investment in question is an apartment building with an expected useful life of fifty years, for example, the forecast of rental returns must be made for a period of half a century. Fortunately, the more distant expected quasi rents are discounted so heavily that they are not very significant in the calculation of present value, while the near-future returns, which are easier to estimate, have more weight in the calculation.

Sources of Funds to the Firm

In preparing a firm's "capital budget," the company officials may make a comparison of investment "requirements" with expected availability of funds over the same period. Like most budgeting, this usually requires a cutting-back on outlays which would be desirable in order to make the budget balance.

The usual sources of investible funds to the firm are depreciation allowances, retained profits, equity financing, and debt financing. Yearly depreciation charges made by a firm have the effect of reserving within the firm assets which are approximately equal to the value of the productive capacity of capital goods which are used up during the year. To the extent that these assets are liquid (rather than being in the form of slow-moving accounts receivable, for example), they can be converted into capital goods in furtherance of the firm's investment program. Similarly, profits earned and retained by the firm during a given year are usually available for investment. This is not always the case, however. If the year's profits show up on the balance sheet in a diminution of liabilities rather than in an increase in assets,

421

no actual funds will have been made available for investment, although it may then be easier to borrow again in order to secure capital assets. If additional equity capital has been raised by selling shares of stock during the year, funds will obviously have been made available for investment by the firm. This will also be the case if bonded indebtedness has been increased, or if there has been short-term borrowing from the banks. Another possible source of investible funds is the drawing-down of unnecessarily large cash balances which have been accumulated in previous periods. Montgomery Ward, under the leadership of Sewell Avery, got out of debt and accumulated $327 million in cash.[1] It seems likely that the new management will utilize a substantial portion of this cash for expansion purposes. If so, their action will illustrate this possible internal source of funds for investment.[2]

Leaving out of consideration the possible existence of an unnecessarily large hoard of cash and the other relatively unimportant sources, one can draw a supply curve for investible funds which incorporates the more usual sources to the firm. Exhibit 1[3] pertains to a definite period of time, such as a year. During this period, funds become available through depreciation reserves, and these are usually reinvested quite automatically by the firm. Consequently, the expected rate of return on these funds need not be very high to induce management to reinvest this amount in the firm rather than in outside opportunities. Replacement of worn-out capital equipment is usually considered a routine matter to a going company. It should be noted that the horizontal axis is labeled "gross investment outlay," since the reinvestment of depreciation allowances does not constitute net new investment.

A somewhat higher prospective rate of return is usually necessary in order to induce officials to "plow back" part of the annual earnings into capital goods. Retention of earnings deprives the stockholders of immediate cash dividends and, consequently, may be unpopular if it does not result in a promising expansion of capacity. It should be recognized, however, that management is often more interested in expan-

---

[1] Charles E. Silberman, "How Much Can Business Borrow?" *Fortune,* June, 1956, p. 134.

[2] In 1947 the reduction in liquid assets provided corporations with $500 million which was devoted to investment, according to Irwin Friend, "Business Financing in the Postwar Period," *Survey of Current Business,* March, 1948, p. 11. In addition to the sources listed above, Friend lists notes payable and increases in tax liabilities. Since corporate income taxes are paid after profits are earned, the reserve for tax payments constitutes quite a permanent source of funds to the firm.

[3] This chart is adapted from that of Edgar M. Hoover, "Some Institutional Factors in Business Investment Decisions," *American Economic Review, Papers and Proceedings,* May, 1954, p. 206.

sion for its own sake than in maximizing the returns to stockholders. New, interesting situations are created through the expansion of activities, and the power and prestige of those who engineer the expansion are likely to be enhanced. Also, as was pointed out in the previous chapter, the salaries of corporation officials tend to be positively correlated with company size.[4]

A still higher prospective rate of return is required to induce the firm to seek outside funds. These may be secured either from the sale

Exhibit 1

SUPPLY OF INVESTIBLE FUNDS—THE THREE MAIN SOURCES

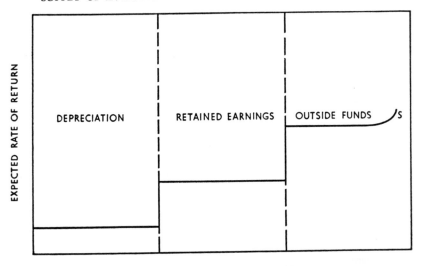

GROSS INVESTMENT OUTLAY

of stock or from the sale of bonds. Stockholders are often skeptical of the desirability of issuing new stock. If the proceeds of a new issue cannot be invested as profitably as the existing equity capital, a reduction in earnings per share will occur; this would be unfavorable to existing stockholders. Similarly, the proceeds from a new bond issue must be invested in a way which promises quite clearly to yield more than enough return to cover the interest cost, even in the event of one or more slumps in general economic activity during the life of the bonds. The supply curve for outside funds is shown as upwardsloping; it may, however, be horizontal over a wide range. The shape of this portion of the supply curve for investible funds depends on what vol-

---

[4] An interesting discussion of business viewed as a game may be found in Frank H. Knight, "The Ethics of Competition," reprinted in a collection entitled *The Ethics of Competition* (New York: Harper & Bros., 1935), pp. 41–75.

ume of new capital funds the potential lenders feel the firm can put to good use. Beyond a certain amount the moneylenders will feel that the riskiness of lending increases; this will cause a higher interest rate to be demanded. There may be an absolute limit to the amount of borrowing which the firm can engage in, and this would cause the supply curve to become vertical at that quantity.

Demand for Investible Funds

In order to place the demand for capital funds on the same chart, it is necessary to think in terms of the percentage returns which can probably be secured from various investments which are open to the firm during the same time period. Usually, businessmen prefer to think in these terms rather than in the analytically preferable terms of calculated present value versus present cost. It should be noted, however, that percentage return is not an entirely suitable criterion, because an investment may yield a very high rate of return on its cost and yet not be worth bothering with because its *absolute* return is so small. An automobile plant, for example, might be able to install peanut-vending machines near all drinking fountains and earn 500 per cent per year on its investment. But this may not be worth while if the absolute return is only a few hundred dollars a year (which is "peanuts" to the automobile company). Also certain "spillover" costs in the form of a need for more sweeping, more handwashing, more drinking of water, etc., would have to be considered. It should be noted that despite the 500 per cent return, the peanut-vending project would not rank high if the investment criterion were present value of the machines less their cost. The dollar magnitude of this difference would not be impressive.

A further advantage of the value-cost comparison is that the calculation can more readily take into account *changing* rather than steady returns. If an accurate average rate of return on an investment is calculated over the life of the capital goods involved, it is necessary to anticipate the amount of the returns above variable costs for each year, just as it is necessary to do in order to calculate present value of expected quasi rents. In addition, it is necessary in the first calculation to assume some sort of depreciation function for the capital good, so that the expected yearly net return *after depreciation* can be calculated. Friedrich and Vera Lutz have pointed out that for the past hundred years, accountants have been searching for a "true" depreciation formula.[5] Such a formula would allocate the cost of a machine over its

[5] *The Theory of Investment of the Firm* (Princeton: Princeton University Press, 1951), p. 7.

lifetime in accordance with the way in which its productive capacity was actually used up. Since no such formula is actually available, an arbitrary depreciation allowance must be made for each year in anticipating the net return which may be secured. However, the alternative method of comparing present value with present cost does not require a deduction of depreciation from expected quasi rents and thus avoids the problem of estimating this slippery cost.

If we assume that management will discard high percentage (but low absolute) returns, that returns will begin to accrue at about the

Exhibit 2

HYPOTHETICAL DEMAND SCHEDULE
FOR CAPITAL FUNDS

Expected Rate of Return	Cost of Project (Millions of Dollars)	Cumulative Demand for Funds (Millions of Dollars)
50%	$ 5	$ 5
46	4	9
35	10	19
24	6	25
15	2	27
10	10	37
8	3	40
6	12	52

same time on different projects (which lessens the need to discount), and that yearly depreciation can be estimated well enough for practical purposes, we can add a demand curve to the supply curve of Exhibit 1. The demand for capital funds can be conceived to be the accumulated sum which can be invested at a given rate of return, or more.[6] Exhibit 2 shows a hypothetical investment demand schedule for a firm. The time period involved is one year. An implicit assumption which is made in constructing the schedule is that each investment opportunity is independent of the others; if this were not the case, the return on previous investments would be affected by consideration of each new project.

A supply schedule of funds for the same year can similarly be drawn. Suppose it is feasible to retain $10 million of earnings and also to issue bonds, but that the issuance of additional capital stock does not meet with the approval of stockholders. The supply schedule

---

[6] This sort of demand schedule is suggested by Joel Dean, *Capital Budgeting* (New York: Columbia University Press, 1951), p. 18. This book is recommended to the reader who is seeking more detailed information on the subject of capital budgeting as practiced by many firms.

Exhibit 3

HYPOTHETICAL SUPPLY SCHEDULE FOR
CAPITAL FUNDS

Expected Rate of Return	Supply of Funds (Millions of Dollars)	Cumulative Supply (Millions of Dollars)	Source
3%	$15	$15	Depreciation reserves
6	10	25	Retained earnings
7	5	30	Bond issue
8	7	37	Bond issue
9	10	47	Bond issue

might look like that of Exhibit 3. This schedule indicates that debt can be placed only at higher interest rates as the amount borrowed increases.

Supply and Demand Together

In Exhibit 4 the hypothetical demand and supply schedules are plotted together. It can be seen that a gross investment outlay of $37 million is desirable, since the curves intersect at this quantity. This volume of funds would be forthcoming at rates low enough to be more than covered by the expected net rate of return on the associated projects. While another $10 million could be borrowed, this does not appear to be desirable, since the funds could not be invested to yield as high a rate of return as would be paid by the firm to obtain the funds.

If the officials directing the firm do not wish to secure investment funds from sources outside the firm—and this is a common situation —only $25 million will be invested during the period under consideration. This sum will permit the exploitation only of investment opportunities which are expected to yield 24 per cent per annum or more; other opportunities which would apparently yield a higher rate of return than would have to be paid on externally secured funds would be excluded by the firm's preference for wholly internal financing.

Although the above analysis has indicated that officials should compare probable rates of yield with interest costs in deciding which investment opportunities to exploit, it should be kept in mind that some investments are not of such a nature as to yield measurable monetary returns. They may still be extremely important, however. Research facilities are an outstanding example. The entire future success of the firm may be dependent on research to develop new products, but it

is difficult to calculate a probable rate of return on investment for research and development purposes. Investments which decrease the
risk of accident or improve employee morale are also of this sort. A
soft-ball diamond, a larger parking area, and a better cafeteria are
examples. Officials must exercise careful, largely nonquantitative

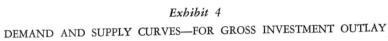

Exhibit 4

DEMAND AND SUPPLY CURVES—FOR GROSS INVESTMENT OUTLAY

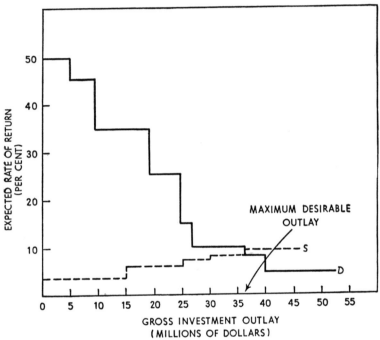

GROSS INVESTMENT OUTLAY
(MILLIONS OF DOLLARS)

judgment in these cases. It is still important, of course, to finance such
improvements as cheaply as possible.

Relative Importance of Internal and External Financing

Internal funds (derived from depreciation reserves and retained
profits) are quantitatively more important than external capital funds
(derived from stock and bond issues). From 1946 to 1949, internal
funds were about three times as large as externally supplied capital
funds.[7] Recently, however, the capital markets have gained in importance. The extremely high level of investment in 1956 has re-

---

[7] Dean, *op. cit.,* p. 42. It should be remembered that these figures pertain to gross
investment rather than net investment; consequently, external financing assumes more
importance as a source of net investment funds.

quired a greater reliance on external financing, since internal sources have become increasingly inadequate.[8] Firms differ greatly in their willingness to enter the capital markets in order to secure funds for expansion. Historically, the Sun Oil Company has been among the firms which has permitted growth to take place only as rapidly as internally supplied funds have permitted.[9] United States Steel has also shown a great preference for internal financing. (The company took advantage of easy money conditions in 1954, however, to borrow $300 million on 10-year bonds.[10]) Du Pont and Sears, Roebuck are among the large firms whose officials have an aversion to debt; on the other hand, Dow Chemical is a willing long-term borrower.[11]

Bonds versus Stocks for External Financing

Economists have generally considered the sale of common stock to be the normal way to raise capital for expansion purposes. Investment by the firm should be based mainly on *anticipated* profits rather than on realized profits. It is theoretically better to have the public voluntarily purchase new shares when the company's outlook is bright than to have management in a position to expand because of its *past* success in earning profits. Actually, however, net stock issues (total issues less retirements) were only about $2 billion in 1955.[12] The sale of additional common stock may jeopardize the control of a corporation, and this may cause corporate officials to seek funds elsewhere. (The device of selling additional stock to the present stockholders through "rights" reduces this risk.) Also, it is difficult to select the proper time to sell new stock because of the rapid price fluctuations which occur. A new issue must be planned well in advance, and market prices may not be as favorable as were anticipated. Existing stockholders are often fearful of a dilution in their equity per share if new shares are issued, since the new investments made by the corporation may be less profitable than existing investments. A further reason for reluctance to use equity financing is found in the high flotation costs of new stock.

In recent years the sale of bonds has been more popular with corporations than the sale of stock. Preferred stock has even less popu-

---

[8] This situation is interestingly described by Charles E. Silberman, "How Much Can Business Borrow?" *Fortune,* June, 1956, p. 131.

[9] Dean, *op. cit.,* p. 54.

[10] Silberman, *op. cit.,* p. 133.

[11] *Ibid.,* pp. 135 and 152.

[12] Securities and Exchange Commission, *Statistical Bulletin,* March, 1956, p. 3.

larity than common stock. Utility companies have, however, made quite substantial use of preferred stock, accounting for about half of the use of this form of security. While public offerings of bonds exceeded the private offerings (to insurance companies, industrial corporations, etc.), the latter exceeded in value all sales of new stock in 1955. (See Exhibit 5.)

An important factor in the preference for selling bonds rather than stock is the high corporate income tax (52 per cent on net income above $25,000). Interest payments on bonded indebtedness are deductible as expenses, thus reducing taxable income, while dividends are considered a distribution of profits. A corporate income tax should,

Exhibit 5

GROSS PROCEEDS FROM SECURITY SALES, ALL CORPORATIONS—1955
(Thousands of Dollars)

Bonds:
Publicly offered..................................$4,175,272
Privately offered.............................. 3,462,215 $7,637,487

Common stock....................................   2,178,342
Preferred stock....................................   637,878

Source: Securities and Exchange Commission, *Statistical Bulletin*, March, 1956, p. 3.

in theory, be levied against economic profit rather than on accounting profit, in order to avoid this discrimination against equity financing. It should be remembered from the first chapter that a "normal" return on capital stock is deductible in calculating economic profit. Unfortunately, this more defensible procedure would be difficult administratively.

The principal danger inherent in debt financing is that interest must be paid even in years of depressed business, whereas dividends on stock can be skipped. (Dividends missed on cumulative preferred stock have to be paid at a later date before common dividends can be paid.) The high level of economic activity in the United States since 1940 has probably diminished the fear of debt on the part of most businessmen—although, as has been noted, some firms still shun debt. Another general economic force has made bonded indebtedness relatively desirable. Our federal fiscal and monetary policy, influenced by the strains of World War II and the Korean War, has for the most part been such as to bring about persistent inflation. Like other debtors, business firms which are net debtors tend to profit from inflation. Since bonded indebtedness is fixed in monetary terms, its *real* burden diminishes with inflation. It has been shown empirically that the market value of stocks of corporations which are net debtors has gone up more in years of inflation than that of the companies which are net creditors.[13]

If year-to-year earnings tend to be relatively steady, there is a particular incentive to raise additional capital by selling bonds rather than stock. Utility companies make much use of bonded indebtedness for this reason. As already noted, utilities also make more use of preferred stock than other corporations. This is because the fixed dividend requirement is not so apt to be bothersome. Most other types of firms have come to consider preferred stock virtually as high-cost debt financing rather than equity financing. While dividends may theoretically be skipped or deferred, they are in practice usually paid and, unlike bond interest, do not reduce a corporation's income tax liability.

Bonds have a special advantage over stock for financing an investment project which promises to be a temporary one, to be followed by a contraction in total investment by the firm. In this situation, equity financing would leave a permanently expanded number of shareholders. If, instead, bonds of relatively early maturity were issued so as to cover the period of temporary need for more capital, the capitalization of the corporation would not have to be permanently increased. This is similar to the well-established practice of borrowing from the banks to meet seasonal or other temporary needs for working capital.

Convertible bonds sometimes offer a worth-while compromise between equity and debt financing. Such bonds may be converted into stock at a specified price. If the corporation's stock rises in market price, many owners of convertible bonds will find it advantageous to exercise the privilege of conversion. Prior to conversion the interest on the bonds will be tax-deductible, and this advantage need not be given up unless a favorable price (as specified on the bond) can be secured. Also, the possibility of substantial capital gain on stock enjoyed by the holder of the convertible bond makes it possible to sell the bonds at favorable interest rates. A special use of the convertible bond is to provide funds during a long period of construction of a plant. If the bonds are made convertible only after two years, for ex-

---

[13] Reuben A. Kessel, "Inflation-Caused Wealth Redistribution: A Test of a Hypothesis," *American Economic Review*, March, 1956, p. 128. Kessel found that in a sample of 30 industrial corporations, shares of the 15 creditor corporations declined in a real value by 13 per cent, while shares of 15 debtor corporations increased in real value by 81 per cent from 1942 to 1948—a period of inflation.

ample, a corporation may utilize low-cost capital to construct the facility, but be in a position to earn dividends on stock by the time con-
versions are made, since the plant will then be in operation. In an
era of chronic inflation (such as we seem to be in), there is much to
be said for using convertible bonds as a method of taking at least
temporary advantage of the tax deductibility of bond interest and also
taking advantage of the popularity of the stock market.

Supply of and Demand for Loanable Funds

The interest rate which must be paid on borrowed funds is, of
course, an important determinant of the feasibility of selling bonds.
While the interest rate varies greatly on bonds of different quality

Exhibit 6

LOANABLE FUNDS THEORY OF INTEREST

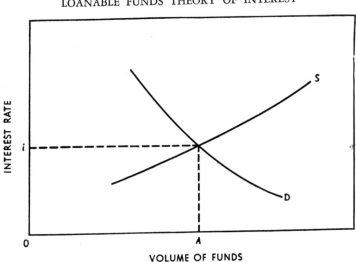

VOLUME OF FUNDS

and different maturity dates, it is instructive to consider this rate, like
other prices, to be determined by demand and supply. The supply
curve of Exhibit 6 rises from left to right, indicating that in a given
time period, lenders are willing to supply a greater volume of funds
at higher interest rates than at lower rates. These lenders consist of
such institutions as banks, building and loan associations, insurance
companies, and some industrial firms, as well as individuals. The
higher the interest rate, the greater the income sacrificed by potential
lenders if they hold on to loanable funds in the form of cash rather
than offering them on the market. Potential borrowers, on the other

hand, find borrowing to be more desirable at lower interest rates, since more investments can then be made which promise to yield a higher rate of return than the rate which must be paid to finance their purchases. The interest rate (i) can be considered to be the rate which equates the demand and supply for loanable funds.[14]

It is important that the corporate officials in charge of finances be extremely well acquainted with the capital markets in both a theoretical and a practical way. Once it has been decided that the firm should secure additional capital by borrowing, it is necessary to decide whether a public or a private offering is more satisfactory, what specific form or forms of bond to sell, and just when and how to float the loan. The executive who is able accurately to feel the pulse of the capital market (or who is lucky) may save his company very important sums of money by securing lower interest rates on borrowed capital. United States Steel, as has been noted, wisely borrowed $300 million in 1954 when interest rates were low, despite its usual policy of internal financing. Whirlpool-Seeger could have saved $60,000 per year in interest charges by selling $30 million in debentures just two weeks earlier in 1955. On the other hand, a two-week delay saved Niagara Mowhawk Power $67,500 a year in interest cost on a $30 million issue.[15] These latter situations arose because of a particularly turbulent capital market during the spring of 1955.

The general state of demand for external financing can, perhaps, be predicted from the surveys of anticipated capital expenditures made by McGraw-Hill, the Securities and Exchange Commission, and the Department of Commerce. A prediction of increased capital expenditures suggests an increased demand for loanable funds and higher interest rates. An upturn in orders for durable producers' goods would carry the same suggestion. Federal Reserve actions must be watched carefully and anticipated whenever possible by the acute vice-president in charge of finance. For example, the rediscount rate was raised five times during the twelve-month period between April 14, 1955, and April 12, 1956, the rate at the Federal Reserve Bank of New York rising from $1\frac{1}{2}$ per cent to $2\frac{3}{4}$ per cent over this period. (The borrowing rate is not always the same at all the Federal Reserve banks.)

[14] Lutz, *op. cit.*, p. 242, points out that the demand curve should be considered to include the funds tied up in old bonds as well as the demand for new loanable funds. The supply curve then should be considered to include funds which security owners are willing to "reinvest," as well as new funds which lenders are willing to invest in bonds.

[15] These examples are from Charles E. Silberman, "The Fine Art of Raising Capital," *Fortune*, July, 1956, p. 97.

This attempt by the central banking authorities to curb inflation raised interest rates on bank loans and on securities by decreasing the supply of loanable funds (shifting the supply curve of Exhibit 6 to the left). An increase in the rate of saving by families would have the opposite effect—i.e., would tend to shift the supply curve to the right, and to lower interest rates.

It should be noted that not only existing, but also anticipated, rates of interest affect the demand and supply curves for loanable funds. The anticipation of higher interest rates causes borrowers' demand to increase in an attempt to beat the cost rise. The same expectation would cause supply to decrease. The expectation of a rise in interest rates would speedily be translated into an actual rise. If demanders and suppliers have contradictory expectations, however, these may cancel one another.

A modern trend in economics is to emphasize the importance of economic growth rather than just the present capability of an economic system to satisfy wants. Similarly, many corporation officials feel that the only way to insure the success of their firms is to keep them growing rather than simply maximizing immediate profits. This penchant for growth has brought the financial expert into a more prominent position in the American corporation. A special vice-president in charge of finance is increasingly common. As a consequence, the intensive study of capital, interest, and securities may ultimately yield rich dividends on "personal capital" built up in the mind of the potential executive.

CASE 11–1: ROBERT C. DAVIS COMPANY

In 1926, Robert C. Davis purchased three variety stores located in small cities in central Ohio. These stores carried the usual line of merchandise handled in the traditional 5- and 10-cent store, and no merchandise was sold at a retail price of more than $1.00. In 1930, Mr. Davis was operating a chain of 11 stores in Ohio and Indiana. These additional stores had been financed out of the earnings of the company.

During the decade of the thirties the Robert C. Davis Company was incorporated and began a period of expansion. Throughout the East and the Middle West, there were a number of small local chains of 10-cent stores, some of which were in financial difficulty as a result of the financial collapse in 1929 and the years of depression immediately following. Mr. Davis had survived this period without severe losses and had observed that, relatively, the 10-cent store was enjoying business better than some firms carrying higher-priced lines of merchandise. Between 1930 and 1938, Mr. Davis acquired nine small chains, which gave his company a total of 73 stores. These acquisitions had been accomplished largely by the issue of cumulative preferred stock in the Robert C. Davis Company. This stock had a par value of $100 and carried an interest rate of $4\frac{3}{4}$ per cent. It was redeemable by the company at $105 per share. Although the rate was considered rather high at the time, Mr. Davis had found that it enabled him to acquire most of these chains at attractive prices and involved little cash in most instances.

As a result of reduced capitalization and overhead on the acquired chains, Mr. Davis was able to realize adequate profits, until 1938, to pay dividends on the preferred stock. In 1938, however, shortly after he had purchased a chain of nine stores, there was a severe setback in business activity, which forced him to pass preferred dividends in 1939. At the time, all of the common stock was held by Mr. Davis personally. In 1940, another chain of 17 stores in Illinois and Kentucky was purchased by a combination of preferred stock, common stock, and cash. About one half of the cash was obtained through a mortgage loan on store properties.

No further dividends were paid on the preferred stock until 1947. During the wartime period of 1941–45 the company introduced higher-priced articles of merchandise, with some items selling as high as $24.95. In spite of restrictions on many types of goods during the war, the company emerged from that period with a substantial surplus. Much of this had been the result of deferred maintenance as well as earnings on sales. As a result of the decline in the market value of the preferred stock, 10,000 shares had been redeemed through purchase in the market. Dividends were resumed in 1947; by 1950, all accumulated dividends had been paid in full. The company had also, by 1950, built and acquired more stores, so that it then had 161 outlets between the Mississippi River and the Atlantic Coast. In order to finance this expansion, the company had issued one million shares of common stock, part of which had been issued to the vendors of stores purchased and part sold in the over-the-counter market. The common stock had a par value of $1.00. Between 1950 and 1954, another one million shares of common stock had been issued to finance additional stores and to provide working capital. In 1954 the stock was selling

at approximately $39 per share. In the same year the dividend was increased to $2.00 per share.

With the development of a boom in the construction of private dwellings in the postwar period, large suburban areas began to appear around the larger cities where the Robert C. Davis Company had many of its stores. Traditionally, the company had located its stores in the heart of the shopping districts in the downtown sections of cities. In the larger cities, stores had also been located in some of the larger outlying shopping areas within the city limits. In 1952 and 1953, there began to appear shopping centers in the suburban areas. These centers were usually promoted by a development company which constructed a complete shopping area consisting of stores of many kinds, one of which was almost invariably a 10-cent store. As large new housing developments were planned, these centers became an integral part of such plans. In some instances the property was built and constructed jointly by stores which became part owners of the project; in other cases the construction was planned and financed by the promoters, and space was leased to stores on a long-term basis.

The Robert C. Davis Company presently had stores in 11 such centers, and, with the exception of one, all were profitable. In nine of these centers, there were no 10-cent stores other than the Davis store. During 1955, many new centers were planned and being built. Mr. Davis believed that stores in the downtown shopping areas would eventually show some declines in operations, especially in those areas where large suburban shopping centers were being developed. He therefore negotiated for the construction of five Davis stores in such centers and for the lease of space on a 25-year basis in 23 other centers. All of these shopping centers were expected to be completed and ready for occupancy by June 1, 1956. It was estimated that the cost of construction of the stores and two warehouses, cost of additional inventory, and provision of additional working capital would amount to $35 million.

The problem of financing this expansion was presented to the board of directors. Exhibit 1 shows the company's balance sheet as of December 31, 1955. Exhibit 2 is the profit-and-loss statement for the period from January 1, 1955, to December 31, 1955. Several plans were presented for raising the necessary funds to meet the anticipated expenditures. As noted in Exhibit 1, the company had $10,005,845 invested in government securities. These bonds were at present yielding an average net of 2.78 per cent. It was recommended that $7.5

Exhibit 1

ROBERT C. DAVIS COMPANY

Statement of Assets and Liabilities, December 31, 1954, and December 31, 1955

Item	1955	1954
ASSETS		
Cash	$19,470,223	$23,439,017
U.S. government securities, at cost and accrued interest	10,005,845	7,832,606
Merchandise inventories, at the lower of cost or market:		
Stores and warehouses	23,939,851	21,138,020
In transit	3,011,905	3,539,826
Total Current Assets	$56,427,824	$55,949,469
Property and equipment, at cost:		
Buildings	$ 7,531,293	$ 7,725,392
Improvements to leased properties	25,377,587	24,542,840
Fixtures and equipment	23,070,003	21,804,529
	$55,978,883	$54,072,761
Less: Allowances for depreciation and amortization	27,614,301	25,509,763
	$28,364,582	$28,562,998
Land	1,734,719	1,532,069
Total Property and Equipment	$30,099,301	$30,095,067
Prepaid expenses	$ 1,013,101	$ 1,159,864
Miscellaneous accounts receivable and sundry investments	591,649	543,507
Total Assets	$88,131,875	$87,747,907
LIABILITIES		
Accounts payable, including merchandise in transit	$ 3,639,541	$ 4,133,699
Taxes withheld or collected	626,856	787,899
Dividend on preferred stock	106,879	106,879
Accrued compensation and other expenses	3,476,833	3,572,519
Accrued state, social security, and other taxes	824,056	1,149,063
Provision for federal taxes on income	7,788,116	9,015,967
Mortgage installments payable within one year	30,252	41,450
Total Current Liabilities	$16,492,533	$18,807,476
Mortgage installments payable after one year	32,208	67,159
Total Liabilities	$16,524,741	$18,874,635
CAPITAL		
Preferred stock, par value $100 per share:		
Authorized, 100,000 shares, issuable in series; issued, 4¾ per cent cumulative series, 90,000 shares (redeemable at $105 per share)	$ 9,000,000	$ 9,000,000
Common stock, par value $1.00 per share:		
Authorized, 3,000,000 shares; issued, 2,129,500 shares	2,129,500	2,129,500
Paid-in surplus	11,917,891	11,917,891
Earnings retained in the business	48,557,743	45,825,881
Total Capital	$71,605,134	$68,873,272
Total Liabilities and Capital	$88,129,875	$87,747,907

million of this amount be used for addition to working capital. The present Cash account was considered the minimum at the present level of operations.

Among the proposals mentioned was an increase in the common stock outstanding. The stock was currently selling around $51 per share. An additional issue of 600,000 shares would yield approxi-

Exhibit 2

ROBERT C. DAVIS COMPANY

Statement of Earnings for January 1–December 31, 1954 and 1955

Item	1955		1954	
Sales..............................		$182,172,687		$187,163,824
Cost of goods sold and operating expenses......................	$160,995,574		$164,072,441	
Provision for depreciation and amortization......................	3,280,294		3,155,520	
Taxes, other than federal taxes on income.......................	1,992,116		2,201,798	
Employees' retirement plan costs.......	1,054,181	167,322,165	1,100,672	170,530,431
		$ 14,850,522		$ 16,633,393
Other income, less other deductions....		290,885		263,021
Earnings before Federal Taxes on Income......................		$ 15,141,407		$ 16,896,414
Provision for federal taxes on income:				
Normal and surtax.................	$ 7,723,000		$ 8,765,000	
Excess profits tax..................		7,723,000	160,000	8,925,000
Net Earnings for the Year.........		$ 7,418,407		$ 7,971,414
Earnings retained in the business, beginning of year...............		45,825,881		42,541,012
Deduct: Dividends paid or declared:				
4¾ per cent preferred stock, $4.75 per share.....................	$ 427,514		$ 427,514	
Common stock, $2.00 per share....	4,259,031	4,686,545	4,259,031	4,686,545
Earnings Retained in the Business, End of Year.............		$ 48,557,743		$ 45,825,881

mately $25 million, after underwriting expenses. Mr. Davis was opposed to this proposal on personal grounds. He presently held 425,375 shares of stock, and to increase the amount outstanding by the proposed amount would dilute his ownership and possibly his control of the company if the larger share were purchased by a small group of individuals or an institutional investor. Another objection raised to the proposal was that the earnings on the additional investment would be subject to income taxes before the payment of dividends.

Still another proposal was the issue of additional shares of preferred stock. This would require an amendment to the charter, but this could be obtained easily. None of this stock had been offered for sale in more than two years. The last transfer had been priced at $114 per share. This met Mr. Davis' argument of dilution of ownership, but the dividend rate was an objection. There was also the tax problem in this instance, as in case of the common stock. Several directors objected to this proposal because of the inflexibility it might impose upon the declarations of dividends on the common stock. One director proposed that this might be the proper time to obtain enough funds to retire the outstanding preferred stock and thus relieve the company of the annual charges to meet the dividends. He pointed out that this stock could be redeemed at $105 per share, as stated in the provisions of its issue.

A third proposal was that the funds be sought from an institutional investor by means of a term loan. The current rate on such loans was about $3\frac{3}{4}$ per cent. If such a loan could be obtained on a 15- or 20-year basis, it would meet the company's needs. Furthermore, the interest on such a loan could be deducted from income before taxes as a business expense. This disadvantage was the fixed charge which the company would have to meet during the lifetime of the loan.

Closely related to the preceding proposal was another that the company issue mortgage bonds or debentures to raise the necessary funds. At present, none of the company properties were indentured except four warehouses which had been built since 1950. Either mortgage bonds or debentures, or a combination of such bonds, would involve the problem of fixed charges, but each had the advantage that the interest was deductible for tax purposes. It was also doubtful if the company possessed enough real property to issue mortgage bonds for the full amount.

A fourth proposal was that the company sell convertible debentures in the amount of $28 million which would be convertible into common stock within two or three years. This arrangement would give the company the advantage of tax deduction for the interest during the life of the debentures; and when conversion took place, the company would be relieved of the liability of the fixed charges. It was anticipated that such debentures could be sold at par if they were offered at a rate of $3\frac{1}{2}$ to 4 per cent. It was proposed that the conversion rate be set at $45 per share of common stock in order to insure conversion.

QUESTIONS

1. Which of the above methods of financing would you recommend? Why?
2. Would you recommend that the new financing include sufficient funds to retire the outstanding preferred stock? Explain.
3. Would you recommend any other method of financing than those proposed? Why?
4. In Exhibit 1, it is shown that earnings retained in the business amount to $48,557,743. Why not use this amount to finance the proposed expansion?

CASE 11–2: DUFF AUTO STORES, INC.

Duff Auto Stores, Inc., operated a nationwide chain of automobile supply stores at retail. The company owned 534 stores of its own and had franchise arrangements with 1,131 independently owned stores. The company-owned stores were located in the larger cities, while the franchise stores were in the smaller cities and towns. All stores carried a fairly complete line of automobile replacement parts and accessories. In addition, a majority of them sold many kinds of hardware and tools. In the postwar period, lines of household appliances had been added.

During the early period of growth and expansion, Duff Stores had sold automobile accessories only. The company began during the depression of the early thirties, when the sales of new cars declined sharply and there was a demand for replacement parts to keep them running over longer periods of time. Until 1937 the company had purchased its entire stock from manufacturers and merchandised many nationally advertised brands of parts and accessories. In 1937, when the firm was operating about 100 stores, it arranged to have tires manufactured under its own brand name. This enabled the company to purchase on more advantageous terms and also permitted it to offer tires at prices under those of the nationally advertised brands. By 1940, it had made arrangements with a number of manufacturers for the production of many replacement parts under the brand name of Duff. Late in 1940 the company began production of its own batteries and several accessories such as points, distributors, spark plugs, floor mats, and seat covers. In 1939 a national advertising campaign was undertaken. All merchandise was sold for cash.

During World War II the firm enjoyed an unprecedented growth of business. The manufacture of new automobiles was halted, so that the demand for automobile replacement parts increased sharply. Under authority of the War Production Board, certain replacement parts were given priority of materials, although production of many accessories was either forbidden or sharply curtailed. In 1945, at the end of the war, Duff Auto Stores had more than 1,000 stores and affiliated dealers. It emerged from this period with a substantial cash surplus.

The period following the war was one of even greater growth and expansion. It was not until 1949 that the production of new cars began to catch up with the pent-up demand. With restrictions removed, the company opened more stores; and to take advantage of the household market, it added a line of appliances and hardware. All appliances and tools were under the Duff brand name. All items, with a few exceptions, were manufactured for Duff by contract with various manufacturers. This rapid growth had, however, raised some problems of finance. In order to obtain supplies of various items, the company had in some cases been forced to finance—both wholly and partially —a number of its suppliers. Many of these suppliers had to build additional facilities in order to produce the desired quantity for Duff.

It had also become necessary to finance partially almost all of the affiliated dealers. A store in a community of 10,000 people required an inventory of approximately $20,000, in addition to costs of leases and property. In some cases, it had been necessary to finance the construction of these stores. In order to obtain as many outlets as possible, the company curtailed the opening of its own stores and encouraged the growth of affiliated stores. Under a franchise arrangement the store was independently owned. The owner or proprietor had to provide at least 35 per cent of the total capital required. Duff Auto Stores, Inc., would finance the balance at current rates of interest, plus 1 per cent of net sales until the balance was repaid. In addition, the owner of the store would agree to purchase all merchandise from Duff. Such a store was known as the local Duff Auto Stores Affiliate.

Shortly after the close of the war, it became apparent that if Duff Auto Stores expected to share in the market for appliances and major automobile accessories and parts, it would be necessary to modify its policy of cash sales only. The growth of installment sales was both rapid and large. In 1947 a program was worked out so that merchandise could be sold for as little as 10 per cent down, with the balance on an installment basis. This meant that some arrangement had to be made to finance the installment sales of all stores. Some affiliated stores made their own arrangements with local banks to carry such paper. At company-owned stores, this paper was accepted in payment of new merchandise. As the amount increased, it was discounted at banks by Duff Auto Stores, Inc., in order to obtain funds.

The postwar expansion of the company had been financed by retained earnings, three sales of common stocks, and two term loans from insurance companies. In 1955, however, it was observed that the amount of installment paper being discounted amounted to more than $200 million. As the sales of the stores had grown, many local banks were unable to accommodate the owners with further advances; and the company had extended, on a selective basis, the privilege of submitting installment paper in payment for new merchandise. It was the inclusion of this group which had caused the rapid growth of the discounting of this paper by Duff Auto Stores, Inc.

The terms of installment sales were the same in all stores. After the required down payment, which varied for different sales, the balance was payable on a monthly basis, not to exceed 24 months. Carrying charges were computed on a block basis—that is, on amounts from $20 to $40 the charge was $3.50 for 24 months. In effect, the charge was about 10 per cent of the total sale for a 24-month period. There were no refunds for prepayment of the account before the end of the payment period. This paper, when forwarded to Duff Auto Stores, Inc., was discounted in various banks throughout the country where the company had established lines of credit. The average rate of discount was $4\frac{1}{2}$ per cent. Although this paper passed in title to banks, payments by customers were still made to Duff Auto Stores, Inc., which redeemed the individual notes from the banks upon payment in full by customers. As payments were received on accounts from customers, they were passed on to the banks. In brief, Duff Auto Stores acted as a collection agency, since all discounted paper was endorsed by Duff, with full recourse.

The vice-president and treasurer of the corporation, after a study of the installment sales program of the company, concluded that the present arrangement was one which did not fully take advantage of potential profit possibilities. He pointed out that while the installment terms were 5 per cent per year on the balances, the company was paying banks $4\frac{1}{2}$ per cent per year, and at the same time assuming all the expenses of collection as well as assuming full liability for payment of the notes to banks. He therefore proposed that the firm set up a wholly owned subsidiary, to be known as Duff Discount Corporation, for the purpose of financing the time sales of Duff Auto

Exhibit 1

DUFF AUTO STORES, INC.

Statement of Assets and Liabilities, December 31, 1955

ASSETS

Cash..		$ 47,469,523.52
Short-term securities............................		24,623,487.00
Merchandise inventory (at lower of cost or market):		
Stores and warehouses.........................	$111,382,779.23	
In transit....................................	15,751,162.55	
On consignment of affiliates....................	56,356,115.67	
In process...................................	8,231,666.51	191,721,723.96
Accounts receivable.............................		5,279,542.75
Total Current Assets........................		$269,094,276.23
Property and equipment:		
Stores.......................................	$ 5,321,154.35	
Factories....................................	17,442,557.91	
Fixtures and equipment........................	43,477,327.50	
	$ 66,241,039.76	
Less: Depreciation............................	15,386,127.33	50,854,912.43
Prepaid expenses...............................		3,652,914.75
Total Assets...............................		$323,601,103.41

LIABILITIES

Accounts payable...............................		$ 7,649,325.51
Notes payable:		
Ten-year term loan at $3\frac{1}{2}$ per cent..................		14,591,781.45
Short-term bank loans.........................		4,122,525.00
Accrued interest................................		421,652.62
Accrued taxes..................................		2,121,579.86
Accrued compensation...........................		8,465,233.72
Provision for federal income taxes................		23,295,742.55
Other accrued expenses..........................		4,661,922.07
Total Liabilities...........................		$ 57,680,437.28
Capital account:		
Preferred stock, Par Value $100:		
Series A, $4\frac{1}{2}$ per cent cumulative, 100,000 shares.......	$ 10,000,000.00	
Series B, $4\frac{1}{2}$ per cent cumulative, 50,000 shares........	5,000,000.00	
Common stock, no-par value, 22,152,475 shares outstanding..................................	154,635,452.75	
Paid-in surplus...............................	11,549,369.45	
Earnings retained in business.....................	84,735,843.93	
Total Capital Account.........................		265,920,666.13
Total Liabilities and Capital....................		$323,601,103.41

Stores, Inc. In order to finance this subsidiary, he recommended that Duff Auto Stores, Inc., acquire the entire authorized issue of common stock of Duff Discount Corporation. In exchange for this stock Duff Auto Stores, Inc., would guarantee the principal and interest of a $3\frac{3}{4}$ per cent debenture offering by Duff Discount Corporation in the amount of $10 million. In addition, lines of credit would be arranged with several banks in the total amount of $150 million, to be used as needed. Under a line of credit the company would be charged interest at the rate of $3\frac{1}{2}$ per cent per year on the amount of credit actually used.

If this recommendation were carried out, Duff Discount Corporation would purchase all of the installment paper of Duff Auto Stores, Inc., for the principal amount of each sale. The carrying charges would remain the same as currently charged, but would be revenues of Duff Discount Corporation. Duff Discount Corporation would not redeem any of the paper currently held by banks but, upon beginning its operations, would finance all new sales, so that within 24 months, all installment paper of Duff Auto Sales, Inc., would be held by it.

Exhibit 2

DUFF AUTO STORES, INC.

Statement of Earnings, January 1, 1955—December 31, 1955

Net sales...			$598,611,352.57
Cost of goods sold................................	$320,377,135.61		
Operating expenses................................	71,325,455.92		
Taxes (other than income).........................	2,732,613.73		394,435,205.26
Earnings before federal income taxes....................			$104,176,147.31
Less: Federal income taxes........................			54,158,596.60
Net earnings.......................................			$ 50,017,550.71
Earnings Retained in Business, Beginning of Year.........			68,622,005.72
			$118,639,556.43
Less: Dividends paid or declared:			
Series A, $4\frac{1}{2}$ per cent preferred........................	$	450,000.00	
Series B, $4\frac{1}{2}$ per cent preferred........................		225,000.00	
Common stock, $1.50 per share.....................		33,228,712.50	33,903,712.50
Earnings Retained in Business, End of Year..............			$ 84,735,843.93

Duff Discount Corporation was organized as proposed and began business on March 1, 1956. On that date the total amount of installment sales held by banks for Duff Auto Stores, Inc., amounted to $201,174,239.64. Exhibits 1 and 2 show the balance sheet and earnings statement for the year ended December 31, 1955.

QUESTIONS

1. Do you think the move was a profitable one? Explain.
2. Do you think Duff Auto Stores, Inc., was "spreading itself too thin" by this proposed arrangement?
3. Should Duff Auto Stores, Inc., have invested more heavily in Duff Discount Corporation than it did? Why?

CASE 11–3: NORTHERN ILLINOIS GAS COMPANY

The Northern Illinois Gas Company provided gas service for approximately 250 communities to the north, south, and west of Chicago.

Exhibit 1

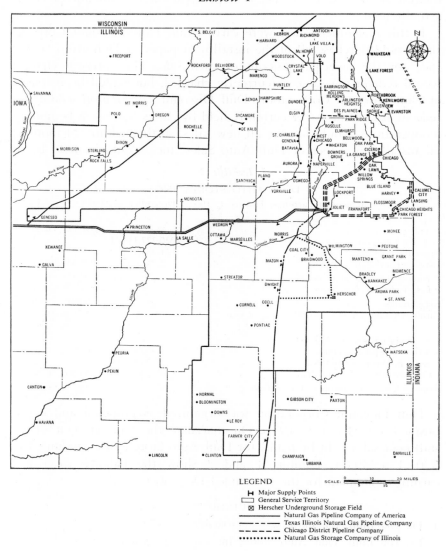

LEGEND   SCALE: 0 5 10 15 20 MILES

⊢ Major Supply Points
☐ General Service Territory
⊠ Herscher Underground Storage Field
———— Natural Gas Pipeline Company of America
– – – – Texas Illinois Natural Gas Pipeline Company
– — – — Chicago District Pipeline Company
••••••••••• Natural Gas Storage Company of Illinois

The territory covered about 10,000 square miles, with an estimated population of 1.85 million persons as of December 31, 1955. The company was franchised and regulated by the Illinois Commerce Commission to provide gas to residential, commercial, and industrial customers. The map in Exhibit 1 shows the geographical area served.

The company obtains the larger part of its gas from two subsidiaries of the Peoples Gas Light and Coke Company—Natural Gas

Pipeline Company of America and Texas Illinois Natural Gas Pipeline Company. Under this contract, Northern Illinois Gas Company has a total firm daily supply of 322 million cubic feet. Gas in excess of this amount may be purchased on an interruptible basis when available. The company also is entitled to approximately 30 per cent of the storage space in the Herscher Dome (see Exhibit 1), a large natural underground storage basin. This is operated by the Natural Gas Storage Company of Illinois, a part of the Peoples Gas system. Under authority of the Federal Power Commission the amount of daily gas withdrawal was increased during 1955. It was anticipated that this amount would be increased slightly, once certain technical difficulties were overcome. It was not expected that any substantial increases in the supply of natural gas would be available before the end of 1957. One of the company's suppliers had proposed the construction of additional pipe-line facilities, which would make an increase possible by that time.

The Northern Illinois Gas Company began operations on February 1, 1954. Its service area was formerly served by the Public Service Company of Northern Illinois, a subsidiary of the Commonwealth Edison Company. Under a contractual arrangement the Northern Illinois Gas Company was established as an independent corporation to serve the prescribed area with gas. The Public Service Company was established to provide electricity to approximately the same area, thus separating the gas and electric operations of the former subsidiary. Under the provisions of the separation contract the Northern Illinois Gas Company acquired the necessary distribution, manufacturing, and service facilities to meet its service obligations.

Exhibit 2 is a statistical summary of the company's operations for the years 1954 and 1955. Of significance in the company's operations is the change in the importance of residential business, which produces relatively greater revenues than the interruptible business it displaces. This is shown as follows for the years 1954 and 1955:

	1955	1954
Residential	64%	60%
Firm commercial and industrial	16	15
Interruptible	20	25

As shown in Exhibit 2, the sale of gas in therms was virtually the same for both 1954 and 1955. It will be noted, however, that firm sales of gas in therms to residential, commercial, and industrial customers increased 14 per cent, and interruptible sales decreased 15 per cent. When gas that has been previously sold on an interruptible

Exhibit 2

NORTHERN ILLINOIS GAS COMPANY,
OPERATIONS FOR THE YEARS 1954 AND 1955

Item	1955	1954
Number of customers (at end of year):		
Residential—without house heating	298,828	286,840
Residential—with house heating	201,436	168,856
Commercial	20,964	19,788
Industrial—other than interruptible	3,006	2,919
Industrial—interruptible	60	57
Public authorities	1,075	996
Other gas utilities	....	....
Total	525,369	479,456
Therms of gas produced, purchased, and sold (in thousands):		
Produced (manufactured and propane)	610	218
Purchased	1,180,576	1,191,860
Total produced and purchased	1,181,186	1,192,078
Losses, company use, net injection into Herscher Storage Field	67,225	57,777
Remainder	1,113,961	1,134,301
Sales:		
Residential—without house heating	81,934	75,337
Residential—with house heating	338,459	290,078
Commercial	36,386	34,197
Industrial—other than interruptible	133,728	116,871
Industrial—interruptible	520,226	614,522
Public authorities	3,228	3,296
Other gas utilities	....	....
Total	1,113,961	1,134,301
Operating revenues (in thousands):		
Residential—without house heating	$11,546	$10,528
Residential—with house heating	32,606	26,564
Commercial	3,329	3,006
Industrial—other than interruptible	7,205	5,945
Industrial—interruptible	13,843	15,298
Public authorities	242	225
Other gas utilities	....	....
Other gas revenues	453	477
Total	$69,224	$62,043
Annual therms per residential customer	886	826
Annual revenue per residential customer	$93.09	$83.88
Annual revenue per residential therm sold	10.50¢	10.15¢
Peak day sendout (in thousands of therms)	3,870	3,552
Therms of gas in Herscher Storage Field at December 31 (in thousands)	36,722	20,023
Miles of gas mains	7,403	6,767
Degree days:		
For the year	5,909	5,541
Percentage of territorial normal (6,310)	93.6	87.8

basis is sold on a firm basis, it commands a much higher price. This trend is expected to continue.

Of great importance is the sharp increase in new residential gas customers. New customers numbering 32,770 were added in 1955, which was 5,057 more than were added in 1954, the highest in the history of both the present company and its predecessor. The favorable trend in number of residential gas customers reflects the continued population growth in the service area. Some of the population increases reported since the last decennial census in 1950 have approached the spectacular. Special census counts taken since 1950 in 79 of the communities served showed a combined population of 809,-681, a gain of 217,670—or 37 per cent—over the 1950 total for

Exhibit 3

NORTHERN ILLINOIS GAS COMPANY,
CONSTRUCTION ESTIMATES AND ESTIMATED
CUSTOMER ADDITIONS, 1956–59

Year	Construction Expenditures	Customer Additions
1956	$21,000,000	37,000
1957	19,500,000	30,000
1958	17,100,000	25,000
1959	16,400,000	

those communities. This increase is greater than the combined population of Evanston, Cicero, and Oak Park, the three largest communities served.

Another area of sharp increase in sales was in gas for house heating. During 1955, two authorizations were made for the installation of gas heating equipment; one authorization was made to 30,000 applicants and the other to 40,000. The demand for this service in 1955 continued to exceed the ability of the company to meet it. Because of the excess of demand over supply, the company found it necessary to establish a waiting list for gas heating service. As gas became available, applicants were authorized to install the necessary equipment. Despite these two authorizations the waiting list at the end of 1955 was 110,-327, compared to 112,235 at the end of 1954.

During 1955, 32,580 gas house-heating customers were added. The installations made in 1955 resulted from the remainder of 37,-000 authorizations granted in 1954 and a portion of the 1955 authorizations. Customers are given one year in which to make their installations, and about two thirds actually complete their installations

Exhibit 4

NORTHERN ILLINOIS GAS COMPANY, BALANCE SHEETS,
DECEMBER 31, 1954 AND 1955

Item	1955	1954
ASSETS		
Utility plan—at original cost or less	$181,039,697	$160,492,445
Less: Provision for accrued depreciation	40,387,658	34,915,811
Utility plant less depreciation	$140,652,039	$125,576,634
Current assets:		
Cash	$ 2,469,412	$ 7,433,974
U.S. government obligations—at cost	3,500,024	9,000,000
Receivables—less reserve	4,996,479	3,953,279
Gas in Herscher Storage Field—at cost	990,340	513,654
Materials and supplies—at cost	2,729,219	2,834,078
Prepaid insurance, taxes, and other expenses	129,316	123,513
	$ 14,814,790	$ 23,858,498
Deferred charges	$ 367,179	$ 269,815
	$155,834,008	$149,704,947
LIABILITIES		
First-mortgage bonds, 3½ per cent series, due 1979; annual sinking fund requirement of $1,200,000 from 1957 to 1977	$ 60,000,000	$ 60,000,000
Preferred stock, cumulative, par value $100; authorized, 250,000 shares:		
5 per cent convertible—authorized and outstanding, 100,000 shares; each share convertible into 10 shares of common stock after January 31, 1957	10,000,000	10,000,000
Common equity:		
Common stock, par value $5.00:		
Authorized, 12,500,000 shares:*		
Outstanding, 6,112,403 and 6,292,484 shares, respectively	30,562,015	31,462,420
Paid-in surplus	35,124,602	32,962,420
Retained earnings	3,112,496	543,919
Total Common Equity	$ 68,799,113	$ 64,968,759
Total Capitalization	$138,799,113	$134,968,759
Current liabilities:		
Accounts payable	$ 4,797,584	$ 4,000,396
Accrued taxes	8,940,666	7,352,137
Dividends declared	1,347,481	1,383,497
Other	1,656,692	2,000,158
	$ 16,742,423	$ 14,736,188
Reserve for deferred federal income taxes	$ 292,472	$..........
	$155,834,008	$149,704,947

* One million shares reserved for conversion of 5 per cent preferred, and 188,666 and 200,000 shares reserved for issuance under the employee stock purchase plan at December 31, 1955, and December 31, 1954, respectively.

within the prescribed period. Out of the open authorizations at the end of 1955, it was anticipated that the company would be serving approximately 30,000 additional customers by the end of 1956. It was doubtful that further authorizations would be made during 1956 because of limitations on the supply of available gas.

Exhibit 5

NORTHERN ILLINOIS GAS COMPANY, STATEMENTS OF INCOME FOR THE YEARS ENDED DECEMBER 31, 1954 AND 1955

Item	1955	1954*
Operating revenues:		
Gas	$69,223,816	$62,042,838
Heating	295,822	296,272
	$69,519,638	$62,339,110
Operating expenses and taxes:		
Gas purchased	$28,982,918	$26,615,724
Other operations	12,778,586	11,732,552
Maintenance	2,255,269	2,479,400
Depreciation	3,791,929	3,486,395
Taxes, other than federal income	4,073,695	3,489,931
Federal income taxes	7,491,274	6,331,000
Deferred federal income taxes	225,726	....
	$59,599,397	$54,135,002
Net operating income	$ 9,920,241	$ 8,204,108
Other income	121,115	125,000
Gross income	$10,041,356	$ 8,329,108
Interest on first-mortgage bonds	2,100,000	2,100,000
Net income	$ 7,941,356	$ 6,229,108
Provision for dividends on preferred stock	500,000	500,000
Net income applicable to common stock	$ 7,441,356	$ 5,729,108
Shares of common stock outstanding at end of year	6,112,403	6,038,569†
Earnings per share	$1.22	$0.95

* Based on the assumption that the company began operations as of January 1, 1954, and issued on that date the securities which were issued on February 9, 1954. The company began operations as of February 1, 1954.

† After deducting 253,915 shares surrendered for cancellation on January 26, 1955, by Commonwealth Edison Company, pursuant to final separation contract.

In order to meet the anticipated growth in demand, both for new customers and for house heating for present applicants, a construction program was projected for the four years 1956–59. This program totaled $74 million. In the gas distribution business, construction expenditures are, to a great extent, dependent upon the number of new customers to be added. Since most of the construction projects represented only several week's work, the program could be altered to meet changing conditions. The present four-year estimates are shown in Exhibit 3.

Of the total amount, it was anticipated that about $45 million of new capital would be required to finance the four-year program. The capitalization of the company at the end of 1955 was as follows:

First-mortgage bonds............................43%
Convertible preferred stock......................... 7
Common stock................................... 50
                                               _____
                                               100%

Exhibits 4 and 5 show the company balance sheets and earnings statements, respectively, for the years 1954 and 1955. Since the firm began business as an independent company in 1954, an annual dividend of 80 cents per share had been paid on the common stock.

QUESTIONS

1. How would you propose that Northern Illinois Gas Company finance the projected new construction? Explain.
2. Would the fact that the company is a regulated public utility have any influence upon the method of financing? Why?

Chapter 12

˄˄˄˄˄˄˄˄˄˄˄˄˄˄˄˄˄˄˄˄˄˄˄˄˄˄˄˄˄˄˄˄˄

LOCATION OF PLANTS

ALTHOUGH the problem of where to locate a new plant arises relatively infrequently for most firms, it is clearly a matter of great importance whenever it must be faced.[1] Economic consultants are often brought in to study the problem of location and to advise management on this subject. While company officials are usually expert in the day-to-day operations of the firm, they may feel much less at home with the problem of finding an optimum location, since this involves such questions as the relative availability and cost of labor, capital, and materials at various places at which they may have had no business experience. Executives employed by large retailing "chains" are more likely than most officials to be in close touch with locational problems because of the frequency with which new outlets are established. There is seldom only one suitable location for a plant; instead, numerous locations are likely to be satisfactory, though some may be decidedly better than others. Some locations, of course, will be so poor that their selection alone would ensure failure.

Location for the Long Pull

A basic assumption which underlies the economic theory of the firm is that executive decisions are motivated by a desire to maximize profits—or more accurately, to maximize the present value of the stream of net profits over the time horizon for which plans are made. Since selection of the best location is one problem which is often associated with new investment by the firm, it can be said that a location should be chosen in such a way as to be consistent with maximization of the present value of the future profits obtainable by the firm on an entire investment project. The optimum location is not necessarily the one which will bring the largest immediate profits. It may, for example, be better to select a suburban site for an apartment building where demand for such housing is presently somewhat inadequate, but on the way up, rather than a place in the city

---

[1] The term "plant" should be understood to include such facilities as stores, apartment buildings, and motels as well as factory buildings.

451

where immediate demand is strong but long-run prospects are poorer. The capitalized value of a similar building in the suburban location might well be larger, because the capitalization process involves anticipating income over the life of the project. Often, however, there is no conflict between securing maximum immediate and long-run returns, perhaps because forecasting the more distant future is so difficult that only near-future prospects are actually weighed.

Importance of Personal Considerations

Personal considerations are sometimes more important factors in the location of small firms, especially, than is the quest for maximum profits. A plant may be located so as to be convenient to the home of the president of the company. Or plants may locate near such cities as New York for the convenience of executives who wish to be within easy reach of urban *divertissement*. Frequently, they are located in Florida or California primarily because of favorable climatic conditions which may be sought by officials for themselves and their employees. When the psychic income of a location is so great to officials as to cause them to accept lower implicit salaries than they could secure at less desirable places, this personal preference can be translated into an actual cost-reducing factor.[2] Similarly, the chief official of a company may have a strong personal preference for a city where he is well known and consequently is more readily able to borrow money, secure materials, and make sales than elsewhere, on account of his personal contacts. While his personal preference for a location may be due to such sales/cost advantages, the same advantages would not accure to another entrepreneur. These personally induced economic gains lie outside the general framework of location theory, which emphasizes the demand/cost situation which would face any firm at a particular place. Nevertheless, personal considerations, and even pure chance, frequently do determine actual locational decisions.

Cost Factors

Both cost and demand considerations are important in the theory of plant location. That is, it is necessary that a site be selected not only where cost per unit is low but also where a sufficient number of units

---

[2] This is pointed out by Melvin L. Greenhut, *Plant Location in Theory and in Practice* (Chapel Hill: University of North Carolina Press, 1956). Greenhut gives an excellent historical survey of location theory (pp. 3–97), a new general theory of plant location (pp. 251–91), and the results of some empirical investigation into actual locational decisions (pp. 295–326).

can be sold. A department store located deep in a woods might have an extremely low daily cost of operation due to low land rent and the need for few sales personnel, but the project would not be successful because of the small sales volume. The cost per unit of sales would be much higher than in a city location.

In the theory of location, main emphasis is usually given to the cost side. The most favorable location for production is usually said to be at the place where the unit cost of gathering materials, processing them, and delivering the finished product is at a minimum. This formulation is somewhat vague, because it does not say *how many* units are produced and sold. If only a few units of finished product could be delivered cheaply from a location, this would be unlikely to make it a desirable one. A fuller explanation of plant location must consider demand as well as the cost of production. In the following discussion, demand will, however, at first be neglected.

Transfer Costs

In those industries where the cost of gathering raw materials and distributing the finished product is an important part of total costs, transportation is a significant locational factor. In order to isolate the significance of the transfer factor, it is necessary to neglect processing costs, the location of competitors, and personal factors. This is the usual analytical technique of relegating to *ceteris paribus* certain variables which are of importance but which must be held constant while the effect of another variable is studied. Also, it is a useful simplification to assume that a plant uses only one raw material and turns out only one product.

The objective of the firm in locating a new plant, under the assumption described, is to minimize the combined material gathering and product distribution cost per unit. Usually, this will call for a location either at the source of the material or at the market for the finished good. The reason for this can be seen most easily by referring to Exhibit 1. Line *G* shows the transportation cost at the different locations between the material source and the market. This "material" transportation cost is based on the rates applicable to the amount of the material which must be used to produce one unit of the finished product. It is lowest, of course, at the material source. It rises for locations more distant from this source, reaching a maximum at the most distant point—namely, at the market for the finished product. Line *P* is similar in nature, pertaining to the cost of transporting one unit of the finished product to market from various locations which might be selected for the plant. This cost would, of course, be lowest if the plant were located at the market and highest if it were at the raw-material source. Line $G + P$ is the sum of the two types of transfer costs, and thus represents the combined material and finished product transfer cost per unit of sales.[3]

As Exhibit 1 is drawn, the total transfer cost would be lowest at the source of the material; consequently, this would be the best loca-

Exhibit 1

TOTAL TRANSFER COST—USUALLY LOWEST AT ONE END

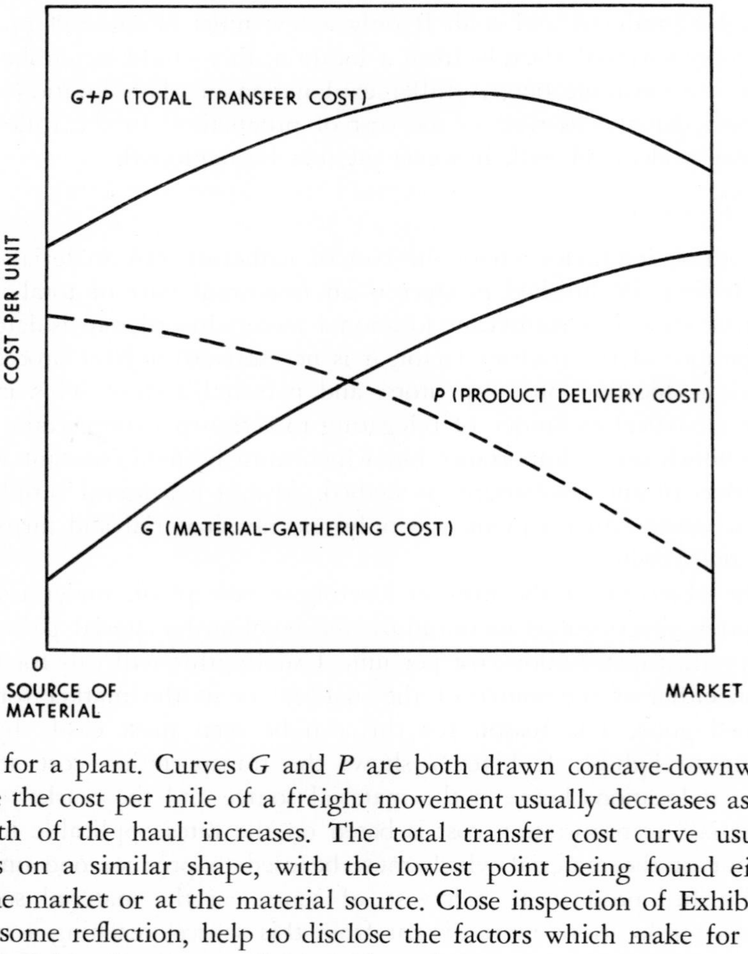

G+P (TOTAL TRANSFER COST)

P (PRODUCT DELIVERY COST)

G (MATERIAL-GATHERING COST)

COST PER UNIT

0

SOURCE OF
MATERIAL

MARKET

tion for a plant. Curves G and P are both drawn concave-downward, since the cost per mile of a freight movement usually decreases as the length of the haul increases. The total transfer cost curve usually takes on a similar shape, with the lowest point being found either at the market or at the material source. Close inspection of Exhibit 1, and some reflection, help to disclose the factors which make for economical location at one place or the other.

The height of curve $G + P$ at the source of the material is de-

[3] This chart is adapted from Edgar M. Hoover, *The Location of Economic Activity* (New York: McGraw-Hill Book Co., Inc., 1948), p. 30.

termined in part by the cost of bringing enough of the (one) raw material to the plant to produce a unit of output, since the G curve intersects the left-hand vertical axis above the zero cost level. Even if the plant is theoretically "at" the source of the material, the assembly of material will require some transport cost. For example, a portland cement mill located right next to a limestone quarry must incur transportation expense in loading the limestone onto a conveyor belt and bringing it into the plant on the belt. A paper mill, while it may be situated right in the forest from which it secures its supply of logs, must incur considerable transportation expense in bringing the logs by truck or railroad to the plant site. Similarly, even if the plant were located at the market, some transfer cost would normally be involved in placing the product in the wholesale or retail outlets. The principal determinant of the best location is usually the relative rise of curves G and P over the range between material source and market. That is, if curve G rises more than curve P over this range (as it does in Exhibit 1), location at the material source is usually more economical; if curve P rose relatively more over this range (and if the curves started at the same height), location at the market would be more economical.

Suppose the material source and the market are 500 miles apart. It is clear that the amount of raw material per unit of product is an important determinant of the relative rise in the two curves over the 500-mile distance. If 10 pounds of material were needed to make one pound of finished product, the material transfer cost curve would go up much more than the product transfer cost curve. That is, the cost of transporting 10 pounds of material 500 miles would probably greatly exceed the cost of moving one pound of product that distance. The smelting of most ores, the ginning of cotton, the crushing of cane sugar, the production of fruit juices, and the canning of crabmeat and salmon are examples of "weight-losing" processes where it would be uneconomical to locate near the market, since this would mean incurring heavy transportation expenses on substances which are wasted or burned up in processing. A dramatic example of extreme weight loss is found in the processing of gold-containing ore, where almost all of the weight is lost. This processing takes place, of course, right at the mines.

Market Orientation

In other cases, it would cost more to move the finished product a long distance than it costs to move the material(s) the same distance. This promotes location at the market. An example is the baking

industry. Flour and other components can be transported quite cheaply
to the city; but bread, pies, and cakes are more costly to transport.
Also, the need for freshness reinforces the desirability of urban location. The farm machinery industry tends to locate in farming areas
rather than near steel mills and other sources of components, because
such bulky machinery is costly to transport compared with components.
The same force has led to the establishment of regional automobile
assembly plants, especially by General Motors and Ford. The form,
perishability, and unit value of finished products have a great influence
on freight rates, and hence on location. For example, the waste space
necessarily involved in transporting tin cans and bottles fosters their
production near the market rather than near sources of materials.

Products which use "ubiquitous" materials—those which are available nearly everywhere—tend to locate at the market. In terms of
Exhibit 1 the principal raw-material source and the market may both
be considered to be at the same place (the market), so that no other
location need be considered. Such products as soft drinks, beer, and
ice are manufactured in cities, since it would obviously be uneconomical to transport the water incorporated in these commodities very far.
At the same time, such manufacturing is usually not carried on in the
very heart of cities because the competition of other uses (clothing
stores, drugstores, banks, etc.) makes rental costs in central areas excessive for businesses which do not sell directly to large numbers of
consumers. Sulfuric acid, an extremely important industrial material,
is weight-gaining in nature and consequently is produced near the
market.

Location near the market is also promoted by the production of
"style goods." The demand for such products as ladies' hats and dresses
is so capricious that producers must be ready to alter the nature of
their output on short notice. By locating in such cities as New York,
the style goods producers are able to reduce inventory losses by keeping their fingers on the pulse of demand. The locational importance
of this factor has been somewhat reduced by the utilization of high-
speed air transportation for style goods.

Location at Both Ends

Where the principal raw material loses very little weight, or where
the higher transportation rate on the finished product quite closely
compensates for the smaller weight of the finished product, it may
make little difference whether processing takes place near the raw-
material source or near the market. In terms of Exhibit 1, the G and

P curves would rise about the same distance, so that the *G* + *P* curve would be at about the same level at the market and at the material source. An example is the oil-refining industry, which has processing facilities both near the oil fields and near the large cities. The utilization of a very large part of the crude oil for a great variety of products means that the processing is not greatly weight-losing; consequently, oil may be refined at the market. At the same time, the finished products are economically transportable (by pipe line, tank car, and tanker, for example), so that processing at the source is also feasible.

The slight weight-losing property of wheat when milled into flour is quite closely compensated for by the higher transportation rate for flour. Consequently, flour milling occurs both near the wheat fields and near the markets. Changes in the relative cost of transporting wheat and flour can quickly alter the relative desirability of milling near the material source or near the market.[4]

Milling-in-Transit Privilege

The tendency which has been noted for location to be most economical either at the source of the principal material or at the market is due to the downward concavity of curves *G* and *P* in Exhibit 1—that is, to the fact that freight rates usually increase less than proportionally with distance. While a location between the material source and the market would secure some of this advantage of rate "tapering" with distance for *both* the material and the product, it would not secure so great a *total* advantage in transfer cost as location at either end. To offset this tendency, the railroads frequently grant "transit" privileges, under which a through-rate is paid on both the raw material (e.g., grain) and the finished product (e.g., flour). This is usually the rate applicable to the raw material. The through-rate replaces the combination of rates which would otherwise be charged; that is, it neglects the fact that a stop is made for purposes of processing.

In terms of Exhibit 1 the transit privilege would cause the total transfer cost line (*G* + *P*) to be horizontal over the entire range. As a consequence, any location between the source of the material and

[4] D. Philip Locklin, *Economics of Transportation* (Chicago: Richard D. Irwin, Inc., 1954), p. 50, points out that the relationship between transportation rates on wheat and flour has at times determined whether flour to be consumed in Europe should be milled in the United States or abroad. Shipping rates for wheat and flour on the Great Lakes greatly affect the desirability of milling flour for the eastern markets in the Midwest or in the East.

the market would be equally feasible from a transportation point of view. It should, however, be noted that from a *social* point of view the transit privilege is not desirable, in that more resources must be devoted to transportation to the extent that location is artificially influenced by this sort of rate. That is, if the concavity of the G and P curves is consistent with the actual cost savings due to long hauls, the transit privilege, by causing the $G + P$ line to be horizontal, distorts "natural" patterns of location. It would also tend to hold down land values at the material source and at the market, and to increase land values at intermediate points.

Transit privileges apply to a large number of commodities and to quite dissimilar forms of "processing." Shippers of livestock may use the privilege to rest their stock and to test the possibilities of local sale. Soybeans and cottonseed may be converted into oil and meal under this rate system. Lumber products may be milled, iron and steel stopped for fabrication of certain kinds, and agricultural products stopped for storage under the transit privilege.

Multiple Sources of Materials

Frequently, a manufacturing process uses two or more materials in large quantities. When both are weight-losing in nature, the optimal location may be between the principal sources of these materials. If one of the materials—e.g., fuel—is more weight-losing in nature than the other, this material will tend to exert more influence on the minimum transfer cost location. At the same time, the attraction of the market may also be significant.

The steel industry provides an interesting example of this situation. It is also an extremely important example because of the attraction of steel itself to a great variety of steel-using manufacturing activities.[5] Steel plants are usually located between deposits of coking coal and iron ore. Much the greater influence has been exerted by coal, in part because of the low-cost water transportation available on the Great Lakes for ore from the Lake Superior region and on the eastern seaboard for imported ore. The market exerts perhaps even greater influence than fuel, especially since cities are the main source of the scrap used in steel making. That is, the best markets are also important sources of a material. Economies recently introduced in the

---

[5] According to Richardson Wood, "Where to Put Your Plant," *Fortune,* July, 1956, p. 101, the existence of the steel belt stretching from Buffalo and Pittsburgh to Detroit and Chicago is the main reason why 70 per cent of the industrial labor force of the country is found in less than 10 per cent of the nation's territory.

use of coal in blast furnaces have somewhat diminished the attraction of fuel as a locational factor for steel mills and have increased the relative locational pull of the markets.[6]

Processing Costs

In many industries, transportation is not highly significant, consituting but a small part of the total cost of putting the product into the hands of the consumer. This may lead to the establishment of a relatively small number of large plants designed to serve national or even international markets. Examples of such commodities are typewriters, alarm clocks and watches, razor blades, and bobby pins. For such goods the location which minimizes processing costs is apt to be optimal. These consist of such expenses as wages and salaries, interest on short-term funds, taxes, utility charges, and the f.o.b. cost of materials and fuel.[7]

If labor were perfectly mobile between different geographical areas, regional differences in wage and salary rates would not be an important factor in plant location.[8] Under this assumption, workers would move until no further advantage in terms of real wages could be secured. (If this is to be strictly true, the real wages must be considered to include as positive or negative items such factors as climate, cultural advantages and disadvantages, traffic congestion, and recreational opportunities.) In the real world, however, labor is notoriously slow to move in adequate numbers. This is a basic reason for the "farm problem" and for the low earnings of many families in the South and Southwest.

The existence of regional differences in the wages of potentially equally productive workers may exert a powerful locational pull in industries where labor costs are a large part of total processing cost. Many textile and woolen mills have moved to the South and to Puerto Rico to take advantage of lower wage rates. The shoe industry has also shown a tendency to establish plants in small communities in the South, especially to utilize female labor. Frequently, firms which move to low-wage areas to take advantage of this cost saving are careful to conceal the fact, in view of the rather general feeling that there is

---

[6] Greenhut, *op. cit.,* p. 117.

[7] The f.o.b. cost of materials and fuel, rather than the delivered price, is considered a processing cost, since the transportation cost was treated as a transfer expense in the previous discussion.

[8] "Perfect mobility" does not necessitate a readiness of *every* worker to move. It implies only such readiness on the part of a sufficient number of laborers to equate wage rates for a given type of work at different places.

something reprehensible in this sort of action. Actually, the only way in which low-wage areas can improve their economic lot rapidly is through the in-movement of capital or the out-migration of labor. Each plant which is located to take advantage of cheap labor helps to raise the real income of workers in that area.

In addition to the wage rate for workers of a given ability level, prospective employers give consideration to turnover, dependability, and local labor laws. Federal minimum-wage legislation, which receives its principal support from congressmen in the high-wage areas, exerts some locational influence, in that it tends to reduce the attraction of surplus-labor areas to new industry. That is, the legislated minimum wage may prevent a regional or local oversupply of labor in relation to employment opportunities from exerting its full effects on wage rates in interstate commerce.

Capital Costs

Although the Federal Reserve System and the Federal Home Loan Bank System do much to increase the mobility of loanable funds, there is still a great deal of difference in interest rates between different parts of the country. This is manifest in the unlike rediscount rates sometimes maintained by the Federal Reserve banks themselves in the various districts. A famous location theorist, August Lösch, whose work included a good deal of empirical investigation of the American economy, found that interest rates in Texas in 1936 were higher the greater the distance from the nearest Federal Reserve Bank.[9] Where communities are not large enough to support a sufficient number of competing financial institutions, there is also a tendency for interest rates to be higher than in the larger cities. Small firms looking for a location for a plant are more likely to be influenced by local interest rates than large firms, since the latter can tap distant sources of loanable funds.

Land Rent

The purchase price which must be paid by a firm for the land on which it erects a plant—or, alternatively, the rent which must be paid on a long-term lease for the use of land—may be an important locational factor. For convenience, we shall speak of the rent on land, since this keeps the cost on an annual or monthly basis comparable to wage and interest payments.

---

[9] August Lösch, *The Economics of Location* (New Haven: Yale University Press, 1954), p. 464.

Land rent, like the return from any factor of production, arises from its value productivity. This productivity stems from the fertility of the soil in agricultural uses, from the minerals which it may contain, and from its location with respect to markets. The last-named factor is of principal importance in location theory.

To the extent that there is active competition for land, and to the extent that landowners are well informed and rational, the rent on better sites will be higher than on poorer ones. Theoretically, the rental value of any piece of land will be determined by the best use of the land from the viewpoint of value productivity. Often, it is to the advantage of the landowner temporarily to hold his land out of use, rather than committing it to a long-term use, if prospects are good for an increase in its value.

A German economist, Johann Heinrich von Thünen,[10] was the first to describe the pattern of land use and rents which would tend to evolve from the unhampered workings of the price system. He considered a large town in the middle of a large plain, where the land was everywhere of equal fertility. The plain was assumed to be isolated from other places of economic activity by a wilderness. The town was considered to supply the farmers with manufactured items in exchange for raw materials and food.

Von Thünen concluded that the rent of land would decline with its distance from the town. Within a circle nearest the town, such commodities as green vegetables and milk would be produced. Intensive cultivation of forest lands for fuel and building materials would take place in the next circle. Such activities as grain and cattle raising would occur in the outer circles. In the most remote zone the most extensive land use—hunting—would take place. The basic principle is that different uses of the land vary in their ability to bear rental costs relative to transportation costs. Such items as milk and vegetables are perishable and are transported to market frequently. They are better able to stand high yearly land rental costs than the high yearly transportation costs which would be associated with more distant hauls to market. Grains, on the other hand, are transported to market less frequently and in larger lots, so they can better bear high transfer costs than high land rents. The aim of each user of land would be to minimize the sum of land rental and transportation charges per time period.

Although based on highly abstract assumptions, the von Thünen

---

[10] *Der isolierte Staat in Beiziehung auf Landwirtschaft und Nationalekonomies* (3rd ed.; Berlin: Schumacher-Zarchlin, 1875).

theory discloses factors which are of importance both for agricultural and for industrial location. If fertility, land contours, and other natural features are fairly uniform, rent per unit of land tends to decline with distance from the market. Since this decline is due basically to the cost of transportation from plant or farm to the market, any change in the structure of transportation charges tends to affect land rents. It was pointed out earlier that the milling-in-transit privilege tends to increase land rents at points more remote from the market and the material source by giving the same through-rate from material source to market regardless of where processing actually takes place. A general increase in freight rates tends to increase rental values near the market and to decrease the value of the more remote sites.

Once the rental value of a piece of land is established, this value can be considered to have the economic function of excluding inferior uses of the land. An ice cream plant, while properly located in the city, is forced by the high rent on downtown property to be situated less centrally. The owner of an orange grove in an area where housing developments are spreading rapidly will find it best to sell the grove to a real estate firm and to relocate his citrus business in an area more remote from the city. A jewelry store, on the other hand, whose sales heavily depend on the number of passers-by, may find it best to pay a high rent in order to secure a downtown location.

Demand Interdependence

A good deal of modern location theory is based primarily on considerations of demand rather than cost. That is, a primary locational objective may be the carving-out of more or less exclusive sales territory by means of securing such proximity to a group of buyers as to be able to undersell competitors. Much of this theory is similar to that of oligopoly pricing, in which the probable reactions of rivals must be considered before a price change is made. That is, in selecting a location, it may be necessary first to determine where rivals will probably locate in response to your decision. It is probable that the theory of games, which was briefly examined in Chapter 7, has useful applications to this sort of locational problem.

Because of the large number of possibilities with respect to the nature of price competition, costliness of changing location, and assumptions which a firm may make as to rivals' reactions, it is necessary to specify clearly the set of assumptions on which any theory of locational interdependence is based. It is also a convenient simplification to consider the market to lie along a straight line rather than having a circular, hexagonal, or irregular shape, as it usually would have in reality. Despite this simplification (or rather *because* of this simplification), it is possible to see some interrelationships of real-world significance.

The following assumptions make possible the study of a simple model of locational interdependence:

1. The market is linear and bounded at both ends.
2. At each point, there can be only one delivered price. The total amount purchased at that point is sold by the firm with the lower delivered

Exhibit 2

OPTIMUM LOCATIONS—TWO-PLANT MONOPOLY

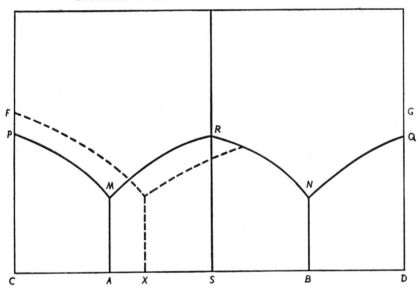

price. The lower the delivered price, the greater the physical volume of sales.
3. There are two rival firms, A and B, selling the same product.
4. Marginal costs are constant, so that the desirability of increasing sales is not limited by rising production costs.
5. Freight rates per unit per mile decline uniformly as the haul increases.
6. Sales are made on an f.o.b. mill basis, so that delivered price at any point is equal to the mill price plus freight.
7. Each plant can be moved to any point, without cost.

Exhibit 2 represents the linear market by the distance CD.[11] If a mill is located at point A, the f.o.b. mill price is AM; delivered prices

---

[11] Chart and analysis are adapted from Arthur Smithies, "Optimal Location in Spatial Competition," *Journal of Political Economy,* June, 1941, p. 426.

to the left and right of *A* are shown by the lines *MP* and *MR*, respectively. These price lines are drawn concave-downward, to reflect the tapering of rates with distance. If a mill is located at point *B* the mill price is similarly represented by *BN,* and delivered prices by *NR* and *NQ.* Points *F* and *G* represent the highest price at which any sales can be made. It is clear that if demand curves are similar and downsloping at all points in the market, greater quantities will be sold near the mills than at a distance, but it will pay to make all additional sales which can be secured, since the consumer is assumed to pay the freight.

If it is assumed that a single firm owns both plants—i.e., that the firm is a monopolist in the market—it is apparent that the locations *A* and *B* are optimal. These locations are at the quartiles, so that distances *CA, AS, SB,* and *BD* are all equal. Maximum sales could be secured by these locations, since lower average delivered prices can be charged than with any other locations. This can be seen by considering what the situation would be if Plant A were closer to *S* than is now shown. Suppose it were located at point *X.* Plant A could then undersell Plant B in the territory just to the right of *S* (as indicated by the dotted price line), but this would not help the firm, since it owns both plants. To the left of *A,* plant A would sell less than before, because delivered prices (as shown by the dotted line) would be higher. While somewhat more than before could be sold between *A* and *X,* this would not make up for the decreased sales to the left of *A.* The firm would, therefore, have a net decrease in total sales, and would be better off with locations at the quartiles instead.

Competition in Location

If the two plants are owned by separate companies, and if each firm believes that the other will match both its price and its location, the quartiles will again be the equilibrium location. Suppose that Plant A considers a move to the center of the market in an effort to control a greater territory. Under this assumption the locator would know immediately that Plant B would also move to the center. If the moves were made, both firms would then still control only half the market (as before) but would have diminished sales, since the long hauls toward *C* and *D* would reduce the quantities which buyers would purchase. The best thing for both plants to do would be to stay at the quartile locations, since they would anticipate poor results from any movement toward the center.

Under altered assumptions as to rivals' reactions the quartiles will no longer be the likely locations. If each competitor believes he can increase his sales territory by moving closer to the center, because his rival will meet price competition but will not change location, both will locate closer than the quartiles to the center. Plant A, for example, may first move from A to X. This will cause Plant A to take sales away from Plant B, which will move a comparable distance toward S, or even farther. (That is, the belief that Plant B would "stay put" turns out to be erroneous.) Plant A will then locate symmetrically, or go even closer to the center. Where the move toward the center will stop depends on how quickly the competitors revise their original expectation of locational independence as they notice declining sales brought on by the rival's movements. Once they have moved toward S, locating at equal distances on either side, they will not retreat to the quartiles, since each would fear that the other would not also move away from the center. The wisest thing for the firms to do would be to come to a cartel-like agreement to move back to the quartiles. In this case a monopolistic agreement as to location (but not as to mill price) would be socially beneficial.

Location along a Highway

Those great modern institutions—the automobile and the highway—create numerous interesting locational problems. In this case the buyers transport themselves to the goods offered by the gift shop, restaurant, filling station, or other roadside facility. The most important consideration is locating and advertising in such a way as to stop a sufficient number of cars. Location at or near the intersection of highways may be advantageous not only because of the greater number of cars passing such a point but also because of the lower speeds which the intersection imposes on drivers.

Gift shops which also sell candy, soft drinks, and other items of interest to motorists often locate along a long stretch of highway well away from all other structures. This permits the purchase or lease of a substantial plot of land with ample parking space, cheaply. At the same time, a large number of passing cars carry potential customers. Where the highway is divided, or where it is a heavily traveled two-lane road, most of the cars will stop only on the right-hand side of the road. A gift shop located along a barren stretch of road will usually advertise heavily for many miles in order to build up demand—which may be the result of pressure from children who have, unfortunately, learned to read. In this situation the optimal strategy for a competitor is to locate on the same side of the road but at a point which will be reached a little sooner by the traffic stream. This permits the invader to take over part of the demand which the other firm's advertising has built up. Adoption of a quite similar name for the shop (Jones's Gift Shop versus Jane's Gift Shoppe) and the handling of similar commodities are also useful. If the first firm then adds a shop on the other side of the highway some miles away, the rival firm can again set up a shop near to it, but reached sooner by the stream of traffic. While the first firm might retaliate by erecting a third facility in front of its rival, this may not be economically feasible, since aggregate capacity could easily become too large for the market. Relocation of an existing shop is likely to be costly, so a situation of being outflanked by a rival is apt to be a serious one.[12]

Agglomeration of Sellers in Informed Markets

Where consumers are poorly informed regarding the relative quality of different goods, there is a strong tendency for sellers to hold back the information which would facilitate rational comparison.[13] Instead, advertisements are confined to generalities, meaningless statements about allegedly useful ingredients with specially coined names, and paid endorsements by famous people who may or may not actually like the product. Similarly, sellers may purposely locate their facilities at a distance from one another in order to decrease the possibility of rational comparison. For example, life insurance companies do not normally locate in the same building with the purpose of fostering easy comparison of policies by potential customers.

On the other hand, sellers who regularly deal with well-informed buyers have a tendency to locate close together, in order to facilitate a comparison of their wares. The seller who chooses to remain outside the wholesale district may find that large buyers will not bother to go out of their way to inspect his goods. The huge Merchandise Mart in Chicago dramatically illustrates the strong tendency of wholesalers to locate very close to one another, in order to facilitate the shopping of the experts.

---

[12] This suggests the roguish possibility of having a mobile gift shop built into a large trailer so that moving the shop would be cheap. It would also be useful if roadside signs were made as readily movable as possible. The whole project involves the further complication of making flexible arrangements with landowners on whose property the trailer and signs would rest.

[13] This is well described by Tibor Scitovsky, *Welfare and Competition* (Chicago: Richard D. Irwin, Inc., 1951), p. 402.

Summary Description of Locational Forces

The forces of location are clearly many. For a firm or industry the governing factors may be transportation costs, processing costs, land-rent expenses, or capital costs. Such special items as waste disposal facilities, availability of water for cooling or other uses, adequacy of police and fire protection, educational facilities, community attitudes, and climate may be vital. The absence, inadequacy, or undesirability of these factors can be offset only through extra expenditure. If these factors are wholly desirable, their existence involves either an explicit or an implicit reduction in cost. (For example, workers may be willing to work for lower real wages if climate is especially good, and a man in business for himself may be less attracted by alternative offers if he is especially satisfied with local educational opportunities for his children.)

But cost factors alone do not determine location. Locational interdependence in some form or another is an ever-present force. In one case, it may be apparent and governing; in another, hidden and secondary. Location which is determined largely by demand considerations often runs the risk, however, of having the demand situation suddenly change for the worse, due to a new facility erected by a rival.

Under f.o.b. pricing, there is a tendency to disperse plants in order to secure regional monopolies. This does not occur under price discrimination of the basing-point variety, except that a small firm may locate at a distance from the nearest basing point in order to secure substantial income in the form of "phantom freight."

Planning commissions and development commissions tend to stress cost saving and tax advantages in their efforts to attract industry. They tend to neglect interdependence on the demand side of the picture. The process of plant location is often an aspect of price practice and hence sales policy, and thereby is part of the over-all competitive philosophy of the firm.

CASE 12–1: REED, WAITE, AND GENTZLER

The firm of Reed, Waite, and Gentzler had for many years been engaged in the production and distribution of a line of work clothes sold under the brand name "RWG." The line consisted primarily of denim overalls and jackets, denim trousers (more popularly known as "blue jeans"), cotton twill trousers and shirts, and plain cotton trousers and shirts. A line of work hosiery was also included. These products were sold nationally, and the line was well known and popular. They were sold by department stores, chains, and specialty shops and, in smaller towns and villages, were found in the "dry goods" stores.

The company operated three plants to supply its market. The shirt factory was located in a city of approximately 80,000 population in New Hampshire. The trouser factory was located in a suburb of Philadelphia, Pennsylvania. This factory produced trousers, overalls, and jackets. The hosiery mill was located in central Pennsylvania in a community of about 110,000 population. The executive and sales offices of the firm were located in New York City. Sales offices were also maintained in Chicago and Los Angeles. The location of headquarters in New York City was dictated by the long-established custom in the trade of buyers converging upon New York. There had been some modification of this practice since 1947; for this reason, sales offices had been opened in both Chicago and Los Angeles.

Like practically all industries in the postwar period, the textile industry had expanded to meet both accumulated demand and new demand resulting from population increases. It appeared, however, that the industry as a whole suffered from chronic excess capacity, which was reflected in keen price competition. A large part of the industry was affected by frequent style changes which, at the manufactured clothing level, sometimes resulted in drastic price cutting. Firms whose products were sensitive to these factors found it essential to maintain locations where such changes in demand could be most quickly perceived. The so-called "work clothes," while not subject to such frequent style changes, were nevertheless highly competitive. There were several large firms competing with Reed, Waite, and Gentzler as well as a number of smaller firms serving regional and local markets.

In addition to the production of RWG-brand clothes, the company produced a number of private brands under contract with department stores and chains. The capacity of the company's plants was, therefore, geared to a demand consisting of RWG products plus private brands produced under contract. Placing of orders for private brands by purchasers was usually handled by competitive bidding. Securing such contracts was almost entirely a problem of competitive costs. Reed, Waite, and Gentzler experienced no more than the usual problems associated with the sales estimates of its own brands of clothing. Production of RWG clothing was planned according to sales estimates plus inventory control, and the balance of capacity was filled to the greatest possible extent by production of private brands. Certain items of work clothing—such as blue jeans, blue cotton shirts, olive-drab twill trousers, and olive-drab cotton and twill shirts—were considered staples. These items could be produced for inventory when there was stability in the market for finished goods. Materials and labor were the two largest components of production. Instability in the finished goods market, however, seriously complicated the inventory problem.

Until 1950, Reed, Waite, and Gentzler had been fairly successful in obtaining sufficient contracts for private brands to keep the trouser factory near Philadelphia operating at or near rated capacity. Early in 1950, there was some noticeable idle capacity which had caused a reduction in the labor force. The outbreak of the Korean War in June of that year had resulted in the procurement of some military contracts which kept the plant occupied until April of 1951. Again, idle capacity began to appear. A similar situation existed among competitors of the company. This condition was reflected in keener competition for bids on private-brand production. Reed, Waite, and Gentzler were unsuccessful bidders on several contracts which they had obtained on many occasions in the past. The company reduced its bids on future contracts but still lost several to its competitors. On the latest contracts which had gone to competitors, the firm felt that it had submitted the lowest possible quotations consistent with its costs of operations. The loss of these contracts was also causing the unit costs of its own brands to rise to such an extent that competition was jeopardizing the market for RWG clothing.

An investigation of the problem was undertaken, and the following facts were revealed:

Labor Costs. It was easily and quickly determined that the labor costs of Reed, Waite, and Gentzler were higher than the costs of several of its larger competitors. Philadelphia had long been known as a "needle trades" city. During the time that a large part of the total labor force of the area had been engaged in the needle trades, the level of wages for the area as a whole had been strongly influenced by wages in the trade. While the supply of labor was adequate, there was little demand on the part of other industries to put upward pressure upon wage rates. The clothing industry had long been unionized except for a number of very small firms, so that the wage structure for the community as a whole had remained fairly stable, although it had tended upward. With the growth of "hard goods" industries in the Philadelphia area, however, the needle trades workers had become a proportionally smaller part of the labor supply, and their influence upon the wage structure had diminished accordingly. The growth of the area as an industrial center during and following World War II had diminished the influence of the trade even further. It was now quite apparent that the rise in wages of textile workers was influenced by the labor demands of other industries rather than exerting an influence upon them. To some extent the pressure of textile workers' unions was an effort to maintain their wage level consistent with that of the area. In the postwar period, growth of new industries and expansion of older ones had placed heavy demands upon the labor supply, in spite of a large population increase in the area.

The same situation existed in other textile areas of the Northeast. This was not true in all areas, however. In some isolated New England textile areas, this condition had not developed, so that some textile mills were able to enjoy a wage advantage due to the local situation. Of greater effect, however, were the differentials in wages within the clothing industry itself. During the decade of the thirties, there had begun a migration of the textile and clothing industry to the southern part of eastern United States. Some of the firms which had relocated in the Carolinas, Georgia, Tennessee, and Alabama were experiencing lower wage scales than plants of the same firms in the north. To some extent, this was because many of the workers in southern plants were not organized by labor unions, and the effects of local labor-supply situations permitted lower wages. The union had at the present time undertaken the organization of southern workers; but even where some workers were organized, there were still wage differentials as compared with the North.

Productivity. Of equal, if not greater, importance was the differential in productivity between southern and northern mills. While the differentials varied between plants and regions, it was clear that productivity was greater, on the average, in southern than in nothern plants. Some of this greater productivity could be traced to more modern plants and equipment, but there were also indications that some was due to the workers themselves. In the North, productivity had actually declined with the growth of more restrictive practices negotiated by collective bargaining.

Materials. There appeared to be little differential in material costs between the two regions. In some cases of individual bargaining between clothing manufacturers and individual mills, there was some shading of prices, but the general practice of price quotations on wide regional bases tended to prevail. There was, however, one notable exception on the Pacific Coast. This area was accessible to Japanese mills, and many kinds of cotton finished goods could be obtained more cheaply than in the eastern United States, although there was some tariff protection.

Markets. Analysis of sales of Reed, Waite, and Gentzler on a regional basis indicated that there had been a considerable shift in the past 25 years. For many years the firm had marketed the greater share of its output in the East, the Northeast, and the Midwest, and since 1947 had moved to the Pacific Coast. The rapid growth of chain stores in smaller cities and towns in rural areas had enabled the company to grow into a national market. With the growth in the production of private brands the output of the firm was further diffused. The chief markets at present were the Atlantic Seaboard, the upper Midwest and the Mississippi Valley, and the Pacific Coast. The company had always sold its merchandise f.o.b. factory. This practice should perhaps be examined, since transportation to the Pacific Coast was an important factor on RWG brands. On private brands, transportation had become more important with the population shift to the Pacific area.

Following this investigation, the company considered the relocation of the trouser factory from Philadelphia to a point which would improve the company's competitive position. Three locations—designated as cities A, B, and C—were suitable as possible choices. Location A was a city of about 55,000 population in western Tennessee. This city was provided with adequate rail and highway transportation, and was within a radius of 200 miles of several textile mills producing the kinds of finished cotton goods used by the trouser factory. Currently, there was in this city a firm producing inexpensive women's dresses. There were also several small firms assembling light electrical goods, and a soap factory. The nearest city of comparable size was 83 miles distant. Surrounding City A was an agricultural area of near-marginal productivity. The city streets, water supply, and similar services were considered adequate for the needs of the immediate future. There was no indication that the city would experience any considerable growth within the next 10 to 20 years. Land was available both within the city and just outside the city limits. The trouser factory in Philadelphia currently employed about 450 persons. It was believed that this number of workers could be recruited from the present population of City A without serious effect upon the existing labor supply.

Location B was located in northeastern Mississippi in a city of approximately 18,000 in an area served by the Tennessee Valley Authority. At present, there was a small hosiery mill located here, as well as a meat-packing firm, a mirror factory, a lumber mill, a small electronics plant, and two canneries. City B was located on the main line of the Illinois Central Railroad and was served by two arterial highways. This city, in contrast to the others, had been actively engaged in a program of attracting industry, and was prepared to offer a number of concessions as to land and taxes. In three instances the city had bonded itself to erect the buildings, and it had leased the buildings to the firms currently occupying them. Upon learning of the interest of Reed, Waite, and Gentzler, similar approaches had been made. City B, however, had grown rapidly within the past 10 years. Its population had increased almost 4,000 within that period, and there were indications that growth would continue, but perhaps at a less rapid rate. About 22 miles distant was another city of 12,000 population and Memphis, Tennessee, was 125 miles away. Jackson, the capital of Mississippi, was a distance of 92 miles. An extensive program of street paving, sewer construction, and schoolbuilding had been projected, but only the early stages had been completed. The area immediately surrounding the city was agricultural, and there appeared to be noticeable migration from this area into City B.

Location C was in Georgia, about 15 miles from Atlanta. City C was also well located as to rail and highway transportation. Since the end of World War II, however, the countryside between City C and Atlanta had developed to such an extent that highway travel between the two areas was regulated by traffic lights and highway patrols. Nearer Atlanta were large housing developments. Toward City C, there were both housing and industry. The population of City C was

Exhibit 1

COMPARISON OF ACTUAL AND ESTIMATED COSTS
OF DENIM TROUSERS
(Per Dozen)

Item	Philadelphia	City A	City B	City C
Materials......................	$ 3.13	$ 3.14	$3.13	$ 3.11
Labor.........................	3.21	1.53	1.49	2.04
Waste........................	0.59	0.61	0.60	0.60
Factory overhead*..............	4.08	2.97	2.27†	2.74
Indirect labor..................	2.01	1.62	1.65	1.81
Administration expense.........	0.40	0.41	0.41	0.41
Total Cost................	$13.42	$10.28	$9.55	$10.71

* Includes amortization of new plant; does not include book value of Philadelphia plant.
† City B proposed certain tax and land concessions, which are taken into account.

approximately 24,000 and was still increasing. To relieve the traffic congestion, a new superhighway had been planned and approved for construction between City C and Atlanta. A number of firms had located their plants in City C in the past 10 years, and several more were currently interested. Beyond City C the area was agricultural. There was evidence of union activity in City C, and many firms in Atlanta and City C were now organized. Where comparisons could be made, there still appeared to be lower unit costs in City C than in plants in the North performing similar operations with organized labor. There was little doubt that the facilities of City C would require improvement and expansion within the next five years.

Exhibit 1 shows costs of producing blue denim trousers at the Philadelphia factory as compared with costs at the three proposed locations. Costs in the proposed locations are estimates based upon surveys of the areas. Exhibit 2 shows the railroad transportation cost from the various points per dozen blue denim trousers. While these costs are not paid by Reed, Waite, and Gentzler, they are part of the delivered cost to the purchaser and thus are a competitive element of delivered price.

Exhibit 2

AVERAGE RAILROAD FREIGHT RATES TO SELECTED CITIES
FROM PHILADELPHIA AND PROPOSED LOCATIONS
(Per Dozen)

Freight Costs to:	From Philadelphia	From City A	From City B	From City C
New York	$0.39	$1.01	$1.14	$0.39
Chicago	0.86	0.99	0.99	0.86
Los Angeles	1.52	1.31	1.49	1.52

The market for Reed, Waite, and Gentzler is divided approximately as follows: 40 per cent is sold in the Atlantic seaboard division, 50 per cent in the Midwest and the Mississippi Valley, and 10 per cent in the Far West and Pacific Coast region.

QUESTIONS

1. Which location would you recommend? Why?
2. Would your answer be the same for both the short and the long run? Explain.
3. Is the lowest-cost location always the best? Elaborate.
4. How would industry-wide bargaining affect the location of firms like Reed, Waite, and Gentzler?
5. What considerations other than those explicitly taken up in the text may influence the choice of a new location for the trouser factory?

CASE 12–2: JAYE AND COMPTON, INC.

The plant of Jaye and Compton was engaged in the printing business. For a number of years, it had confined the major part of its activities to the printing of several national magazines, mail-order catalogs, and city telephone directories. In addition, it filled large color-printing orders on a job basis. Only in certain cases did the company accept any orders for quantities under 10,000 copies.

The firm of Jaye and Compton was located in Chicago; and from the time the partnership was formed until 1937, the company had operated in leased quarters in an industrial building. In that year the partners decided that the rental on the space had reached such proportions that it would be more economical to occupy its own plant. The firm then moved to a building which had been erected in 1928 for a machine-tool company. It was four stories high and had been constructed so that all floors, including the basement, would support heavy equipment. It was equipped with two freight elevators and had its own steam power plant. The machine-tool company had failed during the depression, and the building had been unoccupied for three years prior to its purchase by Jaye and Compton. The purchase price was considerably less than its original cost and, in 1937, the building could not be duplicated at the price paid for it. Considerable renovation had been necessary, and some new equipment was acquired, but it was believed that the building would be adequate for several decades. At the same time, the company had acquired five vacant lots across the street from this building. Upon removal to these quarters the partnership was incorporated.

The present building, which occupied one city block, was fully occupied by the firm in 1953. The vacant lots, which for many years had been used as parking space for employees, were now occupied by three buildings. The company had grown to the point where it now had 4,700 employees, 3,450 of whom were working in the shops on two shifts. One of the buildings constructed on the vacant lots was used entirely for storage, while another had been constructed in 1941 as an employee cafeteria. In addition, two other buildings several blocks away had been leased for storage of paper and supplies, which were transferred by truck to the main building as needed. Four blocks from the main building the company was presently leasing, on an annual basis, a large vacant lot which had been improved for employee parking.

In the main plant itself, printing operations were carried on in the basement and first three floors. The top floor was used for office space. Because of lack of space on any one floor, it had not yet been possible to devise a system where any one job could be initiated and completed on the same floor. In some cases a given job would require operations on all floors. This necessitated a great deal of handling and movement from one floor to another, much of which had to be done in small lots because of the narrow space between machines. Very little power handling equipment could be used because of the crowded conditions.

Since 1947, business had been increasing, and it was anticipated that there would be further increases. Several of the national magazines which the company had printed for many years were increasing in both size of issue and quantity, which further complicated the problems of the already crowded scheduling department. The actual and prospective increases in business volume were also a strain on the apprentice-training program which the company felt it was forced to expand in order to provide adequate trained personnel. After a survey of these operational difficulties, the conclusion was reached that additional space or an entirely new plant would be necessary.

A firm of industrial engineers was retained to make recommendations for a solution. The first step was an investigation of additional space and retention of the present quarters. This line of inquiry was not very promising. There was no space available within 20 blocks of the present plant. The space which was available could be reached only by automobile and truck, and it would be necessary to travel streets which were currently overloaded with traffic. It was feared that additional space at such a distance would result in rising costs per job, a situation which was to be avoided, since it might affect bids on contract jobs. This avenue of investigation was quickly abandoned, and efforts were concentrated upon the location of an entirely new plant.

Quickly discarded was the possibility of moving out of the Chicago area entirely. This was considered, but the chief limitation was the procurement of trained personnel in a new location. A demand for approximately 3,500 printers, pressmen, typesetters, and color-press operators was one which it was felt that no one community could provide immediately. The nature of Jaye and Compton's business was not such as to permit a reduction of any size and a gradual building-up over the long run. There were some communities in which the supply of skilled workers was adequate, but they would have to be drawn away from present employment. This would probably lead to substantial increases in wages in the long run and high turnover in the short run.

A search was undertaken for a location in the Chicago area. The present plant was easily accessible by public transportation as well as private automobile. Employees of the company lived in all sections of Chicago and did not appear to be concentrated in any one particular area. A survey revealed that approximately one half of the workers used public transportation; the remainder used private cars or car pools. The company was completely unionized, except for white-collar workers, and labor problems had been negligible. The average period of service for skilled workers was 14 years. In view of these findings, it was felt that the new location would have to be one of relatively easy access and one which would not materially increase travel time for a substantial majority of the workers.

The industrial engineering firm suggested two possible plant sites. One was located in a suburb northwest of Chicago, approximately 17 miles from the present location, which was on the west side of Chicago about two miles west of the downtown business area. On this proposed location the company could erect a one-story plant, in which machinery could be assembled so as to minimize the amount of material handling. Conveyor belts and power handling equipment could be used. The storage section of the plant would be two or three stories and would also be suitable for power handling equipment. This section would be connected to the printing area by conveyor belts. The office portion would be four stories in height and would also house the cafeteria, lounges, and recreational space. There was adequate space for parking up to 4,000 automobiles. The suburban railroad station was the equivalent of four city blocks distant. The community was primarily residential, although a number of light industries were located there. The larger share of the population of 31,000 was employed in the City of Chicago. One of the features of commuting was that Jaye and Compton employees would be riding on suburban trains at a time when the rush hour was in the opposite direction. This location would, however, entail a journey of approximately $1\frac{1}{2}$ hours for employees living on the south side of Chicago. For employees living on the west side, it would increase their travel time by approximately 20 to 30 minutes. For employees living on the north side, the increased travel time would average about 10 minutes.

The second location was within the city itself, on the far west side and slightly south of the main business section of Chicago, about seven miles distant. This location was much more accessible by public transportation, being served by both bus and train. The difference in travel time for employees, compared to the present location, would be somewhat negligible. The amount of land was limited, however. The printing operations would again be housed in a building of at least three stories, but the layout would be improved so as to reduce a substantial portion of the handling which occurred in the present plant. In order to provide adequate parking space, the storage facilities would be four stories in height; while the office building, with space for the cafeteria and recreational facilities, would be six stories high.

This location would be more accessible for the negotiation of business, a great deal of which originated in the Chicago business area. There would also be easier access to railway transportation, since this site was adjacent to the main line of the Pennsylvania and Santa Fe railroads. The other site would be provided with a railway siding, but because it was on a railroad leading out of Chicago to the Northwest, there would be a delay of one day in delivery of freight cars to rail lines to the east and south of Chicago.

Exhibit 1 is a brief summary of the report of the industrial engineering firm. The net earnings of Jaye and Compton before federal income taxes for the year 1953 were $8,543,291.

Exhibit 1

Item	Northwest Suburban Site	City of Chicago Site
Cost of new plant....................................	$20,400,000	$23,575,000
Property taxes—new plant (per year)....................	961,000	1,315,000
Reduction in miscellaneous costs (per year)..............	1,422,000	978,000
Estimated annual reduction in total payroll at current volume of business*.............................	3,200,000	2,465,000
Estimated number of employees at current volume of business...	4,100	4,275

* This figure includes not only the actual reduction in numbers of employees but also the increased productivity of remaining employees due primarily to new layout and use of additional equipment.

The firm had ample resources to construct either of the proposed new plants without any external financing. It was estimated that the present plant could be sold for approximately $3.25 million.

The president of Jaye and Compton preferred the Chicago site for the new plant. He was quite concerned over employee reaction to the more distant location. Several of the directors, however, preferred the suburban location. They were of the opinion that the distance factor could be overcome to a large extent in the long run. Since it was a suburban community, the workers could be encouraged to move to the suburbs. Two directors even proposed that the company undertake the financing of the purchase of new homes for employees who had five or more years of service with the company. This would involve the commitment of about $10 million of company funds for an average period of approximately 10 years. As an added inducement the interest rate could be set at about 1 per cent below the present mortgage-money market. The company at present had almost $20 million in securities, from which these funds could be taken if necessary. This commitment would not jeopardize the construction of a new plant from internal funds.

QUESTIONS

1. Which location would you recommend? Why?
2. Would you consider it profitable for the company to undertake financing of employee homes, as proposed by the two directors?
3. To what extent do transportation *costs* affect this proposed change of location?
4. Which considerations appear to be more important in this case—long run or short run?
5. Does a publishing firm usually locate near the source of its principal raw materials or near the market? Explain.

Chapter 13

~~~~~~

TAXATION AND THE FIRM

IN AN economy where federal tax collections amount to about $75 billion annually—about one fifth of gross national product—and where state and local taxes are increasing steadily, a great many business decisions are affected strongly by tax considerations. Personal decisions are also based on tax liability to a much greater extent than was the case before World War II. Some well-known motion-picture actors have limited themselves to two new films per year due to the high tax rates on additional income. Recently, the 50-year-old president of a corporation gave up his $50,000-a-year salary because the position netted him only $4,500 after taxes.[1] This was due to his large income from investments which put virtually his entire salary into the top income tax bracket. The federal income tax can in such a case be aptly described as a "subsidy to leisure." It is also a subsidy to home ownership, in that property taxes are deductible from gross income, and because no tax is assessed against income received in the form of housing services from an owner-occupied dwelling.[2] On the other hand, a renter who keeps an equivalent amount invested in securities or other income-earning assets pays an income tax on such income and is unable to deduct property taxes which enter into his rental costs.

Corporation Income Tax

The magnitude of the tax on corporate net income (30 per cent on the first $25,000 and 52 per cent on the remainder) makes it a major factor in many business decisions. It was pointed out in Chapter 1 that, in theory, this tax should be assessed against economic profit rather than against accounting profit. This reform is probably not administratively practicable; but if it could be put into effect, it would discontinue the unfortunate stimulus now given to debt financing in-

---

[1] "Tax Angles: Federal Levies Push More Americans into Unusual Decisions," *Wall Street Journal,* January 3, 1956, p. 1.

[2] The Department of Commerce, however, imputes a value to such housing services in arriving at national income estimates.

479

stead of equity financing, due to the deductibility of explicit interest payments only, in arriving at net income. (It has also been pointed out that the chronic inflation since the outbreak of World War II has tended to make bond issues preferable to stock issues from the point of view of firms in need of capital; that is, a debtor status is desirable if inflation is in the offing.) A more nearly practicable reform in the corporate income tax would consist of eliminating the deductibility of bond interest in arriving at net income for tax purposes. This change would, of course, permit a substantial lowering of the tax rate.

The existence of a high tax on corporate income gives some stimulus to use of the partnership form and to the individual proprietorship as a means of avoiding this impost. Income received under these forms of business organization is taxed only as personal income, while the net profit received by a corporation is first taxed as corporate income and then as personal income, to the extent that it is paid out as dividends. This is frequently criticized as "double taxation," and the criticism has led to recent amendment of the federal tax regulations to permit a limited deduction of dividend income in arriving at taxable personal income. To the extent that income is retained by the corporation through the reinvestment of profits, there is some avoidance of this double taxation; but since plowing back profits tends to increase the market value of stock, a capital gains tax of 25 per cent will eventually have to be paid by the owner when he sells his shares.[3] The advantage of the corporate form in raising capital, its limited liability, and the relative independence of its existence from the life of any individual are of such importance that the corporate form of organization retains its popularity in spite of the high corporate income tax.

The small corporation, however, may be quite seriously hampered by this tax compared with the large corporation. It was pointed out in Chapter 11 that, from 1946 to 1949, incorporated firms secured about three fourths of their capital from the retention of profits. To the extent that the corporate income tax is absorbed by the firm rather than passed forward to the consumer or backward to suppliers of inputs, it directly reduces the profits which can be retained by the corporation. This probably hinders the growth of smaller corporations more than that of larger ones, due to the greater ability of the latter to secure additional funds through the sale of new securities. Also, the growth of

---

[3] If the stock is retained until the death of the owner, no tax on the capital gain need be paid by the estate. This value will, however, enter into the estate and inheritance tax liability, and the need to pay these taxes may require liquidation of some securities.

corporations in the more risky lines of business is probably hampered more than that of other corporations, because the former tend to sell common stock rather than bonds to a greater degree.

This problem has been examined recently by John Lintner and J. Keith Butters.[4] They found through empirical study that the average retained earnings of profitable smaller manufacturing companies regularly constituted a much larger percentage of their net worth than did the retained earnings of larger manufacturers. They point out further that even when outside capital is *available* to small firms, it is often less acceptable to them than to large corporations, because terms may be less favorable, and because there is more fear of weakening the control position by selling additional securities with voting privileges.[5]

Is the Corporate Income Tax Shifted?

Conclusions as to the effect of the corporate income tax generally rest on the assumption that the burden of the tax falls on the corporation rather than upon customers, workers, or others. If, instead, it were possible to shift the tax completely, dividends and retained profits would not be decreased by the existence of the tax. In that event, there would not actually be any impact on the relative rate of growth of small corporations compared with large ones, or on risky activities compared with others. The question of the incidence of the corporation income tax is therefore important, and it is one which has received a good deal of attention from economists. There is little consensus among the experts, however.

The traditional view has been that the corporate income tax is not an element in costs, since it is assessed only on net profit; that it consequently will not affect the inputs or outputs of firms; and that it cannot, therefore, be shifted. That is, if corporations turn out the same volume of goods with the tax in existence as they would in the absence of the tax, selling prices will be the same, so the tax will not be borne by consumers. And if corporations faced with this tax will utilize the same volume of resources as otherwise, they will have to pay the same amount for these inputs and consequently cannot shift the tax "backward." Marginal cost curves of firms are, in this traditional view, unaffected by the income tax. As a consequence, a perfectly competitive industry will have no reason to change output in

---

[4] "Effects of Taxes on Concentration," *Business Concentration and Price Policy* (Princeton: Princeton University Press, 1955), pp. 239–80.

[5] *Ibid.,* p. 258

the short run. Similarly, a monopolistic firm, assuming that it is already charging the most profitable price, will have no incentive to change that price, even though it is forced to share its profits with society.

Most businessmen share the opinion that the corporate income tax is not shifted, according to two surveys by the National Industrial Conference Board.[6] It should be recognized, however, that answers to such a question may be more nearly propaganda than honest conviction. Most people like to claim that their own tax burden is heavier than it should be and to imply that it should therefore be lowered. On the other hand, some businessmen feel that the best attack on the corporation income tax is to claim that it really hits consumers and workers.

A key fact in the analysis of the incidence of the corporate income tax is that it is not assessed against economic profit but rather against accounting profit. That is, not only does it hit windfall profits, innovation profits, and monopoly profits, but it also reduces the net return received by the owners of "self-employed" factors. For example, the greater the extent to which a firm utilizes its own capital—that is, utilizes equity capital rather than borrowed capital—and the greater the extent to which it owns capital assets instead of renting them from others, the larger its corporate income tax liability will be for a given level of sales. The latter point needs explanation. If a corporation owns a building without a mortgage, it can deduct such items as annual depreciation, repairs, and maintenance in arriving at its taxable net income, but it cannot deduct imputed interest on its investment. If, instead, it leases the building from another owner, the rental which it pays will include interest on the capital tied up in the building as well as annual depreciation, repairs, and maintenance. This will reduce the amount of its income tax, provided it is able to rent the building in a highly competitive market, so that there is not also an element of monopoly profit in the annual rent which is paid.

This is a difficult point which is, perhaps, worthy of additional analysis. Suppose a building is owned outright and used by its owner. The value of the services derived from its use (its "quasi rents") normally includes an interest yield on the original cost as well as

---

[6] *The Shifting and Effects of the Federal Corporation Income Tax,* Vol. 1 (New York: National Industrial Conference Board, 1928); and *Effects of Taxes upon Corporate Profits* (New York: National Industrial Conference Board, 1943). Over 75 per cent of the top men in 10,000 corporations surveyed in the earlier questionnaire felt that the tax was not shifted.

covering depreciation. Therefore, an interest element will be included in the *income* of the firm, but not in the costs which are deductible for income tax purposes. If, instead, the use of the building is secured by leasing it from someone else, there will be not only an interest element in the income received from its employment but also a deductible interest cost. This is a separate matter from the deductibility of bond interest and the nondeductibility of a normal return on stock which is outstanding. If a corporation raised most of its capital by selling bonds and, in addition, leased most of its capital equipment from others, it would be able to charge against expenses both the interest on the bonds and the interest on the value of the equipment (since this would be an element in the rent paid), while it would include interest in income only once (since interest would enter into the value of the services of the equipment).

This rather subtle consideration is probably an important reason for the popularity of the "lease-back" arrangement, under which a corporation sells its principal properties to another company and then immediately secures their use on a long-term lease. Some corporations make it their policy always to rent, rather than own, stores and other facilities which they use. If rental charges are reasonable, an income tax advantage can be gained. This raises the question, however, of whether *someone* does not finally have to pay the taxes which can thus be sidestepped. If the firm which owns the property is not incorporated, it will not be subject to the corporate income tax, although a personal income tax will have to be paid. If the firm owning the property is a small corporation, the $25,000 exemption from the surtax will substantially reduce its corporate income tax liability. Thus, a large corporation which sells its buildings to one or more small subsidiary corporations and leases back these buildings may be able to secure a worth-while income tax saving—a saving which derives from reducing the tax on interest income.

To the extent that the corporate income tax reduces the supply of capital to enterprises, it can be said to be shifted forward to consumers through higher prices. That is, output will be lower and prices higher than in the absence of the tax. In the main, however, incidence of this tax appears to rest on stockholders. But this conclusion is not necessarily applicable in the case of oligopoly. If it is the accepted pricing practice in an industry to add to prime cost a certain percentage markup for overhead and another markup for profit, it is probable that the corporate income tax causes the last-named percentage to be larger and thereby causes a shifting of the tax to consumers. On the other hand, if strong organization of an oligopolistic industry makes it possible for all firms to charge a price which approximates that which would be charged by a monopolist in the field, the corporate income tax would fall chiefly on the stockholders, since it would not be desirable to raise price. In this case, since above-normal returns would probably be made on investment, it is doubtful that there would be any serious long-run effects on the industry's growth. The possible patterns of oligopolistic behavior are so numerous that it is difficult to reach very useful generalizations regarding the probable effects of the corporate income tax. The difficulty of assessing its incidence, along with its great importance to the federal government as a revenue raiser, suggests that this tax will be a part of the American business scene for a long time. The major questions for the immediate future seem to be whether to make the tax a progressive one rather than charging a flat 52 per cent on most income, and whether to change the percentage if a single rate is kept in effect.

Taxation and Mergers

Business mergers are motivated by numerous considerations in addition to the tax advantages which may be gained.[7] Tax motives constitute an important and often dramatic reason for mergers, however. This arises mainly from the provisions of the federal tax law which permit the "carry-back" and "carry-forward" of losses incurred in a particular year. A loss incurred in 1956 can be used to secure a refund on 1954 and 1955 corporate income taxes—if those were profitable years—or to reduce the tax during the years 1957 through 1961 if those years are profitable. That is, losses can be carried back two years and forward five years as an offset against profits.

This provision has given a peculiar value to unprofitable operations, increasing the selling value of a firm which has unused tax losses on its books above what it would otherwise be. Frequently, firms with tax losses are advertised for sale—and the existence of the losses is stressed in the advertisements. Profitable firms often run advertisements showing they want to buy unprofitable companies. Also, firms with

---

[7] These are summarized by J. Keith Butters, John Lintner, and William L. Cary, *Effects of Taxation: Corporate Mergers* (Boston: Harvard University, 1951), p. 232, as the "desire for a new product, plant or production organization, for greater vertical integration, including both new marketing outlets and sources of supply, and for financial advantages of various sorts." They found that taxes constituted an important reason for about one fourth of the mergers involving selling companies with assets over $1 million.

tax losses frequently look for profitable companies to buy, so that the loss can be offset against the profits of the merged firms.[8]

It should not be inferred that it is just as good for a corporation to have a loss as a profit, of course. A loss means an impairment in the net asset position of a firm. (The excess of total assets over total liabilities is decreased.) But if there are profits against which the loss can be fully offset, the ill-effects of the bad year on the net assets of the firm can be cut approximately in half.

Assuming, for convenience, a 50 per cent corporate income tax and a two-year carry-back privilege, suppose profits and taxes were as follows:

Year	Income (Millions of Dollars)	Tax (Millions of Dollars)
1954	$2	$1
1955	2	1
1956	− 4	2 (refund)

There would then have occurred no change in the net asset position for the three-year period as a whole. Without the carry-back position, there would have been a $2 million impairment of assets. The damage caused by the 1956 experience has been cut in half by the carry-back possibility.

If a firm has a large tax loss that cannot usefully be carried back, it is especially important that it resume profitable operations quickly and substantially enough to be able to make full use of the loss carry-forward privilege. If it seems unlikely that this can be done, a solution may lie in merger with a company which promises to earn steady profits in the near future. If the latter firm buys the tax-loss firm, the net price which it must pay for the acquisition is, in effect, substantially reduced by the tax saving which will accrue. It is important, of course, that the unprofitable company be made profitable again, or the temporary tax gain to the buying firm can turn into a long-run loss.

In 1954, Congress clarified the rules on tax-loss mergers, making it illegal to merge companies where the action is aimed overtly at tax reduction. Also, the United States Treasury has been working on new regulations, in order to clarify what can and cannot be done for tax-reduction purposes. The whole matter is difficult to handle ad-

---

[8] This is interestingly described in "Tax Loss Mergers Bloom Again," *Business Week,* January 14, 1956, p. 41.

ministratively because tax saving is likely to be only one of several important considerations in a merger, and it is usually hard to show that it is really the basic motive.

Under present tax law the "50 per cent" and "20 per cent" rules are a significant restriction on tax-saving mergers. The former specifies that a purchased company loses its tax-loss credits entirely if it changes its location or business within two years after the purchase and if 50 per cent or more of the stock falls into the hands of ten or fewer unrelated persons. The 20 per cent rule calls for a graduated reduction in the tax-loss credit if the owners of the company with the loss credit do not get at least 20 per cent representation in the successor corporation.

Merger of Curtiss-Wright and Studebaker-Packard

An interesting recent example of a potential merger in which a huge tax loss is involved is that of Curtiss-Wright and Studebaker-Packard.[9] Studebaker and Packard merged in 1954, but the new company continued to secure a diminishing share of the sales of all new cars, their portion being only about 2 per cent in the middle of 1956. In 1955 a net loss of about $29 million was suffered. Continued losses brought the total tax-loss credit of Studebaker-Packard to about $150 million by the fall of 1956.

Officials of Studebaker-Packard were unable to sell the company to or merge with any other automobile manufacturer. Finally, a well-known air-frame and engine manufacturer, Curtiss-Wright (which has large defense contracts), made a deal which may save Studebaker-Packard, but not through immediate merger. Curtiss-Wright leased some of the plants of the automobile firm and agreed to manage Studebaker-Packard for three years. Curtiss-Wright also secured a two-year option to buy five million shares of unissued Studebaker-Packard stock at $5.00 per share.

If this $25 million option is exercised, the companies will be merged, and the new corporation can take advantage of the huge tax loss. Under the 20 per cent rule, holders of Studebaker-Packard stock will have to get at least a 20 per cent equity in the new corporation. Also, it seems probable that the usual requirement that the merged company must stay in the same line of business for two years in order that a tax credit may be valid may be satisfied if Studebaker-Packard produces automobiles for two years after the option

---

[9] Information on this deal has been taken from William B. Harris, "The Breakdown of Studebaker-Packard," *Fortune,* October, 1956, p. 139.

arrangement was made rather than two years after actual merger. As already indicated, Treasury rules regarding tax losses are not entirely clear as of the time of this writing.

Accelerated Depreciation

Since 1913 the income tax laws have permitted a reasonable deduction for depreciation of durable assets. There has been fairly general use of the straight-line formula, where original cost less salvage value is written off at a uniform absolute rate over the life of the asset.[10] The straight-line method is becoming less popular, however, because of a very important change in the law in 1954, which now allows accelerated depreciation according to specified formulas. The principal interesting fact about the new law is that it allows firms to compute depreciation according to either the "declining balance" or the "sum-of-digits" method as well as by the straight-line method. Both provide larger depreciation deductions in the early years of life of a durable asset, and both provide tax savings compared with the straight-line method.[11]

Depreciation Allowances for Defense Facilities

A special sort of accelerated depreciation is allowed for facilities which receive the necessary certification from the Office of Defense Mobilization as important to the national defense. Under the rapid write-off program a portion of the cost of a new project may be charged off in five years. As of July 8, 1956, a total of 21,326 projects had been certified for rapid amortization.[12] This program is based on World War II experience with accelerated depreciation of emergency facilities.[13] A large number of certificates have been issued to

---

[10] William J. Edmonds, "The Effect on Business Decisions of Changes in Tax Depreciation Policy," *National Tax Journal*, March, 1955, p. 99.

[11] The law allows use of the declining balance method at a rate up to twice the straight-line rate. For example, an asset with an estimated life of 10 years could be depreciated at a yearly rate of 20 per cent—this rate being applied each year to the undepreciated balance. If the asset cost $1,000, the first year's depreciation charge would be $200; the second year's $160, etc. The act permits the firm to shift, at any time, to a straight-line basis on the balance of unrecovered costs less salvage. Otherwise, the asset would never be fully written off.

Under the sum-of-digits method a complete write-off does occur. If the asset will last 10 years, the allowable depreciation charge in the first year is 10 divided by the sum of digits from 1 to 10—that is, 10/55; the second year, it is 9/55; and the tenth year, it is 1/55.

[12] *New York Times*, July 8, 1956.

[13] The wartime program is described and analyzed by E. Cary Brown and Gardner Patterson, "Accelerated Depreciation: A Neglected Chapter in War Taxation," *Quarterly Journal of Economics*, August, 1943, p. 630.

utility companies and railroads. Oil companies, metals producers, ship-builders, air lines, freight-car builders, and other industries have also received large numbers of certificates. The effects on tax liability of this sort of emergency amortization are quite similar to the tax re-sults of regular accelerated depreciation as provided in the 1954 Rev-enue Act. Consequently, the effects will not be separately examined.

Interest Saving

The financial newspapers and popular discussions usually emphasize that accelerated depreciation results only in a deferral of tax liability, because the heavy depreciation charges in the early years of an asset's life will be counterbalanced by correspondingly smaller write-offs in later years, thus increasing the tax liability in later years. One error in this observation is that it neglects the permanent saving in interest

Exhibit 1

DEPRECIATION OF A SINGLE PROJECT BY TWO METHODS

Depreciation by:	Year 1	Year 2	Year 3	Year 4	Year 5
Straight-line method........	$300	$300	$300	$300	$300
Sum-of-digits method.......	500	400	300	200	100
Difference.............	+$200	+$100	$ 0	−$100	−$200

which results from accelerated depreciation. Assets which can be tem-porarily retained in a company by reducing early tax liability will normally earn an interest income for the firm—an income due en-tirely to the deferral of taxes. A dollar on hand today is worth more than a dollar which will not be received for a number of years, since if it is on hand today, it can begin immediately to earn interest. Consequently, a tax saving today is better than a tax saving in the future.

The tax benefits from accelerated depreciation are, in practice, usu-ally not limited to the extra interest income which it generates. If only a single investment project is considered, the interest saving is actually the only saving. This is illustrated in Exhibit 1, which shows annual depreciation charges under the straight-line and sum-of-digits methods against a $1,500 project. To keep this calculation simple, a five-year life span is assumed; salvage value is assumed to be zero; and the projects are completed at the beginning of year 1, so that full depreciation can be charged for that year. While annual depreciation is greater in the first two years when the sum-of-digits formula is used, this is exactly counterbalanced in the last two years. The only permanent advantage comes from interest on the early tax saving.[14]

Continuous Investment

If a firm is a progressive one, its yearly gross investment (including the reinvestment of funds made available through depreciation charges) is likely to have an upward trend. Even if the annual gross

Exhibit 2

ANNUAL STRAIGHT-LINE DEPRECIATION WITH CONSTANT RATE OF INVESTMENT

Project No.	Year 1	Year 2	Year 3	Year 4	Year 5	Year 6
1...............	$300	$300	$300	$ 300	$ 300	
2...............		300	300	300	300	$ 300
3...............			300	300	300	300
4...............				300	300	300
5...............					300	300
6...............						300
Annual Total..	$300	$600	$900	$1,200	$1,500	$1,500

Exhibit 3

ANNUAL SUM-OF-DIGITS DEPRECIATION WITH CONSTANT RATE OF INVESTMENT

Project No.	Year 1	Year 2	Year 3	Year 4	Year 5	Year 6
1...............	$500	$400	$ 300	$ 200	$ 100	
2...............		500	400	300	200	$ 100
3...............			500	400	300	200
4...............				500	400	300
5...............					500	400
6...............						500
Annual Total..	$500	$900	$1,200	$1,400	$1,500	$1,500

investment is constant rather than increasing, the results of accelerated depreciation are considerably more favorable than when only an individual investment project is considered.

Exhibits 2 and 3 show yearly depreciation charges under the straight-line and sum-of-digits methods, respectively, when there is a gross investment of $1,500 a year, other assumptions being the same as were

---

[14] The capitalized value of the anticipated tax saving at the beginning of year 1 would be positive, since the negative savings in years 4 and 5 would be discounted more heavily than the positive savings of the first two years.

used in connection with Exhibit 1. It can be seen that in the fifth year and thereafter, the annual depreciation charge will level out at $1,500 under both methods of depreciation. However, the larger total depreciation charges in the first four years under the sum-of-digits method mean not only a saving of interest but a permanent retention of more profits than could have been retained under straight-line depreciation. A similar permanent saving of assets can be shown to take place with utilization of the declining balance formula.

If yearly gross investment tends to increase from year to year, the new accelerated depreciation methods will result in *permanently* higher yearly depreciation charges, and hence tax savings.[15] Firms which are able to grow rapidly and steadily stand to profit most by changing over to accelerated depreciation for tax purposes. Also, firms which are heavy users of fixed capital in relation to sales will gain more by the switch than those which have relatively little fixed capital. In general, such industries as manufacturing, railroads, and utilities seem to have more to gain from the 1954 Revenue Act than retailing, wholesaling, financial, or personal service activities.

Expectations regarding future tax rates also play a part in the making of rational decisions as to whether to switch from straight-line to accelerated depreciation. If it is anticipated by corporate officials that the present 52 per cent rate will probably be lowered in the future, the advantages of accelerated depreciation are even greater. It is then especially desirable to take the largest possible depreciation deductions when tax rates are high. This would be true even if there were only a single investment project, such as was assumed in Exhibit 1.

The main effects of accelerated depreciation under the 1954 Revenue Act have probably not yet been felt. However, accelerated depreciation of the emergency type, which requires special certification, has apparently had a great effect on investment in the postwar period. According to *U.S. News and World Report*,[16] the after-tax profits of all corporations except banks and insurance companies declined from $17.5 billion to $16.7 billion between 1947 and 1954. Yet corporations were able to increase dividend payments by $3.2 billion and to step up the rate of investment of internally generated funds

---

[15] This is pointed out in an excellent article by Robert Eisner, "Depreciation under the New Tax Law," *Harvard Business Review*, Vol. XXXIII (January–February, 1955), p. 70. Eisner says that continued inflation may in itself bring about a growing annual rate of investment by most firms.

[16] "Why Business Spending Is Going to Stay High," May 27, 1955, p. 89.

because bigger depreciation allowances contributed an extra $7.4 billion to such investment.

Excise Taxes

It has been indicated that the corporation income tax poses extremely important problems for management. Another important levy in this respect is the manufacturers' excise tax, which ranks second among business taxes only to the corporate income tax as a revenue raiser for the federal government. Some use is also made of this tax by state and local governments, but these fiscal bodies make greater use of general sales taxes than of imposts directed at particular types of manufacturing. The reason is clear. A state using such a tax is likely to repel new firms and may even lose established ones if it levies such an impost on goods manufactured within its borders, especially when they are sold in interstate commerce. Federal excise taxes on liquor, gasoline, cigarettes, and other tobacco products are well known and very important in this category.

When a new excise tax is levied, or when the rate of an existing one is increased, the firm has to decide whether to attempt to pass the levy on to consumers in whole, in part, or not at all. If the firm is operating in a purely competitive situation, it does not have the option of deciding how much to change its price. Instead, this will be decided for the individual seller by the combined actions of a great many competing enterprises.

Shifting of an Excise Tax by a Competitive Industry

The basic means by which an excise tax can be passed forward to consumers is through a reduction in supply. Assuming that the demand curve for a product will be unaffected by the tax, the only way in which price can be raised is through a decrease in supply. Usually, this reduction will be greater in the long run than immediately, because it takes some time to shift resources to an untaxed use.

Suppose an excise tax of 5 cents a dozen were levied on farmers who produce and sell eggs. This is a highly competitive industry, and the effects of the tax can best be divined through use of the economists' pricing model for perfect competition. Since the farmers would have to pay the government 5 cents for each dozen eggs produced, the marginal costs of each firm would be that much higher than before. The short-run supply curve for the entire egg industry would shift upward by a like amount. Price to the consumer would go up, but not by a full 5 cents per dozen.

The short-run effect of an (unanticipated) excise tax can most easily be seen with the aid of a diagram such as Exhibit 4. Straight-line demand and supply "curves" are used for convenience. The post-tax supply curve S' lies above the pretax supply curve by 5 cents at each possible output. This shift in supply raises the price of eggs from P_1 to P_2 —an amount less than the tax, but only a little less, in view of the

Exhibit 4

TAX SHIFTING UNDER COMPETITION—PART OF TAX SHIFTED
IN SHORT RUN

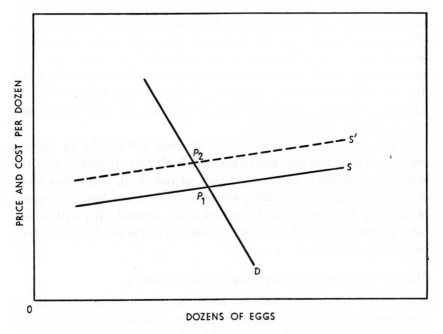

way the chart is drawn. Determinants of the short-run price increase are the size of the tax, the slope of the demand curve, and the slope of the supply curve. The change in price can most conveniently be calculated from the formula

$$\Delta P = \frac{t}{1 + \left(\frac{c}{b}\right)},$$

where ΔP is the price increase, t is the amount of the tax, c is the slope of the supply curve, and b is the slope (disregarding sign) of the demand curve.[17] If the supply curve were horizontal (had a zero

---

[17] For the derivation of the formula, see M. R. Colberg, "Shifting of a Specific Excise Tax," *Public Finance: Finances publiques*, Vol. IX, No. 2, p. 168.

slope), the formula readily shows that price would rise by the full amount of the tax. If the demand and supply curves had equal numerical slopes, the price would rise by one half the amount of the tax. Any other combination of slopes can be as readily handled by means of the formula.

Economic factors which underlie the slopes of the demand and supply curves actually determine the incidence of an excise tax. The more readily consumers will be willing and able to substitute other goods for the taxed one, the smaller will be the slope of the demand curve for the taxed good, and the smaller the proportion of the tax which will be immediately shifted to buyers. That is, the taxed industry will not find it economical to raise price very much if close substitutes are available toward which buyers can divert their custom.

On the supply side, factors which make plant relatively "flexible" are conducive to the ready reduction in amount supplied, and hence to a passing-forward of most of the tax. As was pointed out earlier in this volume, the use of relatively little fixed capital compared with variable inputs makes for flexibility. Also, divisibility of the plant increases flexibility (i.e., makes for relatively horizontal short-run supply curves). In the case of the tax on egg production the plant can be thought of as consisting mainly of a large number of separate egg-producing machines (i.e., chickens). These can quite economically be withdrawn from productive use, reducing the supply of eggs and raising market price. The chickens which are withdrawn from egg production can readily be put to another use—they can be sold as food. Also, the farmer and his family are likely to eat into their capital.

Shifting in the Long Run

In the long run, it is likely that an excise tax levied on a competitively produced commodity will be wholly, or almost wholly, included in the price which consumers must pay. Long-run supply curves are usually horizontal or upsloping only slightly—the latter occurring if some resources are bid up in price by firms within the industry as the industry expands in size.

It can readily be seen by reference to the formula that if the long-run supply curve is horizontal (has a zero slope), the price increase due to the tax will be equal to the full amount of the tax, regardless of the slope of the demand curve.[18] The complete shifting of the tax

---

[18] Substituting zero for c in the formula, we have $\Delta P = \dfrac{t}{1 + \left(\dfrac{0}{b}\right)}$ which equals t

regardless of the amount of slope in the demand curve.

will have been accomplished by means of firms leaving the industry to enter untaxed activities. In addition to being reflected fully in price, the excise tax will be harmful to the owners of resources which are forced into other fields, to the extent that earnings are less favorable in the new occupations. If the long-run supply curve is slightly up-sloping, the price to consumers will be raised by not quite the full amount of the tax.

Shifting under Monopoly

Paradoxically, a monopolistic firm is apt to absorb a greater part of an excise tax than will a competitive firm. This conclusion, however, rests on the assumption that the monopolistic firm was charging a

Exhibit 5

EXCISE TAX ON MONOPOLY—MAY BE LARGELY ABSORBED

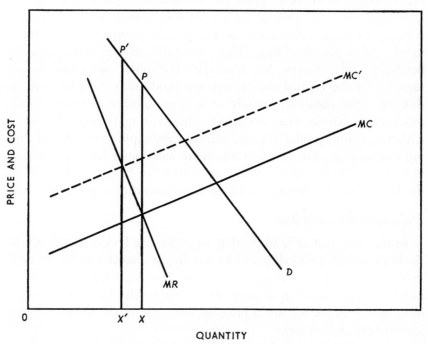

profit-maximizing price before the tax was levied. If his price was be-low this level—due, for example, to fear of antitrust action by the fed-eral government—the tax is likely to be fully passed on to the buyer, since this action would not seem unreasonable.

If it is assumed that an optimum price was in force before the tax, the motive to increase price can be shown in Exhibit 5. Marginal costs will be higher by exactly the amount of the excise tax, since the firm must pay this amount to the government on each unit produced. The upward shift in marginal costs will cause the optimum price to rise from XP to $X'P'$ and the rate of production to fall from OX to OX'. It will be noted that the price increase is considerably less than the tax.

As in the competitive case the change in price due to the tax can most conveniently be stated by means of a formula. Again, it is the relative slopes of the (linear) demand and marginal cost curves which determine the price increase, the formula being

$$\triangle P = \frac{t}{2 + \left(\frac{c}{b}\right)},$$

where the symbols have the same meaning as before, except that c denotes the slope of the marginal cost curve rather than the supply curve.[19] The figure 2 in the denominator causes the price increase under monopoly to be less than it would have been under competition with the same demand and cost curves in existence. If, for example, the marginal cost curve is horizontal (slope of zero), the price increase under monopoly equals half of the tax. Under competition, it is equal to the entire tax.

Miscellaneous Tax Effects

Emphasis has been placed in this chapter on the corporate income tax and on excise taxes. Many other types are, of course, of importance to businessmen. These include general sales taxes, property taxes, licenses, utility taxes, and others. It was pointed out in Chapter 12 that state and local taxes may be an important consideration in locational decisions. This is especially true of levies such as the property tax which are difficult to shift. A property tax does not affect short-run marginal costs of the firm and hence does not cause a reduction in output whereby price can be immediately raised. Over the longer run, however, property taxes on business tend to raise prices to consumers by restricting somewhat the quantity of resources going into business employment and in this way reducing supplies of goods. Fuller analysis, however, requires a consideration of the ways in which government expenditures aid business, alternative ways in which government reve-

---

[19] Under monopoly, there is no supply curve, but the marginal cost curve is influential in determining output. The formula and its derivation can be found in Colberg, *op. cit.*, p. 171.

nue can be raised, and other matters beyond the scope of this brief treatment.

CASE 13–1: HENRY W. SILASH

Shortly after Henry W. Silash moved to Chicago from Buffalo, New York, in 1922, he purchased a 332-acre farm northwest of Chicago, about 23 miles from the center of the city. This farm was situated at the northern edge of the "black belt," a highly fertile area of black soil extending from Ohio into Iowa. While not the best farmland in the area, the soil yielded a living for Mr. Silash and his family as long as it was tilled. Mr. Silash paid $14,000 for this farm. It included a nine-room house, two barns, and a few smaller sheds.

As shown in Exhibit 1, Mr. Silash's farm was bounded on the north by Appleton Road, on the east by Town Line Road, and on the west by Carson Street. Appleton Road was the extension of Appleton Street, which originated in a suburb of Chicago, about five miles to the east. Carson Street was an extension of a street by the same name in the City of Chicago. Town Line Road began at the northern city limits of Chicago and ran directly north, terminating at an east-west highway about 15 miles to the north. The southern boundary of the Silash farm adjoined the farm of Dorson Cronkhite.

During the decade of the twenties, there occurred a housing boom in this particular area. As a result, a number of homes were built west of the suburbs north of Chicago, and to the north of Chicago itself, in the general direction of the Silash farm. Appleton Road became one of the main traffic routes east and west. Both Town Line Road and Carson Street carried increasing traffic loads. No homes were built within a mile or two of the Silash farm, but Mr. Silash did lease a small parcel of his property at the corner of Appleton Road and Town Line Road to an oil company which erected a gasoline service station on the corner in 1928.

As a result of the WPA road-building program in the years of the great depression, Carson Street was reconstructed and became the main highway northwest from Chicago. In 1937, Appleton Street was also improved. In 1939, Town Line Road was widened and became a main route for traffic between Chicago and points in eastern Wisconsin. In 1938, Mr. Silash leased two more parcels of land for commercial purposes and renewed the 1928 lease with the oil company. He leased the parcel at the corner of Carson Street and Appleton Road

Exhibit 1

VICINITY OF HENRY W. SILASH FARM

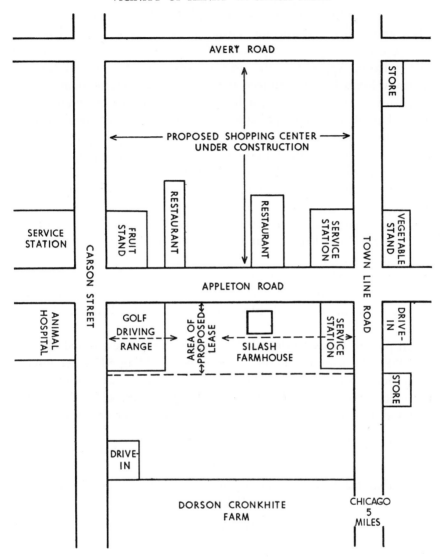

to an individual who constructed a golf driving range and putting green. On Carson Street, where the Silash and Cronkhite farms adjoined, he rented a small parcel to a firm which erected a small restaurant and ice cream stand to serve "drive-in" customers.

While these developments were going on with Mr. Silash, several commercial establishments of relatively small size sprang up on Appleton Road and Town Line Road. These are identified in Exhibit 1.

Following World War II, a housing boom of substantial proportions developed in the general area of the Silash farm. By 1952 the vicinity of the Silash farm was surrounded with new homes, both finished and under construction. Little development of home building had occurred along Carson Street and Town Line Road north of Appleton Road. Apparently, the presence of commercial establishments of many kinds had discouraged the use of this land for home building. Late in 1951, however, a large parcel of land—extending from Town Line Road along Appleton Road to Carson Street, then north to Avery Road, thence east to Town Line Road—was leased by a development company for the purpose of constructing a shopping center to serve the newly developed area. This area contained 97 acres, and the purchase price was $1,271,350. Shortly after the initial construction was begun on this center in 1954, Mr. Silash was approached by a real estate company which wished to lease the entire frontage of his farm on Appleton Road, from Town Line Road to Carson Street, to a depth of 375 feet. This would include the land now leased by the oil company and the golf driving range. The real estate company proposed a 24-year lease at the annual rate of $42,500 per year, with an option to renew for an additional 20 years at a rate to be determined at renewal.

All present leases on the Silash farm had been renewed and ran until 1958. The lease to the oil company was yielding $175 per month for a plot 125 by 110 feet. The golf driving range was yielding $215 per month for an area of approximately nine acres, while the restaurant and drive-in yielded $100 per month. This latter area was not affected by the proposed lease.

Mr. Silash consulted an appraiser to determine the value of the land for which the lease had been proposed. The report of the appraiser stated that the total amount of land involved was 219.4 acres and placed upon it a valuation of $810,000.

QUESTIONS

1. Should Mr. Silash accept the lease as proposed by the real estate company? If not, what amount would you suggest?
2. On the basis of the valuation, would you say that the lessees of the parcels of the Silash farm were getting a bargain? Explain.
3. In order that Mr. Silash can accept the new lease offer, it will be necessary to make a settlement with the driving range lessee and the oil company. What amounts would you suggest for settlement?
4. If Mr. Silash had an offer to sell or lease, which would you recommend? Why?

5. From a tax viewpoint, would it be advantageous for the real estate company to rent the land from Mr. Silash instead of purchasing it from him? Explain.

6. What tax advantages and disadvantages to Mr. Silash would be involved in outright sale of the property to the real estate company compared with renting it to the company on a long-term lease?

CASE 13–2: *NATIONAL CARBIDE CORPORATION* v. *COMMISSIONER OF INTERNAL REVENUE*, 366 U.S. 422

Air Reduction Sales Company, Pure Carbonic, Inc., National Carbide Corporation, and Wilson Welder and Metals Company are wholly owned subsidiaries of Air Reduction Corporation. For the year 1938, these subsidiaries reported income only as stated in their contracts with the parent company. The balance of the income of these subsidiaries was transferred to the parent company, which reported it as income for the purpose of income taxes and declared excess profits taxes for 1938. The Commissioner of Internal Revenue assessed each of the subsidiaries for deficiencies in income tax and declared-value excess profits tax for that year. The Tax Court ruled in favor of the subsidiaries. The Court of Appeals reversed. Appeal was made by the subsidiaries to the United States Supreme Court.

MR. VINSON, C.J.: Petitioners are three wholly owned subsidiaries of Air Reduction Corporation (Airco). They seek a determination of the question whether deficiencies in income and declared value excess profits taxes for the year 1938 found by the Commissioner of Internal Revenue are properly chargeable to them. Their contention is that they are corporate agents of Airco, that the income from their operations is income of Airco, and that income and excess profits taxes must be determined on that basis.

By a series of combinations and dissolutions of previously acquired subsidiary companies, Airco had, prior to 1938, reduced the number of its subsidiaries to four. All operated strictly in accordance with contracts with Airco. The subsidiaries were utilized by Airco as operating companies in the four major fields of operation in which it was engaged. Air Reduction Sales Company carried on the manufacture and sale of the gaseous constituents of air; National Carbide Corporation, the manufacture and sale of calcium carbide; Pure Carbonic, Inc., the manufacture and sale of carbon dioxide; and Wilson Welder and Metals Company, the manufacture and sale of welding machines and supplies.[20]

The contracts between Airco and its subsidiaries provided, in substance, that the latter were employed as agents to manage and operate plants de-

---

[20] Wilson Welder had a net deficit during the year here involved and is not a petitioner in this action.

signed for the production of the products assigned to each, and as agents to sell the outputs of the plants. Airco was to furnish working capital, executive management and office facilities for its subsidiaries. They in turn agreed to pay Airco all profits in excess of six per cent on their outstanding capital stock, which in each case was nominal in amount.[21] Title to the assets utilized by the subsidiaries was held by them, and amounts advanced by Airco for the purchase of assets and working capital were shown on the books of the subsidiaries as accounts payable to Airco. The value of the assets of each company thus approximated the amount owed to Airco. No interest ran on these accounts.

Airco and its subsidiaries were organized horizontally into six overriding divisions: corporate, operations, sales, financial, distribution, and research. Officers heading each division were, in turn, officers of the subsidiaries. Top officials of Airco held similar positions in the subsidiary companies. Directors of the subsidiaries met only to ratify the action of the directors and officers of Airco.

Airco considered the profits turned over to it by the subsidiaries pursuant to the contracts as its own income and reported it as such. Petitioners reported as income only the six per cent return on capital that each was entitled to retain. Similarly, in declaring the value of their capital stock for declared value excess profits tax purposes, the subsidiaries reported only the nominal amounts at which the stock was carried on the books of each. The Commissioner notified petitioners of substantial income and excess profits tax deficiencies in their 1938 returns, having taken the position that they are taxable on the income turned over to Airco as well as the nominal amounts retained. The Tax Court held, however, that the income from petitioners' operations in excess of six per cent of their capital stock was income and property of Airco.

According to the Tax Court's opinion: "The issue which (was decided) in this proceeding is whether, as the respondent has determined, the income from the operations of the three petitioners belonged not to Airco, the parent, but to the petitioners, and was taxable to them; or whether, as the three petitioners contend, the income from the operations of the petitioners in 1938, exclusive of the small amounts paid to petitioners under the contracts, belonged and was taxable to Airco, the parent company, both because the petitioners were in fact incorporated departments, divisions, or branches of Airco's business and because the petitioners operated pursuant to express contract with Airco."

So far as control is concerned, we can see no difference in principle between Airco's control of petitioners and that exercised over *Moline Properties, Inc.,* by its sole stockholder. Undoubtedly the great majority of corporations owned by sole stockholders are "dummies" in the sense that their policies and day-by-day activities are determined not as decisions of the corporation but by their owners acting individually. We can see no significance, therefore, in findings of fact such as, "The Airco board held regular meetings and exercised complete domination and control over the business of Airco and each of the petitioners," and "The chairman, vice chairman, and president of Airco

---

[21] Sales had outstanding 125 shares of stock of $100 par value; Carbide's outstanding capital stock was 50 shares of $100 par value; Carbonic also had 50 shares of $100 par value.

were in charge of the administration and management of the activities of each petitioner and carried out the policies and directives with respect to each petitioner as promulgated by the Airco board." We reversed the Board of Tax Appeals in *Moline Properties* in the face of its finding that "Full beneficial ownership was in Thompson (the sole stockholder), who continued to manage and regard the property as his own individually."

Some stress was placed by the Tax Court, and by petitioners in argument here, upon the form of ownership of assets adopted by Airco and its subsidiaries. Petitioners' capital stock was, as has been stated, nominal in amount. Assets of considerable value, to which title was held by the subsidiaries, were balanced by accounts payable to Airco on the books of each. The Tax Court thought it material that "All assets held by each petitioner were furnished to it by Airco, which paid for them with its own cash or stock. Airco supplied all the working capital of each petitioner."

If Airco had supplied assets to its subsidiaries in return for stock valued at amounts equal to the value of the assets, no question could be raised as to the reality of ownership of the assets by the subsidiaries. Airco would then have been in a position comparable, so far as ownership of the assets of petitioners is concerned, to that of the sole stockholder in *Moline Properties*. We think that it can make no difference that financing of the subsidiaries was carried out by means of book indebtedness in lieu of increased book value of the subsidiaries' stock. A corporation must derive its funds from three sources: capital contributions, loans, and profits from operations. The fact that Airco, the sole Stockholder, preferred to supply funds to its subsidiaries primarily by the second method, rather than either of the other two,[22] does not make the income earned by their utilization income to Airco. We need not decide whether the funds supplied to petitioners by Airco were capital contributions rather than loans. It is sufficient to say that the very factors which, as petitioners contend, show that Airco "supplied" and "furnished" their assets also indicate that petitioners were the recipients of capital contributions rather than loans.[23]

Nor do the contracts between Airco and petitioners by which the latter

[22] As a practical matter, a considerable part of the assets of petitioners was supplied out of profits from their operations. Even though assets were purchased directly out of the earnings of a subsidiary, however, the amount withdrawn was entered in the accounts payable by the subsidiary and in the accounts receivable of Airco, since substantially all profits of the subsidiaries were, by contract, payable only to the parent.

[23] Since petitioners were required to pay all profits except very small amounts to Airco each year, it was obviously impossible for them to pay the accounts payable to Airco. . . . Mr. C. E. Adams, Chairman of Air Reduction Corporation, testified that the assets of the subsidiaries represented by the accounts payable could be realized by Airco only upon dissolution of the subsidiaries. In other words, there was never any expectation that the accounts would be paid prior to dissolution. Since no interest ran on these accounts, the "loans" were identical, except in name, with contributions of capital. . . . The fact that no interest ran on these "loans" is, of course, further indication that they are capital contributions.

Title to gas cylinders used by petitioners, amounting in value to about $13,000,000, was retained by Airco, but the cylinders were used by the subsidiaries without charge. Whether these, too, were capital contributions we find it unnecessary to decide in this case. Free use of the cylinders by petitioners, if they were merely on loan, may have distorted the subsidiaries' income beyond the allocations made by the Commissioner, but that problem is not before us.

agreed to pay all profits above a nominal return to the former, on that account, become "agency" contracts within the meaning of our decisions. The
Tax Court felt that the fact that Airco was entitled to the profits by contract
shows that the income "belonged to Airco" and should not, for that reason, be
taxed to petitioners. Our decisions requiring that income be taxed to those who
earn it, despite anticipatory agreements designed to prevent vesting of the
income in the earners, foreclose this result. . . . Of course one of the duties
of a collection agent is to transmit the money he receives to his principal
according to their agreement. But the fact that petitioners were required by
contract to turn over the money received by them to Airco, after deducting
expenses and nominal profits, is no sure indication that they were mere collection agents. Such an agreement is entirely consistent with the corporation–
sole stockholder relationship whether or not any agency exists, and with other
relationships as well.

What we have said does not foreclose a true corporate agent or trustee from
handling the property and income of its owner-principal without being taxable
therefor. Whether the corporation operates in the name and for the account of
the principal, binds the principal by its actions, transmits money received to the
principal, and whether receipt of income is attributable to the services of employees of the principal and to assets belonging to the principal are some of the
relevant considerations in determining whether a true agency exists. If the
corporation is a true agent, its relations with its principal must not be dependent
upon the fact that it is owned by the principal, if such is the case. Its business
purpose must be the carrying on of the normal duties of an agent.

They claim that they should be taxable on net income aggregating only
$1,350.00, despite the fact that during the tax year (1938) they owned as-
sets worth nearly 20 million dollars, had net sales of approximately 22 million
dollars, and earned nearly four and one-half million dollars net. Their employees number in the thousands. We have passed the questions whether Airco's
interest in these assets is that of owner of the subsidiaries or lender, but whatever the answer, they do not belong to Airco as principal. The entire earnings of petitioners, except for trifling amounts, are turned over to Airco not
because the latter could command this income if petitioners were owned by
third persons but because it owns and thus completely dominates the subsidiaries. Airco, for sufficient reasons of its own, wished to avoid the burdens
of principalship.[24] It cannot now escape the tax consequences of that choice,

---

[24] The two main purposes for the adoption by Airco of the corporate subsidiary
method of operation, as related by Mr. E. E. Adams, Chairman of Air Reduction
Corporation, were these: "Frankly, in 1918 and still, Air Reduction, Inc., was and is a
New York corporation. Even at that early date it became evident, as I already said,
we were going to have plants scattered all over the United States. We didn't want to
domicile the parent company in 48 states of the Union and have us subject to service in all
those states, and that was distinctly a reason for using this corporate setup in connection
with operations to be run as divisions, just as the contract set forth.

"Now, in addition to that, as a practical matter, out in the field and on the firing
line, to have a representative, an officer, we will say, of Pure Carbonic, when trouble
arises with a customer, a vice president of Pure Carbonic, who is not an officer of
Air Reduction, Inc., at all, who goes in and straightens that out with that customer,

no matter how bona fide its motives or long standing its arrangements. When we referred to the "usual incidents of an agency relationship" in the *Moline Properties* case, we meant just that—not the identity of ownership and control disclosed by the facts of this case.

We have considered the other arguments made by petitioners and find them to be without merit. The judgment of the Court of Appeals is *Affirmed.*

QUESTIONS

1. Can you suggest any way in which Airco could retain its present corporate organization but have the income show as that of the parent company?

2. Would the income tax rate and the excess profits tax ever influence the distribution of profits between a parent company and its subsidiaries?

3. What comment would you make as to the capital structure of the subsidiaries in this case for the purpose of the declared-value excess profits tax? Would this arrangement affect the total tax liability for the consolidated companies?

4. From the facts of the case, does it appear that Airco sacrificed profits, as regards the tax liability of showing all profits in the parent company, for the purpose of attempting to establish an agency relationship? Does this mean the company failed to maximize profits under the existing legal framework?

5. How would a change in the tax brackets for a graduated corporate income tax affect the relationships between a parent company and its subsidiaries?

---

increases his kudos, helps him with all his negotiating efforts, with their competitors on the outside."

It is thus apparent that Airco was attempting to avoid the status of principal *vis-a-vis* its subsidiaries. As principal it would have been subject to service of process through its agents, as owner of the subsidiary it was not. . . . The purpose of having officers of subsidiaries who could deal directly with customers does not indicate an agency relationship. On the contrary, the very purpose of the organization adopted was to lead customers to believe that they were dealing with top men in the company actually manufacturing and selling the products they purchased.

Chapter 14

~~~~~~

GOVERNMENT AND BIG BUSINESS

THE SHERMAN ACT of 1890 made the federal government the umpire in the great game of business, giving it the responsibility of preventing monopoly in interstate commerce. Congress used broad language in describing the nature of illegal monopoly, leaving it up to the administrative agencies and the courts to determine more explicitly what will not be permitted. The main provision of the Sherman Act states that "every contract, combination in the form of trust or otherwise, or conspiracy in restraint of trade or commerce among the several states, or with foreign nations is hereby declared to be illegal. . . ."

The Sherman Act was reinforced in 1914 by the Clayton Act, which —in addition to covering such practices as price discrimination (which was described in Chapter 9), interlocking directorates, tying contracts, and exclusive-dealer arrangements—gave the federal government more explicit power over monopoly by merger. The principal provision of this sort (Section 7, as amended in 1950) states that "no corporation engaged in commerce shall acquire, directly or indirectly, the whole or any part of the stock or share capital . . . [or] the whole or any part of the assets of another corporation also engaged in commerce, where in any line of commerce in any section of the country, the effect of such acquisition may be substantially to lessen competition, or to tend to create a monopoly."

For the most part, enforcement of these basic antimonopoly laws has not been very successful, but the constant threat imposed by their existence has probably forestalled many combinations, overt price agreements, and other restraints on competition which would otherwise have been put into effect. The antimonopoly laws have caused some firms to attempt to hold their share of an industry's business to 50 per cent or less [1] and to hold prices below those which would maximize short-run profits. That is, many firms are persuaded to take a long-run view, prospering more moderately and avoiding antitrust prosecution,

---

[1] Fifty per cent is something of a magic number in this connection, since if it is exceeded, it opens the firm to the accusation that it is more powerful than even a combination of all of its rivals.

504

rather than the short-run view of pushing a monopolistic advantage to its utmost.[5]

Dissolution and Divestiture

The most spectacular action which can occur under the Sherman Act is dissolution of a huge corporation. This is, however, an extremely rare event. In 1911 the Supreme Court, in two extraordinarily important decisions, ordered the dissolution of the Standard Oil Company of New Jersey and the American Tobacco Company. The former controlled about 90 per cent of the oil-refining business, while the latter controlled about 95 per cent of the cigarette business as well as high proportions of smoking tobacco, plug tobacco, and snuff production.[2] Standard Oil was broken up into a number of regional companies, while American Tobacco's assets were assigned to three full-line companies and eleven smaller ones. In both cases the previous large stockholders retained control, reducing the power of the dissolution actually to increase competition greatly.

A more recent (1952) dissolution of large magnitude involved the Big Five motion-picture producers. Major producers were forced to sell their affiliated exhibition outlets. The court decrees ordered that about 1,300 theaters be operated by newly formed theater companies, and that more than 1,200 theaters be sold to independent exhibitors.[3] (In view of the difficulties caused by the rapid growth of television around 1952, the sale of many theaters by the producers may actually have been good business, anyway.) The magnitude of the divestiture in the motion-picture industry was unusually great. A well-known antitrust economist has characterized this as "probably the government's greatest economic victory in the 60-year history of antitrust enforcement."[4] Usually, the judgments rendered by the courts require only partial divestiture by large corporations of interests held in other firms. Even partial divestiture judgments are not common, however.

In the United States Steel case of 1920 the Supreme Court decided that "mere size is no offense." No attempt to monopolize was found in this case because of lack of evidence of coercive, predatory, or exclusive tactics.[5] This dictum prevailed for about a quarter century but was

---

[2] Vernon A. Mund, *Government and Business* (2d ed.; New York: Harper & Bros., 1955), p. 208.

[3] *Ibid.*, p. 237.

[4] Walter Adams, "The Aluminum Case: Legal Victory—Economic Defeat," *American Economic Review,* December, 1951, pp. 915–16.

[5] J. B. Dirlam and A. E. Kahn, *Fair Competition: The Law and Economics of Antitrust Policy* (Ithaca: Cornell University Press, 1954), p. 45.

finally reversed in the Alcoa case, which was won by the government after 13 years of litigation. Here, size *was* considered to be the essence of an individual firm's monopoly power. (This decision is probably largely responsible for the popularity in recent years of measures of "concentration" by the Federal Trade Commission, since these relate directly to the problem of bigness of the individual company.) Nevertheless, the Aluminum Company of America was not broken up into smaller units. Instead, it was decided that the War Assets Administration should sell the surplus government-owned aluminum capacity to the Reynolds Metals Company and the Kaiser Aluminum and Chemical Company in order to provide some competition for Alcoa. The latter's market position in primary aluminum was reduced from one of virtually complete monopoly to approximately 50 per cent of the industry's total.[6]

The New View of Monopoly

Lately, there has been a tendency for the administrative agencies and the courts to examine market structures and the behavior of prices in order to find circumstantial evidence of market domination. Specific *intent* to monopolize and the use of predatory practices to achieve market domination may no longer be necessary factors in determining when the existence of monopoly power falls under the Sherman Act's prohibition of restraint of trade.

This tendency was manifest in the Alcoa case, already mentioned, and in the American Tobacco decision of 1946. The court upheld a finding of conspiracy among three separate tobacco companies to fix prices, even though there was no direct evidence of collusion among the companies. The main evidence was circumstantial, in that prices charged by the separate firms tended to move together. The entire practice of price leadership in interstate commerce now appears to run the risk of being determined to be "conscious parallelism of action," even when it is not established by an explicit "agreement to agree" on prices.

The new antitrust attitude seems to have been reflected also in a 1953 case, *United Shoe Machinery Corporation* v. *United States.* This company produced 75 to 95 per cent of the shoe machinery turned out in the country and had followed the policy of leasing rather than selling the machinery. The court found United Shoe Machinery's practices to be "not predatory but instead to be those of a normally aggres-

---

[6] John V. Krutilla, "Aluminum—A Dilemma for Antitrust Aims?" *Southern Economic Journal,* October, 1955, p. 165.

sive firm." The corporation was ordered to offer its machinery for sale on terms that would not substantially favor leasing, and prohibited any lease in excess of five years.

In this case the former refusal to sell outright had prevented the creation of a secondhand market. (As is very evident in the automobile industry, the sellers of used cars may offer substantial competition to the sellers of new ones.) Also, United Shoe Machinery, by tying in repairs with its rental contracts, was found to have prevented the growth of independent repair services.[7]

Economies of Size

In considering the wisdom of dissolution of large corporations holding substantial monopoly power, judging when "big" is "too big" is most difficult. Economies of scale with respect to plant arise from the increased specialization of productive processes and the use of large machines. A machine capable of turning out twice as much output as a smaller one usually does not cost twice as much—at least up to a point. In order to use highly specialized processes of production and the largest available machinery, a plant frequently must be very large. The economies of scale differ greatly, however, from industry to industry.

While economies of scale are most spectacular with respect to plants, they exist also with respect to firms. A large multiplant firm is able to diversify its production so as to secure a stability of profits greater than would be likely with a single line (unless that line had an extremely dependable demand, such as exists for electricity). Also, a large firm usually enjoys substantial economies in purchasing, in marketing its products, and in advertising, financing, and research. (Research cost per unit is lower when a newly discovered product can be sold in large volume.) Integration to insure dependable supplies of materials and components at cost often provides a further economy related to scale of firm.

In any antitrust case, it is possible for the large firm to show the existence of competition, since *some* substitution is always possible. This may come from identical products turned out by other domestic firms, similar products which are substitutes in at least some uses, imports, or the secondhand market. It can also demonstrate economies of scale which could not be secured by a smaller company. Such *diseconomies* as may exist due to the difficulty of co-ordinating a far-flung

---

[7] "The Supreme Court, 1953 Term," *Harvard Law Review*, Vol. LXVIII (1954-55), p. 142.

industrial empire are not likely to be obvious. Also, the greater compulsion toward efficiency which would be brought about by more thoroughgoing competition is not likely to be clearly demonstrable, since even a firm with great monopoly power has the profit motive to spur its efficiency.

Natural Monopolies Treated Differently

When firms are deemed to be "natural monopolies" because of the clear advantages of large-scale company operations in relation to total demand, it is the prevailing public policy not to enforce the antitrust laws but instead to encourage monopoly by means of exclusive franchises, and to regulate maximum rates through administrative commissions as a means of securing for society at least a portion of the benefits of large-scale production. Or direct government ownership may be resorted to, with rates set directly by public authorities, with or without the check of a regulatory commission. In the case of the railroads and truckers especially, public regulation has also taken the form of shielding firms from the full effects of competition by fixing minimum rates as well as maximum rates. The category of "natural monopolies" which are properly subject to regulation is not clean-cut. Some industries (e.g., trucking and taxicabs) have been considered by government to be properly subject to rate regulation, even though price competition might be effective; while in other industries, where cost advantages of very large firms make real price competition unlikely, no public regulation of price exists or is likely to exist in the foreseeable future.

Workable Competition

In recent years the concept of "workable competition" has been improvised to denote a situation in which there are a number of noncolluding firms in each market area, where no one firm occupies a large part of the market, and where new firms can enter on approximately even terms. This situation can provide the consumer with many of the advantages which could be derived from pure competition—as long as rivalry remains genuine in important respects. Unfortunately, the concept of workable competition is a vague one. What will be deemed by one investigator to provide sufficient protection to the consumer may be considered by another to be an intolerably monopolistic situation.

Usually, different firms do not turn out exactly the same product or set of products, making it difficult to say what constitutes the "industry" or "group" within which there is supposed to be a sufficient number of firms to provide workable competition. Also, it is unclear just how many firms are needed within an industry—once a definition has been arrived at—to provide substantial competition. A duopolistic (two-firm) industry may be more competitive than one consisting of a dozen firms if the two are genuine rivals in important matters (especially in price) while the twelve co-operate in some important respects. However, the likelihood of securing substantial competition increases as the number of firms increases, since it is harder to keep all members of a larger group "in line" through trade association activity or other means. As the group becomes larger, the potential gain in sales by a price "chiseler" becomes greater, and the danger to him of retaliatory price cuts by all the other firms becomes smaller. Consequently, antitrust policy which succeeds in establishing or keeping a larger number of firms in any given field may not guarantee that the field will be made or kept workably competitive; but, at least, it tends to decrease the likelihood of full collusion on basic matters.

Mergers

The strong merger movement among American corporations in recent years has greatly increased antitrust interest in the effects of this activity on the competitiveness of industry. It can be readily seen in Exhibit 1 that the number of mergers and acquisitions in manufacturing and mining has been increasing since 1949. The number is still far below that of the late 1920's, however.

Under the law the Federal Trade Commission can institute its proceedings against a merger or acquisition only after it has been consummated. If the Federal Trade Commission is successful, the complications involved in restoring *status quo ante* mean that the order of divestiture must be issued as soon as possible.[8] As a consequence, many antitrust officials are anxious to secure a change in the law which would require the filing of information on mergers prior to their consummation. Under current proposals the mergers themselves would not require prior government approval.

A recent Federal Trade Commission study of the mergers which were consummated between 1948 and 1954 was motivated by the upward trend in consolidations. Time and staff limitations restricted the

---

[8] *Annual Report of the Federal Trade Commission, 1955* (Washington, D.C.: U.S. Government Printing Office, 1956), p. 33.

Exhibit 1

NUMBER OF MERGERS AND ACQUISITIONS IN MANUFACTURING
AND MINING

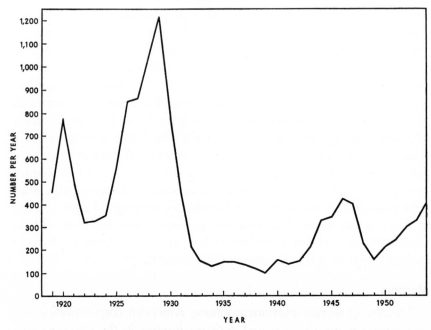

Source: Federal Trade Commission, *Report on Corporate Mergers and Acquisitions* (Washington, D.C.: U.S. Government Printing Office, May, 1955).

Exhibit 2

COMPANIES MAKING TEN OR MORE ACQUISITIONS,
JANUARY 1, 1951—JULY 31, 1954

Company	Number of Acquisitions
Foremost Dairies, Inc.	43
Suburban-Propane Gas Co.	17
General Shoe Corp.	15
Chemical Enterprises, Inc.	12
General Gas Corp.	12
Olin-Mathieson Corp.	12
Sinclair Oil Corp.	11
American Machine and Foundry Co.	10
American Marietta Co.	10
Borden Co.	10
Burlington Industries, Inc.	10

Source: Federal Trade Commission, *Report on Corporate Mergers and Acquisitions* (Washington, D.C.: U.S. Government Printing Office, May, 1955, p. 57).

study mainly to information already in the commission's files. According to this incomplete record, the eleven firms listed in Exhibit 2 were among those which made ten or more acquisitions between January 1, 1951, and July 31, 1954.

Large dairy companies have been extremely active in acquiring other firms in the same field. In addition to Foremost Dairies, Inc., the National Dairy Products Corporation, Borden Company, and Beatrice Foods Company have acquired many incorporated and unincorporated firms. The Federal Trade Commission has recently stated that National Dairy Products Corporation has acquired all or part of the stock or assets of 40 dairy concerns since 1951; Borden is reported to have acquired 80 concerns; and Beatrice Foods Company, 131 companies.[9]

Nature of Gains to Firms

The Federal Trade Commission analysts found six advantages to the acquiring firm which were frequently apparent as important motives in mergers and acquisitions:[10]

1. Additional capacity may be more quickly secured by merger than by new construction.
2. A larger line of products in the same general business is often secured by retaining items already being turned out by the acquired firm.
3. Diversification of products can often be most easily and safely effected by taking over lines which are already successful.
4. Vertical integration is sometimes achieved by merger as a way of assuring dependable supplies of materials and components at cost.
5. Vertical merger, looking instead toward sale of final products, is sometimes advantageous, especially when the existing facilities for distribution can readily handle additional products.
6. Geographic coverage can quickly be expanded by taking over facilities located in regions not already covered.

It is desirable to look at the motivation for mergers from the point of view of the *selling* firm as well as the acquiring firm. Tax motives were discussed in the previous chapter. Among the nontax motives the following have been listed by the author of a recent study of corporate mergers:[11]

1. The desire to retire.
2. Loss of key management personnel by death.
3. Desire to reduce the load of key executives.
4. Inability of top management to keep up with its competition.
5. Desire to become connected with larger companies.
6. Dissension among owner-managers.
7. Anticipation by owners of a decline in the value of their holdings.

---

[9] *Wall Street Journal,* October 16, 1956, p. 3.

[10] *Annual Report of the Federal Trade Commission, 1955,* p. 59.

[11] J. Fred Weston, *The Role of Mergers in the Growth of Large Firms* (Los Angeles: University of California Press, 1953), pp. 72–73. Weston concluded that internal expansion has been of more importance since the turn of the century than mergers in explaining the present size of the large firms studied.

8. Desire to capitalize the value of owner contributions where this value was highly dependent on active owner participation in management.

9. Desire for greater diversification to improve the quality and marketability of investment holdings.

Mergers and the Public Interest

No valid generalization can be made regarding the effects of mergers on the public interest. Each particular acquisition must be separately considered in the light of the market situation which it affects. In the automobile industry, where smaller companies seem to be at a serious disadvantage relative to the Big Three, the merger of small firms has been encouraged by the government as a means of improving their competitive positions. This attitude was manifest in the Nash-Hudson, Kaiser-Willys, and Studebaker-Packard mergers.

Where only small companies are involved, the Federal Trade Commission usually considers that the merger or acquisition does not tend to create a monopoly. Also, the antimerger provisions of the Clayton Act are not applicable to acquisitions by or from noncorporations, or to acquisitions which are made solely for investment. However, when a large corporation shows a disposition to acquire numerous smaller corporations in the same—or nearly the same—line of business, thus removing them as competitors, the Federal Trade Commission is apt to place its activities under close scrutiny for possible antitrust violation.

Even when a large corporation is active in acquiring other corporations, the consequences may range anywhere from no effect on competition to a severe loss of competition, depending on the exact nature of the acquisitions. If a "vertical" acquisition of a parts supplier who has produced exclusively for the acquiring firm occurs, there is no effect on the immediate extent of competition at either level. A certain amount of potential competition may be eliminated, since the "captive" parts supplier will now probably be unavailable as a source of components to any new entry into the field of the acquiring corporation. More immediate and possibly serious repercussions on competition can occur if a vertical acquisition involves a raw-material or parts supplier who also supplies other firms, particularly when the latter are competitors of the acquiring firm. Much depends on the availability of alternative sources of the material or components. If these are available only at higher cost from another source—due, for example, to their having to be shipped a greater distance—the damage to competition may be substantial. The great complexity and variety of market situations which are involved make the commission's job of policing mergers which may be contrary to the public interest an extremely difficult one.

Exclusive-Dealer Contracts

Section 3 of the Clayton Act prohibits exclusive-dealer contracts whenever their effect may be substantially to lessen competition in interstate commerce. The leading case brought under this section was *Standard Oil Company of California et al.* v. *United States in* 1949. The Supreme Court held that exclusive-dealer contracts affecting a substantial amount of business are illegal when utilized by a seller who is of major importance in his market. The decision is obviously not a very clear one because of the difficulty of knowing what a "substantial" amount of business is and when a seller is a "major" factor.

Two recent (1953 and 1954) decisions have weakened the prohibition of exclusive-dealer contracts. They indicate that if a manufacturer establishes exclusive outlets by refusing to sell to dealers handling competing products, it can have such arrangements upheld, even though the effect on competition may be the same as that of exclusive-dealer contracts.[12] That is, even though exclusive-dealer contracts may be illegal in a positive sense, they can sometimes be enforced indirectly by means of a refusal on the part of the manufacturer or wholesaler to deal with the unco-operative retailer. Exclusive-dealership arrangements are difficult to outlaw because of the basic right of a seller to sell to whomever he wishes. (In the case of a common carrier or public utility, however, the seller is obliged to sell to all who wish to buy.)

Interlocking Directorates

Another of the prohibitions of the Clayton Act is directed at interlocking directorates among corporations. Section 8 provides, in substance, that no person may be a director in two or more competing corporations, any one of which has capital, surplus, and undivided profits aggregating more than $1 million, the prohibition not being applicable, however, to banks and common carriers.[13] Antitrust enforcement on this front has not been vigorous, but the existence of the prohibition has probably reduced somewhat the direct use of this device, which

---

[12] "An Interstate Circuit Approach to the Refusal to Deal Dilemma under Section 3 of the Clayton Act," *Yale Law Journal*, Vol. LXIV, p. 581.

[13] *Annual Report of the Federal Trade Commission, 1950* (Washington, D.C.: U.S. Government Printing Office, 1951), p. 27. All of the information on interlocking directorates presented here was obtained from this report.

may, quite obviously, lead to collusive rather than competitive activities. Section 8 does not prohibit interlocks between suppliers and corporate customers, and this is a very common situation.

In 1946, the year to which the Federal Trade Commission study applies, the food industry was one of the outstanding exhibitors of interlocking directorates. For example, three of the ten largest dairies were directly or indirectly interlocked with one another. (Indirect interlocking occurs, for example, when two corporations each have a director who is also on the board of a third corporation.) The three largest dairies were also indirectly interlocked with General Foods Corporation, Standard Brands, and Best Foods. The largest of the diary companies was indirectly interlocked with two large baking companies, which were potential customers, and with a large manufacturer of metal and paper containers.

Heavy interlocking was found to exist among sugar companies. Sixteen of the 23 largest sugar companies had direct or indirect ties. American Sugar Refining alone had direct and indirect interlocks with 16 potential customers.

The nonferrous metals industry was indirectly interlocked through financial institutions and also through some leading industrial corporations. American Metal Company was interlocked with 10 companies within the industry; Kennecott Copper Corporation and Phelps Dodge Corporation, with eight; and Anaconda Copper Mining Company, St. Joseph Lead Company, and American Smelting and Refining Company, with seven.

In the electrical machinery industry, the Big Four manufacturers—General Electric, Westinghouse, Western Electric, and Radio Corporation of America—were indirectly interlocked through six large commercial banks, two of the largest life insurance companies, a public utility, a railroad, and an industrial company. They also had backward interlocks to suppliers and forward ones to customers.

The leading petroleum companies—Standard of New Jersey, Socony-Vacuum Oil Company, Texas Company, Standard of California, Standard of Indiana, Gulf Oil Corporation, and others—were found by the Federal Trade Commission to be closely tied together by means of interlocking directorates or by joint ownership of affiliates. The most significant interlocking directorates were through a leading New York bank.

None of the rubber companies had directors in common in 1946. The most significant of the interlocking relations were apparently those between U.S. Rubber and General Motors, resting on heavy du

Pont investments in both companies and the presence of du Pont directors on both boards. This relationship accounts for the prevalence of U.S. Rubber Company tires on new General Motors cars.

Significance of Interlocking Directorates

The significance of interlocking directorates cannot be simply assessed. Much depends on the power exerted by the directors through whom the relations are established. This may range from great power all the way down to mere observation. Much depends also on the nature of the companies which are thus linked. If the firms are rivals in an industry which has a small number of firms, collusive actions are likely to result. If the firms have related but not identical lines of products, the interlocking is apt to forestall the encroachment of each upon the other through the addition of new products.

Interlocking directorates between a company and its suppliers or customers may bring about preferential treatment in prices, in allocation of materials in short supply because of a strike or other emergency, or in special access to market outlets. When manufacturing companies are linked with financial institutions, they may be given preferred access to credit compared with a newcomer to the field, thus putting a potential competitor at a disadvantage. As was pointed out in the chapter on plant location, the local availability of credit is quite often an important factor in causing a firm to choose one city rather than another as the site of a new facility.

The Fair-Trade Philosophy

At the same time that the federal government seeks to keep business competitive by means of antitrust activity, the "fair-trade" laws tend to have the opposite effect—namely, that of preventing thoroughgoing price competition at the retail level. These laws permit manufacturers to establish resale prices on certain items. Like some other laws affecting price, their effects are not entirely in one direction. There is some validity to the claim that the fair-trade laws actually promote the preservation of competition by preventing large retailers from using well-advertised products as loss leaders to attract business away from smaller firms. The latter cannot use loss leaders so effectively, since they have fewer other products to which to "lead" customers. Also, there is some validity to the argument that use of a nationally advertised brand as a loss leader may "cheapen" the product unduly in the public mind.

Resale price maintenance has been applied most extensively to commodities possessing distinctive characteristics in the minds of consumers. Proprietary items produced under secret formulas and trade-marked items sold directly to consumers are most suitable for this purpose. Durable items like farm machinery, household electrical appliances, radios, and television sets are not very suitable, because effective retail prices can so readily be altered by means of the trade-in allowance given to the buyer. Drugs, toilet goods, cosmetics, liquor, and sporting goods have been subjected extensively to fair-trade pricing.

The driving force behind enactment of the fair-trade laws was the National Association of Retail Druggists. Beginning in 1935, this association made enactment of state resale price-maintenance laws and the passage of a national fair-trade law its main objective; a secondary objective was obtaining at least a 50 per cent markup on drugstore items.[14] Led by California, which passed a fair-trade law in 1931, forty-four other states enacted similar legislation by 1941. In 1937, Congress amended the Sherman Act by passing the Miller-Tydings Resale Price Maintenance Act. This legalized retail price fixing in interstate commerce where a state law existed. The Supreme Court found the Miller-Tydings Act to be unconstitutional in 1951, but passage of the McGuire Act in 1952 again put on the books a federal fair-trade law —with revised wording to meet the objections of the court. Without a federal law exempting firms which use fair-trade contracts from prosecution under the antitrust laws, the state laws would be of very limited significance.

Operation of the fair-trade laws has been hampered very substantially during the past few years by both legal and economic forces. By July, 1955, the highest courts of Arkansas, Florida, Georgia, Michigan, and Nebraska had declared their state laws unconstitutional. Kentucky and Indiana have since joined this group. The Supreme courts of California, New Jersey, New York, Pennsylvania, and Wisconsin have held their acts unenforceable.[15] Colorado was added to the latter group in October, 1956, when the Supreme Court of that state held unconstitutional the "nonsigner" clause of the fair-trade law.[16] This clause has usually been the center of legal attack. The nonsigner clause in a state fair-trade law makes binding on nonsigners a resale price

---

[14] *Report of the Federal Trade Commission on Resale Price Maintenance* (Washington, D.C.: U.S. Government Printing Office, 1945), p. xxxi.

[15] National Industrial Conference Board, *The "Fair Trade" Question* (Studies in Business Economics, No. 48) (New York, 1955), p. 32.

[16] *Christian Science Monitor,* October 12, 1956, p. 12.

specified on a particular item if a contract is signed with just one retailer in the state.

A recent (June 11, 1956) Supreme Court decision has struck a
blow at the use of fair-trade contracts by manufacturers who also do
some wholesaling. This decision directly involved McKesson & Robbins, Inc., the nation's largest drug wholesaler, which also makes and
sells some products under its own brand.[17] It was ruled that McKesson
& Robbins may not have fair-trade agreements with independent
wholesalers with whom its own divisions compete. Since many manufacturers do some wholesaling, this decision may have quite widespread
importance. It is evident that the fair-trade movement has lost much
of the power which it possessed a few years ago.

Economic Forces Hampering Fair Trade

The basic economic force of substitution has been a main detriment
to the fair-traders. The manufacturer who sets a retail price at a high
level on his product invites the entry of technically similar commodities by other manufacturers into the market. These may be fair-traded
at a lower level, or not fair-traded at all. Many manufacturers have
attempted to "have their cake and eat it, too," by selling the same commodity under different brand names, fair-trading one and selling the
other through different outlets without fair-trade contracts. This is a
variety of price discrimination which may be effective to the extent
that consumers do not realize the similarity of the products or to the
extent that they are not careful in spending their money.[18]

Frequently, the lower-priced version of the same good is sold
through "discount houses," which have had a phenomenal rise in recent years. These stores make a feature of selling branded lines at a
large reduction in price. The United States Chamber of Commerce recently estimated that fully 18 per cent of all retail sales were made by
discount outlets of some type.[19] In such cities as New York and Los
Angeles the discount houses sell well over half of the major appliances. In the latter city, gasoline service stations have recently begun
to compete with the discount houses.[20] The motorist can now buy at
cut rates such items as television sets, vacuum cleaners, and nylon

---

[17] "Slow Reaction on Court's Jolt to Fair Trade," *Sales Management,* July 20, 1956.

[18] This is not unlike the practice of some filling stations of selling the same gasoline
at different prices from different pumps under different brand names.

[19] *New York Times,* November 14, 1954.

[20] *Wall Street Journal,* November 11, 1956.

stockings while having his car serviced. The attraction of the discounted merchandise seems also to have increased the volume of gasoline and oil sales.

Retail jewelers have been among the groups to complain that some manufacturers have used them as a "show case stimulus to the business of discount houses." The complaint, which was filed with the Federal Trade Commission, has been that jewelry manufacturers have deliberately sold watches, silverware, and related goods to discount houses without requiring adherence to fair-trade prices while at the same time enforcing fair-trade prices against jewelers. The Federal Trade Commission does not, however, have any definite regulatory duty with respect to the fair-trade laws. The commission's advice to the retail jewelers was to sue for enforcement of the fair-trade prices against the discount houses or, alternatively, to disregard fair-trade prices themselves. A manufacturer who discriminates in the enforcement of his fair-trade prices among different types of sellers is unlikely to win a suit against a seller who disregards fair-trade prices.

Manufacturers' Actions Regarding Fair Trade

To date, some manufacturers have adhered strictly to the fair-trade philosophy; others have fair-traded and not fair-traded at the same time; and still others have completely abandoned the setting of resale prices. Westinghouse, which started fixing retail prices on its appliances in 1949, abandoned fair-trade prices on its line of electric housewares and bed coverings in 1955, being the first major appliance dealer to do so.[21] General Electric did not abandon resale price maintenance but cut retail prices by as much as 30 per cent in order to narrow the gap between prices quoted by regular dealers and by discount houses.[22] General Electric, however, dropped its fair-trade pricing in Michigan after the Supreme Court ruled that only signers of fair-trade pacts were bound by manufacturers' resale prices.[23] Similarly, fair-trading was dropped in Indiana when that state's law was found to be unconstitutional.

The W. A. Sheaffer Pen Company, after a vigorous and costly drive to enforce its fair-trade prices, recently followed the lead of Westinghouse in dropping resale price maintenance.[24] This was done in order

---

[21] *Wall Street Journal,* September 1, 1955, p. 18.

[22] *Wall Street Journal,* December 27, 1955.

[23] *Wall Street Journal,* October 12, 1955.

[24] *Wall Street Journal,* December 5, 1955.

to permit its dealers to meet local competition. Sheaffer continued the use of suggested retail prices as a substitute for legally enforceable fair-trade prices.

A basic lesson to be learned from the recent history of the fair-trade movement is that competition is so vigorous a force in the American economy that legislative attempts to thwart its operation often meet with insuperable obstacles. Also, experience confirms the observation that the courts, in seeking to preserve our constitutional rights, often manifest more economic wisdom than our legislatures. As long as private economic initiative and constitutional government are allowed to flourish, the nation will continue its rapid economic growth.

CASE 14–1: *STANDARD OIL COMPANY OF CALIFORNIA et al.* v. *UNITED STATES,* 337 U.S. 293

Under contracts entered into by an oil company with independent dealers in petroleum products and automobile accessories, the dealer agreed to purchase exclusively from the company all of his requirements of one or more of the products marketed by the company. In 1947 the contracts affected a gross business of $58,000,000, comprising 6.7 per cent of the total in a seven-state area in which the company sold its products. Held: The contracts were violative of Section 3 of the Clayton Act, and the company was properly enjoined from enforcing or entering into them.

MR. JUSTICE FRANKFURTER: This is an appeal to review a decree enjoining the Standard Oil Company of California and its wholly-owned subsidiary, Standard Stations, Inc.,[25] from enforcing or entering into exclusive supply contracts with any independent dealer in petroleum products and automobile accessories.

The Standard Oil Company of California, a Delaware corporation, owns petroleum-producing resources and refining plants in California and sells petroleum products in what has been termed in these proceedings the "Western area"—Arizona, California, Idaho, Nevada, Oregon, Utah and Washington. It sells through its own service stations, and to industrial users. It is the largest seller of gasoline in the area. In 1946 its combined sales amounted to 23 per cent of the total taxable gallonage sold there in that year: sales by company-owned service stations constituted 6.8 per cent of the total, sales under exclusive dealing contracts with independent service stations, 6.7 per cent of the total; the remainder were sales to industrial users. Retail service-station sales by Standard's six leading competitors absorbed 42.5 per cent of the total taxable gallonage; the remaining retail sales were divided between more than seventy small companies. It is undisputed that Standard's major competitors

---

[25] Standard Stations, Inc., has no independent status in these proceedings; since 1944 its activities have been confined to managing service stations owned by the Standard Oil Company of California.

employ similar exclusive dealing arrangements. In 1948 only 1.6 per cent of retail outlets were known as "split-pump" stations, that is, sold the gasoline of more than one supplier.

Exclusive supply contracts with Standard had been entered into, as of March 12, 1947, by the operators of 5,937 independent stations, or 16 per cent of the retail gasoline outlets in the Western area, which purchased from Standard in 1947, $57,646,233 worth of gasoline and $8,200,089.21 worth of other products. Some outlets are covered by more than one contract so that in all about 8,000 exclusive supply contracts are here in issue. These are of several types but a feature common to each is the dealer's undertaking to purchase from Standard all his requirements of one or more products. Two types, covering 2,777 outlets, bind the dealer to purchase of Standard all of his requirements of gasoline and other petroleum products as well as tires, tubes, and batteries. The remaining written agreements, 4,368 in number, bind the dealer to purchase of Standard all his requirements of petroleum products only. It was also found that independent dealers had entered 742 oral contracts by which they agreed to sell only Standard's gasoline. In some instances dealers who contracted to purchase from Standard all their requirements of tires, tubes, and batteries, had also orally agreed to purchase of Standard their requirements of other automobile accessories. Of the written agreements, 2,712 were for varying specified terms; the rest were effective from year to year but terminable "at the end of any such year, by giving to the other at least 30 days prior thereto written notice. . . ." Before 1934 Standard's sales of petroleum products through independent service stations were made pursuant to agency agreements, but in that year Standard adopted the first of its several requirements-purchase contract forms, and by 1938 requirements contracts had wholly superseded the agency method of distribution.

Between 1936 and 1946 Standard's sales of gasoline through independent dealers remained at a practically constant proportion of the area's total sales; its sales of lubricating oil declined slightly during that period from 6.2 per cent to 5 per cent of the total. Its proportionate sales of tires and batteries for 1946 were slightly higher than they were in 1936, though somewhat lower than for some intervening years; they have never, as to either of these products, exceeded 2 per cent of the total sales in the Western area.

Since Section 3 of the Clayton Act was directed to prohibiting specific practices even though not covered by the broad terms of the Sherman Act, it is appropriate to consider first whether the enjoined contracts fall within the prohibition of the narrower Act. The relevant provisions of Section 3 are:

"It shall be unlawful for any person engaged in commerce, in the course of such commerce, to lease or make a sale or contract for sale of goods, wares, merchandise, machinery, supplies, or other commodities, whether patented or unpatented, for use, consumption, or resale within the United States . . . on the condition, agreement, or understanding that the lessee or purchaser thereof shall not use or deal in the goods . . . of a competitor or competitors of the . . . seller, where the effect of such lease, sale, or contract for sale or such condition, agreement, or understanding may be to substantially lessen competition or tend to create a monopoly in any line of commerce."

Obviously the contracts here at issue would be proscribed if Section 3 stopped short of the qualifying clause beginning, "where the effect of such lease, sale, or contract for sale. . . ." If the effect is to be given that clause, however, it is by no means obvious, in view of Standard's minority share of the "line of commerce" involved, of the fact that share has not recently increased, and of the claims of these contracts to economic utility, that the effect of the contracts may be to lessen competition or tend to create a monopoly. It is the qualifying clause, therefore, which must be construed.

The District Court . . . concluded: "Grant that, on a comparative basis, and in relation to the entire trade in these products in the area, the restraint is not integral. Admit also that control of distribution results in lessening of costs and that its abandonment might increase costs. . . . Concede further, that the arrangement was entered into in good faith, with the honest belief that control of distribution and consequent concentration of representation were economically beneficial to the industry and to the public, that they have continued for over fifteen years openly, notoriously and unmolested by the Government, and have been practiced by other major oil companies competing with Standard, that the number of Standard outlets so controlled may have decreased, and the quantity of products supplied to them may have declined, on a comparative basis. Nevertheless, as I read the latest cases of the Supreme Court, I am compelled to find the practices here involved to be violative of both statutes. For they affect injuriously a sizeable part of interstate commerce, or,—to use the current phrase,—'an appreciable segment' of interstate commerce."

The issue before us, therefore, is whether the requirement of showing that the effect of the agreements "may be to substantially lessen competition" may be met simply by proof that a substantial portion of commerce is affected or whether it must also be demonstrated that competitive activity has actually diminished or probably will diminish.

We are dealing here with a particular form of agreement specified by Section 3 and not with different arrangements, by way of integration or otherwise, that may tend to lessen competition. To interpret that section as requiring proof that competition has actually diminished would make its very explicitness a means of conferring immunity upon the practices which it singles out. Congress has authoritatively determined that those practices are detrimental where their effect may be to lessen competition. It has not left at large for determination in each case the ultimate demands of the "public interest.". . . Though it may be that such an alternative to the present system as buying out independent dealers and making them dependent employees of Standard Stations, Inc., would be a greater detriment to the public interest than perpetuation of the system, this is an issue, like the choice between greater efficiency and freer competition, that has not been submitted to our decision. We are faced, not with a broadly phrased expression of general policy, but merely a broadly phrased qualification of an otherwise narrowly directed statutory provision."

In this connection it is significant that the qualifying language was added only after a flat prohibition of tying clauses and requirements contracts had passed both Houses of Congress. The conferees responsible for adding that language were at pains, in answering protestations that the qualifying clause seriously weakened the section, to disclaim any intention seriously to augment the burden of proof to be sustained in establishing violation of it. It seems hardly likely that, having with one hand set up an express prohibition against a practice thought to be beyond the reach of the Sherman Act, Congress meant, with the other hand, to reestablish the necessity of meeting the same tests of detriment to the public interest as that Act had been interpreted as requiring. Yet the economic investigation which appellant would have us require is of the same broad scope as was adumbrated with reference to unreasonable restraints of trade in *Chicago Board of Trade* v. *United States,* 246 U.S. 231. To insist upon such an investigation would be to stultify the force of Congress' declaration that requirements contracts are to be prohibited whereever their effect "may be" to substantially lessen competition. If in fact it is economically desirable for service stations to confine themselves to the sale of the petroleum products of a single supplier, they will continue to do so though not bound by contract, and if in fact it is important to retail dealers to assure the supply of their requirements by obtaining the commitment of a single supplier to fulfill them, competition for their patronage should enable them to insist upon such an arrangement without binding them to refrain from looking elsewhere.

We conclude, therefore, that the qualifying clause of Section 3 is satisfied by proof that competition has been foreclosed in a substantial share of the line of commerce affected. It cannot be gainsaid that observance by a dealer of his requirements contract with Standard does effectively foreclose whatever opportunity there might be for competing suppliers to attract his patronage, and it is clear that the affected proportion of retail sales of petroleum products is substantial. In view of the widespread adoption of such contracts by Standard's competitors and the availability of alternative ways of obtaining an assured market, evidence that competitive activity has not actually declined is inconclusive. Standard's use of the contracts creates just such a potential clog on competition as it was the purpose of Section 3 to remove wherever, were it to become actual, it would impede a substantial amount of competitive activity. . . .

The judgment below is *Affirmed.*

QUESTIONS

1. What alternative method of distribution of Standard's products would you recommend in view of this decision?
2. Is there any difference in the nature of the costs involved in an agency method of distribution as compared with the independent dealer?
3. Is there any difference in the nature of the costs involved in the requirements contracts for independent dealers as compared to that of company-owned stations?
4. Is there any possible relationship between the use of requirements contracts and total unit cost of production? Could the decision in this case have any possible effect upon the price of petroleum products?
5. Assuming that the Standard Oil Company of California was maximizing profits under the requirements contract arrangement, will an alternative

method of distribution probably cost more or less than the present arrangement? In both the long and the short run?

6. If a decision is made to market through company-owned service stations, what kind of corporate organization would you recommend? Why?

CASE 14-2: SCHWEGMANN BROS., INC.

In 1946, Schwegmann Bros., Inc., opened a grocery supermarket in New Orleans, Louisiana. The firm offered for sale to the public a number of items below their advertised "fair-trade" prices. In May, 1951, court injunctions were issued, requiring the company to cease the sale of a number of products below fair-trade prices established under the Louisiana Fair Trade Law, including Seagram's and Calvert's liquors, Bayer's aspirin, International Cellucotton's Kotex and Kleenex, Sterling Drug's Milk of Magnesia, and Lever's Pepsodent. Calvert Distillers Corporation and Seagram Distillers Corporation successfully brought suit in the U.S. District Court to enjoin Schwegmann Bros., Inc., from selling their products at cut-rate prices. Schwegmann Bros., Inc., petitioner in the decision which follows, appealed to the U.S. Supreme Court (*Schwegmann Brothers* v. *Calvert Distillers Corp; Schwegmann Brothers* v. *Seagram Distillers Corp.*, [71 Sup. Ct. 745]).

MR. JUSTICE DOUGLAS delivered the opinion of the Court.

Respondents, Maryland and Delaware corporations, are distributors of gin and whiskey. They sell their products to wholesalers in Louisiana, who in turn sell to retailers. Respondents have a price-fixing scheme whereby they try to maintain uniform retail prices for their products. They endeavor to make retailers sign price-fixing contracts under which the buyers promise to sell at not less than the prices stated in respondents' schedules. They have indeed succeeded in getting over one hundred Louisiana retailers to sign these agreements. Petitioner, a retailer in New Orleans, refused to agree to the price fixing scheme and sold respondents' products at a cutrate price. Respondents thereupon brought this suit in the District Court by reason of diversity of citizenship to enjoin petitioner from selling the products at less than the minimum prices fixed by their schedules.

It is clear from our decisions under the Sherman Act (26 Stat. 209) that this interstate marketing arrangement would be illegal, that it would be enjoined, that it would draw civil and criminal penalties, and that no. court would enforce it. Fixing minimum prices, like other types of price fixing, is illegal *per se*. Resale price maintenance was indeed struck down in *Dr. Miles Medical Co.* v. *Park & Sons Co.*, 220 U.S. 373. The fact that a state authorizes the price fixing does not, of course, give immunity to the scheme, absent approval by Congress.

Respondents however, seek to find legality for this marketing arrangement in the Miller-Tydings Act enacted in 1937 as an amendment to Sec. 1 of the Sherman Act. That amendment provides in material part that "nothing herein contained shall render illegal, contracts or agreements prescribing minimum prices for the resale" of specified commodities when "contracts or agreements of that description are lawful as applied to intrastate transactions" under local law.

Louisiana has such a law. La. Gen. Stat. Sec. 9809.1 *et seq.* permits a "contract" for the sale or resale of a commodity to provide that the buyer will not resell "except at the price stipulated by /the/ vendor". The Louisiana statute goes further. It not only allows a distributor and retailer to make a "contract" fixing the resale price; but once there is a price-fixing "contract", known to a seller, with any retailer in the state, it also condemns as unfair competition a sale at less than the price stipulated even though the seller is not a party to the "contract". In other words, the Louisiana statute enforces price fixing not only against parties to a "contract" but also against nonsigners. So far as Louisiana law is concerned, price fixing can be enforced against all retailers once any single retailer agrees with a distributor on the resale price. And the argument is that the Miller-Tydings Act permits the same range of price fixing.

The argument is phrased as follows: the present action is outlawed by the Sherman Act—the Miller-Tydings Act apart—only if it is a contract, combination, or conspiracy in restraint of trade. But if a contract or agreement is the vice, then by the terms of the Miller-Tydings Act that contract or agreement is immunized, provided it is immunized by state law. The same is true if the vice is a conspiracy, since a conspiracy presupposes an agreement. That was in essence the view of the Court of Appeals, which affirmed by a divided vote a judgment of a district court enjoining petitioner from price cutting.

The argument at first blush has appeal. But we think it offends the statutory scheme.

We note to begin with that there are critical differences between Louisiana's law and the Miller-Tydings Act. The latter exempts only "contracts or agreements prescribing minimum prices for the resale". On the other hand, the Louisiana law sanctions the fixing of maximum as well as minimum prices, for it exempts any provision that the buyer will not resell "at the price stipulated by the vendor". We start then with a federal act which does not, as respondents suggest, turn over to the states the handling of the whole problem of resale price maintenance on this type of commodity. What is granted is a limited immunity—a limitation that is further emphasized by the inclusion in the state law and the exclusion from the federal law of the consigner provision. The omission of the nonsigner provision from the federal law is fatal to respondents' position unless we are to perform a distinct legislative function by reading into the Act a provision that was meticulously omitted from it.

A refusal to read the nonsigner provision into the Miller-Tydings Act makes sense if we are to take the words of the statute in their normal and customary meaning. The Act sanctions only "contracts or agreements". If a distributor and one or more retailers want to agree, combine, or conspire to fix a minimum price, they can do so if state law permits. Their contract, combination, or conspiracy—hitherto illegal—is made lawful. They can fix minimum prices pursuant to their contract or agreement with impunity. When they seek, however, to impose price fixing on persons who have not contracted or agreed to the scheme, the situation is vastly different. That is not price fixing by contract or agreement; that is price fixing by compulsion. That is not following the path of consensual agreement; that is resort to coercion.

Much argument is made to import into the contracts which respondents make with retailers a provision that the parties may force nonsigners into line. It is said that state law attaches that condition to every such contract and that therefore the Miller-Tydings Act exempts it from the Sherman Act. Such a condition, if implied, creates an agreement respecting not sales made under the contract but other sales. Yet all that are exempted by the Miller-Tydings Act are "contracts or agreements prescribing minimum prices for the resale" of the articles purchased, not "contracts or agreements" respecting the practices of noncontracting competitors of the contracting retailers.

It should be noted in this connection that the Miller-Tydings Act expressly continues the prohibitions of the Sherman Act against "horizontal" price fixing by those in competition with each other at the same functional level. Therefore, when a state compels retailers to follow a parallel price policy, it demands private conduct which the Sherman Act forbids. See *Parker* v. *Brown,* 317 U.S. 341, 350. Elimination of price competition at the retail level may, of course, lawfully result if a distributor successfully negotiates individual "vertical" agreements with all his retailers. But when retailers are *forced* to abandon price competition, they are driven into a compact in violation of the spirit of the proviso which forbids "horizontal" price fixing. A real sanction can be given the prohibitions of the proviso only if the price maintenance power granted a distributor is limited to *voluntary* engagements. Otherwise, the exception swallows the proviso and destroys its practical effectiveness.

The contrary conclusion would have a vast and devastating effect on Sherman Act policies. If it were adopted, once a distributor executed a contract with a single retailer setting the minimum resale price for a commodity in the state, all other retailers could be forced into line. Had Congress desired to eliminate the consensual element from the arrangement and to permit blanketing a state with resale price fixing if only one retailer wanted it, we feel that different measures would have been adopted—either a nonsigner provision would have been included or resale price fixing would have been authorized without more. Certainly the words used connote a voluntary scheme. Contracts or agreements convey the idea of a cooperative arrangement, not a program whereby recalcitrants are dragged in by the heels and compelled to submit to price fixing.

The history of the Act supports this construction. The efforts to override the rule of *Dr. Miles Medical Co.* v. *Park & Sons Co., supra,* were long and persistent. Many bills had been introduced on this subject before Senator Tydings introduced his. Thus in 1929, in the Seventy-First Congress, the Capper-Kelly fair trade bill was offered. It had no nonsigner provision. It merely permitted resale price maintenance as respects specified classes of commodities by declaring that no such "contract relating to the sale or resale" shall be unlawful. As stated in the House Report, that bill merely legalized an agreement "that the vendee will not resell the commodity specified in the contract except at a stipulated price." That bill became the model for the California act passed in 1931—the first state act permitting resale price maintenance. The California act contained no nonsigner clause. Neither did the Capper-Kelly bill that was introduced in the Seventy-Second Congress. So far as material here it was identical with its predecessor.

The Capper-Kelly bill did not pass. And by the time the next bill was introduced—three years later—the California act had been changed by the addition of the nonsigner provision. That was in 1933. Yet when in 1936 Senator Tydings introduced his first bill in the Seventy-Fourth Congress, he followed substantially the Capper-Kelly bills and wrote no nonsigner provision into it. His bill merely legalized "contracts or agreements prescribing minimum prices or other conditions for the resale" of a commodity. By this date several additional states had resale price maintenance laws with nonsigner provisions. Even though the state laws were the models for the federal bills, the nonsigner provision was never added. That was true of the bill introduced in the Seventy-Fifth Congress as well as the subsequent one. They all followed in this respect the pattern of the Capper-Kelly bill as it appeared before the first nonsigner provision was written into state law. The "contract" concept, utilized by Capper-Kelly before there was a nonsigner provision in state law was thus continued even after the nonsigner provision appeared. The inference, therefore, is strong that there was continuity between the first Tydings bill and the preceding Capper-Kelly bills. The Tydings bills built on the same foundation; they were no more concerned with nonsigner provisions than were their predecessors. In view of this history we can only conclude that if the draftsman intended that the nonsigning retailer was to be coerced, it was strange indeed that he omitted the one clear provision that would have accomplished that result.

An argument is made from the reports and debates to the effect that "contracts or agreements" nevertheless includes the nonsigner provisions of state law. The Senate Report on the first Tydings bill, after stating that the California law authorized a distributor "to make a contract that the purchaser will not resell" except at the stipulated price said that the proposed federal law "does no more than to remove Federal obstacles to the enforcement of contracts which the States themselves have declared lawful." The Senate Report on the second Tydings bill, which was introduced in the Seventy-Fifth Congress, did little more than reprint the earlier report. The House Report, heavily relied on here, gave a more extended analysis.

The House Report referred to the state fair trade acts as authorizing the maintenance of resale prices by contract and as providing that "third persons with notice are bound by the terms of such a contract regardless of whether they are parties to it"; and the Report also stated that the objective of the Act was to permit the public policy of the states having such acts to operate with respect to interstate contracts for the sale of goods. This Report is the strongest statement for respondents' position which is found in the legislative history. The bill which that Report endorsed, however, did not pass. The bill which became the law was attached by the Senate Committee on the District of Columbia as a rider to the District of Columbia revenue bill. In that form it was debated and passed.

It is true that the House Report quoted above was referred to when the Senate amendment to the revenue measure was before the House. And one Congressman in the debate said that the nonsigner provision of state laws was validated by the federal law.

But we do not take these remarks at face value. In the first place, the House Report, while referring to the nonsigner provision when describing a typical state Fair Trade act, is so drafted that the voluntary contract is the core of the argument for the bill. Hence, the General Statement in the Report states that the sole objective of the Act was "to permit the public policy of States having 'fair trade acts' to operate with respect to interstate contracts for re-sale of goods"; and the fair-trade acts are referred to as legalizing "the maintenance, by contract, of resale prices of branded or trade-marked goods."

In the second place, the remarks relied on were not only about a bill on which no vote was taken; they were about a bill which sanctioned "contracts or agreements" prescribing not only "minimum prices" but "other conditions" as well. The words "other conditions" were dropped from the amendments. Why they were deleted does not appear. It is said that they have no relevance to the present problem, since we are dealing here with "minimum prices" not with "other conditions". But that answer does not quite hold. The question is the amount of state law embraced in the word "contracts or agreements". It might well be argued that one of the "conditions" attaching to a contract fixing a minimum price would be the liability of a nonsigner. We do no more than stir the doubt, for the doubt alone is enough to make us skeptical of the full implications of the old report as applied to a new and different bill.

We look for more definite clues; and we find the following statement made on the floor by Senator Tydings: "What does the amendment do? It permits a man who manufactures an article to state the minimum resale price of the article in a contract with the man who buys it for ultimate resale to the public. . . ." Not once did Senator Tydings refer to the nonsigner provisions of state law. Not once did he suggest that the amendment would affect anyone but the retailer who signs the contract. We search the words of the sponsors for a clear indication that coercive as well as voluntary schemes or arrangements are permissible. We find none. What we do find is the expression of fear in the minority report of the Senate Committee that the nonsigner provisions of the state laws would be made effective if the law passed. These fears were presented in the Senate debate by Senator King in opposition to the amendment. But the Senate Report emphasizes the "permissive" nature of the state laws, not once pointing to their coercive features.

The fears and doubts of the opposition are no authoritative guide to the construction of legislation. It is the sponsors that we look to when the meaning of the statutory words is in doubt. And when we read what the sponsors wrote and said about the amendment, we cannot find that the distributors were to have the right to use not only a *contract* to fix retail prices but a *club* as well. The words they used—"contracts or agreements"—suggest just the contrary.

It should be remembered that it was the state laws that the federal law was designed to accommodate. Federal regulation was to give way to state regulation. When state regulation provided for resale price maintenance by those who contracted and those who did not, and the federal regulation was relaxed only as respect "contracts or agreements", the inference is strong that Congress left the noncontracting group to be governed by pre-existing law. In other words, since Congress was writing a law to meet the specifications of state law, it would seem that if the nonsigner provision as well as the "contract" provision of state law were to be written into federal law, the pattern of the legislation would have been different.

We could conclude that Congress carved out the vast exception from the Sherman Act now claimed only if we are willing to assume that it took a devious route and yet failed to make its purpose plain.

Reversed.

MR. JUSTICE JACKSON, whom MR. JUSTICE MINTON joins, concurring.

I agree with the Court's judgment and with its opinion insofar as it rests upon the language of the Miller-Tydings Act. But it does not appear that there is either necessity or propriety in going back of it into legislative history.

Resort to legislative history is only justified where the face of the Act is inescapably ambiguous, and then I think we should not go beyond Committee reports, which presumably are well considered and carefully prepared. I cannot deny that I have sometimes offended against that rule. But to select casual statements from floor debates, not always distinguished for candor or accuracy, as a basis for making up our minds what law Congress intended to enact is to substitute ourselves for the Congress in one of its important functions. The Constitution, in requiring three readings of an Act in each House before final enactment, intended, I take it, to make sure that Congress knew what it was passing and passed what it wanted, and that what it enacted was formally reduced to writing. It is the business of Congress to sum up its own debates in its legislation. Moreover, it is only the words of the bill that have presidential approval, where that approval is given. It is not to be supposed that in signing a bill, the President endorses the whole Congressional Record. For us to undertake to reconstruct an enactment from legislative history is merely to involve the Court in political controversies which are quite proper in the enactment of a bill but should have no place in its interpretation.

Moreover, there are practical reasons why we should accept whenever possible the meaning which an enactment reveals on its face. Laws are intended for all of our people to live by; and the people go to law offices to learn what their rights under those laws are. Here is a controversy which affects every little merchant in many States. Aside from a few offices in the larger cities, the materials of legislative history are not available to the lawyer who can afford neither the cost of acquisition, the cost of housing, or the cost of repeatedly examining the whole congressional history. Moreover, if he could, he would not know any way of anticipating what would impress enought members of the Court to be controlling. To accept legislative debates to modify statutory provisions is to make the law inaccessible to a large part of the country.

By and large, I think our function was well stated by Mr. Justice Holmes:

"We do not inquire what the legislator meant; we ask only what the statute means". Holmes, Collected Legal Papers, 207. See also *Soon Hing* v. *Crowley,* 113 U.S. 703, 710–711. And I can think of no better example of legislative history that is unedifying and unilluminating than that of the Act before us.

MR. JUSTICE FRANKFURTER, whom MR. JUSTICE BLACK and MR. JUSTICE BURTON join, dissenting.

In 1890, Congress passed the Sherman Law, which declared illegal "every contract, combination in the form of trust or otherwise, or conspiracy, in restraint of trade or commerce among the several States, or with foreign nations". In 1937, Congress passed the Miller-Tydings Amendment. This excepted from the Sherman Law "contracts or agreements" prescribing minimum prices for the resale of trade-marked commodities where such contracts or agreements were valid under State statute or policy. It would appear that insofar as the Sherman Law made maintenance of minimum resale prices illegal, the Miller-Tydings Amendment made it legal to the extent that State law legalized it. "Contracts or agreements" immunized by the Miller-Tydings Amendment surely cannot have a narrower scope than "contract, combination . . . or conspiracy" in the Sherman Law. The Miller-Tydings Amendment is an amendment to Sec. 1 of the Sherman Law. The category of contract cannot be given different content in the very same section of the same act, and every combination or conspiracy implies an agreement.

The setting of the Miller-Tydings Amendment and its legislative history remove any lingering doubts. The depression following 1929 gave impetus to the movement for legislation which would allow the fixing of minimum resale prices. In 1931, California passed a statute allowing a manufacturer to establish resale prices binding only upon retailers who voluntarily entered into a contract with him. This proved completely ineffective, and in 1933 California amended her statute to provide that such a contract established a minimum price binding upon any person who had notice of the contract. This amendment was the so-called "nonsigner" clause which, in effect, allowed a manufacturer or wholesaler to fix a minimum resale price for his product. Every "fair trade" law thereafter passed by any State contained this "nonsigner" clause. By the close of 1936, 14 States had passed such laws. In 1937, 28 more States passed them. Today, 45 out of 48 States have "fair trade" laws.

A substantial obstacle remained in the path of the "fair trade" movement. In 1911, we had decided *Dr. Miles Medical Co.* v. *Park & Sons Co.,* 220 U.S. 373. There, in a suit brought against a "nonsigner", we held that agreement to maintain resale prices was a "contract . . . in restraint of trade" which was contrary to the Sherman Act. To remove this block, the Miller-Tydings Amendment was enacted. It is said, however, that thereby Congress meant only to remove the bar of the Sherman Act from agreements between the manufacturer and retailer, that Congress did not mean to make valid the "nonsigner" clause which formed an integral part of each of the 42 State statutes in effect when the Amendment was passed.

The Miller-Tydings Amendment was passed as a rider to a Revenue Bill for the District of Columbia. The House Conference Report contains only five lines concerning the rider. But the rider was not a new measure. It came as no surprise to the house, which already had before it practically the same language in the Miller Bill, reported favorably by the Committee on the Judiciary. Both the House and Senate, therefore, had before them reports dealing with the substance of the Miller-Tydings Amendment. These reports speak for themselves. . . . Every State act referred to in these reports contained a "nonsigner" provision. I cannot see how, in view of these reports, we can conclude that Congress meant the "nonsigner" provisions to be invalid under the Sherman Act—unless, that is, we are to depart from the respect we have accorded authoritative legislative history in scores of cases during the last decade. In many of these cases the purpose of Congress was far less clearly revealed than here. It has never been questioned in this Court that Committee reports, as well as statements by those in charge of a bill, are authoritative elucidations of the scope of a measure.

It is suggested that we go to the words of the sponsors of the Miller-Tydings Amendment. We have done so. Their words confirm the plain meaning of the words of the statute and of the congressional reports. Senator Tydings made the following statement: "What we have attempted to do is what 42 States have already written on their statute books. It is simply to back up those acts, that is all; to have a code of fair trade practices written not by a national board such as the N.R.A. but by each State, so that the people may go to the State legislature and correct immediately any abuses that may develop." 81 Cong. Rec. 7496.

Representative Dirksen made a statement to the House as a member of its Conference Committee. He referred to the case of *Old Dearborn Co.* v *Seagram Corp.,* 299 U.S. 183, in which this Court had held that the "nonsigner" provision of the Illinois "fair trade" statute did not violate the Due Process Clause. Mr. Dirksen continued: "A question then arose as to whether or not the maintenance of such resale prices under a State fair trade act might not be in violation of the Sherman Anti-Trust Act of 1890 insofar as these transactions sprang from a contract in interstate commerce. This question was presented to the House Judiciary Committee and there determined by the reporting of the Miller bill. It was essentially nothing more than an enabling act which placed the stamp of approval upon price maintenance transactions under State acts, notwithstanding the Sherman Act of 1890." 81 Cong. Rec. 8138.

Every one of the 42 State acts which the Miller-Tydings Amendment was to "back up"—the acts on which the Miller-Tydings Amendment was to place a "stamp of approval"—contained a "nonsigner" provision. As demonstrated by experience in California, the State acts would have been futile without the "nonsigner" clause. The Court now holds that the Miller-Tydings Amendment does not cover these "nonsigner" provisions. Not only is the view of the Court contrary to the words of the statute and to the legislative history. It is also in conflict with the interpretation given the Miller-Tydings Act by the Federal Trade Commission, by the Department of Justice, and by practically all persons adversely affected by the "fair trade" laws. The "fair trade" laws may well be unsound as a matter of economics. Perhaps Congress should not pass an important measure dealing with an extraneous subject as a rider to a revenue bill, with the coercive influence it exerts in avoiding a veto; perhaps it should restrict legislation to a single relevant subject, as required by the constitutions of three-fourths of the States. These are matters beyond the Court's concern. Where both the words of a statute and its legislative history clearly indicate the purpose of Congress, it should be respected. We should not substitute our own notion of what Congress should have done.

QUESTIONS

1. What is the advantage to a manufacturing firm of fair-trading its products? What is the danger from the point of view of the fair-trading manufacturer?

2. What is the advantage to the customer?

3. What effect does the invalidation of a fair-trade law have upon the marketing and distribution arrangements of a company which has been operating under fair-trade agreements?

4. Do you believe fair trade promotes or obstructs competition? Explain.

5. Do the fair-trade laws tend to cause retailing firms to specialize on a limited number of commodities or to move in the direction of becoming "general" stores? Explain.

INDEX

A

Adams, Walter, 505
Allen, Clark L., 54
Arbitrage, 14–15

B

Bacon, Nathaniel T., 118
Bain, Joe S., 172, 211
Basing-point system
  multiple, 333
  other industries, 333–35
  single, 332–33
Bear, J. B., 16
Berquist, Fred E., 248
Borden, Neil H., 253
Boulding, K. E., 8
Break-even analysis, 137–39
Brown, E. Cary, 487
Buchanan, James M., 54
Burck, Gilbert, 295
Burns, Arthur R., 213
Butters, J. Keith, 481, 484

C

Capital
  budget, 421
  equipment, nature of, 379
  funds, sources of, 421–24
Capitalization, 379
Cartels, 214–15
Cary, William L., 484
Clemens, Eli W., 322
Colberg, Marshall R., 54, 300, 492
Colbert, L. L., 335
Competition
  disadvantages of nonprice, 225–26
  effects of nonprice, 223–24
  internal brand, 308–10
  monopolistic, 88, 210
  nonprice, 218
  perfect, 86–87
  pure, 87–88, 210
  quality and style, 218–20
  in service, 222–23
  in terms of trade, 222–23
  workable, 508–9

Concentration
  of American industry, 206–8
  company, 208–9
  plant, 208–9
  ratios, 206–8
Contracts, exclusive dealer, 513
Cost
  average, 135, 137
  as basis for regulation, 134
  control of, 132–33
  in determination of income, 131–32
  fixed, 134–37
  incremental, 135, 137
  marginal, 135–37
  marginal as determinant of output,
    140–41
  related to pricing, 133–34
  role of measurement of, 131
  and size of firm, 175–76
  a statistical study of, 177–87
Cost curves
  average, 139–41
  long-run, 169–72
  marginal, 139–41
  shape of marginal, 143–45
Costs
  joint, 296–99
  joint under monopolistic competition,
    299–302
  variable, 134–37
Cournot, Augustin, 118
Court, Andrew T., 219
Cross-hauling, 337–38

D

Dauten, Carl A., 34
Dean, Joel, 177, 425, 427, 428
Demand
  changes in, 90–92
  complementary, 308
  curve, 80–81
  elastic, 83, 87
  elasticity of, 81–82, 130
  elasticity of and revenue, 82–83
  facing a monopolist, 83–86
  inelastic, 83
  for investible funds, 424–26

533

INDEX OF CASES

This book has been set on the Linotype in 12 and 10 point Garamond No. 3, leaded 1 point. Chapter numbers and chapter titles are in 18 point Lydian Bold. The size of the type page is 27 by 46½ picas.